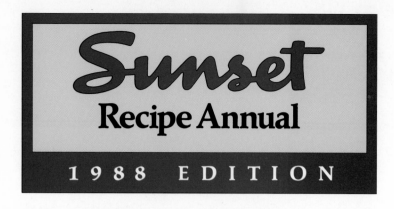

# Sunset
## Recipe Annual
### 1988 EDITION

Every Sunset Magazine recipe and
food article from 1987

By the Sunset Editors

*Moroccan feast (page 222)*

**Lane Publishing Co.** ■ **Menlo Park, California**

# Our Tribute to 1987

*Seviche with Kiwi Fruit (page 296)*

In this collection of over 700 recipes, Sunset celebrates its 1987 harvest of magazine food articles. If you've already sampled *The Best of Sunset,* you'll know the quality of experience to expect from this companion cook book.

As in earlier years, in 1987 *Sunset Magazine* covered a broad and varied spectrum of food topics—from simple soups to fantasies of ice cream and from casual family meals to entertaining on a grand scale. Cooks who participated in our pages ranged from grade-schoolers to professionals and included both men and women.

Also noteworthy in 1987, the magazine paid special tribute to the basic ingredients that compose a great meal. Whether oats for breakfast, pickles and onions with lunch, or standing rib roast as the star attraction at dinner, there was an in-depth article to explain all the how's and why's. We hope you'll enjoy these simple cooking lessons along with the banquet of extraordinary recipes contained in this cook book.

**Cover:** Chilled Avocado Soup (page 13). Photograph by Glenn Christiansen.

**Back cover:** Kumquat Meringue Pie (page 32). Photograph by Norman A. Plate.

Sunset Magazine
    Editor: William Marken
Sunset Books
    Editor: David E. Clark
    Managing Editor: Elizabeth L. Hogan

All material in this book originally appeared in the 1987 issues of *Sunset Magazine* and was created by the following editors, illustrators, and photographers:

**Home Economics Editor, Sunset Magazine**
Jerry Anne Di Vecchio

**Home Economics Staff, Sunset Magazine**
Linda Anusasananan
Sandra Bakko Cameron
Pamela J. Eimers
Paula Smith Freschet
Bernadette Hart
Elaine S. Johnson
Annabel Post
Betsy Ann Reynolds

**Illustrations**
David Broad *(Chefs of the West)*
Alice Harth *(Kitchen Cabinet and pages 266–269, 272–274, 276)*

**Photography**
Glenn Christiansen
Peter Christiansen
Norman A. Plate
David Stubbs
Darrow M. Watt
*(see page 352 for individual credits)*

This Annual was produced by Sunset Books.

**Book Editors**
Cornelia Fogle
Helen Sweetland

**Contributing Editor**
Susan Warton

**Design**
Williams & Ziller Design

# Contents

# The Year at Sunset

Thousands of Western cooks, in each month of 1987, turned to the food pages of Sunset Magazine for bold new ideas, in-depth coverage, a fresh point of view, and mouthwatering recipes. As in earlier years, Sunset in 1987 delivered the full culinary calendar that has made the magazine a respected authority on food, wine, and entertaining for more than six decades.

Whether you're new to our pages or a seasoned subscriber, as you glance through this cook book, you'll immediately see that Sunset approaches its subjects with an appetite for adventure. Where but in Sunset, in 1987 or any other year, were you likely to find buffalo meatballs, kumquat gelato, or "squeeze salads" for skiers? Where else would you find *any* salad recipe for the ski slope?

More down-to-earth stories of 1987 delved into everything from oats to onions to prosciutto to freshly caught trout for breakfast. For serious diners, there was pepper-seasoned standing rib roast. For indecisive hosts, there was a caterer's list of easy entrées. For romantics, there were stuffed squash blossoms; for herb-gardening cooks, burnet; and for sports fans, a giant pretzel sandwich.

Without missing a morsel, this Sunset Recipe Annual recaptures the entire tantalizing year of 1987, including every food story from each of the twelve months and all four regional editions. If you flipped past the microwavable Quick and Easy *Dim Sum* the first time around, it's now yours for keeps and at your leisure. If your family has been asking for Dynamite Dogs, but you've mislaid the recipe, here it is again. Or, if you've never yet seen all these marvelous recipes, photographs, drawings, charts, and possibilities, get ready for a feast.

## BEHIND THE SCENES AT SUNSET

One of the most talked-about stops on visitors' tours of Sunset's Menlo Park, California, offices is the magazine editorial test kitchen. Here, a staff of home economics editors carefully develops every recipe that eventually appears in print. From whimsical fig tulips to oven-smoked meats, every recipe published in 1987—as in every year—was repeatedly tested, tasted, discussed, and im-

proved. Then, it was retested again by non-professionals working in the test kitchen, just to be sure that directions were clear and complete.

Sunset's continuing objective is to produce articles that you can put to use with equipment already in your kitchen, and with the most efficient and satisfying outlay of time, skill, and expense. The ultimate aim is great-tasting, good-looking, and otherwise magnificent recipe results. By definition, for Sunset this also means results that are healthful and light, created from an abundance of fresh ingredients. But, for appropriate occasions, the magazine may also present such rich extravagance as Tartufo (a white chocolate fantasy) or Chewy-gooey Brownies.

**Recipe ideas** reach Sunset from all over the West and beyond. The magazine's home economics editors do not always stay at home in Menlo Park. They get out of the kitchen frequently, traveling in all directions to look for food news and story ideas.

Some of 1987's most intriguing recipes originated quite far afield—*Carnitas* from Mexico, *Feijoada* from Brazil, or the crusty Damper Loaf once baked by convict settlers of Australia. Cuisines around the Pacific Rim receive special neighborly attention from Sunset.

Closer to home, field work also means consulting with specialists in order to keep readers accurately informed of important topics. In 1987, home economics editors tapped the expertise of the Cooperative Extension at the University of California at Davis, the Food and Drug Administration, and the United States Department of Agriculture, as well as such groups as the National Livestock and Meat Board, National Fisheries Institute, and other special boards and councils throughout the country.

In a very different kind of field work, recipe ideas may sprout literally in Western gardens when spring and summer warm the soil. *Mitsuba, shiso,* and other Japanese herbs inspired a 1987 food story that appeared in the same issue with a gardening report on how to grow them. A new taste to most of our readers, the delicate herbs are also available in many Oriental markets.

**Readers contribute** some of our most popular recipes. Recipes mailed by readers are evaluated monthly for possible publication. Many appear in Sunset's regular cooking features: Menus, Kitchen Cabinet, or Chefs of the West.

A longstanding tradition at Sunset, reader contributions date back to the magazine's early issues of 1929, which included the first Kitchen Cabinet "rec-

*Sunset magazine home economics staff (left to right): Paula Freschet, Betsy Reynolds, Annabel Post, Jerry Anne Di Vecchio, Pamela Eimers, Linda Anusasananan, Bernadette Hart, Sandra Cameron, Elaine Johnson.*

ipe exchange." Men who like to cook have been exchanging recipes and wit in Chefs of the West since 1940. (David Broad's delightful Chefs cartoons and Alice Harth's elegant drawings for Kitchen Cabinet are shown in full color for the first time in this cook book.) As for Menus, a relative newcomer, it has remained a perennial favorite with readers since it began in 1955.

Several times each year, Sunset spotlights individual readers whose recipes, party ideas, or cooking techniques are exceptionally newsworthy. Don't miss either the method or the eating of "Steamroller" Chicken, the creation of a thrifty and talented home chef from the Northwest. To go with it, don't overlook his *Pasta alla Puttanesca.*

**Recipe testing** is an exacting as well as an exciting process. All recipes are prepared a minimum of four times—or as often as it takes for us to be assured that you will get excellent results.

Each fraction of a teaspoon, nuance of flavor, and minute of cooking time is evaluated. Testing demands patience, because Sunset does not stint on how much time it may take. Perfect pickles, for example, went through four summers of testing before they were considered ready for you in 1987. But put them out for lunch, and they'll be gone in minutes.

**Taste panels** rate reader-submitted recipes for flavor, appearance, and ease of preparation. The popularity of these panels at Sunset is understandable: interested staff members are invited to sample a collection of these dishes at lunchtime and to record their opinions. The taste panel is composed of two home economics editors and eight changing volunteers from throughout the company. Recipes that eventually appear in print must first win an enthusiastic response from the panel. A score card for rating such recipes is shown above right.

## BALANCING OUR MENU

The twelve months of 1987 spread out a broad spectrum of food articles. As you leaf through the pages of this book, you'll see a rich and appetizing variety of recipes. Like a healthy diet, they offer a balanced selection.

**Celebrating the seasons** has been one of Sunset's time-honored traditions, usually in articles that showcase fruits and vegetables at prime availability. In the fall of 1987, our tribute to persimmons covered everything from botanical details to an elegantly sculptured presentation with hazelnut-flavored liqueur. Earlier, the summer started off with advice on the tender care of baby vegetables, then making a big splash in produce markets.

**Western fruits, vegetables, and herbs** are featured prominently in the magazine all year long. In one of 1987's major articles, Sunset honored the onion with breathtaking close-up photography and an in-depth analysis of the bulb's structure, chemistry, and behavior in cooking. Read it, and you'll never take another onion for granted.

**Breakthrough stories** on other basic ingredients included, in 1987, a 12-page report on lean meats. Accompanied by drawings and charts, as well as photographs, it explored the "lean revolution" that has brought good news to health-sensitive meat shoppers. It also served up succulent ideas for quick-cooking pork, tender yet lean beef, and festive kebabs of lamb. Low calorie counts will astonish you.

**Ideas for entertaining** brighten Sunset's pages frequently in any year. In 1987, there was crisp, wood-smoked pizza cooked on the barbecue, a novel approach and a raving success. It was also a year that emphasized easier entertaining. There were "easy on the waistline" appetizers, an "easy on the cook" brunch, and dozens of quick, simple recipes in between. To top everything off, for Thanksgiving, we mapped out the easiest approach: a potluck feast (with 27 sumptuous recipes from which to choose).

**Still more variety** in Sunset's 1987 menu was provided by smaller stories scattered throughout the year. For a touch of history, there was a report on the original tortilla (from Spain and made with

*Rating the recipes at a taste panel.*

eggs). For young cooks, there were tempting possibilities, from sunflower seed butter to a teen-ager's dream cake (Chocolate Cooky Cheesecake). For steaming the perfect cup of hot milk or cappuccino, a short article surveyed simple to sophisticated equipment. And for 1987's clock-watching bakers, there was a brief scientific study of the fastest possible loaf of yeast bread. Can you beat 50 minutes?

## RELIVING A GREAT YEAR

Though it brings together every food feature of Sunset Magazine in 1987, this cook book is more than a collection of memories. It has been produced for your translation into extraordinary meals, picnics, appetizers, snacks, beverages, and more. We hope that you, with family and friends, will savor every page.

Organized chronologically by month, our Recipe Annual lends itself naturally to use as a seasonal resource. But it will also inspire delicious thoughts at any page as you leaf through it. Favorite recipes, specific main ingredients, and other sub-categories can all be found in the three indices at the end of the book.

Every recipe of the year is worth tasting, but several stand apart as good choices for certain occasions. Here are some that we urge you to try:

- **For young cooks:** Junior Chefs with the Microwave (July)
- **For the family:** Valentine dinner (Menus, February)
- **For a casual summer lunch:** Bones barbecue (Menus, July)
- **For a more formal and elegant dinner:** Sole-wrapped Belgian Endive Rolls (November)
- **For a splashy warm-weather party:** Fish-fry Salad for 8 (September)

- **For a hearty breakfast:** Fruit & Spice Oatmeal Porridge (February)
- **For a hot-weather thirst:** Italian Fruit Fizzes (August)
- **For a new cooking adventure:** Tamale Sausages (May)
- **For hungry snackers:** Pickled Jicama (November)
- **For an intriguing new source of fiber:** Quinoa (November)

- **For meat-and-potato diners:** Braised Venison with Vegetables (October)
- **For a new flavor sensation:** Right-in-the-oven Smoking (March)
- **For bakers:** Sour Sunflower Pumpernickel Bread (October)
- **For a sweet Easter surprise:** Chocolate Easter Eggs (April)

We hope that you'll enjoy these and all the other Sunset Magazine recipes of 1987 as you explore this cook book from the first page of January to the last of December. From all of us at Sunset, have a great year.

# JANUARY

Sopaipillas (page 14)

**A**fter six decades and tens of thousands of recipes, some of Sunset's best have become Western Classics. In January, we featured a dozen classic dishes and photographed them on their home ground. Many of our other January recipes—including a collection of delectable appetizers—offered ways to keep post-holiday fare simple, quick, and light.

7

# Western Classics

I N FEBRUARY 1929, Sunset Magazine adopted the editorial policy that still guides it: a magazine of Western living for people who live in the West. Over the years, the recipes that have appeared in our pages have become a history of Western tastes.

Such factors as climate, geography, and ethnic mixtures have shaped our regional life style. Informality and a willingness to experiment are a large part of everyday experiences in the West.

For years Sunset editors have traveled around the West and around the world, gathering ideas to share with our readers and learning on location how to use the ingredients and seasonings that give regional and ethnic dishes their character.

Sunset's recipes reflect the easy-going way Westerners live. We enjoy the outdoors—and casual, al fresco meals—whatever the weather. We revel in our plentiful, year-round supply of fresh foods—from fruits and vegetables to seafood and cheeses—and feature them in our food pages.

Certain recipes reflect our past—a history that goes back to the Spanish who explored the Southwest in 1540, with overlays from the Indians who were here well before then. Western classics also include dishes based on foods produced primarily in the West, and ones that are exceptionally well suited to our way of living.

On this and the following eight pages, we look at a sampling of those heritage recipes. To photograph them on their home ground, we went to the locations in the West where these recipes claim their roots. We think you'll agree that each has earned its right to be called a Western classic.

## INDIAN-STYLE SALMON BAKE

The coastal Indians of the Northwest have handed down one of the region's grand traditions. It's their method of baking salmon—butterflied, woven on wood, and cooked over an outdoor fire. Since we first published an eyewitness report in the April 1933 Sunset, we've used this technique many times.

- 1 or 2 whole salmon (6 to 8 lb. *each*)
  Light brine (¼ cup salt to each 4 quarts water)
  Wood frame (directions follow)
  Foil
- ¼ cup (⅛ lb.) butter or margarine, melted
- 2 tablespoons lemon juice

Have your fishman remove the salmon head, tail, and back fin, then butterfly the salmon from stomach side (do not separate fillets at back) and bone it; leave skin intact. At home, rinse fish.

Place fish in a deep pan or a heavy plastic bag set in a pan. Cover with brine; let stand for 45 minutes to 1½ hours.

Lay one 6-foot frame piece flat. Wrap foil slightly longer than fish around center of stake. Position three frame pieces (each 18 inches) at right angles to stake; center pieces and space evenly apart.

Lift fish from brine; rinse and pat dry. Align center of fish with long stake; lay fish on top of 18-inch pieces (wide end of fish pointed toward sharpened end of stake). Adjust position of 18-inch pieces so entire edge of fish overlaps them by 2 to 3 inches at top and bottom.

On top of salmon, place remaining two 18-inch pieces, centered between and parallel to the short pieces beneath the fish—in effect, weave the fish in place.

Foil-wrap the second 6-foot stake as you did the first. Lay second stake directly over first, sharpened ends together, with fish and short pieces sandwiched between. Tightly wrap wire around the 2 long stakes above and below fish.

If cooking a second fish, repeat steps.

While you are framing salmon, start fire in a location sheltered from wind.

The ideal fire is made of driftwood and built against the base of a large rock or a big log (for reflected heat, wind protection). Make the firebed at least twice as long as width of fish, placed side by side. Burn fire until you have a solid bed of glowing coals—allow at least 30 minutes. Add wood to keep gently blazing as fish cooks. Push fire around to control heat, particularly if there's a breeze.

Face fish toward heat. With a hammer, pound sharpened ends of stakes into sand or soft ground at least 12 inches from fire until bottom edge of fish is about 2 feet above fire. If fire is against a rock, angle stake at a 60° angle over fire. If fire is in the open, angle stake at a 45° angle over fire. (Control angle by wedging a rock between base of stakes and ground.)

Mix butter with lemon juice. Cook fish for 25 minutes, basting several times with mixture. Then carefully pull out stakes, rotate fish, pound stakes gently back into sand, and cook until fish flakes readily when prodded in thickest part with a fork, about 25 minutes longer; baste often.

Push fire away or move fish back from heat. Pull chunks from frame to eat. Each salmon makes 10 to 12 servings.

**Frame.** For each frame, you'll need 18 feet of milled 1-by-1s and 2 feet of 22-gauge or heavier wire. Use two 6-foot-long 1-by-1s for uprights, and sharpen one end of each. Rip the remaining 1-by-1 and cut five 18-inch-long pieces.

Soak wood in water overnight so it won't burn (you can improvise a trough by draping a large sheet of plastic over two 2-by-4s and filling with water to cover the wood); wrap short pieces with foil.

*Butterflied salmon, held open and supported by wooden frame, angles over driftwood dire to "bake" Indian-style on Puget Sound beach.*

*Cream-enriched broth, lots of potatoes and clams, a few other vegetables, and skillful seasonings are essence of Browny's chowder.*

## BROWNY'S CLAM CHOWDER

*This chowder is a specialty of Browny's Seafood Broiler in Richmond Beach, just north of Seattle. Owner Michael Brown owns up that it's an old Sunset recipe, but he's done significant restyling.*

- 6 slices bacon, chopped
  Prepared vegetables (directions follow)
- 1½ pounds red thin-skinned potatoes, scrubbed and cut into ½-inch cubes
- 2 bottles (8 oz. *each*) clam juice
- 8 cans (6½ oz. *each*) chopped clams
- 1 bay leaf
- ½ teaspoon liquid hot pepper seasoning
- ¼ teaspoon pepper
- 1½ teaspoons Worcestershire
- ¾ teaspoon dry thyme leaves
- 4 cups whipping cream
  Salt

Cook bacon in an 8- to 10-quart pan over medium heat, stirring often, until crisp. With a slotted spoon, lift out bacon and drain on paper towels; discard all but 2 tablespoons of the drippings. Add prepared vegetables and stir often until slightly browned.

Add potatoes and clam juice to pan; bring to a boil, reduce heat, cover, and simmer until potatoes are tender when pierced, about 15 minutes. Stir in clams and their liquid, bay leaf, hot pepper seasoning, pepper, Worcestershire, thyme, cream, and bacon. Season to taste with salt. Heat until steaming, then serve. Makes about 4 quarts, enough for 8 to 10 servings.

**Vegetables.** Thinly slice 2 medium-size **carrots** and 2 stalks **celery**; chop 1 small **onion** and ½ small **green bell pepper** (stemmed and seeded); mince or press 1 clove **garlic**.

## CRUNCH-TOP APPLE PIE

*Apple pie has fared well through the years with Sunset readers. This crumb- and nut-topped one, from January 1953, is among the most requested desserts from our files.*

*Its simplicity may have a lot to do with its longevity.*

- 6 medium-size tart apples, peeled, cored, and sliced
  Unbaked 10-inch pastry shell
- 1 cup *each* sugar and graham cracker crumbs
- ½ cup *each* all-purpose flour and chopped walnuts
- ½ teaspoon ground cinnamon
- ½ cup (¼ lb.) butter or margarine, melted
- 1 cup whipping cream

Arrange apples evenly in pastry shell. Combine sugar, graham cracker crumbs, flour, walnuts, and cinnamon; sprinkle over apples. Pour butter evenly over topping. Bake in a 350° oven until crust is well browned and apples are tender when pierced, about 1 hour. Serve at room temperature or chilled.

Cut in wedges and offer with whipped cream. Makes 8 or 9 servings.

*Crunch-top apple pie, one of Sunset's most requested desserts, is warmed and dappled by the same sun that ripens apples in Wenatchee orchard, beyond.*

*Dungeness crab, captured off the Golden Gate, is essence of San Francisco's great fish stew, cioppino. Serve with sourdough bread.*

their liquid, wine, bay leaf, basil, and oregano. Cover and simmer until slightly thickened, about 20 minutes.

To broth, add clams, shrimp, and crab. Cover and simmer gently until clams pop open and shrimp turn pink, about 20 minutes longer.

Ladle hot broth and some of each shellfish into large soup bowls or soup plates. Makes 6 servings.

## LONDON BROIL

*When Sunset introduced this classic recipe 30 years ago, most Western cooks were serving flank steak well cooked—usually braised. We showed how flank steak, grilled or broiled just until rare, could be flavorful and tender. The name London Broil moved on and is now used to describe steaks from the top round, which are also best grilled rare. Both steaks seem more tender when cut across the grain in thin slanting slices.*

    1 flank steak (about 1½ lb.), trimmed of fat
      Salt and pepper
      Butter or margarine (optional)

Place steak on a grill 4 to 6 inches above a solid bed of hot coals (you should be able to hold your hand at grill level for just 2 to 3 seconds). Cook, turning once, until meat is done to your liking (cut to test): about 10 minutes for rare, 14 minutes for medium-rare.

Put meat on a platter; with a sharp knife, cut meat across the grain into thin, slanting slices.

Season to taste with salt and pepper; top each serving with a pat of butter, if desired. Makes 4 or 5 servings.

## SAN FRANCISCO-STYLE CIOPPINO

*We first presented San Francisco's famous cioppino in 1941, crediting its invention to San Francisco fishermen from the Dalmatian coast. Dungeness crab is the star of this robust shellfish stew; clams and shrimp add their flavors, too. It's traditional to sop up the thick tomato and garlic sauce with lots of extra-sour sourdough bread.*

    ¼ cup olive oil or salad oil
    1 large onion, chopped
    2 cloves garlic, minced or pressed
    1 large green bell pepper, stemmed, seeded, and chopped
    ⅔ cup chopped parsley
    1 can (15 oz.) tomato sauce
    1 can (28 oz.) tomatoes

    1 cup dry red or white wine
    1 bay leaf
    1 teaspoon dry basil
    ½ teaspoon dry oregano leaves
    12 clams in shell, suitable for steaming, scrubbed
    1 pound large shrimp (about 30 per lb.), shelled and deveined
    2 live or cooked large Dungeness crab (about 2 lb. *each*), cleaned and cracked

In a 6- to 8-quart pan over medium heat, combine oil, onion, garlic, bell pepper, and parsley; cook, stirring often, until onion is soft. Stir in tomato sauce, tomatoes (break up with a spoon) and

Baked in Dutch oven, bread is part of a camp meal for Basque shepherd, rancher, and newcomer to Clovis, California.

## SHEEPHERDER'S BREAD

*Basque shepherds who tended flocks on remote Western rangelands baked their bread in Dutch ovens buried in pits. Few follow this routine today. Now updated versions of the dome-shaped loaf are baked in conventional ovens—with much more predictable results.*

*This recipe came from Anita Mitchell of Elko, Nevada; it won her the bread-baking championship at the 1975 National Basque Festival. We published it the following year.*

    3  cups very hot tap water
    ½  cup (¼ lb.) butter or margarine
    ½  cup sugar
    2½ teaspoons salt
    2  packages active dry yeast
       About 9½ cups all-purpose flour
       Salad oil

In a large bowl, combine hot water, butter, sugar, and salt. Stir until butter is melted; let cool to about 110°. Stir in yeast; cover and set in a warm place until bubbly, about 15 minutes.

Beat in about 5 cups of the flour to make a thick batter. Stir in about 3½ cups more flour to make a stiff dough. Scrape dough onto a floured board; knead until smooth and satiny, 10 to 20 minutes, adding as little flour as possible to prevent sticking. Place dough in a greased bowl; turn over to grease top. Cover and let rise in a warm place until doubled, about 1½ hours.

Punch dough down and knead briefly on a floured board to release air; shape into a smooth ball. With a circle of foil, cover the inside bottom of a 5-quart cast-iron or cast-aluminum Dutch oven. Grease foil, inside of Dutch oven, and lid with oil.

Place dough in Dutch oven and cover with lid. Let rise in a warm place until dough pushes up lid by about ½ inch, about 1 hour (watch closely).

Bake, covered with lid, in a 375° oven for 12 minutes. Remove lid and continue to bake until loaf is golden brown, 30 to 35 minutes. Remove bread from oven and turn out onto a rack to cool (you'll need a helper).

Peel off foil and turn loaf upright. Slice loaf in large slabs, or cut in wedges. Makes 1 very large loaf.

## CHILLED AVOCADO SOUP

*This cool, velvety, pale green bisque provides delicious evidence of the long-time popularity of the recipe and avocados in the West. Native to the New World, avocados were introduced into Southern California in 1848. Hass, the buttery thick-skinned variety that now dominates the marketplace almost year-round, used to alternate seasons with the tender-skinned and harder-to-ship Fuerte.*

*This recipe appeared in Sunset's November 1957 Kitchen Cabinet. If you like, slip a spoonful of sour cream into each bowl. A good companion: butter lettuce with sliced oranges, onions, and black ripe olives.*

- 1 **large ripe avocado**
- ½ **cup half-and-half, light cream, or whipping cream**
- 1½ **cups regular-strength chicken broth**
- 1 **tablespoon lemon juice**
  **Salt**
  **Chopped chives**

Halve, pit, and peel avocado. Place avocado halves, half-and-half, broth, and lemon juice in a blender; whirl until smooth. Season to taste with salt. If made ahead, cover and refrigerate up to 24 hours. Sprinkle each serving with chives. Makes 4 to 6 servings.

## ANGEL PIE

*Lemons were part of California's great citrus boom of the 1890s, and it's not surprising that angel pie, perennially popular with Westerners, is filled with a tart lemon curd. Since 1929, at least a dozen versions of this meringue-based dessert have appeared in Sunset's pages.*

- 4 **large eggs, separated**
- ½ **teaspoon cream of tartar**
- 1½ **cups sugar**
  **Grated peel of 2 lemons**
- 3 **tablespoons lemon juice**
- 1 **cup whipping cream**

In the large bowl of an electric mixer, whip egg whites at high speed until frothy. Sprinkle on cream of tartar and continue beating until whites will hold soft peaks. Then gradually add 1 cup of the sugar, 2 tablespoons at a time, until all is incorporated and the whites are glossy and will hold very stiff peaks.

With the back of a tablespoon, spread meringue in a well-greased 9-inch pie pan, pushing meringue high on the pan sides so that it resembles a pie shell. Bake in a 300° oven until meringue feels firm and dry but is not browned, about 40 minutes. Let cool on a rack. If made ahead, cover airtight and let stand as long as overnight.

In the top of a double boiler, beat egg yolks, the remaining ½ cup sugar, lemon peel, and lemon juice until blended. Cook over simmering water, stirring constantly, until sauce is thick, about 10 minutes. Let cool, then cover and refrigerate until chilled, or up to overnight.

Whip cream until it holds soft peaks; fold into chilled lemon sauce. Spoon mixture into meringue shell. Chill at least 2 hours or up to 8 hours to mellow for cutting. Makes 6 to 8 servings.

*Avocado in the soup, oranges in the salad. It's not unusual to see the trees that produce these fruits growing side by side in gardens within view of downtown L.A.*

## CAESAR SALAD

*Nobody knows whether this Western classic was created by, or for, a Caesar. We published our first version in 1945, presenting the salad as it was made in a Coronado, California, restaurant. But our research indicates that the dish probably originated in nearby Tijuana during the town's heyday in the '20s and '30s.*

*This recipe contains all the classic ingredients: crisp romaine, anchovies, croutons, Parmesan cheese—and barely warm eggs to make the dressing cling.*

- 2 **large heads romaine lettuce**
- 1 **clove garlic**
- ¾ **cup olive oil or salad oil**
- 2 **cups ¾-inch cubes day-old French bread**
- 2 **large eggs**
  **Freshly ground black pepper**
- 3 **tablespoons lemon juice**
- 6 **to 8 canned anchovy fillets, chopped**
- ½ **cup freshly grated Parmesan cheese**

Discard coarse outer romaine leaves. Break remaining leaves from head; rinse well and drain. If greens are not as crisp as you like, wrap in paper towels, enclose in plastic bags, and refrigerate for at least 30 minutes or until next day.

Crush garlic in a small bowl, pour oil over it, and let stand for at least 1 hour or up to 8 hours.

Heat ¼ cup of the garlic oil in a 10- to 12-inch frying pan over medium heat. Add bread cubes and stir often until browned on all sides. (Or coat bread cubes with ¼ cup garlic oil, spread in a rimmed 10- by 15-inch baking pan, and toast in a 325° oven until browned; stir occasionally.)

Immerse eggs in boiling water to cover for exactly 1 minute; lift out with a slotted spoon. Use warm or cool.

Tear romaine leaves into bite-size pieces and place in a large salad bowl; sprinkle generously with pepper. Pour remaining ½ cup garlic oil over lettuce; mix until leaves are coated.

Break eggs over salad, sprinkle with lemon juice, and lift with a salad fork and spoon to mix well. Add anchovies and cheese; mix again. Add croutons and mix gently. Serve at once. Makes 10 to 12 servings.

*Caesar salad crossed the border from Tijuana to San Diego, where Sunset first found it. The barely warmed egg makes the seasonings cling.*

## SOPAIPILLAS

*Frances Antencio's version of Southwest fried bread uses a yeast dough flecked with bits of whole-wheat flour. Serve these light, fluffy pillows plain, drizzled with honey or syrup, or sprinkled with cinnamon-sugar or powdered sugar.*

- 1 **package active dry yeast**
- ¼ **cup warm water (110°)**
- 1½ **cups milk**
- 3 **tablespoons lard or shortening**
- 1 **teaspoon salt**
- 2 **tablespoons sugar**
  **About 4 cups all-purpose flour**
- 1 **cup whole-wheat flour**
  **Salad oil**

In a large mixing bowl, dissolve yeast in water. In a 1½- to 2-quart pan, combine milk, lard, salt, and sugar; heat to 110° and add to dissolved yeast. With a dough hook or a spoon, beat in 3 cups all-purpose flour and the whole-wheat flour until dough is stretchy. Add about ½ cup all-purpose flour to form a stiff dough.

*If mixing with a dough hook,* add flour, 1 tablespoon at a time, until dough pulls cleanly from bowl sides.

*If mixing by hand,* scrape dough out on a floured board and knead, adding as little flour as possible to prevent sticking, until dough is smooth. Place hand-mixed dough in a greased bowl; turn over to grease top.

Cover dough (mixed either way) with plastic wrap and let stand 1 hour at room temperature.

Punch down dough and knead on a lightly floured board to expel air. Roll ¼ of the dough out at a time into a rectangle about ⅛ inch thick. Cut 6 equal pieces. Place on lightly floured pans and lightly cover with plastic wrap. If you work quickly, you can let cut sopaipillas stay at room temperature up to 5 minutes; otherwise, refrigerate them until all are ready to fry.

In a deep 3- to 4-quart pan, heat 1½ to 2 inches salad oil to 350° on a deep-fat frying thermometer. Fry 2 or 3 sopaipillas at a time. When the bread begins to puff, gently push the portion where the bubble is developing into hot oil several times to help it puff evenly. Turn several times and cook just until pale gold on both sides, 1 to 2 minutes total. Drain on paper towels.

Serve immediately or keep warm until all are fried. Or if made ahead, cool, cover, and chill up to 2 days; freeze to store longer. To reheat, bake, uncovered, on baking sheets in a 300° oven, turning once, just until warm, 5 to 8 minutes. Do not overheat or they will become hard. Makes 2 dozen.

## PORK STEW WITH PURSLANE OR SPINACH

*Purslane, a weed common in Western gardens in late spring and summer, adds slightly crisp texture and mildly tart flavor to this pork stew. The dish harks back to hacienda days when the cook gathered greens to add to meals' variety. Spinach is an all-year option.*

    4  to 5 pounds boneless pork
       shoulder
    4  cloves garlic
       Water
       Tomatillo sauce (recipe follows)
       Salt
    8  to 10 cups purslane (verdolaga)
       sprigs (about 1½ lb.), coarse stems
       discarded; or 14 cups lightly
       packed spinach leaves (about
       1½ lb.)

Trim fat off pork; reserve for sauce. Cut meat into 1½-inch cubes; place in a 5- to 6-quart ovenproof pan with garlic and 2 cups water. Cover and bring to a boil; reduce heat. Simmer for 45 minutes.

Remove from heat and ladle out 2 cups broth; skim and discard fat, then reserve broth for sauce. Bake meat in pan, uncovered, in a 425° oven until well browned, about 1 hour. Stir often.

Return pan to direct heat; add tomatillo sauce and season to taste with salt. Stir to scrape browned bits free. Simmer, covered, until meat is very tender when pierced, about 1 hour. (At this point, you can let stew cool, then cover and chill for up to 3 days; cook, covered, stirring occasionally over low heat until hot, before continuing.)

Rinse purslane well; drain in a colander. Pour 2 to 4 quarts boiling water over greens to wilt them; drain. Pour stew into a serving bowl; top with greens. Makes 8 to 10 servings.

**Tomatillo sauce.** Remove husks from 2 pounds **tomatillos** (about 8 cups); rinse tomatillos and put into a 10- by 15-inch rimmed baking pan. Bake in a 500° oven until tinged with brown, about 15 minutes. (Or use 3 cans, 13 oz.-size, tomatillos.) In a blender or food processor, whirl tomatillos and 4 stemmed and seeded **fresh** or canned **jalapeño chilies** until puréed. Set aside.

In a 12- to 14-inch frying pan over medium heat, render enough **pork fat** to make ¼ cup; discard fat lumps. Add 4 large **onions,** sliced, and 3 cloves **garlic,** minced or pressed. Stir often until onions are golden. Add reserved **broth;** boil, uncovered, until almost all liquid has evaporated. Pour in tomatillos. Use hot or cold. If made ahead, cover and refrigerate for up to 3 days.

## HUEVOS RANCHEROS

*A long-time Western favorite, huevos rancheros are simply eggs served ranch- or farm-style.*

*Popular for brunch or supper throughout the West, the traditional versions always include eggs, corn tortillas, a sauce or two, and a side dish of beans. Beyond this, the dish is cooked and garnished according to your preference. From Sunset's past, here's one way to go.*

*(Continued on next page)*

*Pork is simmered to succulence with seasonings native to the Americas. In mission and hacienda days, wild greens would have filled in for the spinach.*

## ...HUEVOS RANCHEROS

**Corn tortillas (directions follow)**
**Scrambled eggs (directions follow)**
**Medium hot sauce (directions follow)**
**Garnishes: avocado slices, fresh cilantro (coriander), chopped green onions, shredded jack or mild cheddar cheese, lime wedges**
**Salsa, homemade (directions follow) or purchased**

For each serving, place 1 or 2 tortillas on a plate; top with a serving of scrambled eggs, about ½ cup sauce, and garnish as desired. Accompany with salsa. Serves 6.

**Corn tortillas.** You need 6 to 12 **corn tortillas.** To toast, moisten your hands lightly with **water;** rub over tortillas, 1 at a time. Place tortilla flat in an ungreased heavy frying pan or on a griddle over medium heat; turn frequently until soft and pliable, about 30 seconds. Stack hot tortillas in a covered dish or wrap in foil. Keep hot for up to 2 hours on an electric warming tray or in a 150° oven.

**Scrambled eggs.** Melt 1 to 2 tablespoons **butter** or margarine in a 10- to 12-inch frying pan over medium-low heat. With a fork, blend 6 **large eggs** with 2 tablespoons **water** and ¼ teaspoon **salt,** or 12 large eggs with ¼ cup water and ½ teaspoon salt. Pour eggs into pan. As eggs begin to set, push cooked portions aside with a spatula to let uncooked egg flow underneath. Repeat until eggs are cooked.

**Medium hot sauce.** Mince 2 large **onions.** Combine in a 10- to 12-inch frying pan with 3 tablespoons **salad oil** and ½ cup diced **red** or green **bell pepper.** Cook, stirring, on medium-high heat until soft. Add 1 can (14 oz.) **pear-shaped tomatoes** (break up with spoon) and liquid, 2 cups **regular strength chicken broth,** 2 cans (10 oz. *each*) **red chili sauce,** and ½ teaspoon *each* **dry oregano leaves** and **cumin seed.** Boil, uncovered, stirring to prevent sticking, until sauce is reduced to about 3 cups. If made ahead, let cool, cover, and chill up to 3 days. Reheat to use.

**Salsa.** Core 1 large firm-ripe **tomato** and mince. Also mince 6 to 8 **green onions** (roots trimmed) and most of the green tops. Mix to taste with 2 to 4 tablespoons **canned diced green chilies,** and **salt** and **pepper.** Makes about 1 cup.

*Huevos rancheros is a catch-all term for eggs and tortillas. This version is served in the kitchen of Margaret and Nathaniel Owings in Jacoma, New Mexico.*

# Beef Brisket—Baked Long & Slow

**T**HE EASIEST APPROACH *to beef brisket— long, slow baking—is also an ideal way to get tender, succulent results. Potatoes can bake right alongside to make a warming winter meal.*

*In these two recipes, fresh whole briskets (not corned) bake for about 4 hours. For one dish, port, lemon, and onion flavor the meat as it cooks; later, you reduce the mixture to a shiny marmalade topping. To season the second brisket, use mushrooms, onions, and red wine.*

## BEEF BRISKET WITH ONION-LEMON MARMALADE & SWEET POTATOES

1  beef brisket (5 to 6 lb.)
2  medium-size onions, thinly sliced
2  medium-size lemons, thinly sliced
1  cup port or apple juice
½  cup firmly packed brown sugar
1  tablespoon dry marjoram leaves
1  teaspoon coarsely ground pepper
8  to 10 medium-size sweet potatoes (about 5 lb. total)
   About 8 kale leaves, rinsed and drained, optional

Trim and discard excess fat from brisket. In a 12- by 18-inch roasting pan, place onion slices and ¾ of lemon slices; enclose remaining lemon in plastic wrap and chill. Lay brisket on top of onion and lemon.

Mix together port, brown sugar, and marjoram; stir until sugar dissolves, then pour evenly over brisket. Sprinkle brisket with pepper and cover roasting pan tightly with foil. Bake in a 300° oven until brisket is very tender when pierced, about 4 hours.

Meanwhile, about 1½ hours before brisket is scheduled to be done, pierce each sweet potato with a fork and set on oven rack alongside or above brisket.

When brisket is tender, uncover pan and return it to the oven to brown the meat slightly, about 15 minutes. Remove brisket from pan and place on a platter; keep warm. When potatoes are soft when pressed, remove them from oven, add to brisket platter, and keep warm.

Skim off and discard fat from pan juices. Place the roasting pan over high heat; boil juices, uncovered, stirring often. As the mixture thickens, reduce heat to medium and stir constantly; cook until thick and shiny, and reduced to about 1½ cups, 20 to 30 minutes.

Spoon marmalade over brisket, then garnish with reserved chilled lemon slices. Decorate platter with kale leaves. To serve, slice brisket across grain. Makes 8 to 10 servings.

## BEEF BRISKET WITH MUSHROOMS

1  beef brisket (5 to 6 lb.)
4  teaspoons olive oil or salad oil
1  large onion, thinly sliced
1  tablespoon dry rosemary
3  cloves garlic, minced or pressed
1  pound mushrooms, thinly sliced
1  teaspoon coarsely ground pepper
1  cup dry red wine or regular-strength beef broth
8  to 10 medium-size russet potatoes (about 5 lb. total)
2  tablespoons cornstarch mixed with ¼ cup water
   Italian parsley sprigs, optional

Remove excess fat from brisket. Place meat in a 12- by 18-inch roasting pan.

To a 10- to 12-inch frying pan, add 2 teaspoons oil, onion, rosemary, and garlic. Cook over medium-high heat, stirring often, until onion is limp and light gold, 8 to 10 minutes. Remove from pan and set aside. Add remaining 2 teaspoons oil and mushrooms; cook, stirring often, until juices evaporate and mushrooms are lightly browned, about 8 minutes. Mix mushrooms and onion; spoon over brisket.

Sprinkle brisket with pepper and pour wine over meat. Cover pan tightly with foil. Bake in a 300° oven until brisket is very tender when pierced, about 4 hours.

Meanwhile, about 1½ hours before brisket is scheduled to be done, pierce each potato with a fork and set on oven rack alongside or above brisket.

When brisket is tender, uncover pan and return to oven to brown meat slightly, about 15 minutes. Remove brisket, mushrooms, and onions from pan and place on a platter; keep warm.

*Cut across grain of tender brisket topped with shiny onion-lemon marmalade and lemon slices. Sauce's sweet-tart flavor complements beef and sweet potatoes.*

When potatoes are soft when pressed, remove from oven, add to brisket platter, and keep warm.

Skim off and discard fat from pan juices. Measure juices; if more than 2 cups, place roasting pan over high heat; boil juices, uncovered, stirring often until reduced to 2 cups. Stir cornstarch mixture into juices and bring to a boil. Pour 1 cup of pan juices over brisket and offer remaining sauce to spoon over each serving. Garnish platter with parsley. To serve, slice brisket across grain. Serves 8 to 10.

# Easy-on-the-Waistline Appetizers

**E**ASY ON A COOK'S TIME *and kind to a guest's waistline, most of these lean appetizers take a half-hour or less to prepare, and all can be made well before the party begins.*

*Make one recipe or several. Ingredients are mostly vegetables, seafood, and lean meats, flavored with lively seasonings.*

## SHRIMP WITH TART DIPPING SAUCE

35 **chives,** *each* about 7 inches long
1 **pound cooked, shelled, and deviened medium-size shrimp** (31 to 35 per lb.)
 **Tart dipping sauce (recipe follows)**

Tie a chive around the center of each shrimp. Put shrimp on platter with sauce in a small bowl. If made ahead, cover and chill up to 4 hours. Makes 31 to 35 pieces, about 8 appetizer servings.

**Tart dipping sauce.** Stir together ¼ cup *each* **dry white wine** and **white wine vinegar,** 1 tablespoon *each* minced **shallots** and **chives,** and ½ teaspoon **pepper.**

## GREEN BEAN KNOTS

1 **tablespoon sesame seed**
 **Water**
¾ **pound Chinese long beans or 1½ pounds slender green onions, ends trimmed, cut into 7-inch lengths**
1 **teaspoon ground ginger**
1 **tablespoon Oriental sesame oil**
2 **tablespoons seasoned rice vinegar, or white wine vinegar mixed with 2 teaspoons sugar**
2 **tablespoons soy sauce**
3 **tablespoons sliced green onions**

In a 10- to 12-inch frying pan, cook sesame seed over medium heat until golden, 3 to 5 minutes; shake pan often. Remove from pan and let cool.

In pan, bring ¼ inch water to a boil over high heat. Add beans, cover, and simmer until beans are tender when pierced, about 10 minutes (4 minutes for onions). Drain; immerse in ice water.

In a bowl, stir together ginger, sesame oil, vinegar, soy sauce, and sliced green onions. Add beans and mix to coat evenly. Cover and let stand 1 hour; stir

several times. If made ahead, chill until next day.

Up to 2 hours before serving, drain beans, then very gently tie each into a loose knot (some may break; reserve these for other uses). Sprinkle with sesame seed, and place on a plate. Makes about 40 knots, 10 to 12 appetizer servings.

## LIME & CHILI-SPIKED VEGETABLES

Trim roots from about 24 **radishes,** then remove all but a few of the best-looking leaves from each. Rinse radishes. Scrub and peel 1 pound **jicama;** cut lengthwise into ½-inch-wide, ½-inch-thick sticks. Set vegetables in a dish or basket. If made ahead, cover and chill until the next day.

In a small bowl, mix 3 tablespoons *each* **lime juice** and **tequila** (or all lime juice). In another bowl, mix 2 tablespoons **chili powder** and 1 teaspoon **salt.** To eat, dip vegetables in lime mixture, then in chili salt. Makes 8 to 10 appetizer servings.

*Chive ties dress up purchased cooked shrimp paired with tangy homemade sauce.*

*Dunk radishes and jicama in mixture of lime juice and tequila, then in chili salt.*

## Bell Pepper & Oyster Boats

4 medium-size red bell peppers, stemmed and seeded
1 can (3¾ oz.) small smoked oysters, drained
2 small packages (3 oz. *each*) cream cheese
2 tablespoons lemon juice
1 teaspoon celery seed
64 chive pieces, *each* 4 inches long

Cut each bell pepper lengthwise into 8 equal strips. If necessary, cut larger oysters in half so you have 32 pieces.

In a bowl, beat cream cheese, lemon juice, and celery seed until smooth. Spread about 1 teaspoon of mixture over 1½ inches on an end of each pepper strip. Place 1 oyster piece and 2 chives on cheese. If made ahead, cover and chill until next day. Makes 32 boats, 8 appetizer servings.

## Eggplant & Goat Cheese Rolls

1 pound Oriental eggplant (about 7) or a 1-pound regular globe eggplant, stems removed
1½ tablespoons olive oil
3 ounces soft goat cheese, such as Montrachet
⅓ cup packed watercress sprigs, washed and crisped

Cut eggplant lengthwise into ¼- to ⅓-inch-thick slices; if using globe variety, cut slices in half lengthwise. Place in a single layer in two 10- by 15-inch rimmed baking pans. Lightly brush both sides of eggplant with oil.

Bake eggplant, uncovered, in a 450° oven for 8 minutes. Turn over and bake until very soft when pressed, about 5 minutes more. Remove slices from oven and let cool in the pans.

Place about ½ teaspoon cheese at 1 end of each slice. Top each dollop with an equal portion of watercress; let some leaves hang over edges. Roll up. If made ahead, cover and chill until next day. Makes 20 to 24 rolls, 5 or 6 appetizer servings.

Speckled quail eggs are hard-cooked; peel and season with toasted salt and pepper.

## Quail Eggs with Toasted Pepper

Place 1½ dozen **quail eggs** in a 1½- to 2-quart pan; cover with **water.** Bring to a boil over high heat, then simmer, uncovered, for 6 minutes. Serve warm in shell. Or if made ahead, run cold water over eggs, then chill up to 3 days; serve cold.

In a 7- to 8-inch frying pan over medium heat, cook 2 teaspoons **salt** and 2 tablespoons **cracked pepper** until salt is pale gold, about 5 minutes; shake pan often. Spoon into a small bowl. If made ahead, cover and let stand up to 1 week.

To serve, place eggs in a basket. Guests peel eggs and dip them into pepper mixture to eat. Makes 6 appetizer servings.

## Beef & Broccoli with Horseradish Dip

Cut a ⅔-pound slice of **cooked boneless roast beef** or turkey breast (or some of each) into ½-inch cubes. Arrange on a platter with 3 cups **broccoli flowerets.**

In a bowl, beat 2 small packages (3 oz. *each*) **cream cheese,** ¼ cup **prepared horseradish,** ⅓ cup **unflavored yogurt,** and 1 teaspoon **cracked pepper** until smooth. Add **salt** to taste. Spoon into a small bowl. If made ahead, cover and chill beef, broccoli, and dip until next day. Provide wooden picks for dabbing morsels into dip. Makes 6 appetizer servings.

# More January Recipes

OTHER DISHES *to brighten wintry January menus feature a warming soup reminiscent of minestrone; a home-style slaw crunchy with green peas, cabbage, and pecans; two recipes pairing Stilton cheese with port wine; and a quick-to-make honey-nut spread for breakfast breads.*

## MEDITERRANEAN PASTA SOUP

*A variation on minestrone, this winter-weather soup combines pasta, beans, and vegetables in a light broth. Thyme, lemon peel, and Italian sausage add flavor and a delightful aroma.*

- ¼ pound mild Italian sausage
- 1 small onion, diced
- 2 cloves garlic, minced or pressed
- 1½ teaspoons dry thyme leaves
- ¼ teaspoon pepper
- ½ cup (¼ lb.) dry small white beans
- 3 quarts regular-strength chicken broth
- 1 teaspoon grated lemon peel
- 2 small carrots, peeled and diced
- 2 stalks celery, diced
- 1 cup dry small shell pasta
- 1 medium-size tomato, cored and cut into ½-inch cubes
- 1 cup (3 oz.) lightly packed shredded Swiss cheese, optional

Remove casings from sausage and crumble into a 4- to 5-quart pan. Cook over medium-high heat, stirring often, until lightly browned, about 4 minutes. Add onion, garlic, thyme, and pepper; cook, stirring occasionally, until onions are light gold, about 6 minutes.

Remove any debris from beans; rinse and drain beans. Add beans, broth, and lemon peel to pan. Bring to a boil over high heat. Cover, reduce heat, and simmer until beans are tender to bite, about 2 hours.

Add carrots, celery, and pasta to broth. Bring to a boil over high heat; reduce heat, cover, and simmer until vegetables and pasta are tender to bite, about 15 minutes. Ladle into bowls and offer tomato and cheese to sprinkle on soup as desired. Makes 3 quarts, 6 to 8 servings. —*Mrs. Scott Kemper, Sacramento.*

*Crunchy cabbage slaw with peas and pecans starts dinner the way Grandma used to. Accompany it with chicken and biscuits.*

## PEA & ROASTED PECAN SLAW

*Light and simple, this old-fashioned salad uses a creamy dressing to bind bright green peas, sweet roasted pecans, and shredded cabbage. Serve it with other straightforward dishes—perhaps a roasted chicken and buttermilk biscuits. To drink, offer milk or lime phosphate (lime syrup mixed with sparkling water).*

- 1 package (10 oz.) frozen petite peas, thawed and drained
- 2 cups finely shredded green cabbage
- 3 green onions, thinly sliced
- ¼ cup *each* sour cream and mayonnaise
- 1 tablespoon white wine vinegar
- 1 teaspoon Dijon mustard
- ¼ teaspoon curry powder
- 5 to 7 romaine leaves, washed and crisped
- 1 cup dry-roasted pecan halves
  Salt

In a large bowl, combine peas, cabbage, and onions; set aside. In a small bowl, blend sour cream, mayonnaise, vinegar, mustard, and curry powder. If made ahead, cover and chill vegetables and dressing separately up to 1 day.

Just before serving, arrange romaine leaves on a serving platter or in a bowl. Mix dressing and vegetables. Stir in ½ cup pecans; add salt to taste. Spoon salad onto leaves and sprinkle with remaining nuts. Serve at once. Makes 6 servings. —*June M. Davis, San Anselmo, Calif.*

## PORK TENDERLOINS WITH STILTON, PORT & JALAPEÑOS

*Classic partners—Stilton cheese and port wine—are usually savored unadorned. But combining the flavors is equally successful in a more elaborate presentation.*

*Here, roast pork tenderloin is topped with a creamy Stilton and port sauce.*

- **2 or 3 pork tenderloins (***each* **½ to ¾ lb; 1½ lb. total)**
- **1 tablespoon salad oil**
- **1 cup port**
- **½ cup regular-strength chicken broth**
- **½ cup whipping cream**
- **¼ pound Stilton cheese, crumbled**
- **1 or 2 fresh jalapeño chilies, halved lengthwise, stemmed, seeded, and slivered**

With a small sharp knife, trim surface fat and silvery membrane from pork. In a 10- to 12-inch frying pan over medium-high heat, brown pork in oil, turning to cook evenly. Transfer meat to a 9- or 10-inch-square pan. Bake in a 400° oven until a meat thermometer inserted in thickest part registers 160°, about 15 minutes.

Meanwhile, discard fat in frying pan and add port and broth. Boil over high heat until reduced to ¾ cup, about 3 minutes. Stir in cream and continue to boil until sauce forms large shiny bubbles, about 5 minutes more. Add cheese and chilies; stir until cheese melts. Remove from heat.

Slice meat across the grain; fan equal portions on each of 4 dinner plates. Spoon sauce over meat. Makes 4 servings.—*Michael Roberts, Los Angeles.*

## PORT-POACHED PEARS WITH STILTON CUSTARD

*Stilton is one of the grand cheeses of England. Port originated in Portugal, but it is also produced in this country. For dessert, pair these traditional mates in port-poached pears coated with Stilton custard and port wine syrup.*

- **2¼ cups port**
- **½ cup plus 2 tablespoons sugar**
- **4 firm-ripe pears with stems, peeled**
- **1 large egg yolk**
- **⅓ cup milk**
- **⅓ cup crumbled Stilton cheese**
- **¼ teaspoon vanilla**

In a 3- to 4-quart pan, bring port and ½ cup of the sugar to a boil over high heat. Add pears, cover, and simmer until pears are tender when pierced, 10 to 15 minutes. Turn pears over halfway through cooking. Lift pears from syrup to a bowl.

Over high heat, boil syrup, uncovered, until reduced to ½ cup, 15 to 20 minutes. Pour over pears and let cool. Cover and chill until cold, at least 2 hours or until the next day. After 1 hour, turn pears over in syrup.

In a bowl, lightly whisk together yolk and the remaining 2 tablespoons sugar. In a 1- to 2-quart pan, heat milk until scalding, stirring often. Gradually whisk milk into yolk and sugar. Return mixture to pan. Cook over medium-low heat, stirring constantly, until custard thickly coats the back of a metal spoon, about 3 minutes. Add Stilton; stir just until cheese melts. Remove from heat and stir in vanilla. Let cool, then cover and chill until cold, at least 2 hours or until next day.

To serve, turn pears over in syrup, then lift from syrup and set on 4 small rimmed plates. Carefully spoon syrup over half of each pear and cheese custard over other half. Makes 4 servings.

## WHIPPED HONEY-NUT SPREAD

*To create this crunchy-sweet spread for breakfast breads, you just blend ground toasted nuts with whipped honey. Since it takes only minutes to do, you might want to make several kinds and have them on hand as quick hostess gifts.*

- **1 cup shelled hazelnuts or almonds (or 1½ cups unshelled roasted pistachios)**
- **1 cup (12-oz. container) whipped honey**

Place hazelnuts or almonds in a single layer in a 9- to 10-inch-wide pan and bake in a 350° oven until golden throughout (cut one in half to check color), 10 to 12 minutes. Let nuts cool. (If using pistachios, omit this step.)

Shell pistachios, if used. To skin hazelnuts or pistachios (almonds do not need to be skinned), place nuts in a clean towel and rub gently to remove loose peel; the nuts do not need to be completely skinned. Place nuts in a food processor or blender. Whirl, pulsing on and off, just until finely chopped; do not whirl into a paste.

In a bowl, combine honey and nuts; mix to blend. Serve, or pack into small containers, cover, and store in a cool place up to 1 month. Makes 1½ cups.

*Creamy whipped honey gets crunch from bits of toasted nuts; spread it on English muffins for a breakfast treat.*

## SPINACH & BROCCOLI QUICHE

Pastry for a 10-inch pie shell
6 ounces Swiss cheese, sliced
1 package (10 oz.) frozen chopped spinach, thawed
2 cups lightly cooked broccoli flowerets
1 tablespoon butter or margarine
¼ pound mushrooms, sliced
½ cup chopped green onions
4 large eggs
1 cup milk or half-and-half
1½ teaspoons dry Italian herb seasoning or dry basil
½ teaspoon salt, or to taste

On a floured board, roll pastry large enough to line a 9-inch quiche pan. Line pan with dough, flute edges, and prick bottom with fork. Bake in a 400° oven for 8 minutes (pastry will still be pale); cool.

Lay half the cheese over the crust. Squeeze moisture from spinach; sprinkle spinach and broccoli over cheese. In a 6- to 8-inch frying pan, stir butter, mushrooms, and onion over medium-high heat until moisture evaporates; sprinkle over broccoli. Top mushroom mixture with remaining cheese.

Mix eggs, milk, Italian herbs, and salt; pour over filling. Bake in a 375° oven until golden, about 40 minutes. Serves 6.
—*Emily Connery, Palo Alto, Calif.*

*Roll pastry large enough to line quiche pan; fill with vegetables and cheese.*

## MIXED RICE SALAD

2¼ cups water
1 package (6 oz.) long-grain and wild rice mix
½ cup *each* mayonnaise and unflavored yogurt
½ cup sliced green onions
¼ cup chopped parsley
Salt and pepper
1 cup diced, peeled cucumbers, chilled
1 cup diced tomatoes, chilled
¼ to ½ cup chopped celery, chilled
½ cup frozen peas, thawed, chilled

In a 2- to 3-quart pan, bring water to a boil over high heat. Add rice and return to a boil. (Do not use seasoning packet; if seasoning is mixed with rice, rinse rice in a strainer under cold water to remove seasoning.) Cover pan and cook on low heat until water is absorbed and rice is tender, about 30 minutes. Uncover and let rice cool to room temperature, about 45 minutes.

Fluff room-temperature rice with a fork, then stir in mayonnaise, yogurt, green onion, and parsley. Season to taste with salt and pepper. Pour mixture into a salad bowl. Place cucumbers, tomatoes, celery, and peas on rice mixture. Mix at the table to serve. Makes 6 servings.—*Cynthia Hessin, Denver, Colo.*

*Peas, tomato, crunchy celery, and diced cucumber top a yogurt-dressed rice salad.*

## LAYERED ENCHILADA CASSEROLE

¼ cup chopped onion
1 tablespoon salad oil
1 can (28 oz.) tomatoes, chopped
2 cans (about 2 oz. *each*) sliced ripe olives, drained
1 can (4 oz.) diced green chilies
Salt
9 corn tortillas (6-in. diameter), cut into 1-inch-wide strips
1½ cups sour cream
2 cups (8 oz.) lightly packed shredded cheddar cheese

In a 10- to 12-inch frying pan, add onion to oil and cook, stirring, over medium-high heat just until onion begins to brown, about 5 minutes. Add tomatoes and their juice, olives, and chilies. Bring to a boil on high heat; reduce heat and simmer, uncovered, 10 minutes to blend flavors. Remove from heat. Add salt to taste.

In a shallow 2-quart casserole, layer ⅓ of the tortilla strips, tomato sauce, sour cream, and cheese. Repeat layers, ending with cheese.

Bake casserole, uncovered, in a 350° oven until mixture is hot in center (sauce will bubble at edges), about 35 minutes. Makes 4 servings.—*Audree Jones, San Francisco.*

*Layer tortilla strips, tomato sauce, sour cream, and cheese in this homey casserole.*

## CHINESE PLUM SAUCE

2 cans (1 lb. *each*) plums in heavy syrup, drained; save syrup
¾ cup water
1 tablespoon salad oil
Spice mixture (recipe follows)
½ cup canned tomato sauce
1 medium-size onion, chopped
1 tablespoon *each* soy sauce and Worcestershire
¼ teaspoon liquid hot pepper seasoning
1 tablespoon rice or wine vinegar

Remove pits from plums. Whirl plums with 1¼ cups of their syrup and the water in a blender until puréed; set aside. Discard remaining syrup.

Heat oil in a 3- to 4-quart pan on medium-high heat; stir spice mixture into hot oil. Add plum purée, tomato sauce, onion, soy, Worcestershire, and pepper seasoning. Boil uncovered, stirring often, until reduced to 3 cups, about 25 minutes. Stir in vinegar; serve warm. Or cover and chill up to 3 weeks. Makes 3 cups. —*Kathryn Williams, San Mateo, Calif.*

**Spice mixture.** Blend 1 teaspoon **Chinese five spice** (or ¼ teaspoon *each* ground cinnamon, clove, ginger, and anise seed); ½ teaspoon *each* **ground cinnamon, ground cumin,** and **dry mustard;** and ¼ teaspoon **pepper.**

*Homemade Chinese plum sauce goes well with roasted chicken and watercress.*

## SWEET POTATO MUFFINS

1 cup mashed, cooked, peeled sweet potatoes
About 1 cup sugar
½ cup milk
⅓ cup butter or margarine, melted
1 large egg
1⅓ cups all-purpose flour
2 teaspoons baking powder
About 1¼ teaspoons ground cinnamon
¼ teaspoon ground nutmeg
¼ cup *each* chopped walnuts and raisins
½ teaspoon salt, or to taste

In a bowl, combine sweet potatoes, 1 cup sugar, milk, butter, and egg; smoothly blend with a fork.

In another bowl, mix flour, baking powder, ½ teaspoon cinnamon, nutmeg, walnuts, raisins, and salt. Add potato mixture; stir just until blended.

Spoon batter into 12 buttered muffin cups (2½ inches across), filling each about full. Mix 2 teaspoons sugar with ¾ teaspoon cinnamon and sprinkle evenly over batter.

Bake in a 350° oven until muffins spring back when lightly touched, about 25 minutes. Remove from pan and serve warm. Makes 12 muffins. —*Jill S. Ferst, Lake Forest, Calif.*

*Spicy, raisin-studded sweet potato muffins are great warm for breakfast.*

## MELTED BRIE WITH WINTER FRUITS

¾ cup chopped pitted dates
1 *each* small apple and small firm-ripe pear, peeled, cored, and diced
½ cup currants
½ cup chopped pecans
⅓ cup rosé wine or apple juice
1 wheel (2 lb.) ripe brie, well chilled
Thin baguette slices, toasted, if desired

In a bowl, mix dates, apple, pear, currants, pecans, and wine. Set aside to soften fruit, about 2 hours.

Cut brie in half to make two round layers. Place 1 layer, cut side up, in an attractive 10-inch shallow-rimmed baking dish (such as a quiche pan). Spread cut side with 2¼ cups fruit. Place remaining cheese layer, cut side down, on fruit. Spoon remaining fruit onto center of cheese. If made ahead, cover and chill filled cheese round up to 2 days.

Bake brie, uncovered, in a 350° oven until it melts at edges and center is warm, 25 to 30 minutes. Offer hot brie from baking dish; scoop up cheese with knife to spread on bread. Makes about 16 servings. —*Danielle Lavery, Honolulu, Hawaii.*

*Spread warm brie with wine-macerated fruit filling on thin baguette slices.*

SEDCO HILLS LIES EAST *of Lake Elsinore in Southern California, and, according to Arthur Vinsel—admittedly a temporary resident—it does little more. It just lies there. It has never produced notable achievements in science, art, or literature. In fact, says Vinsel, this recipe will represent the first recognition Sedco Hills has won outside its own neighborhood.*

*Vinsel's vision of his Sedco Hills hog bursting upon world consciousness like a new comet comes to pass below. If the moment of notoriety should prove brief, let Sedco Hills remember that, although Andy Warhol predicted that fame would eventually come to everybody, he also said that it might last only 15 minutes.*

*The name Arturo's Sedco Hills Hog makes a strong statement; if you think the name might put off your guests, simply call it Carnitas Arturo.*

*"Chef Vinson envisions his Sedco Hills hog bursting upon world consciousness like a new comet."*

### ARTURO'S SEDCO HILLS HOG

- 4 large (about ½ lb. *each*) pork shoulder steaks
- 1 large orange
- 1 teaspoon *each* dry oregano leaves, ground cumin, and grated lemon peel
- 1 tablespoon lemon juice
- 2 large onions, chopped
- 3 tablespoons butter or margarine
- 2 large red or green bell peppers, stemmed, seeded, and diced
- 2 cloves garlic, minced or pressed
- ½ cup prepared mild taco salsa
- 1 cup dry white wine
  Cilantro (coriander) sprigs
  Warm soft corn tortillas
  Salt and pepper

Trim excess fat from pork; set steaks aside. Ream the juice from the orange. In a 9- by 13-inch baking dish, combine orange juice, oregano, cumin, lemon peel, and lemon juice. Turn meat in mixture to coat well; set aside. Mix onions with the liquid, then settle meat back into dish, topping with about half the onion mixture. Cover and let stand at least 30 minutes, or cover and chill up to overnight.

Melt 1 tablespoon of the butter in a 10- to 12-inch frying pan over medium-high heat; scrape onions from meat and add steaks to pan. Cook until meat is browned on both sides, 10 to 12 minutes, then lift out and set aside.

Add the remaining 2 tablespoons of butter to pan on medium-high heat. Add onion marinade, bell peppers, and garlic. Cook, stirring occasionally, until onions are soft, about 10 minutes.

Return pork to pan. Add taco sauce and wine, and bring to a boil; cover, reduce heat, and simmer until pork is very tender when pierced, 1 to 1¼ hours. Lift out pork and place on a platter; keep warm. On high heat, boil pan mixture, stirring until most of the liquid has evaporated, 8 to 10 minutes. Pour over pork and garnish with cilantro. Serve with tortillas; add salt and pepper to taste. Makes 4 servings.

*Arthur R. Vinsel*

*Lake Elsinore, Calif.*

IF WE AGREE *that bread is the staff of life, we should make every effort to find an honest, sturdy staff to support us, not a soft, spongy one that will let us down when we lean on it.*

*James Lee's Oatmeal Cracked Wheat Bread is just such a staff. It has all the nutritional content that whole grains bring, along with a high fiber content.*

*More apparent, though, are the taste and the texture. The first complements the flavors of good butter, honey, or jam instead of merely holding them up, while the second can stand up to the butter knife (or your teeth) without flattening into the dough whence it sprang.*

## OATMEAL CRACKED WHEAT BREAD

- 1 package active dry yeast
- 2½ cups warm water (about 110°)
- 5½ to 6 cups unbleached all-purpose flour
- ½ cup bulgur (cracked wheat)
- 1½ cups regular rolled oats
- ⅓ cup wheat germ
- ⅓ cup firmly packed brown sugar
- 2 teaspoons light molasses
- ¾ teaspoon salt

In a large bowl, sprinkle yeast over water and let stand about 5 minutes. Add 2½ cups of the all-purpose flour; beat until well moistened. Cover with plastic wrap and let stand at room temperature until bubbly, at least 6 hours or up to 24 hours.

To this sponge add the cracked wheat, rolled oats, wheat germ, sugar, molasses, and salt.

*To mix with a dough hook,* stir until well combined, then add 2½ cups more all-purpose flour and beat on high speed for about 8 minutes, then add more flour, 2 tablespoons at a time, until dough pulls cleanly from side of bowl. Cover bowl with plastic wrap.

*To mix by hand,* beat sponge mixture until stretchy and well moistened. Stir in 2½ cups all-purpose flour to make a stiff dough. Scrape dough out onto a floured board and knead, adding as little flour as possible to prevent sticking, until dough is smooth and elastic, about 15 minutes. Place dough in a greased bowl and cover with plastic wrap.

Either way, let dough rise in a warm place until doubled, about 1½ hours.

Punch down dough and let rest for 10 minutes; cover with plastic wrap. Divide dough into 3 equal portions; shape each into a loaf and place in a well-greased 4- by 8-inch loaf pan. Cover with plastic wrap and let rise in a warm place until doubled, about 45 minutes.

Bake, uncovered, in a 375° oven until loaves are browned and sound hollow when lightly tapped, 35 to 40 minutes. Let cool in pans for 10 minutes, then turn out onto racks and let cool completely. Makes 3 loaves, each about 1 pound.

*San Mateo, Calif.*

**S**HRIMP COURAGEOUS? *What can it mean? Chef Eric Lie gives us no more hint than the name itself. It could refer to the courage a cook needs to buy shrimp in these inflationary times, but more likely it refers to the boldness of the seasoning, which blends brandy, chili powder, ginger, mustard, pepper, and Worcestershire.*

*Can the delicate shrimp stand up to such treatment without damage to their character? Our tasters agree that they can, and that this curryless curry is a triumph.*

*"Can the delicate shrimp stand up to such treatment?"*

## SHRIMP COURAGEOUS

- 6 tablespoons butter or margarine
- 2 tablespoons lemon juice
- 1 pound medium-size shrimp (31 to 35 per lb.), peeled, deveined, and butterflied
- ¼ cup brandy
- 1 tablespoon Worcestershire
- 1 tablespoon Dijon mustard
- ½ teaspoon chili powder
- ¼ teaspoon *each* ground ginger, dry tarragon, and pepper
- ¼ pound mushrooms, sliced
- 2 tablespoons all-purpose flour
- 2 cups milk
  Salt
  Hot cooked brown rice
  Chopped parsley

Melt 3 tablespoons of the butter in a 10- to 12-inch frying pan over medium-high heat. Add lemon juice and shrimp and stir just until shrimp turn pink, 2 to 3 minutes. Add brandy and, when bubbling, set aflame (not beneath a vent, fan, or anything flammable). Shake pan until flames die. Lift out shrimp with a slotted spoon and set aside.

To pan, add remaining 3 tablespoons butter, Worcestershire, mustard, chili powder, ginger, tarragon, pepper and mushrooms. Cook on medium-high heat, stirring often, until mushrooms are lightly browned, about 5 minutes. Sprinkle flour over mushrooms and stir until mixture is bubbly. Remove from heat; gradually and smoothly stir in milk. Return to medium-high heat and stir until boiling. Add shrimp; stir until hot. Add salt to taste.

Spoon shrimp onto portions of rice and sprinkle with parsley. Makes 4 servings.

*Edmonds, Wash.*

# January Menus

AN INDULGENT LAST HURRAH *for the holidays starts the new year, then belt tightening begins. This month's light, quick-to-prepare meals are in keeping with diet resolutions and back-to-work schedules.*

*Splurge on January 1 with a brunch featuring coffee cake. When calorie counting starts, bowls of borscht, topped with poached eggs, provide slimming but satisfying lunchtime fare. For dinner, swordfish cooks fast under the broiler; follow it with a sweet vegetable tart.*

*Cinnamon-and-sugar bubble cake stars in this informal menu for 6 to 8 people. The rest of the meal needs no cooking.*

*Depending on your schedule, you can shape the coffee cake, refrigerate it overnight, and bake it next day. Or make it the morning you plan to serve it, allowing 2½ to 3 hours for preparation.*

*For 8 people, buy 1 pound each of cheese and meat. Diners can spread meat and cheese slices with a little mustard, roll them up, and eat out of hand. Buy 1½ pounds each of grapes and tangerines.*

## NEW YEAR'S DAY BRUNCH

**Pull-Apart Coffee Cake          Butter
Tangerines          Green Grapes
Jarlsberg, Havarti, or Gouda Cheese
Sliced Ham or Lebanon Bologna
Dijon Mustard
Champagne or Sparkling Cider**

## PULL-APART COFFEE CAKE

  1  **package active dry yeast**
 ¼  **cup warm (110°) water**
 ½  **teaspoon salt**
 ¼  **cup sugar**
 ¼  **cup salad oil**
 ¾  **cup warm (110°) milk**
  1  **large egg**

 About 3½ cups all-purpose flour
  1  **cup raisins**
 ½  **(¼ lb.) butter or margarine, melted
    Cinnamon-nut sugar (recipe
    follows)**

In a large bowl, sprinkle yeast over water; let stand to soften, about 5 minutes. Stir in salt, sugar, oil, milk, and egg until blended. With a dough hook or spoon, stir in 3¼ cups of the flour until smooth.

*To knead with a dough hook,* beat at high speed until dough pulls cleanly from sides of bowl, about 10 minutes. Scrape dough onto a board; knead in raisins.

*To knead by hand,* scrape dough onto a lightly floured board. Knead until smooth and elastic, adding flour as required to prevent sticking, about 10 minutes. Knead in raisins.

Divide dough into 3 equal portions, then cut *each* into 16 equal pieces. Shape segments into balls, roll in butter, then in cinnamon-nut sugar. Stagger balls,

*Pull-apart coffee cake starts the year on a sweet note. Accompany with fruit, meat, cheese, and sparkling cider.*

barely touching, in layers in a greased 9-
to 10-inch ring mold (about 2½-qt. size).
Sprinkle with remaining cinnamon-nut
sugar; drizzle with remaining butter.

Cover lightly with plastic wrap and let
rise in a warm place until puffy, about 45
minutes. (Or chill until puffy, 16 to 18
hours.) Bake in a 350° oven until well
browned, 30 to 35 minutes.

Let cool in pan on a rack for at least 20
minutes or up to 3 hours. Run a knife
between cake and pan sides, then place
a plate on top of pan and turn cake out (if
cake sticks, lightly tap pan to loosen). If
desired, place another plate on top of
cake and gently turn over to serve; if cake
comes apart, restack pieces. Makes 1 loaf
(1 lb.), 6 to 8 servings.—*Mrs. Victor
Greene, Woodland Park, Colo.*

**Cinnamon-nut sugar.** Stir together ¾
cup **sugar,** 1 tablespoon **ground cinnamon,** and ½ cup finely chopped
**walnuts.**

---

### LIGHT LUNCHEON
### BORSCHT

**Red Soup with Poached Eggs**
**Rye Bread      Green Salad**
**Frozen Juice Bars**
**Cabernet Sauvignon or Milk**

---

*Hearty flavors of beets, cabbage, tomatoes,
and red wine make this soup taste richer
than it is. To keep calories low, top it with
yogurt instead of sour cream.*

*You can cook the soup and eggs ahead.
As they reheat, mix salad. If you have a
food processor, use it to cut up the beets.*

### RED SOUP WITH POACHED EGGS

- 1  **medium-size red onion, sliced**
- 2  **tablespoons salad oil**
- 2  **pounds beets (about 10 medium
  size), scrubbed, tops and root ends
  trimmed, and beets cut into
  matchstick-size pieces**
- 2  **cups packed shredded red cabbage**
- 6  **cups regular-strength chicken
  broth**
- ¾  **cup dry red wine, or ¾ cup regular-
  strength chicken broth and 2 tablespoons red wine vinegar**
- 1  **can (about 16 oz.) sliced stewed
  tomatoes**
  **Poached eggs (recipe follows)**
- 1  **to 1½ cups unflavored yogurt**

*Poached egg and rye bread lend substance to
this light beet and cabbage soup.*

In a 5- to 6-quart pan over medium-high
heat, stir onion in oil until golden, about
10 minutes. Stir in beets, cabbage, and
broth. Bring to a boil, then reduce heat
and simmer, covered, until beets are
barely tender when pierced, about 20
minutes.

Stir in wine, then tomatoes and their
liquid. (If made ahead, cool, cover, and
chill until next day.) Return to a simmer
and cook, covered, 10 minutes more.
Ladle soup into bowls, then top with
eggs. Offer yogurt to add to taste. Makes
6 servings.

**Poached eggs.** In a 5- to 6-quart pan,
bring 2 inches **water** to a boil over high
heat. Immerse 6 to 12 **large eggs,** a few
at a time, in water for exactly 8 seconds.
Lift out. Reduce heat so water forms
only very small bubbles on bottom of
pan. Gently break each egg into water,
spacing slightly apart. Cook until set to
your liking, 3 to 5 minutes for soft yolks.
With a slotted spoon, lift out eggs,
drain, and serve.

If made ahead, place eggs in ice water.
Cover and chill up to 24 hours. To reheat,
immerse eggs in hot water for 5 to 10
minutes, until eggs are warm to touch.

---

### QUICK SWORDFISH SUPPER

**Broiled Swordfish with
Tomato-Olive Confetti**
**Steamed Brown Rice**
**Carrot-Parsnip Tart**
**Sauvignon Blanc or Sparkling Water**

---

*Simply prepared fish, with a lime-spiked
tomato and olive relish, offers a healthy
change from rich holiday foods. Serve the
not-too-indulgent carrot-parsnip tart for
dessert.*

*If time is short, make the tart a day
ahead. As rice cooks, wash the watercress,
then prepare the tomato-olive confetti and
broil the fish.*

### BROILED SWORDFISH WITH
### TOMATO-OLIVE CONFETTI

- 1½  **pounds swordfish steaks, about 1¼
  inches thick**
- 1  **tablespoon olive oil or salad oil**
- 3  **cups packed watercress sprigs,
  washed and crisped**
  **Tomato-olive confetti (recipe
  follows)**

Divide fish into 4 equal portions. Place
on an oiled rack in a 12- by 14-inch broiler
pan. Brush top of fish with oil. Broil
about 5 inches below heat for 5 minutes.
Turn fish over and brush with oil. Broil
until fish is no longer opaque in center
(cut to test), 5 to 6 minutes more.

Place an equal portion of watercress
on 4 dinner plates. Set fish on watercress. Spoon equal portions of tomato-
olive confetti over fish and watercress.
Makes 4 servings.

**Tomato-olive confetti.** In a bowl, stir
together 1 medium-size **tomato,** cored
and chopped; ½ cup sliced **pimiento-
stuffed green olives;** 2 tablespoons
drained **capers;** and 3 tablespoons *each*
sliced **green onions, lime juice,** and
**olive oil** or salad oil.

## CARROT-PARSNIP TART

Press-in pastry (recipe follows)
2  cups *each* shredded peeled carrots and parsnips
½  cup water
3  large eggs
1½  teaspoons grated orange peel
1  teaspoon grated lemon peel
2  tablespoons all-purpose flour
⅔  cup sugar
1  cup lemon-flavored yogurt
½  cup pecan halves

Press pastry over bottom and sides of a 9-inch tart pan with removable bottom. Bake in a 325° oven until pale gold, 15 to 20 minutes. Remove from oven.

Meanwhile, place carrots, parsnips, and water in a 10- to 12-inch frying pan over high heat. Bring to a boil, cover, and simmer over low heat until vegetables are very soft to bite and liquid has evaporated, about 12 minutes. Stir occasionally. Remove from heat and let cool.

In a bowl, whisk eggs, orange and lemon peel, flour, sugar, and yogurt until blended. Stir in carrots and parsnips. Pour mixture into the tart shell. Evenly arrange pecans on top in a double row around rim. Bake in a 325° oven until tart no longer jiggles in center when gently shaken, 40 to 45 minutes.

Let cool on a rack for at least 10 minutes; or let cool completely, cover, and chill until next day. Run a knife between crust and pan rim before serving, then remove rim. Makes 8 to 10 servings. — *Roxanne Chan, Albany, Calif.*

**Press-in pastry.** In a food processor or bowl, combine 1 cup **all-purpose flour** and 3 tablespoons **sugar.** Add ⅓ cup **butter** or margarine, cut into small pieces; process or rub with fingers until fine crumbs form. Add 1 **large egg yolk;** process or stir with a fork until dough holds together when pressed.

# FEBRUARY

*Kumquat Meringue Pie (page 32)*

**K**umquats, part of winter's
citrus bounty, were highlighted in the February issue
in pie, jam, gelato, sauce, and other tangy treats. The
confusion of oats—whole, cut, rolled—was tastefully straight-
ened out; shopping tips and a scoopful of recipes offered
some healthy options. A casual dinner party featured boil-as-
you-watch pasta and "steamroller" chicken. We also
showed you how to impress friends with delicate dim
sum *prepared ahead and cooked briefly
in the microwave.*

# Mystery Citrus: Kumquats

**P**RETTY BUT PUZZLING *little gems, kumquats have thin, aromatic skin that's edible and sweet tasting. But the fruit inside is lemon-sour, with few or many seeds.*

*Native to Asia, the kumquat allegedly takes its name from its Chinese title, chin kan, or golden orange. Although closely related to citrus species, kumquats are of the genus Fortunella. The fruit grows on an evergreen shrub or small tree with bright green pointed leaves and orange-perfumed blossoms.*

*There are at least six different kinds of kumquats, but the one you see most in produce markets is the oblong-shaped Nagami, or oval kumquat; it's usually 1 to 2 inches long. Less frequently found is the Meiwa, or large, round kumquat. Other kinds are mostly used as ornamental plants, but fruits of all are edible.*

*Fruit may cling year-round on established plants, but you usually see kumquats in markets from as early as November until as late as June. Kept refrigerated, fruit of good quality keeps well for up to a*

*month after harvest. Late-season fruit is often sweeter.*

*Kumquats are a versatile ingredient in the hands of the creative cook because their sweet-sour flavor suits a number of dishes.*

*We first approach this tasty mystery with a pastry that uses the fruit raw and also cooked as jam.*

*Preserved kumquats do double duty with barbecued pork. You use the syrup from the preserves to make a baste for the meat, and also season the preserves to make a relish to go with the pork.*

*If you like lemon meringue pie, kumquat meringue pie will tempt you. Bananas and kumquats achieve exotic balance in gelato. And kumquat marmalade is another way to enjoy the fruit post-season.*

## KUMQUAT PASTRY TART

> 1 **sheet frozen puff pastry (½ of a 17¼-oz. package)**
> ¾ **cup microwave kumquat jam (recipe follows) or kumquat marmalade (recipe page 32)**
> ½ **cup whipping cream Ginger cream spread (recipe follows)**
> ½ **pound (about 2 cups) kumquats, sliced about ⅛ inch thick (discard seeds and end pieces)**
> 2 **tablespoons orange-flavored liqueur**

Lay puff pastry on a 12- by 15-inch baking sheet. Cover and let stand at room temperature until pliable, 20 to 30 minutes. Unfold pastry and roll out to make a 10-inch square. Brush evenly with 2 tablespoons of the jam. Bake on lowest rack of a 425° oven until well browned, 12 to 14 minutes (pastry may puff unevenly). Remove from oven and let cool.

Up to 1 hour before serving, beat whipping cream until it will hold soft peaks; fold gently into ginger cream. Spread evenly over baked pastry. Arrange kumquat slices on cream, overlapping slices slightly.

Melt remaining jam in a 2- to 3-cup pan over low heat; stir often. Mix in liqueur. Gently brush jam over sliced kumquats. Serve, or chill up to 1 hour. Cut in rectangles. Makes 8 or 9 servings.

**Ginger cream spread.** In a 1½- to 2-quart pan, stir together ¼ cup *each* **sugar** and **all-purpose flour.** Smoothly blend in 1 cup **milk** and add 4 slices, each quarter-size, **fresh ginger.** Bring to boil, stirring, over medium-high heat.

*Sparkling kumquat jam is brushed over sliced kumquats on baked puff pastry spread with ginger cream.*

In a small bowl, beat 2 **large egg yolks** to blend. Stir ¼ cup hot milk mixture into eggs, then stir all back into pan. Stir on low heat until thickened, about 5 minutes; remove ginger and discard. Let cool, cover, and chill at least 1 hour or up to 3 days. Stir to use. Makes about 1⅓ cups.

## MICROWAVE KUMQUAT JAM

> 1 **pound (about 3½ cups) kumquats**
> 1½ **cups sugar**

Rinse kumquats and cut into ⅛-inch slices; discard seeds and end pieces. Chop fruit very coarsely. Mix fruit with sugar in a 2½- to 3-quart nonmetal bowl.

Cook, uncovered, in a microwave oven on full power until mixture begins to boil, about 6 minutes; stir down bubbles. Continue to cook in microwave, stirring every 2 to 3 minutes, until fruit mixture is thick enough to spread, about 10 minutes. Jam will thicken slightly as it cools. Serve warm or cool; to store, cover and chill up to 2 months. Makes about 2 cups.

*Bright yellow-orange kumquats look like tiny thin-skinned oranges. Skin tastes sweet; fruit is puckery-tart. Eat fruit with skin.*

*Microwave kumquat jam takes 15 minutes to cook. Use it with breakfast breads or on the pastry tart on page 30.*

## GLAZED LOIN OF PORK WITH KUMQUATS

2 cups preserved kumquats (recipe follows), drained
1 cup syrup from preserved kumquats
1 tablespoon honey
1 tablespoon Dijon mustard
2 cloves garlic, minced or pressed
1 teaspoon minced fresh ginger
2 tablespoons minced shallots
¼ teaspoon freshly ground pepper
1 boned, rolled, and tied center-cut pork loin, 3½ to 4 pounds
½ cup regular-strength chicken broth
   Salt

Reserve 6 or 7 whole preserved kumquats for garnish. Cut remaining fruit into halves, discarding seeds. Set fruit aside. In a 1½- to 2-quart pan, stir together syrup, honey, mustard, garlic, ginger, shallots, and pepper; bring to a boil over high heat, then set aside.

In a barbecue with lid (uncovered), ignite 50 charcoal briquets on fire grate. When briquets are lightly covered with gray ash (30 to 40 minutes), push half the coals to each side of the grate and place a 9- by 13-inch foil drip pan in center. Position grill 4 to 6 inches above the coals.

Place roast, fat side up, on grill over pan. Cover barbecue and open dampers.

Roast the pork until meat thermometer inserted in center registers 155°, 55 to 65 minutes. Brush roast with kumquat syrup mixture 7 or 8 times as it cooks. Transfer roast from grill to a platter; loosely cover and keep warm.

Pour remaining syrup into a 10- to 12-inch frying pan. Add broth and any juices that accumulate with the cooked pork. Boil mixture over high heat until reduced by half; stir in reserved kumquat halves and cook until hot.

Garnish roast with reserved whole kumquats. Slice meat and offer the hot preserved kumquat sauce and salt to add to taste. Makes 8 to 10 servings.

## PRESERVED KUMQUATS

2½ pounds (about 8 cups) kumquats
   Water
3 cups sugar

Rinse kumquats. With a sharp knife, cut a small cross in the blossom end of each fruit. Put kumquats in a 3- to 4-quart pan, adding enough water to cover.

Bring to a boil, cover, and simmer over low heat for 3 minutes. Drain off water immediately.

Add sugar and 3 cups water to pan; set over high heat. Bring to boiling, stirring occasionally. Reduce heat and simmer gently, uncovered, until fruit is very tender when pierced but holds its shape well, about 10 minutes; remove from heat.

Pour kumquats and syrup into a jar (about 2 qt.) and let cool. Serve, or cover and chill up to 3 weeks.

To store longer, pour hot kumquats and syrup into hot, sterilized pint- or half-pint-size jars. Syrup should cover fruit and come to within ¼ inch from top of each jar. Wipe rims clean. Top with hot, sterilized lids and screw ring bands on firmly. Place filled jars on a rack in a deep 7- to 8-quart pan. Cover completely with boiling water. Hold at simmering (180°) for 10 minutes. Lift jars from water and let cool on a towel. Press lids: if they stay down, jars are sealed; if they pop up, jars are not sealed and should be kept in the refrigerator. Makes about 3 pints.

*Preserved kumquats make relish to accompany barbecued pork loin. The meat is glazed with sauce from the fruit.*

## KUMQUAT MERINGUE PIE

- 1 to 1¼ pounds (3 to 4 cups) kumquats
- 1½ cups sugar
- 6 tablespoons cornstarch
- 1½ cups water
- 4 large eggs, separated
- 3 tablespoons butter or margarine
- 1 baked pastry shell for a single-crust 9-inch pie
- ½ teaspoon vanilla

Rinse kumquats. Thinly slice 6 fruit, discarding seeds; set fruit aside. Cut the rest of the fruit in half and squeeze (pinch between fingers) to extract juice. Pour juice through a fine strainer to measure: you should have ½ cup (if not, squeeze more kumquat halves). Discard seeds.

In a 2- to 3-quart pan, whisk 1¼ cups of the sugar with cornstarch to mix. Gradually whisk in kumquat juice and water, blending until smooth. Cook over medium-high heat, stirring, until mixture thickens and comes to a full boil.

In a small bowl, beat egg yolks to blend, then whisk into yolks about ½ cup of the hot filling; pour yolk mixture back into pan. Cook, stirring, over very low heat for 2 more minutes. Remove from heat and stir in sliced kumquats and butter; let cool slightly, then pour into pastry shell.

Beat whites at high speed in large bowl with electric mixer until frothy. Gradually add remaining sugar, 1 tablespoon at a time, beating until whites will hold stiff, glossy peaks. Beat in vanilla.

Pile meringue onto filling. With a spatula, push meringue over filling and up against edge of pastry shell; use spatula to make decorative swirls in meringue. Bake at 375° until meringue is tinged with gold, 5 to 7 minutes. Let cool at least 3 or up to 12 hours. Makes 8 or 9 servings. —*Nathan C. Smith, Pomona, Calif.*

*Cool gelato combines kumquats, mellow bananas, and orange liqueur.*

## KUMQUAT-BANANA GELATO

- 3 cups milk
- 1 cup sugar
- 6 large egg yolks
- ½ teaspoon vanilla
- ¼ cup orange-flavored liqueur
- 1¼ pounds (about 4 cups) kumquats
- 1 medium-size ripe banana
- 2 tablespoons lemon juice

In a 3- to 4-quart pan, combine milk and sugar. Stir over medium heat until milk is scalding.

In a bowl, gradually whisk 1 cup of the hot milk into egg yolks, then whisk egg mixture into pan. Cook, stirring constantly, over medium-low heat until custard coats back of a spoon in a smooth, thin layer, 10 to 12 minutes. Stir in vanilla and liqueur; let cool, then cover and chill.

Rinse kumquats and slice thinly; discard seeds. In a blender or food processor, whirl kumquats with banana until very smoothly puréed; add lemon juice. Stir into chilled custard.

Pour mixture into container of an ice cream maker (self-refrigerated, or use 8 parts ice to 1 part salt) and freeze according to manufacturer's directions or until the dasher or stirring paddle will no longer rotate.

Serve gelato softly frozen. Or, to mellow and firm, remove lid and dasher of ice-chilled maker, cover container with plastic wrap, top with lid, and repack with 4 parts ice to 1 part salt for 2 hours; or transfer gelato to the freezer until very firm. To store, cover and freeze up to 1 month. Makes about 2 quarts.

## KUMQUAT MARMALADE

- 2 pounds (about 7 cups) kumquats
- 1 lemon, thinly sliced (discard seeds)
- 8 cups water
- 4½ cups sugar

Rinse kumquats and slice ⅛ inch thick; discard seeds.

In a 5- to 6-quart pan, combine kumquats, lemon, and water; bring mixture to a boil. Reduce heat, cover, and simmer for 25 to 30 minutes or until peel is translucent. Stir in sugar. Cook, stirring often, over medium heat, uncovered, until marmalade thickens and reaches 220° on a candy thermometer—about 1 hour. Let cool before serving. Or store, covered and chilled, up to 2 months.

To store longer, pour hot marmalade into hot, sterilized pint or half-pint jars to within ¼ inch of rim; wipe rims clean. Top with hot sterilized lids and screw ring bands on firmly. Process in a hot water bath as directed for preserved kumquats, preceding (see page 31). Lift jars from water and let cool on a towel. Press lids: if they stay down, jars are sealed; if they pop back up, jars are not sealed and should be stored in the refrigerator. Makes about 3 pints.

# Oats—in Cookies, Oatmeal, Breads & More

**D**O OATS HAVE LIFE *beyond cookies and porridge? Surprisingly, this member of the grass family has many guises beyond the familiar rolled oats, and its nut-like flavor is good in both savory and sweet preparations. Here, we explore different oat forms and present classic recipes, as well as some unexpected choices.*

## ARE ALL OATS CREATED EQUAL?

Processing makes the difference. After harvesting, oats are dried and toasted to enhance their flavor, then hulled. At this point, they're called *groats*. From here, the groats can be *steel-cut* or *rolled*.

Steel-cut oats resemble cracked wheat and, like groats, cook more slowly than rolled oats; they're also chewier—ideal for pilaf or hearty porridge.

Rolled oats come in varying thicknesses that determine how fast they cook. The commonest—from thickest to thinnest—are regular, quick-cooking, and instant. Quick-cooking and instant have been cut up to hasten cooking. Rolled oats are popular in porridge and also in baked goods, such as breads and cookies.

Processed oats are available whole, with hulls removed, as groats (in scoop). They can be further refined to make steel-cut oats (top) or rolled oats in varying thicknesses: regular (bottom right), quick (bottom center), instant (above groats).

## WHAT'S IN A NAME? SHOPPING TIPS

Grocery stores usually stock rolled oats. At health-food stores, you're likely to find oat groats, steel-cut oats, and thick and regular rolled oats. Trips to gourmet and British and Irish import stores should uncover additional choices—Scotch and Irish, which may be steel-cut or rolled. The oats we found ranged from 60 cents to $2.50 per pound; imports were generally the most expensive.

For a traditional start on the day, we give you some variations on wholesome oatmeal porridge. The first two have a slightly chewy texture; if you prefer creamier porridge, use the instant or creamy oatmeal porridge recipes that follow. Scottish oatcakes are a great cracker alternative for cheese or jam. Our basic oatmeal cooky recipe offers chewy or crisp options. The oatmeal-buttermilk bread is quick to make, as is the crunchy topping for apple crisp. Steel-cut oats or groats are the basis for a flavorful pilaf.

## FRUIT & SPICE OATMEAL PORRIDGE

- 2¾ cups water
- 1 teaspoon ground cinnamon
- ¼ teaspoon *each* ground nutmeg and ground allspice
- ⅓ cup raisins
- ½ cup chopped pitted dates
- 1⅓ cups regular or quick-cooking rolled oats, or oat groats
  Milk or half-and-half (light cream)

In a 3- to 4-quart pan, bring water, cinnamon, nutmeg, allspice, raisins, and dates to a boil over high heat. Stir in oats. Cover and simmer until almost all water is absorbed, about 8 minutes for regular oats, 1 to 1½ minutes for quick-cooking, or 35 to 40 minutes for groats. Spoon into bowls; add milk. Serves 4.

## STEEL-CUT OATMEAL PORRIDGE

Follow directions for **Fruit & Spice Oatmeal Porridge,** preceding, but increase water to 3¼ cups and use 1⅓ cups **steel-cut oats** instead of rolled oats. Cook, covered, until almost all the water is absorbed, 15 to 20 minutes; stir occasionally. Makes 4 servings.

## INSTANT OATMEAL PORRIDGE

Follow directions for **Fruit & Spice Oatmeal Porridge,** preceding, but do not cook. Instead, in a large bowl, mix 4 packages (1 oz. *each*) **regular-flavor instant rolled oats** with the raisins, dates, and only ½ teaspoon cinnamon and ⅛ teaspoon *each* nutmeg and allspice. Decrease water to 2½ cups; bring water to a boil, then stir thoroughly into the oat mixture. Let stand 2 minutes before serving. Makes 4 servings.

## CREAMY OATMEAL PORRIDGE

Follow directions for **Fruit & Spice Oatmeal Porridge,** preceding, but use **regular** or quick-cooking **rolled oats.** Add oats, cinnamon, nutmeg, allspice, raisins, and dates to *cold* water. Bring to a boil, then cook, covered, stirring often, until almost all the water is absorbed, about 5 minutes for regular oats, 1½ minutes for quick-cooking. Makes 4 servings.

## SCOTTISH OATCAKES

- ½ cup steel-cut oats
- 1 cup regular rolled oats
- ½ cup all-purpose flour
- ¾ teaspoon sugar
- ¼ teaspoon salt
- ¼ teaspoon baking powder
- 2 tablespoons melted butter or margarine
- ⅓ cup hot water

In a blender or food processor, whirl steel-cut and rolled oats until coarsely ground.

Place all but 2 tablespoons of the oats in a bowl with flour, sugar, salt, and baking powder; stir until combined. Add butter; stir until evenly distributed. With a fork, mix in water until evenly moistened. Pat dough into a ball, then flatten slightly.

Sprinkle reserved oats on a board. Roll dough out 1/16 inch thick. With a 2½- to 3-inch round cutter, cut dough into rounds. Reroll and cut scraps. Place oatcakes about 1 inch apart on 2 greased 12- by 15-inch baking sheets.

Bake in a 325° oven until oatcakes are golden, about 25 minutes. Let cool on a rack. Serve, or store airtight at room temperature up to 2 days. Makes 26 to 30.

## TAILOR-MADE CHEWY OATMEAL COOKIES

- 1 cup (½ lb.) butter or margarine
- ½ cup granulated sugar
- 1½ cups firmly packed brown sugar
- 2 large eggs
- 1½ teaspoons vanilla
- 1½ cups all-purpose flour
- ¼ teaspoon salt
- 1 teaspoon baking soda
- ¼ teaspoon *each* ground allspice and ground cloves (optional)
- ½ teaspoon ground nutmeg (optional)
- 1½ teaspoons ground cinnamon (optional)
- 3 cups regular or quick-cooking rolled oats
- 1 cup raisins (optional)
- ¾ cup chopped walnuts (optional)

In large bowl of an electric mixer, beat butter and granulated and brown sugars until creamy. Beat in eggs until well blended, then mix in vanilla. Stir together flour, salt, soda, allspice, cloves, nutmeg, and cinnamon. Add to butter mixture; stir well. Stir in oats, raisins, and walnuts until evenly moistened.

Drop dough by rounded tablespoons onto greased 12- by 15-inch baking sheets, spacing about 2 inches apart. Bake in a 375° oven until cookies are golden but centers are still soft, 10 to 12 minutes. If using 1 oven, switch position of pans halfway through cooking. Transfer cookies to racks to cool. Serve, or store airtight up to 3 days. Makes about 4 dozen.

## TAILOR-MADE CRISP OATMEAL COOKIES

Follow directions for **Tailor-Made Chewy Oatmeal Cookies,** preceding, but decrease flour to 1 cup and omit baking soda.

Drop dough by rounded tablespoons onto greased 12- by 15-inch baking sheets, spacing about 2 inches apart. Pat dough into ¼-inch-thick rounds. Bake cookies in a 350° oven until well browned, about 12 minutes. If using 1 oven, switch position of baking sheets halfway through cooking. Let cool on pans for 1 minute, then transfer cookies to racks to cool completely. Serve, or store airtight up to 3 days. Makes about 4 dozen.

*Fresh-from-the-oven treats include oat-topped quick bread, oatmeal cookies, and thin Scottish oatcakes that go well with butter, jam, or cheese.*

*Thin or thick? Crisp or chewy? Tailor our basic recipe to create your favorite style of oatmeal cookies.*

## QUICK OATMEAL-BUTTERMILK BREAD

1¼ cups regular or quick-cooking rolled oats
   About 1½ cups all-purpose flour
½ teaspoon *each* salt and baking soda
1½ teaspoons baking powder
1 tablespoon sugar
2 tablespoons melted butter or margarine
1 large egg
¾ cup plus 3 tablespoons buttermilk

In a blender or food processor, whirl ½ cup of the oats until finely ground. Place in a large bowl with ¼ cup more of the oats, 1½ cups flour, salt, baking soda, baking powder, and sugar. In a small bowl, whisk butter, egg, and ¾ cup of the buttermilk until blended. Add to flour mixture and stir until moistened.

Scrape dough onto a lightly floured board and knead until smooth, about 1 minute. Shape into a smooth round and place in a greased 8-inch round cake pan. Press lightly so bread is evenly thick and almost touches pan rim.

In a small bowl, mix remaining ½ cup oats and 3 tablespoons buttermilk. Evenly pat oats on top of dough. Bake in a 375° oven until bread is well browned, 45 to 50 minutes. Serve hot or let cool on a rack. Cut into wedges. If made ahead, wrap airtight and let stand overnight; freeze to store longer. Makes 1 loaf, 1⅓ pounds.

## OAT PILAF

1 large onion, thinly sliced
3 tablespoons butter or margarine
1 cup steel-cut oats or oat groats
1¾ cups regular-strength beef broth (2¼ cups if using oat groats)
   Parsley sprigs

In a 10- to 12-inch frying pan over medium-high heat, cook onion in butter until onion is limp, about 10 minutes; stir often. Add oats and stir for 1 minute. Add broth.

Bring to a boil over high heat, then simmer, covered, until liquid is absorbed, about 15 minutes for steel-cut oats, 40 minutes for oat groats. Stir occasionally. Garnish with parsley. Serves 4 or 5.

*Oats and onions? Add toasted oat groats (or steel-cut oats) to sautéed onions, then cook with beef broth for flavorful pilaf.*

*Sprinkle topping of oats, butter, and brown sugar over sliced apples; bake to make homey and satisfying apple crisp.*

## APPLE-OATMEAL CRISP

4 large (about 2 lb.) Golden Delicious or Granny Smith apples, peeled if desired, cored, and sliced ⅓ inch thick
2 tablespoons lemon juice
   Oat-streusel topping (recipe follows)
   Whipped cream or ice cream (optional)

In a shallow 2-quart baking dish, mix apples with lemon juice. Pat fruit into an even layer. Sprinkle evenly with streusel. Bake in a 375° oven until apples are tender when pierced, 35 to 40 minutes.

Serve warm or cool; or let cool completely, then cover and hold at room temperature up to overnight. Accompany with cream, if desired. Makes 6 to 8 servings.

**Oat-streusel topping.** In a bowl, rub with your fingers until crumbly ⅔ cup **butter** or margarine, 1¼ cups **regular** or quick-cooking **rolled oats,** and 1 cup firmly packed **brown sugar.**

# "Steamroller" Chicken

A THRIFTY COOK, *Bob Peterson buys whole birds and bones the breasts himself to make a specialty dish he calls steamroller chicken. The breasts—with a portion of the wings attached—look considerably flattened, and so the name.*

*The breasts are the entrée following a pasta dish Mr. Peterson serves his guests at a comfortable cooking island in his Seattle kitchen. He reserves legs and thighs for family meals; carcasses go into a stockpot.*

*Bob Peterson calculated that purchased boned breasts cost as much as the whole bird. But if time is crucial, you can buy the breasts boned—minus the wing joint.*

*As the water comes to a boil for the pasta, heat the oven to finish chicken.*

## PASTA ALLA PUTTANESCA

1 cup salty black olives, rinsed and pitted
1 can (2 oz.) anchovy fillets, rinsed, patted dry, and diced
2 tablespoons drained capers
1 can (7 oz.) solid-pack tuna in water, drained
¾ cup chopped parsley
  Tomato sauce (recipe follows)
  Water
1 pound dry linguini or vermicelli

In a 10- to 12-inch frying pan over medium heat, combine olives, anchovies, capers, tuna, parsley, and tomato sauce; cook until hot, stirring occasionally.

Meanwhile, in a 4- to 5-quart pan, bring 3 quarts of water to a boil on high heat. Add linguini and cook, uncovered, until tender to bite, about 10 minutes. Drain pasta well and mix with sauce. Serve in bowls or wide soup dishes. Makes 8 servings.

**Tomato sauce.** In a 5- to 6-quart pan, combine ¼ cup **olive oil** or salad oil; 1 medium-size **onion,** chopped; 6 cloves **garlic,** minced or pressed; 1 teaspoon *each* **dry basil** and **dry oregano leaves;** and ½ teaspoon **crushed dried hot red chilies.** Cook on medium-high heat, stirring often, until onion is slightly browned, about 10 minutes. Add 2 cans (1 lb. 12 oz. *each*) **pear-shaped tomatoes with basil;** mash to break up pieces. Boil on high heat, uncovered, until reduced to 3 cups, about 30 minutes; stir often.

*First he browns steamroller chicken, then Bob Peterson completes the cooking in the oven.*

*Guest gets recruited to help serve first course of linguini mixed in a tomato sauce with tuna, olives, and anchovies.*

*Party group enjoys pasta at kitchen island while chicken finishes in the oven. Then they move to the dining room for the main course.*

*Serve chicken with pan-dripping sauce, pear-shaped tomatoes with basil garnish, and green beans.*

## STEAMROLLER CHICKEN

- **4 whole chickens (about 3 lb. *each*) or 4 whole chicken breasts (about 1 lb. *each*), boned and cut in half**
- **1 tablespoon coarse ground pepper**
  **About 1 teaspoon salt**
- **4 tablespoons (⅛ lb.) butter or margarine**
- **¼ cup *each* lemon juice and regular-strength chicken broth or water**

With a sharp knife, cut off chicken legs and thighs; reserve for other uses. With your hands, force chicken wings back at shoulders until wings pop loose in sockets. Following steps 1 through 4 at right, cut breasts and wings from carcass. If desired, lay breast halves skin up; trim edges slightly to even shape. Sprinkle chicken on all sides with pepper.

Sprinkle about ½ teaspoon salt into a 10- to 12-inch frying pan on medium-high heat. Fill pan with 1 layer of breasts, skin down; cook until browned, about 3 minutes. Turn over breasts, add 1 table-spoon butter, and cook until browned, about 3 minutes. Transfer browned breasts, skin up and in a single layer, to a 10- by 15-inch baking pan; scrape drippings over the chicken. Repeat steps until all breasts are browned. (If done ahead, you can let chicken stand at room temperature up to 1 hour.)

Put breasts in a 400° oven and bake until no longer pink in center (cut to test), about 6 minutes, or 10 minutes if cooled to room temperature.

Stir lemon juice and broth into the frying pan. When chicken is baked, lift from baking pan, add drippings to lemon and broth mixture, and bring to boiling on high heat; stir in remaining butter. Pour into a small bowl. Put a piece of chicken on each dinner plate. Offer pan sauce to spoon onto chicken. Serves 8.

## How to "Steamroll" a Chicken

**1** *Lay bird breast down. Remove legs; reserve. Cut wing joints free at back; do not cut off wing or pierce skin on other side.*

**2** *To free meat, slip small sharp knife along ribs down to the keel. Also cut flesh from wishbone. Do not pierce skin.*

**3** *Turn chicken over. Cut along the keel to separate breast half from carcass and lay piece flat, skin up.*

**4** *Cut off wing at the second joint, removing wing tip. Repeat these steps on remaining breast half.*

# Squeeze Salads

**H**OW ABOUT A SQUEEZABLE MEAL? Here, we suggest wholesome spreads that are the base for quick-to-prepare lunches you can carry onto the ski slopes or enjoy during cross-country ski trips.

You transport the spreads in flexible plastic tubes—sold for about $1 in sporting goods or camping equipment stores (make sure clip is included). Simply add the filling through the bottom of the tube, then seal with clip (see photo below); or use a small plastic container that seals securely, and bring a spoon for serving.

To fill the tubes, we've devised a selection of hearty salad mixtures fine-textured enough to squeeze through the tube's narrow opening onto bread, crackers, celery stalks, or cucumber slices. These combinations make satisfying meals that pack easily into a backpack or fanny pack.

Flavor choices for the salads are egg, garbanzo-based hummus, pizza, and refried bean.

Additional luncheon treats can include sweet, chewy popcorn-and-peanut balls or bran-and-apricot sticks; recipes follow. Also bring individual-size containers (boxes, cans, pouches) of fruit and vegetable juices and whole fruits that travel well: apples, oranges, firm pears.

**To transport squeeze salads,** keep them cold in an insulated bag. Or, if carrying lunch in an uninsulated pack close to the body, plan to eat salads within 4 hours.

## WINTER EGG SALAD

- 3 large hard-cooked eggs
- 2 tablespoons sweet pickle relish
- 1 tablespoon *each* mayonnaise and finely chopped green onion
- 2 teaspoons Dijon mustard
  Salt and pepper
- 4 to 6 slices dense-textured pumpernickel bread, or 1 dozen crisp rye crackers

In a food processor or blender, combine eggs, pickle relish, mayonnaise, onion, and mustard. Whirl until coarsely puréed. Add salt and pepper to taste. Cover; chill at least 1 hour or up to 2 days.

Spoon salad into a flexible plastic tube (about 1-cup size). Slide on end clip to close. Or spoon salad into a leakproof plastic container (about 1-cup size). To transport, follow preceding directions.

To serve, squirt or spoon the salad onto bread or crackers. Makes about 1 cup, enough for 1 tube or 2 servings.

## HUMMUS SALAD

- ½ cup garbanzo beans plus ¼ cup bean liquid
- 2 tablespoons lemon juice
- ⅓ cup tahini (sesame seed paste)
- 1 teaspoon ground cumin
- 1 clove garlic, pressed or minced
  Salt and pepper
- 4 to 6 slices dense-textured pumpernickel bread, or 1 dozen crisp rye crackers

In a food processor or blender, combine beans and liquid, lemon juice, tahini, cumin, and garlic; whirl until smooth. Add salt and pepper to taste. Cover and chill at least 1 hour or up to 3 days.

Spoon salad into a flexible plastic tube (about 1-cup size) and slide on end clip to close. Or spoon salad into a leakproof plastic storage container (about 1-cup size). To transport, follow preceding directions.

To serve, squirt or spoon salad onto bread or crackers. Makes about 1 cup, enough for 1 tube or 2 servings.

## PIZZA SALAD

- 1 small onion, finely chopped
- 1 tablespoon olive or salad oil
- ¼ pound mushrooms, finely chopped
- 1 can (14 oz.) stewed tomatoes
- ⅓ cup tomato paste
- 1 teaspoon *each* dry basil and dry oregano leaves
- 1 ounce dry salami, finely chopped
  Salt and pepper
- ¼ pound parmesan or romano cheese, thinly sliced (optional)
  Crusty rolls (at least 2) or hardtack crackers (8 to 12)

In a 10- to 12-inch frying pan set over medium-high heat, cook onion in olive oil, stirring occasionally, until translucent, about 5 minutes. Add mushrooms and stir often until all liquid evaporates, about 3 minutes longer. Add tomatoes and their liquid, tomato paste, basil, and oregano. Cook, stirring occasionally, until very thick, 20 to 25 minutes.

Remove from heat and stir in salami; let cool. Season with salt and pepper. Cover and chill pizza salad at least 1 hour or up to 3 days.

Spoon salad into 2 flexible plastic tubes (about 1-cup size) and slide on end clips to close. Or spoon salad into a leakproof plastic storage container

With cap on plastic squeeze tube, spoon filling through open bottom to within 1 inch of end.

To seal tube, fold plastic over ½ inch, then slide on end clip. Tube can be washed and used again.

(about 2-cup size). Put cheese in a plastic bag and seal. To transport, follow preceding directions.

To serve, squirt or spoon salad onto slices of the roll or crackers; top with a slice of cheese, if desired. Makes about 2 cups, enough for 2 tubes or 4 servings.

## MEXICAN REFRIED BEAN SALAD

    1   tablespoon olive or salad oil
    1   small onion, chopped
    1   can (4 oz.) diced green chilies
    1   teaspoon *each* chili powder and
        ground cumin
    ¼   teaspoon ground coriander
    ¾   cup refried beans
    ¼   teaspoon liquid hot pepper
        seasoning
    ½   cup firmly packed shredded
        cheddar cheese
    ½   to ¾ pound tortilla chips, or
        4 to 6 pocket bread rounds (about
        5-in. size)

In a 10- to 12-inch frying pan over medium heat, cook olive oil and onion, stirring occasionally, until onion is translucent, about 5 minutes. Add green chilies, chili powder, cumin, and coriander; stir about 2 minutes. Mix in the refried beans and pepper seasoning; stir until hot. Let cool, then mix in the cheese. Cover and chill bean salad at least 1 hour or up to 3 days. To transport, follow preceding directions.

Spoon salad into 2 flexible plastic tubes (about 1-cup size) and slide on end clips to close. Or spoon salad into a leakproof plastic storage container (about 2-cup size). To transport, follow preceding directions.

To serve, squirt or spoon salad onto tortilla chips or into portions of pocket bread. Makes about 1¾ cups, enough for 2 tubes or 4 servings.

## PEANUT-SPECKLED SNOWBALLS

        About 2 quarts popped popcorn
    1   cup salted roasted peanuts
    ½   cup cream-style peanut butter
        About ½ cup (¼ lb.) butter or
        margarine
    1   package (10 oz., or 4 cups firmly
        packed) marshmallows

In a large buttered bowl, combine popcorn and peanuts; set aside.

In a 2- to 3-quart pan on medium heat, combine peanut butter and ¼ cup of the

*Space-age ski lunch from a tube! Enjoy pizza or winter egg salads soft enough to squeeze onto bread or crisp vegetables. Tube salads travel well in fanny packs, can be made ahead.*

butter; stir until melted. Add marshmallows and stir until they melt and are well mixed with the butter mixture, about 5 minutes.

At once, pour hot mixture over popcorn and peanuts. Stir gently to coat all pieces.

Let stand until popcorn is just cool enough to touch. Coat hands with butter (to prevent sticking) and firmly mold popcorn mixture into 1- to 2-inch-diameter balls. Set balls slightly apart on waxed paper. Individually seal each popcorn ball in foil or clear plastic wrap; store airtight up to 5 days. Makes 24 balls.

## BRAN & DRIED FRUIT STICKS

    2   cups bran cereal
    ½   cup *each* raisins and slivered
        dry apricots
        About ½ cup (¼ lb.) butter or
        margarine
   30   large (3 cups firmly packed)
        marshmallows

In a large buttered bowl, mix together bran, raisins, and apricots; set aside.

In a 1- to 2-quart pan over medium heat, combine butter and marshmallows; stir until mixture is melted and blended, about 5 minutes.

At once, pour hot mixture over bran and fruit, then stir gently to mix well.

Let mixture stand until just cool enough to touch. Coat hands with butter (to prevent sticking) and firmly pat mixture into 1- by 3-inch sticks. As you shape each stick, set it on waxed paper; pieces should not touch. When all are shaped, seal each piece in foil or clear plastic wrap; store airtight up to 5 days. Makes 12 sticks.

# Dim Sum Quick & Easy

**T**HESE CONTEMPORARY *Chinese* dim sum *are quicker and easier to make than the more traditional versions of these appetizer-like morsels. They are based on one versatile puréed shrimp mixture that tops cabbage squares, shiitake mushrooms, and scallops.*

*With help from time-saving equipment, preparation is simple and fast. The shrimp paste—customarily hand minced—goes together quickly with a food processor. Cooking, usually done in a steamer, takes only a few minutes in a microwave oven.*

*All three appetizers can be prepared a day ahead, needing only to cook the day of the party. If your microwave isn't full size, you may need to cook the appetizers half at a time on two plates; reduce suggested cooking times by about a third.*

## FRESH SHRIMP PASTE

| | |
|---|---|
| ½ | **pound medium-size shrimp (40 to 50 per lb.), shelled and deveined** |
| 2 | **large egg whites** |
| 1 | **tablespoon dry sherry** |
| 1 | **tablespoon minced fresh ginger** |
| 1 | **clove garlic, pressed or minced** |
| 2 | **teaspoons cornstarch** |
| 1 | **teaspoon sugar** |
| | **About ½ teaspoon salt, or to taste** |
| ½ | **teaspoon Oriental sesame oil or salad oil** |
| ⅛ | **teaspoon white pepper** |

In a food processor, combine shrimp, egg whites, sherry, ginger, garlic, cornstarch, sugar, salt, oil, and pepper. Whirl until smoothly puréed and paste-like. Or with a knife, finely mince shrimp. In a bowl, combine shrimp and remaining ingredients; beat until well blended and sticky.

Use in the following recipes. Makes 1⅓ cups.—*Henry and Judy Chan, Yank Sing Restaurant, San Francisco.*

## SHRIMP ON CABBAGE SQUARES

| | |
|---|---|
| 10 | **large napa cabbage leaves** |
| | **Fresh shrimp paste (recipe precedes)** |
| 48 | **julienne strips (*each* about 1 inch long) thinly sliced cooked ham** |
| 24 | **fresh cilantro leaves (coriander)** |
| | **Soy sauce** |

Cut off leafy portions of cabbage, then cut thick stems into 24 squares (1½-inch *each*). Reserve leaves and trimmings for another use. Place cabbage pieces in a nonmetal bowl; cover with plastic wrap. In a microwave oven, cook at full power for 2 minutes. Rotate bowl a half-turn; continue cooking just until cabbage is slightly wilted, 1 to 2 minutes longer. Drain well.

On each cabbage piece, mound an equal portion of shrimp paste (about 1½ teaspoons). Lightly press 2 strips of ham and a cilantro leaf into paste on each piece.

Place slightly apart on an 11- to 12-inch plate. Cover with plastic wrap. If made ahead, cover and chill, up to overnight.

In a microwave oven, cook at full power for 1½ minutes. Rotate plate a half-turn; continue cooking at full power till shrimp paste is firm when lightly pressed, 1½ to 2½ minutes longer. Let stand, covered, about 5 minutes. Uncover plate. Serve with soy sauce for dipping. Makes about 24 squares, 8 appetizer servings.

## SHRIMP ON SHIITAKE MUSHROOMS

| | |
|---|---|
| 24 | **small (1½ in. diameter) dried shiitake mushrooms** |
| | **Water** |
| 2 | **tablespoons soy sauce** |
| 1 | **tablespoon minced fresh ginger** |
| 2 | **teaspoons sugar** |
| 1 | **teaspoon Oriental sesame oil or salad oil** |
| 1 | **green onion, thinly sliced** |
| | **Fresh shrimp paste (recipe precedes)** |
| | **About 2 tablespoons frozen green peas, thawed** |

Soak mushrooms in warm water until soft, about 30 minutes; lift from water. Cut off and discard tough stems.

In a nonmetal bowl, mix mushrooms, 2 tablespoons soy sauce, ginger, sugar, oil, onion, and 1 cup water. Cover bowl with plastic wrap. In a microwave oven, cook at full power until mushrooms are very tender when pierced, 8 to 10 minutes. Drain mushrooms; press out excess liquid.

On gill side of each mushroom, mound an equal amount of shrimp paste (about 1½ teaspoons). Lightly press 2 or 3 peas into the paste. Place mushrooms, filled side up, slightly apart on an 11- to 12-inch plate. Cover plate with plastic wrap. If made ahead, chill up to overnight.

In a microwave oven, cook at full power for 2½ minutes. Rotate plate a half-turn; continue cooking at full power until shrimp feels firm when gently pressed, 1½ to 2½ minutes longer. Let stand, covered, about 5 minutes. Uncover plate; offer soy sauce for dipping. Makes 24 mushrooms, about 8 appetizer servings.

## SHRIMP ON A SCALLOP PEDESTAL

| | |
|---|---|
| 1 | **teaspoon sugar** |
| 1 | **teaspoon cornstarch** |
| 1 | **large egg white** |
| | **Soy sauce** |
| ⅛ | **teaspoon white pepper** |
| ¾ | **pound sea scallops (1½ in. diameter), rinsed and drained** |
| | **Fresh shrimp paste (recipe precedes)** |
| | **About 30 fresh cilantro leaves (coriander)** |

In a bowl, mix sugar and cornstarch. Stir in egg white, 1 teaspoon soy sauce, and pepper. Cut scallops into ⅓- to ½-inch-thick rounds; mix into egg mixture. Cover and chill 15 minutes or up to 1 hour.

Drain off excess marinade from scallops. Set scallops slightly apart on an 11- to 12-inch plate. On each round, mound an equal portion of shrimp paste (1 to 1½ teaspoons); garnish with a cilantro leaf. Cover with plastic wrap. If made ahead, cover and chill up to overnight.

In a microwave oven, cook at full power for 2½ minutes. Rotate plate a half-turn. Continue cooking at full power until shrimp paste feels firm when gently pressed, 2 to 3 minutes longer. Remove from oven. Let stand, covered, about 5 minutes. Uncover; drain off excess liquid or transfer scallops to a clean plate. Serve with soy sauce for dipping. Makes about 30 rounds, about 10 appetizer servings.

# Spanish Vegetable Dishes

To ADD INTEREST to winter menus, consider these three Spanish vegetable dishes.

At Alambique, a Madrid cooking school, director Clara Maria Llamas serves the first dish chilled to begin a light lunch; it's a salad of oven-roasted peppers, eggplant, and onion, with lemon-caper dressing and a scattering of olives. It's also good as an accompaniment to fish and meats.

The second dish is an intriguing salad of cooked potato wedges drenched with a light dressing and topped with a chopped mixture of apple, bacon, olives, and red onion.

The last dish uses mint and raisins in a refreshing balance with sweet carrots.

## ESCALIBADA

    About 2 tablespoons olive oil
 2  medium-size onions, peeled and
    cut into quarters
 1  medium-size (about 1 lb.) egg-
    plant, stem removed
 2  large red bell peppers, cut in half,
    stems and seeds removed
 1  large yellow or green bell pepper,
    cut in half, stem and seeds
    removed
 4  cloves garlic, unpeeled
    Lemon-caper dressing (recipe
    follows)
 1  can (6 oz.) pitted green or black
    ripe olives, drained
    Salt and pepper

Brush a 10- by 15-inch baking pan or shallow casserole with 2 tablespoons olive oil. Separate onion layers and scatter in pan. Cut eggplant into 1-inch chunks; add to pan. Stir vegetables to coat lightly with oil. Cover pan with foil and bake in a 350° oven until eggplant is tender when pierced, about 45 minutes.

Meanwhile, lay peppers, cut side down, with garlic on a lightly oiled 10- by 15-inch baking pan. Place in oven alongside (or on rack above) onion and eggplant.

Bake until peppers begin to soften and collapse and skin loosens, about 30 minutes. Remove from oven and set garlic aside. Cover pan with foil and let peppers cool, then pull off and discard skins. Slice peppers into ¼-inch strips. Add to cooked eggplant and onions. With a spatula, gently turn vegetables. Bake vegetables, uncovered, until eggplant is lightly browned, about 20 minutes more.

Peel garlic; mash pulp. Stir into dressing and pour over baked vegetables.

Add olives; mix gently. Add salt and pepper to taste. Spoon onto a platter or salad plates. Makes 6 to 8 servings.

**Lemon-caper dressing.** Mix 3 tablespoons **lemon juice;** 2 tablespoons **capers,** drained; and 2 tablespoons **olive oil.**

## SPANISH POTATO SALAD

 3  medium-size (1½ lb.) thin-skinned
    potatoes, scrubbed
    Water
    Marinade (recipe follows)
 1  small apple
 ⅓  cup crisp-cooked crumbled bacon
    or finely chopped cooked ham
 1  can (2 oz.) chopped black ripe
    olives
 ¼  cup finely chopped red onion

Put potatoes into a 3- to 4-quart pan; fill pan with water to cover potatoes by about 1 inch. Bring to a boil over high heat; reduce heat, cover, and simmer until potatoes are tender when pierced, about 30 minutes. Drain.

Cut each potato lengthwise into 1-inch-wide spears. Put potatoes in a 9- by 13-inch baking dish. Reserve 1 tablespoon marinade; pour remainder over potatoes and turn gently to coat evenly. Set aside until potatoes are tepid, 30 to 40 minutes; or cool, cover, and chill up to overnight. Bring to room temperature to serve.

Arrange potato spears on a serving platter or on 6 to 8 salad plates. Core apple and finely chop; add to reserved marinade. Stir in bacon, olives, and onion. Spoon over potatoes. Makes 6 to 8 servings.

**Marinade.** In a bowl, combine ⅓ cup **white wine vinegar;** 3 tablespoons **olive oil;** 2 cloves **garlic,** pressed or minced; ½ teaspoon **pepper;** and **salt** to taste. Makes about ½ cup.

## MINTED CARROTS

 1½  pounds carrots, peeled
  2  tablespoons butter or margarine
  ½  cup golden raisins
  ½  cup regular-strength chicken broth
  ¼  cup firmly packed fresh mint
     sprigs
  2  teaspoons firmly packed brown
     sugar
     Salt and pepper

*Carrot spears are cooked briefly in broth with raisins and mint; garnish with more mint.*

Cut carrots into matchstick pieces 3 to 4 inches long and about ¼ inch square.

Melt the butter in a 10- to 12-inch frying pan over medium heat. Add carrots, raisins, chicken broth, half the mint, and sugar. Bring to boiling; reduce heat, cover and simmer until carrots are tender-crisp when pierced, about 10 minutes. Uncover and boil on high heat until liquid evaporates, 5 to 10 minutes longer; shake pan frequently.

Meanwhile, strip leaves from all but 1 or 2 mint sprigs. Finely sliver the leaves.

Discard cooked mint sprigs and season the carrots with salt and pepper to taste. Pour onto a platter and sprinkle with slivered mint; garnish with mint sprigs. Makes 4 to 6 servings.

# More February Recipes

ADD VARIETY to your February meals with this lively quartet. These recipes range from soup—a flavorful oyster bisque—to spiced nuts. Rounding out the selection are a hearty whole-wheat bread and an elegant dessert to serve for Valentine's Day.

## HONEST-TO-GOSH 100% WHOLE-WHEAT BREAD

*Extra yeast gives this whole-wheat bread a light, bouncy texture more commonly associated with white breads.*

    2  packages active dry yeast
 1½  cups warm water (110°)
    5  tablespoons honey or molasses
4¾  to 5¼ cups whole-wheat flour
   ¼  cup (⅛ lb.) butter or margarine, melted
    2  teaspoons salt
    2  large eggs

*Homemade whole-wheat loaf rises tall during baking. Use a serrated knife to slice thinly for sandwiches, toast.*

In a large bowl, combine yeast, water, and 1 tablespoon of the honey; let stand about 5 minutes. Add 1½ cups of the whole-wheat flour. Beat until smoothly blended. Cover and let stand in a warm place until doubled, 20 to 30 minutes.

Stir in butter, remaining ¼ cup honey, salt, and eggs. Add 2 cups whole-wheat flour and beat until thoroughly moistened. Stir in another 1¼ cups flour.

*If using a dough hook,* beat on high speed until dough pulls cleanly from sides of bowl, 5 to 8 minutes; add flour, 1 tablespoon at a time, if needed.

*If mixing by hand,* scrape dough out onto a whole-wheat-floured board and knead until dough is smooth, about 10 minutes; add just enough flour to board to prevent sticking. Place dough in an oiled bowl.

Cover dough with plastic wrap. Put in a warm place and let rise until doubled, about 1 hour. Punch dough down and knead lightly on a board to release air bubbles. Cut dough into 2 equal portions. Shape each portion into a loaf and place each in a greased 4- by 8-inch loaf pan. Cover lightly with plastic wrap and let rise in a warm place until almost doubled, 20 to 30 minutes.

Bake in a 375° oven until bread is golden brown and sounds hollow when tapped, 35 to 40 minutes. Turn out onto racks to cool. Makes 2 loaves, each 1¼ pounds.—*Alison Conner, Mercer Island, Wash.*

## OYSTER BISQUE WITH STEAMED VEGETABLES

*Oyster shells are the surprising ingredient that adds extra flavor intensity to this oyster bisque. The shells are wisely discarded before the bisque is served with potatoes, Jerusalem artichokes, and napa cabbage to make a handsome entrée.*

*If you have a microwave oven, use it as an easy way to open oysters at home.*

    2  dozen medium-size (about 4 in. long) Pacific or Eastern oysters
   ½  cup (¼ lb.) butter or margarine
    2  tablespoons all-purpose flour
    3  bottles (8 oz. *each*) clam juice
    2  cups water
    1  cup whipping cream
    8  to 12 small (about 1½ in. diameter) thin-skinned potatoes, scrubbed
    1  pound Jerusalem artichokes, scrubbed and cut into ¼-inch-thick slices
    3  cups (about 1 lb.) finely shredded napa cabbage
        Lemon wedges
        Salt and pepper

Have oysters shucked at the market and put in a container with their juices; bring shells home, too, and scrub them well with a stiff brush under cool running water.

Or use a microwave oven to open shells. Buy unshucked oysters and scrub shells as directed. Arrange 7 or 8 scrubbed oysters at a time around the edge of a 9- or 10-inch nonmetal dish. Cook on full power until shells open slightly, 30 to 45 seconds. Cut oysters free from shells and set oysters and juices aside; reserve shells.

In a 6- to 8-quart pan, melt butter over medium-high heat. Stir in flour until blended; then gradually stir in clam juice, water, and cream. Add shells. Bring to a boil over high heat. Cover, reduce heat, and simmer for 30 minutes.

At the same time, steam potatoes on a rack in a covered 5- to 6-quart pan over about 1 inch boiling water for 15 minutes. Add Jerusalem artichokes and steam, covered, until potatoes are tender when pierced, about 15 minutes more. Push vegetables to one side and add cabbage (and water, if needed). Cover and steam just until cabbage wilts, about 5 minutes.

Pour shells and broth into a colander set in a large bowl; discard shells. Rinse pan and slowly pour broth back into it; discard shell bits at bottom of bowl. Bring broth to boil; add oysters. Cook just until oyster edges curl, about 1 minute. Spoon equal portions of vegetables, oysters, and broth into wide soup bowls. Offer lemon, salt, and pepper to add to taste. Serves 4 to 6.

Stir syrup and pecans often to develop thick glaze for nuts in microwave.

## RUM-SPICE NUTS

*Sugar- and spice-crusted pecans or walnuts, bathed first in rum, make a simple confection to offer with fruit or ice cream for a quick dessert.*

*With a microwave oven, they're quick to make, but the nuts need to steep in their liqueur bath for at least an hour.*

- 1½ cups pecan or walnut halves or pieces
- ⅓ cup rum
- 3 tablespoons butter or margarine, cut into small pieces
- ⅓ cup sugar
- 2 teaspoons pumpkin pie spice

In a 9- to 10-inch round glass baking dish, mix pecans with rum and cover tightly with plastic wrap. Let sit 1 to 24 hours; stir often the first hour.

Add butter, sugar, and pumpkin pie spice; mix and spread nuts evenly. Cook uncovered in a microwave oven on full power for 1½ minutes. Stir well, spread evenly, and repeat. Reduce cooking time to 1 minute and repeatedly cook, stir, and spread until a thick syrup coats nuts, a total of 5 or 6 minutes more.

Scrape nuts onto baking parchment or foil, separate with a spoon, and let cool completely. Serve, or store airtight up to 2 weeks. If nuts soften, recrisp in the baking dish in a microwave on full power for 2 minutes; stir once. Let cool before serving. Makes about 2 cups.

## ORANGE-SPICE NUTS

Follow directions for **Rum-Spice Nuts** (left), but omit rum and use ⅓ cup **orange-flavored liqueur.**

## VANILLA CREAM WITH RHUBARB-STRAWBERRY SAUCE

*Pink and pretty, the delicate sauce for this cool vanilla cream dessert gets its rosy color from hothouse rhubarb and early strawberries. Serve the festive mold and topping for a romantic conclusion to your Valentine's Day dinner.*

*Hothouse rhubarb, also called strawberry rhubarb, is super-sour and technically an herb with an edible stalk. Its fruity flavor develops and its sharpness gets toned down when you combine it with strawberries and a little sugar to make the sauce. If you like, make both cream and sauce ahead.*

- 1 package unflavored gelatin
- ¼ cup water
- 3 large eggs
- ½ cup sugar
- 1 teaspoon vanilla
- 1 cup whipping cream
- 1 or 2 perfect strawberries, rinsed and hulled
  Rhubarb-strawberry sauce (recipe follows)

In a 1- to 2-cup pan, sprinkle gelatin over water; let stand until softened, about 5 minutes.

In the small bowl of an electric mixer, beat eggs on high speed until frothy. Gradually add sugar and vanilla, beating until eggs are about double in volume.

At the same time, set gelatin over medium heat and stir frequently until it liquefies; remove from heat and beat into the eggs.

At once, in another bowl whip the cream until it will hold soft peaks. Thoroughly but gently fold egg mixture into cream; if inadequately mixed, the gelatin will not thicken the mixture evenly. Pour into a 1-quart plain or decorative mold. Cover and chill until firmly set, at least 3 hours or up to 2 days.

To unmold, immerse pan up to rim in hottest tap water just until edges of dessert begin to melt. To help release suction, insert the blade of a table knife at the pan rim and push to bottom. Remove knife and lay a rimmed serving dish on top of the mold; holding dish

and mold together, invert and shake gently to dislodge dessert. Serve, or cover without touching dessert and chill as long as overnight.

Pour about half the rhubarb-strawberry sauce over and around the dessert. Spoon dessert into individual bowls with some of the sauce and add remaining sauce to taste. Makes 8 servings.

**Rhubarb-strawberry sauce.** Rinse, drain, and hull 4 cups (about 1 lb.) **strawberries.** Put fruit in a blender or food processor, add ¼ cup **sugar,** and whirl until smooth.

Rinse ½ pound **rhubarb;** trim off dried out ends, if necessary. Cut stalks into 1-inch pieces; you should have 2 cups.

Place strawberry mixture and rhubarb in a 2- to 3-quart pan. Bring to a boil on high heat, stirring occasionally to prevent sticking. Reduce heat and simmer, covered, just until rhubarb is tender when pierced, 8 to 12 minutes. Whirl in a blender or food processor until smoothly puréed. Serve warm or cool; if made ahead, cover and chill up to overnight.

Poured over and around berry-topped vanilla cream dessert, sauce has tang of rhubarb, fruitiness of strawberries.

*Spicy sausage, lentils, and vegetables are the basic makings for flavorful gumbo.*

## FRESNO SMOKED SAUSAGE & LENTIL GUMBO

- ¾ pound smoked sausage (andouille or Polish), sliced ¼ inch thick
  About ⅓ cup salad oil
- ⅓ cup all-purpose flour
- 4 stalks celery, finely chopped
- 3 cloves garlic, pressed or minced
- 2 medium-size onions, diced
- 2 large carrots, finely chopped
- 2 quarts regular-strength chicken broth
- 1¾ cups (¾ lb.) lentils
- 1 tablespoon Worcestershire
- ¼ teaspoon pepper
- ¼ teaspoon cayenne

In a 5- to 6-quart pan over medium heat, cook sausage, stirring, until brown. Spoon from pan; reserve. Add oil to drippings in pan to make ⅓ cup fat. Add flour; stir until mixture is red-brown, about 10 minutes.

Add celery, garlic, onion, and carrots; cook, stirring, until vegetables begin to soften, about 3 minutes. Add reserved sausage, chicken broth, lentils, Worcestershire, pepper, and cayenne. Bring to boiling over high heat; reduce to simmer, cover, and cook until lentils are soft when pressed, about 40 minutes. Makes 6 to 8 servings. —*Mrs. Anne Dobrinen, Fresno, Calif.*

*Canned roasted peppers give a quick start on sandwiches topped with cheese, avocado.*

## ROASTED RED PEPPER SANDWICHES

- 4 whole-wheat English muffins
- 8 thin slices red onion
- 1 large ripe avocado
- 8 thin slices jack cheese, *each* about 2½ inches square
- 2 jars (7 oz. *each*) roasted red bell peppers or pimientos, drained
- 3 tablespoons grated parmesan cheese

Split English muffins in half and arrange, cut sides up, on a 12- by 15-inch baking sheet. Set sheet about 6 inches below the broiler and toast muffins until golden, about 2 minutes.

Place 1 slice onion on each muffin. Peel and pit avocado; slice each half into 8 wedges. Top each onion slice with 2 avocado wedges and 1 slice jack cheese, then an equal amount of red peppers. Sprinkle each muffin with an equal amount of parmesan cheese.

Return to oven and broil until jack cheese melts slightly, 2 to 3 minutes. Makes 4 to 8 servings. —*Janet Moore, Beulah, Colo.*

*Broccoli steams atop cooked mushrooms and barley for an easy one-pan dish.*

## BROCCOLI WITH MUSHROOMS & BARLEY

- 3 tablespoons butter or margarine
- 1 pound mushrooms, sliced
- 1 small onion, chopped
- 1½ cups regular-strength beef broth
- ½ cup barley, rinsed
- 4 cups (about 1 lb.) broccoli flowerets
  Water
- 2 tablespoons grated parmesan cheese (optional)

In a 10- to 12-inch frying pan over medium heat, melt butter. Add mushrooms and onion; cook, stirring occasionally, until liquid evaporates and vegetables are light golden, about 20 minutes. Add broth and barley. Heat to boiling, then reduce to simmer; cover and cook until barley is tender to bite, about 30 minutes.

Spread broccoli evenly on barley. If broth has cooked away, add ¼ cup water; cover and cook until broccoli is tender when pierced, about 10 minutes. Remove cover and cook until liquid evaporates. Lift broccoli from pan and arrange alongside barley on a platter. Sprinkle barley and mushrooms with parmesan, if desired. Serves 4 to 6. —*Peggy Deen, Corvallis, Ore.*

## HEARTY HEALTHY HOTCAKES

⅓ cup *each* regular rolled oats, cornmeal, and all-purpose flour
2 tablespoons sugar
1 teaspoon baking powder
½ teaspoon baking soda
¼ teaspoon salt, or to taste
2 large eggs, separated
1 cup buttermilk
   Salad oil

In a bowl, combine oats, cornmeal,
flour, sugar, baking powder, baking
soda, and salt. In another bowl, whisk
egg yolks and buttermilk to combine.
Pour liquid into dry ingredients; stir just
to evenly moisten.

With an electric mixer, beat egg whites
on high speed until soft peaks form.
Gently fold whites into batter.

Heat an electric griddle to 375° (or heat
a 10- to 12-inch frying pan over medium-
high heat until a drop of water sizzles on
it). Brush griddle lightly with oil. Spoon
about ⅓ cup batter per pancake onto
griddle; cook until top of pancake is set
and bottom is medium brown, about 1
minute. Turn pancake over; cook until
medium brown, about 30 seconds more.
Repeat with remaining batter. Makes
about 8 pancakes.—*Mickey Strang,
Ridgecrest, Calif.*

*Oats and cornmeal add rich flavor; whipped egg
whites increase lightness of tender pancakes.*

## MEDITERRANEAN SQUASH SALAD

1 medium-size (about 3 lb.) spaghetti squash
⅓ cup currants
2 tablespoons white wine vinegar
2 tablespoons orange juice
2 tablespoons firmly packed brown
   sugar
1 teaspoon grated orange peel
¼ cup pine nuts
   Salt and pepper

Cut squash in half lengthwise; scoop out
and discard seeds. On a rack in a 5- to
6-quart pan, place squash cut side
down; halves can overlap. Fill pan with
no more than 2 inches water, or to just

below rack. Bring to boiling. Cover pan
and boil steadily until pulp is tender
when pierced, about 25 minutes (add
boiling water to pan, if needed).

When squash is cool to touch, scoop
out pulp and separate strands with 2
forks. Mix squash with currants, vinegar, orange juice, sugar, and orange
peel. Cover and chill until cold, 2 hours,
or up to overnight. Stir pine nuts into
squash mixture. Add salt and pepper to
taste. Makes 6 to 8 servings.—*Roxanne
Chan, Albany, Calif.*

*Separate strands of cooked squash with a fork;
mix with currants and seasonings, then chill.*

## CHOCOLATE-PEPPERMINT VALENTINE CAKE

2½ cups all-purpose flour
2 cups sugar
⅔ cup unsweetened cocoa
⅔ cup crushed peppermint candy
1½ teaspoons baking soda
¼ teaspoon salt
2 large eggs
1½ cups canned applesauce
¾ cup (⅜ lb.) butter or margarine,
   at room temperature
½ cup water

In large bowl of an electric mixer put
flour, sugar, cocoa, ½ cup of the peppermint candy, baking soda, and salt; mix

on low speed to combine. Add eggs,
applesauce, butter, and water; beat until
smooth, about 2 minutes.

Cut waxed paper to fit the bottoms of 3
heart-shaped or round baking pans, *each*
8 to 9 inches in diameter. Butter pan
sides and paper; dust with flour. Spread
batter equally in each pan.

Bake in a 350° oven until a slender
wooden skewer inserted in the center of
each comes out clean, about 40 minutes.
Let stand 10 minutes; invert cakes onto
racks to cool. Place on dishes and sprinkle cakes with remaining candy. If made
ahead, cover and chill up to 2 days.
Makes 3 cakes, 6 to 8 servings each.—
*Sheryl Kindle Fullner, Everson, Wash.*

*Say "Be my valentine" with a sweetheart pepper-
mint-chocolate cake and ice cream.*

THE 20TH CENTURY *may well be remembered as the age of the acronym. World War II gave us jeep (from GP, or general purpose vehicle), radar, sonar, and snafu. International relations contributed UNESCO and NATO, and financial institutions introduced the IRA. Extending the trend to naming food, Frank McMillan developed PANDA bread.*

*He got the idea for his recipe from the San Francisco Zoo, where the giant pandas on loan from China ate—in addition to bamboo—a supplement called panda bread. Concocted to provide important nutrients, the bread was also designed to appeal to panda palates.*

*Chef McMillan's bread, designed to appeal to human tastes, contains pumpkin, applesauce, nuts, dates, and apricots. Put the initials—and the ingredients—together, and you get PANDA bread. It's delicious warm or cool, and you can freeze any surplus for later use. Already a COW (Chef of the West), Mr. McMillan gets an apron to go with his toque.*

*"He got the idea for his recipe from the San Francisco Zoo, where the giant pandas ate a supplement called panda bread."*

## PANDA BREAD

- ⅔ cup solid shortening
- 1¼ cups *each* granulated sugar and firmly packed brown sugar
- 4 large eggs
- 1 cup canned applesauce
- 1 cup canned pumpkin
- 2 cups all-purpose flour
- 1½ cups whole-wheat flour
- 2 teaspoons baking soda
- ½ teaspoon baking powder
- ½ teaspoon salt
- ½ teaspoon ground cinnamon
- ¼ teaspoon *each* ground mace, ground nutmeg, and ground cloves
- ⅔ cup *each* chopped dried apricots and pitted dates
- 1 cup chopped walnuts

In a large bowl, beat shortening, granulated sugar, and brown sugar with an electric mixer until well blended. Add eggs, 1 at a time, and beat until well mixed. Beat in applesauce and pumpkin.

Stir together all-purpose flour, whole-wheat flour, baking soda, baking powder, salt, cinnamon, mace, nutmeg, and cloves. Add dry ingredients to pumpkin mixture; stir until flour is moistened, then beat until well blended. Stir in apricots, dates, and nuts.

Spoon batter equally into 2 well-greased 5- by 9-inch loaf pans. Bake in a 350° oven until a slender wooden pick inserted in each loaf's center comes out clean and bread just begins to pull away from pan sides, about 1 hour.

Let cool in pans for 10 minutes, then turn loaves out onto a rack to cool further. Serve warm or at room temperature. If made ahead, wrap airtight and refrigerate for up to 1 week, or freeze to store longer. Makes 2 loaves, *each* about 2 pounds.

*Frank McMillan*

*Orinda, Calif.*

A BIG WHITE CIRCLE *of pizza dough is to a cook what a blank canvas is to a painter. But most pizza makers use a conventional style and limited palette, working largely with deep red tomato sauce and pale cheeses, with pointillist touches of olive and sausage. Along comes W. J. Wirth with a radical new set of ingredients for his concept—breakfast pizza.*

*This spectacular creation resembles a technicolor Aztec calendar stone. It has an outer circlet of thin tomato slices (just enough to satisfy an Englishman's morning craving for a grilled tomahto) and is brightened by a bacon center and the sunny sides of 6 eggs. These nest in a bed of sausage on a pizza dough foundation. To complete this breakfast, all you add is coffee.*

## BREAKFAST PIZZA

- 1 package active dry yeast
- ¾ cup warm water (110°)
- 1 teaspoon sugar
- 1 tablespoon olive oil or salad oil
- ¼ teaspoon salt
- 2 cups all-purpose flour
- 6 slices bacon (optional)
- 1 pound bulk pork sausage
- 1 large firm-ripe tomato, cored, seeded, and very thinly sliced
- 6 large eggs
- 1 cup (4 oz.) shredded mozzarella cheese

In a large bowl, sprinkle yeast over water and let stand for 5 minutes to soften. Stir in sugar, oil, and salt, then mix in flour and beat until stretchy. Cover bowl with plastic wrap and let stand in a warm place until dough doubles, about 30 minutes. If made ahead, don't let dough rise; instead, cover and chill overnight.

Meanwhile, in a 10- to 12-inch frying pan, cook bacon over medium heat until crisp; drain on paper towels. When cool enough to touch, crumble bacon; discard fat. Add the sausage to the pan, breaking it into chunks (about ½ inch) with a spoon; stir often over medium heat until meat is well browned, 12 to 15 minutes. Lift out sausage with a slotted spoon and drain well on paper towels; discard fat.

Punch down dough, then roll or pat it to fit in a greased 14-inch pizza pan, pushing the dough up the sides to form a slight rim. In a 450° oven, bake dough on the bottom rack until lightly browned, about 15 minutes.

Remove crust from oven and evenly sprinkle with sausage. Then sprinkle the crumbled bacon in a 3-inch circle in the center of the crust. Arrange tomato slices around outside edge of crust.

Mentally divide the pizza into 6 wedge-shaped pieces; carefully break an egg onto each wedge, then evenly sprinkle cheese over all.

Return pizza to oven and continue to bake just until egg whites are set but yolks are still soft, 12 to 15 minutes more. Remove from oven and cut into wedges. Serve at once. Makes 6 servings.

*Thornton, Colo.*

---

ALONE, EGGPLANT IS UNASSERTIVE, *but in the proper company, this retiring vegetable grows bold. David Horowitz, a man devoted to seeing that products deliver as advertised, uses an admixture of Mediterranean flavorings—olive oil, garlic, tomato, herbs, and feta cheese—to give his eggplant recipe the flair its name implies.*

## EGGPLANT À LA DAVID

- 2 tablespoons olive oil or salad oil
- 1 medium-size onion, thinly sliced
- 1 clove garlic, minced or pressed
- 1 medium-size eggplant (about 1 lb.), stemmed and cut into 1-inch cubes
- 1 teaspoon dry basil
- 1 medium-size (6 to 8 oz.) zucchini, ends trimmed and cut into ½-inch-thick slices
- 1 large firm-ripe tomato, cored, seeded, and chopped
- ¾ cup crumbled feta cheese
  Salt and pepper

In a 10- to 12-inch frying pan over medium heat, combine oil, onion, and garlic; stir often until onion is golden, 12 to 15 minutes.

Stir in eggplant and basil; cover and cook for 10 minutes. Add zucchini and cook covered, stirring often, until eggplant is very soft when pressed, 15 to 20 minutes more. Add tomato and cheese, then stir gently just until hot. Season to taste with salt and pepper. Makes 4 to 6 servings.

*david horowitz*

*Burbank, Calif.*

*"Golfer's special: there's always a beef when you shank one."*

---

CHEF JULES GREENBERG *creates with words as well as ingredients and uses a pun to introduce his stew-soup. Referring to the recipe, which combines lamb shanks and oxtails, he says, "I call it my golfer's special. There's always a beef when you shank one."*

## LAMB SHANKS WITH OXTAILS

- 4 lamb shanks, cracked
  About 2 pounds small oxtails
  All-purpose flour
- 3 tablespoons salad oil
- 1 can (10½ oz.) condensed consommé
- 1 cup dry red wine
- 1 can (1 lb.) tomatoes
- 2 cloves garlic, minced or pressed
- 1 tablespoon Worcestershire
- ½ teaspoon *each* dry rosemary, dry oregano leaves, and pepper
- 1 bay leaf
- 4 small (about 1½ in. diameter) thin-skinned potatoes, peeled and halved
- 4 small carrots, peeled and cut into 1½-inch lengths
- 2 small stalks celery, cut into 1½-inch lengths
- ¼ pound mushrooms, sliced
  Chopped parsley
  Salt

Coat shanks and oxtails with flour, then shake off excess. Pour oil into a 6- to 8-quart pan on medium heat; add meat and cook until browned on all sides. Discard fat. To the pan add consommé, wine, tomatoes (break up with a spoon) and their liquid, garlic, Worcestershire, rosemary, oregano, pepper, and bay leaf. Bake, covered, in a 350° oven for 2 hours.

Add potatoes and carrots; cover and bake 30 minutes longer. Then add celery and mushrooms; cover and bake until meat is very tender when pierced, 45 minutes to 1 hour more.

Lift meat and vegetables from pan with a slotted spoon and serve into wide soup dishes. Skim fat from broth and discard, then ladle equally into dishes. Sprinkle soup with parsley and add salt to taste. Makes 6 servings.

*Bakersfield, Calif.*

# February Menus

MIDWINTER PRODUCE *is far more plentiful and varied than some shoppers believe. This month, our menus take advantage of old standbys and a few unusual offerings. For breakfast or brunch, embellish buckwheat crêpes with some of the fine winter pears. The Comice variety is especially luscious and sweet.*

*Leeks, potatoes, and carrots simmer in a light broth with fish for a simple pot-au-feu. Butter lettuce and purple salad savoy (an ornamental kale) make a colorful salad accompaniment.*

*For supper, an oven-baked hash of jicama, yams, lima beans, and bright peppers forms a flavorful bed for Cornish game hens, which nestle in the vegetable mixture as they cook.*

Spoon sour cream onto buckwheat crêpes topped with pecans and juicy pears.

## BUCKWHEAT BREAKFAST

**Buckwheat Crêpes with Pears**
**Sliced Canadian Bacon**
**Hot Spiced Cider**

*For a morning meal, combine buckwheat-flecked crêpes with succulent pears, maple syrup, sour cream, and nuts.*

*Use readily available buckwheat pancake mix or pure buckwheat flour (found in health-food stores) for the crêpes. Those made with the mix will be a bit more tender and possess a milder flavor than those prepared with the flour.*

*Make the crêpes in the morning or up to a day ahead. Brown bacon (you'll need 8 to 12 oz.) and slice pears just before serving.*

## BUCKWHEAT CRÊPES WITH PEARS

1⅓ cups milk
4 large eggs
1 cup buckwheat pancake mix or buckwheat flour
About 2 tablespoons butter or margarine
12 to 15 pecan or walnut halves
4 or 5 small, soft-ripe Comice or Anjou pears, cored and sliced
Sour cream
Warm maple syrup

In a blender, combine milk, eggs, and buckwheat; whirl until smooth. Place a 7- to 8-inch crêpe pan or a frying pan measuring 7 to 8 inches across the bottom over medium-high heat. When hot, add ¼ teaspoon butter and swirl to coat surface. Stir batter and pour in about ¼ cup, quickly tilting the pan so batter flows evenly over bottom. Cook until top is dry and edge is lightly browned, about 1 minute. Turn with a spatula and brown other side, about 30 seconds more. Turn out onto a plate and fold in quarters to make a triangle. Place on a platter in a warm oven; cover platter lightly with foil. Repeat to make remaining crêpes.

In the same pan over medium-low heat, melt butter, then quickly add the nuts, shaking often until lightly toasted, 2 to 3 minutes. Scatter nuts over crêpes.

(If made ahead, place folded crêpes in a single layer on two 12- by 15-inch baking sheets. Scatter nuts over crêpes. Cool, cover, and chill up to 1 day. To reheat, bake, covered, in a 400° oven until hot, 5 to 8 minutes. Transfer to a serving plate.)

Offer pears, sour cream, and syrup to top each portion. Makes 16 crêpes, 4 or 5 servings.

## VALENTINE DINNER

**Green & Purple Salad**
**Fish Pot-au-Feu**
**Baguette      Butter**
**Sauvignon Blanc      Sparkling Water**
**Chocolate Hearts      Espresso**

Start this elegant meal with green and purple salad greens lightly coated with a creamy garlic dressing. Follow with vegetables and fish poached in a simple broth. Then delight your valentine with cool, melt-in-your-mouth chocolate hearts.

Make the chocolate hearts in advance; they store in the freezer for a couple of weeks. Wash and crisp salad greens and prepare the dressing up to a day ahead. The main dish goes together quickly.

## GREEN & PURPLE SALAD

4 cups (about 6 oz.) lightly packed small butter lettuce leaves, washed and crisped
3 cups (3 to 4 oz.) lightly packed small purple salad savoy or red cabbage leaves, washed and crisped
⅓ cup olive oil or salad oil
2 tablespoons white wine vinegar
1 clove garlic, pressed or minced
1 tablespoon mayonnaise
Salt and pepper

Arrange butter lettuce and salad savoy in a wide, shallow serving bowl. Whisk together oil, vinegar, garlic, and mayonnaise. Pour over greens and mix. Add salt and pepper to taste. Serves 4.

Simple, light pot-au-feu features fish and vegetables in a tarragon-laced broth. Serve with a vibrant mix of salad leaves.

## FISH POT-AU-FEU

5 cups regular-strength chicken broth
1 cup dry white wine (or 1 cup regular-strength chicken broth and 3 tablespoons white wine vinegar)
½ teaspoon dry tarragon
4 small (1½ in. diameter) thin-skinned red potatoes, scrubbed
4 medium-size carrots, peeled and cut in half
4 medium-size leeks (about 2 lb. total), roots and most of the dark green tops trimmed
1½ pounds lean white fish fillets, such as lingcod or sea bass

In a 5- to 6-quart pan, combine broth, wine, and tarragon. Bring to boiling over high heat. Add potatoes and carrots, return to boiling, then cover pan and reduce heat. Simmer 10 minutes.

Meanwhile split the leeks lengthwise and rinse well; add to pan. Cover and simmer vegetables 10 minutes longer. Pierce vegetables to check tenderness and lift from broth with a slotted spoon when done. Cover cooked vegetables and keep warm. Cut fish into 4 equal portions. Add to broth after most of the vegetables are tender and have been removed from pan; simmer gently until fish is opaque in thickest part (cut to test) and remaining vegetables are tender when pierced, 7 to 10 minutes.

With a slotted spatula, carefully lift out fish and place a piece in each of 4 wide, shallow bowls. Lift out remaining vegetables. Place equal portions of each vegetable in the bowls. Ladle hot broth over servings. Serves 4.

## CHOCOLATE HEARTS

6 ounces semisweet chocolate, finely chopped, or baking chips (about 1 cup)
¼ cup whipping cream
2 tablespoons crème de menthe (or ½ teaspoon mint flavoring and 2 tablespoons whipping cream)
2 tablespoons cocoa

In a 1- to 2-quart pan, combine chocolate and cream. Stir over lowest possible heat until chocolate melts and is blended with cream, 2 to 3 minutes. Remove from heat and stir in crème de menthe.

Line the bottom and about 1 inch up the sides of a 4- by 8-inch pan with foil. Pour chocolate mixture into pan. Freeze until firm enough to cut, 45 to 60 min-

Cocoa-dusted chocolate candies will melt your valentine's heart. Serve with flowers, espresso.

utes. Lift out of pan and peel off foil. Place chocolate slab on a piece of waxed paper dusted with cocoa. With a small (1- to 1½-inch) heart-shaped cooky cutter, quickly cut chocolate, spacing hearts close together and wiping cutter often (or cut around a cardboard heart-shaped pattern with a knife). Cut the excess chocolate into bite-size pieces.

Roll each chocolate piece in cocoa to coat heavily. Serve, or if made ahead, arrange chocolates in a single layer in a shallow pan; cover and freeze up to 2 weeks. Makes about 9 hearts (1½-inch size) and 10 to 12 odd-size pieces (8 oz. total).

### GAME HEN SUPPER

**Cherry Tomatoes in Parsley Vinaigrette**
**Roasted Cornish Game Hens with Vegetable Hash**
**Ice Cream Sundaes**
**Coffee**     **Milk**

Split Cornish game hens roast on a bed of diced vegetables.

While the vegetable hash bakes, cut about 3 cups cherry tomatoes in half and mix with about ⅓ cup basic oil-vinegar dressing; for color, add approximately 2 tablespoons chopped parsley. Cover and chill salad until ready to serve.

Offer ice cream sundaes for dessert.

(Continued on next page)

## ROASTED CORNISH GAME HENS WITH VEGETABLE HASH

2 Cornish game hens
   (*each* 1¼ to 1½ lb.)
3 tablespoons lemon juice
3 tablespoons olive oil or salad oil
2 teaspoons minced fresh or
   crumbled dry rosemary
1 clove garlic, pressed or minced
1 small jicama (1 lb.), peeled and cut
   into ½-inch cubes
2 large yams or sweet potatoes
   (1 lb. total), scrubbed and cut into
   ½-inch cubes
1 large red or yellow bell pepper,
   stemmed, seeded, and diced
1 large onion, coarsely chopped
1 package (10 oz.) frozen baby lima
   beans, thawed
   Salt and pepper
   Fresh rosemary sprigs (optional)

With scissors or a knife, split game hens in half lengthwise. Rinse and pat dry.

In an 11- by 17-inch roasting pan, mix lemon juice, oil, minced rosemary, and garlic. Turn the split birds in oil mixture to coat; lift out and set aside. Add jicama, yams, bell pepper, and onion to pan; stir to coat with the oil and rosemary mixture.

Bake vegetables, uncovered, in a 425° oven for 30 minutes. Stir in lima beans. Lay game hens, cut side down, on vegetables and continue baking until birds are browned and meat is no longer pink in thickest part of breast (cut to test), 30 to 45 minutes longer.

Lift out the birds and place on a large platter; spoon vegetables alongside. Sprinkle with salt and pepper to taste. Garnish with rosemary sprigs. Makes 4 servings. —*Carla Olsten, Ketchum, Idaho.*

*Pretzel-Shaped Sandwich Loaf (page 52)*

**H**ale and hearty fare for March
included a quartet of colorful chilies and a super-sized, pretzel-
shaped loaf that makes a grand sandwich for an informal
party. Oven smoking was presented as a simple way to obtain
succulent, smoke-flavored foods without a fire. Our March
issue also featured timesaving dishes enhanced with exotic
touches—dressy ways to wrap up ground beef, a custard that
bakes in five minutes in a microwave oven, a speedy
stir-fry featuring tortellini, and quick desserts
using winter citrus.

# Giant Pretzel Sandwich Loaf

**S**PORTS FANS *will appreciate this varia-tion on standard game-watching fare.*

*You shape beer- and rye-flavored yeast dough into a giant pretzel, then bake it, split it, and layer cold cuts inside. Serve the sandwich at home, or wrap in foil to trans-port to the field. The loaf is also a good pot-luck choice. You can bake the pretzel ahead, if you like. It also freezes well; simply thaw and fill to serve.*

## PRETZEL-SHAPED SANDWICH LOAF

  1  **bottle (12 oz.) dark beer**
 ⅓  **cup cornmeal**
 ¼  **cup dark molasses**
  1  **package active dry yeast**
 ¼  **cup warm water (110°)**
  2  **tablespoons salad oil**
  1  **teaspoon table salt**
  1  **cup rye flour**
3¾  **to 4 cups all-purpose flour**
  1  **large egg, lightly beaten**
     **Coarse salt (optional)**
     **Sandwich ingredients (directions follow)**

In a 1- to 2-quart pan, stir together beer, cornmeal, and molasses. Bring to a boil over high heat, then let cool to 110°.

In a large bowl, sprinkle yeast over water; let stand to soften, about 5 min-utes. Stir in beer mixture, oil, table salt, and rye flour until blended. With a dough hook or spoon, stir in 3½ cups of the all-purpose flour until smooth.

*To knead with a dough hook,* beat until dough pulls cleanly from sides of bowl, about 10 minutes; add a little all-purpose flour at a time if dough still sticks to bowl.

*To knead by hand,* lightly coat a board with all-purpose flour; scrape dough onto it. Knead until smooth and elastic, 12 to 15 minutes, adding as little flour as possible to prevent sticking.

Place dough in a greased bowl, turn over, cover with plastic wrap, and let rise in a warm place until doubled in volume, 1 to 1¼ hours. Punch down, then knead briefly to release air.

On a lightly floured board, roll dough with your hands into a smooth rope about 1½ inches thick and 46 inches long. Ease rope onto a greased 14- by 17-inch baking sheet, placing middle of the rope 2 inches from the center of 1 long pan edge.

To shape rope into a pretzel (as shown below), pick up ends of rope and form about ½ of the dough into a circle with a center opening approximately 11 inches in diameter. Cross ends at top of circle, twist twice, then lay ends over bottom of circle and tuck under. Cover pretzel loosely with plastic wrap and let rise in a warm place until puffy, about 30 minutes.

Brush dough with egg, then sprinkle lightly with coarse salt. Bake in a 350° oven until well browned, about 30 min-utes. Transfer to a rack and let cool com-pletely. (If made ahead, cover and store at room temperature up to 1 day. Freeze for longer storage; thaw to use.)

With a serrated knife, carefully split bread horizontally. Gently lift off top and turn cut side up. Fill with sandwich ingredients. Cut into wedges to serve. Makes 1 loaf (2¼ lb. without filling), enough for 6 to 8 servings.

**Sandwich ingredients.** Spread cut side of 1 bread half with ⅓ cup **mayonnaise.** Spread cut side of other half with ½ cup **mustard.** Over bottom half, layer ½ pound *each* **thinly sliced cooked turkey, thinly sliced cooked ham,** and **thinly sliced Swiss cheese;** 8 large **butter let-tuce** leaves, washed and crisped; and 2 large **tomatoes,** thinly sliced. Place up-per half of bread cut side down on filling.

*To shape pretzel, cross dough rope ends at top of circle, twist twice, then lay ends over bottom of circle and tuck under.*

*Carefully split cooled bread through center with long knife; lift off pretzel top and fill to make sandwich loaf.*

*Giant pretzel loaf, filled with cold cuts, lettuce, and tomatoes, feeds a hungry group. Serve in generous wedges.*

# Choose-the-Color Chili

A STANDBY FAVORED *for generations, chili has a new look these days. You'll find it takes beautifully to variations, as in these different-hued, different-tasting choices.*

*Three of the chilies are hearty. Indian curry seasonings flavor the white bean chili, made with lamb for substance. Black beans give dark color to the second; Polish sausage enriches its taste. Red chili con carne gets color and medium fire from sweet peppers and ground New Mexico chilies (instead of standard chili powder, a blend of seasonings).*

*The quick green chili is all-vegetable, with lots of peppers and chilies; you add jalapeño cheese for heat and protein.*

*Serve the Indian-style chili with pappadums—spiced lentil wafers—available in well-stocked supermarkets, or Middle Eastern markets; fry as package directs.*

*Look for ground New Mexico or California chilies in well-stocked supermarkets or Mexican groceries; their flavors are similar.*

## INDIAN-STYLE BROWN CHILI

- 2 pounds lean, boned lamb for stew, fat trimmed, cut into 1½-inch pieces
- ¼ cup salad oil
- 2 large onions, sliced
- 3 cloves garlic, minced or pressed
- 1 tablespoon minced fresh ginger
- 1 tablespoon *each* cumin seed and mustard seed
- 2 cinnamon sticks (*each* 3 inches long)
- 3 bay leaves
- 4 small dried hot red chilies
- ½ teaspoon ground cloves
- 1 teaspoon ground cardamom
- 1 tablespoon ground coriander
- 7 cups regular-strength beef broth
- ¾ pound (2 cups) dried Great Northern beans, sorted of debris and rinsed
  Small dried hot red chilies

In a 5- to 6-quart pan over high heat, brown meat half at a time, stirring, in 1 tablespoon of the oil. Lift out and set aside. Reduce heat to medium. Add remaining oil, onions, garlic, and ginger. Cook, stirring occasionally, until onions are very limp, 10 to 15 minutes.

Add cumin, mustard seed, cinnamon, bay leaves, and the 4 chilies; stir for 3 minutes. Add cloves, cardamom, and coriander; stir 1 minute. Stir in broth, beans, lamb, and any juices.

Bring to a boil over high heat; simmer, covered, until beans are very tender to bite, about 3 hours; stir often. If made ahead, cool, cover, and chill up to 2 days. Reheat to serve. Garnish with dried chilies. Makes 2½ quarts, 5 or 6 servings.

## MELLOW BLACK BEAN CHILI

- ¼ cup olive oil
- 4 large onions, sliced
- 4 cloves garlic, minced or pressed
- 3 large stalks celery, chopped
- 1 tablespoon ground cumin
- 1 pound (2½ cups) dried black beans, sorted of debris and rinsed
- 1 can (7 oz.) diced green chilies
- 8 cups regular-strength chicken broth
- ½ cup dry sherry
- ¼ cup lemon juice
- 1½ pounds kielbasa (Polish sausage), thinly sliced
  Sour cream or unflavored yogurt
  Prepared hot red salsa

In oil in a 6- to 8-quart pan over medium-high heat, cook onions, garlic, and celery until very limp, about 20 minutes; stir often. Add cumin and stir for 1 minute.

Stir in beans, chilies, and broth. Bring to a boil over high heat, then simmer, covered, until beans are tender to bite, about 2½ hours. Stir in sherry and lemon juice. In a blender, whirl half the soup, a portion at a time, until smooth. Return to pan.

Stir in sausage. Simmer, covered, for 10 minutes more. If made ahead, cool, cover, and chill up to 2 days; reheat to serve. Offer sour cream and salsa to add to taste. Makes 4 quarts, 8 servings.

## NEW MEXICAN RED BEAN CHILI

- 2 jars (7 oz. *each*) roasted red peppers or canned pimientos
- 1 large red onion, chopped
- 2 pounds ground lean beef
- 3½ cups regular-strength beef broth
- 1 can (28 oz.) tomatoes, cut up
- 1 teaspoon ground allspice
- 2 teaspoons *each* ground cumin and ground coriander
- 4 teaspoons dry oregano leaves
- ½ cup ground dry New Mexico or California chilies
- 3 cans (about 16 oz. *each*) kidney beans, drained

In a blender, whirl red peppers and their liquid until smooth; set aside.

In a 5- to 6-quart pan over high heat, cook onion and half of beef until onion is limp, 6 to 8 minutes; stir often. Remove from pan. Cook remaining beef until well browned; stir often. Skim and discard fat.

Return beef and onion to pan with puréed peppers, broth, tomatoes and liquid, allspice, cumin, coriander, oregano, ground chilies, and beans. Bring to a boil over high heat, then simmer, covered, for 45 minutes; stir often. Uncover and simmer until thickened to your liking, 15 to 30 minutes, stirring often. If made ahead, cool, cover, and chill up to 2 days. Reheat to serve. Makes 3 quarts, 6 servings.

## GREEN, GREEN PEPPER CHILI

- 4 large green bell peppers, stemmed, seeded, and halved
- 2 cans (7 oz. *each*) whole green chilies, split lengthwise
- 3 tablespoons salad oil
- 4 large onions, sliced
- 2 cloves garlic, minced or pressed
- 1 tablespoon dry oregano leaves
- 2 cans (13 oz. *each*) tomatillos
- 6 cups regular-strength chicken broth
- 4 fresh jalapeño chilies (3 inches *each*), stemmed, seeded, and minced
- ½ cup chopped fresh cilantro leaves
- 2 cups (½ lb.) shredded jalapeño jack cheese
  Sour cream or unflavored yogurt
  Fresh cilantro sprigs

Thinly slice bell peppers and green chilies crosswise; set aside. In oil in a 6- to 8-quart pan over medium-high heat, cook onions and garlic, stirring often, until very limp and golden, about 30 minutes.

Stir in oregano, tomatillos and their liquid, broth, bell peppers, green chilies, and jalapeños. Bring to a boil over high heat, then simmer, covered, until bell peppers are very tender to bite, about 15 minutes. If made ahead, cool, cover, and chill up to 2 days; reheat to serve. Stir in chopped cilantro. Offer cheese, sour cream, and cilantro sprigs to add individually. Makes 4 quarts, 8 servings.

*Four chili colors, four different flavors. Clockwise from lower left: black bean chili and corn tortilla; brown, Indian-style lamb chili with crisp pappadums; New Mexican red bean chili; all-vegetable green chili with cilantro and cornbread.*

# Right-in-the-Oven Smoking

A HINT OF HICKORY SMOKE *in the air makes most mouths water in anticipation of a succulent treat from the barbecue. But you can have the same effect—and achieve similar flavor—without a fire, using just your oven.*

*We call the technique oven-smoking, and the ingredient that makes it possible is "liquid smoke." This preparation flavors foods, but it does not preserve them as true smoking—brining followed by partial drying—does.*

*This pale chestnut-color liquid, sold in small bottles alongside seasoning sauces in the supermarket, is actually made from smoke. As hickory wood burns, the smoke is captured in tubes, where it cools and condenses, then is filtered and bottled. You may also find it in flavors made with other woods, such as mesquite, in gourmet food stores and mail-order catalogs.*

*Oven-smoking is actually a combination of baking and steaming. The equipment is simple: a 5- to 6-quart pan or casserole with a tight lid and a rack that will fit inside.*

*Essentially, all you do is pour a small amount of liquid smoke in the pan, set foods you want to cook and flavor on the rack in the pan, cover the pan, and bake. As the liquid smoke evaporates, it permeates the food. You can control the intensity of the flavor by changing the amount of liquid smoke you use. Remember: a little goes a long way, and the smoke flavor tastes stronger when the foods are cold.*

*Smaller cuts of meat and pieces of fish or seafood, maximum of 2 inches thick, work best. Those suggested in the chart on page 58 can help you get started with your own experiments. If you want to smoke-flavor more than one food at a time or make a larger quantity, use more than one pan.*

*Although no real smoke is generated, the evaporating liquid smoke has a very penetrating odor. It will fill the kitchen and cling to your hair and clothes. If you prefer not to greet guests with these aromas, do your oven-smoking early in the day, or even the day before, and serve the smoked food chilled or at room temperature.*

*Oven-smoked foods will keep well for at least two days. To store, wrap securely to prevent the smoke flavor from permeating other items in the refrigerator.*

*Obvious foods to select for oven-smoking are those that are delicious when smoked by conventional methods: salmon, trout, shellfish, poultry, and pork. However, this process lends itself to more imaginative possibilities, such as oven-smoked potatoes—delicious and useful hot or cold.*

*You can serve these foods straight from the oven, tepid, or chilled. The recipes here give you some examples of each way: the mussels are tasty hot or cold, chicken breast and potatoes can go into salads, and salmon is best warm with linguine.*

## SMOKED MUSSELS WITH LEMON MAYONNAISE

**Smoked mussels (see chart on page 58), hot or cold**

½ **cup lemon mayonnaise (recipe follows)**

Arrange mussels on a platter with a small bowl of lemon mayonnaise. Pluck mussels from shell with a small fork or wooden pick and dip into mayonnaise. Makes 3 or 4 appetizer servings.

*Oven-smoked chicken breast has a pale amber surface; for salad, cut chicken in slanting slices, arrange alongside mixed salad greens, and add orange vinaigrette over greens and chicken.*

**Lemon mayonnaise.** In a blender or food processor, whirl 2 tablespoons **lemon juice,** 2 cloves **garlic,** 1 **large egg,** and ⅛ teaspoon **paprika** until blended. With motor running, slowly pour in 1 cup **salad oil** until combined. Add **salt** and **pepper** to taste. If made ahead, cover and chill up to 2 days. Makes 1¼ cups.

## SMOKED CHICKEN BREAST SALAD

 1 **tablespoon butter or margarine**
 ¾ **cup pecan halves**
 1½ **quarts mixed salad greens (such as butter and romaine lettuce, watercress), washed and crisped**
 4 **smoked chicken breast halves (see chart on page 58), chilled**
 **Orange vinaigrette (recipe follows)**

Melt butter in an 8- to 10-inch frying pan over low heat. Add pecans and stir until nuts darken slightly and have a toasted flavor, about 6 minutes. Pour onto paper towels to drain.

Arrange an equal amount of salad greens on 4 dinner plates and sprinkle greens equally with the pecans.

Cut each half-breast in slanting slices ¼ inch thick. Arrange overlapping slices of each half on a plate alongside greens. Spoon vinaigrette over greens and chicken. Makes 4 servings.

**Orange vinaigrette.** In a bowl, combine ¼ cup **orange juice,** 2 tablespoons **white wine vinegar,** 2 tablespoons **salad oil,** 1 tablespoon thinly slivered or shredded **orange peel** (colored part only), 2 teaspoons **honey,** 2 teaspoons **Dijon mustard,** and ½ teaspoon **coarsely ground pepper.**

## SMOKED POTATO SALAD

 1½ **pounds cold smoked thin-skinned potatoes (see chart on page 58), cut into ½-inch cubes**
 2 **large celery stalks, thinly sliced**
 2 **green onions (roots trimmed), thinly sliced**
 1½ **tablespoons drained capers**
 ⅓ **to ½ cup lemon mayonnaise (recipe precedes)**
 **Salt and pepper**

In a bowl, gently mix together the potatoes, celery, onions, and capers. Stir in ⅓ cup lemon mayonnaise; add more mayonnaise if desired. Season with salt and pepper to taste. Serve, or cover and chill up to 2 days. Makes 4 to 6 servings.

*Mmmm! Hickory smoke aroma rises from pan as she checks progress of mussels in the shell; they're on a rack over liquid smoke.*

*Served hot or cold to dunk in lemon mayonnaise, smoked mussels make tasty appetizers.*

## PASTA & SMOKED SALMON

¾ pound salmon fillet, skin removed, and fish cut into ½-inch-wide strips
2 quarts water
¾ pound dry linguine or spaghetti
2 tablespoons white wine vinegar
½ cup finely chopped onion
1 cup whipping cream
¾ cup dry white wine
1 tablespoon Dijon mustard
¼ cup grated parmesan cheese
½ cup fresh parsley sprigs
Salt and pepper

Smoke salmon strips as directed in chart at right for salmon fillet, but reduce time to 10 to 12 minutes; let stand.

Bring water to boiling in a 4- to 6-quart pan over high heat. Add linguine and cook, uncovered, until tender to bite, about 10 minutes. Drain.

As linguine cooks, boil vinegar with onion in a 10- to 12-inch frying pan over high heat until vinegar evaporates, about 2 minutes. Add cream, wine, and mustard. Boil uncovered, stirring often, until sauce is reduced to 1¾ cups. Add hot drained linguine; lift with forks to coat with sauce.

Divide linguine and sauce evenly among 4 dinner plates; sprinkle each serving with 1 tablespoon cheese. Arrange an equal amount of salmon beside each serving of linguine. Garnish with parsley. Mix salmon with linguine; season to taste with salt and pepper. Makes 4 entrée servings.

*Spoon chutney onto oven-smoked pork chop; it's an easy dinner with rice and cucumbers.*

# Foods You Can Oven-Smoke

## *Basic directions for oven-smoking:*

Pour 3 tablespoons **liquid smoke** into a 5- to 6-quart pan. Set a perforated or wire rack in the pan. Arrange **food** (select from chart, below) in a single layer on rack and tightly cover the pan. Bake in a 350° oven until food tests done (see chart). Serve hot, tepid, or chilled. If made ahead, let cool, cover, and chill up to 2 days. Makes 2 to 4 servings.

| Foods to try | Maximum amount or size | How do you know when they're done? |
| --- | --- | --- |
| Whole chicken breasts (1 lb. *each*), boned, skinned, and cut in half | 4 half-breasts | White in center (cut to test), 20 to 25 minutes |
| Chicken legs (thigh with drumstick) | 4 legs (1½ to 2 lb. *total*) | No longer pink at thigh bone (cut to test), 40 to 50 minutes |
| Whole broiler-fryer chicken | 3 to 3½ lb. | No longer pink at thigh bone (cut to test), 1¼ to 1½ hours |
| Game hens | 2 (2½ to 3 lb. *total*) | No longer pink at thigh bone (cut to test), 1 to 1¼ hours |
| Pork tenderloin | (1 to 2 lb. *total*) | Meat thermometer inserted in thickest part reads 160° and meat is no longer pink in center (cut to test), 35 to 45 minutes |
| Pork chops | 4, each cut 1 inch thick | No longer pink in center (cut to test), 25 to 30 minutes |
| Mussels, well scrubbed and beards removed | 18 (about 1 lb. *total*) | Shells open, about 15 minutes |
| Clams, suitable for steaming, well scrubbed | 18 (about 1½ lb. *total*) | Shells open wide, 15 to 25 minutes |
| Trout, whole | 10 to 11 in. long *each* (about 1 lb. *total*) | Fish is opaque in center of thickest part (cut to test), about 20 minutes |
| Salmon, steak or fillet (skin removed) | 1-inch-thick steaks; ¾ lb. fillet | Fish is opaque in center of thickest part (cut to test), 15 to 25 minutes |
| Thin-skinned potatoes, scrubbed and cut in half lengthwise | 3 or 4 large (1½ to 2 lb. *total*) | Tender when pierced, about 45 minutes |

# Spanish Soup

**M**EDITERRANEAN COOKS *have long favored the dry fava bean, but it's not that familiar a vegetable on most Western dining tables. On a recent visit to Spain, we enjoyed a light soup of dry favas and fresh clams. Back home, we went in search of sources so we could duplicate the soup and develop a creamy variation.*

*You'll find the dry beans sold in bulk in health-food stores or in Italian and Middle Eastern markets. As with fresh favas, which appear sporadically in markets April through June, the dry beans have tough skins that can discolor the cream-colored beans during cooking. To remove them, simply soak favas overnight, then pull off loosened skins. The soaked favas cook surprisingly fast, and fall apart if overcooked.*

*If you're allergic to favas or can't find them, use dry lima beans from your neighborhood market.*

To serve, ladle steamed clams into bowls, adding clam-flavored broth filled with fava beans and red and green peppers.

## FAVA BEAN & CLAM SOUP

1½ cups (½ lb.) dry fava beans or dry
    lima beans, sorted of debris and
    rinsed
    Water
2 tablespoons olive oil
1 large green bell pepper, stemmed,
    seeded, and sliced into ¼-inch
    strips

Peel tough skin from dry fava beans after soaking them overnight.

5 cloves garlic, pressed or minced
1 large leek, white part only, slit
    lengthwise, rinsed well, and
    thinly sliced
1 jar (7 oz.) roasted red bell peppers
    or pimientos, drained and sliced
2 cups bottled clam juice
2 cups regular-strength chicken
    broth
20 clams, suitable for steaming, well
    scrubbed
2 tablespoons dry sherry

In a large bowl, combine beans with 1 quart water; let stand overnight. Drain beans and discard water. Pull off and discard tough skins. (If using lima beans, soak them overnight but don't skin them.)

In a 5- to 6-quart pan over medium-high heat, combine oil and green bell peppers; cook, stirring, until peppers are limp. Add garlic and leeks; cook, stirring, until leeks are limp. Add red peppers, clam juice, and broth. Bring to boiling over high heat; reduce to simmer, add clams, cover, and cook until clams open, 3 to 10 minutes. Lift out clams as they open and set aside.

Add beans to broth and simmer, covered, until tender to bite, about 10 minutes (20 to 30 minutes for limas); stir in sherry. Transfer soup to a serving container, set clams on top, then ladle into bowls; or put clams in bowls and spoon the soup over them. Makes 4 or 5 servings.

## FAVA CREAM SOUP

Make **Fava Bean & Clam Soup** (preceding), omitting clams. Whirl soup, half at a time, in a blender until smoothly puréed. If desired, thin with hot **regular-strength chicken broth.** Serve with purchased or homemade **garlic croutons.** Makes 4 or 5 servings.

# Celery Root—The Winter Cook's Friend

**D**RAB, GNARLED, ROUGH—*not adjectives suggestive of beauty, but they do describe celery root. Although ugly, it's packed with culinary potential, and this great favorite of European cooks is in its prime these cool months.*

*Is this vegetable the root of green celery stalks? No. It's the root of celeriac, a member of the same family grown just for the root. The thin-stemmed sprigs of leaves taste similar, and both plants evolved from a wild celery native to Mediterranean marshlands.*

*Wholesome, satisfying, and with a pronounced celery flavor, celery root is good raw or cooked. Used raw in a salad, its subtle nutlike flavor is accented by wild rice. Shredded celery root combined with chilies makes an intriguing salsa. And when baked, or simmered and whipped, with carrots and potatoes, celery root makes a fine vegetable dish. The carrots add a pleasing blush of color.*

## WILD RICE & CELERY ROOT SALAD

- ⅔ **cup wild rice**
  **Water**
- ¼ **cup lemon juice**
- ¼ **cup *each* cider vinegar and olive or salad oil**
- 1 **tablespoon Dijon mustard**
- 1 **medium-size (about ¾ lb.) celery root**
- 3 **large stalks celery, thinly sliced**
  **Watercress sprigs, optional**
  **Salt and pepper**

Rinse rice in a fine strainer under hot running water. Pour rice into a 1½- to 2-quart pan and add 2 cups water. Bring to a boil; reduce to simmer, cover, and cook until tender to bite, about 45 minutes. Drain rice; let stand until cool.

Meanwhile, in a large bowl, combine lemon juice, vinegar, oil, and mustard; stir well. Scrub celery root; cut off coarse skin and any dark spots, then cut into ⅛- by 1-inch sticks; as cut, mix with dressing in bowl to prevent discoloration. Add sliced celery and rice; mix well.

Serve, or cover and chill up to overnight. Pour salad onto a platter and garnish with watercress; add salt and pepper to taste. Makes 4 to 6 servings.

## CELERY ROOT SALSA

- 1 **large (about 1 lb.) celery root**
- ⅓ **cup lime juice**
  **Tomatillo sauce (recipe follows)**

Scrub celery root. Cut off coarse skin and any dark spots. Shred by hand or with a food processor. In a large bowl, mix shredded celery root with lime juice and tomatillo sauce.

Cover and chill at least 1 hour or up to 3 days; mix before serving. Makes about 4 cups; allow ⅓ to ½ cup per serving.

*White slivers of celery root, green celery slices, and wild rice make an intriguingly textured salad suited to rare roasts and game entrées.*

*Grated cheese? No, it's shredded celery root—in a salsa with tomatillos and chilies. Try this salsa with grilled lamb.*

*Cut brown skin off celery root. Dice root and potatoes; shred carrots. Boil, then whip together for a tasty vegetable purée.*

**Tomatillo sauce.** In a bowl, mix 2 cans (13 oz. *each*) **tomatillos,** drained and chopped; 2 **green onions** (roots trimmed), including part of green tops, thinly sliced; 1 small can (4 oz.) **diced green chilies;** and 1 fresh **jalapeño chili** or serrano chili, stemmed, seeded, and minced.

## A Trio of Whipped Roots

1 medium-size (about ¾ lb.) celery root
  About 1¼ cups regular-strength chicken broth
¼ cup chopped shallots
2 large (about 1 lb.) russet potatoes, peeled
2 medium-size carrots, peeled
2 tablespoons butter or margarine
1 tablespoon honey
  Salt and pepper

Scrub celery root. Cut off coarse skin and any dark spots; cut into ½-inch cubes. Put cubes in a 4- to 6-quart pan and add 1 cup broth and shallots. Bring to boiling on high heat; cover and cook 5 minutes.

Meanwhile, cut potatoes into ½-inch cubes. Shred carrots by hand or with a food processor. Add potatoes and carrots to celery root. Bring to a boil over high heat; reduce to simmer, cover, and cook until vegetables are very tender when pierced, about 15 minutes.

With a hand-held electric mixer (you can use a potato masher, though texture will be coarser, but do *not* use a food processor), whip vegetables with butter, honey, and remaining broth until smooth. If you like a softer mixture, whip in a little more broth. Season to taste with salt and pepper, and serve. Makes 5 to 7 servings.

## A Trio of Baked Roots

Following directions for **A Trio of Whipped Roots** (preceding), cut up **celery root, carrots, shallots,** and **potatoes.** Use only ½ cup **chicken broth.** Also measure the **honey** and **butter.**

In a well-buttered, shallow 2-quart casserole, mix celery root, carrots, shallots, potatoes, broth, and honey. Spread vegetables out in an even layer and dot with butter, cut into small pieces. Cover casserole tightly with foil. Bake in a 400° oven until vegetables are tender when pierced, about 1½ hours. Uncover and bake until vegetables are lightly browned on top, about 30 minutes. Sprinkle with 2 tablespoons minced **green onions** or parsley. Season with salt and pepper to taste. Serves 4 to 6.

# Dressy Wrappers for Ground Beef

**D**RESSY WRAPPERS *and international seasonings turn humble, economical ground beef into party fare in these two recipes.*

*In a dish inspired by Thai and Chinese cuisines, lettuce encloses curry-flavored beef. To assemble the dish, diners spoon seasoned bits of warm beef into a lettuce leaf. The crisp, cool wrapper contrasts with the warm meat. If you like, accompany this with rice or thin noodles to eat separately or in the meat packet. Offer tropical fruit for dessert.*

*The savory ground beef and pork mixture bound with cheese has Mexican flavors, but you wrap it using the Middle Eastern technique of rolling it in buttered fila dough. Present slices with crisp greens.*

## CURRY BEEF WRAPPED IN LETTUCE

- 1 medium-size onion, chopped
- 1 tablespoon salad oil
- 2 tablespoons *each* curry powder, tomato paste, and sugar
- ¾ pound coarsely ground lean beef
- ⅛ pound mushrooms, chopped
- 2 tablespoons distilled white vinegar Salt
- 1 medium-size head (about ¼ lb.) butter lettuce, washed and crisped

In a 10- to 12-inch frying pan, cook onion in oil over medium-high heat, stirring,

until edges begin to brown, about 5 minutes. Mix in curry powder, tomato paste, and sugar. When mixture bubbles, cook, stirring, 1 minute. Add meat, mushrooms, and vinegar, breaking up meat with a spoon. Cook, stirring, until juices begin to evaporate and meat is no longer pink but still moist enough to hold together, about 8 minutes; add salt to taste.

Spoon meat mixture into a serving bowl. Arrange lettuce leaves in a basket or platter. Spoon hot meat into leaves to roll up and eat. Makes 6 to 8 appetizer servings, 3 or 4 entrée servings. —*Grace Kirschenbaum, Los Angeles.*

## GROUND MEAT IN A FILA ROLL

- 1 pound ground lean beef
- ½ pound bulk pork sausage
- 1 medium-size onion, chopped
- 1 large clove garlic, minced or pressed
- ¼ teaspoon pepper
- ½ pound fila dough
- ½ cup (¼ lb.) butter or margarine, melted
- 3 cups (¾ lb.) lightly packed shredded jack cheese
- 1 can (4 oz.) diced green chilies
- 1 can (about 2 oz.) sliced ripe olives Salt
- 1 cup sour cream
- 1 medium-size firm-ripe avocado, peeled, pitted, and sliced
- 1 medium-size tomato, cored, seeded, and diced

Crumble beef and sausage into a 10- to 12-inch frying pan. Add onion, garlic, and pepper. Cook, stirring occasionally, on medium-high heat until meat browns and onion is limp, about 12 minutes. Drain off and discard fat; set mixture aside.

Cut a piece of plastic wrap or foil about 1 inch longer and wider than a sheet of fila. Lay plastic wrap on a flat surface. Working quickly, lay 1 sheet fila on the wrap and brush with about 1 teaspoon melted butter. Repeat process, stacking and buttering all fila sheets.

Combine meat mixture with cheese, chilies, and olives; add salt to taste. Center the meat in a band down the length of the fila. Use plastic wrap to support fila as you lift 1 side over filling. Brush edge with butter, then lift other edge of fila over buttered edge to seal. At each end of the log, press fila edges together to enclose filling. Slide an 11- by 17-inch

rimless baking sheet under edge of log. Using the plastic wrap as support, roll the log onto the baking sheet so the seam is on the bottom. Brush log with butter.

With a sharp knife, make decorative diagonal slashes, about 2 inches apart, across fila; do not cut through to filling. If made ahead, cover airtight and chill up to overnight; return to room temperature before baking. Bake log, uncovered, in a 350° oven until pastry is flaky and golden, about 1 hour.

Present log on a board and cut into 6 to 8 slices. Accompany slices with sour cream, avocado slices, and diced tomato. Makes 6 to 8 servings. —*Toni Pruitt Bouman, Los Angeles.*

*Guide fila with plastic wrap as you roll pastry over Mexican-flavored ground beef.*

*Serve slice of fila roll with sour cream, avocado wedge, and diced tomato.*

*Spoon well-seasoned, cooked ground beef into crisp lettuce cups. Roll up wrappers and eat as an appetizer or entrée.*

# Microwave Custard

Single portion of custard, cooked in a microwave, has strawberry garnish. Serve warm or cold for dessert or breakfast.

**B**AKED CUSTARD IN MINUTES? *With a microwave oven, you can reduce conventional baking time by at least half and eliminate the traditional water bath. Simply mix the ingredients, heat until warm, then cook in custard cups or small ramekins until softly set.*

*Because microwaves cook food very quickly, you must watch the custard carefully, especially the last minute or two—a few seconds can make the difference between a smooth dessert and a rubbery one.*

*When done, a microwave-cooked custard appears set but jiggles when gently shaken; it firms up a bit upon cooling. If results are softer than you expect, consider the flowing portion a complementary sauce. For a more even but firmer texture, cook custard slightly longer at 50 percent power, and use the same test for doneness.*

*We give choices of custards made individually or by fours. With just one custard in the oven, put a cup of water alongside to absorb some of the energy and slow the cooking rate so the dessert sets more gradually and evenly.*

*Use milk, whole eggs, and vanilla for a simple, firm custard. If you'd like a richer version, use half-and-half, egg yolks, and liqueur.*

## MICROWAVE-BAKED CUSTARD FOR 1

In a 1-cup glass measuring cup, combine ½ cup **milk** or half-and-half (light cream), 1 **large egg** or large egg yolk, 1½ tablespoons **sugar,** ¼ teaspoon **vanilla** or 2 teaspoons orange-flavored liqueur; beat until blended.

Place the cup in a microwave oven and cook the mixture, uncovered, at full power (100 percent), stirring every 30 seconds until warm, 1 to 1½ minutes. Pour through a fine strainer into a nonmetal custard cup or ramekin (about ¾ cup size). Sprinkle lightly with **ground nutmeg,** if desired.

Place in a microwave oven. Set a 1-cup glass measuring cup containing 1 cup lukewarm **water** alongside. Cook, uncovered, at 50 percent power; rotate custard cup a quarter turn every minute, just until custard appears barely set and jiggles slightly all over when gently shaken, 3 to 5 minutes. Remove from oven and let cool at least 10 minutes. Serve warm, cool, or cold (if made ahead, cover and chill up to overnight). Makes 1 serving.

## MICROWAVE-BAKED CUSTARD FOR 4

- 1½ **cups milk or half-and-half (light cream)**
- 4 **large eggs or 4 large egg yolks**
- 6 **tablespoons sugar**
- 1 **teaspoon vanilla or 2 tablespoons orange-flavored liqueur**
  **Ground nutmeg (optional)**

In a 1-quart glass measuring cup, combine milk, eggs, sugar, and vanilla; beat lightly until blended. Place in a microwave oven and cook, uncovered, at full power, stirring every minute, until warm to touch, 3 to 4 minutes. Pour through a fine strainer into 4 nonmetal custard cups or ramekins (about ¾ cup *each*). Sprinkle custards lightly with nutmeg.

Set cups in a circle in a microwave oven and cook, uncovered, at 50 percent power. Every 2 minutes, move each cup a quarter turn and rotate its position in the circle. Cook just until custard appears set but still jiggles slightly all over when gently shaken, 6 to 8 minutes total. Remove each custard when it looks done. Let stand at least 10 minutes. Serve warm, cool, or cold (if made ahead, cover and chill up to overnight). Serves 4.

# Quick Desserts with Winter Citrus

WINTER CITRUS FRUITS—*now readily available—lend their refreshing flavors to these quick-to-assemble desserts.*

*In the first, grapefruit and candied peel spill over ice cream for a creamy-tart contrast. In our second recipe, simple cornstarch pudding gains stature when mixed with tangerine slices and juice.*

## GRAPEFRUIT & CREAM

**2 medium-size pink grapefruit**
**¼ cup orange-flavored liqueur**
**About 2 cups water**
**1½ tablespoons *each* honey and sugar**
**About 1 quart vanilla ice cream**

With a vegetable peeler, pare golden part of peel from 1 grapefruit. Cut peel into very thin shreds; set aside.

With a knife, cut remaining peel and white membrane from both grapefruit. Holding fruit over a bowl, cut parallel to membrane to free segments. Squeeze juice from membrane into bowl; discard membrane. Drain off juice and reserve.

Stir 3 tablespoons liqueur into fruit.

In a 1- to 1½-quart pan over high heat, bring 1 cup water and peel to a boil. Boil, uncovered, for 2 minutes; drain. Repeat with 1 more cup of water.

Measure reserved juice; add water if needed to make ½ cup. To drained peel in pan, add the juice, honey, and sugar. Bring to a boil over high heat and boil, uncovered, stirring occasionally, until peel is translucent and syrup is reduced to 2 tablespoons, 5 to 8 minutes. Remove from heat. Stir in remaining liqueur.

In 6 dessert bowls, place 1 scoop of ice cream. Spoon grapefruit segments and liqueur over ice cream. Top equally with peel and syrup. Serves 6.

## TANGERINE PUDDING PARFAIT

**6 medium-size tangerines (about 1½ lb.)**
**3 large egg yolks**
**3 tablespoons lemon juice**
**⅔ cup sugar**
**¼ cup cornstarch**
**¾ cup milk**
**1 cup water**
**Citrus flowers and leaves (optional)**

Grate enough peel from tangerines to make 2 teaspoons; then ream enough fruit to make ½ cup juice. Cut off remaining peel and white membrane from unreamed tangerines. Cut fruit in half lengthwise; thinly slice crosswise. Remove and discard seeds. Set aside fruit.

In a bowl, mix yolks, tangerine peel, and tangerine and lemon juices. Set aside.

In a 1½- to 2-quart pan, mix sugar and cornstarch. Whisk in milk and water. Cook, stirring, over medium heat until mixture thickens, about 10 minutes. Whisk in yolk mixture and continue to cook, stirring, until pudding bubbles, about 5 minutes.

(If made ahead, cover with plastic wrap touching pudding; chill until next day.)

To serve, layer warm or cold pudding in 4 tall glasses with sliced fruit. Garnish with citrus flowers and leaves. Serves 4.

*Grapefruit segments and strands of candied peel offset sweetness of ice cream.*

*Layer tangerine pudding and fruit in glass.*

# More March Recipes

ETHNIC-INSPIRED DISHES *are featured in this collection of March recipes. We suggest Chinese crab claw appetizers, a Latin-style black bean salad flecked with colorful vegetables, and a hearty stir-fried pasta entrée combining ideas from Italy and the Orient. Other recipes include a hearty salad, sautéed fruits to accompany roasted meats, and an unusual dessert we call Bird Seed Cake.*

## CHINESE CRAB CLAW APPETIZERS

*If you've wondered what to do with the cooked crab claws you see occasionally in markets, the Chinese have an idea: turn them into appetizers that have their own handle, the pincers.*

*These crab claws, from a variety of species, have their pincers intact but most of the remaining shell has been cut off to expose a plump bite of meat. The claws usually come frozen, but occasionally you'll find them thawed, displayed with fresh fish in fish markets, particularly Oriental ones. A pound of claws—about 24—costs $10 to $15.*

*To cook them Chinese-style, you coat the meat portion of the claws with a paste of seasoned sole and more crab, then brown them in hot oil. Let the claws cool briefly, just until you can pick up the pincers comfortably, then eat.*

*Although claws are best hot from the oil, you can cook them ahead and reheat.*

- 1 large egg white
- ¼ cup sliced green onion (including tops)
- 1 tablespoon *each* dry sherry and minced fresh ginger
- 2 teaspoons cornstarch
- ¼ teaspoon *each* pepper and Oriental sesame oil
- ¼ pound *each* boned, skinned sole fillet and shelled, cooked crab
- 12 to 14 (about ½ lb.) cooked crab claws, including pincers, with part of the shell sawed off; thaw if frozen
  Salad oil
  Lime sauce (recipe follows)

In a food processor or blender, whirl egg white, green onion, sherry, ginger, cornstarch, pepper, sesame oil, and sole until smoothly puréed. Scrape into a bowl and mix in shelled crab. With a spoon, spread an equal portion of purée evenly over meat on each claw, using all the purée. Set the coated claws slightly apart on waxed paper.

Heat 1½ inches oil in a deep 2- to 3-quart pan to 350° on medium-high heat. Add 3 claws at a time and cook, uncovered, until fish purée is golden brown, 3 to 4 minutes. Lift out with a slotted spoon; drain on paper towels. Keep warm until all claws are cooked.

Serve when pincers are cool enough to touch. If made ahead, let claws cool; arrange in a single layer in a 10- by 15-inch pan, cover, and chill overnight. Uncover and bake in a 275° oven until hot, 5 to 10 minutes; fish will be firmer than if freshly cooked. Dip claws in sauce to eat. Makes 4 to 7 servings, 2 to 3 claws per person.

**Lime sauce.** Mix 3 tablespoons *each* **soy sauce** and **lime juice** with 1 **fresh small hot green chili** (such as jalapeño or serrano), seeded and minced.

*Dip hot crab claws into a lime and chili sauce to eat; pincers serve as handles.*

## BLACK BEAN SALAD

*Flavorful bits of red, yellow, and green— bell pepper, lemon peel, and green onion—give visual impact to this black bean salad. Black beans, long popular in Latin dishes because of their mild but distinctive flavor, are now available in many supermarkets. To preserve color and texture, drain and rinse the beans after they're cooked.*

*Cooked black beans combine with bell pepper, lemon, and green onion to make a colorful salad.*

- 1¾ cups (½ lb.) black beans, sorted of debris and rinsed
- ½ teaspoon cayenne
- 2 quarts regular-strength chicken broth or water
- 1 small red bell pepper, stemmed, seeded, and finely chopped
- ½ cup diagonally sliced green onions
- 2 tablespoons balsamic vinegar or red wine vinegar
- 1 tablespoon lemon juice
- 1 tablespoon very thinly slivered lemon peel, yellow part only
- ½ cup firmly packed cilantro sprigs, rinsed and drained
  Salt

Combine beans, ¼ teaspoon of the cayenne, and broth in a 4- to 5-quart pan. Bring to boiling over high heat. Reduce heat to simmer, cover, and cook until beans are tender to bite, about 45 minutes. Pour beans into a colander, discarding liquid. Rinse beans under cold water until water runs clear and beans are cool (bite to test), about 3 minutes. Drain well.

Mix remaining cayenne, bell pepper, onions, vinegar, lemon juice, and lemon peel with beans. Set aside several cilantro sprigs; chop remaining. Stir chopped cilantro into beans. Add salt to taste. Serve, or cover and chill up to overnight. Garnish with cilantro sprigs. Makes 4 cups, 6 to 8 servings.

*Cooked tortellini and gorgonzola mingle with sliced chicken and broccoli in this hearty stir-fried entrée. Sprinkle with nuts before serving.*

## TORTELLINI WITH BROCCOLI & GORGONZOLA

*Italy and the Orient marry in this robust pasta and stir-fry dish. The base is loop-shaped tortellini, available dry, freshly made, or frozen; fillings vary, but any will do here. Keep in mind that dry tortellini about double in size when cooked; fresh (or frozen) get only slightly larger.*

*The ingredients that transform this recipe into a hearty main dish are stir-fried nuts, chicken, and broccoli in a sauce of broth and gorgonzola. Although the dish can be made quickly, we offer make-ahead steps.*

- 1 whole chicken breast (1 lb.)
- 3 tablespoons butter or margarine
- ¾ cup walnuts or pecans (halves or large pieces)
- 5 cups broccoli flowerets (from about 1¼ lb. broccoli)
- About 1½ cups regular-strength chicken broth
- ½ cup finely chopped onion
- 4 teaspoons cornstarch
- ½ cup firmly packed crumbled gorgonzola or other blue-veined cheese
- ½ teaspoon coarsely ground pepper
- About 4 cups cooked tortellini (hot or cold)
- 1 tablespoon white wine vinegar

Bone and skin chicken breast; discard bones and skin. Cut breast crosswise into ¼-inch-thick slices.

In a wok, 10- to 12-inch frying pan, or 5- to 6-quart pan, melt 1 tablespoon of the butter over medium heat. Add walnuts and stir until nuts are crisp to bite, about 10 minutes (take care not to scorch). Pour nuts onto paper towels to drain. (If made ahead, cover and chill overnight.)

Wipe pan clean; place over high heat. Add 1 tablespoon butter; when melted, add chicken and stir frequently until meat just turns white in center (cut to test), about 3 minutes. Pour into a bowl.

To pan, add broccoli and 2 tablespoons broth. Cover and cook until broccoli stems are tender when pierced, 8 to 10 minutes; stir several times. To prevent sticking, add more broth, 1 tablespoon at a time. Lift broccoli from pan with slotted spoon and add to chicken. (If made ahead, let cool, cover, and chill overnight.)

Wipe pan clean again. Add remaining butter and onion; stir until onion is limp, about 5 minutes. Sprinkle cornstarch over onion; stir to mix. Add 1¼ cups broth; stir until boiling. Turn heat to low; add ¾ of the cheese and stir until smooth. Add pepper, chicken, broccoli, and tortellini; mix gently until hot (cut a tortellini to test), about 5 minutes. Stir in vinegar, pour into a serving bowl, and sprinkle with walnuts and remaining cheese. Makes 4 servings.

## TRICOLOR SALAD

*The earthy flavors of Jerusalem artichokes and beets team up with tart green apples in this bold salad. Both vegetables are in plentiful supply now. For the apple, try a Newtown Pippin or a Granny Smith. Because beets will stain the other ingredients, you dress and arrange the components separately.*

- ½ pound Jerusalem artichokes (sunchokes), scrubbed
- 1 pound medium-size beets with tops
- 1 large tart green apple
- ¼ cup currants
- ¼ cup thawed frozen orange juice concentrate
- ¼ cup white wine vinegar
- 2 tablespoons salad oil
- 1 tablespoon minced fresh mint or 1 tablespoon dry mint leaves, crumbled
- Salt and pepper

Shred artichokes and place in a bowl. Cut leaves from beets; discard stems and bruised leaves. Wash tender leaves and pat dry. Scrub beets, trim ends, shred, and place in a second bowl. Core and chop apple; mix with currants in a bowl.

Mix orange concentrate with vinegar, oil, and mint; add 2 tablespoons to apple, ¼ cup to artichokes, and remainder to beets. Stir each to mix. Arrange beet greens on a platter. Place beets, artichokes, and apples in rows over greens. Add salt and pepper to taste. Makes 6 servings. —*Roxanne Chan, Albany, Calif.*

## SAUTÉED FRUITS

*Thickly sliced apples or bananas, quickly sautéed in onion- and ginger-spiked butter, make an interesting spicy-sweet accompaniment for roasted meats or poultry.*

- 3 tablespoons butter or margarine
- 1 small onion, coarsely chopped
- 1½ teaspoons finely chopped fresh ginger
- About 1½ cups prepared fruit (see below)
- 1 to 2 tablespoons lime juice
- 2 to 4 tablespoons firmly packed brown sugar

Melt butter in a 10- to 12-inch frying pan over medium heat. Add onion and ginger; cook, stirring, until onion is barely soft, about 1 minute.

Add prepared fruit and turn gently to coat with butter. Cover and cook, turning occasionally, until fruit is heated through and very tender when pierced (2 to 5 minutes for most fruits).

Season fruit with lime juice and sugar; mix gently to blend well. Serve hot as an accompaniment to roasted poultry, pork, ham, or lamb. Makes about 3 cups.

**Prepared fruit.** For apples, peel and core **apples,** then cut into ½-inch-thick slices.

For bananas, peel **bananas** and cut into ½-inch-thick slices; coat with **lemon juice.**

## BIRD SEED CAKE

*Ingredients traditional in bird-seed mixtures—millet, sunflower seed, and sorghum—give this moist cake a pleasantly chewy texture and wholesome flavor. Serve it plain or frosted.*

*Look for millet in health food stores.*

- ½ cup **millet**
  **Water**
- 1½ cups **whole-wheat flour**
- 1 teaspoon **ground cinnamon**
- 1 teaspoon **baking soda**
- ¼ teaspoon **salt** (optional)
- 1 cup **sorghum syrup** or **light molasses**
- 2 large **eggs**
- ½ cup **salad oil**
- 2 cups **unsalted sunflower seeds**
  **Orange-cheese frosting** (recipe follows), optional
- 2 tablespoons finely shredded **orange peel** (optional)

In a 1- to 2-quart pan, combine millet and 1½ cups water. Bring to boiling over high heat, then reduce heat and simmer over low heat, uncovered, until water is absorbed, 10 to 15 minutes. Remove from heat and add ¾ cup water.

In a bowl, mix flour, cinnamon, soda, and salt. Add sorghum syrup, eggs, and oil, stirring to blend. Stir in millet-water mixture and sunflower seeds. Spread batter in a greased 8- by 12- or 9- by 13-inch baking pan or dish.

Bake in a 350° oven until top springs back when lightly touched in center, 30 to 35 minutes. Let cool in pan on rack.

Spread orange-cheese frosting over cooled cake. If desired, sprinkle orange

Millet and sunflower seeds (nutrients found in bird seed) add chewy texture to dark, cinnamon-spiced dessert cake.

peel evenly over frosting. (If made ahead, cover and chill up to 1 day.) Cut cake in squares and lift out of pan to serve. Makes 12 servings. —*Nancy Van der Velde, Santa Barbara, Calif.*

**Orange-cheese frosting.** In a small bowl, beat with an electric mixer at high speed 1 large package (8 oz.) **cream cheese** (at room temperature), 1 teaspoon grated **orange peel,** and 1 teaspoon **vanilla** until smooth. Add 2 cups **powdered sugar;** beat until smooth. Makes 1½ cups.

*Ginger-yogurt dressing goes on salad of strawberries, asparagus, carrots, apples.*

## FRUIT, VEGETABLE & GINGER SALAD

12  medium-size asparagus spears (about 1½ lb.)
Water
2  medium-size carrots, peeled and thinly sliced
2  cups strawberries, rinsed, hulled, and cut in half
1  medium-size apple, cored and cut into ⅛- by 1½-inch sticks
1  cup unflavored yogurt
1  tablespoon honey
1  tablespoon minced fresh ginger

Snap off and discard tough ends of asparagus; rinse spears well. In a 10- to 12-inch frying pan, bring about 1 inch water to boiling on high heat; lay spears in water. Cook, uncovered, until tender when pierced, about 6 minutes. Lift from water with a slotted spoon and submerge at once in ice water. Add carrots to boiling water and cook until tender when pierced, about 4 minutes. Lift from water with a slotted spoon and add to asparagus. When vegetables are cold, drain.

Arrange asparagus, carrot, strawberries, and apple sticks equally on 6 salad plates. Mix together yogurt, honey, and ginger; serve dressing in a small cup with each salad. Serves 6.—*Roxanne E. Chan, Albany, Calif.*

*Two peas—dried and frozen—team up in a vegetable soup with Oriental touches.*

## DOUBLE PEA SOUP ORIENTAL

¾  cup (about ½ oz.) dried shiitake mushrooms
Water
1  cup dried split green peas
1  tablespoon salad oil
1  small onion, diced
2  cups thinly sliced celery
1  medium-size carrot, thinly sliced
2  tablespoons minced fresh ginger
6  cups regular-strength chicken broth
1  package (10 oz.) frozen peas
½  to 1 teaspoon *each* liquid hot pepper seasoning, Oriental sesame oil, and salt (optional)

In a bowl, combine mushrooms and 1½ cups warm water; let stand until softened, about 20 minutes. Discard water. Cut off and discard stems; mince caps. Sort split peas for debris and rinse.

To a 4- to 5-quart pan over medium heat, add salad oil, onion, celery, carrot, and ginger; stir often until vegetables are limp, about 10 minutes. Add mushrooms, split peas, broth, and 2 cups water. Bring to boiling; cover and simmer until peas are soft to bite, about 1½ hours. Add frozen peas and cook until hot, about 5 minutes. Add to taste the hot pepper seasoning, sesame oil, and salt. Serves 8.—*Grace Kirschenbaum, Los Angeles.*

*Sauté strips of bell pepper and onion, then cook tofu cubes; finish with cheese.*

## SAUTÉED TOFU WITH PEPPER STRIPS

About 2 tablespoons salad oil
1  small onion, thinly sliced
1  *each* large green and red bell peppers (or 2 of 1 color), stemmed, seeded, and cut lengthwise into thin strips
2  cloves garlic, minced or pressed
1  pound medium or firm tofu, drained, patted dry, and cut into ¾-inch cubes
1  tablespoon soy sauce
¼  cup shredded parmesan cheese

To a 10- to 12-inch frying pan over medium-high heat, add 2 tablespoons oil, onion, bell peppers, and garlic. Cook, stirring often, until vegetables are limp, about 10 minutes. Pour onto a small platter; cover and keep warm.

Add tofu to frying pan and pour soy sauce evenly over the cubes. Cook over medium-high heat, turning with a wide spatula to lightly brown all sides, about 7 minutes. Add a little more oil to pan, if needed, to prevent tofu from sticking.

Transfer tofu with the spatula onto the cooked vegetables. Sprinkle tofu with the cheese and serve. Makes 2 or 3 servings.—*Diane McPherson, Maui, Hawaii.*

## BAKED CHICKEN BREASTS WITH PEARS

    3  whole chicken breasts (about 1 lb.
       *each*), boned, skinned, and halved
    3  tablespoons soy sauce
    4  teaspoons cornstarch
    1  cup pear-flavored schnapps or
       apple juice
    2  medium-size firm-ripe pears
       Parsley sprigs (optional)
       Lime wedges (optional)
       Salt and pepper

Rub chicken with soy sauce, then lay breasts side by side in a 9- by 13-inch pan. Bake in a 425° oven just until meat is no longer pink in the center (cut to test), about 15 minutes.

Meanwhile, put cornstarch in a 1½- to 2-quart pan; smoothly stir in the schnapps. Peel and core pears, then cut fruit lengthwise into ½-inch-thick slices; add to pan. Mixing gently, bring to a boil on medium-high heat; cover and simmer until pears are tender when pierced, about 5 minutes. When chicken is done, add pear mixture; shake pan to mix gently. Transfer chicken, fruit, and sauce to a platter and garnish with parsley. Offer lime, salt, and pepper to add to taste. Serves 4 to 6.—*Carmela M. Meely, Walnut Creek, Calif.*

*Chicken breasts bake with soy sauce; pears poached in schnapps go on top.*

## SALMON & PASTA ENTRÉE SALAD

    3  medium-size pink grapefruit
       Dressing (recipe follows)
    3  cups cooked shell-shaped pasta
    1  cup sliced celery
    1  cup ¼-inch-thick carrot sticks, *each*
       about 1½ inches long
    ½  cup chopped parsley
    ½  cup slivered green onion
    6  to 12 large lettuce leaves, washed
       and crisped
    1  can (15½ oz.) pink salmon
       Salt and pepper

Cut skin and white membrane from grapefruit. Hold fruit over a bowl and cut segments free. Squeeze juice from membrane into bowl (save for dressing); discard membrane.

In another bowl, mix dressing, pasta, celery, carrot, parsley, and onion. Cover salad and chill at least 1 hour; or chill salad and fruit, covered, up to overnight. Arrange lettuce leaves on 6 dinner plates; spoon salad onto leaves. Drain salmon; break into chunks. Lay fish and fruit around salad; add salt and pepper to taste. Serves 6.—*Mrs. Bud Reynolds, Federal Way, Wash.*

**Dressing.** Measure **grapefruit juice** (preceding); you should have about ½ cup. Mix with ¼ cup **vinegar**, 2 tablespoons *each* **salad oil** and **lime juice**, and 1½ teaspoons **dry dill weed.**

*Canned salmon and grapefruit make lively additions to main-dish pasta salad.*

## MOLASSES CRUNCH COOKIES

    ½  cup (¼ lb.) butter or margarine, at
       room temperature
    6  tablespoons dark molasses
    6  tablespoons firmly packed brown
       sugar
    1  large egg
    ½  teaspoon vanilla
    1  cup all-purpose flour
    ½  teaspoon baking soda
    ¼  teaspoon salt (optional)
    ½  cup chopped walnuts

In large bowl of an electric mixer, beat butter, molasses, sugar, egg, and vanilla at high speed until light and fluffy, about 4 minutes.

Mix flour with soda, salt, and nuts. At low speed, thoroughly blend flour mixture into creamed mixture.

On well-greased 12- by 15-inch baking sheets, spoon dough in rounded 1 teaspoon size mounds 1½ inches apart; cookies spread as they bake. Bake in a 350° oven until slightly darker brown at edges, 8 to 10 minutes.

Transfer with a spatula to racks to cool; cookies crisp as they cool. Serve, or store airtight at room temperature up to 3 days; freeze to store longer. Makes about 4 dozen cookies, each about 2 inches in diameter.—*Linda Twitchell, Bellingham, Wash.*

*Thin molasses-flavored crisps go with milk for an afternoon or evening snack.*

CATTLE AND SHEEP *require large areas of pasture for feeding. The pig, on the other hand, is an opportunistic feeder, like its master, and can thrive on whatever the village provides in the way of food and shelter. It is no wonder, therefore, that pork is a key protein in the diet of crowded China. Naturally, the Chinese have become masters at cooking pork.*

*Paul Burnworth acknowledges his debt to the Chinese in this recipe for barbecued pork. The marinade is a simple one, with an important added seasoning blend— Chinese five spice. If you use the optional red food coloring, the pork slices will have an attractive red rim as commonly seen on Chinese restaurant barbecued pork.*

## CHINESE BARBECUED PORK

⅓ cup sugar
3 tablespoons soy sauce
2 tablespoons dry sherry
¼ teaspoon Chinese five spice (or ⅛ teaspoon *each* ground allspice and crushed anise seed)
1 clove garlic, minced or pressed
3 to 4 drops red food coloring (optional)
2 or 3 pork tenderloins (about 2 lb. total)
Toasted sesame seed (optional, directions follow)
Prepared Chinese-style hot mustard

In a 7- by 12-inch baking dish, stir together sugar, soy sauce, sherry, Chinese five spice, garlic, and red food coloring. Lay pork in dish and rotate pieces to coat with marinade. Cover meat and chill at least 1 or up to 2 days; turn pork in marinade several times.

On the fire grate in a barbecue with a lid, ignite about 40 charcoal briquets. When briquets are covered with gray ash (about 30 minutes), bank half on each side of the grate and put a foil or metal drip pan in the center. Position grill 4 to 6 inches above the coals.

Meanwhile, lift pork from marinade; fold and tie thin ends underneath so each tenderloin is evenly thick. Place

"*The Chinese have become masters at cooking pork.*"

pork on grill over the coals and quickly brown on all sides, 5 to 8 minutes total. Then set meat over drip pan, put lid on barbecue, and open dampers. Cook pork until a meat thermometer inserted into center reaches 155° to 160°, 30 to 40 minutes. Baste often with marinade. Cut pork into thin slices. Serve with sesame seeds to sprinkle over meat; offer mustard alongside. Makes 4 to 6 servings.

**Toasted sesame seed.** Pour 2 to 3 tablespoons **sesame seed** into a 7- to 8-inch frying pan. Shake often over medium heat until seeds are golden, 5 to 8 minutes. Use warm or cool; store airtight at room temperature up to 2 weeks.

*Paul L. Burnworth*

*Okanogan, Wash.*

ERMA'S SOUP, *also known as Erma's Mexican Soup, began as a hasty improvisation some 50 years ago, when Allen Peel's mother-in-law put together a soup using whatever she could find in the pantry. The result has been revised and amended over the years by a host of friends and relations, and the currently accepted Peel version is printed here.*

*This soup can be marvelously comforting on a blustery day. It can also admit endless variations; pepper lovers will add more green chilies, while others may want to add body with potatoes or corn. Garbanzos or kidney beans are other possible extras. Let your fancy be your guide.*

## ERMA'S SOUP

2 large cans (28 oz. *each*) tomatoes
2 pounds Polish sausage (kielbasa), thinly sliced
3 large onions, coarsely chopped
6 large carrots, cut into ¼-inch-thick slices
2 cans (7 oz. *each*) diced green chilies
½ pound small mushrooms (1- to 1½-in. caps), halved
Salt and pepper

Slice through tomatoes in the cans to cut them into chunks. Pour tomatoes and their liquid into a 6- to 8-quart pan. Add sausage, onions, carrots, chilies, and mushrooms. Bring to a boil over high heat; cover, reduce heat, and simmer until carrots are very tender to bite, about 35 minutes.

Season soup with salt and pepper to taste and ladle into wide soup plates. Makes 5 quarts, 10 to 12 servings.

*Allen Peel*

Studio City, Calif.

**T**HE GERMANS *have given us two classic cabbage preparations, sauerkraut and red cabbage. The latter is always prepared in sweet-sour style. Lamar Parker's Bavarian version draws sweetness from Golden or Red Delicious apples, acidity from vinegar or red wine, and both from red currant jelly. Serve it with sauerbraten (another great German sweet-sour creation) or with a white sausage such as bratwurst. Potato pancakes and applesauce are also good companions.*

"Bavarian Red Cabbage draws sweetness from apples, acidity from vinegar or red wine."

## BAVARIAN RED CABBAGE

- 1 **large head (about 2½ lb.) red cabbage**
- 3 **tablespoons salad oil**
- 1 **large onion, chopped**
- 2 **medium-size Red or Golden Delicious apples, peeled, cored, and diced**
- ½ **cup red wine vinegar or dry red wine**
- 1 **bay leaf**
  **Water**
- ½ **cup red currant jelly**
  **Salt**

Cut out and discard cabbage core, then, in a food processor or with a sharp knife, finely shred cabbage.

Pour oil into an 8- to 10-quart pan and place on medium heat; add onion and stir often until limp, about 10 minutes. Add cabbage and stir often until cabbage begins to wilt, about 10 minutes. Add apples, vinegar, and bay leaf; mix well.

Cover, reduce heat to low, and simmer until cabbage is very tender to bite and develops a mellow, sweet flavor, about 2 hours; stir occasionally. If necessary to keep cabbage from scorching, add water, 1 tablespoon at a time. Add jelly and mix until melted. Turn heat to high and cook, uncovered and stirring frequently, until liquid has evaporated. Discard bay leaf; add salt to taste. Cabbage tends to get juicy on standing and may require additional cooking to evaporate the liquid. Makes 6 or 7 servings.

*Lamar L. Parker*

Tempe, Ariz.

**D**O YOU HAVE ANY IDEA *how hard an oyster works to ready itself for your table? Allowing the oyster an average age of two years and assuming that while searching for food it filters a minimum of 25 gallons of sea water a day, it has filtered 18,250 gallons during its lifetime. Some estimates place its filtration rate at 8 gallons an hour, which yields an astonishing 140,160 gallons for two years. If you were to work as hard, you would have to multiply these figures by 2,000—roughly the factor by which you outweigh the oyster. The mind boggles.*

*Fortunately the oyster has no mind (at least we have not detected one), so it merely continues to strain sea water and make*

"An oyster filters a minimum of 25 gallons of sea water a day."

*delicious protein out of whatever detritus floats its way.*

*B. J. Nichols cooks and serves his oysters with a subtle sauce, which enhances their flavor without in the least overpowering it. An absorbent bed of toast ensures that nothing of the oyster shall be lost.*

## OYSTERS LE GRANDE

- 4 **to 6 slices firm-textured white bread**
- ½ **cup (¼ lb.) butter or margarine**
- 2 **jars (10 oz. *each*) small Pacific oysters**
- 2 **tablespoons catsup**
- 1 **tablespoon *each* Worcestershire and lemon juice**
  **Chopped parsley**
  **Salt and pepper**

Arrange bread on a rack in a 10- by 15-inch baking pan and place in a 300° oven until bread is dry and lightly browned, 20 to 25 minutes. Spread each slice with some of the butter and keep warm.

Melt remaining butter in a 10- to 12-inch frying pan over medium heat; add the oysters and their liquid, catsup, Worcestershire, and lemon juice. Cook, turning oysters over several times until the edges are curled and oysters are plump, about 5 minutes.

With a slotted spoon, ladle oysters evenly onto toast; keep warm. Boil pan juice over high heat until reduced to about ½ cup. Evenly spoon juice over oysters, garnish with parsley, add salt and pepper to taste, and serve at once. Makes 4 to 6 servings.

*B. J. Nichols*

Eugene, Ore.

# March Menus

TIMESAVING AND FAMILIAR MEALS *en-hanced with exotic touches high-light this month's menus. All are suitable for those midweek evenings when you rush home to cook for the family. And you can plan to sit down in 45 minutes or less.*

*One supper converts easily to a weekend breakfast, too.*

In this eclectic menu, sourdough toast forms the base for hamburgers glazed with Chinese oyster sauce—a lively alternative to catsup. The same sauce and mustard make excellent dipping for the oven-fried potato and carrot sticks.

*Preserved ginger on the sundaes carries Oriental flavors right through to dessert.*

*While the potato and carrot oven-fries bake, cook the hamburgers and assemble condiments. You can chop the ginger ahead, but plan on making the sundaes just before serving. Children can scoop the ice cream while you whip the cream.*

---

### SAN FRANCISCO HAMBURGER SUPPER

San Francisco Burgers
Potato & Carrot Oven-fries
Oyster Sauce      Mustard
Ginger Cream Sundaes
Sparkling Water with Lime

---

### SAN FRANCISCO BURGERS

1½  pounds ground lean beef
Salad oil
About ½ cup purchased oyster sauce

4  slices (each ¾ in. thick) sourdough bread, cut from a long loaf
About 2 tablespoons Dijon mustard

4  large butter lettuce leaves, washed and crisped

3  tablespoons minced parsley

Divide beef into 4 equal portions and shape each into a round patty ¾ inch thick. Lightly coat bottom of a 12- to 14-inch frying pan with oil; set over medium-high heat. Add patties to the hot pan and cook, uncovered and turning once, until brown on the outside and

*Open-face beef burgers with a twist; they're seasoned with oyster sauce, not catsup. Potato and carrot oven-fries get the same treatment.*

pink in the middle, about 10 minutes. Lift patties from pan and discard fat.

Spread each patty with about ½ tablespoon oyster sauce; return patties to pan and cook, oyster sauce side down, just enough to glaze, about 30 seconds. Meanwhile, spread tops of patties with the same amount of sauce. Turn and cook meat enough to glaze, about 30 seconds.

While the meat is browning, lightly toast bread slices in a toaster or toaster oven. Spread each slice with 1 teaspoon mustard and 2 teaspoons oyster sauce. Top each toast slice with 1 lettuce leaf.

Transfer hot patties onto lettuce-topped toast; garnish with parsley. Eat with a knife and fork; offer oyster sauce and mustard to add to taste. Makes 4 servings.

## POTATO & CARROT OVEN-FRIES

    3  large (1½ to 1¾ lb.) thin-skinned
       potatoes, scrubbed
    6  medium-size carrots, peeled
    2  tablespoons salad oil
       Salt

Cut potatoes and carrots into sticks about ½ inch thick and 4 inches long. Put vegetables in a 10- by 15-inch rimmed pan; pour oil over vegetables and mix with hands to coat. Divide vegetables equally and put half of them in another 10- by 15-inch pan; spread vegetables out in pans.

Bake, uncovered, in a 400° oven until vegetables are lightly browned and tender when pierced, 45 to 50 minutes; switch pan positions halfway through baking. Sprinkle with salt to taste. With a wide spatula, transfer vegetables to a basket lined with a paper or cloth napkin; serve at once. Makes 4 servings.

## GINGER CREAM SUNDAES

Beat ½ cup **whipping cream** with 1 tablespoon **sugar** until cream holds soft peaks. Measure ½ cup **preserved ginger in syrup;** dice ginger, saving syrup.

Divide about 1 pint **vanilla ice cream** equally among 4 dessert bowls or sundae dishes. Spoon an equal amount of whipped cream, then ginger and its syrup, over the ice cream. Makes 4 servings.

| TWO-WAY CHICKEN DINNER |
| :---: |
| **Sake-Steamed Chicken Breasts with Rice** |
| **Cucumber Salad** |
| **Fresh Kiwi Fruit or Bananas** |
| **Hot Green Tea      Apple Juice** |

*This quick menu caters to tastes of young and old. For adults, a dipping sauce offers sophisticated flavors from Japanese cuisine. The same menu without the sauce suits more finicky eaters. In all, this meal is very calorie conscious.*

*Steam chicken in a microwave oven, or use a steamer; both are quick.*

*Give children the option of seasoning the chicken with sauce or making the chicken and rice into lettuce sandwiches with mustard and mayonnaise. Adults might want to try their dexterity at eating with chopsticks.*

*Thinly slice cucumbers for the salad, and mix with dressing of white vinegar slightly sweetened with sugar and salt to taste.*

*Offer peeled sliced kiwi fruit or bananas for dessert; adults can add a splash of orange-flavored liqueur.*

## SAKE-STEAMED CHICKEN BREASTS WITH RICE

    ½  cup sake or rice vinegar
    ½  teaspoon salt
    6  skinned and boned chicken breast
       halves (about 1½ lb. *total*)
    1  small head (about 1¼ lb.) iceberg
       lettuce, washed and crisped
       About ⅓ cup soy sauce
    1  tablespoon prepared horseradish
       Slivered green onion or black sesame seed
       Lemon wedges
       Hot cooked rice
       Mustard and mayonnaise (optional)

In a bowl, stir together sake and salt until salt dissolves. Turn chicken in the mixture. Cover and chill at least 30 minutes or up to 2 hours; discard marinade.

Arrange chicken in a single layer on a 10- or 11-inch round nonmetal plate or pie dish; place thickest ends toward rim. Cover chicken with clear plastic wrap. Cook in a microwave oven on full power until meat is no longer pink in center (cut to test), 6 to 8 minutes. For even cooking, rotate dish ¼ turn every 2 minutes.

*Two-generation meal: adults dip chicken in soy sauce spiked with horseradish; children can wrap chicken in lettuce with rice and cucumbers to munch plain.*

(Or cover chicken with waxed paper or foil, and set dish on a rack in a slightly larger pan. Cover and steam over boiling water until meat is no longer pink in center, about 12 minutes; cut to test.)

While chicken cooks, place 1 or 2 large lettuce leaves on each of 4 to 6 dinner plates. Finely cut the remaining lettuce into long thin shreds and pile equally onto leaves.

Also, for each adult's plate (or child's plate, if desired), pour about 2 teaspoons soy sauce into a tiny bowl and add ½ teaspoon horseradish; set dish on plate.

Cut chicken breasts crosswise into ½-inch-wide strips. Spoon rice on or alongside lettuce and divide chicken strips among the dinner plates; sprinkle with onion or sesame seed, and garnish with a lemon wedge.

To eat, squeeze lemon into soy mixture and dip chicken into sauce. Or tear lettuce leaves into large portions and wrap bits of chicken, rice, and shredded lettuce in them to eat out of hand; season if you like with mustard and mayonnaise. Makes 4 to 6 servings.

## A LAZY-COOK MENU FOR MORNING OR EVENING

**Grits Cake with Corn & Asparagus**
**Baked Sausages**
**Pineapple Cooler**

*This meal comes together with little attention, since almost everything cooks in the oven.*

*Start the hearty grits cake on top of the stove. Finish in the oven, with the sausages alongside. Allow about 1 pound pork link sausages for 6 people; bake, uncovered, in a 7- by 11-inch pan until brown, 30 to 40 minutes.*

*While these foods bake, stir together the pineapple drink.*

## GRITS CAKE WITH CORN & ASPARAGUS

- ¾ **to 1 pound asparagus, rinsed**
- 2 **cups regular-strength chicken or beef broth**
- 1½ **cups water**
- 1 **cup quick-cooking hominy grits or regular polenta**
- 1 **cup frozen corn kernels**

Snap off tough ends of asparagus. Cut spears crosswise in half. Cut stem ends into ½-inch-thick rounds.

In a 2- to 3-quart pan, bring broth and water to a boil on high heat. Add asparagus tips and return liquid to a boil; then simmer, uncovered, until asparagus is just tender when pierced, 4 to 6 minutes. Remove pan from heat; with a slotted spoon, scoop out tips and set aside to drain.

Slowly pour grits into broth, stirring. Add corn and asparagus rounds and return broth to a full boil on high heat, stirring. Pour into a buttered shallow 2-quart casserole. Bake, uncovered, in a 350° oven until mixture is firm, 30 to 40 minutes.

Remove from oven; top cake with cooled asparagus tips. Serve at once, spooning grits onto dinner plates. Makes 6 servings.

## PINEAPPLE COOLER

- 3 **cups refrigerated, reconstituted, or canned pineapple juice**
- 1½ **cups unflavored yogurt**
- ½ **cup water**
- 2 **tablespoons sugar**
  **Cracked ice**

In a 1½- to 2-quart pitcher, stir pineapple juice, yogurt, water, and sugar until mixed. To serve, pour into tall glasses over cracked ice. Makes 5 cups, or 6 servings.

# APRIL

*Chocolate Easter Eggs (page 80)*

**E**nticing aromas welcomed
guests to a brunch party that's easy on the cook; all the food
cooks in the oven, and most can be ready when friends arrive.
Our Easter eggs cracked open to reveal a delicious surprise:
chocolate filling. International dishes featured in April included
a two-course Vietnamese dinner of beef fondue followed by
soup; a spicy, fruit-studded bread from Costa Rica; creamy
risotto from Italy; and a Spanish tortilla that
combines eggs with potatoes.

75

# All-in-the-Oven Brunch

THE ENTICING AROMAS of *warm ham and freshly baked apples linger in the air, soon joined by the fragrance of sizzling potatoes and the tantalizing smell of an egg-rich Dutch baby turning golden brown. These scents all come from the oven, and they're a calculated part of the welcome, as friends arrive for brunch.*

*Apples join the ham as it finishes roasting; they bake at the same temperature. Both can be in the last stages of cooking as guests arrive (or they can be prepared ahead). Then you turn up the oven temperature and slip in the potatoes to brown—while guests temper hunger pangs with warm muffins and a frothy milk punch. When the potato cake is half-done, the Dutch baby goes in to bake alongside it at the same temperature.*

*This is a meal that Mary Lou and Robert Block serve from their large, well-equipped kitchen that's often the center of activity in their Seattle house; the couple's philanthropical projects frequently focus on parties at home. This popular party menu can expand to serve a large group: they just order a larger ham and use more than one oven. But you need only one oven to adapt their brunch for an intimate party of six.*

*Brunch host Bob Block takes "Dutch baby" pancake from oven as guests wait to serve themselves.*

---

## BLOCK BAKED BRUNCH

Milk Punch
Bran Muffins      Butter
Herb-Crusted Ham
Tender Dutch Baby
Oven-Crisp Potato Cake
Crunch-Top Baked Apples
Champagne

---

*You could bake muffins earlier on, using a favorite recipe, and reheat them. Or, like the Blocks, you might pick them up at a good muffin shop or bakery.*

*Serve the apples freshly baked or cook them the day before; the clarified butter, an optional ingredient for the potato cake, can also be made well ahead.*

*The ham, coated with an herb-seasoned crust, can be served hot, or baked up to 4 hours ahead and served at room temperature. Portions are generous for six, so you will probably have leftovers to enjoy later. You could also buy baked ham and serve it cold and thinly sliced. Allow about 3 ounces of cooked meat for a serving.*

*The blender-whizzed milk punch must be served at once to be at its best.*

*To get started, whirl up milk punch, a batch at a time, to sip as you nibble warm bran muffins. Whether you make muffins ahead or buy them (allow 2 per person), set them slightly apart on 1 or 2 baking sheets and heat in a 350° oven until hot, about 10 minutes. Serve muffins with the meal, too.*

*Garnish plates liberally with sprays of watercress. You might also offer a sweet-hot mustard or a sweet-tart chutney.*

### MILK PUNCH

  2  cups milk
     Ice cubes
  2  tablespoons powdered sugar
  1  teaspoon vanilla or 4 to 6 tablespoons bourbon
     Ground nutmeg

Pour milk into a 4-cup glass measure; add enough ice cubes to make 3 cups. Add the sugar and pour into a blender. Holding on lid, whirl mixture at high speed until it's a smooth slush. Add vanilla or bourbon (to taste) and whirl to blend. At once, pour punch into 2 or 3 glasses (at least 8-oz. size). Sprinkle each serving lightly with nutmeg. Makes 2 or 3 servings; repeat to serve 4 to 6.

### HERB-CRUSTED HAM

  1  shank end picnic ham (5½ to 6½ lb.)
  ¼  teaspoon *each* fennel seed, black peppercorns, dry thyme leaves, and dry rubbed sage
  ¼  cup fine dry bread crumbs

Rinse ham and pat dry. Set on a rack (with thickest layer of fat under skin on top) in a 12- by 15-inch roasting pan. Bake in a 350° oven until a meat thermometer inserted to the bone in thickest part of ham registers 140°, about 2 hours.

Meanwhile, whirl fennel, peppercorns, thyme, sage, and crumbs in a blender until spices are coarsely ground (or crush spices with a mortar and pestle or a rolling pin and mix with crumbs).

When meat thermometer reaches 140°, remove ham from the oven and let cool about 30 minutes; it will still be quite warm, but you should be able to touch it. With scissors and a sharp knife, cut hard skin on top of ham from fat; break the skin into pieces to eat while warm, or later, if desired.

Pat seasoned crumbs evenly over fat on ham. Return to oven and continue baking until meat thermometer registers 160°, about 45 minutes. If crumbs begin to darken more than you like, lay a piece of foil over dark area. Let ham stand at least 15 minutes or until cool, then carve. Makes 6 servings (with leftovers).

### TENDER DUTCH BABY

  3  large eggs
  6  tablespoons all-purpose flour
  1  tablespoon granulated sugar
  6  tablespoons milk
  3  tablespoons butter or margarine
     Powdered sugar
  1  lemon, cut into wedges

In a blender or food processor, whirl eggs with flour, granulated sugar, and milk until smoothly mixed, scraping down sides of container several times. If made ahead, mixture can be covered and chilled overnight; stir before baking.

Put butter into a 10- to 12-inch frying pan that can go into the oven. Set pan in a 425° oven on a rack placed slightly above center. Let butter melt; it takes about 4 minutes. Tilt pan to coat bottom with butter, then quickly pour in the batter. Bake until pancake puffs at edges (it may also puff irregularly in the center) and is golden brown, about 15 minutes.

Working quickly, cut into 6 wedges and transfer to dinner plates, using a wide spatula; the wedges may deflate somewhat after cutting. Sprinkle wedges liberally with powdered sugar and squeeze on lemon juice to taste. Makes 6 servings.

## OVEN-CRISP POTATO CAKE

3 large (about 1½ lb. total) russet potatoes
4 tablespoons clarified butter (directions follow) or melted margarine (or use 2 tablespoons *each* melted butter and salad oil, mixed together)
Salt and pepper

Peel potatoes and carefully cut into slices about ⅛ inch thick (use a manual slicer or food processor slicing blade, applying even pressure to get desired thickness). Coat the inside of a 10- to 12-inch oven-proof nonstick frying pan with some of the butter. Neatly overlap potato slices in an even layer in the pan. Evenly drizzle remaining butter over potatoes; brush lightly with your fingertips to coat slices without disturbing them.

Bake on the bottom rack of a 425° oven until potatoes on bottom are well browned (lift with a spatula to check), about 45 minutes. Remove from oven. Invert a rimmed pan that's larger than the frying pan (such as a 12- to 14-inch pizza pan) over the frying pan. Using potholders to protect your hands, quickly flip potatoes onto the rimmed pan; be careful not to drip hot fat on yourself. With spatula, push cake back in shape, if necessary. (If made ahead, cover potatoes and let stand up to 4 hours.)

Return potatoes to oven and bake until the cake is browned on the bottom, about 20 minutes (potatoes partially cooked ahead take the same amount of time).

Invert potato cake onto a small platter. Use a spoon to break cake into portions, or cut in wedges. Add salt and pepper to taste. Makes 6 servings.

## CLARIFIED BUTTER

In a 1- to 1½ quart pan, melt ½ cup (¼ lb.) **butter** over low heat; do not disturb as it melts. Carefully skim crusty-looking surface from butter and discard. Gently pour clear liquid, the clarified butter, from pan into a small container, such as a jar. When it is difficult to pour out only the clarified butter, spoon off as much more as you can. Reserve the opaque white liquid to use to season vegetables (store, covered, in the refrigerator as long as 1 week).

You should have at least 5 tablespoons clarified butter; use to cook crisp potato cake, or for sautéing foods on high heat. Cover and chill up to 2 weeks.

## CRUNCH-TOP BAKED APPLES

6 Golden Delicious, Winesap, or McIntosh apples, *each* about 3 inches in diameter
1 cup granola cereal
¼ cup (⅛ lb.) butter or margarine, at room temperature
3 tablespoons firmly packed brown sugar
½ cup apple juice
Whipping cream or half-and-half (light cream), optional

Rinse apples and core, using an apple corer. Mix cereal with butter and sugar, then press ⅙ of the mixture into the center of each apple, mounding any extra on top. Set apples slightly apart in a shallow baking dish (9- by 13-inch, or 10- by 14-inch oval). Add apple juice to pan.

Bake, uncovered, in a 350° oven until fruit is tender when pierced, about 30 minutes. Serve warm or at room temperature, spooning fruit into individual bowls with some of the baking juices. If made ahead, you can let apples stand, covered, at room temperature overnight. Offer cream to pour over apples, as desired. Makes 6 servings.

*Full spread includes, clockwise from top, bran muffins, sugar-dusted Dutch baby, baked ham, crisp potato cake, and baked apple.*

# Costa Rican Spice Bread

A SPIRALED FRINGE *decorates this soft, springy, flavorful loaf we discovered in Limón, Costa Rica. Richly scented with spices and studded with dried fruit, the loaf indeed lives up to its name:* pan bon—*good bread.*

*Caramelized sugar and cheddar cheese give the loaf its warm hue. A strip of dough cut like a fringe decorates the top.*

*The recipe makes two loaves. Serve them freshly baked, or wrap and freeze. To reheat, thaw bread unwrapped, then place on a sheet of foil and cover lightly with foil; bake in a 350° oven until warm, 15 to 20 minutes.*

## COSTA RICAN FRINGED SPICE BREAD

- 1 **cup sugar**
- 1¾ **cups water**
- ½ **cup (¼ lb.) butter or margarine, cut into pieces**
- 1 **tablespoon vanilla**
- 2 **packages active dry yeast**
- 5 **to 5½ cups all-purpose flour**
- 1½ **teaspoons** *each* **ground ginger and ground cinnamon**
- ½ **teaspoon** *each* **ground nutmeg and salt**
- 1 **cup (4 oz.) firmly packed shredded sharp cheddar cheese**
- ½ **cup raisins**
- ½ **cup chopped dried apricots**

Pour sugar into a 10- to 12-inch frying pan and cook over high heat, shaking pan often, until sugar liquefies and turns a dark amber color (do not scorch), about 4 minutes. Add 1½ cups hot water and butter. Reduce heat to low. Stir until all sugar dissolves and butter melts. Remove from heat. Let cool to 110°. Add vanilla.

In a large bowl, soften yeast in ¼ cup 110° water, about 5 minutes. Add cooled sugar mixture, 4 cups flour, ginger, cinnamon, nutmeg, and salt.

Using an electric mixer with a dough hook or heavy spoon, beat dough until flour is incorporated.

*If using a dough hook,* mix in 1 cup flour. Beat at high speed until dough is stretchy and pulls cleanly from bowl, about 3 minutes; if needed, add more flour, 1 tablespoon at a time. Remove 3 tablespoons dough; cover and set aside at room temperature. Beat cheese, raisins, and apricots into remaining dough just until incorporated.

*Starting at edge of loaf, coil slashed strip around top; fringe will overlap slightly as it spirals toward center.*

*If mixing by hand,* stir in 1 cup flour with a heavy spoon. Scrape dough onto a floured board. Knead, adding as little flour as possible, until dough is smooth and elastic, about 10 minutes. Remove 3 tablespoons of dough; cover and set aside at room temperature. Gradually knead cheese, raisins, and apricots into remaining dough until distributed. Place in an oiled bowl; turn to grease top.

Cover dough with plastic wrap; let rise in a warm place until almost doubled, 2 to 2½ hours.

Punch down dough. Divide into 2 equal portions. On a lightly floured board, knead to shape each portion into a ball. Place each on a greased 12- by 15-inch baking sheet and press to form a flat 6-inch round.

Divide reserved dough into 2 equal portions. On a floured board, roll each portion into a thin 2- by 14-inch strip. Along 1 side, make 1½-inch-long slashes about ¼ inch apart. Coil a strip over top of each loaf. Cover loaves lightly with plastic wrap; let rise in a warm place until almost doubled, 1½ to 2 hours.

Bake in a 325° oven until top springs back when gently pressed in center, 40 to 45 minutes. (If using 1 oven, switch pan positions halfway through baking.) Transfer to racks. Serve warm or cool. Makes 2 loaves (about 1½ lb. each).

*Roll small piece of spice bread dough into a long, thin strip. Along one side of strip, make 1½-inch-long slashes about ¼ inch apart to create "fringe" for the loaf.*

*Amber loaf gets its color and sweet-savory flavor from caramelized sugar and cheddar cheese. The aromatic bread is studded with dried fruit.*

# Chocolate Easter Eggs

WHO'S BEEN TEACHING *the Easter bunny new tricks? Huguette Dumas, a master of chocolate from Le Belge Chocolatier in San Rafael, California, has. Here we share her delicious secrets.*

*Instead of a hen's egg inside a real eggshell, a chocolate one takes its place—not by magic, but in a series of simple, carefully executed steps; you have to wait minutes to hours between each. First you empty the eggshells, then sterilize them and, if you like, decorate with color. The shells need at least a day to dry.*

*Next, you swirl melted chocolate inside the shell to create a thin wall, then chill. When the wall is firm, pipe in mousse or truffle filling and chill again for an hour or up to a week.*

To empty eggshell so you can use it as a realistic mold for chocolate eggs, blow raw egg through punctured end of shell.

Pipe chocolate mousse or truffle filling into sterilized shells that have already been lined with a hard layer of chocolate.

## CHOCOLATE EASTER EGGS

    6  large eggs
       Easter egg dye (optional), prepared
       as package directs
    6  ounces (about 1 cup) chopped bit-
       tersweet or semisweet chocolate
       Gianduia mousse or chocolate truf-
       fle filling (recipes follow)

Using an ice pick or a cooking fork tine, carefully pierce the shell through membrane at each end of 1 egg. On the wide end of the egg, carefully break shell away from hole to make an opening about ¼ inch in diameter. Place your lips over the smaller hole and blow to force the raw egg out the large hole and into a bowl. Repeat to empty remaining shells. (Use eggs in recipes that call for whole eggs; 1 egg equals 3 tablespoons. Eggs spoil quickly: cover, refrigerate, and use right away.)

In a 2- to 3-quart pan, place eggshells and water to cover; push shells beneath water until they fill and sink. Bring water to a gentle boil; to sterilize, simmer, uncovered, at least 15 minutes. Remove shells with a slotted spoon and drain.

When cool enough to handle, gently shake shells to remove remaining water and any loose bits of cooked egg white. Immerse in cool water to fill shells again; drain well. If desired, color shells. Set shells, large holes up, in egg carton and let stand at room temperature to dry overnight. Store dry shells, covered, up to 3 days.

When shells are thoroughly dry inside, place a piece of transparent tape over the small hole on each shell; return shells to carton, large holes up. If shells are not dry inside, chocolate lining (next step) will not stick to form a smooth interior shell.

In the top of a double boiler, occasionally stir chocolate over hot (not simmering) water until chocolate is smoothly melted. Remove pan from heat. At once, spoon chocolate into a plastic-lined pastry bag fitted with a plain tube (¼-inch opening or slightly smaller), and pipe 1 to 2 tablespoons chocolate into a shell through large hole. Quickly shake and roll shell to coat interior evenly; peek inside to be sure no light patches remain. Turn large hole down over pan and shake excess chocolate into it. Set shell, large hole up, in the egg carton and at once refrigerate until chocolate is firm, at least 30 minutes or up to 3 days. Repeat to coat remaining shells.

Squeeze any remaining chocolate in pastry bag back into pan. Pour extra chocolate onto a sheet of foil to cool; reserve for other uses. Rinse and dry the pastry bag.

Fit pastry bag with the same tip, and spoon in filling; pipe into shells, filling completely. To avoid creating air bubbles while filling shells, squeeze bag with steady pressure and shake shell gently to settle filling into it. Wipe surfaces clean with a damp cloth, then chill filled shells. Keep extra filling at room temperature. After 1 hour, filling in shells may settle; if so, pipe in more, bringing flush with rim. Wipe shells clean and chill until filling at openings is firm, about 1 hour (eggs keep up to 1 week in the refrigerator). To disguise big hole, wrap eggs with ribbon or push the stem of a small fabric flower into filling. Pull tape off small hole.

*To serve chocolate mousse eggs,* tap shells of cold eggs to crack around top. Peel off top part of shell and place in egg cups and let warm to room temperature before eating with a spoon.

*To serve truffle eggs,* tap shells of cold eggs to crack; peel off shell. Eat eggs out of hand or cut into bite-size pieces.

Recipe makes 6 eggs.

**Gianduia mousse filling.** Fill base of a double boiler with enough water to surround top unit of the pan. Heat water to 140°. In top pan, combine 7 ounces (1¼ cups) chopped **bittersweet,** semisweet, or milk **chocolate,** ¼ cup **hazelnut-flavored liqueur,** and 1 tablespoon **whipping cream;** set into hot water and remove entire unit from heat. Stir just until chocolate is smoothly melted. Remove top pan from water. Stir smoothly into chocolate ¼ cup room temperature **butter** or margarine (cut up), then 1 **egg yolk.**

With an electric mixer, whip 2 **large egg whites** on high speed until frothy. Add 1 tablespoon **powdered sugar** and beat until whites hold soft peaks. Stir ¼ of the whites into chocolate mixture; fold in the remaining whites. Use at once; hold extra filling up to 1 hour at room temperature.

*Pastel-tinted eggshells filled with hidden sweet chocolate make a charming spring holiday dessert. Tuck them into a grass-and posy-filled basket and top each with ribbon or tiny fabric flower blossoms.*

**Chocolate truffle filling.** Fill base of a double boiler with enough water to surround top unit of the pan. Heat water to 140°. In top pan, combine 9 ounces (1½ cups) chopped **bittersweet,** semisweet, or milk **chocolate,** ¼ cup **orange-flavored** **liqueur,** and 3 tablespoons **whipping cream**; set into the hot water and remove entire unit from heat. Stir just until chocolate is smoothly melted. Remove top pan from water. Stir smoothly into choc- olate 3 tablespoons room-temperature **butter** or margarine (cut up) and 2 table- spoons **superfine** or powdered **sugar** (powdered sugar doesn't dissolve as well). Use at once; hold extra filling up to 1 hour at room temperature.

# "Two-Jewel" Dinner: Asian Fondue & Soup

**O**N SPECIAL OCCASIONS in Vietnam, families celebrate with a dinner composed of seven small courses—"seven jewels"—all made with beef. Chef Kim Quy Tran of San Francisco's Golden Turtle restaurant proposes a Western variation on the meal, featuring two of the principal dishes; the combination works very well if you're entertaining 6 to 8 people at home.

You start with a light Asian version of beef fondue with accompaniments of crisp fruit, vegetables, herbs, and a lively sauce. You end, Asian fashion, with soup.

All the ingredients are arranged well ahead and presented at the table.

For the fondue, set a container of the boiling, pungent broth on a portable burner within easy reach of everyone at the table, and keep it simmering. With 6 guests, 1 burner is adequate; with 8, it is more convenient to have 2 burners.

Each guest, using chopsticks or a fork with a long handle, passes one or two thin slices of beef at a time through the hot broth—the meat is cooked in seconds.

Then the cooked meat is wrapped in moistened edible rice paper along with lettuce, mint, and slivers of carrots and apples; the roll is dipped in the sweet-tart-hot sauce and eaten. Guests need to

moisten each round of dry rice paper with water just before using.

To serve the soup, bring cooked-ahead rice-ginger broth to boiling and pour over raw meat. The hot broth cooks the beef.

End dinner with sliced tropical fruit to eat plain or with coconut ice cream.

You may need to shop in an Asian market for the dried rice paper rounds, fish sauce, daikon, carambola, and lemon grass. If they are unavailable, use the alternatives suggested. Use lettuce leaves alone as wrappers if you can't find the rice paper.

It is easiest to buy 1 piece of eye of round for the 2 courses. Ask your butcher to thinly slice the meat for the fondue. You can mince some of the slices for the soup in the food processor or with a knife.

*Set up at home, here's how Vietnamese beef fondue works: you dip beef slices in pot of simmering vinegar broth; place on moistened rice paper with lettuce, carrot, daikon, apple, mint; then roll up and dip in sauce to eat.*

## VIETNAMESE BEEF FONDUE WITH VINEGAR
### (Bo Nhung Giam)

- ¼  cup *each* sugar, white distilled vinegar, and water
- 1  piece daikon (about 3 inches long), peeled (optional)
- 1  large carrot, peeled and cut into matchstick-size sticks
- 1½  pounds beef eye of round, trimmed of fat and sliced across the grain as thinly as possible
- 1  large head (¾ lb.) red leaf lettuce, washed and dried
- 1  small cucumber, cut into matchstick-size sticks
- 1  large tart green apple, cut into matchstick-size sticks and dipped in lemon or lime juice; or 2 small star fruit (carambola), thinly sliced crosswise
- 1  cup lightly packed fresh mint sprigs
- 1  cup lightly packed fresh coriander (cilantro) sprigs
  Dipping sauce (recipe follows)
  Cooking broth (recipe follows)
- 30  to 40 pieces edible rice paper (6- or 8-inch diameter), about ½ pound

In a bowl, stir together sugar, vinegar, and water until sugar dissolves. Cut ¼-inch-deep notches down the length of the daikon, spaced about ½ inch apart, then thinly slice daikon crosswise. Mix daikon and carrot with vinegar mixture; cover and chill, stirring occasionally, for at least 1 hour or up to 4 hours.

Arrange beef slices in overlapping layers on 1 or 2 platters. Drain daikon and carrot. On 1 or 2 additional platters or in shallow baskets, cluster piles of daikon, carrot, lettuce, cucumber, apple, mint, and coriander. (If done ahead, cover and chill platters up to 4 hours.)

To serve, pour dipping sauce into 6 to 8 small bowls. Bring cooking broth to a boil, place over portable tabletop burner, and keep simmering (if you use 2 burners, double the amount of cooking broth and place in 2 pans). Place platters of foods alongside burners.

Using a spray bottle with water, or a bowl of water with brush, lightly moisten both sides of 6 to 8 pieces of rice paper and place each on a dinner plate or in a single layer on a tray (paper will stick if stacked); let stand until pliable, about 30 seconds. Moisten more paper as needed.

To eat, place a small piece of lettuce and a few pieces of daikon, carrot, cucumber, apple, mint, and coriander on the moistened paper. With chopsticks, drop a slice of meat into cooking broth and cook just until it loses its pinkness on the outside but is still rare inside, about 30 seconds. Lift out meat and place on vegetables. Fold bottom of rice paper up and sides in. Pick up and dip in sauce to eat. Makes 6 to 8 servings.

**Cooking broth.** In a 2- to 3-quart pan, combine 2 cups **white distilled vinegar,** 2 cups **water,** 2 tablespoons chopped **fresh lemon grass** (optional), 3 tablespoons **sugar,** 2 tablespoons **salad oil,** 1 tablespoon **salt,** 6 thin slices (*each* about the size of a quarter) **fresh ginger,** 8 thin slices **yellow** or white **onion,** and 2 **green onions,** roots trimmed off and cut into 1-inch lengths.

**Dipping sauce.** Mix ¾ cup *each* water, **fish sauce** (*nuoc mam*) or soy sauce, **white distilled vinegar,** and **sugar** with ¼ cup finely shredded **carrot,** 2 tablespoons **lime juice,** 4 teaspoons minced seeded **fresh hot chili** (jalapeño, or red chili paste, or crushed dried hot red chilies), and 12 cloves **garlic,** pressed or minced.

## BEEF RICE SOUP
### (Chao Bo)

- 2 **quarts water**
- ½ cup **long-grain white rice**
- 6 **thin slices** (*each* about the size of a quarter) **fresh ginger**
- 2 **tablespoons fish sauce** (*nuoc mam*) **or soy sauce**
- 4 **teaspoons sugar**
  **Salt**

- 2 **tablespoons salad oil**
- 1 **teaspoon finely chopped garlic**
- 1 **tablespoon minced fresh lemon grass, or 1 teaspoon grated lemon peel (yellow part only)**
- ½ **cup thinly sliced green onion**
- ½ **pound lean beef such as eye of round or flank steak, minced**
- 1 **tablespoon chopped fresh coriander (cilantro)**
- ¼ **teaspoon pepper**
  **Dipping sauce (recipe above)**

In a 3- to 4-quart pan, combine water, rice, and ginger. Bring to boiling and simmer, covered, until rice is very tender to bite, about 30 minutes. Add fish sauce, sugar, and salt to taste. Set aside as long as 4 hours.

Meanwhile, in a 6- to 8-inch frying pan, combine oil, garlic, and lemon grass. Stir over low heat just until garlic is golden; set garlic oil aside.

Mix green onion and beef in a tureen. To serve, bring broth to boiling and add garlic oil. Pour boiling hot soup over meat and stir. Sprinkle with coriander and pepper. Offer dipping sauce to season as desired. Makes 6 to 8 servings.

*Pour simmering broth, flecked with tender grains of rice, over minced beef; the very hot liquid quickly and lightly cooks the meat to make a refreshing soup.*

# Cheese Soups

COOL SPRING DAYS *invite soup. Whether it's served alone in generous bowls, with a salad or sandwich as a main course, or in smaller portions to start a meal, hot soup is appropriate for this time of year.*

*These three recipes capitalize on cheese to lend smoothness, rich flavor, and protein.*

*Carrots and cream cheese, punctuated with caraway seeds, create a thick, flavorful blend in the first soup. Offer with warm rye bread or breadsticks.*

*Apples and cheddar cheese are natural companions in our second choice, making a slightly sweet soup reminiscent of the old American favorite, apple pie with cheese. Spoon chutney into the soup or spread this condiment on whole-grain crackers.*

*Chili lovers will relish the heat in the corn and pepper soup; you can temper it slightly with jalapeño jack cheese or add more fire to taste with prepared salsa. Serve with corn chips or hot corn bread.*

## CARROT & CREAM CHEESE SOUP

2½ cups regular-strength chicken broth
4 cups (about 2 lb.) peeled and sliced carrots
½ cup chopped onion
¾ teaspoon caraway seed
1 large package (8 oz.) cream cheese
⅓ cup shredded carrot

In a 3- to 4-quart pan over high heat, bring broth with sliced carrots, onion, and ½ teaspoon caraway seed to a boil; cover and simmer until carrots are tender when pierced, about 15 minutes.

Pour broth and carrots into a blender or spoon carrots and some broth into a food processor and whirl until smooth, 3 to 5 minutes. Return to pan; stir often over medium-high heat until boiling. Meanwhile, cut cheese in half lengthwise, then into thin slices crosswise. Reserve 1 slice for each serving; add remaining cheese to soup and whisk until smooth.

Ladle soup into 3 to 5 bowls; sprinkle with shredded carrot, reserved cheese slices, and remaining caraway seed. Makes 3 to 5 servings, 1 to 1⅔ cups each.

## APPLE CHEESE SOUP

2 cups regular-strength chicken broth
4 cups (about 3 large) cored, peeled, and chopped apples
¼ cup slivered almonds
2 tablespoons butter or margarine
2 tablespoons all-purpose flour
1 cup apple juice
1 cup (4 oz.) firmly packed shredded cheddar cheese
½ cup chutney

In a 3- to 4-quart pan over high heat, bring 1 cup chicken broth to a boil with apples. Turn heat to low, cover pan, and simmer until apples are tender when pierced, about 10 minutes.

Meanwhile, spread almonds in a single layer in an 8- or 9-inch cake or pie pan. Bake in a 350° oven until nuts are lightly browned, about 10 minutes; shake occasionally. Set aside.

Scrape apples and broth into a blender or food processor; whirl the mixture until smoothly puréed.

In the same 3- to 4-quart pan over medium-high heat, melt butter. Add flour and stir until bubbly. Remove from heat and slowly whisk in the apple juice and remaining chicken broth. Cook, stirring, until boiling, about 5 minutes.

Remove pan from heat. Reserve ¼ cup of the cheese; whisk the rest into the hot broth, stirring until smooth. Add apple purée and place over medium-high heat; stir until boiling. Pour into a tureen or 4 soup bowls; sprinkle with reserved cheese and then with almonds. Offer chutney to stir into each portion to taste. Makes 4 servings, each about 1 cup.

## CORN & JALAPEÑO CHEESE SOUP

2 tablespoons butter or margarine
1 small onion, minced
½ teaspoon ground cumin
3½ cups regular-strength chicken broth
1 tablespoon cornstarch
2½ cups (1 lb.) frozen corn kernels
1 large red bell pepper, stemmed, seeded, and chopped
½ to ¾ cup prepared salsa
2½ cups (about 9 oz.) lightly packed shredded jalapeño-flavored jack cheese

In a 4- to 5-quart pan over medium-high heat, melt butter. Add onion and cumin, and cook, stirring often, until onion is soft but not brown. Smoothly blend 1 to 2 tablespoons of the broth with cornstarch. Pour cornstarch mixture and remaining broth into pan; add corn, pepper, and ¼ cup salsa. Bring to a boil over high heat, stirring. Pour soup into a tureen or 4 wide bowls. Offer cheese and salsa to taste. Makes 4 servings, about 1⅓ cups each.

*Smooth texture of sweet carrot soup comes from cream cheese. Caraway seed, shredded carrot, and more cheese garnish each bowl.*

# Spanish Tortilla—An Egg-Potato Omelet

SPANIARDS *brought the word* tortilla *to Mexico. The Mexicans, in turn, used it to describe their flat corn and flour cakes with which we are so familiar. Yet in Spain today, you'll find that the original meaning still holds: a tortilla is an omelet. It is also this combination of eggs with potatoes.*

*In tapas bars, the egg-potato dish, or Spanish tortilla, is often served at room temperature as a snack with sherry. The tortilla is also very popular for supper at home, where it is often served with fruit or salad (supper is typically eaten long after 8 in the evening).*

*For Westerners, the Spanish tortilla and suggested variation are also excellent choices for a weekend brunch.*

## SPANISH TORTILLA

- 3 tablespoons olive oil
- 1 small onion, finely chopped
- 2 cloves garlic, pressed or minced (optional)
- 2 medium-size (about 1 lb.) thin-skinned potatoes, scrubbed and cut into ¼-inch cubes
- 1 can (6 oz. drained weight) pitted black ripe olives, drained
- 1 jar (7 oz.) roasted red peppers or pimientos, drained; or 1 can (7 oz.) diced green chilies, drained
- 9 large eggs
  Sour cream (optional)

In a 10- to 12-inch nonstick frying pan over medium heat, combine 1 tablespoon oil, onion, and garlic; cook, stirring often, just until onion is limp, about 5 minutes. Add remaining oil and potatoes; turn with a wide spatula to coat evenly with oil.

Cook over medium-high heat, turning often, until potatoes are golden and tender to bite, about 15 minutes. Coarsely chop olives and peppers; stir into potatoes.

In a bowl, whisk eggs until blended. Reduce heat under potatoes to low; add eggs. Cover and cook until eggs are set about 1 inch around edge but still look liquid in the center, about 8 minutes. Uncover; tilt pan and, with a spatula, slightly lift edges of tortilla to let uncooked egg flow under. Cover and cook until egg is set on top but still looks moist, 5 to 10 minutes.

Ease a spatula down sides and under the tortilla to be sure it is not stuck. Lay a flat plate or a rimless baking sheet, wider than the frying pan, over the top of the pan. Holding plate and pan together, invert tortilla onto the plate. With your hand or a spatula, slide tortilla back into pan, cooked side up. Cook, uncovered, until eggs are set on bottom, about 1 minute more; lift with spatula to test.

Slide tortilla onto a serving platter. Cut into wedges and serve hot, warm, or at room temperature, with sour cream to spoon on portions. Makes 4 to 6 servings.

## BACON TORTILLA

Cook ½ cup firmly packed chopped **bacon** in a 10- to 12-inch nonstick frying pan over medium heat; stir often until browned. Follow directions for **Spanish Tortilla,** preceding, but omit the first 1 tablespoon of olive oil, adding onion and garlic to pan with bacon. Omit olives and peppers.

Also stir ½ cup lightly packed shredded **cheddar cheese** into whisked eggs.

*From bar snack to brunch fare: in Spain this tortilla is a familiar and popular combination of potatoes and eggs. Serve wedges with sour cream; offer fresh fruit.*

# Fennel—A Flavorful Base for Salads

**B**ULBOUS HEADS *of fresh fennel have a crisp, celery-like texture and slight licorice taste. Also called sweet anise or finocchio, fennel makes a flavorful base for salads. In the following three dishes, raw slices of the aromatic vegetable combine with oranges, watercress, or steamed clams.*

## FENNEL SALAD WITH ORANGE

- 3 tablespoons pine nuts or slivered almonds
- 4 large oranges
- ¼ cup salad oil
- 2 tablespoons white wine vinegar
- 1 teaspoon minced fresh rosemary or crumbled dry rosemary
- 2 large heads (1½ to 2 lb. total) fresh fennel, ends trimmed
- 6 large butter lettuce leaves, washed and crisped
  Salt and pepper

In a 6- to 8-inch frying pan over medium-low heat, toast nuts until golden, 4 to 5 minutes; stir often. Let cool.

Grate enough peel from 1 orange to make ¼ teaspoon. Ream 1 orange to make ⅓ cup juice. Cut peel and white membrane from remaining 3 oranges. Thinly slice fruit crosswise.

Stir together grated orange peel, orange juice, oil, vinegar, and rosemary.

Remove and reserve fennel leaves. Trim bruises from fennel, then cut heads into quarters lengthwise; remove and discard core and tough stems. Thinly slice sections crosswise to make 4 cups. Mix slices with dressing; cover and chill 15 minutes.

Place a lettuce leaf on each of 6 dinner or salad plates; top equally with fennel slices and dressing, oranges, nuts, and fennel leaves. Add salt and pepper to taste. Makes 6 servings.

## FENNEL & WATERCRESS SALAD

- 1 large carrot, peeled
- ⅓ pound watercress
- 2 medium-size heads (1 to 1½ lb. total) fresh fennel, ends trimmed
- 2 ounces parmesan cheese
- 6 tablespoons olive or salad oil
- 3 tablespoons white wine vinegar
- 1 teaspoon Dijon mustard
  Salt and pepper

With a vegetable peeler, evenly pare 16 to 20 long, thick, wide strips down length of carrot; reserve remaining carrot

*Slivers of crisp white fennel, toasted pine nuts, and orange dressing make this salad— embellish with orange slices, feathery fennel leaves.*

for another use. Tightly curl carrot strips and place in ice water; chill 15 minutes or up to 1 hour.

Pluck off tender watercress sprigs to make 4 cups; wash, dry, and chill to crisp, 15 minutes or up to overnight.

Trim bruises from fennel, then cut heads into quarters lengthwise; remove and discard core and tough stems. Thinly slice sections crosswise to make about 3 cups.

Cut cheese into very thin shavings with a cheese slicer or knife.

Drain carrots. In a bowl, mix oil, vinegar, and mustard. Add carrots, fennel, and watercress; mix well and place on 4 salad or dinner plates. Add cheese and salt and pepper to taste. Serves 4.

## FENNEL SALAD WITH CLAMS

- 4 green onions, ends trimmed
- 1 cup dry white wine
- 1 cup water
- ½ teaspoon fennel seed
- 24 clams suitable for steaming, well scrubbed
- 3 tablespoons lemon juice
- 2 large heads (1½ to 2 lb. total) fresh fennel, ends trimmed
  Lemon wedges

Thinly slice white part of onions; reserve green tops for garnish. In a 5- to 6-quart pan, combine sliced onion, wine, water, and fennel seed. Cover and bring to boil over high heat. Add clams; cover and simmer until clams pop open, 5 to 10 minutes. Lift out clams, pouring juices back into pan. Let clams cool. Meanwhile, boil liquid, uncovered, over high heat until reduced to ⅓ cup, 10 to 12 minutes. Let cool. Add lemon juice.

Remove and reserve fennel leaves. Trim bruises from fennel, then cut heads into quarters lengthwise; remove and discard core and tough stems. Thinly slice sections crosswise to make 4 cups. Remove clams from shells. In a bowl, mix clams, fennel slices, and reduced clam juice. Cover and chill about 15 minutes. Lay onion tops across 4 dinner plates. Mound salad on onions. Garnish with lemon wedges and fennel leaves. Serves 4.

# Worldwide Companions: Beans & Rice

A COMMON PAIR *in much of the world, beans and rice complement each other nutritionally to form high-quality protein.*

*Here we offer them as an entrée and two side dishes. First, spicy sausage and ham hocks simmer with red beans to form a thick sauce you spoon over rice. Next, pungent fermented black beans (sold in Oriental markets) season short-grain rice. In the third dish, from Costa Rica, red beans cook with rice and coconut milk to make a creamy companion to chicken.*

## SPICY RED BEANS, SAUSAGE & RICE

- 2 **tablespoons salad oil**
- 1 **pound andouille or linguisa sausage, cut into ¼-inch slices**
- 2 **large yellow onions, chopped**
- 2 **stalks celery, chopped**
- 1 **large green bell pepper, stemmed, seeded, and chopped**
- 6 **green onions, thinly sliced**
- 2 **quarts water**
- 1 **teaspoon cayenne**
- ½ **teaspoon dry thyme leaves**
- 4 **dry bay leaves**
- 1 **or 2 ham hocks (about 2 lb. total)**
- 1 **pound (2⅓ cups) dry small red beans**
- 2 **to 4 tablespoons cider vinegar**
  **Salt and pepper**
- 8 **to 10 cups hot cooked rice**

In a heavy 8- to 10-quart pan, combine oil and sausage; stir often over medium-high heat until meat is browned. Add yellow onions, celery, bell pepper, and green onions; stir until vegetables are limp, about 5 minutes.

Add water, cayenne, thyme, bay leaves, and ham. Sort through beans and discard debris. Rinse and drain beans, then add to pan. Bring to boiling; reduce heat, cover, and simmer over low heat until ham is very tender when pierced, 1½ to 2 hours. Lift out ham; let cool. Skim off and discard fat from bean mixture, then continue simmering, uncovered, while meat cools. When ham is cool enough to handle, about 15

minutes, remove and discard fat and bones; tear meat into bite-size chunks. Return meat to pan.

Simmer, uncovered, over low heat, stirring occasionally, until most of the liquid evaporates, 20 to 30 minutes longer. (If made ahead, cool, cover, and chill. Reheat, covered, over low heat, stirring occasionally, until hot; if mixture becomes too thick, add a little water.) Add vinegar, salt, and pepper to taste.

To serve, spoon hot rice onto plates or into shallow bowls, then pour bean mixture over top. Makes 2¾ quarts, 8 to 10 servings. — *Bruce Aidells, Kensington, Calif.*

## FERMENTED BLACK BEANS & RICE

- ½ **cup fermented black beans**
  **Water**
- ¼ **cup (⅛ lb.) butter or margarine**
- 1 **small onion, chopped**
- 1 **cup short-grain white (pearl) rice**

Rinse black beans, drain, and place in a bowl. Add water to cover. Let soak for 30 minutes. Drain.

In a 3- to 4-quart pan, melt butter over medium heat. Add onion and stir until limp. Add rice and stir until light gold. Add 1¾ cups water; boil over high heat, uncovered, until most of the water evaporates, 6 to 8 minutes. Reduce heat to low and stir in beans; cover and cook until rice is tender to bite, about 15 minutes longer. Makes 3½ cups, 4 servings. — *Michael Roberts, Los Angeles.*

## COCONUT RED BEANS & RICE

- 1 **cup dry small red beans**
- 1 **large onion, chopped**
- 2 **cloves garlic, pressed or minced**
- 1 **small dried hot red chili**
- 1 **can (12 to 14 oz.) coconut milk, thawed if frozen**
  **About 1 quart regular-strength chicken broth or water**
- 2 **cups long-grain white rice**
  **Salt**

Pick out any debris from beans. Rinse beans and drain. In a 5- to 6-quart pan, combine beans, onion, garlic, chili, coconut milk, and 1 quart broth. Bring to boiling, then reduce heat and simmer, covered, until beans are almost completely soft when pressed, 1¼ to 1½ hours.

*Combine dry red beans with ham hock, spicy sausage, vegetables, and spices; simmer until thick and tender. Then ladle the chunky, flavorful bean and meat sauce over hot cooked rice.*

Stir in rice. Cover and cook over low heat until rice is tender and most of the liquid is absorbed, about 30 minutes longer (add a little broth if needed to prevent sticking). Discard chili. Add salt to taste. Makes 7½ cups, 8 to 10 servings.

# Breakfast & Brunch Spreads

SIMPLE, EFFECTIVE WAYS *to dress up mar-malade and jam bring zest to these spreads. You add to them white or dark chocolate, along with a compatible liqueur.*

*When you spread this mixture on warm breads or toast, the liqueur intensifies the fruit flavor, and the chocolate softens slightly into melting nuggets.*

*Since these mixtures go together quickly, you might make several kinds to have on hand as hostess gifts.*

## RASPBERRY & DARK CHOCOLATE JAM

Mix together 1 cup (12-oz. jar) **raspberry jam,** ¼ to ⅓ cup **orange-flavored liqueur** (to taste), and ½ cup finely chopped **semi-sweet chocolate.** Serve, or cover and chill up to 2 months. Makes 1⅔ cups.

## STRAWBERRY & WHITE CHOCOLATE JAM

Mix together 1 cup (12-oz. jar) **straw-berry jam,** ¼ to ⅓ cup **black raspberry-flavored liqueur** (to taste), and ½ cup finely chopped **white chocolate.** Serve, or cover and refrigerate up to 2 months. Makes 1⅔ cups.

## BLACKBERRY & WHITE CHOCOLATE JAM

Mix together 1 cup (12-oz. jar) **black-berry jam,** ¼ to ⅓ cup **blackberry-fla-vored liqueur** or currant liqueur (to taste), and ½ cup finely chopped **white chocolate.** Serve, or cover and chill up to 2 months. Makes 1⅔ cups.

## RASPBERRY & WHITE CHOCOLATE JAM

Mix together 1 cup (12-oz. jar) **raspberry jam,** ¼ to ⅓ cup **black raspberry-fla-vored liqueur** or blackberry-flavored liqueur (to taste), and ½ cup finely chop-ped **white chocolate.** Serve, or cover and chill up to 2 months. Makes 1⅔ cups.

## ORANGE & WHITE CHOCOLATE MARMALADE

Mix together 1 cup (12-oz. jar) **orange marmalade,** ¼ to ⅓ cup **almond-flavored** or orange-flavored **liqueur** (to taste), and ½ cup finely chopped **white chocolate.** Serve, or cover and refrigerate up to 2 months. Makes 1⅔ cups.

*Dress up orange marmalade with white chocolate chunks and almond-flavored liqueur to serve with hot breads. Or try other combinations of jams, liqueurs, and chocolates.*

# Prunes Poached in Red Wine

HUMBLE DRIED PRUNES *acquire a richer, deeper flavor when gently poached in red wine with cinnamon and lemon. Unadorned, they make a simple but elegant dessert. Or use them to embellish a buttery biscuit cake or an oven pancake.*

*You can store poached prunes in their syrup in the refrigerator for several weeks.*

## PRUNES IN WINE SYRUP

- ½ **pound pitted dried prunes**
- 2 **cups dry red wine**
- ½ **cup sugar**
- 1 **cinnamon stick (3 to 4 inches long)**
- 2 **strips (*each* ½ by 3 inches) pared lemon peel, yellow part only**
- 2 **tablespoons lemon juice**

In a 3- to 4-quart pan, combine prunes, wine, sugar, cinnamon, and lemon peel and juice. Bring to a boil, reduce heat, cover, and simmer until prunes are soft and plump, about 30 minutes. Cool, cover, and chill until cold, at least 1 hour; refrigerate as long as 2 weeks.

Serve prunes with syrup in small glasses or bowls. Or use in following recipes. Makes 6 servings.

## BUTTER BISCUIT & WINE PRUNES

- 1 **cup (½ lb.) butter or margarine**
  **About ¾ cup sugar**
- 1 **teaspoon vanilla**
- 4 **large eggs**
- ½ **teaspoon baking powder**
- 1¾ **cups all-purpose flour**
  **Prunes in wine syrup (recipe precedes)**
- 1 **cup whipping cream, softly whipped**

With an electric mixer at high speed, beat butter in a bowl until creamy. Add ¾ cup sugar and beat until well blended. Add vanilla. Add eggs, 1 at a time, beating well after each addition. Beat in baking powder. Add flour; mix just until blended. Spread batter into a greased 9-inch round cake pan. Sprinkle evenly with about 1 teaspoon of the sugar.

Bake in 350° oven until a slender wooden pick inserted in center comes out clean, 30 to 35 minutes. Cool in pan on a rack for about 10 minutes; invert cake onto a rack. Set cake, sugar-crusted side up, on a serving platter.

Serve cake warm or cool, cut in wedges. Offer prunes and cream to spoon over portions. Serves 8 to 10.

## PRUNE & ALMOND PASTE PANCAKE PUFF

- ¼ **cup (⅛ lb.) butter or margarine**
- 1 **cup all-purpose flour**
- 2 **tablespoons sugar**
- 3 **large eggs**
- 1 **cup milk**
  **Prunes in wine syrup (recipe precedes), drained well (reserve syrup)**
- ½ **cup (5¼ oz.) packed almond paste or marzipan**
  **Powdered sugar**

Set oven at 425°. Place butter in a shallow 2-quart baking dish; put in heating oven until butter melts, 5 to 10 minutes.

Meanwhile, whirl flour, sugar, eggs, and milk in a blender or food processor until smooth. Remove dish from oven. Arrange prunes evenly in a single layer in dish. Crumble almond paste evenly over prunes. Pour flour batter over prunes.

Bake until puffy and golden brown, 30 to 35 minutes. Dust with powdered sugar. Serve at once, spooned into bowls. Offer reserved syrup to pour over each serving. Makes 6 to 8 servings.

*Spooned over a cream-topped wedge of butter biscuit cake, syrup-steeped prunes make an appealing dessert. Prunes in syrup keep several weeks.*

# More April Recipes

FRESH FLAVORS *for spring include a sweet-tart variation on aïoli to serve with fruit; nutlike spreads made from sunflower seed; and a spinach salad with orange segments and red onion rings. Our basic risotto recipe uses pearl barley or one of five varieties of rice.*

## APPLE AÏOLI

*Fruity overtones from apple and lemon create a sweet-tart variation on aïoli. This garlic dip brings out the natural sweetness of vegetables such as carrots and broccoli, as well as apples and pears. Pack it for a picnic dip or offer it as a casual appetizer.*

*Dip apple wedges, pear wedges, carrot sticks, and broccoli flowerets into sauce flavored with apple, lemon, and garlic.*

5 tablespoons lemon juice
2 tablespoons thawed frozen apple juice concentrate
2 large egg yolks
1 clove garlic, minced or pressed
About ½ teaspoon ground cinnamon
1 cup salad oil
1 *each* large red, yellow, or green apple and ripe pear, cored and sliced into ¼-inch wedges
4 cups broccoli flowerets
3 large carrots, peeled and cut into 3-inch sticks

In a blender or food processor, combine 3 tablespoons lemon juice, apple juice concentrate, egg yolks, garlic, and ½ teaspoon cinnamon; whirl until blended. With the motor on high, slowly pour in the oil; mixture will thicken. Scrape mixture into a small serving bowl; if made ahead, cover and chill up to overnight.

Sprinkle sauce lightly with ground cinnamon and set bowl on a serving platter. Mix apple and pear wedges with remaining lemon juice to preserve color. Arrange fruit and vegetables around bowl. Makes 1⅓ cups sauce, 8 to 10 servings. —*Roxanne Chan, Albany, Calif.*

## SUN BUTTER

*It sticks to the roof of your mouth, like peanut butter. But butter made from sunflower seeds has its own nutty taste. If you like the seeds, you'll enjoy the butter.*

2 cups unsalted roasted sunflower seeds (directions follow), or purchased salted roasted sunflower seeds
1 to 3 teaspoons salad oil (optional)
1 to 2 tablespoons powdered sugar (optional)
Salt (optional)

Whirl seeds in a food processor until smooth, 5 to 7 minutes. Or whirl at high speed in a blender; if necessary, add oil a little at a time to help form a smooth butter. If desired, add sugar or salt to taste; mix well. Serve, or cover and chill up to 3 weeks. Makes 1 cup.

**Unsalted roasted sunflower seeds.** Spread 2 cups **raw sunflower seeds** in an even layer in a 10- by 15-inch baking pan. Bake in a 350° oven, stirring occasionally, until most seeds are golden brown, 15 to 20 minutes. Let cool; if made ahead, store airtight up to 2 weeks.

## CHOCOLATE SUN BUTTER

Make **Sun Butter,** preceding, but omit salt and use only ½ cup **powdered sugar** and 1 tablespoon **salad oil.** Stir in ¼ cup **unsweetened cocoa** and ½ teaspoon **vanilla.** Use, or cover and chill up to 3 weeks. Makes 1¼ cups.

## BARBECUE HERB BLENDS

*Outdoor chefs gearing up for another season will appreciate these aromatic blends for flavoring grilled foods. Purchased dry herbs are the base; just grind them in a blender to make seasonings for meat, poultry, or fish and vegetables.*

*To use herb blends for smoke, soak 3 tablespoons barbecue herbs (choices follow) in warm water to cover for 15 minutes. Drain in a fine strainer. Scatter wet herbs on coals as you cook foods in a covered barbecue.*

*To use herb blends as seasonings, lightly sprinkle foods with the dry herbs before barbecuing.*

## HERBS FOR MEAT

In a blender, whirl until coarsely ground 1½ tablespoons *each* **dry basil** and **dry oregano leaves;** and ¼ cup *each* **crushed dry bay leaves, juniper berries, dry rosemary,** and **dry savory leaves.** Use as directed, preceding, on beef, lamb, or pork, or store airtight as long as 4 months. Makes ¾ cup.

## HERBS FOR POULTRY

In a blender, whirl until coarsely ground 4 teaspoons *each* **cracked pepper** and **dry savory leaves;** and ¼ cup *each* **dry basil, rubbed sage, dry thyme leaves,** and **dry lavender** (optional). Use as directed, preceding, or store airtight up to 4 months. Makes ¾ cup.

## HERBS FOR FISH OR VEGETABLES

In a blender, whirl until coarsely ground 1 tablespoon **fennel seed,** 2 tablespoons *each* grated fresh **lemon peel** and **dry tarragon,** and ⅔ cup **pickling spice.** Use as directed, preceding, or store airtight up to 1 month. Makes ¾ cup.

## RISOTTO

*The celebrated creaminess of risotto, the Italian rice dish, comes from the way it's made rather than the type of rice used.*

*Italians favor the special variety of rice called arborio, but here we explore using other grains: short-, medium-, and long-grain white and brown rice and pearl barley. Though these grains don't duplicate the results of the arborio, each has its own distinctive flavor and texture.*

*First you lightly toast the grains in butter with onion; this keeps them from sticking together as you later stir them to release some of their starch, which thickens the cooking broth and creates the creaminess. Because the risotto is cooked uncovered, the cooking liquid is concentrated. If using canned broth, dilute it as directed; otherwise the risotto may be too salty.*

- 3 **tablespoons butter or margarine**
- 1 **medium-size onion, chopped**
- 1 **cup grain (choices follow)**
- 3 **to 5 cups regular-strength beef or chicken broth (if using salted broth, use half water, half broth)**
- ¼ **to ½ cup shredded or grated parmesan cheese**

In an 8- to 10-inch frying pan, cook butter and onion over medium heat, stirring, until onion is translucent, about 5 minutes. Add grain and stir until opaque or faintly golden, about 2 minutes. Add broth and bring to a boil over high heat.

Reduce heat and simmer, uncovered. Stir occasionally at first; then, as liquid is almost absorbed, stir frequently until grain is tender to bite (approximate cooking times for each grain follow). You may have to add more liquid, ¼ cup at a time, to prevent sticking. Just before serving, stir in desired amount of cheese. Makes 4 to 5 servings.

**Short-grain white rice:** use 3 cups broth; takes about 20 minutes.

**Medium-grain white rice** (including arborio): use 3½ cups broth; takes about 25 minutes.

**Long-grain white rice:** use 3¾ cups broth; takes about 30 minutes.

**Short-grain brown rice:** use 5 cups broth; takes about 1¼ hours.

**Long-grain brown rice:** use 5 cups broth; takes about 1¼ hours.

**Pearl barley:** use 4½ cups broth; takes about 50 minutes.

## SPINACH SALAD WITH SWEET-SOUR DRESSING

*A new version of an old favorite, this spinach salad successfully plays off the texture and flavor of its ingredients. A creamy sweet-sour dressing coats crisp greens, tangy oranges, and hot red onion.*

- 1½ **pounds spinach, stemmed, coarse leaves discarded, and washed; or ¾ pound curly endive, washed**
- 2 **large oranges**
- ½ **small red onion, thinly sliced**
- 3 **tablespoons sugar**
- ¼ **cup cider vinegar**
- ½ **teaspoon *each* dry mustard, celery seed, and paprika**
- ½ **cup salad oil**
  **Salt**

Wrap spinach leaves in paper towels and chill to crisp, at least 1 hour or up to 1 day. With a sharp knife, cut peel and white membrane from oranges, then cut fruit segments from inner membranes. Separate onion slices into individual rings.

In a small bowl, mix sugar, vinegar, mustard, celery seed, and paprika until sugar dissolves. Add salad oil, whisking until dressing is the consistency of honey.

*Creamy, sweet-tart dressing clings easily to spinach, oranges, and onions.*

Combine spinach, oranges, and onion in a serving bowl. Pour dressing over salad, then mix lightly to coat; add salt to taste. Serve at once. Makes 6 to 8 servings. —*Hazel Bullock, Laguna Hills, Calif.*

## ASPARAGUS BRUNCH

1 long loaf (1 lb.) sourdough bread
4 tablespoons olive oil
1 medium-size onion, thinly sliced
1 pound asparagus, tough ends removed
½ pound cooked ham, cut into thin strips
4 hot large poached or soft-cooked eggs (optional)

Cut 4 diagonal slices from center of bread, *each* ½ inch thick and about 7 inches long. Reserve remainder of bread for other uses. Lightly brush both sides of bread slices with 2 tablespoons of the oil. In a 12- to 14-inch frying pan over medium-high heat, brown bread on both sides, about 10 minutes. Place 1 slice on each of 4 dinner plates; keep warm.

Add remaining oil to pan with onion, asparagus, and ham. Cook, stirring often, until asparagus is tender-crisp to bite, 8 to 10 minutes. Arrange equal portions of asparagus, ham, and onion on each plate. Accompany each serving with a poached egg or a soft-cooked egg cut in half and scooped from the shell. Makes 4 servings.—*J. Heflin, Kirkland, Wash.*

*Whole-meal brunch combines toast, asparagus, ham, and soft-cooked egg.*

## ORANGE-CURRANT SCONES

About 3 cups all-purpose flour
About ¾ cup sugar
½ teaspoon baking powder
1 teaspoon baking soda
2 teaspoons grated orange peel
½ cup (¼ lb.) butter or margarine
¾ cup currants
¾ cup buttermilk
Orange butter (recipe follows)

In a large bowl, stir together 3 cups of the flour, ¾ cup of the sugar, baking powder, baking soda, and orange peel. With pastry blender or fingers, work in butter until fine crumbs form. Stir in currants. Add buttermilk and mix until evenly moistened.

Scrape dough onto a lightly floured board and knead 10 turns. Pat into a 9-inch round, then place in a greased 9-inch round cake pan. Sprinkle lightly with sugar. Bake in a 400° oven until golden brown, about 40 minutes.

Turn out of pan; invert onto a plate. Cut into 8 wedges and serve with orange butter. Makes 8 servings.—*Susan Dalton, San Jose, Calif.*

**Orange butter.** In a small bowl, beat ½ cup (¼ lb.) **butter** or margarine with 1 teaspoon grated **orange peel** and 1 tablespoon **powdered sugar** until creamy.

*Serve orange-scented, currant-studded breakfast scones with orange butter.*

## LAYERED SPINACH CASSEROLE

2 cups water
1 cup long-grain brown rice
¾ pound spinach
4 large eggs
¼ teaspoon *each* celery seed, dry oregano, and pepper
2 tablespoons soy sauce
2 tablespoons minced parsley
1½ cups (6 oz.) shredded cheddar cheese
¼ cup (⅛ lb.) melted butter
¾ cup toasted wheat germ

Bring water to a boil in a 1½- to 2-quart pan over high heat. Add rice; cover and simmer until rice is tender to bite, about 35 minutes.

Meanwhile, discard coarse spinach leaves and roots. Rinse remaining leaves well, pat dry, and mince. In a large bowl, whisk eggs with celery seed, oregano, pepper, 1 tablespoon soy sauce, and parsley. Stir in spinach.

Mix cheese with rice and pat into a greased 10-inch quiche or pie pan. Spread evenly with spinach mixture. Stir together butter, wheat germ, and remaining soy; pat evenly over spinach. Bake, uncovered, in a 325° oven until topping feels set when lightly pressed, about 25 minutes. Makes 6 servings.—*Chris Peterson, Moscow, Idaho.*

*Make brown rice and cheddar base; top with eggs and fresh spinach, then bake.*

## Chicken-Rice-Tomatillo Bake

- 1 broiler-fryer chicken, about 3½ pounds, cut up
- 2 tablespoons salad oil
- 1 medium-size onion, chopped
- 1 clove garlic, minced or pressed
- 1 cup long-grain white rice
- 1 can (13 oz.) tomatillos
  About 1 cup regular-strength chicken broth
- 1 can (4 oz.) whole green chilies, thinly sliced crosswise
- 1 teaspoon ground cumin
- 2 tablespoons minced fresh cilantro (coriander)
  Cilantro sprigs

In a 10- to 12-inch frying pan over medium-high heat, brown chicken in oil, a portion at a time. Remove chicken from pan; set aside. Add onion, garlic, and rice to pan; stir often until rice is golden, about 5 minutes. Set aside.

Drain liquid from tomatillos; add broth to make 2 cups. Halve tomatillos. In a shallow 2-quart baking dish, mix broth, tomatillos, chilies, cumin, minced cilantro, and rice; top with chicken. Bake, uncovered, at 350° until meat at thigh bone is no longer pink (cut to test), 40 to 45 minutes. Garnish with cilantro sprigs. Serves 4. — *Robin Warren, Fort Bragg, Calif.*

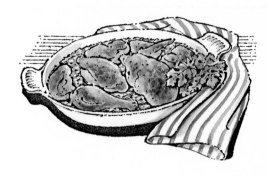

*Chicken pieces bake atop rice pilaf flavored with tomatillos and chilies.*

## Guacamole Pasta Salad

- Water
- 1 cup mixed colors dry spiral-shape pasta
- ½ pound green beans, ends trimmed, cut into 1-inch lengths
- 1 small carrot, chopped
- 3 tablespoons minced onion
- 1 tablespoon salad oil
- 3 tablespoons lemon juice
  Butter lettuce leaves, washed and crisped
- 1 large ripe avocado
  Salt and pepper

Fill a 2- to 3-quart pan ¾ full of water and bring to a boil over high heat. Add pasta and boil until just tender to bite, about 5 minutes. Drain and let cool.

Meanwhile, in a 1- to 2-quart pan, bring ¼ inch water to a boil over high heat. Add beans and carrot; cover and simmer until beans are tender-crisp to bite, about 4 minutes. Drain; let cool. In a bowl, combine pasta, beans and carrot, onion, oil, and 1 tablespoon of the lemon juice. Arrange in equal portions on lettuce leaves on 4 salad plates. Pit, peel, and mash avocado with remaining lemon juice. Spoon equal portions onto salads. Season to taste with salt and pepper. Serves 4. — *Marie Mitchell, Lake Oswego, Ore.*

*Fresh vegetables blend with curls of bright cooked pasta on lettuce.*

## Whole-Wheat Poppy Seed Pound Cake

- ¾ cup (⅜ lb.) butter or margarine
- 1 cup firmly packed brown sugar
- 3 large eggs
- ½ teaspoon *each* baking soda and salt
- 1 tablespoon grated lemon peel
- 3 tablespoons poppy seed
- 1 cup unflavored yogurt
- 2¼ cups whole-wheat flour
  Lemon glaze (recipe follows)

In large bowl of an electric mixer, cream butter and sugar until smooth. Add eggs, 1 at a time, beating well after each addition. Mix in soda, salt, peel, and poppy seed. Add yogurt; beat well. Stir in flour. Pour evenly into a greased and floured 5- by 9-inch loaf pan. Bake in a 350° oven until a slender wooden pick inserted in center comes out clean, about 1 hour.

Let the cake cool in the pan on a rack for 15 minutes, then invert from pan onto a plate.

Evenly drizzle glaze on top of cake. Serve warm; or let cool, then store, covered, at room temperature until next day. Makes 12 servings. — *Ceil Anderson, Menlo Park, Calif.*

**Lemon glaze.** In a small bowl, mix 1 cup sifted **powdered sugar** with 1½ tablespoons **lemon juice** until smooth.

*Whole-wheat and poppy seed cake, with lemon glaze, makes a wholesome dessert.*

*"What do you call the hybrid offspring of a hamburger, a taco, and a burrito?"*

WHAT DO YOU CALL *the hybrid off-spring of a hamburger, a taco, and a burrito? Hamburrito, perhaps, or Mac-Tac? Gary Stephens, exercising admirable restraint, merely calls his creation a Cal-Mex Burger. The Chefs of the West taste panel called it inspired. A Renaissance painter might have rendered it as the apotheosis of the hamburger: a meat patty swathed in a soft, warm flour tortilla and crowned with cilantro, ascending into heaven like Elijah in his chariot.*

*You can control the chariot's fire by varying the amount of chilies and sauce.*

## CAL-MEX BURGERS

1½ pounds ground lean beef
1 medium-size white onion, chopped
6 slices (1 oz. *each*) jack cheese
¼ cup canned diced green chilies
¼ cup drained canned pinto beans
6 flour tortillas (7- to 8-inch size)
Butter or margarine
Prepared taco sauce
Fresh cilantro (coriander) leaves
Thinly sliced firm-ripe tomatoes (optional)

Mix beef and onion together, then divide into 6 equal portions and shape each into a patty about 6 inches in diameter. Cut cheese slices diagonally in half to make triangles. Arrange 1 triangle on each meat patty so a long edge lies along center of patty; if cheese extends beyond patty, fold over onto meat.

Spoon chilies equally onto cheese on meat, and top equally with beans. Lay remaining cheese triangles over beans.

Fold plain half of each patty over filling and gently pinch edges together to seal, forming a half-moon.

Lightly spread tortillas with butter, stack, and wrap in foil.

Arrange stuffed beef patties on a barbecue grill 4 to 6 inches above a solid bed of hot coals. (You should be able to hold your hand at grill level for only 2 or 3 seconds.) Cook, turning as needed, to brown both sides, until meat is done to your liking, 10 to 12 minutes for medium-rare (cut to test). About 5 minutes before meat is done, set packet of tortillas on grill to warm, turning packet several times to heat evenly.

To serve, place each meat patty on a tortilla, top with taco sauce, cilantro, and tomato, then fold tortilla to enclose meat. Eat out of hand. Makes 6 servings.

*Gary P. Stephens*

*Monrovia, Calif.*

CHOPPED AND SEASONED, *chicken liver is a standby on many an hors d'oeuvre tray. But true fanciers often prefer less gussying-up than is usual and might wish to promote this meat from appetizer to entrée status. Chef Lemoise Angier's stir-fry satisfies both requests.*

## STIR-FRIED CHICKEN LIVERS WITH CHINESE PEA PODS

1 pound chicken livers
3 tablespoons soy sauce
3 tablespoons dry sherry
3 teaspoons minced fresh ginger
1 teaspoon sugar
1 teaspoon cornstarch
2 tablespoons salad oil
½ pound Chinese pea pods, ends and strings removed
6 medium-size green onions, including tops (roots trimmed off), cut into 2-inch lengths
Hot cooked rice

Rinse chicken livers and pat dry. Cut into bite-size pieces and mix with 1 tablespoon soy sauce, 1 tablespoon sherry, and 2 teaspoons of the minced ginger; let stand 15 minutes.

For the cooking sauce, combine 2 tablespoons soy sauce, 2 tablespoons sherry, sugar, and cornstarch; stir until cornstarch is dissolved. Set aside.

Pour oil into a 10- to 12-inch frying pan or wok and place on high heat; when oil is hot, add the peas, the remaining 1 teaspoon ginger, and the green onion; stir-fry until peas are tender-crisp to bite and bright green, 1 to 2 minutes. Lift out with a slotted spoon and set aside.

Add livers and the marinade to the pan; stir-fry until livers are browned but still pink in the center (cut to test), 3 to 4 minutes. Return vegetable mixture to pan with cooking sauce; stir-fry just until blended and sauce has thickened. Serve with rice. Makes 3 or 4 servings.

*Lemoise Angier*

*Aptos, Calif.*

**G**REGORY YASINITSKY'S *mostaccioli and Swiss is really just macaroni and cheese in another guise. But what a guise! On a scale of 1 (spartan) to 10 (sybaritic), it certainly rates a 9, and diners with simple but refined tastes will not even miss the truffle that might raise it to a 10.*

*You begin with the conventional white sauce but add Swiss instead of cheddar cheese. Then come the surprises: ham and spinach for color and contrast, and Dijon mustard and hot pepper seasoning to point up flavors without disguising them.*

## MOSTACCIOLI & SWISS

**Water**
8 ounces dry mostaccioli (short tube-shaped pasta)
¼ cup (⅛ lb.) butter or margarine
¼ cup all-purpose flour
2 cups milk
3 cups (12 oz.) shredded Swiss cheese
¼ teaspoon liquid hot pepper seasoning
1 tablespoon Dijon mustard
½ pound cooked ham, cut into thin slivers
1 package (10 oz.) frozen chopped spinach, thawed
**Salt and pepper**

In a 5- to 6-quart pan, bring 3 to 4 quarts water to boiling over high heat. Add pasta and boil, uncovered, just until barely tender to bite; drain. Put pasta in a bowl and cover with cold water.

Melt butter in the 5- to 6-quart pan over medium heat; stir in flour and cook until bubbly. Remove from heat and smoothly stir in milk; return to medium-high heat and stir until boiling. Add 2 cups of the cheese, hot pepper seasoning, and mustard, stirring until cheese melts; remove from heat.

Drain mostaccioli well and add to sauce along with ham; mix gently.

With your hands, squeeze as much moisture from spinach as possible; stir into pasta mixture.

Pour into a shallow 2-quart casserole; if made ahead, cover and chill up to 24 hours. Cover and bake in a 350° oven for 20 minutes, about 30 minutes if chilled. Uncover, sprinkle casserole with the remaining 1 cup cheese, and continue to bake until cheese melts and mixture is bubbly, about 10 minutes longer. Add salt and pepper to taste. Serves 4 to 6.

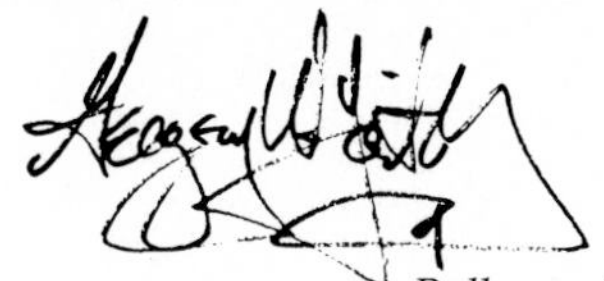

*Pullman, Wash.*

**S**OPHISTICATES MAY *look down their noses at gelatin desserts as childhood relics. On the other hand, they regard nonsweet gelatin preparations (such as Walter Greenway's tomato aspic) with respect, and the shimmering aspic around their paté with something like veneration.*

## TOMATO ASPIC

1 tablespoon *each* **instant beef bouillon, sugar, and Worcestershire**
¼ teaspoon dry basil
**About 3 cups water**
2 envelopes unflavored gelatin
1 can (6 oz.) tomato paste
2 tablespoons white wine vinegar
½ cup *each* **thinly sliced celery, finely chopped green bell pepper, and peeled and finely chopped cucumber**
¼ cup minced parsley
¼ pound small cooked and shelled shrimp (optional)
**Large lettuce leaves, washed and crisped**

In a bowl, combine bouillon, sugar, Worcestershire, and basil with ¼ cup of the water; sprinkle on gelatin and let stand to soften, about 5 minutes.

Spoon tomato paste into a measuring cup and slowly blend in enough water to make 2 cups *total*. Heat another 1¾ cups water to boiling, stir into gelatin mixture, then add vinegar and diluted tomato paste; pour into a 7- to 8-cup mold.

Cover and chill until syrupy, about 1½ hours. Stir in celery, bell pepper, cucumber, parsley, and shrimp. Cover with plastic wrap and chill until set, at least 6 hours or up to overnight.

To serve, dip mold into hottest tap water up to pan rim just until edges of aspic begin to melt slightly, 10 to 15 seconds, then invert onto a lettuce-lined serving plate. Makes 6 to 8 servings.

*Walter Greenway*

*San Rafael, Calif.*

**L**AMAR PARKER'S *Coffee Liqueur Ice Cream Cake requires the combined arts of the baker, the confectioner, the distiller, and the ice cream maker, yet transcends them all. It's true no one really needs anything so rich and complex. But what is civilization if not the sum of things we don't really need?*

## COFFEE LIQUEUR ICE CREAM CAKE

½ gallon vanilla ice cream
1 quart chocolate ice cream
**Butter**
24 ladyfingers (3-oz. package)
¼ cup coffee-flavored liqueur
2 tablespoons instant coffee powder or granules
**About 8 ounces chocolate-covered hard toffee candy bars, coarsely chopped**
**Whipped cream (optional)**

Set out the ice creams at room temperature to soften for 10 to 15 minutes.

Butter a 9-inch cheesecake pan that's at least 3 inches deep and has a removable bottom; line sides with ladyfingers standing vertically with flat sides facing in.

Stir together the liqueur and instant coffee. In a large bowl, combine ice creams and liqueur mixture. Beat with an electric mixer until well blended. Then stir in the candy. Scrape mixture into lined pan. Cover and freeze until firm, at least 12 hours; cover airtight to store longer (up to 2 weeks).

To serve, remove sides from pan and place cake on a serving plate. Decorate top with whipped cream, if desired. Let stand at room temperature until you can cut to serve, 15 to 20 minutes. For easier cutting, dip a sharp knife into hot water before each cut. Makes 16 to 20 servings.

*Lamar L. Parker*

*Tempe, Ariz.*

# April Menus

N O TIME TO COOK? *One solution is to take advantage of foods that are ready to eat (or close to it) and available at your supermarket or delicatessen. Menus this month equip you with one-stop shopping plans for four busy days. All are the means to meals that can be on the table in 30 minutes or less.*

*Roast chicken, pasta sauces, and a large variety of salads—all staples at most delis—are the starting point for these quick meals. Round out main courses with supermarket basics.*

Supper for two: buy Oriental noodle salad from the deli and shrimp, fruit, cookies, and beverages from the supermarket. Quickly stir-fry the shrimp, then serve the prepared salad with crisp Asian pear wedges alongside.

---

## SHRIMP & NOODLE SUPPER

Stir-fried Shrimp & Salad Platter
Lemon Sorbet    Almond Cookies
Hot Tea    Warm Sake

---

*Serve freshly cooked shrimp with purchased noodle salad. To save more time, buy peeled and deveined shrimp. Also, buy a noodle salad with Oriental seasonings if available and, for dessert, sorbet and cookies.*

### STIR-FRIED SHRIMP & SALAD PLATTER

1 tablespoon butter, margarine, or salad oil
1/16 teaspoon cayenne
1/2 pound medium-size shrimp (40 to 50 per lb.), shelled and deveined
1 to 2 teaspoons Oriental sesame oil
2 cups prepared noodle salad with Oriental-style seasonings or oil and vinegar dressing
   Fresh cilantro (coriander) sprigs (optional)
1 large Asian pear, cored and cut into wedges

In an 8- to 10-inch frying pan over high heat, melt butter with cayenne. Add shrimp and stir-fry until opaque in center (cut to test), about 3 minutes. Add sesame oil to taste and pour shrimp onto a platter or 2 plates. Accompany with noodle salad, and garnish with cilantro and Asian pear wedges. Makes 2 servings.

---

## BUILD-YOUR-OWN TACO SUPPER

Roast Chicken Tacos
Cucumber Slices    Cherry Tomatoes
Fresh Papaya with Lime
Sparkling Mineral Water

---

*Gather the elements for these soft tacos, then let diners assemble their own.*

*Serve the chicken warm from the store, cool, or reheated; also warm the tortillas in the oven or, for faster results, in a microwave oven. While those foods heat, pull together the taco extras. Also rinse and slice 1 small cucumber and rinse about 2 cups cherry tomatoes to serve with the meal.*

*Seed papaya halves, and accompany with lime wedges to squeeze over fruit.*

*For a Chinese variation on chicken tacos, omit salsa and cheese and offer prepared hoisin sauce instead.*

## ROAST CHICKEN TACOS

1 whole cooked broiler-fryer chicken (about 2 lb.), warm or cool

8 to 12 flour tortillas (7- to 8-inch diameter)

1 medium-size ripe avocado, peeled, pitted, and thinly sliced

1 to 2 tablespoons lemon juice

2 medium-size green onions, ends trimmed, thinly sliced

2 cups (6 oz.) lightly packed shredded cheddar cheese

½ cup fresh cilantro (coriander) leaves, rinsed and drained

About ¾ cup purchased salsa

To serve the chicken warm, wrap in foil or in the ovenproof bag in which deli-cooked chickens are often sold. Put in a 325° oven while warming the tortillas.

Stack tortillas, seal in foil, and place in a 325° oven; allow 15 to 30 minutes to heat tortillas and chicken.

(To use a microwave oven, put chicken on a nonmetal plate and drape with paper towels. Heat in a microwave oven on full power for 3 to 4 minutes, reversing position of chicken after 2 minutes. Wrap stacked tortillas in paper towels and cook on full power for about 2 minutes.)

Place chicken on platter or cutting board. Moisten the avocado with lemon juice to keep from turning brown. In small bowls or separately around the chicken, arrange the avocado, onions, cheese, and cilantro. Serve salsa in a small bowl alongside. Put warm tortillas in a napkin-lined basket beside chicken.

To eat the chicken, tear or cut off pieces of meat. Put some of the chicken in a tortilla and add to taste some of the onion, avocado, cheese, cilantro, and salsa. Fold the tortilla over the filling; eat out of hand. Serves 4.

---

### LASAGNA PACKETS FOR DINNER

Lasagna Packets
Salads-by-the-Pound
Breadsticks      Butter
Coffee Gelato    Biscotti
Chianti          Apple Juice

---

*Instant lasagna, a new dry pasta product, is speedy—you need only moisten it to use. Egg roll wrappers are an alternative.*

*Build your own soft taco with purchased roast chicken and quickly assembled condiments from the supermarket. Offer tomatoes and cucumbers to munch alongside. For dessert, serve papaya halves to eat with a squeeze of lime.*

*Buy about 2 pounds total of 1 or 2 ready-made salads, such as mixed greens with a dressing and marinated artichoke hearts. You can also buy olives, breadsticks, gelato, and Italian-style cookies.*

## LASAGNA PACKETS

2 quarts hottest tap water

4 to 6 sheets (about 7 inches square) instant lasagna noodles or 8 egg roll wrappers (about 6 in. square)

1 package (10½ oz.) thawed frozen chopped spinach

2 cloves garlic, pressed or minced

1 teaspoon dry mixed Italian herbs (optional)

1½ cups purchased (fresh or canned) pasta sauce, such as marinara, bolognese, roasted red pepper, or shrimp sauce

1 pint ricotta or small-curd cottage cheese

½ cup grated parmesan, romano, or asiago cheese

Put water in a 5- to 6-quart pan. Add lasagna and let stand until pliable, about 5 minutes; drain. (Don't soak egg rolls.)

While the pasta softens, squeeze the chopped spinach to remove as much liquid as possible. Stir spinach, garlic, herbs, ½ cup pasta sauce, ricotta, and ¼ cup parmesan until well mixed.

Lay sheets of pasta flat; scoop equal amounts of ricotta mixture onto center of

each sheet. Fold 4 corners of each sheet into center over filling, pulling together to make packets snug. Grease a 9- by 13-inch baking dish or casserole. Set packets, folded side down, in dish.

Moisten top of packets evenly with remaining sauce; sprinkle with remaining parmesan. Bake, uncovered, in a 400° oven until lasagna is hot in center

*(Continued on next page)*

*Precooked noodles and store-bought pasta sauce are the components for lasagna packets.*

## ...LASAGNA PACKETS

(cut to test), 10 to 15 minutes. Makes 4 to 6 servings.

### PITA SALAD SANDWICH PICNIC

Pita Salad Sandwiches
Pickles
Apples    Shortbread Cookies
Chocolate-covered Raisins
Dry Red Wine    Lemonade

*Pack up utensils—plates, cups, flatware, and blanket. Select the food and individual portions of beverages at a market on your way to the picnic. The site can be urban, rural, or in your own garden.*

*Choose a selection of vegetable salads to add variety to each sandwich. Purchase either whole-wheat or white pocket bread, or a combination of both. Don't limit yourself to just cucumber pickles, but choose pickled peppers or onions, as well.*

*At the picnic site, drain off thin salad dressings before assembling the sandwiches.*

## PITA SALAD SANDWICHES

2 packages (4 oz. each) herb-flavored cheese spread

4 to 6 pocket (pita) bread rounds (about 7-inch diameter), cut in half

1 cup alfalfa sprouts

2 to 2½ pints *total* of prepared salads; choose several, such as marinated cucumbers, bean salad, mixed vegetable salad

Spread about 1 tablespoon of the cheese in each pita bread half. Add alfalfa sprouts and 1 or 2 kinds of salad. Makes 8 to 12 sandwiches, 4 to 6 servings.

# MAY

*Mother's Day breakfast (page 106)*

$\mathbf{T}$he mighty onion claimed the
May spotlight; we explored its structure and chemistry, how to
control its behavior, and cooking techniques and recipes that
show off its flavorful qualities. We also tested short cuts to
speed up yeast bread-making. Other features included an easy-
to-prepare breakfast for Mother's Day, an array of appetizers
and healthy snacks, appealing main dish soups, recipes using
ground buffalo meat, tamale-like sausages wrapped in corn-
husk packets, and six varieties of chewy-gooey brownies.

# What Makes an Onion Work?

**L**IKE A BOMB, *an onion holds power, heat, surprise. Cut it, and it explodes with strong smells, hot flavors, and irritating vapors. But detonate the firepower, and it can be meek and mild—even sweet.*

*The key is understanding an onion's structure. With this knowledge, any cook can manipulate this versatile bulb to achieve pleasingly specific results. With help from Dr. Ruth Tanner, chemistry professor at the University of Lowell, Massachusetts, and a professional chef, we explain how this works and give cooking techniques for dry onions.*

*The variety of possible tastes and textures is impressive. Onions have been cultivated as a food since at least 3000 B.C. Mexicans like the hot bite of raw onions as a condiment, the Chinese stir-fry them, the Danes deep-fry them, and Indians use them as a mellow base for curries.*

## ONION STRUCTURE & ONION CHEMISTRY

Onions come in many different colors and sizes, but all are the same species. The dry bulbs, the vegetable we're exploring here, are 89 percent water and 8 to 9 percent soluble sugars; the rest is minerals, fats, proteins, and sulfur compounds.

The sulfur compounds produce dis-

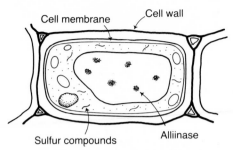

*Elements of an onion's taste are within each cell. When you cut into cell, enzyme alliinase starts chain of chemical responses, sulfur gives distinctive flavor and aroma.*

tinctive flavor and an aroma that can be difficult to disguise once you've eaten or touched onions. These oil-soluble compounds remain in the oils on your skin. They're blood-soluble and so can be detected in breath and perspiration.

Some onion compounds do not form until you break cell membranes. As soon as a cell is broken, as by peeling, bruising, or cutting, a sequence of reactions follows. A key component is the enzyme alliinase (see drawing above). The degree to which this enzyme is activated affects the intensity of the response.

First, sulfur-containing compounds are produced; these are responsible for irritating vapors, one of which stimu-

lates a tear response, and for a biting astringency. These compounds quickly break down into others, which ultimately yield the onion flavor and aroma. In raw or partially cooked onions, these compounds mask sugars and dominate taste.

## HOW TO CONTROL ONION BEHAVIOR

Cutting or breaking the cell membranes develops compounds associated with flavor, aroma, and bitterness. With more disruption, more of these compounds—including lachrymator (tear producer)—will be formed. To minimize this effect, peel onions under running water so you rinse away vapors and lachrymator as they are created. Chilling onions before you cut also slows the release of tear producer.

When you chop onions in a food processor, more cells are bruised than when you mince onions by hand—so the flavor is stronger and more bitter.

Cooking time and heat intensity both affect flavor. A short period of high heat brings out strong onion characteristics more quickly. But long cooking over low heat diminishes the strong taste, enhancing the onion's natural sweetness. Using too high a temperature for

*Regardless of color or size, dry onions have similar structure and chemical composition and behave the same way when you use them for cooking. But the flavors that develop depend on how you physically handle onions and how you use them.*

too long a time develops bitterness, which is somewhat different from a burnt flavor.

An onion's natural acidity affects color. If you soak it in water or cook it in butter, acidity outside may be less than inside, causing its own acid to leach out and its color to change. This is a problem only with red onion: if you pour an acid like vinegar over it, it turns bright pink; in an alkaline solution (such as one containing baking soda), it turns yellow-green. To preserve the red color, outside acidity should match the onion's own natural acidity of about 0.3 percent; use a solution of 1 tablespoon vinegar to 2 cups water. Use more vinegar if the onion is to be cooked for a long time (heat accelerates loss of color) or soaked in a large quantity of water for a long time, or if you prefer a brighter pink color.

Following are five sure-fire techniques for cooking onions and ways to tone down the harshness in raw onions.

## SAUTÉ: MOST FLAVOR (NOT HOT)

*Sautéing or stir-frying cut onion over medium-high heat brings out the most flavor. The high temperature volatilizes the*

Onion bulb consists of concentric shells of leaf bases swollen with stored water and sugars. Cells also hold small amounts of minerals, fats, protein, sulfur compounds.

# ...What Makes an Onion Work?

**1. Chop, sauté for definite onion flavor**
*Sauté onions over medium-high heat until limp, then add wine to make topping for steak (recipe below).*

**2. Slice, then cook slowly for sweet mellowness**
*Cook sliced onions over moderate heat until limp, golden, and sweet. Pile atop ham and cheese on toasted rye for sandwich (page 103).*

first set of compounds, then speeds production of other compounds associated with onion flavor and aroma. Sugars in the onion caramelize, which lends color and flavor to sauces and stocks.

Heat also drives out the air between the cells, making onion pieces translucent. When vinegar or spices are cooked with them, as for béarnaise sauce, a curry base, or the onion-wine topping for steak, the collapsed onion cells soak up the added seasonings like a sponge.

Serve these mild but richly aromatic onions over meats, as a seasoning starter for sauces, and to flavor vegetables.

## SAUTÉED ONIONS

1 tablespoon butter, margarine, or salad oil
1 large onion (3 to 3½ in. diameter), chopped

In a 10- to 12-inch frying pan, melt butter over medium-high heat. Add onion and cook, stirring often, until onion is translucent and edges are lightly browned, 5 to 7 minutes. Serve hot. Makes about ¾ cup.

## STEAK WITH SAUTÉED ONIONS

*Here, chopped onions are sautéed to develop a toasty sweetness, then cooked in red wine. The onions sop up the wine, making a delicious sauce for steak.*

1 tablespoon butter or margarine
1 tablespoon salad oil
4 tender boneless beef steaks (about 6 oz. each) such as loin or rib, cut 1 to 1½ inches thick
1 large onion (3- to 3½-in. diameter), chopped
½ cup dry red wine
Salt and pepper

**3. Boil whole for sweetness**
*Boiling gives onions mild sweetness. Try them cooked in broth (recipe at right).*

In a 10- to 12-inch frying pan, melt butter with oil over medium-high heat. Add meat and cook, uncovered, until well browned on each side, about 4 to 6 minutes a side for rare meat (cut in thickest part to test). Transfer meat to a serving platter and keep warm.

Add onion to pan drippings and cook, stirring often, over medium-high heat until soft, 5 to 6 minutes. Add wine and boil, uncovered, until most of liquid evaporates, about 1½ minutes. Spoon over steaks. Sprinkle with salt and pepper to taste. Makes 4 servings.

## SLOW-COOK:
## SWEET, MILD, LIMP

*Slow-cook sliced onions in fat over moderate heat until they become very limp and golden. Slicing brings forth flavor components; long gentle cooking dissipates them, unmasking natural sweetness. Some of the soluble onion sugars caramelize during cooking, deepening and enriching flavor.*

*Use the sweet onions as a base for soup, as a condiment for plain roasted or sautéed meats or poultry, or in sandwiches.*

### SLOW-COOKED ONIONS

> 4 large onions (3 to 3½ in. diameter)
> 4 tablespoons butter or margarine

Thinly slice onions crosswise and separate into rings. In a 12- to 14-inch frying pan, melt butter over medium-high heat. Add onions. Cook, stirring occasionally, until they are very limp, taste sweet, and turn golden, 20 to 30 minutes. If onions begin to brown, reduce heat to medium-low and stir more often. Serve hot.

If made ahead, cool, cover, and chill up to 2 days. To reheat, stir onions in an 8- to 10-inch frying pan over low heat until hot. Makes 3 to 4 cups.

### SLOW-COOKED
### ONION SANDWICH

*Onions turn remarkably sweet and mellow when cooked long on low heat. Pile the golden, limp slices on toasted rye for open-faced sandwiches. Eat them with a knife and fork.*

> 6 slices dark rye bread
>   Dijon or German mustard
> 6 thin slices (6 oz. total) Black Forest, Westphalian, or baked ham
> 6 slices (4 to 5 oz.) Swiss cheese
> 4 cups hot slow-cooked onions (recipe above)
>   Coarsely ground pepper or chopped parsley

Place bread in a single layer on a 12- by 15-inch baking sheet. Broil about 4 inches from heat until toasted, then turn

and toast other side, about 2 minutes total. Spread top of each slice with mustard and lay ham and cheese equally on each slice. Return to oven and broil until cheese melts, about 1 minute. Spoon an equal amount of onions on each slice. Sprinkle with pepper or parsley. Makes 6 open-faced sandwiches.

## BOIL WHOLE:
## SWEET, MILD

*When small, whole, peeled onions are boiled in water, the onion produces a compound much sweeter than sugar. As with baked whole onions, alliinase's hot flavor doesn't develop.*

*Serve small boiled onions with butter or in a cream sauce or buttery broth glaze.*

### BOILED WHOLE ONIONS

>   Water
> 16 to 18 small peeled onions (1½ in. diameter)
>   Butter or margarine
>   Salt and pepper

In a 3- to 4-quart pan, bring 1½ to 2 quarts water to boiling. Add onions and simmer, covered, until tender when pierced, about 20 minutes. Drain. Add butter, salt, and pepper to taste. Makes 4 to 6 servings.

### GLAZED ONIONS

*Simmered in broth and water, onions lose their hot taste and develop a compound that is much sweeter than regular sugar. Then, as juices—enhanced by soluble sugars from the onion—are reduced, they form a sweet, rich glaze.*

> 2 tablespoons butter or margarine
> 16 small onions (1- to 1½-in. diameter), peeled
> 1 cup regular-strength beef broth
> ½ cup water

In a 10- to 12-inch frying pan, melt butter. Add onions, broth, and water. Cook, covered, over medium-low heat, shaking pan often, until onions are tender when pierced, about 20 minutes. Uncover pan and boil over high heat, shaking pan often until pan juices thicken and lightly glaze onions, about 5 minutes. Serves 4.

## ROASTED ONION HALVES

Cut 3 large **onions** (3 to 3½ in. wide) in half lengthwise. If desired, pour ¼ cup **balsamic** or red wine **vinegar** into a 9- by 13-inch pan. Place onions, cut sides down, in pan.

Bake in a 350° oven until soft when pressed, 30 to 45 minutes. Serve with **butter** or margarine and **salt** and **pepper** to taste. Makes 3 to 6 servings.

## GRILLED ONIONS

Place 6 large **onions** (3 to 3½ in. wide) on a grill 4 to 6 inches above a solid bed of medium-hot coals (you should be able to hold your hand at grill level only 3 to 4 seconds).

Cook, turning often, until onions feel very soft when pressed, 1 to 1¼ hours. Cut in half to serve with **butter** or margarine and **salt** and **pepper** to taste. Makes 6 to 12 servings.

**4. Bake whole for mildness**
*Bake onions in skins for mild flavor; halve to serve plain or with butter (recipes below, right).*

**5. Deep-fry for crisp rings**
*Fry rings until crisp and golden. Use as a garnish for sandwiches (see page 105).*

## DEEP-FRY: CRISP, SWEET, GOLDEN

*Cut onion into thin shreds, lightly dust with flour, and fry in a generous amount of oil. The large surface area exposes sulfur compounds. The hot oil drives off many of them and much of the onion's moisture, leaving crisp sweet shreds.*

*Serve fried onions for a snack, on grilled meat patties or chops, or on open-faced sandwiches. They can be cooked ahead and reheated.*

## CRISP-FRIED ONIONS

    2  **large onions (3 to 3½ in. diameter)**
  ½  **cup all-purpose flour**
      **Salad oil**
      **Salt**

Peel and thinly slice onions. Separate into rings. Pour flour into a bag. Add onions and shake to coat evenly with flour.

In a deep 2½- to 3-quart pan, bring 1½ inches oil to 300° on a thermometer. Add onions, shaking off excess flour, about ¼ at a time, and cook, stirring often, until golden, about 5 minutes. Regulate heat to maintain it at 300°.

## BAKE WHOLE: MELLOW & MILD

*If onion is cooked uncut, hot flavor from its enzyme, alliinase, never develops; you get only mild-sweet onion flavor.*

*A whole onion can be roasted or grilled. If it is peeled or cut in half, the sugars caramelize slightly on the outer surfaces, and a richer flavor develops. With roasted onion halves, you can add a little vinegar to the pan; its tartness counterbalances the onion's sweetness.*

*Eat whole onions in their skins with roasted or grilled meats; they can cook alongside for a simple vegetable accompaniment. Slice in halves to serve; allow one or two halves for each portion.*

## WHOLE ROASTED ONIONS

Place 6 large **onions** (3 to 3½ in. wide) in a shallow 3-quart baking pan or 9- by 13-inch pan. Bake in a 350° oven until they feel soft when pressed, 50 to 60 minutes. Cut in half and serve with **butter** or margarine and **salt** and **pepper** to taste. Makes 6 to 12 servings.

With a slotted spoon, lift out onions and drain on paper towels (discard any scorched bits). Sprinkle lightly with salt. Serve warm or cool. If made ahead, package airtight and chill up to 3 days. To reheat, spread in a single layer in a 10- by 15-inch pan and bake in a 350° oven until warm and crisp, 2 to 3 minutes. Makes 5 to 6 cups.

## EGG SALAD SANDWICH WITH CRISP ONIONS

⅓ cup mayonnaise
1 tablespoon Dijon mustard
6 hard-cooked large eggs, peeled and coarsely chopped
  Salt and pepper
  Butter or margarine
4 slices pumpernickel bread
1 small cucumber, thinly sliced
6 cups crisp-fried onions (recipe on page 104)

In a bowl, mix mayonnaise and mustard. Gently mix in eggs and salt and pepper to taste. Butter 1 side of each bread slice. Arrange a single layer of cucumber slices on each piece of bread, overlapping slightly. Mound equal portions of egg salad on cucumber. Garnish each sandwich with a handful of crisp-fried onions. Offer remaining onions and cucumber slices to eat alongside. Makes 4 servings.

## RAW: CRISP & HOT, OR CRISP & NOT SO HOT

*Many people like the mild bite of crisp, raw onion in salads or with hamburgers. To minimize harshness, it helps to use a variety generally recognized to be sweet, such as Maui, Vidalia, or Walla Walla. Many of these are as much as 12 percent sugar—as sweet as an orange.*

*Because sweet varieties develop little or no lachrymator, they cause no tears and develop relatively weak onion flavor. They are best raw; cooked, they taste so mild as to seem neutral. In most onions, the lachrymator produces antibacterial and antifungal qualities that account for the long storage life. But the kinds without lachrymator potential spoil quickly when bruised. To minimize bruising, wrap onions individually in paper. Keep them in a cold place, at just above freezing.*

*High-sugar onions have a short season, so it's helpful to know how to use other varieties raw. But how do you select an onion to eat raw? Shape, color, size: none of these is a consistent indicator of mildness. Even within a single onion, flavor can vary. Growing conditions appear to affect taste more: generally, onions grown with little water tend to taste hotter. Appearance is no clue.*

*We've found two ways to tone down harsh flavor in any onion, and also preserve crisp texture. Immerse thin slices in ice water until crisp, 20 to 30 minutes, to rinse away some of the hot flavor and tear-producing compounds. The result will be pretty, crisp slices. But when you bite into them, you will again break cell walls, initiating a new set of reactions. A hot onion will still have some heat.*

*Or squeeze the slices in water to break up cells and wash away more of the stronger-tasting compounds. Drain, then chill in ice water; water plumps crushed cells and gives crisp texture. These somewhat battered-looking slices will have milder, more consistent flavor, because more of the cells have been broken, releasing and washing away harsh flavor.*

*Prepared either way, the slices have definite onion flavor with a degree of bite, if not harshness, that depends on the individual onion. Use in salads, sandwiches, and relishes.*

## CRISP RAW ONION SHREDS

1 large onion (3 to 3½ in. diameter)
  Water
2 cups ice cubes
¼ cup vinegar

Peel and thinly slice onion. Place slices in a bowl and add tepid water to cover. For milder flavor, squeeze with your hands until onions are almost limp. Drain, rinse, and return to bowl. Add ice, vinegar, and about 2 cups water. Let stand until crisp, 20 to 30 minutes. Drain well. Lift out onion. Makes 3 to 4 cups.

## ONION-MINT RELISH

*The onion flavor in this crisp relish is tempered slightly by the addition of mild tart-sweet mint marinade. Serve with barbecued meats or in sandwiches, or add to green salads.*

**Rinse, then chill—to eat raw**
*Squeeze, wash, and crisp slices to eat raw, as in relish (recipe below).*

¼ cup rice vinegar (or white wine vinegar with 1 teaspoon sugar)
2 teaspoons sugar
2 tablespoons minced fresh mint leaves
3 to 4 cups crisp raw onion shreds (recipe at left)
½ cup shredded carrot
  Salt

Mix vinegar and sugar until sugar dissolves. Mix in mint, onion shreds, and carrot, and add salt to taste. Serve, or cover and chill up to 4 hours. Makes 3 to 4 cups, 6 to 8 servings.

# Wake-Up Breakfast for Mom

CHILDREN CAN COOK for Mother's special day. And offering her a special Sunday breakfast on that day is a way many enjoy showing off their skills.

But what to make? The young cooks we interviewed said that it ought to look pretty fancy, but not be too hard to make. They also mentioned that dishes that make a big mess have obvious drawbacks if part of the treat includes cleanup by the kitchen crew.

Here are two recipes that might just fit the bill. The first is a dressy-looking crisp pastry with ham, cheese, almonds and frozen puff pastries. If Mom is a chocolate lover, she'll be delighted with chocolate waffles topped with ice cream and strawberries; the cooks are apt to like them a lot, too.

Our young cook pours chocolate waffle batter into hot waffle iron to bake. She tops cakelike waffles with ice cream and strawberries—and a smile.

## HAM & ALMOND PASTRY SPIRALS

- 1 package (3 oz.) sliced cooked ham, finely chopped (⅔ cup)
- ½ cup slivered almonds
- ½ cup shredded Swiss cheese
- 1 sheet thawed frozen puff pastry (½ of a 17¾-oz. package)
- 1½ tablespoons butter or margarine, melted

In a bowl, mix together ham, nuts, and cheese; set aside.

Lay pastry sheet flat on an unfloured board. Brush top lightly with butter, then evenly scatter the ham mixture over the pastry.

Lift 1 edge of the pastry square and roll to enclose the filling. Place the pastry log seam side down and use a sharp knife to cut it into 1-inch slices. Lay slices about 1 inch apart in a 10- by 15-inch baking pan. Brush tops of spirals with remaining butter. If made ahead, cover with plastic wrap and chill up to overnight.

Bake the spirals, uncovered, in a 400° oven until rich golden brown, 25 to 30 minutes. With a wide spatula, carefully transfer hot pastries to plates or a basket and serve. Makes 9 or 10; allow 2 per serving.

## CHOCOLATE WAFFLE RAFTS

- 2 ounces unsweetened or semisweet baking chocolate
- 3 cups strawberries, rinsed and hulled
  About 1 cup sugar
- 2 large eggs
- 1 cup milk
- ½ cup (¼ lb.) melted butter or margarine
- 1 teaspoon vanilla
- 1¼ cups all-purpose flour
- ¼ teaspoon baking soda
  Salad oil
- 1½ to 2 pints (3 to 4 cups) ice cream— vanilla, chocolate, strawberry, or your favorite flavor

Fill the bottom of a double boiler with enough water to come up a little around the bottom of the top part. Put on high heat until water is boiling. Take pan off the heat. Put the chocolate in top of double boiler and let stand to melt.

While chocolate melts, cut strawberries in half and put into a bowl; sweeten the berries with about 1 teaspoon of the sugar.

In a large bowl, combine the eggs, chocolate, 1 cup sugar, milk, butter, and vanilla; beat with an electric mixer until all the ingredients are well blended, about 1 minute. (Or beat with a heavy spoon until the ingredients are well blended.) Add the flour and baking soda; mix slowly with the electric mixer until the flour is moistened, then beat until batter is smooth. (Or stir in flour and then beat with heavy spoon until batter is smooth.)

Heat a waffle iron on medium heat, or set an electric waffle iron to medium or 350°. Open grids and brush both sides lightly with the salad oil. Pour about ⅓ cup batter in the center of the bottom iron; close lid. Cook waffle until it looks dry, about 3 minutes; take a peek when it stops steaming. Lift waffle from pan with a fork and put it on a rack to cool. (The waffle will be soft, so you may need to use 2 forks to lift it from the waffle iron without tearing it.) Repeat to cook remaining batter.

(If you make the waffles ahead, let cool, then wrap airtight and hold at room temperature up to overnight. Cover the strawberries and put them in the refrigerator. Or wait until just before serving to wash, drain, cut, and sweeten berries.)

Place a whole waffle on each plate. Scoop out about ½ cup ice cream and put this amount on top of each waffle. Spoon an equal amount of strawberries and their juices onto each waffle. Makes 6 to 8 waffles, or 6 to 8 servings.

Danny rolls pastry log filled with cooked ham, Swiss cheese, and slivered almonds.

*"Surprise, Mom!" Danny and Jenny rolled and baked pastry spirals to go with Mother's Day breakfast of scrambled eggs, asparagus, strawberry yogurt, strawberries—and flowers.*

# Bacon & Eggs Tostada

A BAKED TOSTADA *for breakfast is definitely a break from traditional fare. Here, south-of-the-border flavors dominate, while Western streamlined techniques allow you to assemble the tostada with ease.*

*You oven-crisp flour tortillas, dipping them first in water. Then bake an egg bordered with bacon and cheese on top until it's done as you like.*

## BACON & EGG BREAKFAST TOSTADAS

- 12 slices bacon (about ¾ lb.), cut into ½-inch-wide pieces
- 1 can (15 oz.) refried beans
- 4 flour tortillas, 7- to 8-inch size
  Water
- 2 teaspoons salad oil
- 2 cups (8 oz.) shredded cheddar cheese
- 4 large eggs
- ¼ cup chopped green onion
- 1 small cantaloupe (about 2 lb.), seeded and cut into thin wedges

1 large orange, peel and white membrane cut off, and fruit thinly sliced
  Red sauce (recipe follows)

In an 8- to 10-inch frying pan, cook bacon over medium heat until crisp; stir often. Drain bacon on paper towels. (If made ahead, cover and chill up to 2 days.)

A few minutes before serving, place refried beans in a 1- to 1½-quart pan and cook over low heat until hot; stir occasionally. (Or place beans in a 1- to 1½-quart nonmetal bowl and cook, uncovered, in a microwave oven on full power until hot, 4 to 5 minutes; stir several times.)

Meanwhile, immerse 1 tortilla at a time in water; drain briefly. At once, lay tortillas flat in 2 lightly oiled baking pans, each 10 by 15 inches, and bake in a 500° oven until pale gold, 3 to 4 minutes.

Remove from oven and sprinkle ¼ of the cheese and ¼ of the bacon evenly around outer edge of each tortilla; be sure to cover edges of tortilla completely

*Spoon mellow red chili sauce over hot, crackly breakfast tostada. Serve with melon and orange slices sprinkled with slivered peel.*

to prevent excess browning. Break an egg onto the center of each tortilla. Immediately return pans to oven and bake until eggs are set the way you like; allow 4 to 5 minutes for soft yolks with firm whites.

At once, carefully loosen tostadas from pans with a wide spatula. Transfer 1 tostada to each dinner plate. Accompany with beans and sprinkle with green onion. Serve with melon and orange slices, and spoon red sauce to taste onto each tostada. Makes 4 servings.

**Red sauce.** In a 10- to 12-inch frying pan over medium-high heat, combine 2 tablespoons **olive oil** or salad oil, 1 medium-size **onion** (chopped), and 2 cloves **garlic** (minced or pressed). Stir occasionally until onion begins to brown lightly, about 7 minutes. Stir in 1 tablespoon **chili powder,** ½ teaspoon **ground cumin,** ¼ teaspoon **ground oregano,** 1 can (15 oz.) **tomato purée,** and 1 cup **regular-strength chicken broth.** Bring to a boil, then reduce heat and simmer, uncovered, until reduced to 2½ cups, 20 to 25 minutes. Serve hot. If made ahead, cover and chill up to 3 days. To rewarm, stir over low heat until hot. Makes about 2½ cups.

*Break an egg onto the center of oven-crisped tortilla; cheese and bacon border holds the egg in place and prevents tortilla edges from becoming too brown.*

# Quick-Method Yeast Breads

AKING YEAST BREAD *has tradition-ally been a time-consuming project. Yeast manufacturers, however, have responded to busier life styles with a new, fast-acting dry yeast that, when used with a modified method for mixing and handling dough, will cut bread-making efforts in half.*

*But does this new yeast work appreciably faster? And how does it compare to doubling the quantity of regular yeast? What happens if you let dough rise only once? Most important, do timesaving techniques produce loaves as delicious as those made by traditional methods?*

*Spurred by these questions, Sunset editors took to the test kitchen. What we discovered (many dozens of loaves later) will help you to turn out a loaf of tender bread in less than 60 minutes and definitely within 1½ hours—about half the time required to make yeast breads by conventional methods.*

*The texture of these quick-method breads (see recipes for white and whole-wheat following) is slightly coarse, rather like whole-wheat bread, but the crumb (bite) is tender. Regardless of which short-cut method you use, the loaves' texture and flavor will be similar.*

## WHAT YOU CAN DO TO SPEED UP BREAD MAKING

If you want to speed up standard yeast-bread recipes, you have two ways to go: make changes in the yeast or alter the way you put the dough together.

**Changing the yeast.** One choice is to substitute 1 package fast-acting dry yeast for 1 package regular active dry yeast; both kinds cost about the same. A different strain, quick yeast is also more finely ground and thus absorbs moisture faster, rapidly converting starch and sugars to carbon dioxide, the tiny bubbles that make the dough expand and stretch.

To speed things up even more, you can double the amount of regular yeast. The air bubbles tend to be slightly larger and less even; the yeast aroma and taste are a bit stronger, particularly in white bread.

**Changing the method.** Another timesaving step is to skip softening the yeast in water. Instead, combine regular or fast-acting dry yeast directly with the dry ingredients. All the liquids (including fat) are then heated to 130°

*Mix (½ to 5 min.)*

*Knead (0 to 10 min.)*

*Rest (0 to 15 min.)*

*Shape (5 min.)*

*Rise (15 to 45 min.)*

*Bake (30 min.)*

*Warm slices of freshly baked bread—made in about 50 minutes by taking all the shortcuts—await butter and honey.*

(higher than the 110° optimum for softening yeast) and mixed with the dry ingredients. The dry ingredients cool the liquids enough to protect the yeast.

Conventional yeast dough rises or proofs twice, doubling in size each time. After the first proofing, usually about 1 hour, you knead the dough to force out the air bubbles, then shape it and let it proof again, usually at least 30 minutes. The second round of bubbles tends to be

smaller and more even, and the bread bakes light and tender. Skipping the first proofing—or reducing it by 75 percent—also saves time; the term for this shorter process is *resting*. With less proofing (resting), the breads we baked were a little denser; with no rest, they had a slightly "gummy" chew like English muffins. However, tasters approved the results of these shortcuts.

## OTHER CONSIDERATIONS OR TIMESAVERS

**Heating liquids.** A thermometer is desirable. Or program a microwave oven and temperature probe to heat the liquids; you don't have to watch them.

**Salt.** Up to a certain point, salt inhibits yeast activity and makes the bread texture finer. Add too much salt (usually an inedible amount), and the yeast barely works. With no salt at all, the dough rises faster, often overproofing before you expect; as a result, bread falls slightly when baked. Unsalted bread can have larger, uneven holes; the dough tends to feel stickier, too, and is harder to handle.

The recipes that follow call for minimal salt, for flavor. You can double this quantity for taste, or leave it out.

**Kneading.** You knead dough to develop gluten, the elastic protein that permits wheat-flour bread to hold its shape when baked. Kneading takes only seconds in the food processor. Next fastest is a dough hook. If kneading by hand, you can beat the soft dough first with an electric mixer to help develop the gluten, then stir in the rest of the flour and knead by hand.

**Rising.** To rest or to rise, the dough should be placed in a warm, draft-free spot so the temperature will stay constant. If it's too hot, the dough rises so fast the texture is uneven. You can measure proofing by the look and feel of the dough: at the perfect state, tiny bubbles appear under the surface, although the dough looks smooth and firm. When you press the dough with your fingertip, it will hold the impression but not settle; underproofed dough springs back.

When the dough is overproofed, you will see more and bigger bubbles, and the surface will look rough or strained and ready to collapse. When you make an impression in the dough, it will sag.

**Oven spring.** With the first blast of heat in the oven, steam from moisture in the dough causes the dough to swell before it is set. This is called oven spring and gives the loaf a full, rounded appearance. If overproofed, the loaf settles and sags after the oven spring.

## FAST YEAST WHITE BREAD

*This recipe gives you options at every step; the fastest way is first. You can apply these techniques to other standard yeast-bread recipes and the whole-wheat recipe on page 111.*

  3  to 3⅓ cups all-purpose flour
  1  package active dry yeast, 1 package fact-acting yeast, or 2 packages active dry yeast
  1  tablespoon sugar
  ½  teaspoon salt
1¼  cups milk
  1  tablespoon butter or margarine

**Container.** Combine 3 cups of flour, yeast, sugar, and salt in 1 of the following:
**1.** *Food processor* with dough or metal blade.
**2.** *Large bowl* of electric mixer with a dough hook.
**3.** *Large bowl* of electric mixer with rotary beaters (start with 2 cups flour).
**4.** *Large bowl* if making bread by hand.

**Heating liquids.** Choose from two methods:
*Microwave oven.* Pour milk into a glass or plastic measuring cup; add butter. Insert the microwave oven temperature probe, place cup in the oven, and plug in the probe. Set the temperature for 130°.
*On the stove.* Melt butter in a 1- to 2-quart pan over medium heat. Add the milk, then heat until it registers 130° on a thermometer.

**Mixing.** Choose one of these four ways:
**1.** *Food processor.* Whirl the flour mixture just to blend. With the motor running, pour the warm liquid through the feed tube. Shut the processor off when dough forms a ball and pulls from container side, 30 to 45 seconds. If dough is sticky, add 1 tablespoon flour at a time and mix in short bursts. Do not knead.
**2.** *Dough hook.* Pour the warm liquid into flour mixture. Mix on low speed until dry ingredients are wet. Then beat at high speed until dough pulls from sides of bowl and forms a ball, about 5 minutes. If dough sticks, add flour 1 tablespoon at a time until dough pulls free. Do not knead.
**3.** *Rotary mixer.* Start with 2 cups flour; add remaining dry ingredients. Pour warm liquid into flour mixture. Mix slowly until dry ingredients are moistened. Beat on high speed until dough is stretchy, 1 to 2 minutes. Remove beaters and stir in 1 cup flour. Scrape dough onto lightly floured board to knead.
**4.** *By hand.* Pour warm liquid into flour mixture; beat with heavy spoon until dough is stretchy, 5 to 7 minutes. Scrape dough onto lightly floured board to knead.

**Kneading.** If you combine the dough by rotary mixer or by hand, you must knead it. These pointers are useful:

Lightly dust dough with flour to make surface less sticky to touch. Always handle dough gently; you want to avoid tearing or breaking the thin, nonsticky skin that develops on the dough. For a light, evenly textured loaf, avoid working in any more flour than absolutely necessary.

The kneading process involves lifting the edge of dough opposite you over the center of the dough. In a forward motion with the palm of your hand, press dough gently to hold together; rotate a quarter-turn and repeat. Continue until dough feels smooth and satiny, about 10 minutes.

**Resting.** Cover the dough in the bowl or on a board with plastic wrap and let rest (stand undisturbed) 10 to 15 minutes. (If resting is omitted, the loaf will be a little moister.) Uncover the dough and flatten it with the heels of your hands to press out as many air bubbles as possible (if using a dough hook, beat out air).

**Shaping.** On a lightly floured board, knead dough (omit quarter-turns) into a smooth, evenly shaped roll about 10 inches long; pinch ends and fold under roll to form a loaf about ½ to ¾ inch shorter than the pan (dimensions given below).

**Rising.** Put loaf, smooth side up, in a greased 4- by 8-inch or 5- by 9-inch loaf pan. Cover lightly with plastic wrap. Set in a warm place away from drafts until loaf just about doubles in size.

To determine if dough has risen enough, flour your little finger and gently press it about ¼ inch into a corner of the loaf; the indentation should hold its shape. If not proofed enough, it will spring back; if overproofed, it will settle further (if so, knead out air and repeat rising).

*Kneading and resting. After resting 15 minutes, rounds of kneaded dough have increased to different volumes (numbers refer to number of packages of yeast used). Dough made with 2 packages regular yeast is so active that bubbles show on the surface.*

*Shaping and rising. After shaping, double-yeast dough is ready to bake in about 20 minutes; within another 20, the remaining loaves will reach the same volume—even the one on the right, which skipped the resting step.*

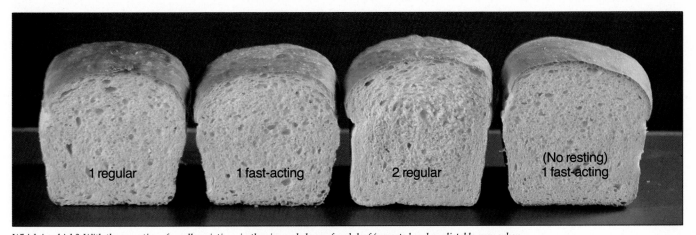

*Which is which? With the exception of small variations in the size and shape of each loaf (expected and predictable even when you use the same method every time), all of these breads look, feel, smell, and taste about the same.*

**Baking.** Uncover loaf and bake in a 425° oven until well browned on top, about 30 minutes. Turn loaf out onto a rack to cool. Slice and serve, or wrap airtight and store at room temperature up to overnight. Makes 1 loaf, 1¼ to 1½ pounds.

## FAST YEAST WHOLE-WHEAT BREAD

Make **Fast Yeast White Bread**, preceding, but omit 1 cup of the all-purpose flour and add 1 cup **whole-wheat flour.**

Combine whole-wheat flour with 1 to 2 cups all-purpose flour, yeast, sugar, and salt, according to mixing method. Rising will take a little longer.

# Tamale Sausages

HEY LOOK LIKE TAMALES, *but when you open them up and sample the contents, the corn-husk packets reveal sausages of well-seasoned meat or fish.*

The dry husks take the place of sausage casings, providing a simple and handsome way to enclose ground mixtures. Unlike casings, husks require no special equipment for stuffing. Just wrap the damp, pliable husk around the filling and tie the ends; then steam sausages until firm.

Husks are available in Mexican markets and the Mexican section of many supermarkets. They are sometimes called hojas or ojas and usually come in 8-ounce bags for about $1.50; leftover dry husks keep almost indefinitely.

The easy-to-make fillings are based on fish (minced by hand or in a food processor) or purchased ground meat. Choose from fish seasoned with chili and cilantro, pork with spicy ground New Mexico chilies (available in Mexican stores and some supermarkets), and veal with herbs.

The sausages can be assembled a day ahead, then cooked to serve hot.

## FISH CORN-HUSK SAUSAGES

> **About 3 ounces dried corn husks**
> **Water**
> **Fish filling (recipe follows)**
> **Sour cream**
> **Green taco salsa or sauce, prepared or homemade**
> **Lime halves**

Separate and sort through dried corn husks, discarding silk and other extraneous material. In a large bowl, cover husks with warm water and let stand until pliable, at least 20 minutes or as long as overnight. Lift husks from water when ready to use and shake off excess water. Tear 1 husk along the grain to make ¼-inch-wide ties as needed.

For each sausage, select a wide, pliable, drained corn husk. Lay flat on work surface. Spoon ¼ cup filling along 1 long side of husk, forming filling into a 4-inch log; there should be about 2 inches of the husk exposed on each end. Starting on the filled side, roll husk up, then tie ends with husk strips to secure filling (if the husk is not wide enough to wrap around filling, set another husk alongside, overlapping edges). Repeat with remaining husks and filling. If made ahead, cover and chill up to overnight.

Place half of the sausages, overlapping slightly, on a rack that fits into a 5- to 6-quart pan. Or arrange in a 10- to 12-inch steaming basket. If you have a steamer that allows you to cook on more than 1 level at a time, stack racks or baskets when filled. Otherwise, steam half of the sausages at a time.

Pour ½ to 1 inch water in base of 5- to 6-quart pan, steamer, or a wok if using steaming baskets. Set sausages over water; water should not touch bottom rack or basket. Cover and bring water to boiling; steam until filling is firm to

*Steam sausages in stacked baskets (or other steamer) until firm to touch.*

touch and fish is opaque in center (cut to test), about 10 minutes; add boiling water as required.

Pile sausages in a basket or plate, or offer from steaming baskets. To eat, untie husk strips or slide them off; fold back or peel off husk to reveal sausage. Serve with sour cream, salsa, and lime. Makes about 24 sausages, 6 to 8 servings.

**Fish filling.** Trim crusts from 5 to 6 slices **white bread** (reserve crusts for another use or discard). Tear bread into small pieces and whirl in a food processor or blender until fine crumbs form. Measure crumbs; you need 1½ cups.

In a food processor, combine the 1½ cups crumbs; 2 pounds boned and skinned **white fish fillets** (such as seabass or rock fish), cut in about 1-inch chunks; 1 cup thinly sliced **green onion;** ½ cup **whipping cream;** ⅓ cup **dry white wine;** ¼ cup chopped fresh **cilantro** (coriander); 1½ to 2 tablespoons minced seeded **jalapeño chili;** 2 **large eggs;** 2 cloves **garlic,** minced or pressed; ½ teaspoon **ground white pepper;** and 1 to 1½

*Shape ¼ cup filling into a 4-inch log, centering it along edge of husk.*

*Roll up to enclose filling (right); tie ends with narrow strips of husk.*

teaspoons **salt.** Whirl until smoothly puréed. (Or, with a knife, finely chop fish. Add crumbs, onion, cream, wine, cilantro, chili, eggs, garlic, pepper, salt; stir until well blended.) Poach a spoonful to taste for salt.

## SPICY PORK CORN-HUSK SAUSAGES

Follow directions for **Fish Corn-Husk Sausages** (recipe precedes), except use this pork filling instead of fish:

Mix together 2 pounds **ground lean pork;** 1 medium-size **onion,** minced; 1 cup **fine dry bread crumbs;** 2 **large eggs;** ¼ cup **ground New Mexico** or California **chilies;** ⅓ cup **red wine vinegar;** 3 large cloves **garlic,** pressed or minced; 2 teaspoons **cumin seed;** 1 teaspoon **dry oregano leaves;** and 1½ to 2 teaspoons **salt.** Poach a spoonful to taste for salt.

Steam as directed until firm to touch and no longer pink in center (cut to test), 10 to 15 minutes. Serve plain or with **sour cream** and **prepared red taco sauce.** Makes about 24 sausages, 6 to 8 servings.

## HERB VEAL CORN-HUSK SAUSAGES

Follow directions for **Fish Corn-Husk Sausages** (recipe precedes), except use this veal filling instead of fish:

Mix together 2 pounds **ground veal;** 2 **large eggs;** ½ cup **fine dry bread crumbs;** ½ cup chopped **parsley;** ⅓ cup **dry white wine** or regular-strength chicken broth; 2 large cloves **garlic,** pressed or minced; 2 teaspoons **dry thyme leaves;** 1 teaspoon **rubbed sage;** ¼ teaspoon **ground nutmeg,** ¼ teaspoon **ground white pepper,** and 1½ to 2 teaspoons **salt.** Poach a spoonful to taste for salt.

Steam as directed until firm to touch (meat remains slightly pink even when done), 10 to 15 minutes. Serve plain or with **Dijon mustard.** Makes 20 to 22 sausages, 5 or 6 servings.

*Ladle green salsa onto moist fish sausages seasoned with cilantro and chili; offer sour cream and lime to season. Serve with tomatoes and boiled beans.*

# "Centerpiece" Soups

WHAT'S THE DIFFERENCE *between soup and a sauce? In the case of these three soups, the flavorful "sauce" is actually a light broth that surrounds the focal ingredient of each dish.*

*One features salmon and another chicken. Both are appealing supper or luncheon main dishes.*

*Hot sautéed salmon fillets, complemented by two kinds of radish and hot wasabi, rest in a mellow sake broth; you could add hot cooked rice, serve rice on the side, or follow soup with a rice or pasta salad.*

*The chilled chicken breast is bathed in a refreshing pineapple-cilantro broth; serve with crisp toast or warm tortillas.*

*In a still lighter "soup," a mint-and-lemon broth gently warms tiny peas and tender lettuce leaves. Offer as a first course, or serve for lunch with bread and cheese or thin ham sandwiches.*

*All three soups go together quickly, but each has make-ahead possibilities. Two of the lean broth bases need a brief time to steep and capture flavor from the seasonings, but both can be reheated; the broth for the chicken soup needs time to cool before final steps.*

*Pan-browned salmon fillet, in sake broth, is complemented by crisp daikon and radish shreds, lemon, and dill. Approach green mound of hot wasabi (Japanese horseradish) with caution.*

## SALMON IN SAKE BROTH WITH TWO RADISHES

- 2 tablespoons salad oil
- ½ cup minced shallots or onions
- 3 cups regular-strength chicken broth
- 1½ cups sake or regular-strength chicken broth
- 1½ tablespoons sugar
- 1 tablespoon chopped fresh dill (or 1½ teaspoons dry dill weed)
- 2 tablespoons lemon juice
- 4 salmon fillets (⅓ to ½ lb. each), skin and bones removed
- 1 piece (about 6 oz.) daikon, peeled and finely shredded
- 4 medium-size red radishes (ends trimmed), finely shredded
  Wasabi cones (directions follow)
- 1 lemon, cut into wedges
  Fresh dill sprigs

In a 3- to 4-quart pan, combine 1 tablespoon of the oil and the shallots. Cook, uncovered, on medium heat, stirring often, until shallots are limp, about 7 minutes. Add broth, sake, sugar, and chopped dill. Cover and bring to a boil over high heat; add lemon juice. Reduce heat to low and keep warm up to 30 minutes; if made ahead, let cool, cover, and chill up to 1 day. Reheat to continue.

In a 10- to 12-inch frying pan, warm remaining 1 tablespoon oil on medium-high heat. Add salmon fillets to pan and cook, uncovered, until brown on each side, 5 to 7 minutes total. Cover and cook on medium-low heat until salmon has almost lost its translucency in the thickest part (cut to test), about 2 minutes longer.

Place 1 salmon fillet in each of 4 wide, shallow soup bowls. Equally mound daikon shreds next to fillets; top daikon with red radish shreds. Top each fillet with a wasabi cone; garnish with lemon wedges and dill sprigs. Ladle broth equally around fish. As you eat with fork and spoon, mix wasabi and squeeze lemon juice into broth to taste. Makes 4 servings.

**Wasabi cones.** Thoroughly mix 2½ tablespoons **wasabi powder** (Japanese horseradish) with 4 teaspoons **water.** With your fingers, shape into 4 equal-size cones.

*Both a soup and a salad, petite peas and lettuce leaves infused with lemon and mint make a handsome first-course dish.*

## PEAS & LETTUCE IN MINT BROTH

4 cups regular-strength chicken broth
1¼ cups firmly packed fresh mint leaves
Strips of yellow peel pared from 1 medium-size lemon
2 cups frozen petite peas
1 teaspoon lemon juice
1 tablespoon slivered mint leaves
1 teaspoon shredded lemon peel
4 medium-size butter lettuce leaves, washed and crisped

In a 2- to 3-quart pan over high heat, bring broth, mint leaves, and strips of lemon peel to a boil. Cover, remove from heat, and let stand for mint to flavor broth, about 15 minutes or up to overnight. With a slotted spoon, scoop out mint and discard.

Bring broth to boiling; add peas and stir until hot, 1 to 2 minutes. Add lemon juice. Pour broth through a strainer equally into each of 4 wide, shallow bowls. Quickly mix peas with slivered mint and shredded lemon peel. Lay a lettuce leaf in each bowl and spoon pea mixture into leaves, dividing equally. Eat with knife, fork, and spoon. Makes 4 servings.

*Ladle chilled pineapple-cilantro broth around cold chicken breast; nasturtium adds peppery bite to luncheon entrée.*

## CHILLED CHICKEN IN PINEAPPLE BROTH

4½ cups regular-strength chicken broth
⅓ cup firmly packed brown sugar
1 tablespoon minced fresh ginger
1 fresh jalapeño or serrano chili, stemmed, seeded, and minced
1 small (3 lb.) pineapple
⅓ cup cilantro sprigs (coriander)
1¼ cups lemon or lime juice
6 cold cooked chicken breast halves, skinned and boned
Cilantro sprigs
6 nasturtium blossoms, rinsed, stems trimmed (optional)
1 lemon, cut into wedges

In a 3- to 4-quart pan over high heat, bring broth, sugar, ginger, and chili to a boil; set aside.

Meanwhile, trim ends off pineapple; also cut off 3 thin crosswise slices. Peel remaining pineapple and coarsely chop enough fruit to make 3 cups. Whirl fruit with the ⅓ cup cilantro in a food processor or blender until smoothly puréed, about 10 minutes.

Stir purée and lemon juice into chicken broth; cover and chill until cold, about 2 hours or up to 1 day. Cover pineapple slices and chill, too.

Place 1 piece of chicken in each of 6 wide, shallow soup bowls. Cut pineapple slices into quarters and add to bowls as garnish, along with cilantro sprigs and nasturtiums. Stir broth mixture and ladle around breasts. Offer lemon wedges to season soup to taste. Eat with knife, fork, and spoon. Makes 6 servings.

# Crisp Asian Appetizer Rolls

IN MANY ASIAN CUISINES a popular appetizer is a crisp roll filled with a seasoned meat and vegetable mixture. Filipinos call it lumpia, and the wrapper they use has the same name. The Chinese know it as spring roll or egg roll, the Vietnamese as imperial roll. While wrappers and fillings may differ, the preparation and end results are very similar.

Usually the appetizers are deep-fried. Here, they're baked to crispness: they're easier to cook and don't have added fat.

Asian markets and some supermarkets sell a variety of frozen or refrigerated wrappers that work well with lumpia.

Since the wrappers differ in thickness, the number of sheets per pound varies.

Roughly, a 16-ounce package of the thin lumpia and rice paper wrappers has 30 or more sheets, while packages of thicker egg roll and spring roll wrappers have fewer. Our recipe uses about 30 wrappers, so count the number in a package before you buy.

When exposed to air, the wrappers dry quickly and become brittle, so cover tightly except when shaping or baking.

## BAKED LUMPIA ROLLS

¾ **pound ground lean pork**
1 **medium-size carrot, peeled and minced**
1 **medium-size onion, chopped**
1 **can (8 oz.) water chestnuts, drained and chopped**
1 **can (8 oz.) bamboo shoots, drained and minced**
8 **cloves garlic, minced or pressed**
2 **tablespoons soy sauce**
1 **teaspoon pepper**
**About 30 lumpia wrappers (about 10-in. diameter), spring roll wrappers (about 8 in. square), egg roll wrappers (about 6 in. square), or rice paper rounds, (6½- or 8½-in. diameter—see following directions for preparation)**
1 **large egg, beaten**
**Dipping sauce (recipe follows)**

In a large bowl, combine pork, carrot, onion, water chestnuts, bamboo shoots, garlic, soy sauce, and pepper. Stir mixture until thoroughly combined. (If made ahead, cover and chill up to overnight.) Except when working with wrappers, keep them covered with plastic wrap to prevent drying. For round and square wrappers, mound 2 tablespoons of filling in an even band across the edge of wrapper closest to you, starting 2 inches in and leaving a ¾-inch margin on each end. Fold the 2-inch flap over the filling; tuck under to secure. Roll over once, then fold in ends.

Brush edge of wrapper opposite you with beaten egg. Continue rolling to make a cylinder. Set lumpia, seam side down, in a 10- by 15-inch baking pan; cover with plastic wrap until ready to bake. Repeat to use all the filling; place lumpia slightly apart on the pan. You will need 2 or more pans; or use 2 pans in sequence.

Bake rolls in a 450° oven, turning once or twice with a wide spatula, until golden brown, about 20 minutes. If using 1 oven and 2 pans, switch pan positions halfway through for even browning. With the spatula, transfer rolls to a board and cut them in half. Serve hot.

If made ahead, let uncut lumpia cool; cover and chill up to 3 days, or freeze up to 4 weeks. To reheat (thaw if frozen), bake on baking pans in a 450° oven until hot, about 10 minutes. Turn rolls to keep color even.

Accompany hot lumpia with dipping sauce. Makes about 60 pieces, enough for 15 appetizer servings.

**To prepare rice paper rounds.** With your hands or a pastry brush, lightly moisten both sides of **rice paper rounds,** 2 or 3 at a time, with **water.** Place rounds in a single layer on racks and let stand until pliable, 2 to 3 minutes. Keep remaining rounds covered airtight until ready to use.

**Dipping sauce.** In a 2- to 3-quart pan, mix ¼ cup firmly packed **brown sugar,** ½ cup **distilled white vinegar,** and 1 tablespoon **soy sauce.** Stir over high heat until sugar dissolves. Mix 1 teaspoon **cornstarch** with 2 tablespoons **water;** add to sugar mixture and stir until sauce boils. Remove from heat and add 2 tablespoons minced **fresh ginger.** Makes ⅔ cup. —Rosemarie Cruz, Vista, Calif.

Dip rolled lumpia appetizers in the flavorful tart-sweet ginger sauce; pork and vegetable filling soaks it up readily.

# Seafood Appetizers

ONE CLASSIC, ONE CONTEMPORARY, these two fish appetizers are refreshing to serve with beverages or to start a meal. The first is Mediterranean-style taramasalata to serve as a dip or a spread. It's made with the pink, rather salty carp roe (tarama in Greek). Aside from the roe, the main ingredients are humble—bread, olive oil, and lemon juice.

The second is a piquant lime ice with cooked shrimp—served at room temperature; tequila lends an intriguing overtone to both the ice and the shellfish.

Refrigerated jars of tarama are sold in Greek or Middle Eastern markets and sometimes turn up in specialty delicatessens. It's relatively inexpensive—around $2 for a 10-ounce jar. Once opened, it keeps about a month in the refrigerator.

You can make this party-size appetizer to serve on crackers or crisp lettuce leaves. If desired, cut the recipe in half for a smaller occasion, or use extra taramasalata to accompany cold poached fish, stuffed grape leaves, or sliced tomatoes.

## TARAMASALATA APPETIZER

10 ounces (⅝ of a 1-lb. loaf) unsliced sweet French bread, crust trimmed off
    Water
1 jar (10 oz., 1 cup) tarama (salted carp roe)
1½ cups olive oil
½ cup lemon juice
3 to 4 tablespoons drained capers
2 lemons, cut into wedges or very thin slices
    Sesame crackers
    Tender inner romaine lettuce leaves, washed and crisped

Slice bread into 1-inch-thick pieces and place in a large bowl; add water to cover. When bread is saturated, about 5 minutes, lift from water and squeeze tightly to remove as much moisture as possible.

Empty bowl, dry, and put bread in it; add tarama. Using a pestle or potato masher, mash the mixture thoroughly. With a fork, whisk in oil, adding it in a slow stream. Stir in lemon juice. If made ahead, cover and chill up to 1 week.

Spoon taramasalata into a serving bowl. Garnish with a few of the capers and a lemon wedge or slice. Alongside, present the remaining capers and lemons, with crackers and romaine. Spoon or scoop taramasalata onto crackers or romaine; top with a few capers and a squeeze of lemon. Or top a cracker with a lemon slice, then add taramasalata and capers. Makes 3½ cups, 20 to 30 servings of 2 to 3 tablespoons each.—Sophie Tsachres, San Mateo, Calif.

**Taramasalata for a small party.** Make **Taramasalata Appetizer,** preceding, using half the quantity for each ingredient. Serves 10 to 15.

## TEQUILA-LIME ICE WITH SHRIMP

1½ teaspoons grated lime peel
1 cup sugar
2 cups lime juice (about 14 fresh limes; or use bottled juice)
½ cup tequila
1 cup water
    Stir-fried shrimp (recipe follows)
    Ice cubes
    Lime peel strips (optional)

In a 9- by 13-inch pan, stir together grated peel, sugar, juice, tequila, and water until sugar is dissolved; cover. Freeze until firm, overnight or up to 1 month.

About 30 minutes before serving, prepare shrimp and set aside. Arrange ice cubes in 5 to 8 small bowls. Nest 5 to 8 smaller bowls (about ¾-cup size) in the ice; put in freezer. (Or omit cubes and put smaller bowls in the freezer.)

With a heavy spoon, break lime ice into chunks. Whirl in a food processor or beat with an electric mixer until a thick icy slush forms. Immediately spoon into chilled bowls; garnish with strips of peel. Accompany with shrimp. Makes 4 cups ice, or 5 to 8 first-course servings.

**Stir-fried shrimp.** Shell and devein 1 pound **large shrimp** (about 35 per lb.). Heat 2 tablespoons **salad oil** in a wok or 10- to 12-inch frying pan over high heat. Add shrimp and stir-fry until bright pink, about 2 minutes. Stir in 2 tablespoons **tequila;** ignite with a match (away from any overhang) and shake until flames die. Add 2 tablespoons **lime juice.** Serve at room temperature.

*Caper-dotted taramasalata—carp roe appetizer salad—goes on crackers or romaine. Add lemon or capers; eat with olives.*

# Cooking with Dried Tomatoes

**I**NTENSE AND COMPLEX *in flavor, chewy-textured dried tomatoes give distinctive seasoning to certain dishes.*

*Here they appear as an appetizer with cream cheese, a vegetable dish, with shrimp to serve over pasta, and a seasoned butter for toast or grilled foods. Dried tomatoes come in two forms: dried and then packed in oil, or just dried. These recipes use the oil-packed ones. Look for domestic or imported brands in fancy food sections of supermarkets, specialty food stores, and delicatessens. They are costly (about $1 an ounce), but a little goes a long way.*

## DRIED TOMATO TORTA

1 cup (½ lb.) *each* cream cheese and unsalted butter, at room temperature

1 cup (5 oz.) freshly grated parmesan cheese

½ cup dried tomatoes packed in oil, drained (reserve oil)

2 tablespoons oil from dried tomatoes packed in oil

About 2 cups fresh basil leaves, lightly packed

Pocket bread toast triangles (directions follow)

With an electric mixer or food processor, beat cream cheese, butter, and parmesan cheese until very smoothly blended.

Cut 4 tomatoes into thin strips; set aside. Whirl remaining tomatoes, oil, and about ½ cup of the cheese mixture in a blender until tomatoes are very smoothly puréed; scrape purée back into bowl with cheese mixture and beat to blend. Cover bowl and chill for about 20 minutes, or until firm enough to shape.

Mound cheese on a platter. If made ahead, cover with an inverted bowl (don't let it touch cheese) and chill up to 3 days; serve at room temperature.

Arrange reserved tomato strips and basil leaves around torta; present with toast triangles. To eat, spread cheese on toast; top with a basil leaf and a tomato strip. Makes 8 to 10 appetizer servings.

**Pocket bread toast triangles.** Split 6 rounds **pocket bread** (6-in. diameter) in half. Cut each round into 6 triangles. Place in a single layer in 2 baking pans, each 10 by 15 inches. Bake in a 400° oven for 3 minutes, switch pan positions, and continue baking until lightly toasted, about 2 minutes longer. Let cool. If made ahead, store airtight up to 3 days.

## ARTICHOKE HEARTS TOSCANA

2 tablespoons oil from dried tomatoes packed in oil

2 cloves garlic, minced or pressed

1 large onion, chopped

1 pound mushrooms, sliced

2 ounces sliced prosciutto, chopped

½ teaspoon dry sage leaves

¼ cup dried tomatoes packed in oil, drained (reserve oil) and chopped

¾ cup dry white wine

½ cup water

Artichoke hearts (directions follow)

Salt and pepper

In a 10- to 12-inch frying pan over medium-high heat, combine oil, garlic, onion, mushrooms, and prosciutto.

Dried tomatoes give rich cheese torta unique flavor and color. For extra wallop, put a basil leaf and a strip of dried tomato on cheese-topped wedge of pocket bread.

Cook, stirring occasionally, until onion is golden and mushrooms are brown and glazed, 15 to 20 minutes. Mix in sage, tomatoes, wine, water, and artichokes; bring to a boil. Simmer, covered, until artichokes are tender when pierced, about 45 minutes; stir occasionally. Season to taste with salt and pepper. Makes 4 to 6 servings.

**Artichoke hearts.** Mix 1 quart **water** and 1 tablespoon **lemon juice** in a large bowl. Break off and discard tough leaves from 15 small **artichokes** (2-in. diameter or less) down to tender, all-edible pale green leaves. Cut off thorny tips and trim stems flush with bottoms. Drop into water as trimmed.

*Roma-type tomato weighed 3 to 4 ounces fresh. Dried, it's shrunk a lot, but its flavor is intensely concentrated.*

*Lively sauce of dried tomatoes, shrimp, basil, and cream flavors hot linguini.*

## PASTA WITH SHRIMP IN TOMATO CREAM

- 2 **tablespoons oil** from dried tomatoes packed in oil
- 1 **clove garlic,** minced or pressed
- 1 **pound large** (31 to 35 per lb.) **shrimp,** shelled and deveined
- ¼ **cup thinly sliced green onion**
- 1½ **tablespoons chopped fresh basil** or 1 teaspoon dry basil
- ⅓ **cup dried tomatoes packed in oil,** drained (reserve oil) and cut into slivers
- ¼ **teaspoon ground white pepper**
- 1 **cup regular-strength chicken broth**
- ¾ **cup dry vermouth**
- 1 **cup whipping cream**
- 10 **ounces dry linguini**
  **Water**
  **Freshly grated parmesan cheese**

In a 10- to 12-inch frying pan over medium-high heat, combine oil and garlic. When hot, add shrimp and cook, stirring often, until opaque in center (cut to test), about 6 minutes. Lift out and set aside.

To the pan, add onion, basil, tomatoes, pepper, broth, vermouth, and cream. Boil on high heat, uncovered,

until reduced to about 1½ cups, about 10 minutes. Add shrimp and stir until hot.

Meanwhile, in a 4- to 5-quart pan, cook pasta in 3 quarts boiling water until just tender to bite, about 8 minutes; drain well. Add cooked pasta to sauce and lift with 2 forks to blend and serve. Offer cheese individually. Serves 4.

## DRIED TOMATO-SHALLOT BUTTER

- 1 **cup** (½ lb.) **butter** or margarine, at room temperature
- ¼ **cup dried tomatoes packed in oil,** drained (reserve oil for other uses) and minced
- 2 **tablespoons minced shallots**
- ½ **teaspoon coarsely ground black pepper**

In a bowl, beat butter, tomatoes, shallots, and pepper until blended. Serve at room temperature. If made ahead, cover and chill up to 3 days. Makes about 1 cup.

# Tofu Snacks

YOU DON'T LIKE TOFU? *You may end up eating your words—along with these spinach and almond-filled cakes of golden-baked tofu. You marinate tofu slices in a ginger-spiked soy-vinegar sauce, sandwich them around a filling, coat with crumbs, and bake until crisp. Chili-seasoned vegetables round out the meal. To save time, omit the filling; bake single layers of breaded, marinated tofu; serve on spinach and sprinkle with almonds.*

## MARINATED TOFU STACKS

>    About 2 pounds regular- or firm-style tofu, drained
> ½  cup seasoned rice vinegar or ⅓ cup rice vinegar and 2 teaspoons sugar
> ½  cup water
> ⅓  cup oyster sauce or soy sauce
> 2  tablespoons soy sauce
> 1  tablespoon chopped fresh ginger
> 1  quart lightly packed, washed, and crisped spinach leaves
>    Toasted almonds (directions follow)
> 1  large egg
> ½  cup fine dry bread crumbs
>    About 2 tablespoons melted butter or margarine
>    Chili vegetables (recipe follows)

Cut tofu into 2- by 4-inch rectangles about ½ inch thick. Lift slices with a wide spatula and set in a single layer in 1 or 2 baking dishes, 9- by 13-inch size.

Mix vinegar, water, oyster sauce, soy, and ginger; pour over tofu. Cover and chill at least 4 hours, or up to 2 days. Chop enough of the spinach leaves to make ¼ cup; reserve remaining leaves.

Lift half of tofu from marinade and place on a double layer of paper towels. Arrange an equal amount of almonds on center of each slice, leaving a ¼-inch border. Repeat with spinach. With a

Baked crisp in its crumb coating, ginger-seasoned tofu cake has filling of chopped almonds, shredded spinach. Chili-seasoned vegetables make it a light but flavorful meal.

wide spatula, lift remaining tofu from marinade and carefully place over spinach.

Cover tofu stacks with a double layer of paper towels. Set a 12- by 15-inch baking sheet on top. Place a 2- to 3-pound weight (such as food cans) in center of pan. Let stand 10 to 15 minutes.

In an 8- or 9-inch pie pan, mix egg with a fork until well blended. Scatter bread crumbs in another pan of equal size. Dip tofu stacks, one at a time, in egg, coating all sides completely; then coat in bread crumbs. Set on a lightly buttered 12- by 15-inch baking sheet. Lightly drizzle tops of tofu stacks with melted butter.

Bake in a 450° oven until crumbs are golden, about 20 minutes. Serve with

reserved spinach leaves and chili vegetables. Makes 3 to 6 servings.

**Toasted almonds.** In an 8- or 9-inch pie pan, scatter ¼ cup **almonds.** Bake in a 350° oven until light gold inside (cut to test), about 15 minutes. Chop coarsely.

**Chili vegetables.** In a 10- to 12-inch frying pan, melt 1 tablespoon **butter** or margarine over medium-high heat. Add 1 large **red bell pepper,** stemmed, seeded, and thinly sliced. Cook, stirring, until pepper is tender-crisp, about 5 minutes. Add 1 can (15 oz.) **straw mushrooms,** drained; 1 can (15 oz.) **baby corn ears,** drained; and ⅛ teaspoon **hot chili oil** or cayenne. Cook, stirring occasionally, until vegetables are heated through, about 5 minutes. Makes 3 to 6 servings.

**1** *Sprinkle almonds and shredded spinach on marinated tofu slices.*

**2** *Set a weight on baking sheet over tofu stacks to press layers together.*

**3** *Dip filled tofu cakes in egg, coat with crumbs, then bake until golden.*

# Dried Snacks

THE OLD-FASHIONED ART *of drying makes these contemporary refreshments. Your oven or a food dehydrator turns corn, bananas, fruit yogurt, and tomatoes into long-lasting snacks, perfect for lunch boxes or nibbling any time.*

*Preparation is simple. Spread liquids on baking sheets or dehydrator trays lined with plastic wrap; lay out foods as directed in the following recipes.*

*Most snacks dry overnight, but time varies with the amount of food and method used. You can use the oven, but dehydrators work faster and require less attention; just follow manufacturer's directions.*

*In the oven, to achieve the optimum drying temperature of 140° to 150°, turn the thermostat to its lowest setting and prop the door open to let air circulate. Check temperature with a thermometer placed at the back of the oven. If the lowest setting is above 150° or temperature rises above 150°, turn the oven off and on periodically for best drying results.*

*On baking sheet covered with plastic wrap, spread puréed corn mixture in thin layer to dry. Break brittle sheet of dried corn purée into chunks for a wholesome snack.*

## CORN CHIPS

Husk, rinse, and dry 3 large **ears corn.** With a sharp knife, cut kernels from cobs; you should have about 2 cups. Discard cobs. Stem and seed 2 **fresh** or canned **jalapeño chilies** or 1 fresh Anaheim (California) chili. Cut chilies into small pieces. In a blender or food processor, purée corn and chilies; scrape purée from container sides often with a rubber spatula. Add **salt** to taste, if desired.

Smoothly cover a 12- by 15-inch baking sheet with plastic wrap; tape excess to underside of pan. Pour corn mixture onto plastic wrap and tilt pan so mixture flows to make a ¼-inch-thick layer.

Set pan, uncovered, in a 140° to 150° oven; prop door open about 2 inches. Leave corn mixture in oven until it feels dry in the center and breaks into brittle pieces, 12 to 17 hours. Near the end of the drying time, if necessary, pull the sheet of corn off the plastic wrap and turn it over to dry the underside. Let cool. Break sheet into bite-size pieces. Serve, or store airtight in the refrigerator up to 2 months. Makes about 3 ounces, 4 or 5 servings.

## BANANA NUT NUGGETS

Peel 3 large **firm-ripe bananas** (about 1½ lb.) and slice into 1-inch-thick diagonal pieces. Put 1¼ cups minced **almonds** in a 9- to 10-inch pie pan. Roll fruit in nuts, pressing lightly to make nuts adhere. Arrange banana pieces, slightly apart, on a 12- by 15-inch baking sheet. Place, uncovered, in a 140° to 150° oven. Prop oven door open about 2 inches and dry bananas until pieces shrivel but give slightly when gently pressed, 12 to 18 hours. Let cool. Serve, or store airtight in the refrigerator up to 1 month. Makes about 10 ounces, 3 or 4 servings.

## YOGURT SUEDE

Smoothly cover a 12- by 15-inch baking sheet with plastic wrap; tape excess to underside of pan.

Stir 2 cups **fruit-flavored yogurt** until smooth; pour onto plastic wrap. Tilt pan so yogurt forms an ⅛-inch-thick layer.

Set pan, uncovered, in a 140° to 150° oven. Prop oven door open about 2 inches. Let liquid dry until yogurt peels off plastic wrap easily, 12 to 15 hours. Let

cool. To eat, peel yogurt off plastic and tear into pieces. To store, roll yogurt suede in plastic wrap; if brittle, return to oven to warm slightly, then roll. To store, seal airtight and chill up to 3 weeks. Makes 4 to 5 ounces, 2 to 4 servings.

## TOMATO CHIPS

Cover an oven rack with a double layer of cheesecloth and tape it to the rack.

Core 2 large **firm-ripe tomatoes** (about 1 lb.). Cut tomatoes crosswise into ¼-inch-thick rounds; discard end slices or save for other uses. Lay remaining rounds in a single layer on the cheesecloth. If desired, sprinkle lightly with 2 teaspoons **dry basil.** Slide rack into oven and set temperature at 140° to 150°; prop door open about 2 inches. Keep tomatoes in oven until they feel dry and snap when broken, 12 to 24 hours. Let cool. Serve, or store airtight in the refrigerator up to 2 months. Makes 1 to 1½ ounces, 3 or 4 servings.

# A Little Thinly Sliced Prosciutto

I T TAKES 10 MONTHS *for prosciutto to develop its firm texture and fragrant sweet-salty taste. The long curing and drying process—originally devised in Parma, Italy—concentrates the flavor of this premium-priced ham, so it can be used effectively in small amounts.*

*In these recipes, you stretch the flavor of the ham, adding just a few ounces to accent other foods. Wrap the thin slices around bitter Belgian endive and grill for a first course. Use it to flavor pasta. Or for an attractive salad, sprinkle crisp-cooked prosciutto shreds over creamy avocado or sweet pear.*

## GRILLED ENDIVE WITH PROSCIUTTO

2  heads Belgian endive (4 oz. each) or 1 head radicchio (about 12 oz.)
8  thin slices prosciutto (about ¼ lb.)
¼  cup extra-virgin olive oil
   Lemon wedges
   Salt and pepper

Cut each endive head lengthwise in quarters. Or cut each radicchio head through the core into 8 equal wedges. Roll each piece with the prosciutto; secure end with a wooden pick.

Place on a grill 4 to 6 inches above a solid bed of medium coals (you should be able to hold your hand at grill level 4 to 5 seconds). Cook, turning, to brown lightly on all sides, 4 to 5 minutes. Transfer to 4 salad plates. Remove picks. Drizzle each serving equally with oil. Garnish with lemon. Add salt and pepper to taste. Serves 4.

## LINGUINI WITH PROSCIUTTO & OLIVES

   Water
8  ounces dry linguini
2  ounces thinly sliced prosciutto, cut into ¼-inch-wide strips
¼  cup olive oil or salad oil
½  cup thinly sliced green onion
1  jar (3 oz.) pimiento-stuffed Spanish-style olives, drained
1  cup cherry tomatoes, cut in halves
   Grated parmesan cheese

In a 5- to 6-quart pan, bring about 3 quarts water to boiling over high heat. Add linguini and boil, uncovered, until noodles are just barely tender to bite, about 9 minutes. Drain well. Pour into a warm serving bowl.

Meanwhile, in an 8- to 10-inch frying pan, stir prosciutto in oil over medium-high heat until lightly browned, about 4 minutes. Add onion; stir until limp. Add olives and tomatoes; shake pan often until olives are hot, about 2 minutes. Pour over noodles and mix. Add cheese to taste. Makes 3 or 4 servings.

## AVOCADO WITH CRISP PROSCIUTTO SHREDS

2  ounces thinly sliced prosciutto, cut into ¼-inch-wide strips
⅓  cup olive oil
⅓  cup chopped shallots
1  tablespoon Dijon mustard
¼  cup red wine vinegar
2  large ripe avocados or firm-ripe pears
   Watercress sprigs, rinsed and crisped
   Salt and pepper

In an 8- to 10-inch frying pan, stir prosciutto in oil over medium-high heat until prosciutto is crisp, 7 to 8 minutes. Lift out of pan with a slotted spoon; drain on paper towels. If made ahead, cool, cover, and chill up to overnight.

Add shallots to pan; stir over medium heat until soft. Remove from heat; whisk in mustard and vinegar. If made ahead, cool, cover, and chill up to overnight.

Cut avocados in half lengthwise. Remove and discard pits and peel. (Cut pears in half lengthwise and core.) Lay each avocado or pear half, cut side down, on a salad or dinner plate. Starting at blossom end, make lengthwise cuts about ⅓ inch apart to within ½ inch of top. Gently press avocado (or pear) to fan out slices. Spoon warm, reheated, or cool dressing over avocados; sprinkle with prosciutto strips and garnish with watercress. Add salt and pepper to taste. Serves 4.

*Embellish avocado fan with crisp prosciutto shreds and shallot dressing.*

# Ground Buffalo

MORE OFTEN *than you might expect, buffalo meat shows up in supermarkets—as ground patties, usually in the freezer case. (Sometimes you can special-order other cuts as well.)*

*Ground buffalo is similar in flavor to lean ground beef, but it has the edge on intensity of taste. Like lean beef, it is priced between $2 and $4 a pound and, ranging from 10 to 14 percent fat, also needs special handling to avoid tasting dry.*

*If you hesitate to enjoy meat from an animal that was once near extinction, take comfort: today, farm-reared herds total about 60,000 head. This is in addition to buffalo sheltered in national parks and game refuges.*

*To take advantage of buffalo's fuller flavor, try the patties coated with crushed pepper and a touch of honey, then broiled. Or shape the ground meat into sweet-tart meatballs, reminiscent of sauerbraten, to go with noodles. We also feature the meat in a variation on Southwest Indian pozole, which usually uses lamb (unlike the Mexican pozole from Jalisco based on pork).*

## PEPPERED BUFFALO PATTIES WITH RELISH

1 **pound ground buffalo**
3 **to 4 tablespoons whole black peppercorns**
2 **tablespoons honey**
1 **tablespoon hot water**
**Black-eyed pea relish (recipe follows)**

Divide buffalo meat into 4 equal portions and shape each into a 1-inch-thick patty; set on waxed paper.

Crush peppercorns with a mortar and pestle or with the bottom of a flat, heavy glass or small pan. Put crushed pepper on paper alongside meat, and pat each patty on all sides in pepper, using all. Set patties well apart on a rack in a broiler pan, about 12- by 14-inch size.

Mix honey with hot water; drizzle some of the liquid over top and sides of patties. Broil meat about 5 inches from the heat until lightly browned, 4 to 6 minutes. Turn with a wide spatula and drizzle top and sides of patties with the honey liquid; for medium-rare, broil until lightly browned (cut to test), about 5 minutes longer.

Pour the remaining honey liquid over meat and serve. Accompany with the black-eyed pea relish. Makes 4 servings.

**Black-eyed pea relish.** Drain 1 can (15 oz.) **black-eyed peas.** In a bowl, combine peas with 1 small **onion,** diced; 3 cloves **garlic,** minced or pressed; ¼ cup *each* **olive oil** or salad oil and **cider vinegar;** and **salt** and **pepper** to taste. Mix well. Serve, or cover and chill up to 4 days, stirring several times. Makes 2 cups.— *Clara Megraw, Santa Ana, Calif.*

## BUFFALO MEATBALLS WITH NOODLES

1 **tablespoon olive or salad oil**
1 **small onion, chopped**
2 **cloves garlic, minced or pressed**
1 **small can (8 oz.) crushed pineapple, drained**
¼ **cup raisins**
1 **tablespoon ground ginger**
1 **pound ground buffalo**
1 **large egg**
¼ **cup fine dry bread crumbs**
 **Water**
½ **pound dry wide egg noodles**
¾ **cup** *each* **regular-strength beef broth and dry red wine**
2 **tablespoons butter or margarine**
 **Italian parsley, optional**
 **Salt and pepper**

In an 8- to 10-inch frying pan over medium heat, combine oil, onion, garlic, pineapple, and raisins. Stir until liquid evaporates (take care not to scorch), about 10 minutes. Remove from heat and stir in ginger; set aside to cool.

In a large bowl, thoroughly mix buffalo with fruit mixture, egg, and crumbs. Shape meat mixture into 1¼-inch balls. Set balls slightly apart in a 10- by 15-inch rimmed pan. Bake, uncovered, in a 450° oven until meatballs are lightly browned and still slightly pink in center when cut, about 12 minutes.

Meanwhile, in a 4- to 5-quart pan, bring 3 quarts of water to boiling on high heat. Add noodles and cook, uncovered, until tender to bite, about 8 minutes. Drain quickly, then pour noodles onto a warm platter. Set meatballs on noodles; cover loosely and keep warm.

Working quickly, add broth, wine, and butter to meat pan, stirring over high heat to release browned bits as mixture comes to a full, rolling boil; stir and boil 2 to 3 minutes to reduce slightly, then pour sauce over meatballs. Garnish with parsley and season to taste with salt and pepper. Makes 4 or 5 servings.

*Southwest Indian–style stew includes ground buffalo meat, hominy, tomatillos, and baby corn.*

## BUFFALO POZOLE

2 **tablespoons olive or salad oil**
2 **large onions, chopped**
¾ **pound mushrooms, thinly sliced**
1 **pound ground buffalo**
2 **cans (13 oz.** *each***) tomatillos**
1 **can (15½ oz.) hominy, drained**
1 **can (15 oz.) baby corn, drained; or 1 package (8 oz.) frozen baby corn**
¼ **cup chopped fresh cilantro (coriander)**
1 **tablespoon dry oregano leaves**
5 **small dried hot red chilies**

In a 5- to 6-quart pan over medium heat, combine 1 tablespoon oil and onion; stir often until onion is lightly golden and sweet to taste, about 20 minutes. Add the mushrooms and stir occasionally until liquid evaporates, about 10 minutes. Pour mixture out of pan and set aside.

Add 1 more tablespoon oil to pan along with the buffalo; stir frequently on high heat until meat is well browned and crumbly, about 10 minutes.

Return onion mixture to pan along with tomatillos and juice (break up tomatillos with spoon); stir to free browned bits. Add hominy, corn, cilantro, oregano, and red chilies; bring to a boil. Cover and simmer for about 15 minutes, stirring occasionally, to blend flavors. If made ahead, let cool, cover, and chill up to overnight; stir over medium heat until hot. Spoon out and discard hot chilies. Makes 6 servings.

# Start with Three Dozen Steamers

THESE NO-FUSS ONE-BOWL ENTRÉES each begin with about three dozen steamer clams. The clams, steamed in flavorful broths, enhance the liquids as they simmer. To make a meal, just team any of the three soups with crusty bread to dunk into the seasoned juices and a simple salad.

Use clams suitable for steaming—such as littlenecks or Manilas from the Pacific, little necks or cherrystones from the Atlantic. Scrub them well, then add to the broth of your choice.

Spicy linguisa sausage seasons the soup speckled with tiny pasta and red bell pepper. A second version is subtly imbued with orange juice, fennel seed, and sautéed leeks. In the third, a light ginger-infused broth with a zesty undertone is finished with bits of garlic, thin ginger shreds, green onion, and crushed dried hot red chilies.

## STEAMED CLAMS WITH LINGUISA & PASTA

- 2 tablespoons salad oil
- ⅓ pound linguisa sausage, cut into ¼-inch-thick slices
- 1 medium-size onion, chopped
- 1 large red bell pepper, stemmed, seeded, and diced
- 3 cups water
- 1½ cups regular-strength chicken broth
- ¾ cup dry white wine
- ¼ cup rice-shaped pasta, or other tiny pasta
- ½ teaspoon dry basil
- 32 to 36 clams suitable for steaming, well scrubbed
  Minced parsley (optional)

In a 5- to 6-quart pan, combine oil and sausage; stir over medium-high heat until lightly browned. Add onion and pepper; stir until onion is limp. Add water, broth, wine, pasta, and basil. Cover and simmer until pasta is tender to bite, about 10 minutes.

Skim off and discard all fat. Add clams. Cover and bring to boiling, then reduce heat and simmer until clams open, 5 to 7 minutes.

With a large spoon, lift out clams and distribute equally in 4 wide, shallow bowls. Pour broth over clams. Sprinkle each bowl lightly with minced parsley. Makes 4 servings.

## STEAMED CLAMS IN ORANGE-LEEK BROTH

- 3 large leeks (about 1 lb. total)
- 2 tablespoons butter or margarine
- 2 strips orange peel (orange part only, ½ by 3 in. each)
- 1 cup orange juice
- 1 can (14 oz.) pear-shaped tomatoes
- 1½ cups regular-strength chicken broth
- 1½ cups water
- ½ teaspoon fennel seed, crushed
- 32 to 36 clams suitable for steaming, well scrubbed
  Orange slices (optional)

Trim roots and tops off leeks; reserve a few tender sections of the green tops for garnish, if desired, and discard remainder. Split leeks in half lengthwise and rinse well between layers; also rinse reserved tops. Thinly slice leeks crosswise.

In a 5- to 6-quart pan, combine butter and leeks. Stir often over medium heat until leeks are limp, about 7 minutes. Add orange peel, orange juice, juices drained from tomatoes, chicken broth, water, and fennel. Dice the tomatoes and add them to the pan. Bring to a boil; cover and simmer over low heat 10 minutes.

Add clams. Cover and bring to boiling; reduce heat and simmer until clams open, 5 to 7 minutes.

With a large spoon, lift out clams and place equally in 4 wide, shallow bowls. Pour broth over clams. Garnish each bowl with an orange slice and leek top, if desired. Makes 4 servings.

## STEAMED CLAMS IN GINGER BROTH

- 2½ cups regular-strength chicken broth
- 2½ cups water
- 8 thin slices fresh ginger (each about the size of a quarter)
- 1 small dried hot red chili
- 1 medium-size cucumber
- 32 to 36 clams suitable for steaming, well scrubbed
- 2 tablespoons salad oil
- 1 tablespoon minced garlic
- 2 tablespoons slivered fresh ginger
- ¼ cup thinly sliced green onions
- ¼ to ½ teaspoon crushed dried hot red chilies (optional)
- 2 limes, cut in halves

In a 5- to 6-quart pan, combine broth, water, ginger slices, and whole chili. Cover and simmer 15 minutes. Peel cucumber and cut in half lengthwise. Scrape out and discard seeds. Cut cucumber crosswise into ¼-inch-thick slices.

Add cucumbers and clams to broth. Cover and bring to boiling over high heat. Reduce heat and simmer until clams pop open, 5 to 7 minutes.

While clams steam, put oil and garlic in a 6- to 7-inch frying pan over medium-low heat and stir just until golden. Remove from heat; stir in ginger slivers, onion, and crushed chilies.

Lift out clams and cucumbers and distribute equally in 4 wide, shallow bowls. Discard ginger slices and whole chili. Pour hot broth over clams. Spoon seasoned oil mixture into each bowl of soup. Offer lime to squeeze over each serving. Makes 4 servings.

*Orange and leeks add a light fresh fragrance to clams in broth.*

*Spoon ginger, green onions, and garlic into soup with steamed clams and cucumber.*

# Chewy-Gooey Brownies

IN AN UNSCIENTIFIC POLL, *people who declared a fondness for brownies also clearly indicated that they liked them chewy-gooey. Chocolate led as the most popular flavor, but votes were divided as to the kind of chocolate used—and, indeed, is chocolate the only choice?*

*Defining the perfect brownie is obviously a subjective proposition. Rather than enter a no-win fray with our own opinion, we offer you six very different chewy-gooey brownies.*

## DARK CHOCOLATE CHEWY BROWNIES

- ½ cup (¼ lb.) butter or margarine, cut into chunks
- 3 ounces unsweetened chocolate
- 1⅓ cups sugar
- 2 large eggs
- 1 teaspoon vanilla
- ½ cup all-purpose flour
- ½ cup of one of the following optional choices: chopped walnuts or almonds, chopped semisweet or white chocolate, or semisweet or white chocolate baking bits
  Fudge sauce (recipe follows), optional

In a 2- to 3-quart pan over low heat, combine butter and unsweetened chocolate; when ingredients begin to soften, stir until melted and blended. Remove from heat; add sugar, eggs, and vanilla and mix well. Add flour and mix well.

Butter an 8-inch square or round baking pan. Scrape batter into pan and spread evenly; sprinkle with nuts. Bake in a 350° oven until brownie feels firm at edges and springs back in center when gently pressed, about 25 minutes. Let cool in pan on rack. To frost, pour fudge sauce over brownie and spread evenly. Serve, or cover and store at room temperature up to 2 days. Cut into 6 or 9 squares or wedges. Makes 6 or 9 servings.

**Fudge sauce.** In a 1- to 2-quart pan over low heat, combine ⅓ cup **whipping cream** and 1 cup (6 oz.) chopped **semisweet chocolate** or semisweet chocolate baking bits; stir until chocolate is melted. Stir in 1 teaspoon **vanilla** or 2 tablespoons mint-flavored liqueur or rum.

Use warm as a sauce. To frost brownies (preceding), let sauce cool until thick enough to spread, about 1 hour. Makes about ¾ cup.

## ROCKY ROAD BROWNIES

Make **Dark Chocolate Chewy Brownies,** preceding, stirring 1 cup **miniature marshmallows** into batter. Sprinkle batter with ½ cup chopped **walnuts.**

## BUTTERSCOTCH-PECAN BROWNIES

Make **Dark Chocolate Chewy Brownies,** preceding, but omit granulated sugar and use 1⅓ cups firmly packed **brown sugar;** omit unsweetened chocolate and increase **all-purpose flour** to 1 cup. Sprinkle batter with ½ cup **pecan halves.** Bake about 40 minutes.

## PEANUT BUTTER BROWNIES

Make **Dark Chocolate Chewy Brownies,** preceding, but reduce **butter** or margarine to 5 tablespoons and omit unsweetened chocolate; instead, stir ¾ cup **peanut butter** into melted butter. Reduce **sugar** to 1 cup and add ¼ teaspoon **baking powder.**

## MILK CHOCOLATE BROWNIES

Make **Dark Chocolate Chewy Brownies,** preceding, but decrease **sugar** to ¾ cup. Omit unsweetened chocolate and use ⅔ cup (4 oz.) chopped **milk chocolate** or milk chocolate baking bits. Increase **all-purpose flour** to ¾ cup. Bake about 30 minutes.

## WHITE CHOCOLATE BROWNIES

Make **Dark Chocolate Chewy Brownies,** preceding, but decrease **butter** or margarine to 6 tablespoons. Omit unsweetened chocolate; instead, use 1⅓ cups (½ lb.) chopped **white chocolate** or white chocolate baking bits and, off the heat, stir 1 cup of the chocolate into melted butter. Decrease **sugar** to ½ cup and increase **vanilla** to 1½ teaspoons. Sprinkle batter with remaining white chocolate and, if desired, ⅓ cup chopped **toffee candy.** Bake about 40 minutes.

*Fudge sauce meanders down ice cream to chewy brownie for super sundae.*

## ULTIMATE BROWNIE SUNDAE

- Your choice brownie (recipes preceding)
- 1½ pints vanilla ice cream, or other favorite flavor
- Fudge sauce, warm (recipe precedes, or use ¾ cup purchased sauce)

Cut brownie into 6 equal pieces. Set each piece on a dessert plate and top with a ½-cup-size scoop of ice cream. Ladle fudge sauce onto ice cream. Makes 6 servings.

# Making Steamed Milk

**H**OT AND FOAMY, *steamed milk by itself or with flavorings makes a warm, soothing drink. Using a steamer—such as the one on some espresso makers—you can create frothy concoctions quickly.*

*Sold at cookware, coffee, and department stores, steamers range from simple cork-and-tube assemblies (about $6) to espresso machines (from $75) with steam tubes. All work about the same way.*

*Steam under pressure can be dangerous, so you must operate the machines as directed. Do not leave them untended unless they have automatic thermostats. Sealed units should be equipped with a safety device that will release pressure if the temperature gets too hot.*

## STEAMED MILK

Fill compartment of steamer or espresso machine with recommended amount of water; close steam tube (see units 2, 3, and 4, below). Or fill a lidless teakettle about half full and insert cork-and-tube steamer (unit 1, below). Heat water over direct heat or turn on heating element. As water boils, steam pressure builds up (unit 1, in teakettle, is always open).

Fill a deep, narrow heat-resistant cup or pan halfway with **milk**. Push tip of steam tube about halfway down into milk (exception: the cork-tube steamer has side vents that should be held at the surface to create froth). Open valve to let steam flow through tube into milk until milk is hot, about 1 minute for 1 cup milk—the cup or pan will feel hot. To

*Steam forced into milk comes through tube that penetrates a cork; the cork plugs spout of a lidless teakettle (the kind that whistles when water boils).*

create foam, bring tip of spout just to surface of milk and hold until milk is frothy. Serve to sip or add to coffee.

**Liqueur-flavored steamed milk.** Steam 1 cup **milk** as directed, preceding. Add to it 1 to 1½ tablespoons **almond-, coffee-, or hazelnut-flavored liqueur.** Serves 1.

**Mocha steamed milk.** Steam 1 cup **milk** as directed, preceding. Add 1½ to 2 tablespoons **chocolate-flavored drink powder** or syrup, 1½ tablespoons **coffee-flavored liqueur** (optional), and 1 teaspoon **instant coffee powder** or granules. Serves 1.

*Simple to elaborate, steamer choices include (1) a cork-and-tube assembly for a whistling teakettle, about $6; (2) a stovetop steamer, $20 to $40; (3) an electric espresso maker with steam tube attachment, about $300; (4) a stovetop espresso maker with steam tube, $75 to $125.*

# More May Recipes

OTHER MAY RECIPES *included a rich, puréed vegetable soup, a colorful mussel and potato salad, and a handsome leg of lamb garnished with glazed oranges and fresh mint. Three make-ahead desserts round out the collection: a spicy marinated berry compote to ladle over ice cream, dessert tostadas topped with lemon cream, and a dense and creamy cheesecake with a chocolate cooky crust.*

## GOLDEN GARDEN SOUP

*Smooth and rich tasting, this soup is thickened by vegetables puréed with their cooking broth; buttermilk adds tang but a minimum of calories. Enjoy warm or cool, perhaps with toasted onion bread and low-fat string cheese torn into thin strands.*

- 1 large onion, chopped
- 2 tablespoons salad oil
- 2 medium-size ripe Roma-type tomatoes, cored and chopped
- 1½ pounds (about 5 medium-size) yellow crookneck squash
- 3 cups regular-strength chicken broth
- 1 cup buttermilk
- ¼ cup loosely packed fresh basil leaves, minced
  Basil sprig
- 1 or 2 tomato slices (optional)

In a 4- to 5-quart pan on medium heat, cook onion in oil until golden, about 10 minutes; stir onion frequently. Add chopped tomatoes and stir often until tomatoes are soft and fall apart, about 5 minutes longer.

Trim ends off squash. Chop squash and add to the pan with the chicken broth. Bring mixture to a boil on high heat; cover and simmer until squash is very tender when pierced, about 15 minutes.

In a blender, whirl vegetable mixture with buttermilk until smoothly puréed. Stir in minced basil. Serve warm or cold. To serve cold, cover and chill up to 1 day.

Pour soup into a tureen and garnish with basil sprig and tomato slices. Makes 4 light entrée or 8 first-course servings. —*Mickey Strang, China Lake, Calif.*

*Nestled in ice, serving bowl of puréed vegetable soup stays chilled on a buffet.*

## MUSSEL & POTATO SALAD

*Tender steamed mussels turn this light potato salad into a fine luncheon main dish. You can prepare it a day ahead.*

- 1½ pounds (1½ in. wide or less) red thin-skinned potatoes, scrubbed
  Water
  Basil vinaigrette (recipe follows)
- 2 pounds mussels in shells, scrubbed and beards pulled off
- 1 jar (7 oz.) roasted red peppers, drained and cut in ¼-inch strips
  Fresh basil leaves

Place potatoes in a 3- to 4-quart pan; add enough water to cover potatoes by 1 inch. Bring water to boiling. Cover, then simmer until potatoes are tender when pierced, about 25 minutes; drain. Cut warm potatoes in half, put in a large bowl, and mix with basil vinaigrette; let stand.

While potatoes cook, place mussels in a 10- to 12-inch frying pan. Add about ¼ inch water. Cover and bring to a boil on high heat; reduce heat to low and cook until mussels open, about 5 minutes. When cool enough to touch, remove mussels from shells and add to potatoes; discard shells and any mussels that don't open. Save liquid for other uses like soups.

Add peppers to potatoes and mussels, mixing gently; cover and chill until cool, at least 30 minutes or up to overnight. Pour salad onto a platter and garnish with basil leaves. Makes 5 or 6 servings.

**Basil vinaigrette.** In a bowl, combine ⅓ cup **seasoned rice vinegar** (or ⅓ cup white wine vinegar and 1 teaspoon sugar), ⅓ cup finely chopped **fresh basil leaves,** 2 tablespoons **olive** or salad **oil,** 1 tablespoon **Dijon mustard,** 1 clove **garlic** (pressed or minced), and ½ teaspoon **pepper.**

*Steamed mussels, boiled potatoes; mix both with red peppers and basil for a cool salad.*

## ORANGE-GLAZED LAMB WITH MINT

*The impact of fresh oranges adds a new twist to the traditional partnership of lamb and mint.*

*To begin, you poach whole unpeeled oranges, then cut them into wedges and simmer in an orange syrup; both fruit and peel are good to eat. The syrup makes a glaze for the lamb and caramelizes the oranges as they bake with potatoes.*

*Mint enters the picture when you add it to the roast drippings along with vinegar, broth, and any extra orange glaze. This makes the thin but flavorful sauce that goes with the lamb, oranges, and potatoes.*

*(Continued on next page)*

## ...ORANGE-GLAZED LAMB WITH MINT

1 leg of lamb (about 5½ lb.)
2 cloves garlic, cut into thin slivers
6 medium-size (about 2 lb.) thin-skinned potatoes
Poached oranges (recipe follows)
½ cup red wine vinegar
½ cup regular-strength beef broth
¼ cup chopped fresh mint
Fresh mint sprigs
Salt and pepper

Trim and discard excess surface fat on leg of lamb. Rinse leg and pat dry. With a thin-bladed knife, pierce 1-inch slits 2 inches apart around the entire leg; push a garlic sliver into each slit. Place leg, fattiest side up, in a V-shaped rack in a 12- by 17-inch roasting pan.

Scrub potatoes and pierce each in several places with the thin-bladed knife; arrange in pan around rack. Bake the lamb and potatoes, uncovered, in a 325° oven until meat thermometer inserted in thickest part of leg (not against bone)

Carve orange-glazed lamb to serve with potatoes and baked glazed orange wedges; mint-orange sauce goes with everything.

registers 140° for rare or 150° for medium, and potatoes give readily when pressed, 1¾ to 2 hours.

About 30 minutes before lamb is done, push potatoes to one side of pan and spoon poached oranges into the open space. Baste leg and fruit with about ⅓ of the syrup from the poached oranges. Continue to bake, basting meat and fruit with syrup about every 10 minutes, until lamb is cooked to the desired temperature.

Place lamb on a platter and potatoes and oranges in another dish; keep all the foods warm while finishing the sauce.

Set roasting pan on high heat and add vinegar, broth, and remaining orange syrup; scrape browned bits free. Boil rapidly until reduced to 1 cup, 5 to 8 minutes. Drain any juices from lamb platter into the roasting pan. Remove pan from heat; stir chopped mint into sauce.

To serve, surround lamb with potatoes and oranges; garnish with mint sprigs. Pour sauce into a pitcher or bowl to ladle onto individual servings of sliced lamb, potatoes, and oranges; add salt and pepper to taste. Makes 5 or 6 servings. — *Helen Hall, Port Angeles, Wash.*

**Poached oranges.** Put 4 medium-size **oranges** in a 4- to 5-quart pan and cover with **water;** bring to boiling on high heat. Cover and simmer until oranges are soft when pressed, about 15 minutes; drain and let cool. Cut each orange in half, then each half into 4 triangular wedges.

In the same pan, combine 1 can (6 oz.) **frozen orange juice concentrate,** ½ cup **sugar,** and ½ cup **water.** Bring to a boil on high heat, stirring.

Add orange pieces to pan. Cook, uncovered, on medium-high heat, stirring occasionally, until approximately ⅓ cup syrup is left, about 20 minutes. Lift oranges from pan with a slotted spoon and drain; set aside, leaving syrup in pan. If made ahead, cover and chill up to overnight; warm syrup to use.

## HERBAL WINE BERRY COMPOTE

*Herbs and spices impart interesting flavor complexities to this red wine and orange juice marinade for berries.*

*Make the mellow-flavored marinade ahead, if you like; reheat and add strawberries. Spoon over ice cream.*

Spoon strawberries steeped in herbal wine syrup over ice cream for dessert.

2 or 3 large oranges
1 cup dry red wine
½ cup sugar
½ cup lightly packed fresh mint leaves
1 bay leaf
1 cinnamon stick (3 in. long)
½ teaspoon black peppercorns
3 cups strawberries, rinsed, drained, hulled, and cut in half
3 to 4 cups vanilla ice cream

With a vegetable peeler, pare 3 thin strips peel (½ by 4 in., orange part only) from 1 orange. Ream enough juice from oranges to make 1 cup. In a 3- to 4-quart pan, combine orange peel, orange juice, wine, sugar, mint, bay leaf, cinnamon, and pepper. Bring to boiling over high heat, stirring until sugar dissolves, then reduce heat to medium-low and simmer, uncovered, until reduced to 1 cup, 20 to 30 minutes. Pour syrup through a fine strainer set over a bowl. Discard spices. (If made ahead, cool, cover, and chill up to 2 weeks; to proceed, reheat to simmering.)

Stir strawberries into hot syrup. Let stand at least 30 minutes; or cool, cover, and chill up to 2 hours. In each of 4 to 6 bowls or glasses, place an equal portion of ice cream. Ladle berry mixture over each serving. Makes 4 to 6 servings. — *Hervé Lebiavant, San Francisco.*

## DESSERT TOSTADA WITH LEMON CREAM

*Crisp and flaky flour tortillas double as serving containers and spoons in this dessert tostada. First fry tortillas, sinking them in hot oil with a ladle to shape and crisp them; you can do this well ahead.*

*Fill the tortilla bowls with lemon cream (also made ahead)—or your favorite ice cream and sauce—then crack off chunks of the bowl to scoop up filling.*

> Salad oil
> 6 flour tortillas (7- to 8-in. diameter)
> ¾ cup whipping cream
> 1 cup lemon curd (recipe follows) or purchased curd (11-oz. jar)
> 3 tablespoons semisweet chocolate curls or grated semisweet chocolate
> 12 to 18 medium-size perfect strawberries, rinsed

In a deep 3- to 4-quart pan, heat 1½ inches salad oil to 375° on a thermometer. Float 1 tortilla on top of the oil. With the bowl of a metal ladle, press down on the center of the tortilla until it touches the bottom of the pan and oil bubbles up around tortilla edges.

Hold tortilla down until it is a golden brown, about 2 minutes; tip ladle from side to side to tilt tortilla so edges brown evenly. Lift tortilla from oil with tongs or a slotted spoon, draining over pan.

Let tortillas cool and drain on paper towels. Repeat to cook remaining tortillas. If made ahead, cover airtight and hold up to overnight.

In a small bowl, beat whipping cream until it holds soft peaks. In another bowl, stir lemon curd with a spoon until smooth; fold into whipped cream. Use, or cover and chill up to overnight.

Set tortillas on dessert plates; spoon about ⅓ cup of the lemon-cream mixture into each. Sprinkle with chocolate and garnish with strawberries. As you eat, break off chunks of the tortilla to scoop through filling. Makes 6 servings.

**Lemon curd.** In the top of a double boiler, melt ¼ cup (⅛ lb.) **butter** or margarine. Add ½ teaspoon grated **lemon peel**, ¼ cup **lemon juice**, ¾ cup **sugar**, and 2 **large eggs;** whisk until blended. Cook over simmering water, stirring, until thickened and smooth, about 20 minutes. Let cool, cover, and chill until cold, at least 2 hours or up to 2 weeks. Makes 1 cup.

## CHOCOLATE COOKY CHEESECAKE

*A dense and creamy New York-style cheesecake loaded with popular chocolate sandwich cookies seems a teen-ager's dream come true. If the batter is thin (as a result of being made in a food processor), cookies float up to make a bumpy-looking top. A thicker batter (made with an electric mixer) holds the cookies in the middle.*

> 1 package (1¼ lb.) chocolate sandwich cookies
> ⅓ cup butter or margarine, melted
> 4 packages (8 oz. each) cream cheese, cut into chunks
> 1 cup sugar
> ⅓ cup whipping cream
> 6 large eggs
> 2 tablespoons all-purpose flour
> 2 teaspoons vanilla

In a food processor, whirl ½ package of the cookies, including filling, until they form fine crumbs (or place cookies in a paper or plastic bag and crush with a rolling pin); mix in butter. Scoop crumbs into a 9-inch cheesecake pan with removable bottom and press crumbs evenly over bottom of pan and about ½ inch up sides. Chill crust to firm, about 20 minutes.

In a food processor or bowl of an electric mixer, whirl or beat cream cheese, sugar, and whipping cream at medium speed until smooth. Add eggs, flour, and vanilla; whirl or beat again to blend.

Pour ½ of the cream cheese mixture over the chilled crust. Break remaining cookies in half and scatter over mixture, using all of them. Pour remaining mixture over cookies. (If you whirl cream cheese mixture in a food processor, filling will be thin enough to allow cookies to float to the top during baking. If prepared in the electric mixer, filling will keep cookies in place.)

Bake the cake in a 300° oven until cheesecake is golden on top and jiggles only slightly in center when gently shaken, about 1 hour and 20 minutes.

Take cake from oven and let cool on a rack. Cover and chill until cold, at least 4 hours or up to overnight. Before serving, run a knife between cake and pan sides; remove rim. Cut cheesecake into slender wedges to serve. Makes 12 to 16 servings. —*Nicole Perzik, Saratoga, Calif.*

*Break up filled tostada, bite by bite, using tortilla chunks as spoons for lemon cream.*

## CURRY-YOGURT-SHRIMP DIP

    1   small zucchini, shredded
        About 1 teaspoon salt
    1   cup unflavored yogurt
    ½   teaspoon curry powder
    ¼   cup thinly sliced green onions
    ½   pound tiny cooked, shelled shrimp
    ¼   cup chopped fresh cilantro
        (coriander)
        Cayenne
        About 2 pounds trimmed raw vege-
        tables: choose one or more—celery
        sticks, cucumber or zucchini slices,
        bell pepper strips

In a bowl, mix shredded zucchini with 1 teaspoon salt. Let stand until zucchini is limp and water comes out of it, 20 to 30 minutes. Rinse and drain, squeezing as much liquid as possible out of zucchini.

Rinse and dry the bowl. In it gently mix together zucchini, yogurt, curry powder, green onions, shrimp, and cilantro; add salt and cayenne to taste. Pour mixture into a small bowl. Sprinkle top with cayenne, if desired. Offer raw vegetables alongside to scoop up the yogurt mixture. Makes 2⅓ cups, about 8 appetizer servings.—*Paula Tuerk, Los Altos, Calif.*

*Make this light yogurt dip just before serving; it gets runny as it stands.*

## BRAN-WHEAT REFRIGERATOR MUFFINS

    2   large shredded-wheat biscuits
    1½  cups boiling water
    1   cup (½ lb.) butter or margarine
    1½  cups sugar
    3   large eggs
    1   tablespoon baking soda
    3½  cups all-purpose flour
    1½  cups buttermilk
    2½  cups whole bran cereal
    1   teaspoon salt, or to taste

Place shredded wheat in a bowl. Pour boiling water over wheat and let stand until cool, about 15 minutes.

Meanwhile, in large bowl, beat butter and sugar with an electric mixer at medium-high speed until creamy. Beat in eggs, 1 at a time. Beat in wheat and water mixture. Add soda and flour; beat until blended. Mix in buttermilk, then stir in bran and salt. If made ahead, store in an airtight container in the refrigerator up to 1 month.

To bake, fill greased or paper-lined muffin cups (about 2½-in. size) to the top with batter. Bake in a 400° oven until tops are browned and a wooden pick inserted in a muffin's center comes out clean, 20 to 25 minutes. Turn out of pans onto racks. Serve warm or cool. Makes about 2½ dozen.—*Julie Hack, Yes Bay, Alaska.*

*Bran-wheat batter waits in refrigerator, ready to use for fresh-baked muffins.*

## ROAST LAMB WITH CHILI RICE

    1   leg of lamb, 5 to 5½ pounds
    3   tablespoons olive oil
    1½  teaspoons cumin seed
    1½  cups thinly sliced green onion
    1   cup long-grain white rice
    2   large carrots, peeled and diced
    2   large thin-skinned potatoes (about
        1 lb.), peeled and diced
    1   or 2 jalapeño chilies, stemmed,
        seeded, and minced
    3   cups regular-strength chicken
        broth

Rub lamb with 1 tablespoon oil and 1 teaspoon cumin. Set lamb on a rack in a 12- by 14-inch roasting pan. Roast in a 350° oven until thermometer inserted in center of thickest part registers 140°, about 1½ hours.

About 30 minutes before lamb is done, combine in a 5- to 6-quart pan 2 tablespoons oil, green onion, and rice. Stir over medium-high heat until onion is soft. Stir in ½ teaspoon cumin, carrots, potatoes, chilies to taste, and broth. Bring to boiling. Reduce heat to low, cover, and simmer until potatoes are tender when pierced, 25 to 30 minutes.

Transfer lamb to a platter. Discard fat from juices; stir juices into rice and serve with lamb. Makes 6 to 8 servings.— *Monia Ibarra, Eugene, Ore.*

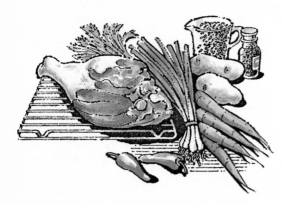

*As lamb roasts, cook rice-and-vegetable pilaf spiced with hot chili and cumin.*

## GRILLED ORANGE-CORIANDER STEAKS

1 teaspoon grated orange peel
¾ cup orange juice
1 small onion, chopped
3 cloves garlic, pressed or minced
¼ cup white wine vinegar
1½ tablespoons ground coriander
1 teaspoon cracked black pepper
1 teaspoon dry basil leaves
4 tender beefsteaks such as New York strip or loin (each about 8 oz. and about 1 in. thick)
Watercress sprigs
Salt

Mix orange peel, juice, onion, garlic, vinegar, coriander, pepper, and basil.

Cover and chill ½ cup of the mixture until serving. In a 9- by 13-inch pan, coat steaks with remaining marinade. Cover and chill, turning meat once, 4 hours or up to overnight.

Lift steaks from marinade and place on a grill, 4 inches from heat, over a solid bed of hot coals (you can hold your hand at grill level for only 2 to 3 seconds). Cook, turning once, until browned on outside and pink inside (cut to test), 14 to 18 minutes total. Place steaks on warm plates. Garnish with watercress. Offer reserved marinade to spoon over each piece. Sprinkle with salt to taste. Makes 4 servings. —*Kazuko Nakane, Seattle.*

*Marinate beefsteaks in orange juice, pepper, coriander, and onion mixture.*

## GREEN BEAN & JICAMA SALAD

⅔ cup thinly slivered red onion
Water
5 tablespoons white wine vinegar
¾ pound green beans, ends trimmed
1 pound jicama, peeled
⅓ cup olive oil or salad oil
2 teaspoons Dijon mustard
Salt and pepper

Place onion in 1½ cups cold water mixed with 2 tablespoons vinegar; let stand 20 to 30 minutes.

Pull beans through a French bean cutter, or cut them with a knife into thin julienne strips. Set beans on a rack above ½ inch boiling water in a 5- to 6-quart pan. Cover and steam over high heat just until beans are tender-crisp to bite, 3 to 4 minutes. Immerse in ice water. When cool, drain. Cut jicama into thin matchstick-size strips.

In a large bowl, whisk together 3 tablespoons vinegar, oil, and mustard. Drain onions. Add onions, beans, and jicama to dressing. Mix to coat vegetables. Add salt and pepper to taste. Serve at once, or cover and chill up to 2 hours. Makes 7 cups, 6 to 8 servings. —*Annette Burden, Santa Barbara, Calif.*

*Mix French-cut beans with slivered jicama, onion, and mustard vinaigrette.*

## OAT-NUT CHOCOLATE CHIP CRISPS

1 cup (½ lb.) butter or margarine
¾ cup firmly packed brown sugar
½ cup granulated sugar
2 large eggs
1 teaspoon vanilla
1 teaspoon baking soda
1¾ cup all-purpose flour
2 cups rolled oats
1 cup finely chopped nuts
1 cup (6 oz.) miniature semisweet chocolate baking bits

In large bowl of an electric mixer, beat butter and brown and granulated sugars until creamy. Beat in eggs, 1 at a time, until blended. Beat in vanilla, baking soda, and flour. Stir in oats, nuts, and chocolate bits until well blended. Drop rounded tablespoons of dough onto greased 12- by 15-inch baking sheets, spacing them about 2 inches apart.

Bake in a 375° oven until golden, 12 to 14 minutes; switch pan positions halfway through if baking more than 1 panful at a time. Cool cookies on pans about 2 minutes, then transfer to racks to cool. Serve warm or cool. Store airtight at room temperature up to 2 days; freeze for longer storage. Makes about 4½ dozen. —*Betty Jane Morrison, Lakewood, Colorado.*

*Rolled oats and chopped nuts add texture to these drop cookies.*

**T**HE WATER-SMOKER *hereinafter referred to is not a hookah or hubble-bubble—that Oriental device for filtering and cooling smoke, made famous by B-movies based on* Arabian Nights *fables and by Alice's supercilious Wonderland caterpillar.*

*It is, instead, a complicated-sounding cooking instrument that moderates the heat and heightens the humidity of the smoke that does the cooking. (We showed them in the August 1983* Sunset.)

*You'll need such a smoker to produce Sheldon Jacobs' succulent, aromatic lamb shanks—which require long, slow cooking. Are the results worth the time and trouble? Chef Jacobs thinks they are—and so is just about every other critter he has smoke-cooked this way. In fact, he is so enamored with the technique that he has invented a commercial-size water-smoker.*

### SMOKED-BRAISED LAMB SHANKS

    6  lamb shanks, about 1 pound each
    ¾  cup salad oil
    ½  cup red wine vinegar
    2  cloves garlic, minced or pressed
    ½  teaspoon coarsely ground pepper
    ¼  teaspoon dry rosemary
    2  or 3 hickory wood chunks, each
       about 2 to 3 inches square
       Water

Place lamb shanks in a large plastic bag. Stir together the oil, vinegar, garlic, pepper, and rosemary. Pour over lamb and seal bag. Refrigerate for at least 1 day or up to 3 days. Turn bag over several times to coat meat evenly with marinade.

Arrange shanks in an 11- by 17-inch pan, pouring marinade over lamb. Cover tightly and bake in a 400° oven for 1½ hours. Remove from oven and uncover pan (meat can cool down).

Also place hickory chunks in a deep bowl and pour in water to cover. Chunks float, so turn them occasionally; let soak at least 45 minutes or up to 3 hours.

If your water-smoker runs on gas or electricity, follow manufacturer's directions.

If its fuel is charcoal briquets, pour 8

pounds of briquets into the fire pan and fit pan into water-smoker. Ignite charcoal; when barely covered with gray ash, about 30 minutes, spread to make level. Lift wood from water and set on coals. Immediately fit water pan in place and add 3 quarts boiling water; add to water any remaining lamb marinade.

Then set cooking rack in place. Pat shanks dry with a paper towel and place slightly apart on rack. Cover the water-smoker; if there are dampers, open them. If temperature gauge on smoker goes above 200° (or medium), close dampers slightly (or remove a few hot coals) to slow rate of cooking. Water-smoke shanks until meat pulls easily from bones, 3 to 3½ hours. Check water

*"Chef Jacobs is so enamored with smoke-cooking that he has invented a commercial-size water-smoker."*

pan after 3 hours; if it is going dry, refill by pouring boiling water through racks (not on meat) into pan.

Serve the shanks hot or at room temperature. Makes 6 servings.

*Shelly Jacobs*

*San Francisco, Calif.*

**M**ICHAEL GALASSO *does not explain why he calls his brunch specialty* Haitian French Toast; *a reasonable hunch is that tropical French equals Haitian. The tropical element is orange juice, which is added to the cream and eggs in which the bread soaks before frying. (Its presence in the batter need not deter you from having your usual orange juice as an eye-opener.)*

### HAITIAN FRENCH TOAST

    1  long loaf (1 lb.) French bread
    1  cup orange juice
    ½  cup whipping cream
    2  large eggs
    1  teaspoon ground cinnamon
    ¼  cup granulated sugar
       Dash of ground nutmeg
    3  tablespoons butter or margarine
       Powdered sugar
       Maple syrup (optional)

Cut loaf ends from bread and reserve for other uses. Cut remaining loaf crosswise into 1½-inch-thick slices and let stand, uncovered, 4 hours to overnight.

In 9- by 13-inch pan, combine orange juice, cream, eggs, cinnamon, granulated sugar, and nutmeg. With a wire whip, whisk until well blended.

Lay bread in pan. Turn several times until all the liquid is absorbed, 3 to 5 minutes. Melt butter in a 12- to 14-inch frying pan over medium heat. Put soaked bread into the frying pan. Cook, turning as needed, until slices are richly browned on both sides, about 5 minutes.

Liberally dust the toast with powdered sugar. Offer maple syrup to add to taste. Makes 4 to 8 servings.

*Michael Galasso*

*Costa Mesa, Calif.*

CRUNCHY GRANOLA *wasn't a tough but outclassed welterweight from South Philadelphia with a wicked left and a glass jaw. Rather, it was the pemmican of the Sixties—a high-energy, low-cost trail food that could be prepared in bulk, stored indefinitely, and substituted, in case of need, for a balanced diet. Like the American Indian pemmican, granola has many formulations which depend on the availability of materials and the taste of the cook. Unlike pemmican, which was usually bound together with bear or deer fat, Eric Lie's Washington Granola—using cinnamon, honey, and nuts—tastes so good that you can easily forget how healthy it is.*

stir to mix well. Spread evenly in 2 baking pans, each about 10 by 15 inches. Bake, uncovered, in a 250° oven, until mixture looks and smells richly toasted, about 2¼ hours; stir 3 or 4 times as the granola bakes.

Let granola cool completely. Store airtight up to 2 weeks. Serve with milk or munch plain. Makes 15 to 16 cups.

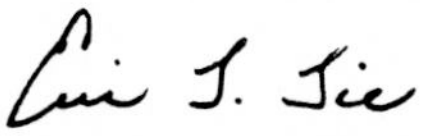

*Eric T. Lie*

Edmonds, Wash.

"His brisket is a decisively flavored pot roast that can be a whole meal or a centerpiece."

NEW MEXICAN BEEF BRISKET *is an accurate name for Jeffrey Clark's creation, but calling it that is about as descriptive as calling Beethoven's Ninth a tune. His brisket is a decisively flavored pot roast that, with garnishes, can be a whole meal or the centerpiece of a Mexican feast.*

*The meat roasts sealed in a bag with seasonings for 5 hours, followed by another hour with a mellow chili purée.*

## New Mexican Beef Brisket

<table>
<tr><td>2</td><td>teaspoons celery salt</td></tr>
<tr><td>4</td><td>cloves garlic, minced or pressed</td></tr>
<tr><td>2</td><td>teaspoons coarsely ground pepper</td></tr>
<tr><td>1</td><td>teaspoon liquid smoke</td></tr>
<tr><td>⅓</td><td>cup Worcestershire</td></tr>
<tr><td>1</td><td>piece beef brisket, 3½ to 4 pounds, trimmed of excess fat</td></tr>
<tr><td>4</td><td>ounces dried red New Mexico or California chilies<br>Water</td></tr>
<tr><td>1</td><td>tablespoon salad oil</td></tr>
<tr><td>2</td><td>tablespoons all-purpose flour</td></tr>
<tr><td>½</td><td>teaspoon each ground cumin and dry oregano leaves</td></tr>
<tr><td>1</td><td>medium-size onion, thinly sliced</td></tr>
<tr><td>10</td><td>to 12 warm flour tortillas (10-in. size)<br>About 6 cups shredded iceberg lettuce<br>About 3 cups (1½ lb.) shredded sharp cheddar cheese</td></tr>
</table>

In a small bowl, stir together celery salt, 2 cloves of the garlic, pepper, liquid smoke, and Worcestershire. Place the meat in a large plastic bag, pour in Worcestershire mixture, and seal the bag. Refrigerate for 24 hours, turning bag over several times.

Remove meat from bag and place on a sheet of heavy foil that is large enough to fold over and completely seal the meat. Pour marinade over meat and seal in the

foil. Set packet in a 10- by 15-inch baking pan. Bake in a 300° oven for 5 hours.

Meanwhile, remove and discard stems and seeds from chilies. Place chilies in a bowl and pour 2 cups boiling water over them. Let soak at least 20 minutes. In a blender, smoothly purée chilies and water.

Place a 1½- to 2-quart pan over medium heat; add oil and stir in flour. Cook, stirring, until flour is lightly browned. Stir in remaining 2 cloves garlic, cumin, and oregano. Remove from heat. Firmly rub purée through a fine strainer into pan; discard residue. Return pan to medium-high heat and stir until boiling.

Remove brisket from oven. Open packet carefully; drain off, cover, and chill drippings. Spread the chili mixture over the meat in the foil and place onion slices on meat. Reseal foil and return to oven; bake until meat is very tender when pierced (test by cutting into meat through foil on top of packet), about 1 hour longer.

Open packet carefully. Lift out brisket and put on a platter; cut across the grain into ¼-inch-thick slices; keep warm. Pour chili sauce into the 1½-quart pan. Lift or skim and discard fat from reserved drippings. Add drippings to chili sauce and bring to boil. To eat, spoon some of the meat into a warm tortilla; add chili sauce, lettuce, and cheese; fold to enclose; and hold over a plate as you eat (it will drip). Or just spoon chili sauce onto portions of meat. Makes 10 to 12 servings.

*Jeffrey Clark*

Denver

"A tough but outclassed welterweight from South Philadelphia."

## Washington Granola

<table>
<tr><td>5</td><td>cups regular rolled oats</td></tr>
<tr><td>1⅓</td><td>cups nonfat dry milk</td></tr>
<tr><td>1</td><td>cup sweetened, shredded coconut</td></tr>
<tr><td>1</td><td>cup soy flour</td></tr>
<tr><td>1</td><td>cup untoasted or lightly toasted wheat germ</td></tr>
<tr><td>1</td><td>cup bran cereal</td></tr>
<tr><td>1</td><td>cup chopped walnuts</td></tr>
<tr><td>1</td><td>cup sesame seed</td></tr>
<tr><td>1</td><td>cup unsalted sunflower seeds</td></tr>
<tr><td>1</td><td>cup unsalted pumpkin seeds</td></tr>
<tr><td>½</td><td>cup salad oil</td></tr>
<tr><td>½</td><td>cup soy oil (or ½ cup more salad oil)</td></tr>
<tr><td>1</td><td>cup honey</td></tr>
<tr><td>2</td><td>teaspoons ground cinnamon<br>Milk</td></tr>
</table>

In a large bowl, stir together the rolled oats, dry milk, coconut, soy flour, wheat germ, bran, nuts, sesame seed, sunflower seeds, and pumpkin seeds.

In a small bowl, stir together the salad oil, soy oil, honey, and cinnamon until blended, then pour over the oat mixture;

# May Menus

**W**ARM, COMFORTABLE *May days are signals that summer is fast approaching. You can feel fairly secure about planning a dinner barbecued outdoors.*

*On cooler evenings, you'll be putting the oven to work. One choice is the pasta and chicken dinner.*

*When you want to stay flexible, the brunch menu is easy to transport for indoor or outside dining. And the same menu makes a good supper.*

## SPRING ITALIAN SUPPER

**Roma Tomatoes & Cheese Pasta with Baked Chicken Legs**
**Mixed Green Salad**
**Pineapple Wedges    Powdered Sugar**
**Black Raspberry Liqueur**

*Timing this menu is easy, because the pasta and the chicken come out of the oven at the same time.*

*As the combination main dish cooks, assemble the salad.*

*For dessert, serve sweet, fresh pineapple wedges plain or with powdered sugar; adults might like to spoon a little berry-flavored liqueur onto the fruit.*

## ROMA TOMATOES & CHEESE PASTA WITH BAKED CHICKEN LEGS

- 4 to 6 chicken legs with thighs (about 2½ lb.)
  Water
- ½ pound dry pasta such as small rounds or shells (about 2 cups)
- 1 tablespoon olive or salad oil
- 1 large package (8 oz.) neufchâtel or cream cheese, at room temperature
- ½ cup (¼ lb.) unsalted butter or margarine, at room temperature
- ⅓ cup finely shredded or freshly grated parmesan cheese
- 3 medium-size (about ¾ lb.) firm-ripe Roma-style tomatoes, cored and chopped
- 1 tablespoon chopped fresh basil or 1 teaspoon dry basil
  Basil sprigs, optional
  Salt and pepper

*Diced tomatoes, whipped neufchâtel cheese, and parmesan cheese perch on top of cooked pasta. Heat in oven with baking chicken.*

Arrange chicken legs in a single layer in a shallow pan about 10 by 14 inches. Bake, uncovered, in a 400° oven for 30 minutes.

As chicken bakes, bring 2 quarts water to boiling in a 3- to 4-quart pan. Add pasta; cook, uncovered, over medium-high heat, until pasta is tender to bite, about 9 minutes. Drain and mix with the oil; pour pasta into a shallow 1½- to 2-quart baking dish or pan; set aside.

With an electric mixer or food processor, whip neufchâtel cheese, butter, and ¼ cup parmesan cheese until well mixed. Mound cheese mixture on top center of pasta and scatter tomatoes over the cheese.

When chicken has cooked 30 minutes, put the pasta, uncovered, in the oven with it. Bake until chicken is no longer pink at thigh bone (cut to test) and pasta is hot in center, about 10 minutes. Sprinkle chopped basil and remaining parmesan over pasta; garnish with basil sprigs and serve with chicken. Add salt and pepper to taste. Makes 4 to 6 servings.

## STEAK & VEGETABLE DINNER FROM THE BARBECUE

**Cucumber & Jicama Sticks**
**Horseradish Yogurt**
**Mineral Water with Bitters & Lime**
**Barbecued Flank Steak & Beet Dinner**
**Citrus Sherbet**
**Chocolate Cookies**

*Horseradish-seasoned yogurt sauce plays a double role. While the main course cooks on the grill, munch raw vegetables dipped into the sauce. Then spoon the same sauce over grilled steak and beets.*

*For a refreshing beverage to serve before and during dinner, splash enough bitters to give a hint of pink into glasses of sparkling mineral water with ice; also add a squeeze of lime juice.*

*You can prepare the appetizer vegetables ahead. Peel 1 large cucumber and 1 small (about 1½ lb.) jicama, and cut into finger-size sticks. Cover and chill up to 3 hours.*

*You'll need a covered barbecue to cook the beets, vegetable packet, and bread that all go on the grill with the flank steak. About 2 hours before serving, ignite the briquets. First cook vegetables over indirect heat, then grill steak directly over hot coals and toast bread alongside.*

### HORSERADISH YOGURT

Stir together 2 cups **unflavored yogurt,** ¼ cup minced **green onions,** ½ teaspoon *each* **mustard seed** and **cumin seed,** and 1 to 2 tablespoons **prepared horseradish** (to taste). Cover and chill at least 1 hour, or up to 3 days. Makes about 2½ cups.

## Barbecued Flank Steak & Beet Dinner

6 medium-size beets, scrubbed, with tops trimmed about 1 inch above stem end
**Vegetable packet (directions follow)**
1 flank steak (about 2 lb.)
1 long loaf (1 lb.) French bread, cut diagonally into 1½-inch-thick slices
**Horseradish yogurt (recipe precedes)**
**Salt and pepper**

Ignite about 40 charcoal briquets on fire grate of a barbecue with lid. When coals are coated with gray ash, about 30 minutes, mound all briquets on 1 side of the grate; add 8 briquets to top of mound. Place grill 5 to 6 inches above grate.

Lay beets and vegetable packet on grill but not over coals. Cover barbecue and open dampers. After 30 minutes, add 6 more briquets to the coals. Cook vegetables until beets are very tender when pierced, about 45 minutes total.

Transfer beets to a platter and set aside. Pull open top of vegetable packet and fold foil back to make a deep rimmed container and keep warm on cool area of grill. If vegetables are juicier than you like, slide packet near coals to boil and reduce some of the liquid; stir often. Lay steak directly over the coals (they should be so hot you can hold your hand at grill level for only 2 to 3 seconds).

Lay bread close to, but not directly over, coals; cook, turning often, until lightly toasted, about 5 minutes. Move toasted bread to cooler area of grill to keep warm. Cook meat until well browned but still pink in thickest part (cut to test), 6 to 8 minutes on a side; turn once or twice.

Place meat on platter and let rest about 5 minutes. Meanwhile, cut beets in half. Put vegetable packet on the platter, or leave on cool area of grill and serve from there along with bread. Slice meat across grain into thin, slanting slices; serve with horseradish yogurt, beets (scoop out of peel or cut it away to eat), vegetables from packet, and toast. Add salt and pepper to taste. Makes 4 servings.

**Vegetable packet.** Lay flat a 12- by 30-inch piece of heavy foil. Center on the foil 2 medium-size **onions,** thinly sliced; 1 pound **mushrooms,** washed and sliced; 1 medium-size **yellow** or red **bell**

*(Continued on next page)*

*Grill flank steak to complete meal on barbecue; bread and vegetables cook alongside. Open packet and keep vegetables warm on grill while slicing steak.*

## ...BARBECUED FLANK STEAK & BEET DINNER

**pepper,** stemmed, seeded, and chopped; pour ¼ cup **olive** or salad **oil** over vegetables. Bring cut ends of foil together and make a double fold to seal. Also double-fold each end to seal. Pat packet to level vegetables.

---

## TORTILLA BRUNCH WITH CRUNCH

**Sugar-Cinnamon Crisps**
**Tortilla-Crust Quiche**
**Fresh Strawberries**
**Coffee      Orange Juice**

---

*One package of large flour tortillas (the kind used for burritos) makes both the crust for the quiche and the sugar-cinnamon crisps.*

*Make the crisps first, in successive batches. While guests munch them, assemble quiche with remaining tortilla and bake. Save leftover crisps for snacks.*

## SUGAR-CINNAMON CRISPS

In a 1- to 2-quart pan, melt ½ cup (¼ lb.) **butter** or margarine over low heat. Add ½ cup firmly packed **brown sugar** and 1½ teaspoons **ground cinnamon;** stir until blended.

Brush 1 side of 9 **flour tortillas** (10-in. size) equally with butter-sugar mixture. Set tortillas, sugar side up, on 12- by 15-inch baking sheets, 1 to a pan. Bake tortilla in a 450° oven until puffed and slightly brown, about 5 minutes. Watch closely to avoid scorching. Slide hot tortilla off sheet. Repeat with remaining tortillas. You can bake 1 or 2 pans at a time.

Let tortillas cool at least briefly for topping to harden. Serve whole or break into pieces; pile into a basket. Serve warm or at room temperature. Store leftover crisps airtight at room temperature up to 1 day. Makes 4 to 8 servings.

## TORTILLA-CRUST QUICHE

- 1  flour tortilla (10-in. size)
- 6  ounces bulk pork sausage
- 1  small onion, diced
- 1  clove garlic, minced or pressed
- 1  small can (4 oz.) diced green chilies
- ½  teaspoon ground cumin
- 3  large eggs
- 1  cup sour cream
- 1  cup (4 oz.) shredded cheddar cheese
- ¼  teaspoon liquid hot pepper seasoning
- 1  small ripe avocado, pitted, peeled, sliced, and dipped in lemon juice

Press tortilla into 9-inch pie pan. Place in a 375° oven to crisp tortilla evenly, about 6 minutes; set aside.

In a 10- to 12-inch frying pan, stir sausage, onion, and garlic over medium-high heat until meat is lightly browned. Stir in chilies and cumin; set aside.

In a bowl, beat to blend eggs, ¾ cup sour cream, cheese, and hot pepper seasoning. Stir in meat mixture and pour into tortilla shell. Bake until center jiggles only slightly when gently shaken, about 30 minutes. Lay avocado slices on quiche and spoon remaining sour cream in center. Cut into wedges. Makes 4 or 5 servings. —*Lucille K. Supple, Laguna Beach, Calif.*

# JUNE

*Carnitas (page 138)*

Casual entertaining moved into June's summer spotlight: we suggested a Mexican-inspired fiesta featuring build-your-own carnitas. For other dinner parties, four professional caterers offered a selection of easy, make-ahead entrées. Baby vegetables, fresh from the garden or greengrocer, were presented in two simple but eye-catching recipes suitable for leisurely nibbling. More of June's international inspiration came from Australia: meat pies to enjoy hot or cold.

# Build Your Own Carnitas

CARNITAS AND SPICED BEANS *plus a trio of lively salsas are Mexico's rousing way of serving pork and beans. Here, we feature a convivial party menu well suited to summer weather.*

The meal focuses on the barbecue, but not on barbecued foods. You use the grill only to heat the tortillas and keep pork and beans warm. Guests manage the tortillas, add fillings and salsas, and eat at their own pace.

Greet guests with cool glasses of agua fresca *made with bright watermelon, one of many fruits used as a base for these thirst-quenching Mexican "cool waters." You can serve* agua fresca *during the meal, or offer beer or* agua minerale—*sparkling water with lime on ice.*

For a light and refreshing conclusion to the carnitas fiesta, serve a light meringue dessert. You firm the whipped meringue by baking it in a loaf pan; when it cools, frost the loaf and serve it with fresh raspberries and two sauces—mango and raspberry. Canned mangoes and frozen raspberries simplify preparation of the sauces.

When you invite guests to serve themselves, suggest various ways they can assemble the meal: spoon meat, beans, sauces, and cheese onto a plate and enjoy with warm tortillas; or roll the tortillas around the dinner elements for a soft taco, enchilada, or flute-shaped flauta.

To assemble filled tortillas, fire-warm 1 or 2 and put on your plate. Spoon meat and beans onto each tortilla and roll to enclose filling; lay tortillas seam down so they won't pop open. Spoon green tomatillo salsa on 1 side of the rolls, red chili salsa on the other, then top with salsa cruda and cheese.

To serve, tear off chunks of pork and place on tortilla; add beans if you like.

Rolled tortillas surrounded with salsas get topped with salsa cruda and tangy cheese.

## SUMMER CARNITAS FIESTA

Watermelon Agua Fresca
Carnitas    Spiced Black Beans
Fire-Warmed Corn Tortillas
Crumbled Cotija Cheese (or Feta)
Green Tomatillo Salsa
Red Chili Salsa
Salsa Cruda    Fiesta Green Salad
Mango & Raspberry Meringue Torte

*You'll find most ingredients in well-stocked supermarkets. If not, shop at a Mexican food market, which also carries cotija, a crumbly sharp cheese, and may even sell freshly made tortillas.*

You'll need at least 16 to 20 corn tortillas (7-inch size) and about ⅓ pound cotija or feta cheese. The cheese is served to sprinkle over the hot foods; crumble cheese between your fingers.

Try to shop at least 2 days ahead. Everything except for the salsa cruda can hold a day or 2 in the refrigerator.

If you're in a hurry, an alternative is to buy ready-to-serve carnitas, red chili salsa, and green tomatillo salsa from Mexican markets.

If you're making your own carnitas, save the broth and fat to use in other recipes in this menu.

## WATERMELON AGUA FRESCA

1 small watermelon or 1 piece of watermelon, about 8 pounds
2 quarts water
1 cup *each* lime juice and sugar
  Ice (optional)

Cut rind off melon and discard. Cut out seedless center, cut in chunks, and whirl in a blender or food processor, a portion at a time, until smoothly puréed. Pour purée into a large jar (at least 1 gallon).

Cut remaining melon with seeds into chunks, picking out and discarding seeds, if desired; reserve a few black seeds if you want the drink to look authentically Mexican. Finely chop

melon; scoop pulp and juices into the jar. (For a smoother drink, purée all the melon.) Add water, lime juice, sugar, and, if desired, the reserved seeds. Stir until sugar is dissolved.

To serve, ladle agua fresca into glasses partially filled with ice. Or cover and chill until cold, at least 2 hours or up to 1 day; serve with ice as an option to add to glasses. Makes 10 servings, 1¾ cups each.

## CARNITAS

1 bone-in pork shoulder or butt (about 7 lb.)
1½ quarts regular-strength chicken broth
1 large onion, quartered
1 tablespoon *each* coriander seed and cumin seed
2 teaspoons fresh oregano leaves, or 1 teaspoon dry oregano leaves
4 canned chipotle chilies in sauce (*chili chipotle en diable*)
2 tablespoons sauce from canned chipotle chilies in sauce
2 bay leaves
  Water
  Salt

To a 7- to 8-quart pan, add pork, broth, onion, coriander, cumin, oregano, chilies in sauce, sauce, and bay leaves. Add at least 2 quarts water, or enough to cover the pork. Cover the pan and bring to a boil on high heat, then reduce heat and simmer until meat pulls apart easily with a fork, 5 to 6 hours.

Carefully support meat with 2 large spoons and lift from broth into a pan (9 by 13 inches or 10 by 15 inches); meat tends to fall apart, but try to keep it in large chunks. Let stand until cool enough to touch. Pour broth accumulated in pan back into cooking pan. Skim fat from broth (or chill broth and lift off solid fat); reserve fat. Pour broth through a fine strainer into another bowl; discard residue and reserve broth and fat to use in other recipes in this menu. If made ahead, cover and chill broth and fat up to 2 days.

Cut off and discard large sections of fat on pork. If made ahead, let meat cool, then cover and chill up to 2 days.

Bake pork, uncovered, in a 450° oven until lightly browned and sizzling, about 20 minutes. To keep pork warm, put pan on a cool area of barbecue grill—not over coals but near them (see fire-warmed tortillas, following), or transfer meat to a heatproof metal platter and place on barbecue grill.

Pull off chunks of meat to serve. Add salt to taste. Makes about 3½ pounds cooked, fat-trimmed meat, enough for 8 to 10 servings.

## SPICED BLACK BEANS

2 large onions, chopped
¼ cup fat from carnitas broth (preceding) or salad oil
1½ quarts broth from carnitas or regular-strength chicken broth
1 quart regular-strength chicken broth
¾ pound dry black beans, sorted for debris and rinsed
1 can (6 oz.) tomato paste
6 cardamom pods; pull off pods and use seeds
2 tablespoons mustard seed
1 teaspoon fresh oregano leaves, or ½ teaspoon dry oregano leaves
1 teaspoon cumin seed
1 cinnamon stick, about 1½ inches long
Salt

In a 4- to 5-quart pan over medium-high heat, cook onions in fat until they are limp and lightly browned, about 20 minutes; stir frequently. Add carnitas broth,

*Use the barbecue serving station to warm, not cook, foods. Tortillas heat on the grill, meat and beans keep warm as guests assemble carnitas.*

chicken broth, beans, tomato paste, cardamom seed, mustard seed, oregano, cumin seed, and cinnamon. Cover the beans and bring to a boil over high heat; reduce heat and simmer until beans mash easily, about 3½ hours.

Uncover and boil beans on high heat, stirring occasionally, until reduced to about 5½ cups, about 30 minutes; stir frequently as mixture reduces to prevent scorching. If made ahead, let cool in pan; cover and chill up to 2 days. To reheat, let beans come to room temperature. Warm on low heat, covered, until hot, about 20 minutes; stir occasionally. Pour beans into a heatproof serving container.

To keep warm, put bean container on cool section of a barbecue grill—not over hot coals, but near them (see fire-warmed tortillas, following). If beans are in a ceramic bowl, you can set them on pork platter (see preceding recipe) to keep warm. Add salt to taste. Makes about 5½ cups, or 8 to 10 servings.

## FIRE-WARMED CORN TORTILLAS

On the firegrate of a barbecue, ignite 40 to 50 charcoal briquets and let them burn until coated with gray ash, about 30 minutes. Push the coals to one side, leaving at least half the grate empty. Lay 4 or 5 briquets on the hot coals, and also add this number every 30 minutes, if needed, to maintain even heat. Set the grill 4 to 6 inches above the coals; let coals burn until they are medium-hot (you should be able to hold your hand at grill level 4 to 5 seconds).

To warm **corn tortillas** (allow 1 or 2 tortillas, 7-inch size, for a serving), lay on grill directly over coals just before you eat them; there's room for several at a time. Turn tortillas several times with your fingers or tongs just until they're warm and pliable (if you warm them too long, they get tough).

## GREEN TOMATILLO SALSA

1¼ **pounds tomatillos**
⅓ **cup chopped fresh cilantro (coriander)**
½ **small hot chili (such as jalapeño or serrano), stemmed, seeded, and minced**
¾ **cup regular-strength chicken broth**
⅓ **cup lime juice**
**Salt**

Pull husks off tomatillos and discard. Place tomatillos in a 9- by 13-inch baking pan, then roast them, uncovered, in a 400° oven until spotted with brown, about 30 minutes. Let cool.

In a food processor or blender, whirl tomatillos and their juices, cilantro, and chili until smoothly puréed. Stir in broth, lime juice, and salt to taste.

Serve the tomatillo salsa at room temperature. If made ahead, cover and chill up to 2 days. Makes 3 cups, enough for 8 to 10 servings.

## RED CHILI SALSA

1 **package (4 oz.) dried ancho chilies**
2 **large onions, chopped**
2 **tablespoons fat reserved from carnitas (preceding) or salad oil**
**About 2 cups carnitas broth (preceding) or regular-strength chicken broth**
1½ **cups water**
½ **teaspoon cumin seed**
1 **teaspoon fresh oregano leaves, or ½ teaspoon dry oregano leaves**
**Salt**

Wipe chilies with a damp cloth to remove dust. Place chilies in a single layer in a 10- by 15-inch baking pan. Roast in a 400° oven until chilies smell toasted, about 4 minutes. Remove from oven and let cool; pull off and discard stems and shake out seeds.

In a 10- to 12-inch frying pan over medium-high heat, cook onions in fat until limp and lightly browned, about 5 minutes; stir often.

Add chilies, 2 cups broth, water, cumin seed, and oregano. Bring to a boil over high heat; reduce heat and simmer, uncovered, until chilies are soft when pierced, about 15 minutes.

With a slotted spoon, transfer chilies and onions to a food processor or blender; add ¼ cup cooking liquid. Whirl until chilies and onions are smoothly puréed. Rub purée firmly through a fine strainer into bowl; discard residue.

Mix chili purée with cooking liquid and measure; you should have 4 cups. If less, add broth to make 4 cups; if more, boil sauce on high heat, stirring frequently, until reduced to 4 cups. Add salt to taste. Serve at room temperature. If made ahead, let the sauce cool, cover, and chill up to 3 days. Makes 4 cups, enough for 8 to 10 servings.

## SALSA CRUDA

2 **medium-size firm-ripe tomatoes, cored, seeded, and diced**
1 **medium-size onion, diced**
½ **cup lime juice**
¼ **cup chopped fresh cilantro (coriander)**
**Salt and pepper**

In a bowl, mix tomatoes, onion, lime juice, and cilantro; add salt and pepper to taste. Serve at room temperature or chilled. If made ahead, cover and chill up to 3 hours; stir before serving. Makes about 2½ cups, enough for 8 to 10 servings.

## FIESTA GREEN SALAD

6 **cups loosely packed washed, drained, and chilled red leaf lettuce**
2 **cups** *each* **loosely packed washed, drained, and chilled dandelion greens, watercress sprigs, and fresh cilantro (coriander) sprigs**
1 **cup thinly sliced red radishes**
**Herb dressing (directions follow)**
**Salt and pepper**

Tear or cut lettuce and dandelion greens into bite-size pieces. Place in a large bowl with watercress, cilantro, and radishes. If made ahead, cover and chill up to 1 day.

Pour dressing over the salad and mix; add salt and pepper to taste. Makes 8 to 10 servings.

**Herb dressing.** Mix together ½ cup **salad oil;** 1½ tablespoons *each* **raspberry vinegar** and **balsamic vinegar** (or 1½ tablespoons *each* lemon juice and red wine vinegar); 2 tablespoons minced **onion;** 1 clove **garlic,** minced or pressed; ¾ teaspoon **fresh oregano leaves,** or ¼ teaspoon dry oregano leaves; and ½ teaspoon **anise seed,** crushed.

## MANGO & RASPBERRY MERINGUE TORTE

5  egg whites
½  teaspoon cream of tartar
1  cup sugar
1  teaspoon vanilla
1  cup whipping cream
1  tablespoon orange-flavored liqueur
1  to 2 cups raspberries, rinsed
   Mango sauce (recipe follows)
   Raspberry sauce (recipe follows)

With an electric mixer on high speed, beat egg whites with cream of tartar in a large bowl until frothy. Continue beating at high speed, slowly adding sugar, until whites will hold stiff peaks. Beat in the vanilla.

Butter and flour-dust a 5- by 9-inch loaf pan. Scoop the meringue into the pan and spread it to make the surface level. Bake in a 275° oven until surface no longer feels sticky, about 40 minutes. Remove cake from oven and place it on a rack; immediately run knife blade around edge of pan to loosen cake. Let cake cool in pan 5 minutes, then turn it out onto a serving platter and let cool.

Beat cream until it holds soft peaks; stir in liqueur. Swirl cream over top and sides of meringue cake. Serve; if made ahead, invert a large bowl over the torte and chill up to 3 hours. Use paper towels to absorb any sugar syrup that weeps from the meringue.

To serve, slice torte into 8 to 10 equal slices. Offer fresh raspberries, and mango and raspberry sauces to add to individual portions. Makes 8 to 10 servings.

**Mango sauce.** Drain 1 can (15 oz.) **sliced mangoes.** In a blender, whirl mango pieces until puréed with 3 tablespoons *each* **lime juice** and **water,** and 1 tablespoon *each* **orange-flavored liqueur** and **sugar.** Rub sauce through a fine strainer into a bowl; discard fibers. Pour into a small serving bowl or pitcher. Serve at room temperature. If made ahead, cover and chill up to 3 days. Makes 1⅓ cups.

**Raspberry sauce.** In a blender, whirl 1 package (10 oz.) thawed **frozen raspberries in light syrup** until puréed. Rub purée through a fine strainer into a bowl; discard seeds. Pour sauce into a small serving bowl or pitcher. Serve at room temperature. If made ahead, cover and chill up to 3 days. Makes 1⅓ cups.

*Spoon brilliant purées of mango and raspberry onto ethereal cream-frosted meringue dessert; accompany with fresh, plump raspberries.*

# The Golden Age of Salads

I N AN AGE *fascinated by both fitness and good food, salads have naturally come into their own. The abundance and variety of produce in Western markets provide continuing inspiration.*

*No longer a predictable plate of greens, salads today combine familiar ingredients with innovative vegetables and fruits found in well-stocked produce departments. Some of the foods are indigenous to the Americas, some arrived with settlers, and the trendiest may even be imported.*

*The appearance of salads has great flexibility: ingredients may simply be lightly mixed, or they may be artfully composed.*

*On these pages you'll find an old Western favorite, Cobb Salad, and three newer combinations: a crisp slaw featuring shredded zucchini and tart apples; a colorful fruit salad with a piquant dressing; and a radicchio-butter lettuce combination enhanced by orange slices and a warm bacon dressing.*

Shredded zucchini and chopped crisp apples with a tart caraway dressing make this unusual slaw.

## ZUCCHINI-APPLE SLAW

- ½ cup mayonnaise
- 3 tablespoons cider vinegar
- 1 tablespoon sugar
- 1 teaspoon caraway seed
- 4 cups coarsely shredded zucchini
- ¼ cup thinly sliced green onions
- 2 or 3 medium-size red- or green-skinned tart apples
  Salt and pepper

Combine the mayonnaise, cider vinegar, sugar, and caraway seed; mix until well blended. In a large bowl, combine shredded zucchini and sliced green onions.

Core apples, peel if desired, and cut into ½-inch chunks (you should have about 3 cups). Add apples to zucchini mixture; pour dressing over salad and mix lightly until well coated. Season with salt and pepper to taste.

Cover and refrigerate for at least 2 hours or up to 4 hours. With a slotted spoon, transfer salad to a serving bowl. Makes 6 servings.

## KIWI FRUIT SALAD

*This salad has seasonal overtones. Enjoy it now, minus the bright orange Fuyu persimmons—the kind you eat while crisp. Then, when the persimmons are in season, add them to the dish.*

- 1 medium-size pineapple, peeled, cored, and cut into 1-inch cubes
- 3 ripe bananas, sliced diagonally
- 2 firm-ripe crisp persimmons, such as Fuyu, thinly sliced (optional)
- 1 cup red grapes (about ½ lb.)
- 6 kiwi fruit, peeled and sliced crosswise
  About 1 cup chopped pecans or walnuts
  Honey-yogurt dressing (recipe follows)

In a large salad bowl, combine pineapple, bananas, persimmons, grapes, and kiwi fruit; mix gently.

If you want to serve the salad slightly chilled, cover and refrigerate for 30 minutes. Place nuts and honey-yogurt dressing in separate bowls; offer with each portion. Makes 6 servings.

**Honey-yogurt dressing.** In a small bowl combine 1½ tablespoons grated **orange peel,** 1 teaspoon grated **fresh ginger,** ¾ cup *each* **mayonnaise** and **plain yogurt,** 2 tablespoons **honey,** and 1 tablespoon **lemon juice.**

Mix the dressing until well blended. If made ahead, cover and refrigerate until next day.

## Cobb Salad

1 pound sliced bacon
1 large ripe avocado
1 tablespoon lemon juice
1 medium-size head iceberg lettuce, thinly shredded
6 tablespoons white wine vinegar
½ teaspoon salt
⅛ teaspoon *each* garlic powder and freshly ground pepper
3 tablespoons chopped chives
½ cup salad oil
⅔ cup (about 3 oz.) finely crumbled blue-veined cheese
1 large tomato, seeded and chopped
1½ cups diced cooked chicken
2 hard-cooked eggs, chopped
Watercress sprigs (optional)

In a 10- to 12-inch frying pan over medium heat, cook bacon until crisp. Lift out, drain, and crumble; set aside. Pit, peel, and dice avocado; moisten avocado with lemon juice and set aside.

Place lettuce in a large, wide salad bowl. In a medium-size bowl, combine vinegar, salt, garlic powder, pepper, chives, and oil; mix until well blended. Pour dressing over lettuce and mix slightly until well coated. Arrange lettuce in an even layer in bowl.

Place cheese in center of lettuce; surround with wedge-shaped sections of bacon, avocado, tomato, chicken, and eggs. Garnish with watercress. Serve immediately. Makes 4 servings.

## Radicchio with Butter Lettuce

3 slices bacon
Salad oil (optional)
1 tablespoon *each* red wine vinegar and minced shallots
½ teaspoon Dijon mustard
1 medium-size orange
2 cups lightly packed coarsely torn or small butter lettuce leaves, washed and crisped
3 cups lightly packed radicchio leaves, washed and crisped
Salt and pepper
Whole chives or long slivers of green onion tops (optional)

In a 10- to 12-inch frying pan, cook bacon over medium heat until crisp. Lift out bacon, reserving drippings; drain bacon and break into 1-inch pieces.

Measure drippings and add enough salad oil, if necessary, to make 3 tablespoons. Return drippings to pan with bacon, vinegar, shallots, and mustard.

(At this point, you can cover the salad dressing mixture and refrigerate it until the next day.)

Cut off peel and white membrane from orange; cut between inner membranes, removing orange segments. In a large bowl, combine lettuce, radicchio, and orange segments.

Heat bacon mixture to simmering over medium heat. Immediately pour the hot dressing over salad and mix gently but quickly until well coated. Season with salt and pepper to taste.

Arrange salad on individual plates. Garnish with a spray of chives, if desired. Serve immediately. Makes 4 servings.

*Cobb salad, a Hollywood favorite, combines lettuce, bacon, avocado, chicken, tomato, egg, and cheese.*

*Sweet orange slices, tender butter lettuce, and red, slightly bitter radicchio get warm bacon dressing.*

# Showing Off Baby Vegetables

**B**ABY VEGETABLES *are what restaurants and produce markets call immature versions of vegetables traditionally harvested when more fully developed. Gardeners often call them thinnings.*

*Whatever you call them, these Lilliputians of the greengrocer's shelf are appealing to look at. But are they worth paying a higher price, or accepting a diminished harvest? For looks, yes. For taste, it's a matter of opinion: many people find immature vegetables as flavorful as full-grown ones, but more tender. They're definitely sweeter, because sugar content is higher.*

*June, July, and August are the months when the most varieties of baby vegetables are available. But because more growers are experimenting with them, almost anything might show up at any season. If you don't see baby vegetables in your market, ask your produce dealer to order them for you.*

*To show off these tiny gems, we suggest two simple but eye-catching presentations. One is an eat-at-your-own-pace melted cheese raclette to serve indoors or out. The other works as a handsome party appetizer—or you could add some little ham sandwiches and consider it a meal.*

*From a basket of petite vegetables, select bite-size crudités to swirl through toasted almond mayonnaise. Serve as an appetizer or salad lunch.*

## RACLETTE WITH BABY VEGETABLES

- **3 to 4 quarts cooked mixed baby vegetables (for choices, see directions on page 146)**
- **2 to 2½ pounds raclette, fontina, or jarlsberg cheese**
  **Freshly ground pepper**
  **Cornichons**

Arrange vegetables (warm or at room temperature) on a platter.

Cut cheese into ½-inch-thick slices. Fit a single layer in a heavy 8- to 10-inch frying pan. Place pan over medium to medium-high heat (use a portable burner, or a barbecue or hibachi with a solid bed of medium coals: you should be able to hold your hand at grill level for 4 to 5 seconds). Cook until cheese melts, then scoop cheese from pan and pour, a bit at a time, onto plates to eat with individual servings of the vegetables. If you like, grind pepper onto melted cheese; serve with cornichons. As cheese is eaten, add more to pan to melt. Slide off heat if cheese starts to scorch. Makes 6 entrée servings.

## BABY VEGETABLES WITH TOASTED ALMOND SKORDALIA

- **2 large egg yolks**
- **2 cloves garlic, minced or pressed**
- **1½ tablespoons lemon juice**
- **½ teaspoon sugar**
- **1 to 4 tablespoons dry white wine**
- **1 cup olive oil or salad oil**
  **Ground toasted almonds (directions on page 146)**
  **Salt**
- **3 to 4 quarts raw or cooked baby vegetables (for choices, see directions on page 146)**

In blender or food processor, whirl yolks, garlic, lemon juice, sugar, and 1 tablespoon wine to blend. With motor running, pour in oil in a slow, steady stream; mixture will thicken to form a mayonnaise. Stir in almonds; if you want a thinner consistency for dipping, add more wine. Add salt to taste. Serve at once, or cover and chill up to 2 days.

Arrange the vegetables in a basket or on a platter; put sauce in a bowl alongside. Dip vegetables into sauce to eat. Makes 1½ cups sauce, 12 appetizer servings.

*(Continued on next page)*

*For a small party, here's a delectable variation on the cheese-and-potatoes of Swiss raclette; melt cheese on a burner or hibachi,*
*then spoon it onto your choice of cooked baby vegetables.*

## ...Baby Vegetables with Toasted Almond Skordalia

**Ground toasted almonds.** In a 350° oven bake ⅓ cup **whole unblanched almonds** in a 9- to 10-inch-wide pan until nuts are golden under skin (break 1 to test), about 8 minutes. Let cool. Whirl nuts in a food processor or blender until finely ground.

## Baby Vegetable Basics... Boiling & Steaming

It's important to start with vegetables of the best quality. Select ones that are fresh-looking, bright in color, firm, and free of blemishes. Eat as soon as possible; if it's necessary to store them, wrap in paper towels and seal in plastic bags, then refrigerate up to a day or two.

Two basic ways to cook baby vegetables are to boil or steam; see listings for individual vegetables for doneness tests and cooking times.

**To boil.** Add cleaned vegetables (up to 1 lb. at a time) to a pan filled with enough boiling water to cover. Boil green vegetables uncovered, other vegetables covered, just until tender when pierced. Drain. Serve hot or cool. If desired, immerse green vegetables in ice water until cool (to hold color); drain before serving.

**To steam.** Place vegetables (no more than 3 layers deep) on a steamer rack placed about ½ inch above gently boiling water; cover. Cook until vegetables are tender when pierced, then lift them out. Serve hot or cool. If desired, immerse green vegetables in ice water until cool (to hold color); drain before serving.

**Beans** (green, yellow). Choose beans 3 to 4½ inches long, about ¼ inch wide. Rinse; trim off stem ends. Serve raw, boiled (takes 3 to 4 minutes), or steamed (takes 5 to 6 minutes).

**Corn.** Choose unhusked ears 5 to 7 inches long, ¾ to 1 inch wide. Pull off and discard husks and silks; trim stem end off cob. Serve raw, boiled (takes 3 to 5 minutes), or steamed (takes 6 to 8 minutes).

**Fennel** (also called finocchio or sweet anise). Choose fennel about 2 inches wide; lengths may vary, depending on method of harvesting. Rinse well, flushing out stalks. Trim off root ends. Leave whole or trim tops to fit cooking pan. Serve raw (break off stalks; tops are tough), boiled (takes 7 to 9 minutes), or steamed (takes 9 to 15 minutes).

**Okra** (red, green). Choose okra 1 to 2 inches long, ½ inch wide. Rinse; cut off stem ends. Boil (takes 3 to 4 minutes) or steam (takes 5 to 6 minutes).

Beans, corn, fennel, and okra are available early and midsummer. Other vegetables you're likely to find in cooler seasons. Some are available all year.

**Beets** (gold, red). Year-round. Choose beets about 1 inch or less across. Trim outer stems off root, leaving just a few tender center stems to serve as a handle. Or cut off stems about 1 inch above the root's crown. Scrub root; rinse well. Serve boiled (takes 20 to 25 minutes) or steamed (25 to 30 minutes). Pinch skins off cooked beets.

**Bok choy, baby.** Year-round. Choose bok choy that are 1 to 2 inches thick and about 6 inches long. Trim off and discard root ends, leaving heads whole. Rinse leaves well, flushing out stalks. Serve raw (whole, breaking off stalks to eat), boiled (takes about 4 minutes), or steamed (4 to 5 minutes).

**Carrots** (long or round; orange, red, or white). Year-round. Choose tapering carrots ½ to ¾ inch wide and 2 to 5 inches long; choose round carrots about ¾ inch in diameter. Clean as for beets. Serve raw, boiled (takes about 4 minutes), or steamed (about 7 minutes).

**Cauliflower.** Winter and spring. Choose heads about 3 inches across. Rinse. Serve raw, boiled (takes about 7 minutes), or steamed (9 to 10 minutes).

**Leeks.** Year-round. Choose leeks about ½ inch across and 12 to 14 inches long with crisp tops. Trim off roots; tops are tender. Wash, flushing out leaves. Serve raw, boiled (takes 1 to 2 minutes), or steamed (3 to 4 minutes).

**Potatoes** (red thin-skinned, also called new potatoes). Late winter through summer. Choose potatoes 1 to 2 inches across. Rinse and scrub. Boil (takes 20 to 30 minutes) or steam (35 to 40 minutes).

**Squash** (many have flowers attached). Late winter through early fall. Green or yellow pattypan should be 1 to 1½ inches wide; green or yellow zucchini about 3 inches long; green emerald about 1¼ inches wide; yellow crookneck about 3 inches long; green or yellow scallopini ¾ to 1½ inches wide; green or gold acorn 1½ inches wide.

Rinse and trim off ends; leave flowers on. Serve raw, boiled (takes 3 to 6 minutes), or steamed (5 to 8 minutes).

**Turnips** (purple, white, gold). Year-round. Tops should be fresh and green; turnips should be ¾ to 1 inch wide and feel firm and dry. Clean as for beets (preceding). Serve raw, boiled (about 5 minutes), or steamed (about 8 minutes).

# Giving Albacore the Swedish Treatment

INCREASINGLY AVAILABLE *fresh or frozen from our coastal waters, albacore has a delicate texture that lends itself to a Swedish treatment most often used for salmon to create gravlax, or gravad (cured) lax (salmon).*

*Gravad albacore is cured and firmed by the dehydrating effect of salt and sugar on the raw fish. The process takes place in the refrigerator over a 24-hour period.*

*Serve gravad albacore as is or, as a variation, cook it briefly on the barbecue to add subtle smoky overtones.*

*To present gravad albacore as an appetizer, slice it thinly and serve with soy sauce and regular prepared horseradish or Japanese hot green horseradish paste, wasabi.*

*As a Swedish-style entrée, use plain or barbecued gravad albacore with a sweet mustard sauce, or create a Japanese-style dish with the elements of sashimi—adding daikon and a sharp soy dressing.*

## GRAVAD ALBACORE APPETIZER SALAD

- 4 **thin slices red onion**
  **Water**
  **About 4 teaspoons golden or salmon caviar**
- 1 **medium-size ripe avocado**
  **About 6 ounces daikon, peeled and finely shredded**
  **Half of a 1½- to 2-pound chilled gravad or barbecued gravad albacore loin (directions follow), cut cross-grain into ⅛- to ¼-inch-thick slices**
  **Soy rice vinegar (recipe follows)**

*Texture contrasts add interest to salad of tender gravad albacore, crisp daikon shreds, onion rings, and smooth avocado.*

Place onion in bowl of cold water, separate into rings, and chill to crisp, 5 to 15 minutes. Put caviar in a fine strainer and rinse under cool running water; let drain in strainer on paper towels. Cut avocado in half lengthwise; pit and peel. Cut each half crosswise into ¼-inch slices. Drain onion and pat dry.

For each serving, mound ¼ of the daikon on a dinner plate. Lean ¼ of albacore slices, overlapping, against the daikon; spoon 1 teaspoon of the caviar on top. Arrange ¼ of the avocado slices and ¼ of the onion rings near daikon mound. Serve at once, offering soy vinegar to add to taste. Makes 4 first-course servings.

**Soy rice vinegar.** In a 1- to 1½- quart pan, bring to a boil ¾ cup **rice vinegar** and 2 tablespoons *each* **soy sauce, slivered fresh ginger;** let stand until ginger flavors vinegar, about 10 minutes. Discard ginger. Cover; chill 30 minutes or up to 3 days.

## GRAVAD ALBACORE WITH MUSTARD-DILL SAUCE

**Gravad albacore loin, or barbecued gravad albacore loin (directions follow)**
**Mustard-dill sauce (recipe follows)**
2 **or 3 thin lemon slices**
**About ½ teaspoon drained capers**
**Fresh dill sprigs**

Place loin on a board. With a very sharp knife, cut gravad albacore loin across grain into ⅛-inch-thick slices, barbecued loin into ¼-inch-thick slices; keep slices in place to retain loin shape. With a wide metal spatula, transfer to a large platter.

Pour half the mustard-dill sauce around the loin. Garnish with lemon slices, capers, and dill. Slide fish through sauce as served. Accompany with remaining sauce. Makes 4 to 6 main-dish servings.

**Gravad albacore loin.** Purchase 1 skinned or unskinned **albacore loin** (1½ to 2 lb.). If fish is fresh (never frozen), freeze at least 7 days at 0° before curing to destroy any dangerous parasites. If you buy frozen (or frozen and thawed) albacore, this step isn't necessary. Set loin in a glass dish large enough to hold fish flat. Rub fish with 2 tablespoons **salad oil.**

Mix together ⅓ cup **sugar,** 3 tablespoons **salt,** and 1½ tablespoons coarse-

*Barbecued, cooled, and thinly sliced, gravad albacore in classic mustard-and-dill vinaigrette makes a handsome entrée.*

ly crushed **black peppercorns;** rub mixture evenly over fish (if not coated, the fish turns very dark, but the discoloration is harmless). Cover dish tightly with plastic wrap. Chill 12 hours, basting fish 2 or 3 times with the accumulating juices. Turn fish to rest on another side; cover. Chill another 12 hours, basting several more times.

After 24 hours, rinse sugar brine from fish; leave peppercorns embedded. The fish is ready to serve. Or refrigerate airtight up to 4 days.

**Barbecued gravad albacore loin.** Lay **gravad albacore loin** (preceding) on a clean barbecue grill over a solid layer of hot coals that extends several inches beyond fish; you should be able to hold your hand at grill level only 2 to 3 seconds.

Cook fish just until it's opaque about ⅛ inch beneath surface (cut to check), about 5 minutes total; turn carefully as needed, using 1 or 2 wide metal spatulas. Lift from grill and let cool. Chill, covered, before slicing; it's easier to cut cold.

**Mustard-dill sauce.** In a bowl, mix ⅓ cup **vinegar,** 2 tablespoons **Dijon mustard,** 1½ tablespoons chopped **fresh dill,** and 1½ teaspoons *each* **dry mustard** and **sugar.** Whisking, slowly pour in 1 cup **salad oil.**

# Easy Dinner Party Entrées

WHAT SHOULD I SERVE *at my dinner party? We asked this question of professional caterers, who regularly solve this puzzle. Like home cooks, they, too, are concerned with make-ahead steps, ease in preparation, and presentation.*

*Rack of lamb is naturally elegant and easy to cook and carve. Peter Higginson dresses it with a red pepper mustard.*

*For guests with diverse tastes, Kate Tremper suggests skewered entrées. You can make several kinds and grill them all at the same time. Guests choose their favorite. One choice is pork with chili.*

*For a quick, easy entrée, Gretchen Mather coats chicken breasts in mustard and bread crumbs to bake. They are deliciously moist.*

*Chicken with pesto, served on a tomato and porcini mushroom sauce, is a showstopper choice. It takes time to assemble the parts, but Patra Cianciolo often makes them ahead. You can substitute fresh button mushrooms for dry porcini.*

## RED PEPPER MUSTARD RACK OF LAMB

- 2 medium-size red bell peppers
- 2 tablespoons port
- 2 tablespoons honey
- 1½ tablespoons dry mustard
- ½ cup Dijon mustard
- 1 teaspoon minced fresh or dry rosemary
- 3 racks of lamb (1½ to 2 lb. each), French cut (rib ends stripped) with chine bones removed

Cut peppers in half and set, cut side down, in a 10- by 15-inch pan. Broil about 4 inches from heat until skin is charred and blistered all over, about 10 minutes. Let cool; peel off blistered skin, remove stem and seeds. In a food processor or blender, whirl pepper, port, honey, dry mustard, Dijon, and rosemary just until pepper is finely chopped; do not purée.

Trim fat from lamb, leaving about ¼ inch on surface. Coat lamb with ⅓ of the pepper mustard sauce; cover and chill at least 4 hours or up to overnight. Also cover and chill remaining sauce until ready to serve.

Place lamb racks, bone side down, in a greased 11- by 17-inch roasting pan. Roast in a 475° oven for 15 minutes. Turn racks fat side down and return to oven.

Rack of lamb is a good choice for elegant entrée. Red pepper mustard coats lamb as it cooks, also serves as a sauce for the meat.

Reduce temperature to 350°; continue cooking until a thermometer inserted in center of thickest part reaches 140° for medium-rare, 10 to 15 minutes longer.

Let meat rest in a warm place 5 to 10 minutes. Cut racks in half or into individual chops; allow a half rack or 3 or 4 chops for each serving. Offer reserved cool pepper mustard to eat with the lamb. Makes 6 to 8 servings. —*Peter Higginson, Ambrosia Caterers, Venice, Calif.*

## SANTA FE PORK BROCHETAS

- 3 pounds boneless pork shoulder or butt, trimmed of excess surface fat and cut into 1-inch chunks
  Red chili purée (recipe follows)
  Water
- 10 red thin-skinned potatoes (about 2 inches wide)
- 1 large onion, cut into 1-inch cubes and layers separated

In a bowl, mix pork chunks with red chili purée. Cover and chill at least 4 hours or up to overnight.

In a 3- to 4-quart pan, bring about 2 quarts water to boiling. Add potatoes. Return to boiling and simmer, covered, until potatoes are just tender when pierced, 15 to 20 minutes. Drain, cool, then cut potatoes into quarters.

On metal skewers, alternate pieces of pork, onion, and potato. Brush any remaining chili purée over vegetables. If made ahead, cover and chill up to 4 hours.

Place on a grill 4 to 6 inches above hot coals (you can hold your hand at grill level only 2 to 3 seconds). Cook, turning, until meat is well browned on all sides and no longer pink in thickest part (cut to test), 15 to 20 minutes. Serves 8 to 10. —*Kate Tremper, Massee's, Sante Fe.*

**Red chili purée.** Remove stems from 6 large (about 3 oz. total) **dry New Mexican** or California **chilies.** Rinse chilies. In a bowl, combine chilies and 2 cups **hot water.** Soak until chilies are soft, about 15 minutes. Rinse chilies (reserve soaking water) and remove seeds.

In a blender or food processor, combine chilies, 2 tablespoons **salad oil,** 2 cloves **garlic,** 1 teaspoon **dry oregano leaves,** 1 teaspoon **cumin seed,** 1 teaspoon **salt** or to taste, and 1 cup of the soaking water; whirl to purée.

## Parmesan Dijon Chicken

- 2 **to 3 slices white bread**
- 1 **cup lightly packed grated parmesan cheese**
- ⅓ **cup melted butter or margarine**
- ⅔ **cup Dijon mustard**
- 3 **tablespoons dry white wine**
- 8 **boned and skinned chicken breast halves (3 to 4 oz. *each*)**

Tear bread in pieces. Whirl in a blender or food processor until coarse crumbs form. Pour 1½ cups of crumbs into an 8- or 9-inch-wide pan; mix with cheese and butter. In another 8- or 9-inch-wide pan, mix mustard and wine. Coat chicken in mustard mixture; dip rounded side of each breast in crumb mixture. Set chicken, crumb side up, slightly apart in a greased 10- by 15-inch pan. Bake in a 500° oven until golden and chicken is white in thickest part (cut to test), about 15 minutes. Makes 8 servings. —*Gretchen Mather, Gretchen's of Course, Seattle.*

## Pesto Chicken with Tomato Porcini Sauce

- 6 **boned and skinned chicken breast halves (each about 4 oz.)**
  **Salt and pepper**
  **Pesto sauce (recipe follows)**
- ½ **cup fine dry bread crumbs**
- ¼ **cup grated parmesan cheese**
- ¼ **cup chopped parsley**
  **Tomato and porcini sauce (recipe follows)**
  **Basil or parsley sprigs**

Place a chicken breast between pieces of plastic wrap and pound evenly with a flat mallet until about ¼ inch thick. Repeat with remaining chicken. Sprinkle chicken lightly with salt and pepper. Spread 1 tablespoon of pesto sauce over each piece. Starting at one end of the breast, roll up neatly. (If made ahead, place chicken, seam side down, in a buttered 10- by 15-inch pan. Cover and chill up to overnight. Freeze to store longer; thaw to continue.)

In an 8- or 9-inch-wide pan, mix bread crumbs, cheese, chopped parsley. Pour remaining pesto into an 8- or 9-inch-wide pan. Coat rolls with pesto, then crumb mixture. Set chicken, seam side down, slightly apart in a buttered 10- by 15-inch pan. Bake in a 400° oven until meat is white in center (cut to test), about 20 minutes.

Pour hot tomato and porcini sauce equally onto 6 dinner plates. Carefully cut each roll on the diagonal in ½-inch slices and arrange on sauce. Garnish with basil sprigs. Makes 6 servings. — *Patra Cianciolo, Creative Catering, San Francisco.*

**Pesto sauce.** In a 6- to 8-inch frying pan, stir 2 tablespoons **pine nuts** or chopped walnuts over low heat just until lightly browned, 3 to 5 minutes.

In a blender or food processor, combine toasted nuts, 3 cloves **garlic,** ½ cup lightly packed **fresh basil leaves** (washed and dried), and ⅓ cup **olive oil.** Whirl to purée. Stir in ¼ cup grated **parmesan cheese** and ¼ cup **sour cream.** Use, or cover and chill up to overnight. Freeze to store longer (thaw to use). Makes about ¾ cup.

**Tomato and porcini sauce.** Soak 2 ounces **dried porcini mushrooms** in 3 cups hot **water** until soft, 20 to 30 minutes. Squeeze and rub mushrooms to work out any grit. Lift out mushrooms and coarsely chop. Pour the soaking water (be careful not to disturb sediment on bottom of bowl) through a fine strainer into glass measure to equal 1 cup; set aside. Discard remaining water. (If dried porcini are not available, use ½ lb. fresh button mushrooms, chopped; do not soak.)

In a 3- to 4-quart pan, bring 1½ quarts **water** to boiling. Add 6 large **Roma-type tomatoes.** Boil until skins crack, 1 to 2 minutes. Lift out tomatoes. Peel, core, cut in half, and squeeze out seeds. Coarsely chop tomatoes.

In a 10- to 12-inch frying pan, combine ⅓ cup **olive oil,** 3 cloves **garlic,** 8 sprigs (4 in. long) **fresh mint** (or 1 teaspoon dry mint), 4 sprigs (3 to 4 in. long) **fresh thyme** (or ¼ teaspoon dry thyme leaves), 4 sprigs **fresh basil** (or ¼ teaspoon dry basil), and 4 sprigs **parsley.** Stir over low heat until garlic is golden, about 5 minutes. Lift out fresh herbs and garlic (spoon off as much of the dry herbs as possible).

Add fresh or dry mushrooms and 1 **chicken bouillon cube.** Stir over low heat until mushrooms are lightly browned. Add tomatoes and the 1 cup reserved porcini soaking liquid or water. Simmer, uncovered, over low heat until sauce is reduced to 1½ cups, 10 to 15 minutes. Add **salt** and **pepper** to taste. Use, or cool, cover, and chill up to overnight. Freeze to store longer; thaw to use. Reheat, covered, over low heat until hot, adding a little **water** if mixture sticks. Makes 2 cups.

*Sliced pesto-stuffed chicken breast is served with tomato and porcini mushroom sauce, hot pasta.*

# Australian Meat Pies

AUSTRALIANS' PASSION *for meat pies equals Americans' love for hamburgers. In fact, Australia's major commercial manufacturer (of almost 6,000 companies) bakes 2.6 million such pies a week for the country's 15.3 million people. Pies are firmly entrenched in the country's cuisine.*

*Here we present a tailor-your-own pie recipe: it makes 12 individual pies or 1 big one; choose white or whole-wheat crust, and fill with beef and lamb, rabbit, or vegetables. Enjoy hot or cold.*

*The rabbit pie was inspired by one served at the Pokolbin Cellar restaurant.*

## SUIT-YOURSELF AUSSIE MEAT PIES

Pastry for 9-inch or individual pies (recipes follow)
All-purpose flour
Beef-lamb, rabbit-madeira, or vegetable filling (recipes follow)
Water
1 large egg mixed with 1 tablespoon water

*For a large pie,* divide pastry for 9-inch pie in half. On a lightly floured board, roll each half into a 12-inch round; trim edges if necessary to make even. Evenly fit 1 pastry round into a 9-inch pie pan; let edges hang over rim. Spoon filling into pan. Lay second round on filling. Pinch together top and bottom pastries extending over rim. Fold pinched edge underneath so dough is flush with pan rim; then crimp. Cut 6 slits through top pastry.

*For small pies,* divide pastry for individual pies into 12 equal portions. For each, roll pastry into a 7-inch round on a lightly floured board; trim edge to make even. Spoon filling in equal portions onto half of each round, to within ¾ inch of the edge. Lightly brush edge with water.

Fold pastry over filling. Press together curved edge of pastry, then fold edge over itself up to the filling. Crimp edge. Cut 3 slits through top. Place pastries slightly apart on two 12- by 15-inch baking sheets.

Brush tops of pies with egg mixture. Bake in a 400° oven until a rich golden brown, about 50 minutes for 9-inch pie, 25 to 30 minutes for small ones (switch pans halfway through baking time). Let cool in or on pan on a rack for at least 20 minutes. Serve warm; or let cool and serve cold. To store, cover and chill up to 2 days. Makes 8 to 12 servings.

**Pastry for 9-inch pie.** In a bowl or food processor, combine 2 cups **all-purpose flour** (or use 1 cup *each* all-purpose and whole-wheat flour) and ½ teaspoon **salt** (optional). With a pastry blender or food processor, mix in ⅓ cup **butter** or margarine (cut in pieces) and ⅓ cup **solid vegetable shortening** until fat particles are the size of small peas. Gradually add ⅓ cup **cold water,** mixing with a fork or processor until dough clings together. Pat dough into a ball; cover and chill 1 hour.

**Pastry for individual pies.** Prepare **pastry for 9-inch pie** (recipe precedes),

*Bloke in insect-repelling outback hat samples meal-size individual pie filled with beef, lamb, and vegetables.*

1 *Meat pie ingredients include chard, celery, red wine, broth, mushrooms, onion, beef and lamb, and pastry.*

2 *On lightly floured board, roll chilled pastry dough for individual pies into 12 rounds, each about 7 inches wide.*

3 *Spoon cooked filling onto pastry rounds. Moisten pastry rims, then fold dough in half to cover meat.*

4 *Crimp pastry edges with fingers to seal. Next, brush with egg for shine, cut slits in top to let steam escape.*

increasing flour to 4½ cups, salt to ¾ teaspoon (optional), butter and shortening to ¾ cup *each*, and water to ¾ cup.

**Beef-lamb pie filling.** Trim and discard fat from ½ pound **boned lamb shoulder** or neck and 1½ pounds **boned beef chuck;** cut meat into ½-inch chunks. In a 10- to 12-inch frying pan with 3 tablespoons **salad oil,** brown half of meat at a time over high heat; stir often. Lift out meat and set aside. Reduce heat to medium-high.

To pan, add 1 large **onion,** chopped; ⅓ pound **mushrooms,** thinly sliced; ½ cup chopped **celery;** and 2½ cups finely chopped **Swiss chard.** Cook, stirring often, until onion is limp, about 8 minutes. If needed, add 1 tablespoon salad oil to prevent sticking. Add 2½ cups **regular-strength beef broth,** ½ teaspoon **pepper,** and meat. Bring to boil; cover and simmer until meat is tender to bite, about 1 hour.

In a small bowl, mix 1 tablespoon **cornstarch** and ⅓ cup **dry red wine.** Mix into meat mixture and stir until boiling.

**Rabbit-madeira filling.** Remove and discard giblets from a 2¾- to 3-pound **fryer rabbit.** Quarter rabbit; place in a 4- to 5-quart pan with 5 cups **water** and 1 medium-size **onion,** chopped. Bring to a boil over high heat; cover and simmer until meat is opaque in thickest part (cut to test), about 30 minutes.

Pour broth through a strainer and save; discard onion. When rabbit is cool enough to touch, cut meat from bones into 1-inch chunks; discard bones. Return broth to pan; boil, uncovered, until reduced to 1¼ cups, 25 to 30 minutes.

Meanwhile, in a 10- to 12-inch frying pan over medium heat, cook 1 cup *each* ½-inch chunks **carrots, celery,** and **onion** in 3 tablespoons **butter** or margarine; stir often until carrots are tender to bite, 15 to 20 minutes. Stir in 1¼ teaspoons **dry rosemary leaves** and ½ teaspoon **pepper.**

In a small bowl, mix 1½ tablespoons **cornstarch** and ⅓ cup *each* **madeira** and **marsala.** Add to frying pan with broth. Stir until boiling. Add rabbit meat and mix well. Season to taste with **salt.**

**Vegetable filling.** In a 12- to 14-inch frying pan over medium-high heat, cook in 3 tablespoons **butter** or margarine 1 large **onion,** chopped; ⅓ pound **mushrooms,** sliced; ½ cup chopped **celery;** 2½ cups minced **Swiss chard;** and 1¼ cups *each* ½-inch cubes **carrots** and peeled **rutabaga.** Stirring often, cook until onions are very limp, about 20 minutes.

Add 1¼ cups **potatoes** cut into ½-inch cubes and 1¼ cups **regular-strength chicken broth.** Bring to a boil; cover and simmer until potatoes are tender when pierced, 8 to 10 minutes. Uncover; stir in ⅓ cup **dry white wine** mixed with 1½ tablespoons **cornstarch.** Stir till boiling.

# Japanese Nibble-Food

A POPULAR JAPANESE SNACK, *inari sushi* is an edible pocket of fried bean curd filled with seasoned rice and bits of vegetable. In this version, peas accompany the rice. Two filling options offer variety: one features spinach, the other chicken and water chestnuts. All make refreshing appetizers or snacks.

Japanese-style fried bean curd comes in several shapes: a rounded oblong about 2 by 4½ inches, a flat rectangle about 3 by 5 inches, and a square about 2½ inches. Packages weigh just a little over an ounce and contain 2 to 4 pieces each. Look for them in refrigerated cases at Asian markets and well-stocked supermarkets; at home, keep them chilled or frozen.

Simmer the fried bean curd in seasoned broth to add flavor. Cut them in half and separate sides gently with your fingers to open pockets for stuffing. Both pockets and fillings can be prepared ahead; assembled sushi can be held several hours.

## INARI SUSHI

- 2½ cups regular-strength chicken broth
- ½ cup seasoned rice vinegar (or ½ cup rice vinegar and 2 tablespoons sugar)
- 2 tablespoons sugar
- 2 tablespoons mirin (sweet rice wine) or cream sherry
- 2 tablespoons soy sauce
- 4 to 5 ounces Japanese-style fried bean curd (choices precede)
  Filling (choices follow)

In a 10- to 12-inch frying pan, combine broth, vinegar, sugar, mirin, soy sauce, and fried bean curd. Over high heat, bring to a boil. Reduce heat and simmer, uncovered, turning casings occasionally, until liquid cooks away, about 30 minutes. Continue cooking, turning pieces until they begin to brown, about 10 minutes more; watch to avoid sticking. Remove from pan and let cool.

To remove excess liquid, press pieces of bean curd between your palms. Use, or cover and chill up to 2 days.

Cut casings in half crosswise, on a slight diagonal if you wish.

With your fingers, ease apart cut sides of each half and press filling firmly into pocket, mounding it slightly higher than pocket sides. Serve, or cover and chill pockets of sushi rice or spinach up to 6 hours, those holding the chicken-water chestnut mixture up to overnight. Makes 16 to 24 pieces, 8 appetizer servings.

For an appetizer or snack, serve inari sushi with sake. Black sesame seeds dot the rice and pea filling in bean curd pockets. A rose of pickled ginger decorates the plate.

**Sushi rice filling.** In a 2- to 3-quart pan over high heat, bring 1¼ cups **water** and 1 cup **short-grain white rice** to a boil; reduce heat to low, cover pan, and simmer until water is absorbed, 6 to 8 minutes. Let cool, uncovered. Stir in ⅓ cup **seasoned rice vinegar** (or ⅓ cup rice vinegar and 1 tablespoon sugar); 3 tablespoons **pickled ginger,** cut into very thin strips; and 1½ teaspoons **black sesame seed** (optional) . Use, or cover and chill up to overnight. Just before filling pockets, stir in ½ cup **frozen petite peas.**

**Spinach filling.** Thaw 3 packages (10 oz. each) **frozen chopped spinach;** squeeze firmly to remove excess liquid. In a bowl, combine spinach, 1 cup minced **red onion,** and 3 tablespoons **seasoned rice vinegar** (or 3 tablespoons rice vinegar and ½ teaspoon sugar).

**Chicken–water chestnut filling.** In a bowl, combine 2 tablespoons *each* **seasoned rice vinegar** (or 2 tablespoons rice vinegar and 1½ teaspoons sugar) and **sweet-hot mustard.** Add 2½ cups shredded **cooked chicken;** 1 cup (5-oz. can) **water chestnuts,** drained and chopped; and ¾ cup sliced **green onions.**

# Summer Sorbets

**F**RUITS WITH FRESH HERBS *are the base for these sorbets. Choose from tart grapefruit-basil or lemon-tarragon, or mellower orange-rosemary and melon-mint. Use one of two methods to freeze them.*

With an ice cream maker. *Use a self-refrigerated machine or ice and salt (1 part salt to 8 parts ice) in a hand-cranked ice cream maker. Pour the sorbet mixture into the maker's container (at least 1-qt. size); cover and freeze according to manufacturer's directions until dasher is hard to turn or stops.*

In your freezer. *Pour sorbet mixture into a 9- by 13-inch pan; cover and freeze until hard (at least 2 hours or up to 1 month). Break into small chunks and whirl in a food processor or beat with an electric mixer until a smooth slush.*

*Either way, serve at once, or cover and freeze up to 1 month.*

## GRAPEFRUIT-BASIL SORBET

1 cup *each* water and sugar
2 cups grapefruit juice
2 tablespoons finely chopped fresh basil leaves

In a 1- to 2-quart pan, bring water and sugar to a boil over high heat; stir to dissolve sugar. Chill. Add juice and basil to syrup. Freeze as directed above. Makes about 3½ cups, 4 to 6 servings.

## LEMON-TARRAGON SORBET

2½ cups water
1 cup *each* sugar and lemon juice
1 tablespoon chopped fresh tarragon

In a 1- to 2-quart pan, bring water and sugar to a boil over high heat; stir to dissolve sugar. Chill. Add juice and tarragon. Freeze as directed above. Makes about 3 cups, 4 to 6 servings.

## ORANGE-ROSEMARY SORBET

½ cup water
2 tablespoons sugar
1 teaspoon finely chopped fresh rosemary leaves
2 cups orange juice

In a 1- to 2-quart pan, bring water, sugar, and rosemary to a boil over high heat; simmer until reduced to ⅓ cup, about 3 minutes. Chill. Add orange juice to syrup. Freeze as directed above. Makes about 3 cups, 4 to 6 servings.

*Fresh basil and grapefruit sorbet is a surprising, refreshing light dessert or snack. Fruit-and-herb sorbets are easy to make, ready to serve from the freezer.*

## MELON-MINT SORBET

⅓ cup *each* water and sugar
1 medium-size honeydew melon (about 2¾ lb.) or 3 small cantaloupes (about 4½ lb. total), cut in half and seeded
2 tablespoons *each* lemon juice and finely chopped fresh mint leaves

In a 1- to 2-quart pan, bring water and sugar to a boil over high heat; stir to dissolve sugar. Chill.

Scoop melon from rind. Smoothly purée in a food processor or blender; you should have about 3 cups. Add purée and mint to syrup. Freeze as directed above. Makes about 3½ cups, 4 to 6 servings.

# Kuchen Made with Fresh Apricots

FRAMED SNUGLY by a golden almond batter that swells up around them in the oven, fresh apricots make an appealing tart-sweet topping for this handsome kuchen.

Brown sugar, sprinkled on the fruit before baking, gives the apricots a glossy shine. Almond slivers add crispness.

For eating, you'll want apricots that are fully ripe—they're soft enough to give when gently pressed. For the kuchen, the fruit can be a little firmer (or fully ripe), because heating brings out the flavor and softens the fruit. To ripen apricots, loosely enclose in a paper bag and leave at room temperature, checking daily.

### APRICOT-ALMOND KUCHEN

Toasted almonds (directions follow)
½ cup (¼ lb.) butter or margarine, at room temperature
½ cup granulated sugar
3 large eggs
1 teaspoon grated lemon peel
1 tablespoon lemon juice
½ teaspoon vanilla
½ cup all-purpose flour
12 to 14 medium-size ripe apricots, cut into halves and pitted
3 tablespoons firmly packed brown sugar
¼ cup slivered almonds

In a food processor (or half at a time in a blender), whirl toasted almonds until very finely ground (but not to a paste), scraping sides of container frequently; set aside ground nuts.

In large bowl of an electric mixer, beat butter and granulated sugar until creamy. Add eggs, 1 at a time, beating well after each addition. Beat in lemon peel, lemon juice, and vanilla. On low speed, mix in flour and ground almonds until thoroughly blended.

Butter and dust with flour an 11-inch tart pan with fluted or plain rim and removable bottom. Scrape batter into pan and spread evenly. Arrange apricot halves closely together, cut side up; press lightly into batter. Sprinkle apricots with brown sugar and slivered almonds.

Bake in a 375° oven until batter is golden brown and feels firm in center when lightly pressed, 35 to 40 minutes (it will swell up around fruit). Let kuchen cool about 10 minutes on a rack. Carefully remove pan rim and serve kuchen warm, or let cool completely and serve at room temperature; cut into wedges. Makes 10 to 12 servings.

**Toasted almonds.** Spread 1 cup **unblanched** or blanched **almonds** in an 8- or 9-inch-wide pan. Bake in a 350° oven until golden brown (if unblanched, break a nut open to test), 10 to 15 minutes; shake pan occasionally. Let cool.

*Fresh apricot halves, sprinkled with slivered almonds, become juicy and more flavorful when baked in a tender almond cake; serve unadorned for a summer brunch. For dessert, offer with vanilla ice cream.*

# More June Recipes

In June *the fruit of the ornamental plum tree was featured in a tasty jam and in individual pastries. A French cook contributed a tarragon-accented lamb soup filled with spring vegetables.*

## ORNAMENTAL PLUM JAM

*The pits from this popular garden tree can be tedious to remove. The fruit is small and doesn't yield much substance. So why bother with ornamental plums? One good reason: great jam.*

*The cherry plum (Prunus cerasifera) and its many purple-leafed varieties bear a light to heavy crop of fruit. The small fruit is actually a plus for jam. It means a high proportion of sour skin to meat for a full-flavored and sweet-tart product.*

*To pit plums as quickly as possible, forgo a knife and, over a bowl, simply squeeze the fruit off the pit with your fingers.*

> **About 3½ quarts cherry plums**
> 1 **package (2 oz.) dry pectin**
> 7½ **cups sugar**

Wash and rinse 5 pint-size canning jars, rings, and new lids. Immerse jars and rings in boiling water to cover. Hold at gentle simmer for at least 10 minutes to sterilize. Sterilize lids as directed by manufacturer. To use, drain jars on a towel.

Wash and drain the plums. Hold fruit over a bowl and squeeze, 1 at a time, to pop out pits, catching juices. Discard pits. Coarsely chop fruit in a food pro-

*Ruby red jam brightens breakfast muffins and has full, tangy plum flavor.*

cessor or with a knife, saving juice. Measure fruit and juice; you should have 6½ cups. If not, prepare more fruit to make this amount.

In an 8- to 10-quart pan, combine plums and pectin. Bring to a rolling boil over high heat, stirring constantly. Stir in sugar and bring to a boil that cannot be stirred down; boil for exactly 2 minutes. Remove from heat; skim, discard foam.

Ladle jam into hot, drained jars, leaving ¼-inch headspace. Wipe rims clean. Set canning lids and bands on jars; screw on tightly, but don't force.

Place jars on a rack in a canning or other deep kettle of water at 180°. Add hot water, if necessary, to cover jars by 1 to 2 inches. Return the water to 180° and hold at that temperature, uncovered, for 10 minutes.

Lift jars from water (do not tip, or you may disturb a partially formed seal) and set on a towel. Let stand until cool. Press center of lids to test seal; if lids stay down, jars are sealed. Serve jam, or store sealed jars in a cool, dark place up to 2 years. Refrigerate unsealed or opened jars up to 3 months. Makes 5 pints.

## PLUM-CREAM CHEESE PASTRIES

On a floured board, roll out each of 6 thawed, **frozen puff pastry shells** to a 5-inch round. Pinch each pastry to form a ½-inch-tall rim. Place pastries 2 inches apart on a 12- by 15-inch baking sheet. In a bowl, beat until smooth 2 small packages (3 oz. each) **cream cheese**, 1 tablespoon **sugar**, ½ teaspoon grated **lemon peel**, and 1 **large egg**. Spread an equal portion in bottom of each pastry. Bake in a 400° oven for 15 minutes.

In a 1- to 1½-quart pan over medium heat, stir ½ cup **Ornamental Plum Jam** (recipe precedes) until bubbling. Spoon equally over puffed cheese in pastries. Bake until pastries are golden, about 5 minutes more. Transfer to a rack and let cool for 10 minutes; serve. Serves 6.

## SPRING LAMB SOUP

*Sweet vegetables combine to refreshing effect with lamb and tarragon in this French whole-meal soup. Rose-Marie Vassallo-Villaneau of Tregastel, France, contributed the recipe.*

*Ladle lamb soup, studded with artichoke hearts, asparagus, and peas, into bowls.*

> 2 **pounds lean boned lamb shoulder or neck (fat trimmed), cut into ½- to 1-inch chunks**
> 3 **tablespoons olive oil or salad oil**
> 3 **medium-size onions, sliced**
> 3½ **cups regular-strength chicken broth**
> 1 **teaspoon dry tarragon**
> 1 **pound tiny artichoke hearts (2-inch diameter or smaller)**
> 1 **package (10 oz.) frozen peas**
> 1 **pound asparagus (tough ends removed), cut into 1-inch slices**
> ¼ **cup chopped fresh mint or 3 tablespoons dry mint leaves**
> 2 **tablespoons lemon juice**
>   **Salt and pepper**

In a 5- to 6-quart pan over high heat, brown lamb, half at a time, in oil. Lift lamb from pan; set aside. Reduce heat to medium-high. Add onions to pan; stir often until limp, about 10 minutes. Mix in lamb, broth, and tarragon. Bring to a boil, then simmer, covered, until lamb is very tender to bite, 1 to 1¼ hours.

Just before lamb is tender, cut thorny tips from artichokes and peel off the coarse leaves (bracts) down to the all-edible pale green inner leaves. Trim stems from artichoke bottoms. Cut artichokes in half lengthwise and add to lamb. Bring to a boil over high heat; cover and simmer for 7 minutes. Stir in peas, asparagus, and mint; simmer, uncovered, until artichokes are tender when pierced, about 5 minutes. Mix in lemon juice and salt and pepper to taste. Makes 8 cups, 4 to 6 servings.

Cool salad of pineapple, strawberry, and papaya has green peppercorns, mint.

## TROPICAL SALAD WITH GREEN PEPPERCORNS

- 1 medium-size (4 lb.) ripe pineapple
- 2 teaspoons drained green peppercorns in brine
- 2 tablespoons *each* honey and orange-flavored liqueur (or orange juice)
- 2 tablespoons chopped fresh mint (or 2 teaspoons dry mint leaves)
- 1 medium-size ripe papaya, peeled, seeded, and cut into wedges
- 6 large strawberries, rinsed
- 6 mint sprigs

Cut peel and top from pineapple. Trim out any "eyes" that remain in fruit, then cut out core. Cut fruit into ¼- to ½-inch dice (you should have about 5 cups) and put into a bowl. Chop peppercorns and add to fruit along with honey, orange liqueur, and chopped mint; mix gently. Cover and chill fruit to blend flavors, 1 hour or up to overnight. Mix salad several times.

To serve, fan an equal number of papaya wedges on each of 6 salad or dinner plates. Spoon pineapple salad equally in mounds alongside. Garnish with strawberries and mint sprigs. Makes 6 servings. —*Randy Rumbell, Reno.*

Assemble and cut up foods, then cook. Sweet-sour sauce coats succulent morsels.

## HAWAIIAN PORK

- 2 pounds boned, lean pork butt or shoulder
- 1 *each* small green and red bell pepper, stemmed and seeded
- 1 small onion
- ¼ pound edible-pod peas
- 1 large egg, beaten
  About ½ cup cornstarch
  About 6 tablespoons salad oil
  Sauce (directions follow)

Cut pork into ¾-inch cubes; cut peppers and onion into 1-inch squares. Separate onion into layers. Remove ends and strings from peas.

Dip pork chunks in egg, then roll in cornstarch, shaking off excess. Pour 2 tablespoons oil into a 10- to 12-inch frying pan on high heat. Add half the pork, turning until browned, 5 to 7 minutes. With a slotted spoon, lift out pork and set aside. Repeat to cook remaining meat.

Add remaining oil to pan. Add peppers and onions; stir-fry until vegetables are tender-crisp, about 2 minutes. Add peas and sauce; stir until boiling. Add pork and stir until hot. Serves 6 to 8. —*Shana Gregory, Santa Clara, Calif.*

**Sauce.** Blend ½ cup *each* **cider vinegar,** firmly packed **brown sugar,** and **catsup;** ¼ cup *each* **cornstarch** and **pineapple juice;** and 2 tablespoons **soy sauce.**

Potatoes and eggplant are base of dish. Serve with a crisply roasted chicken.

## SPICY POTATOES IN COCONUT SAUCE

- 1 large eggplant (about 1¼ lb.)
- 4 medium-size thin-skinned potatoes (about 1¼ lb. total)
- 2 small red bell peppers, stemmed, seeded, cored
  Spices (directions follow)
- 2 tablespoons salad oil
- 1 cup regular-strength chicken broth
- 1 can (12 oz.) thawed frozen coconut milk
  Salt
- 2 green onions, thinly sliced

Peel eggplant and potatoes and cut into 1½-inch chunks. Cut peppers length-wise into ⅛-inch-wide strips. In a 12- to 14-inch frying pan on high heat, stir peppers and spices in oil until peppers are just limp, about 2 minutes. Remove from pan and set aside.

To pan, add eggplant, potatoes, and broth. Cover and simmer until vegetables mash easily, about 30 minutes; stir often. Add peppers and coconut milk. Simmer until sauce thickens, about 5 minutes, stirring often. Add salt to taste. Garnish with onions. Serves 4 or 5. —*Sonia Ottusch, Berkeley.*

**Spices.** Mix 2 cloves **garlic** (minced or pressed), 2 teaspoons minced **fresh ginger,** and 1 teaspoon *each* **cumin seed, ground coriander,** and **ground turmeric.**

## CHICKEN ADOBO

1 broiler-fryer chicken (3¼ to 3½ lb.), cut up
1 medium-size onion, quartered
½ cup *each* distilled white vinegar and water
1 tablespoon pickling spice
2 tablespoons soy sauce
1 clove garlic, minced or pressed
1 medium-size firm-ripe tomato, cored and cut into wedges
Parsley sprigs

In a 4- to 5-quart pan, combine chicken, onion, vinegar, water, pickling spice, soy sauce, and garlic. Bring to a boil over high heat. Reduce heat, cover, and simmer, stirring often, until thigh is no longer pink when cut at the bone, about 30 minutes.

With a slotted spoon, lift chicken and onion from broth; set aside. Spoon off fat and reserve. Boil broth, uncovered, on high heat until reduced to ¾ cup. Return onion to broth; keep warm.

Add reserved chicken fat to a 12- to 14-inch frying pan on medium-high heat. Brown chicken on all sides in fat; this takes about 5 minutes total.

Place chicken in a shallow bowl; pour onion and broth over meat. Garnish with tomatoes and parsley. Serves 4.— *Mary Lou Sanelli, Sequim, Wash.*

*Brown the chicken after braising it. Pickling spice is short-cut seasoning.*

## YELLOW RICE STICKS

¾ cup regular-strength chicken broth
3 tablespoons lime juice
2 tablespoons honey
1 tablespoon slivered fresh ginger
1½ teaspoons curry powder
2 tablespoons salad oil
1 cup broccoli flowerets, thinly sliced diagonally
2 medium-size carrots, peeled and cut in matchstick-size pieces
Yellow sticks (directions follow)
Lime wedges

Mix broth with lime juice, honey, ginger, and curry; set aside.

Place a wok or 12- to 14-inch frying pan over medium-high heat. Add oil; when hot, add broccoli and carrots. Stir-fry until tender-crisp, about 3 minutes. Add broth mixture. Bring to a boil on high heat. Add yellow sticks, mix with vegetables and broth, and pour into a bowl. Garnish with lime wedges. Serves 6 to 8.— *Betty Storrey, Kerman, Calif.*

**Yellow sticks.** To 2 quarts boiling **water** in a 4- to 5-quart pan, add ½ pound **rice sticks** (*mai fun* or thin rice noodles) or dry vermicelli and 2 teaspoons **ground turmeric.** Boil, uncovered, until tender to bite—5 minutes for rice sticks, 8 minutes for vermicelli; drain.

*Stir-fry vegetables; boil rice sticks (or pasta) with bright orange turmeric; mix.*

## MAPLE SYRUP PIE WITH RASPBERRIES & CREAM

Purchased pastry for a 9-inch deep-dish shell
½ cup all-purpose flour
½ cup firmly packed brown sugar
3 tablespoons butter or margarine, cut into chunks
½ cup maple or maple-flavored syrup
½ cup whipping cream, whipped
1 to 2 cups raspberries

Roll out pastry on a floured board and fit into a 9-inch tart pan with removable bottom. Bake in a 325° oven for 10 minutes; color will be pale.

Meanwhile, rub flour, sugar, and butter with your fingers until fine crumbs form. In a 1½- to 2-quart pan, bring syrup to a boil on high heat. Remove from heat and stir in flour mixture; pour into the pastry.

Bake tart in a 375° oven until crust is golden brown, about 35 minutes. Remove from oven; let cool until just warm to touch. Remove pan rim and slide a knife between crust and pan bottom to free; leave tart on pan.

To serve, spoon cream and some berries onto center of tart; accompany with remaining berries. Cut tart into wedges. Makes 8 to 10 servings.— *Nina Cimon, Phoenix.*

*Serve caramel-dense maple syrup tart topped with whipped cream, raspberries.*

**A**N ALMOST INCREDIBLY *efficient package, the egg is as fraught with possibilities as a crystal ball. Stare at one long enough and you may see a cake, a meringue, an omelet, a zabaglione—or, down the road, perhaps even a chicken. But breakfasts and brunches require eggs as eggs, whether they be sunny-side up on toast (the counterman's classic "Adam and Eve on a raft, eyes open"), over easy, scrambled soft, or soft- or hard-cooked in the shell. You can embellish them with salsa and tortillas if your palate requires a stronger stimulus, or give them a benediction—so to speak—with ham, hollandaise, and English muffin.*

*For something wholly different, though, try Pete Vassler's Dear Eggs. Mr. Vassler leaves the origin of the name shrouded in mystery, but he eagerly shares the recipe.*

## DEAR EGGS

  1  **tablespoon butter or margarine**
  3  **tablespoons dry sherry**
  ¼  **cup water**
  1  **chicken bouillon cube**
  1  **clove garlic, minced or pressed**
  2  **small onions, thinly sliced**
  1  **fresh green Anaheim (California) chili, seeded and chopped**
  3  **tablespoons finely chopped fresh basil leaves, or 1 tablespoon dry basil**
  3  **tablespoons chopped parsley**
  ⅛  **teaspoon cayenne (optional)**
  1  **large firm-ripe tomato, cored, peeled, and diced**
  4  **large eggs**
     **Lemon pepper seasoning, or salt and pepper**
  2  **split English muffins, toasted and buttered**

In a 10- to 12-inch frying pan, melt the butter over medium-high heat. Add sherry, water, bouillon cube, and garlic and stir until bouillon cube is dissolved.

*"Stare at an egg long enough and you may see a cake, a meringue, an omelet, a zabaglione—or even a chicken."*

Add onions, chopped chili, basley, and cayenne. Bring to a boil, cover, reduce heat, and simmer until onion is limp and liquid evaporates, 8 to 10 minutes. Stir in the tomato.

Push all the vegetables into a mound on 1 side of the pan. Carefully crack eggs into cleared space in pan. Cover and cook over low heat until done to your liking, 3 to 4 minutes for soft yolks and firm whites.

With a wide spatula, transfer 1 egg onto each muffin half; spoon vegetable sauce over eggs and serve. Add lemon pepper to taste. Serves 2 or 4.

*Pete Vassler*

*Aloha, Ore.*

**I**RA TURNER *has passed away, but we are fortunate to be able to share his recipe for salsa. Although a few of our tasters characterized it as a reasonable simulation of trial by fire or burning at the stake (Mr. Turner would have liked that), the majority proclaimed it the best salsa they had ever tasted. Pointing fingers, they called the dissenters candy-mouths who would be just as happy with ketchup. This salsa will indeed bring little beads of moisture to your brow, but you can always use just a little less of it.*

The fuel that feeds its flame is the jalapeño, the highly flavored and very hot sausage-shaped chili (usually about 3 inches long) that takes its name from Jalapa (or Xalapa), appropriately in the tropical Mexican state of Tabasco.

To avoid painful and prolonged burning, which results when you get jalapeño seeds under your fingernails or touch your hands to your eyes (or any tender tissue), wear rubber or disposable plastic gloves while handling chilies.

If you want to know much, much more about peppers—a family that includes the hot chilies crucial to this salsa—read Peppers: The Domesticated Capsicums, by Jean Andrews (University of Texas Press, Austin, 1984; $40). Dr. Andrews is not only a fine botanist, historian, gardener, and cook, but an artist as well; her 32 paintings in the book are outstanding—as are her descriptions, which help unscramble the pepper world.

## SALSA

1 can (28 oz.) tomatoes
1 medium-size green bell pepper, stemmed, seeded, and coarsely chopped
2 cloves garlic
8 cups (about 2¼ lb.) fresh jalapeño chilies (green—immature, hottest; or red—ripe, mellower; or both), stemmed and seeded
1 medium-size onion, cut into chunks

"Ira Turner's salsa is a reasonable simulation of trial by fire."

1 can (29 oz.), or 3 cups tomato purée
2 cups dry red wine
3 tablespoons sugar
2½ tablespoons red wine vinegar
2½ tablespoons distilled white vinegar (or red wine vinegar)
1½ teaspoons pepper
1½ teaspoons dry basil
1 teaspoon cayenne (optional)
1 tablespoon Worcestershire
2 teaspoons salt, or to taste

Place about half of the tomatoes and their liquid, bell pepper, garlic, jalapeños, and onion in a blender or food processor and whirl until finely chopped. Pour into a 5- to 6-quart pan. Finely chop remaining tomatoes, bell pepper, garlic, jalapeños, and onion, and add to pan.

Stir in tomato purée, wine, sugar, wine vinegar, distilled vinegar, pepper, basil, cayenne, and Worcestershire. Bring to a boil over high heat; reduce heat and simmer, uncovered, stirring often until mixture is reduced to about 3 quarts, about 30 minutes. Add salt to taste. Let cool, then serve. Or store to use as needed: ladle salsa into refrigerator or freezer containers (1- to 2-cup size) and cover. Store in the refrigerator up to 2 weeks, or freeze for longer storage. Makes about 11 cups.

*Tucson*

FRUIT SOUPS *seem strange to most Americans, although they're staples of northern European cuisine. Westerners may find the avocado, although a fruit, more palatable in soup than cherry or plum because the buttery avocado is familiar in roles that are savory rather than sweet.*

*Even when not thought strange, soups are rarely considered beautiful (except by Lewis Carroll's Mock Turtle, who sang of soup's beauty in Alice's Adventures in Wonderland), but this soup has the color and smooth opacity of pale green jade.*

"The Mock Turtle sang of soup's beauty."

## CHILLED AVOCADO SOUP

2 tablespoons butter or margarine
¼ cup chopped onion
1 small clove garlic, minced or pressed
1 tablespoon all-purpose flour
2 cups (or 1 can, 14½ oz.) regular-strength chicken broth
2 large ripe avocados (about 1½ lb. total)
½ teaspoon chopped fresh tarragon, or ¼ teaspoon dry tarragon
1 tablespoon tarragon wine vinegar
2 cups half-and-half (light cream)
Salt and white pepper
Chopped chives
Lime wedges

Melt butter in a 3- to 4-quart pan over medium heat. Add onion and garlic and stir often until onion is faintly browned, about 5 minutes. Add flour and stir until bubbly. Gradually stir in broth; turn heat to high and stir until boiling. Set aside to cool slightly.

Pit, peel, and cut avocados into chunks into a blender. Add broth mixture, tarragon, and vinegar. Whirl until smooth. Pour into a large bowl, stir in cream, and salt and pepper to taste. Cover and chill until cold, about 3 hours or up to overnight. Stir to obscure any darkening.

Ladle soup into small bowls and sprinkle with chives. Squeeze in lime juice to taste. Makes 5 or 6 servings, about 1 cup each.

*Bradbury, Calif.*

# June Menus

OUTDOOR DINING *figures prominently in this month's menus. For lunch on the patio, serve crêpes made with seasonal ingredients. Celebrate school's summer recess with a whimsical picnic in the park. Use the barbecue to turn out Indian-style shish kebabs.*

## LUNCHTIME GARDEN CRÊPES

**Fresh Corn Crêpes with Goat Cheese & Sautéed Vegetables**
**Greek Olives**
**Tomato & Butter Lettuce Salad**
**Strawberries, Blueberries & Raspberries**
**Sauvignon Blanc or Iced Tea**

*Indulge in summer produce: corn, zucchini, and carrots for the entrée; lettuce and ripe tomatoes for the salad; and a small mountain of berries for dessert.*

*The crêpe dish can be made in stages over several days, depending on your schedule; heat filled crêpes just before serving.*

*Allow 1 tomato per person; turn each into a flower by cutting wedges about ¾ of the way through. Serve on lettuce with oil-vinegar dressing.*

## FRESH CORN CRÊPES WITH GOAT CHEESE & SAUTÉED VEGETABLES

- 2 small packages (3 oz. each) cream cheese, at room temperature
- 11 ounces (1¼ cups packed) soft unripened goat cheese, such as Montrachet
- ⅓ cup milk
- 3 medium-size zucchini, ends trimmed
- 4 medium-size carrots
- 3 tablespoons butter or margarine
- ¾ teaspoon dry thyme leaves
  Fresh corn crêpes (recipe follows)

In a bowl, beat cream and goat cheeses with milk until smooth; set aside.

Cut zucchini and carrots into pieces about ¼ inch thick and 7 inches long. (Or cut into long shreds using the widest blade of an Oriental or regular shredder.)

*Alfresco lunch features summer's bounty. Fresh corn crêpe filled with carrots, zucchini, and goat cheese goes with a simple salad. Berries warm in the sun for dessert.*

In a 10- to 12-inch frying pan over medium-high heat, cook carrots with butter and thyme, stirring often, for 4 minutes. Add zucchini and cook, stirring occasionally, until carrots are tender-crisp to bite, 3 to 5 minutes longer.

Choose the 12 best-looking crêpes and lay them flat with rough, corn-textured side facing down (reserve any remaining crêpes for other uses). Spread each crêpe with an equal amount of cheese mixture, then spoon an equal amount of vegetables on half of each crêpe, letting vegetables extend a little beyond crêpe edges. Fold crêpes in half over filling.

Arrange crêpes slightly apart on 2 greased 10- by 15-inch rimmed baking pans. (At this point, you can cover and chill up to 2 days.) Bake, uncovered, in a 350° oven until vegetables are hot in center (lift top of crêpe to test), about 15 minutes. Makes 12 crêpes, 6 servings.

**Fresh corn crêpes.** Husk 2 medium-size **ears of corn** and discard silk. Cut kernels off cobs; discard cobs. In a 10- to 12-inch frying pan over medium-high heat, cook corn in 2 tablespoons **salad oil,** stirring often, until tender-crisp to bite, 5 to 10 minutes. Season to taste with **salt.**

In a blender or food processor, whirl until smooth 1½ cups **milk, 3 large eggs,** ½ teaspoon **dry thyme leaves,** ¼ cup **cornmeal,** and ¾ cup **all-purpose flour.** Add corn kernels; whirl just to mix.

Heat a 7- to 8-inch crêpe pan or frying pan over medium heat. To make each crêpe, lightly brush pan with melted **butter** or margarine (you'll need 1½ to 2½ tablespoons total). Stir batter, then all at once ladle about 3 tablespoons batter into pan. Quickly tilt pan to coat bottom completely with batter. Cook until surface looks dry, about 30 seconds. Turn crêpe with a wide spatula; cook bottom side until speckled brown (lift to check), about 20 seconds. Turn out of pan; stack crêpes as they're cooked.

Use; or to store, restack cooled crêpes between pieces of plastic wrap. Wrap airtight and chill up to 2 days or freeze up to 1 month. Makes 13 to 18 crêpes.

---

## SCHOOL'S-OUT PICNIC

**Grilled Hot Dogs & Buns**
**German Mustard      Pickle Relish**
**Mayonnaise      Catsup or Salsa**
**Watermelon**
**Gingerbread Cupcakes in Cones**
**Peach-Almond Ice Cream**
**Lemonade**

---

*Celebrate summer vacation with a hot dog barbecue. While the coals heat, churn peach-almond ice cream. For a surprise, scoop ice cream onto cones that have gingerbread baked inside.*

*Buy a few extra cones to avoid using any with cracks or holes—cake batter leaks out of these.*

*Three-part treat: scoop homemade peach ice cream onto gingerbread cupcake baked in cone; serve to eager recipient.*

## GINGERBREAD CUPCAKES IN CONES

½  cup sugar
1¼  cups all-purpose flour
1  teaspoon *each* baking soda, ground ginger, and ground cinnamon
¼  teaspoon *each* ground nutmeg and ground allspice
½  cup *each* salad oil and dark molasses
1  large egg
½  cup hot water
12  flat-bottom, plain ice cream cones (about 3 in. tall, without cracks or holes)

In a bowl, mix sugar, flour, soda, ginger, cinnamon, nutmeg, allspice. Add oil, molasses, egg, water; mix until well blended.

Spoon batter equally into ice cream cones. Place cones upright and slightly apart in a 9- by 13-inch baking pan. Bake in a 350° oven until a slender wooden pick inserted in center of a cupcake comes out clean, about 20 minutes.

Place cupcake cones on a rack and let cool completely. If made ahead, store uncovered at room temperature up to 1 day. (Cones soften if covered.) Makes 12.

## PEACH-ALMOND ICE CREAM

1  tablespoon lemon juice
2  large eggs
½  cup sour cream
1  cup firmly packed brown sugar
¼  teaspoon almond extract
2  teaspoons vanilla
1½  pounds ripe peaches, peeled, pitted, and cut into chunks
2  cups half-and-half (light cream)

Place lemon juice, eggs, sour cream, brown sugar, almond extract, and vanilla in a blender or food processor; whirl until smoothly blended. Add peaches and whirl just until small pieces of fruit remain.

Pour mixture into container of a ½-gallon-capacity ice cream maker—self-refrigerated or using 1 part salt and 8 parts ice. Stir in half-and-half until well combined.

Freeze according to manufacturer's directions or until dasher or stirring paddle will no longer rotate. Serve ice cream; or to firm, repack container with 1 part salt to 4 parts ice, or store airtight in freezer up to 1 month. Makes 2 quarts. — *Beth Gouveia, Roseville, Calif.*

---

## INDIAN-STYLE BARBECUE

**Calcutta Kebabs**
**Steamed Brown Rice**
**Melon-Chutney Salad**
**Crisp Sugar Cookies      Cherries**
**Yogurt-Mint Cooler**

---

*A cumin-garlic marinade flavors barbecued lamb and bell pepper skewers. Honeydew melon with chutney and lime dressing makes a simple, refreshing accompaniment. Offer the savory yogurt and mint drink to sip during the meal.*

*The 12 skewers will fit all at once on the grill of a kettle barbecue. If your barbecue has less grill space, barbecue the lamb and peppers in stages: cook the peppers first and keep them warm in the oven while you grill the lamb. Or serve the peppers at room temperature.*

## CALCUTTA KEBABS

¼ cup lemon juice
½ cup salad oil
3 cloves garlic, minced or pressed
1 tablespoon ground cumin
2 pounds boned leg of lamb (fat trimmed), cut into 1½-inch chunks
2 *each* medium-size green, red, and yellow bell peppers (or 6 of 1 kind), stemmed, seeded, and cut into 1½-inch pieces

In a large bowl, combine the lemon juice, oil, garlic, and cumin. Add the lamb; stir to coat. Cover and chill at least 4 or up to 24 hours.

Ignite 60 charcoal briquets on firegrate of a barbecue; let burn until coals are just covered with gray ash, about 30 minutes. Spread coals into an even layer and put grill in place 4 to 6 inches above them.

Meanwhile, thread equal portions of lamb, slightly apart, on 6 slender 10- to 12-inch metal or wooden skewers. Thread equal portions of peppers, slightly apart and alternating colors, on 6 more skewers. Brush peppers all over with the cumin marinade.

Place peppers and lamb on grill. Cook, turning and basting once with cumin marinade, until peppers are tender when pierced and meat is done to your liking (cut to test), 10 to 15 minutes for medium-rare. Makes 6 servings. —*Roxanne Chan, Albany, Calif.*

## MELON WEDGES WITH CHUTNEY DRESSING

Cut 1 large **honeydew melon** (about 4 lb.) in half lengthwise; scoop out and discard seeds. Cut each half into 6 equal wedges, then cut off and discard peel. Arrange wedges on a platter.

Strain liquid from ⅓ cup **Major Grey chutney** into a bowl; stir in 2 tablespoons **lime juice.** Finely chop chutney pieces and stir into lime mixture. Spoon evenly over melon. Makes 6 servings.

## YOGURT-MINT COOLER

In a blender, whirl just until blended 3 cups *each* **unflavored yogurt** and **water,** and 3 tablespoons *each* finely chopped **mint** and **green onion.** Pour into glasses over **ice cubes;** garnish with **mint sprigs.** Makes 6 servings.

# JULY

*Pizza on the Barbecue (page 164)*

**S**ummer meals have a
special appeal, as cooks seek easy-to-prepare dishes using
the season's bountiful produce. For leisurely July entertaining,
we suggested a simple method for cooking pizza on the
barbecue, homemade hot dogs, salmon salads, and scoop-and-
serve ice cream spectaculars. Junior chefs took over the kitchen
to cook their specialties in the microwave oven. We shared the
results of our in-depth pickling experimentation and some
sweet-hot Mexican discoveries from Acapulco.

# Pizza on the Barbecue

**B**ARBECUED PIZZA? *Isn't that carrying a good idea a little too far? Not if you want to turn out pizza similar to that baked in a big pizza oven—really crisp on the bottom, slightly aromatic from the smoldering wood embers, and, for summer cooks, blissfully out of the kitchen.*

*We first came upon the idea when we reported a barbecue cooking contest in Sebastopol, California.*

*The process is simple and effective. Stoke the barbecue with a measured number of charcoal briquets, then arrange the ignited briquets to frame the pizza. Cover the barbecue, open the drafts, and let the heat build up. Then sprinkle the soaked wood chips on the coals and set the pizza on the grill to give the wood-oven taste. Cover the barbecue and let the pizza bake.*

*Here, we present a good basic sausage pizza made with thawed bread dough, as well as a somewhat more sophisticated alternative with artichokes and roasted peppers. Or you can use your own favorite recipes for dough and topping.*

*The technique works with any unbaked, ready-to-cook pizza, including ones you buy refrigerated or frozen (follow package directions for thawing first).*

*Want to bake more than one pizza? Cook them in sequence; we give directions.*

## PIZZA ON THE BARBECUE

  1 **jar (about 1 lb.) marinara sauce**
  2 **cups hickory or mesquite wood chips (optional)**
    **Water**
  1 **pound mild Italian sausage**
    **Olive oil**

  1 **tablespoon cornmeal**
  1 **loaf (1 lb.) frozen white bread dough, thawed**
  ½ **pound mozzarella cheese, shredded**
  ¼ **pound jack cheese, shredded**
  ½ **small onion, thinly sliced crosswise**
  ½ **medium-size red bell pepper, stemmed, seeded, and thinly sliced crosswise**
  ¼ **to ⅓ cup calamata or Niçoise olives (optional)**
  1 **cup loosely packed basil leaves**

Bring marinara sauce to a boil in a 5- to 6-quart pan; over medium-high heat, stir frequently to prevent sticking until reduced to about ¾ cup. If made ahead, cover and chill up to 3 days.

Mix wood chips with about 2 cups warm water and let soak at least 30 minutes or up to 4 hours.

Peel casing off sausage and break meat into bite-size pieces in a 10- to 12-inch frying pan. Cook over medium-high heat, stirring occasionally, until brown, about 15 minutes.

On the firegrate of a barbecue with lid, ignite charcoal briquets—use 50 briquets for 23-inch-diameter round barbecue, 75 for 18- by 32-inch rectangular barbecue. When covered with ash, about 30 minutes, push coals in a circle or rectangle just larger than the pizza pan. (If you plan to cook more than 1 pizza, at this time add 10 briquets to the round barbecue, 20 to the rectangular one; space evenly.) Set grill 4 to 6 inches above coals.

Cover barbecue, open drafts, and heat until temperature in barbecue is 400° to 450° (set an oven thermometer in center

of grill, not over coals; or refer to thermostat on barbecue, which should read hot), about 15 minutes.

Meanwhile, oil a 14-inch-diameter pizza pan or a 10- by 15-inch shallow rimmed pan. Sprinkle with cornmeal. Roll out dough on a lightly floured board: for pizza pan, roll dough into a 15- to 16-inch-diameter round; for rectangular pan, make dough about 11 by 16 inches. Lift dough into pan; dough tends to shrink, so pat firmly out to pan edge.

Evenly spread marinara sauce over dough, leaving about 1 inch of dough uncoated at the edge. Mix the mozzarella and jack cheeses, and scatter over sauce. Top the cheese with sausage, onion, bell pepper, and olives. Let stand until barbecue is ready.

Drain wood chips and sprinkle over coals. Place pizza on grill within (not over) rim of coals; cover barbecue. Cook with drafts open until crust is well browned on bottom (lift with a wide spatula to check) and cheese is melted, about 15 minutes; check crust after 10 minutes. Remove from barbecue, top with basil leaves, and cut into wedges to serve. Makes 4 to 6 servings.

## ARTICHOKE & ROASTED PEPPER PIZZA

Make pizza as directed (preceding), omitting the sausage, onion, and bell pepper; olives are optional. Top the cheese with 1 jar (6 oz.) **marinated artichoke hearts,** drained; ⅓ cup crumbled crisp-cooked **bacon** ( ¼ lb. uncooked); and 1 jar (7 oz.) drained **roasted red peppers.**

**1** *Arrange pizza toppings on dough in pan; at the same time, start second pizza.*

**2** *Ring firegrate with hot coals; to prevent burning, pizza pan goes on grill in center of coals.*

**3** *With grill in place, add damp wood chips, then pizza to bake.*

*Savor each slice: barbecued crust is crisp and the flavor woodsy — just like the authentic pizza baked in a woodburning Italian oven but requiring much less effort.*

# Making Perfect Pickles

"WHAT'S A PERFECT PICKLE?" "How do I make old-fashioned fermented pickles?" "Can I make pickles quickly, without processing?" "Do I have to use all that salt?" "I've made pickles for years, but this year they spoiled. What happened?"

Prompted by these and other reader questions, we embarked on in-depth pickling experimentation; 475 pints and 22 gallons later, we share the results. They will surprise even experienced picklers and ensure success for pickling newcomers.

In addition to pickling logic and logistics, we give recipes for two basic kinds of dill pickles—quick and fermented—and for refrigerated pickles (these don't require water-bath processing). If you're watching your salt intake, you can reduce or omit salt from quick (but not from fermented) pickles, or use a salt substitute. For more on salt, answers to pickling questions, and an equipment check list, see the boxes on this page and pages 169 and 171.

## WHAT IS A PICKLE?

By reputation, a pickled cucumber is sour and salty, with just enough crunch. It's an unparalleled sandwich partner and a satisfying low-calorie snack.

Practically any food can be cured in acidified brine—"pickled." And because people have been pickling for centuries, there are dozens of methods for doing it. Our report is confined to two methods—quick and fermented (sometimes called kosher). Also, we're concerned here with sour pickles only—not sweet ones, such as bread-and-butters.

From a scientific standpoint, pickles are made by increasing the acidity of cucumbers. This produces the typical sour flavor and is essential in preservation. You can increase acidity in two ways: by adding acetic acid (vinegar), which is called quick pickling, or by causing lactic acid formation, which is called fermenting.

Quick pickles taste rather sharp and vinegary. Fermented ones have a mellower, more rounded flavor.

## What Equipment Do You Need?

IF YOU'VE CANNED BEFORE, chances are you already have most of the equipment you need to pickle. Two of our recipes require no canning equipment, just containers. Here are checklists to get you going.

For **Refrigerator Quick Dill Pickles,** you need *pint-size jars or plastic containers.*

For **Old-Fashioned Fermented Dill Pickles** that you plan to store in the refrigerator, you need *gallon-size glass or food-grade plastic jars.* They're available from some hardware, garden supply, and bottle stores. Or ask a restaurant for an empty one.

To process fermented pickles, or to make **Quick Dill Pickles** (whole or spears), **Low-Salt, Salt-Substitute,** or **No-Salt Quick Dill Pickles,** you need:

*Canning jars: quarts or pints, depending on recipe*

*Canning lids and bands to fit jars*

*Nonmetal knife to remove air bubbles*

*Canning or other kettle that's at least 2 inches taller than jars*

*Rack that fits in bottom of kettle to support jars*

*Thermometer to check water bath*

*Tongs to handle hot lids and bands*

*Jar lifter (we like ones with rubber grips)*

## WHAT'S INVOLVED?

**Quick pickles.** You start by adding seasonings, vinegar, and water to jars of cucumbers. Then, either refrigerate jars or process them in a water bath to store. Refrigeration has the advantage of speed, and pickles stored this way will keep up to six months. Refrigerated pickles are crisper than processed pickles and have more of a fresh cucumber flavor.

Water-bath processing mellows flavors, kills enzymes that would cause pickles to soften, and seals jars so you can keep them without refrigeration. Water temperature is critical: 180° is best; if much lower (under 175°), jars don't seal consistently. Higher temperatures overcook pickles and make them too soft.

**Fermented pickles.** This method isn't time-consuming in itself, but the cucumbers do need to sit 7 to 14 days at room temperature for fermentation to take place. Then they need to "cure"; this can take several weeks more.

Four stages are involved in making fermented pickles. The first takes one to two days. You submerge cucumbers in a brine; helpful bacteria found naturally on the cucumbers begin multiplying, changing the cucumbers' color from bright green to olive.

Stage two, "bubbly fermentation," usually lasts three to five days. Bacteria break down sugars in the cucumbers, producing lactic acid (responsible for the good sour flavor), some acetic acid (vinegar—this gives a sharp flavor), and carbon dioxide (you'll see bubbling). It's much like what happens when you make sourdough bread or sauerkraut. Cloudiness in the brine is bacteria in suspension.

This stage of fermentation is over when bubbling stops and the acidity increases to a $pH$ of 4.2 to 4.6 ($pH$ is a measurement of relative acidity, and lower numbers mean a *more* acidic solution). Watch for bubbles to disappear, or buy some $pH$ paper from a scientific supply store and use it to check.

During stage three, "quiet fermentation," more lactic acid is produced, and the $pH$ drops to 3.3 to 3.7. This takes three to seven days. There are two ways to tell when this stage is over. You can check with $pH$ paper. Or let the pickles progress to stage four *at room temperature* and produce one batch of scum yeast (it appears as an opaque film on the brine's surface), then carefully remove all the scum yeast. Chemically, scum yeast can't produce in quantity until fermentation is over. *It's important not to rush stage three, because if the brine is not acidic enough and you go ahead and process pickles, any botulinum bacteria present could form toxins.*

Stage four is curing. Now pickle color and texture stabilize and flavor mellows, much as when you age a fine wine. No more fermentation is taking place; to keep scum yeasts from taking over and pickles from spoiling, you must either refrigerate or process the pickles. Curing is complete when you cut into a pickle and find it's an even, dark, translucent green to the center (step 4 on page 169).

Curing time depends on the variety and maturity of the cucumbers you use and the temperature at which fermentation occurs. The process can overlap with fermentation and be done by the time fermentation is complete (about 10 days). Or the fermentation-plus-curing period can last up to seven weeks. Most of our pickles fermented in six to nine days and took another two to seven days to cure, but it's unpredictable. If you get tired of waiting, you can eat the pickles early—they just won't have full flavor.

Some cucumbers contain more natural pectin than others and are extra-firm; they cure more slowly. Smaller (younger) cucumbers often cure more quickly than larger ones.

Fermentation temperature is important, and 65° to 70° is ideal. Below that, fermentation will be considerably slower. Above, it will proceed too quickly, producing excessive carbon dioxide, which can break cucumber cell walls and result in hollow pickles. Softening and spoilage can also occur at higher temperatures.

To foster the growth of helpful microorganisms during fermentation and curing, and to inhibit scum- and mold-producing organisms, you need an anaerobic (airless) environment. The bag of water you see in the pictures on page 168 accomplishes this: it holds cucumbers submerged in brine and keeps air out.

## INGREDIENTS: CUCUMBERS & WHAT ELSE?

Basic pickling ingredients are cucumbers, flavorings, and water. For quick pickling, you also need vinegar. Salt may or may not be needed, depending on pickle type.

*Snacker's special is pickle from a jar of quick dills.*

**Cucumbers.** Choose pickling cucumbers, the fresher the better: extra-fresh cucumbers make extra-crisp pickles. Cukes should be firm and bright green, with no soft or yellow spots, and no shriveling, which would indicate they'd been stored too long or were picked old. Older, larger (longer than 5 inches) cucumbers may have formed tunnels; if possible, cut one to check a batch before buying. (If you can, taste before buying: bitter cucumbers make bitter pickles.) Very large cukes are more likely than small ones to become hollow during or after pickling.

Cucumbers, especially young ones, are very susceptible to shriveling. Once you pick or buy them, pickle them as soon as possible. If you can't use the cucumbers right away, cover them with damp towels and refrigerate up to two days.

**Flavorings.** Use fresh seed-head dill, sold in markets with pickling cucumbers.

**Water.** Tap water is fine, unless your water has an extremely high iron level, which could cause pickles to darken. In that case, use bottled distilled water.

**Vinegar.** Much of a pickle's flavor comes from vinegar and/or lactic acid. The acidity also helps prevent the growth of spoilage organisms.

Quick pickles gain acidity from commercial vinegar, which is 4 to 6 percent acid. *Do not use homemade vinegars,* which can vary widely in acidity. Our recipes call for distilled white vinegar. You can use cider vinegar if you like its flavor, but pickles will be somewhat darker in color.

Fermented pickles create their own acidity in the form of lactic acid and vinegar, so you needn't add commercial vinegar.

**Salt.** A certain level of saltiness is associated with a good pickle. In quick pickling, salt's only function is flavor; if you're watching your salt intake, you can omit it or use a salt substitute (but note: some testers felt pickles made with salt substitute had a bitter aftertaste). By omitting salt, you may taste more of the cucumber's natural sweetness.

In fermented pickling, salt inhibits the growth of spoilage organisms, while allowing good microbes to multiply. *Do not make fermented pickles without salt.*

## OLD-FASHIONED FERMENTED DILL PICKLES

*Making fermented pickles is not an exact science, especially in terms of timing. It's a little tricky to know when the second stage of fermentation is complete (see fermented pickles, page 166). Consider buying a box of pH paper ($4 to $6.50) from a scientific supply store. With it, you'll be sure fermentation is complete when the paper reads pH 3.7 or less. Buy paper with a scale of about pH 3.0 to 5.5.*

*Curing—the final stage of pickling—may be complete by the time fermentation is over, or it may take several weeks more (see page 167). Be patient; the results are worth the wait.*

> About 3½ pounds small (3- to 4-inch) pickling cucumbers, about 30
> Water
> 4 large fresh dill seed heads (each about 5-inch diameter)
> 4 to 6 cloves garlic, peeled and cut in half
> 12 black peppercorns
> 1 dry bay leaf
> 1 teaspoon whole allspice
> 4 small dried hot red chilies (optional)
> ¼ cup table salt

Wash cucumbers in cool water (do not scrub); pick off and discard any blossoms. Drain cucumbers and put into a clean 1-gallon glass or food-grade plastic jar with dill, garlic, peppercorns, bay leaf, allspice, and chilies.

In a container (at least 2½ qt.), stir salt with 2 quarts water until salt dissolves. Pour over cucumbers in jar.

Fill a pint-size plastic bag ½ full with water; close with a wire twist. Put bag into a second plastic bag; close with another wire twist. Set bag over cucumbers to hold them under brine. (Brine level should be near top of jar; if it's low,

## FERMENTED PICKLES, STEP BY STEP

**1** *For fermented pickles, pour brine into jar over cucumbers, dill, garlic, and spices.*

**2** *Push water bag into jar so brine covers cukes, creates airless environment for fermentation.*

**3** *Once a day during fermentation (7 to 14 days), check brine top and inside of jar for scum; remove any you see.*

# What About Salt & the Different Kinds of Salt?

**S**ALT IS SALT. Or is it? We discovered a confusing array of salts on grocery shelves: plain and iodized table salt; kosher, pickling, rock, popcorn, and sea salts; salt substitutes. Which to choose? Does it matter? Is salt even needed?

Salt's a necessary component of fermented pickles. For other styles, salt is a matter of taste, as well as whether you are limiting your salt intake. To separate salt fact from fiction, we talked to experts and tested different salts in pickling.

**Grain size.** Whether salts are from the ocean or the earth, one difference is grain size. Popcorn salt is one of the finest grades; table salt is a fine grade; kosher, pickling, and sea salts are a little coarser; rock salt is the coarsest.

Testing showed grain size is not important in pickling: table salt works as well as coarser salts. But measured amounts of different salts are not equal in weight. *For every tablespoon of table salt called for in our recipes, you can substitute ½ ounce of another salt.*

**Additives.** Different additives also distinguish salts. Most of these are anti-caking agents, used to keep salt free-flowing. Iodized salt may also contain dextrose (sugar) and sodium bicarbonate (baking soda) to keep iodine from degrading.

Additives might concern you because they don't all dissolve completely in pickle brine. *Sodium silico-aluminate* (the anti-caking agent used in most table salt) and *sylox* (used in some table salt) leave a very small amount of harmless precipitate in brine. Our recipes call for table salt — it's readily available, and the precipitate is not significant. (Though popular belief holds that "canning" or "pickling" salt has no additives, some has sodium silicoaluminate.)

If you want perfectly clear brine, use salt without additives. Or buy salt containing these completely soluble anti-caking agents: *magnesium carbonate* (used in table salt sold in health-food stores), *yellow prussiate of soda* (used in some kosher salts), and *tricalcium phosphate*

(used in some popcorn salts).

Iodized salt leaves slightly more precipitate in brine than plain (uniodized) salt; you can use either. One myth is that iodized salt darkens pickles. In fact, pickles made with iodized salt are no darker than ones made with plain salt. With any pickling, cucumbers turn from bright to olive green.

**Cloudiness.** Fermented-type pickles naturally develop a small amount of white, cloudy deposit at the bottom of the jar as helpful bacteria settle. This is unrelated to the type of salt used.

**Salt substitutes.** These products are made of potassium chloride instead of sodium chloride, which some people restrict for health reasons. ("Light" salts are a combination of potassium chloride and sodium chloride.) You can use a salt substitute instead of regular salt for quick pickles (see recipe, page 171). Fermented pickles require salt to keep undesirable microbes in check; *do not make fermented pickles with a salt substitute.*

---

fill plastic bag ¾ full of water.) Cover jar with a lid or plastic wrap and a rubber band. Set in a cool (60° to 70°), dry place (not in the dark, and not on a wood surface, which could be ruined if brine spills).

Together, the two fermentation stages

(see discussion, page 166 and 167) can take 7 to 14 days. During the first stage, remove lid and bag of water once a day and examine top of brine; if you see any white scum on the surface, skim it off with a spoon and discard. Wipe off any scum inside jar. Rinse any scum off the

plastic bag and return bag to jar; cover. (Scum is unlikely to form during this stage, but check anyway.)

The brine will bubble and may foam slightly; it will also turn cloudy. With bubbling, a little brine may spill out of jar; this is normal.

The first stage of fermentation is complete when spontaneous bubbling (don't shake jar when you check) subsides. Bubbles may be small, so look carefully.

During the second stage of fermentation (3 to 7 days), you'll see no bubbling. But continue to check brine, jar, and bag for scum. Fermentation is over when $pH$ paper dipped in brine reads lower than 3.7. If you don't have $pH$ paper, let the pickles stand at room temperature and produce one batch of scum yeast to indicate the end of fermentation; then carefully remove all the scum yeast.

At this point, you must *either* refrigerate the jar *or* process pickles as directed at right to keep the pickles from spoiling.

*(Continued on next page)*

**4** *Cukes on left just went into brine, are white inside. Olive ones in middle have fermented; dark green edges mean start of curing. Cured pickles at right are green throughout.*

## ...OLD-FASHIONED FERMENTED DILL PICKLES

Then the pickles must cure to develop their full flavor (see page 167). They may be cured by the time fermentation is over or take up to 5½ weeks; usually, curing takes about 1 week.

To determine whether curing is complete, cut into a pickle. It should be an even, translucent dark green throughout (see step 4, page 169). If pickles are not yet cured to the center, refrigerate opened jar. About once a week, cut into a pickle to check curing. (You can eat cucumbers that aren't completely cured: they just won't have full flavor.)

In the refrigerator, pickles keep up to 1 year if immersed in brine with water bag. Check jar about once a month; remove any scum on brine or bag.

**To prepare for water-bath processing,** set an 18- to 22-quart kettle filled about ⅔ full of water on high heat; cover and bring to simmering. Into kettle, put a canning or other rack that fits in pan. Also have a 2- to 3-quart pan of water at about 180° to replenish kettle water as needed.

While water heats, wash, rinse, and drain 3 wide-mouth quart-size canning jars, free of nicks or cracks. Heat 3 rings and new lids as manufacturer directs.

Pack pickles into jars with dill and spices. (Discard water bag.) Pour brine over pickles, leaving ½ inch headspace. Discard any extra brine; also trim any pickles that stick up into the top ½ inch of jar. Run a plastic or wooden knife around inside of jars to release trapped air. Wipe rims clean. Set hot lids and bands on jars and screw on tightly, but don't force.

**To process pickles,** lower jars onto rack in kettle of water. If needed, add more hot water to cover jars by 1 inch. Bring water to 180°, then process, uncovered, at 180° for 20 minutes. Lift out jars with a jar lifter (do not tip jars or you may break a partially formed seal); set on a towel to cool completely.

Press centers of lids; if they stay down, jars are sealed. Remove bands from sealed jars; wipe jars clean to remove any brine. Eat, or store in a cool, dark place up to 2 years. Store unsealed jars and opened pickles, chilled, up to 6 months. Makes 3 quarts. — *Selma Bloch, Seattle.*

## QUICK DILL PICKLE SPEARS

*Amount of cucumbers varies, depending on size and how you pack them into jars.*

    Water
  7 small cloves garlic, peeled and cut
    in half

  2 or 3 fresh dill seed heads (each
    about 4-inch diameter)
3½ teaspoons mustard seed
 28 whole allspice
3¼ to 3¾ pounds small (3- to 4-inch)
    pickling cucumbers, 25 to 35
  1 quart distilled white vinegar
  2 tablespoons table salt

Set an 18- to 22-quart kettle filled about ⅔ full of water on high heat, covered, and bring the water to simmering. Into kettle, put a canning or other rack that fits the pan. Also have a 2- to 3-quart pan of water at about 180° to replenish the kettle water as needed.

While water heats, wash, rinse, and drain 7 wide-mouth pint-size canning jars, free of nicks or cracks. Heat 7 jar rings and new lids as manufacturer directs.

In each jar, put 2 garlic pieces, ¼ to ⅓ of a dill head (6 to 10 flowerets), ½ teaspoon mustard seed, and 4 whole allspice.

Wash cucumbers in cool water; pick off and discard any blossoms. Drain cucumbers; quarter lengthwise. Vertically pack spears compactly (don't force) into jars. Leave top ½ inch of jars clear; if spears stick up into this area, cut them off.

In a container (at least 2½ qt.), combine vinegar, 1 quart water, and salt; stir to dissolve salt. Pour over cucumbers in

## QUICK PICKLES, STEP BY STEP

**1** *For quick pickles, first pack cucumber spears vertically in pint canning jars with spices, then add vinegar brine.*

**2** *Run a plastic knife between cucumbers and jar to release air bubbles. Put on lids and bands; tighten.*

**3** *Lower pickle-filled jars into 175° to 180° water; cook 20 minutes. Lift out; let stand undisturbed until cool.*

jars, leaving ½ inch headspace. Run a plastic or wooden knife around inside of jars to release trapped air. Wipe rims clean. Set hot lids and bands on jars and screw on tightly, but don't force. Process as directed in preceding recipe (page 168). Makes 7 pints. — *Beverly Hartman, Fresno, Calif.*

## LOW-SALT OR SALT-SUBSTITUTE QUICK DILL PICKLES

Follow preceding directions for **Quick Dill Pickle Spears,** but use only 1 tablespoon **table salt;** or use 1 to 2 tablespoons salt substitute (potassium chloride).

## NO-SALT QUICK DILL PICKLES

Follow preceding directions for **Quick Dill Pickle Spears,** but omit salt.

## REFRIGERATOR QUICK DILL PICKLES

Follow preceding directions for **Quick Dill Pickle Spears,** using 1 to 2 tablespoons salt. Use pint-size jars or plastic containers. Pack spears horizontally if using plastic containers. Cover and refrigerate at least 24 hours or up to 6 months. Do not process in water bath.

## WHOLE QUICK DILL PICKLES

Follow directions for **Quick Dill Pickle Spears,** Low- or No-Salt Quick Dill Pickles, or Refrigerator Quick Dill Pickles, but use 3 or 4 wide-mouth quart-size canning jars, free of nicks or cracks. In each jar, put 2 cloves **garlic,** ½ of a **dill head** (12 to 16 flowerets), 1 teaspoon **mustard seed,** and 7 to 9 whole **allspice.**

Pack whole cucumbers into jars. Pour in brine, leaving ½ inch head space, and process in water bath as directed for 20 minutes. (Do not process refrigerator pickles.) Makes 3 or 4 quarts.

# Pickling Qs & As

PICKLING SEASON brings reader questions. Here are answers to common queries.

**Can I salvage bitter cucumbers?**
No. If they taste bitter when raw, they'll be bitter when pickled. It's best to get a new batch of good-tasting cucumbers.

**Should I remove cucumber blossoms?**
Yes. If blossoms are moldy, which usually occurs only in very humid climates, an enzyme in the mold can break down cucumber tissues and cause softening. Grape leaves counteract this enzyme, so you may see them in some recipes.

**For extra-crisp pickles, should I use alum or slaked lime?**
No. For crisp pickles, use very fresh cucumbers, and, if you process them, keep the water bath at 175° to 180°. (Higher temperatures soften pickles.)

Our quick pickles made with alum and slaked lime were no more snappy than ones without these so-called crisping agents. Alum slowed down the progress of fermentation and left pickle skins tough. Slaked lime seemed to prevent fermentation from taking place.

**Why does garlic turn turquoise in brine?**
There's a chemical naturally present in immature garlic that turns it blue in an acid medium. The garlic is fine to eat.

**Is it safe to hot-pack pickles?**
Yes, you can process pickles by the open-kettle method (pour boiling vinegar-water over cucumbers packed in sterilized jars, then attach sterilized lids and rings). But we found quick pickles made this way had a harsh garlic-vinegar flavor, whereas water-bath processing mellows flavor.

**Why did pickles get soft?**
There are a number of possibilities. For all types of pickles, blossoms might be attached to cucumbers (see above). Cucumbers might have been overmature or held too long after picking. Pickles might be processed too long or at too high a temperature. The jar's seal might be incomplete. The jar might have been stored in too warm a place (over 100°).

For fermented pickles, you probably didn't skim off scum (seen as white film on top of brine or water bag) or mold from the brine's surface. Or pickles might have been exposed to air (not covered with brine).

A soft pickle may not be safe to eat; discard it. If the rest of the jar smells all right and other pickles aren't soft or slimy, they're safe to eat.

**Why did I get hollow pickles?**
Usually, hollow pickles start with hollow cucumbers—from plants watered insufficiently while growing.

Large cucumbers can become hollow during pickling; tissues are more fragile than in smaller cucumbers and can break when carbon dioxide is produced. Pickles that ferment at too high a temperature (over 70°) may also become hollow because carbon dioxide is produced too quickly and ruptures cell walls. Pickles stored in too warm a place (over 100°) may get hollow.

**What are kosher pickles?**
Pickle manufacturers disagree on the meaning of "kosher." In some cases, kosher pickles are manufactured in accordance with Jewish religious laws; these pickles don't differ from others in flavor. Other times, kosher means a classic flavor, usually with garlic. In home use, the term kosher is sometimes used for fermented pickles and sometimes for any pickle containing garlic.

**Why do some cucumbers never ferment?**
You've probably either overwashed the cucumbers or used alum or slaked lime. Rinse dirt off, but don't scrub. Micro-organisms present on cucumber skins help fermentation start.

**Is it best to ferment in the dark?**
No. Toward the end of fermentation, scum yeasts and mold can easily grow; they like dark places. A kitchen counter is a good spot for fermenting pickles.

**The brine of my fermented pickles turned cloudy. Is this okay?**
Yes. The cloudiness is caused by helpful bacteria suspended in brine.

**What's the white sediment that forms at the bottom of the jar in fermentation?**
Dead bacteria. As lactic acid increases, it kills some bacteria.

# Dynamite Dogs

KIN TO THE CLASSIC FRANKFURTER, *these juicy sausages can be made mild to hot. But it's only with maximum seasoning that they merit the name of "dynamite dogs."*

*Once you assemble the ingredients and equipment, the sausage-making process is fairly simple. You grind the meat and fat, season the mixture, then vigorously beat the mixture with ice to create a modified emulsion that makes the sausages juicy. Next, fill the sausage casings and twist at intervals to form dogs.*

*Poach the sausages right away (important for food safety) and serve; or chill and reheat. Once the sausages have been poached, you can also pan-brown or barbecue them.*

*From the meat counter, you'll need to purchase soft pork fat (from the pork back) and natural sausage casings, so call in your order several days ahead. Casings cost about 50 cents a yard and are sold either in a salt solution or dry salt and need to be washed before using. Both the fat and casings can be frozen.*

*For equipment, you'll need a food chopper (electric or manual) to grind the meat and a sausage-stuffing attachment, but you can improvise the latter. Make a stuffing tool with a plastic-lined pastry bag fitted with the plastic tube of a gravy baster (tip and part of end sawed off to create a 5-inch-long nozzle); slide tube into pastry bag, leaving 1 inch of the tube in the bag; secure bag to the neck of the tube by wrapping securely with sturdy tape.*

*To stuff the casings, recruit a helper. Have one person operate the food chopper or pastry bag while you guide the meat mixture into the casings.*

*The amount of salt looks high, but it is necessary to create the emulsion of fat and ice for moist, firm-textured sausages with a minimum of fat.*

## DYNAMITE DOGS

1½ **pounds boneless beef chuck**
   **About 1½ pounds boneless pork butt or shoulder**
   **About 1 pound pork back fat with skin (trim off skin and discard); or use about ½ pound pork fat pieces, trimmed of all meat membrane**
2 **large eggs**
½ **cup nonfat dry milk powder**
   **Seasoning paste (recipe follows)**
1 **tablespoon salt**
2 **cups crushed ice**
   **About 4 yards natural sausage casings, 1¼-inch diameter**
   **Water**
   **About 3 yards thin cotton string**

Cut beef and pork into 1-inch cubes. Trim off and discard fibrous membranes and tough gristle; you need 2 cups packed cubes of each meat. Cut the pork fat into 1-inch cubes; you need 1 cup packed fat. Mix meat and fat together.

With an electric or manual food chopper fitted with the fine blade, grind the mixture of meat and fat, putting it through the chopper 3 times.

Put eggs in a bowl and beat to blend. Add meat mixture, dry milk, seasoning paste, and salt. .Using your hands or a heavy spoon, mix well. (If made ahead, cover and chill mixture as long as overnight.)

In a food processor or small bowl of a heavy-duty electric mixer with mixing attachment (not a whip), whirl or beat at high speed ½ of meat mixture with ½ of the crushed ice just until the mixture looks creamy in consistency. This takes about 40 seconds in a processor, 1 minute in a mixer (if you overbeat, mixture looks fibrous and sausages will have a mealy texture). Transfer sausage to a large bowl. Repeat process with remaining meat and ice. To avoid spoilage, keep meat mixture cold whenever you are not working with it.

Cut casings into 4- to 5-foot-long sections and let soak in warm water for 10

Grind meat, trimmed of all fibrous membrane and gristle, and fat together three times with an electric or manual food chopper.

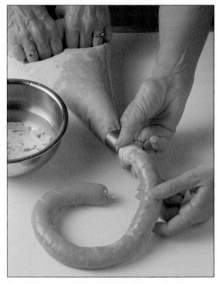

Squeeze meat mixture into casing, and form a solid sausage; two pairs of hands make job easier. Pastry bag is one tool you can use.

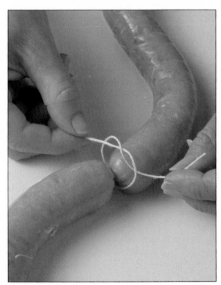

Twist filled casing every 7 inches and tie twist with string to form fuse for a dynamite-stick sausage.

minutes. Slide 1 end of a length of casing onto a smooth-tipped faucet. Run warm water through the casing to rinse out salt and check for holes; repeat with each section. Let casings stand in cool water until ready to use. Just before using, drain and strip off excess water with your fingers.

Apply sausage-stuffing attachment to food chopper according to manufacturer's directions. (Or improvise with a pastry bag as suggested preceding.)

Ease end of 1 piece of casing onto the stuffing tube, allowing the last 2 inches of the casing to hang free. (Or ease casing onto the plastic baster tip fitted into the pastry bag.) Get a second pair of hands to help from this point on.

Force meat mixture through the food chopper, using chopper plunger to keep flow of meat even. (If using the pastry bag, fill bag with the meat, fold bag shut, and roll or twist to force meat into casings.) For the first few inches, hold casing closed at tip as meat fills it; let out air, then knot casing tip. For the rest, pierce casing with a needle to release air. Fill casings so they feel plump.

If casings tear (they're tougher than they look), force meat away from tear, cut casing, twist, and set aside. Continue with remaining casing.

As each section of casing is stuffed, tie ends in knots. Twist sausage at about 7-inch intervals to form individual dogs; tie at each twist with a piece of string to secure. Repeat until all the meat is used; keep sausages cold.

Fill an 8- to 10-quart pan with 5 quarts of water; bring to a rapid boil over high heat. Turn off heat and immediately add sausages (to keep submerged, place a wire rack or slightly smaller pan on top). Cover and let stand until sausages feel firm to touch, about 30 minutes. Drain, then cut sausages apart. You can serve

*Heat-seasoned with cayenne, mustard, horseradish, and garlic, dynamite dog (complete with fuse) attracts a big bite.*

the sausages hot or, if made ahead, let cool, cover, and chill up to 3 days. Freeze for longer storage, then thaw in refrigerator.

*To brown sausages on barbecue* after poaching, place on a grill 4 to 6 inches above a solid layer of medium coals (you should be able to hold your hand at grill level for about 4 to 5 seconds). Cook until sausages are brown, turning as needed, about 15 minutes total.

*To pan-brown sausages* after poaching, cook over medium heat in a single layer, uncovered, in a lightly greased frying pan, turning as needed, about 7 minutes.

*To reheat in water,* immerse in enough simmering water to cover, turn heat to low and cook about 6 minutes.

Makes 11 or 12 sausages, each about ¼ pound. — *Lydia Raymond, Oakland.*

**Seasoning paste.** In a 10- to 12-inch frying pan, combine 2 tablespoons **salad oil;** 1 medium-size **onion,** minced; and 2 tablespoons minced or pressed **garlic.** Stir occasionally over medium-high heat until onion is limp, about 5 minutes. Remove from heat and add ¼ cup **paprika,** 2 teaspoons **ground nutmeg,** 1½ to 2 teaspoons **dry mustard,** and ½ to 1 teaspoon **cayenne.** Stir until spices are combined. Pour in ½ cup **water,** ½ cup **catsup,** and 2 teaspoons to 1 tablespoon **prepared horseradish.** Return to heat, stir, and cook until mixture is dry, about 6 minutes; set aside to cool. (For the dynamite-hot flavor, use maximum amounts of dry mustard, cayenne, and horseradish.)

# Ice Cream Spectaculars

SCOOP AND SERVE. *That's about all you do to make these ice cream spectaculars. They're hang-the-calories rewards at the end of a meal or on their own.*

*For the party-size treats—the fruit split and cooky platter—ice cream teams with fresh fruits. Both are easy and fast to arrange if you scoop the ice cream ahead and return it to the freezer till serving time.*

*The sundae and dunce caps feature rich ice creams complemented by toppings with contrasting textures and flavors.*

## DOUBLE PEANUT BRITTLE SUNDAE

- ½ pound peanut brittle
- ¾ cup salted peanuts, coarsely chopped
- ¾ cup purchased caramel sauce
- 1 quart rich vanilla ice cream
  About 1 cup whipped cream

Break off and set aside 4 large chunks of the brittle, *each* about 2½ inches wide. Coarsely crush remaining brittle.

Put 1 tablespoon *each* crushed brittle, peanuts, and caramel into each of 4 deep dessert dishes (at least 1½-cup size). Place a big scoop of ice cream in each dish. Repeat layers; top equally with remaining crushed brittle, nuts, caramel.

*Chunk of peanut brittle tucked into vanilla ice cream is topped by whipped cream puff, salty peanuts, and buttery smooth caramel.*

Mound ¼ of the cream onto each sundae, and stick a chunk of brittle into ice cream. Serve at once. Serves 4.

## COOKY PLATTER WITH PEACHES & CREAM

- ½ gallon (2 qt.) toasted almond ice cream
  Cooky platter (recipe follows)
- 3 to 4 large ripe peaches, peeled and sliced
- 1 cup purchased caramel sauce
- ¼ cup toasted almonds (directions follow)

Let ice cream stand at room temperature to soften slightly. Quickly scoop it into large balls and set them side by side in a chilled 10- by 15-inch pan; at once set pan in the freezer. If done ahead, wrap pan airtight and hold up to 4 days.

Stack ice cream on cooky platter, mounding slightly. Tuck peach slices around ice cream, drizzle with caramel, and sprinkle with almonds. At once, use a sharp knife to cut in wedges. Serves 8 to 10.

**Toasted almonds.** Scatter ¾ cup **sliced almonds** in an 8- or 9-inch-wide pan. Bake nuts in a 350° oven until lightly toasted, about 8 minutes; let cool. Use ¼ cup of the nuts to top the dessert (preceding) and ½ cup for cooky platter (following).

**Cooky platter.** In a food processor or with fingers, whirl or rub together 1 cup **all-purpose flour;** ½ cup (¼ lb.) **butter** or margarine, cut up; ½ cup **toasted almonds** (see preceding); ¼ cup firmly packed **brown sugar;** and ¼ teaspoon **almond extract** until dough holds firmly together. Press dough evenly over bottom and sides of a 10- or 11-inch tart pan with a removable bottom. Bake in a 325° oven until golden brown, about 25 minutes. Let cool.

## GIANT SUNBURST FRUIT SPLIT

- ½ gallon (2 qt.) rich vanilla ice cream
  About ½ of a 2-pound cantaloupe, seeded, peeled, and cut into ¾-inch-thick wedges
- 2 medium-size firm-ripe bananas, cut in half lengthwise and crosswise
- 2 to 3 ripe medium-size nectarines, peeled and sliced

*Large almond-flavored cooky, mounded with toasted almond ice cream, peaches, and toppings, sparkles with candles.*

- 1 cup raspberries, rinsed and drained
  Strawberry sauce (recipe follows)

Let ice cream stand at room temperature to soften slightly. Quickly scoop it into large balls and set them side by side in a chilled 10- by 15-inch pan; at once set pan in the freezer. If done ahead, wrap pan airtight and hold up to 4 days.

Chill a large, shallow platter. Arrange cantaloupe, banana, and nectarine pieces on outer rim to create a sunburst effect. Mound ice cream balls in the center of the platter and sprinkle with raspberries. Drizzle 1 cup strawberry

*Golden spikes of cantaloupe and nectarine and pale rays of banana surround mound of vanilla ice cream topped with raspberries.*

*Sugar cone hats top chocolate ice cream scoop nested in toasted hazelnuts and coffee ice cream resting in chopped chocolate.*

sauce over ice cream. Spoon portions of fruit and ice cream into dessert bowls. Add remaining sauce to taste. Serve at once. Makes 8 to 10 servings.

**Strawberry sauce.** In a blender or food processor, purée 2 cups rinsed and hulled **strawberries**, ¼ cup **orange juice**, and 1 tablespoon **sugar.** Makes about 2 cups.

## DUNCE CAPS

½  cup coarsely chopped hazelnuts

½  cup coarsely chopped semisweet chocolate

1  pint *each* coffee and rich chocolate ice cream

8  purchased sugar ice cream cones

Scatter hazelnuts in an 8- or 9-inch-wide pan. Bake in a 350° oven until lightly toasted, about 7 minutes; let cool.

On each of 4 dessert plates, make equal, separate mounds of nuts and chocolate. Spread each mound to make about a 2-inch circle. Top each circle of chocolate with a rounded scoop of coffee ice cream; on each circle of nuts, put a rounded scoop of chocolate ice cream. Cap each ball with a cone and serve. Serves 4.

# Junior Chefs Use the Microwave

**C**HILDREN SEEM TO HAVE *an instinctive aptitude for using the microwave oven. Its safety factors, speed, and cleanup-saving potential also make it a good choice when junior chefs decide to whip up treats for friends or family.*

*These four microwaved dishes are child-tested for taste and ease of preparation: a salad with a hot ground beef and taco-filling topping, a warm open-faced tortilla snack, a flavorful cheese and pasta dish with turkey and Chinese pea pods, and a gooey brownie-like dessert.*

*Although microwave ovens work fastest with small amounts of food, these recipes—which make enough for four to six servings—come together quickly.*

*Remember that although microwave oven surfaces don't get warm, potholders are essential when handling the containers, which absorb heat from the food cooked inside. Also, when foods are covered for* some steps to make cooking more even, remove the cover very carefully to prevent steam from harming your hands or face.

*Because a minimum of utensils are put to work, tidying up is less dreary.*

## ZAPPED TACO SALAD

1 pound ground lean beef
1 medium-size onion, chopped
1 can (15 oz.) kidney beans, drained
1 can (15 oz.) stewed tomatoes
1 can (4 oz.) diced green chilies
2 tablespoons chili powder
1 medium-size head iceberg lettuce, washed, crisped, and shredded
2 medium-size firm-ripe tomatoes, cored and cut into wedges
½ pound (about 5 cups) corn chips
1 cup (4 oz.) shredded cheddar cheese

Crumble beef into a 9- by 13-inch non-metal shallow dish; add the onion, and cover the dish tightly with plastic wrap. Cook in microwave oven on full power (100 percent) for 6 minutes; stir after 3 minutes (be careful of steam when lifting cover). Uncover and cook at full power until meat starts to brown lightly, about 13 minutes; stir every 3 minutes. Spoon out fat and discard.

Mix beans, tomatoes, chilies, and chili powder with meat mixture. Cook at full power, lightly covered with a paper towel, until mixture is bubbling, about 10 minutes; stir every 2 to 3 minutes.

Meanwhile, divide lettuce evenly among 4 dinner plates. Lay tomato wedges and corn chips around the lettuce, dividing equally. Spoon ¼ of the hot meat mixture onto lettuce on each plate and top each with ¼ of the cheese. Makes 4 servings.

*Taco salad is a team effort, and the rewards are speedy. Steps to delegate: cutting tomatoes, slicing lettuce, shredding cheese, stirring beef.*

*Crisp tortilla is topped with vegetables and cheese for a nutritious snack.*

## FLOPPY DISKS

4 flour tortillas (7 to 8 inches wide)
1 tablespoon butter or margarine
1 medium-size onion, chopped
½ pound mushrooms, sliced
½ pound mozzarella cheese, shredded
1 medium-size firm-ripe tomato, cored and thinly sliced
1 teaspoon ground nutmeg

Lay 1 tortilla on a nonmetal plate in a microwave oven. (To puff, the tortillas need to come from a freshly opened package.) Cook, uncovered, on full power (100 percent) until top of tortilla puffs, about 1 minute. Turn tortilla over and continue to cook until top puffs, about 1 minute more. Set aside; tortilla crisps more on cooling. Repeat with remaining tortillas.

In a shallow 9- by 13-inch nonmetal dish, combine butter, onion, and mushrooms. Tightly cover with plastic wrap and cook in microwave oven on full power for 6 minutes; stir after 3 minutes. Uncover and continue to cook at full power, stirring every 3 to 4 minutes, until all the liquid from the mushrooms has evaporated, about 10 minutes.

Place each tortilla on a nonmetal plate. Spoon onion-mushroom mixture in equal amounts onto each tortilla, spreading almost to the rim with the spoon. Scatter cheese equally over vegetable topping and top equally with tomato. Sprinkle each "disk" with ¼ teaspoon nutmeg.

One at a time, put a plate with a tortilla in the microwave oven and cook, uncovered, on full power until cheese melts, 1½ to 2½ minutes each. Makes 4 servings.

## PEA POD & TURKEY PASTA

1 package (6 oz.) frozen Chinese pea pods
8 to 10 ounces fresh pasta, such as fettuccine
1 can (14½ oz.) regular-strength chicken broth
1 cup whipping cream
2 cups ¼- by 1-inch strips cooked turkey
2 cups (8 oz.) shredded Swiss cheese

Set package of pea pods in a microwave oven and cook on full power (100 percent) for 1 minute. Let stand 3 minutes; turn package over and cook on full power for 1 minute. Pour peas into a colander and let them drain.

Lay pasta level in a shallow 2- to 2½-quart nonmetal casserole; pour broth and cream over pasta. Tightly cover casserole with plastic wrap. Cook in microwave oven on full power until pasta is tender to bite, about 9 minutes; stir every 3 minutes (be careful of steam when lifting plastic).

Mix in the turkey and cook, uncovered, on full power for 2 minutes. Add cheese and pea pods and mix with 2 forks to blend. Cook on full power until cheese melts, about 1 minute. Makes 4 to 6 servings.

## CHOCOLATE-PEANUT BROWNIE CUPS

½ cup *each* all-purpose flour and sugar
3 tablespoons cocoa
¼ teaspoon baking soda
6 tablespoons cream-style peanut butter
2 tablespoons milk
1 large egg
½ cup semisweet chocolate baking bits
1 cup miniature marshmallows

In a bowl, combine flour, sugar, cocoa, and soda. Stir in peanut butter, milk, and egg, mixing until well blended. Stir in chocolate bits and marshmallows.

Divide mixture equally among 6 non-metal custard cups (¾-cup size). Evenly space cups in a circle in microwave oven. Cook desserts, uncovered, at full power (100 percent) for 1½ minutes. Rotate cups, trading each with the one directly across from it; continue cooking on full power for 1½ minutes more.

Let desserts stand in oven for 3 minutes to finish cooking (centers will be soft). The cups will be hot; use potholders to remove from oven. Serve hot or warm. Makes 6 servings.

*Use potholders when taking hot food from the microwave. Here, oven surfaces are not hot, but the chocolate-peanut brownie cups are.*

# Sweetness & Heat — A Mexican Secret

THE INTERPLAY of sweetness and heat is basic to many of Mexico's most popular dishes. To add another dimension to these tastes, the tartness of lime or other fruit is often present as well.

In a summer cooking program we previewed at the Acapulco Princess Hotel, chefs shared their recipes, including two classics using sweet-hot as a flavoring element. These recipes, for chilies rellenos and pico de gallo, are given here.

Chilies rellenos, or stuffed chilies, are filled many ways, but a picadillo filling of browned and seasoned ground pork with raisins teams the sweet and the hot deliciously. Our instructor selected stubby, dark green poblano chilies to stuff because of their generous cavities. The chili flavor, though warm, is palatable even to the timid. The dish's sweetness comes from raisins in both filling and sauce, and from pineapple in the salsa.

(Poblano chilies are gaining a significant foothold in Western markets; if you don't see them, you can probably order them through your produce market.)

Pico de gallo — literally "rooster's beak" — has many forms. Typically, it's a salad-like mixture or snack of jicama, cucumber, and orange, most often seasoned with chilies and lime juice — but there are many other kinds.

The cooking school's version starts with sliced jicama and cucumber, and adds pineapple, carrots, and papaya or mango. Slices are arranged on a platter and drenched with a refreshing sweet-hot mixture of orange and lime juices flavored with jalapeño chilies. Because the dressing contains no fat, calories are minimized, and the colorful salad, with its wide range of textures, qualifies as exceptional flavor value.

Pudgy poblano chilies, encased in a puffy egg batter, are filled with pork, raisins, and nuts, topped with minced salsa.

## CHILIES RELLENOS

- 1 **pound ground lean pork**
- 1 **small onion, chopped**
- 2 **cloves garlic, minced or pressed**
- ½ **cup raisins**
- ⅓ **cup *each* slivered almonds and chopped pecans**
- 2 **tablespoons minced fresh mint leaves, or 1 tablespoon dry mint**
- 2 **tablespoons minced fresh basil leaves or 2 teaspoons dry basil**
- 1 **can (8 oz.) tomato sauce**
  **Salt**

- 6 **medium-size poblano chilies (about 1 lb. total) or small green bell peppers (about 3 inches wide)**
  **About ⅓ cup all-purpose flour**
  **Egg batter (recipe follows)**
  **Minted salsa (recipe follows)**

In a deep 10- to 12-inch frying pan, combine pork, onion, garlic, raisins, almonds, pecans, mint, and basil. Cook, stirring to crumble meat, on medium-high heat until meat is browned, about 20 minutes. Add tomato sauce and salt to taste. If made in advance, let cool, cover, and chill up to overnight.

Rinse chilies. Leaving stems on, slit each chili (or pepper) lengthwise and pull out seeds and ribs. Fill chilies equally with pork mixture, packing in firmly. Roll chilies in flour; shake off excess.

Rinse and dry frying pan; add ¾ to 1 inch oil. Place on high heat until oil is 425° on a deep-frying thermometer.

When oil is hot, hold a chili by the stem and dip into the egg batter, turning to coat well all over; as you use up the batter, you will need a spoon to ladle batter evenly over chilies. Lift chili, still holding by the stem, from batter and gently slide it into the hot oil; the pan will accommodate about 3 chilies at a time. Cook, basting chilies with hot oil, until golden brown on bottom, then turn and brown other sides.

Lift chilies from oil with a slotted spoon and drain on paper towels; keep warm. Repeat to cook remaining chilies. Serve chilies with salsa to spoon over them. Makes 6 servings.

**Egg batter.** Separate whites and yolks of 4 **large eggs.** In a large bowl, whip whites until short peaks hold when beater is lifted. With the same beater, whip yolks to blend. Fold yolks into whites; use at once.

**Minted salsa.** In a 10- to 12-inch frying pan, cook 1 cup chopped **onion** in 1 tablespoon **salad oil** over medium heat until onion is limp and golden, about 10 minutes; stir often.

Meanwhile, core, seed, and chop enough **ripe tomatoes** to make 2½ cups. Add tomatoes to frying pan with ½ cup chopped **fresh** or canned **pineapple;** ¼ cup packed chopped **fresh mint leaves** or 2 tablespoons dry mint; ⅓ cup **raisins;** ¾ cup **tomato juice;** and 1 **chicken bouillon cube.**

Bring salsa mixture to a boil on high heat; reduce heat to a simmer. Cook, stirring occasionally, until bouillon cube has dissolved and mixture is reduced to 3 cups, about 10 minutes. If made ahead, cool, cover, and chill up to 2 days. Reheat salsa to serve. Makes about 3 cups.

## PICO DE GALLO SALAD

- 1 **piece ripe pineapple, 2¼ to 2½ pounds, peeled**
- ¾ **pound jicama, peeled and rinsed**
- 2 **large carrots, peeled**
- 1 **medium-size cucumber, peeled**
- 1 **large firm-ripe papaya or mango (10 to 12 oz.)**
  **Fresh mint sprigs (optional)**
  **Chili lime juice (recipe follows)**
  **Salt**

*Low-calorie pico de gallo combines sliced papaya, cucumber, jicama, pineapple, and carrots with chili, lime juice, and mint.*

Cut pineapple crosswise into ¼-inch-thick slices. Cut jicama into ¼-inch slices. Cut carrots diagonally into ⅛-inch slices.

Cut cucumber diagonally into 3 pieces; with an apple corer or slender knife, cut out center with seeds if desired. Then cut each cucumber section diagonally into ¼-inch slices.

Peel papaya, cut in half lengthwise, seed, and cut crosswise into ¼-inch slices. Or slit mango peel just through to fruit, pull off peel, and cut fruit off the seed into ¼-inch slices.

Group each element of the salad separately on a large platter. (If made ahead, cover and chill up to 4 hours.) Garnish platter with mint. Pour chili lime juice over salad; serve, adding salt to taste. Makes 8 to 10 servings.

**Chili lime juice.** Stem and seed 1 small **fresh serrano** or jalapeño **chili.** Whirl in a blender with ⅓ cup **lime juice** and ¼ cup **orange juice** until chili is puréed.

# Squash Blossoms — Cooked or Raw

**D**O AS ITALIAN GARDENERS *have done for generations and enjoy the prolific production of a squash vine by eating the blossoms as well as the fruit.*

*If you don't have a garden, order blossoms from your produce market.*

*Good raw or cooked, flowers from any squash vine—winter or summer, acorn to zucchini—will do.*

*The only distinction that matters is the sex of the blossom: male flowers, which grow directly from the stem, tend to stay open whether used raw or fried. These blossoms don't produce fruit, but you should leave about half of them on the vine for pollinating female blossoms.*

*Female blossoms, which grow at the end of immature squash (some cooks use the tiny squash and flowers together), are only open briefly when they're young. You can carefully separate these blossoms from the young squash, and the fruit will continue to develop on the vine.*

*Pick blossoms soon after they open. They need to be handled gently but are more durable than you might suppose. To clean them, reach into the well of the flower and pinch out the stem in the middle, then rinse thoroughly with gently running water to wash away any bugs and dirt. Drain flowers cup side down on paper towels.*

*Use the blossoms right away or, if you want to save them until you have more to use at one time, refrigerate them for up to three days. Before refrigerating, lay the washed and drained blossoms cup side down or on their sides in a single layer on a pan lined with paper towels; cover lightly, but airtight, with plastic wrap.*

*Our recipes give four approaches. The most dramatic presentations use raw flowers, as in the mango-laced rice salad and with cold poached fish.*

*A real surprise is to find sautéed blossoms as a filling in cheese-flavored crêpes.*

*A favorite Italian way to serve squash flowers is dusted with flour, coated with egg, and quickly fried. Here we offer them with a light tomato relish.*

## SQUASH BLOSSOMS WITH RICE SALAD

- 1 large ripe mango (about ¾ lb.), peeled
- ½ cup salad oil
- 3 tablespoons white wine vinegar
- 2 tablespoons *each* minced onion and minced fresh cilantro (coriander)
- 1 tablespoon minced fresh or canned seeded jalapeño chilies
- 3 cups cold, cooked long-grain white rice
  Salt and pepper
- 12 large (3- to 4-inch-long) squash blossoms
  Fresh cilantro sprigs

Cut mango from pit; discard pit and dice the fruit. Stir together mango, oil, vinegar, onion, minced cilantro, and chilies. (If desired, cover and chill up to 2 days.)

Just before serving, stir together the rice and the mango mixture; season rice salad with salt and pepper to taste.

Pinch and discard stems from centers of blossoms. Rinse blossoms gently; drain cup side down. Lightly fill each squash blossom with 2 to 3 teaspoons of the rice salad. Gently mix half the blossoms into the salad and mound it on a serving platter; garnish with the remaining blossoms and cilantro sprigs. Serves 4 to 6.

## STUFFED SQUASH BLOSSOMS & SEABASS

- 18 medium-size (2- to 3-inch-long) squash blossoms
- 1½ tablespoons (1 oz.) canned black whitefish or lumpfish caviar
- 3 pounds very fresh, firm white-flesh fish, such as white seabass, rockfish, or lingcod, boned, skinned, and cut into 6 equal pieces, each about 1 inch thick
- 2 ounces smoked salmon
- 1 tablespoon lemon juice
- ½ cup whipping cream
  Pesto (recipe follows)

Pinch and discard stems from centers of blossoms. Rinse blossoms gently; drain cup side down. Spoon caviar into a fine strainer and rinse under cold running water until water runs clear; set aside.

Rinse fish; trim equally from each piece enough to make ¼ cup total. In a food processor or blender, purée trimmings with salmon and lemon juice.

Whip cream until it holds soft peaks. Add puréed fish and caviar; fold together to blend. Spoon about 1 tablespoon of the seafood cream into each squash blossom. Leave blossom open or gently twist petal ends together to shut. Set blossoms in a single layer on a plate lined with paper towels; cover and chill up to 4 hours.

*Tender, uncooked blossoms cradle a mousse of smoked fish and caviar to serve with cold poached seabass. Female blossoms, such as these, are usually closed.*

Bring 3 inches of water to boiling in a 5- to 6-quart pan. Add fish; cover and remove from heat; let stand 8 minutes. Cut a slit to center of thickest part of a piece of fish; if done, the fish will look opaque in center; if not, let stand 2 to 5 minutes longer. Drain fish, cover, and chill at least 1 hour or up to 4 hours.

To serve, place 1 piece of fish on each dinner plate; spoon pesto equally onto each piece. Place 3 stuffed blossoms on each plate alongside the fish. Serves 6.

**Pesto.** In a food processor or blender, coarsely purée ¾ cup lightly packed **fresh basil leaves,** ½ cup **olive oil,** and 2 tablespoons *each* grated **parmesan cheese** and **lemon juice.**

## SQUASH BLOSSOM CRÊPES

    20  to 30 medium (2- to 3-inch-long)
        squash blossoms
    3   tablespoons butter or margarine
    10  crêpes (recipe follows)
    5   ounces (about ⅔ cup) chèvre (goat)
        cheese or camembert cheese
    10  tablespoons chopped chives or
        green onion
    30  whole chives or 10 stems from the
        tops of green onions, each 10 to 12
        inches long

Pinch and discard stems from centers of blossoms. Rinse blossoms gently; drain cup side down.

In a 10- to 12-inch frying pan over medium-high heat, melt 1 tablespoon of the butter. Add blossoms all at once and stir occasionally until lightly wilted, about 2 minutes; set aside.

Lay crêpes out flat, one at a time. Top each with 1 tablespoon cheese, 1 tablespoon chives, and 2 or 3 sautéed squash blossoms. Fold crêpe ends in slightly, then roll each crêpe to enclose filling; put aside, seam side down.

Cluster 3 whole chives or use 1 green onion stem to wrap around middle of each filled crêpe and tie in a knot; trim ends. Repeat for each crêpe. Lay crêpes, seams down and side by side, in a 9- by 13-inch oval or rectangular baking dish.

Melt remaining 2 tablespoons butter and pour over tops of crêpes. (If made ahead, cover and chill up to 1 day.)

Bake, covered, in a 350° oven until crêpes are steaming hot when uncovered, 15 to 20 minutes from room temperature, 30 minutes if chilled. Serve as a first course with 1 or 2 as a portion. Serves 5 to 10.

*Lightly coat blossoms with flour, dip in egg, fry quickly, and drain on paper towels.*

**Crêpes.** In a blender or food processor, whirl 3 **large eggs** and 1 cup **all-purpose flour.** Add 1½ cups **milk** and whirl until smooth.

Place a 7- to 8-inch crêpe pan or frying pan over medium-high heat; melt about 2 teaspoons **butter** or margarine, tilting pan to coat bottom. Remove pan from heat, pour in about ¼ cup of batter, and immediately tilt pan to coat bottom evenly. Return pan to heat and cook until crêpe surface feels dry, about 30 seconds. Turn with a wide spatula; cook bottom side until speckled brown (lift to check), about 20 seconds. Turn out of pan onto a plate.

Repeat, adding **butter** each time, to make each crêpe; stack as cooked. To store, restack cooled crêpes between pieces of plastic wrap; wrap airtight and chill for up to a week or freeze for up to a month. Before separating to reuse, bring crêpes back to room temperature; they tear if cold. Makes 10 to 13.

## FRIED SQUASH BLOSSOMS WITH FRESH TOMATO RELISH

    6   large (3- to 4-inch-long) or 12
        medium-size (2- to 3-inch-long)
        squash blossoms
        About 2 tablespoons all-purpose
        flour
    2   large eggs
        Salad oil
        Fresh tomato relish (recipe follows)
    6   or 12 sprigs fresh tarragon or
        watercress

*Unusual first course: tomato relish fills fried blossoms; garnish with tarragon sprig.*

Pinch and discard stems from centers of blossoms. Rinse blossoms gently; drain cup side down.

Put flour in a bowl or bag; in another bowl or an 8- or 9-inch-wide pan, beat eggs to blend. Coat 1 blossom at a time lightly with flour; shake off excess. Dip blossom into egg, lift out, and drain briefly. With your fingers, spread petals open, if desired. Add coated flowers to about 1 inch salad oil heated to 400° in an 8- to 10-inch frying pan and cook until light golden brown, about 30 seconds; turn as needed or push down into oil. If you want to preserve the open shape of the flowers, cook blossoms in about 2 inches of oil in a deep 2- to 3-quart pan. Drain fried flowers on paper towels.

Serve hot or at room temperature. (If made ahead, let stand at room temperature, lightly covered, up to 8 hours; to reheat, arrange in a single layer in a 10- by 15-inch pan and place, uncovered, in a 450° oven until hot, about 5 minutes.)

Accompany fried blossoms with fresh tomato relish; if desired, fill each blossom with ½ to 1 tablespoon of the relish. Garnish servings with tarragon sprigs. Allow 1 large or 2 medium blossoms as a portion. Makes 6 first-course servings.

**Fresh tomato relish.** Core, seed, and finely chop 1 large firm-ripe **tomato.** Mix with 1 tablespoon *each* **olive** or salad **oil, red wine vinegar,** and minced **shallot;** ¾ teaspoon chopped **fresh tarragon** (or ¼ teaspoon dry tarragon); and **salt** and **pepper** to taste.

# Quick Summer Salmon Salads

SALMON'S RICH FLAVOR *shows off in these two quick-to-fix summer salads. For the first, you roll up slightly smoky-tasting lox into fanciful roses to serve with piquant cilantro sauce. This simple but effective first course comes from The Grange restaurant, Adelaide, Australia.*

*Use fresh salmon steaks—now in good supply—for the second salad; poach over direct heat or in a microwave oven.*

## LOX ROSES
### WITH CILANTRO SAUCE

½  **pound thinly sliced lox or cold-smoked salmon**
2  **medium-size ripe tomatoes, peeled and seeded**

1½  **cups firmly packed fresh cilantro (coriander) sprigs**
2  **tablespoons lemon juice**
2  **tablespoons salad oil**
1  **tablespoon drained green peppercorns**
   **Fresh cilantro sprigs**

Divide lox into 4 equal portions. Loosely roll each portion into a spiral to form one large or several small roses; set aside.

In a blender or food processor, whirl tomatoes, the 1½ cups cilantro sprigs, lemon juice, oil, and peppercorns until smoothly puréed. Pour an equal portion onto 4 salad plates. Set roses in sauce, flattening bottoms slightly so roses will stand up. Garnish with cilantro sprigs and serve at once; sauce separates on standing. Makes 4 first-course servings.

## POACHED SALMON SALAD
## WITH TARRAGON VINAIGRETTE

4  **salmon steaks, each about ½ pound and 1 inch thick, poached (directions follow)**
2  **medium-size heads Belgian endive (about 4 oz. each), leaves separated**
4  **cups lightly packed curly endive leaves (about 8 inches long), rinsed and crisped**
2  **cups lightly packed watercress sprigs, rinsed and crisped (or use 6 cups total curly endive)**
½  ***each* medium-size red and green bell peppers (or use 1 of 1 color), stemmed, seeded, and thinly sliced crosswise**
   **Tarragon vinaigrette (recipe follows)**

Place 1 salmon steak on each of 4 dinner plates. Arrange equal portions of Belgian and curly endive, watercress, and bell peppers next to salmon. Offer vinaigrette to top salads. Makes 4 main-dish servings.

**Poached salmon.** *Over direct heat:* in a 12- to 14-inch frying pan, combine 1 quart **water,** ½ cup **dry white wine,** 10 **black peppercorns,** 4 **whole allspice,** 1 **bay leaf,** and 3 tablespoons **lemon juice.** Bring to a boil over high heat, then cover and simmer for 15 minutes. Add salmon steaks, cover, return to simmer, and cook until fish is no longer translucent in center (cut to test), about 8 minutes.

*In the microwave:* in a 10-inch round nonmetal dish, combine poaching ingredients (see direct heat instructions, preceding), except use only 1¾ cups water. Cook, uncovered, on high power (100 percent) for 8 minutes. Add salmon steaks with thickest portions toward rim, and cook, uncovered, on high for 4 minutes. Turn steaks, give dish ¼ turn, and cook, uncovered, on high until fish is just opaque in center (cut to test), 1 to 2 minutes.

Lift salmon from liquid and let cool (reserve liquid for other uses). Serve cold; if made ahead, cover and chill overnight.

**Tarragon vinaigrette.** In a bowl, mix ⅓ cup **white wine vinegar,** 1 tablespoon **Dijon mustard,** 1½ tablespoons minced **fresh tarragon,** and 1 teaspoon **sugar.** Whisking rapidly, gradually add ⅔ cup **salad oil.**

*Spoon tarragon vinaigrette over main-dish salad of poached salmon steak, watercress, Belgian and curly endive, red and green bell pepper strips.*

# Adventures with Avocados

**W**HEN AVOCADOS *are abundant and well priced, it's a good time to experiment with using them in unexpected ways. A variation on gazpacho, the cold soup uses avocados instead of tomatoes. As a dessert, try folding mashed avocado into a velvety meringue — South Americans have long favored such treatment.*

## COOL AVOCADO GAZPACHO

- 1 **large cucumber, peeled**
- 3 **cups regular-strength chicken broth**
- ¼ **cup firmly packed fresh cilantro (coriander) leaves**
- 2 **tablespoons lime juice**
- 2 **medium-size firm-ripe avocados**
- 1 **small red onion**
  **Curry-garlic croutons (recipe follows)**
  **Fresh cilantro sprigs (optional)**
- 2 **medium-size limes, cut into wedges**

Chop cucumber; whirl in a blender with 2 cups of the chicken broth, cilantro, and lime juice until smoothly puréed. Pit, peel, and coarsely chop avocados. Add to cucumber mixture; whirl very briefly to coarsely purée avocado, leaving some chunks. Cover and chill until cool, at least 2 hours or up to overnight.

Peel onion and cut several thin slices crosswise; set slices aside. Mince enough remaining onion to make ¼ cup. Mix minced onion and remaining broth with soup.

Pour equal portions of soup into 6 soup bowls. Separate onion slices into rings. Garnish each bowl with a few croutons, onion rings, and cilantro sprigs. Offer lime wedges to squeeze and more croutons to add individually. Makes 6 servings, 1 cup each.

**Curry-garlic croutons.** Cut day-old **French bread** (about half of a 1-lb. loaf) into ½-inch cubes to make about 5 cups total. Spread cubes evenly in a 10- by 15-inch baking pan. Bake in a 300° oven for 15 minutes.

Meanwhile, in a 6- to 8-inch frying pan over medium heat, melt ½ cup (¼ lb.) **butter** or margarine. Stir in 2 cloves **garlic,** minced or pressed, and 1½ teaspoons **curry powder.** Stir until garlic turns golden, about 2 minutes.

After croutons bake 15 minutes, pour seasoned butter over them and mix gently. Reduce oven to 275° and bake croutons until light brown and crisp, about 45 minutes; stir occasionally. Cool completely. Serve, or store airtight at room temperature up to 5 days.

## AVOCADO CREAM PARFAIT

- 1 **small orange**
- 2 **large firm-ripe avocados, pitted and peeled**
- 2 **tablespoons lime juice**
- 3 **tablespoons orange-flavored liqueur (optional)**
- 2 **large egg whites**
- ½ **cup sugar**

Grate enough peel from orange to make 1½ teaspoons; wrap orange and chill.

In a large bowl, coarsely mash avocados with a fork or potato masher; mix in lime juice, orange liqueur, and orange peel. Cover with plastic wrap and refrigerate until cold, at least 1 hour or up to 4 hours.

In a deep bowl, whip egg whites with an electric mixer on high speed until a thick froth. Continue to whip at high speed and slowly sprinkle in sugar; beat until whites hold stiff, glossy peaks when beaters are lifted. Add avocado mixture and fold smoothly into whites.

Evenly divide avocado mixture among 4 to 6 tall, stemmed glasses. Cover and chill until cold, at least 1 hour or up to 4 hours.

Cut 4 to 6 thin slices crosswise from unpeeled orange; tuck a slice into each dessert to garnish. Makes 4 to 6 servings.

*Squeeze lime juice into chilled avocado gazpacho; serve cold soup with curry-garlic croutons and lime wedges.*

# Savory Madeleines

TYPICALLY, *the petite French dessert cakes called madeleines are prepared from a sweet butter-rich batter, then baked in special pans that give them a pretty, shell-shaped form. But here is a moist, cheese-laced variation, with zucchini for texture and delicate flavor.*

*Serve the moist baked madeleines hot or at room temperature, as an appetizer or to accompany soup or salad.*

## ZUCCHINI MADELEINES

- 3 medium-size zucchini (about 1½ lb. total), shredded
- 2 teaspoons salt
- 6 tablespoons olive oil
- 1 medium-size onion, chopped
- 1 cup all-purpose flour
- 1 tablespoon baking powder
- 5 large eggs
- 2 tablespoons milk
- 1¼ cups (about 5 oz.) freshly grated parmesan cheese
- 1 clove garlic, minced or pressed
- 2 tablespoons chopped fresh basil leaves or 1 teaspoon dried basil
- ¼ teaspoon pepper

In a large bowl, mix shredded zucchini with salt. Let stand until zucchini is limp and liquid has drained from it, about 30 minutes. Rinse zucchini well and

Shell-shaped zucchini madeleines take their form from a madeleine pan; as an option, bake in tiny muffin pans.

Spoon egg-tender batter, generously speckled with zucchini shreds, into buttered, flour-dusted madeleine pans.

drain, squeezing out as much water as possible.

Meanwhile, pour 2 tablespoons of the oil into an 8- to 10-inch frying pan on medium-high heat. Add onion and cook, stirring occasionally, until limp and lightly browned, about 10 minutes; set aside.

In a large bowl, stir flour with baking powder. In a separate bowl, whisk together until blended eggs, milk, remaining oil, cheese, garlic, basil, and pepper; add zucchini and onion and mix well. Stir zucchini mixture into flour mixture just until evenly moistened.

Butter and flour madeleine pans (1½- to 2-tablespoon size) or tiny muffin pans (about 1½-inch diameter). Spoon batter into pans, filling to rims. Bake in a 400° oven until puffed and lightly browned,

about 15 minutes for 1½-tablespoon size, 18 minutes for 2-tablespoon size, 20 minutes for small muffins. Cool about 5 minutes, then invert pans to remove madeleines; use a spatula to loosen them gently, if necessary. (If you have only 1 pan, wash, dry, butter, and flour it again before baking the next batch.)

Serve madeleines hot or at room temperature. If made ahead, let cool, then wrap airtight and chill up to 24 hours, or freeze to store longer.

To reheat, lay madeleines (thawed, if frozen) in a single layer on 2 baking sheets, 12- by 15-inch size, and place in a 350° oven until warm in centers, about 5 minutes. Makes 3 dozen.

# Light Desserts

CAN YOU REALLY *have your cake and eat it, too? The answer is yes. Here are three satisfying low-calorie desserts, all prepared without using reduced-calorie ingredients. The Ricotta Cheesecake has 206 calories per serving, Oranges in Ginger Champagne 207, and Chaudeau 68.*

## RICOTTA CHEESECAKE

- 2 teaspoons butter or margarine, at room temperature
- ¼ cup toasted wheat germ
- 3 large eggs
- 1½ pounds (3 cups) ricotta cheese
- ⅔ cup sugar
- ⅓ cup sour cream
- ⅓ cup cornstarch
- 1 teaspoon baking powder
- 1 teaspoon vanilla
- 3 tablespoons butter or margarine, melted and cooled
- 2 teaspoons grated lemon peel
- 2 cups fresh fruit, such as raspberries, strawberries, and/or sliced peaches or nectarines
- Mint sprigs (optional)

Spread the 2 teaspoons of room-temperature butter over bottom and sides of a 9-inch cake pan with a removable bottom, then sprinkle with wheat germ. Set aside.

In a food processor or blender (or in large bowl of an electric mixer), combine eggs, ricotta cheese, sugar, and sour cream. Whirl (or beat) until smooth. Stir together cornstarch and baking powder; add to cheese mixture along with the vanilla, melted butter, and lemon peel. Whirl (or beat) until well blended. Pour into prepared pan.

Bake in a 325° oven until cake looks firm when gently shaken, 55 to 60 minutes. Let cool on a rack, then cover and refrigerate until cold.

To serve, remove pan sides. Arrange some of fruit on top of cake; garnish with mint. Offer remaining fruit to accompany individual servings. Makes 12 servings.

## ORANGES IN GINGER CHAMPAGNE

- ¾ cup *each* sugar and water
- 2 tablespoons minced crystallized ginger
- 4 large oranges
- 1 bottle (750 ml.) dry champagne or 3 to 4 cups ginger ale

*Ricotta gives this smooth, calorie-light cheesecake a refreshing finish. Summer nectarines and raspberries embellish it.*

In a 2- to 3-quart pan, combine sugar, water, and ginger. Stir over medium heat until sugar dissolves, then bring to a boil over high heat and continue to boil, uncovered, for 5 minutes. Let cool, then refrigerate until cold or up to 1 day.

Using a sharp knife, cut peel and all white membrane from oranges. Hold oranges over pan of cold ginger syrup to catch juice; cut segments free, lift out and add to cold syrup. Stir gently. Cover and refrigerate for about 3 hours.

To serve, spoon oranges and syrup equally into 6 to 8 champagne or wine glasses. Pour champagne over fruit to fill glasses. Makes 6 to 8 servings.

## CHAUDEAU

- 2 large eggs
- ¼ cup sugar
- 1 cup fruity white wine (such as Gewürztraminer, Chenin Blanc, or Johannisberg Riesling)

In a 2½- to 3-quart pan, combine eggs, sugar, and wine. Set over high heat and beat constantly with a portable electric mixer until mixture is foamy and has increased 3 to 4 times in volume, about 5 minutes. Pour into wine glasses at once to sip. Makes 6 to 8 servings.

*Cook tender scallops and shrimp quickly with wine, mushrooms, garlic, onions.*

## SEAFOOD & MUSHROOMS

- 3 tablespoons butter or margarine
- 2 cups thinly sliced mushrooms
- 2 cloves garlic, pressed or minced
- ½ pound scallops, rinsed
- ½ pound medium-size shrimp (43 to 50 per lb.), shelled and deveined
- ¼ cup dry white wine
- ½ teaspoon paprika
- 2 tablespoons chopped green onions
- 1 tablespoon chopped fresh chives (or green onion tops)
- 2 to 3 cups hot cooked rice

Melt butter in a 10- to 12-inch frying pan over medium heat. Add mushrooms and garlic; cook, stirring occasionally, until mushrooms are lightly browned and liquid has cooked away, 8 to 10 minutes.

If scallops are more than 1 inch thick, slice crosswise in half; if more than 1 inch across, cut in half. Add scallops, shrimp, wine, and paprika to mushrooms; cook, stirring, until scallops and shrimp are opaque in center (cut to test), about 3 minutes. Stir in green onions and chives. Serve over hot rice. Makes 3 or 4 servings. — *L. Lum, Tacoma, Wash.*

*Showing off Western produce is salad of avocado, artichoke, orange, macadamias.*

## AVOCADO–MACADAMIA NUT SALAD

- 3 tablespoons orange juice
- 1 tablespoon Dijon mustard
- 1 teaspoon soy sauce
- 1 package (9 oz.) frozen artichoke hearts, thawed and drained
- 2 large ripe avocados
- 1 tablespoon lemon juice
- ¼ cup salted macadamia nuts, coarsely chopped
- 1 tablespoon finely chopped or shredded orange peel (orange part only)

In a bowl, combine orange juice, Dijon mustard, and soy sauce. Add artichoke hearts, stirring to coat evenly with dressing; set aside.

Pit and peel avocados; slice lengthwise into ¼-inch wedges. Dip wedges into lemon juice. Arrange an equal number of wedges on 4 to 6 salad plates. Drain artichoke hearts; reserve dressing. Arrange an equal amount of artichoke hearts on each plate with avocados. Spoon remaining dressing over avocados. (If prepared ahead, cover and chill up to 4 hours.)

Sprinkle avocados with equal amounts of macadamia nuts and orange peel. Makes 4 to 6 servings. — *Gladys Kent, Port Angeles, Wash.*

*No messy frying: batter on wings bakes crisp in the oven. Glaze goes on last.*

## CHICKEN WINGS ORIENTAL

- ½ cup cornstarch
- 2 teaspoons water
- 2 pounds chicken wings, rinsed and patted dry
- 1 large egg, lightly beaten
- 1 tablespoon salad oil
- ½ cup *each* sugar, regular-strength chicken broth, and rice vinegar or white wine vinegar
- ¼ cup catsup
- 1 teaspoon soy sauce
- 2 cloves garlic, pressed or minced

Stir 2 teaspoons cornstarch with 2 teaspoons water; set aside. Dip wings in egg, then in remaining cornstarch to coat lightly. Pour oil into a 10- by 15-inch rimmed pan. Put in a 450° oven to heat. Add wings to pan, meaty side down. Bake until light brown on bottom, 25 to 30 minutes. Turn wings; bake until light brown, 20 minutes.

In a 1½- to 2-quart pan, mix sugar, broth, vinegar, catsup, soy, and garlic; boil on high heat, stirring, until reduced to ¾ cup. Still stirring, add cornstarch mixture; bring to a rolling boil.

Brush all the sauce over wings. Continue baking, uncovered, until sauce bubbles, about 5 minutes. Makes 4 servings, about 3 wings each. — *Mrs. Ann Andersen, Sitka, Alaska.*

## Banana-Oatmeal Pancakes

¾ cup quick-cooking rolled oats
⅔ cup whole-wheat flour
¼ to ½ teaspoon salt (optional)
1 teaspoon baking powder
½ teaspoon baking soda
1 medium-size ripe banana
1 large egg
¾ cup buttermilk
About 2 tablespoons salad oil

In a bowl, combine oats, flour, salt, baking powder, and baking soda.

In another bowl, mash the banana with an electric mixer or a fork (you should have about ¾ cup).

With mixer or fork, beat egg with the mashed banana until blended. Add buttermilk and 2 tablespoons oil; mix until smooth. Add the dry ingredients and stir until blended.

Heat an electric griddle to 350° (or place a 10- to 12-inch frying pan over medium heat until a drop of water sizzles on it). Brush griddle lightly with oil. Spoon 3 tablespoons batter per pancake onto griddle; cook until top of pancake is set and bottom is medium brown, about 2 minutes. Turn pancakes; cook until medium brown, 1½ minutes more. Repeat with remaining batter. Makes 10 pancakes. — *Lois Anderson, Truckee, Calif.*

*Start the morning with banana-oatmeal pancakes; drizzle them with warm syrup.*

## Twisted Pasta Salad

4 quarts water
2 cups dry curled pasta twists
2 tablespoons sliced almonds
¼ cup firmly packed chopped bacon
⅓ cup mayonnaise
1 tablespoon honey
¼ teaspoon pepper
½ cup finely chopped celery
½ cup finely chopped or shredded carrot
1 thinly sliced green onion

In a 5- to 6-quart pan over high heat, bring water to boiling; stir in pasta. Cook, uncovered, until pasta is tender to bite, 8 to 10 minutes; drain. Rinse in cold running water until pasta is cool, about 2 minutes; drain and set aside.

Meanwhile, in a 10- to 12-inch frying pan over medium heat, cook almonds, stirring, until light golden, 6 to 8 minutes. Pour from pan and set aside. Add bacon to pan and cook, stirring often, until browned. Drain on paper towels.

In a large bowl, stir together mayonnaise, honey, and pepper. Add pasta, bacon, celery, carrots, and onion; stir to coat evenly with dressing. Sprinkle with toasted almonds. Makes 4 to 6 servings. — *Linda E. Martin, San Bernardino, Calif.*

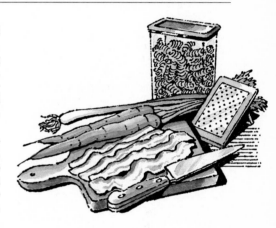

*Bacon, crisply cooked, and vegetables season pasta salad; dressing has honey.*

## Italian Cream with Raspberries

1 small package (3 oz.) cream cheese, at room temperature
¼ cup (⅛ lb.) butter or margarine, at room temperature
⅔ cup powdered sugar
1 tablespoon lemon juice
1½ teaspoons vanilla
¼ cup dried currants
3 cups raspberries, rinsed and drained

In a bowl of an electric mixer (or in a food processor), beat cream cheese and butter until smooth. Add sugar, lemon juice, and vanilla; beat or whirl to mix. Stir in currants. Cover and chill the mixture until cold, about 1 hour, or up to 1 week.

Meanwhile, whirl 1½ cups of the raspberries in a food processor or blender until smoothly puréed; if desired, press purée through a fine strainer to remove seeds. Spoon an equal amount of purée into 5 to 8 small bowls or on dessert plates. Put 2 to 3 tablespoons berries on purée; save a few for garnish. Spoon 2 to 3 tablespoons Italian cream on berries; top with remaining berries. Makes 5 to 8 servings. — *Carmela Meely, Walnut Creek, Calif.*

*Italian cream has whipped icing texture and a flavorful affinity for raspberries.*

NO DELICATESSEN PLATTER, *church sup-per, picnic, or potluck is complete with-out potato salad. Everyone has a favorite recipe; most like it cold, but some like it hot. Some prefer sweet, others sour. The only constant factor is that when most cooks eventually discover a recipe they like, they never swerve from it thereafter.*

*Rolla Boughan's Walla Walla Onion Potato Salad just might be the blend to shake these conservatives out of their rut. Unusual ingredients—apple, sweet relish, and stuffed green olives—elevate the salad to a new plane.*

## WALLA WALLA ONION POTATO SALAD

- 3 pounds medium-size red thin-skinned potatoes
- 1 large Walla Walla onion or other mild red or white onion
- 1 cup thinly sliced celery
- 1 large Golden Delicious apple, cored and diced
- 12 pimiento-stuffed Spanish-style green olives, sliced
- ⅓ cup chopped sweet pickle
- 1½ cups mayonnaise
- 1 teaspoon Dijon mustard
- 2 tablespoons distilled white vinegar
- 1 teaspoon bottled steak sauce or soy sauce
  Salt and pepper

In a 4- to 5-quart pan, place potatoes in 1 inch of boiling water, cover, and boil over medium heat until tender when pierced, 25 to 30 minutes. Drain well and let cool. Peel potatoes, if desired, then dice; place in a large bowl.

Cut onion into quarters and slice thin; add to potatoes along with celery, apple, olives, and pickle.

In a small bowl, stir together the may-onnaise, mustard, vinegar, and steak sauce. Spoon over potato mixture and mix gently. Season to taste with salt and pepper. Cover and refrigerate for at least 2 hours or until the next day. Makes 10 to 12 servings.

*Rolla Boughan*

*Portland*

HOW DO YOU GIVE GUESTS *the greatest quantity of barbecued lamb with the lowest amount of bone and the least waste? Our suggestion: lay the burden on your meatman; have him bone and butterfly a leg of lamb. Once he's finished, you can take over: marinate, barbecue, and serve it forth as Sid Goldstein does—sliced and adorned with his crowning touch, home-made chutney.*

*Chutney is the name given to that pre-serve in which ingredients not ordinarily thought to go well with each other—fruit, onions, vinegar, and spices hot, sweet, and sour—coexist peaceably. It was born in India, where, classically, mango serves as its base. Mr. Goldstein's version uses cur-rants—those tiny dried grapes that re-semble miniature raisins. They should not be confused with true currants, the acidic red, white, or black fruits of currant bushes* (Ribes).

## GRILLED BUTTERFLIED LEG OF LAMB WITH CURRIED CURRANT CHUTNEY

- 1½ cups dry red wine
- 2 teaspoons curry powder
- 1 teaspoon dry tarragon
- ¼ teaspoon lemon pepper seasoning
- 1 leg of lamb (6 to 7 lb.), boned and butterflied
- 3 tablespoons butter or margarine
- ½ cup finely chopped onion
- 1 small red bell pepper, stemmed, seeded, and diced
- ½ cup dried currants
- ¼ cup black currant liqueur (crème de cassis)
- ⅛ teaspoon cayenne
- 1 beef bouillon cube
- 2 teaspoons red wine vinegar

In a shallow 11- by 14-inch roasting or broiler pan, combine ½ cup of the wine, 1 teaspoon of the curry powder, ½ tea-spoon of the tarragon, and the lemon

*"Every cook has a favorite recipe for potato salad."*

pepper seasoning. Trim and discard excess fat from lamb. Lay lamb out in pan and turn several times to coat with the marinade; cover and chill at least 2 hours or up to overnight. Turn meat several times.

Melt butter in a 10- to 12-inch frying pan over medium heat; add onion and bell pepper and stir often until onion is limp, about 8 minutes. Add the remaining 1 teaspoon curry powder and the currants and stir until fruit puffs slightly. Add remaining 1 cup red wine, remaining ½ teaspoon tarragon, the black currant liqueur, cayenne, bouillon cube, and vinegar. Bring to a boil over high heat; reduce heat and simmer until mixture is reduced to about 1¼ cups, about 30 minutes. Pour into a blender or food processor and whirl until smooth. Set aside; if made ahead, cover and chill up to overnight.

To barbecue lamb, lift from marinade, draining briefly. Lay meat out flat, boned side up, on a grill 4 to 6 inches above a solid bed of medium-hot coals (you should be able to hold your hand at grill level 3 to 4 seconds). Basting frequently with remaining marinade, cook, turning as needed to brown evenly and avoid flare-ups, until meat is rare in thickest portion (a meat thermometer inserted in the center reads 130°, or meat is still red—cut to test), 40 to 45 minutes. Thinner sections will be medium to well done.

Place lamb on a board and slice thin; accompany with the chutney. Makes 7 or 8 servings.

*Menlo Park, Calif.*

**W**ESTERN CHEFS *seem to focus on barbecues, chilies, and chowders. Only rarely do they favor us with dessert recipes. Even so, we remain convinced that desserts are a little bit like tax shelters: people who deplore them in public are likely to enjoy them in private. Virgil Newell's Chocolate Almond Ice Cream is actually as much a frozen mousse as it is an ice cream, and its flavor is sensational. You need not take his word for it, or ours; the Oregon State Fair has awarded it two first prizes.*

*We can't think of a better way to top off a Fourth of July picnic or barbecue.*

## CHOCOLATE ALMOND ICE CREAM

⅔ cup slivered almonds
2 cups sugar
¼ cup all-purpose flour
⅔ cup unsweetened cocoa
2 large eggs
3 cups half-and-half (light cream)
4 cups (1 qt.) whipping cream
1 tablespoon vanilla

Spread almonds in an 8- or 9-inch-wide pan; toast in a 350° oven until nuts are lightly browned, about 8 minutes. Set nuts aside.

In a 2- to 3-quart pan, combine sugar, flour, and cocoa. Stir in eggs and half-and-half. Place over medium heat and cook, stirring, until mixture comes to a gentle boil, about 12 minutes.

Let mixture cool to lukewarm, then blend in whipping cream and vanilla. Cover and chill until cold, at least 2 hours or up to overnight.

Pour chilled mixture into an ice cream freezer container (1-gal. size, or freeze in batches). Freeze in a self-refrigerated or ice-and-salt maker (use 1 part salt to 8 parts ice) until mixture is partially frozen (dasher will be hard to turn). Add almonds; continue to freeze until dasher no longer turns. Serve softly frozen. Or repack with 1 part salt and 2 parts ice, or place in a container in the freezer and firm for 1 or 2 hours. To store, package airtight and freeze up to 1 month. Makes about 2 quarts.

*Salem, Ore.*

**T**HERE ARE THOSE *who believe that salmon needs no adornment except (just possibly) a little butter or a squeeze of lemon juice. Such purity of approach is perhaps to be admired, but it cannot be forgotten that we live in a pluralistic society which must also tolerate the opinions of chefs who would dress their fish more elaborately—with spinach, sorrel, or any of a variety of sauces. Alan Kunz favors baking his fillets with cilantro salsa.*

*Salsa on salmon? Like the music of Wagner, as Mark Twain once said, it is better than it sounds. The essential flavoring ingredient is cilantro, the flavor of which is not far removed from that of citrus peel—and, as even the purest purist will*

*attest, citrus and salmon have a relationship on the platter more meaningful than any they will ever enjoy in life.*

## SALMON WITH CILANTRO SALSA

2 salmon fillets (equal size, about 4 lb. total)
¾ cup lime juice
⅔ cup green onions, including tops, thinly sliced
2 pickled jalapeño chilies, stemmed and finely chopped
1½ cup loosely packed fresh cilantro (coriander) leaves, minced
⅓ cup olive oil
Salt and pepper

Lay fillets skin side down in a 9- by 13-inch baking pan. Evenly drizzle 2 tablespoons lime juice over the fillets. In a small bowl, combine remaining lime juice, onions, jalapeños, cilantro, and olive oil. Spread ½ cup of the cilantro salsa over 1 fillet. Lay the other fillet, skin side up, atop the first, fitting together neatly. If made ahead, cover and chill salmon up to overnight.

Bake, uncovered, in a 350° oven until fish is opaque in thickest portion (make a small cut to test), 35 to 45 minutes.

If desired, pull off top skin and cut fish crosswise through the 2 fillets, making 6 to 8 slices. Offer remaining cilantro salsa and salt and pepper to add to taste. Makes 6 to 8 servings.

*Walnut Creek, Calif.*

*"We must also tolerate the chefs who dress their salmon more elaborately."*

TAKE TO THE OUTDOORS *with this month's menus. They're suited to warm-weather entertaining and dining.*

*Two menus use the barbecue. On the Fourth, grill chicken wings and big, bony beef ribs for celebrants to gnaw. Or roast an* herb-crusted pork loin to succulent tenderness in a covered barbecue.

*Arrange cool, cooked fish and vegetables on a platter for a one-pan, make-ahead meal. Take it to a favorite picnic spot, or serve for patio entertaining.*

*Celebrate the Fourth with a barbecue featuring mustard-grilled beef ribs and chicken wings, corn with chive butter, toasted bread, vegetables, watermelon.*

---

### BONES BARBECUE

**Raw Vegetable Relishes**
**Grilled Mustard Ribs & Wings**
**Corn on the Cob      Chive Butter**
**Chive Butter Toast**
**Lemonade      Beer**
**Watermelon Wedges**

---

*For eating grilled beef ribs and chicken wings, hands are your best utensils. Other foods in this happily informal meal require no cutlery either.*

*Marinate the ribs and wings at least 4 hours before cooking.*

*For an appetizer salad, offer crisp, raw vegetables. Choose from cucumber spears, small whole carrots, celery stalks, bell pepper strips. You'll need about 2 pounds of vegetables for 6 to 8 servings. Prepare the vegetables, cover, and chill up to several hours before serving. Offer them plain or with your favorite dip.*

*Shortly before meat is done, cook the corn. When meat is ready, toast bread on the grill, then brush with butter. The remaining chive butter goes on the corn.*

### GRILLED MUSTARD RIBS & WINGS

> 3  **pounds beef ribs, cut into separate ribs**
> 3  **pounds chicken wings**
>    **Mustard marinade (recipe follows)**

Place ribs and wings in separate large plastic bags. Pour half of the marinade over each. Seal each bag, mix to coat, and set bags in a 9- by 13-inch pan. Chill, turning meat occasionally, at least 4 hours or up to overnight.

Place meat on a grill 4 to 6 inches above a solid bed of medium-hot coals (you should be able to hold your hand at grill level only 3 to 4 seconds). Cook wings, turning and basting with remaining marinade, until browned and no longer pink near bone (cut to test), 20 to 25 minutes; cook ribs, turning and basting, until browned but still slightly pink near bone (cut to test), 15 to 20 minutes. Makes 6 servings.

**Mustard marinade.** Stir together 1 cup **Dijon mustard,** 1 cup **dry white wine** or regular-strength chicken broth, 2 tablespoons **salad oil,** 2 tablespoons **honey,** 2 teaspoons **dry tarragon,** and 2 cloves **garlic,** pressed or minced.

## CHIVE BUTTER TOAST

Split 1 **round loaf** (1½ lb.) **French bread** in half horizontally to make 2 rounds. Mix together ½ cup (¼ lb.) melted **butter** or margarine; 2 cloves **garlic,** pressed or minced; and 2 tablespoons minced **chives** or green onions (including tops).

Place bread, cut side down, over medium coals (you should be able to hold your hand at grill level only 4 to 5 seconds); cook until lightly toasted, 3 to 5 minutes. Brush cut surfaces with chive butter (use remaining butter to brush on hot cooked corn; see menu). Cut bread in wedges and serve warm. Makes 6 to 8 servings.

---

### DAD'S TURN AT DINNER

Mixed Greens with Vinaigrette
Barbecued Pork Loin with Herbs
Pepper & Eggplant Stew
Crusty Bread      Butter
Gamay Beaujolais    Apple Juice
Raspberry Sorbet & Vanilla Ice Cream
Ginger Crisps

---

*Let the men take charge of this meal. If two families get together, two chefs could share the job.*

*Start the barbecue fire about 2 hours before serving.*

*While the pork roasts to moist succulence in a covered barbecue, cook the vegetable stew and prepare salad greens to mix with your favorite dressing.*

## BARBECUED PORK LOIN WITH HERBS

1  **bone-in pork loin roast (4½ to 5 lb.), backbone cracked**
3  **tablespoons** *each* **minced fresh oregano, fresh thyme, fresh rosemary, and fresh sage leaves (or 1 tablespoon of each dry herb)**
2  **cloves garlic, pressed or minced**
2  **tablespoons olive oil**
   **Sprigs of fresh herbs (optional)**
   **Salt and pepper**

Ignite 60 charcoal briquets on the firegrate of a covered barbecue.

Trim and discard surface fat from pork. Slash meaty side of roast diagonally to make a crisscross pattern about ¼ inch deep. Mix oregano, thyme, rosemary, sage, garlic, and oil; rub ovdr roast.

*Team cooking: one chef trims fat from pork loin, then coats it with fresh herbs; the other prepares the vegetable stew.*

When coals are covered with gray, 30 to 40 minutes, bank equally on each side of grate, leaving space for a metal or foil drip pan in center; set pan in place. Scatter 5 or 6 briquets over each bank of coals. Lay pork on grill over drip pan, cover barbecue, and open dampers. Every 30 minutes, add 5 or 6 briquets to coals on each side to maintain heat. Cook until a thermometer inserted in thickest part at bone reads 150° to 155° and meat is white in center (cut to test), 1¼ to 1½ hours.

Let the meat rest in a warm place for about 10 minutes. Cut between ribs to separate them; serve. Garnish with herb sprigs. Add salt and pepper to taste. Makes 8 servings. — *Jeff Fields and Patrick Jamon, Santa Monica, Calif.*

## PEPPER & EGGPLANT STEW

3  **tablespoons olive oil**
1  **large onion, chopped**
3  **large red bell peppers, stemmed, seeded, and cut in julienne strips**

1  **teaspoon** *each* **chopped fresh rosemary, fresh thyme, fresh sage, and fresh oregano leaves (or ¼ teaspoon of each dry herb)**
4  **cloves garlic, pressed or minced**
3  **large firm-ripe tomatoes, cored and cut in 1-inch cubes**
1  **large eggplant (1¼ to 1½ lb.), peeled and cut in ½-inch cubes**
   **Salt and pepper**

Pour oil into a 5- to 6-quart pan and place over medium-high heat. Add onion and red peppers and cook, stirring often, until lightly browned, about 10 minutes. Stir in rosemary, thyme, sage, oregano, garlic, tomatoes, and eggplant. Cover and simmer over low heat, stirring occasionally, until eggplant is very soft when pressed, about 25 minutes. Add salt and pepper to taste. Makes 8 servings.

---

### SUMMER PICNIC PLATTER

Cool Salmon Steaks & Vegetables
with Radish Tartar Sauce
Grapes      Iced Tea

---

*Spoon a lean tartar sauce, crunchy with radishes, over salmon and vegetables.*

*Cook the beans, salmon, and potatoes in sequence in the same pan of water. They can be prepared up to 1 day ahead. Add the chopped vegetables to yogurt or sour cream shortly before serving.*

*(Continued on next page)*

*A calorie-lean sauce of radish-seasoned yogurt goes over salmon and vegetables.*

## COOL SALMON STEAKS & VEGETABLES WITH RADISH TARTAR SAUCE

Water
1 pound green beans, ends trimmed
4 salmon steaks (6 to 8 oz. each)
8 to 12 red thin-skinned potatoes
4 butter lettuce leaves (1½ inches wide), washed and crisped (optional)
1½ cups cherry tomatoes
Radish tartar sauce (recipe follows)
Lemon wedges

In a 5- to 6-quart pan, bring 3 quarts water to boiling over high heat. Add beans; boil, uncovered, just until bright green and barely tender to bite, about 5 minutes. With tongs, lift out beans and immerse in ice water to cool.

Return water to boiling. Add fish. Cover pan tightly and remove from heat. Let stand until fish is opaque in thickest part (cut to test), 10 to 14 minutes. Remove steaks and immerse in ice water to cool.

Return water in pan to boiling; add potatoes and simmer, covered, until tender when pierced, 20 to 25 minutes. Drain and immerse in ice water to cool. Drain cool beans, fish, and potatoes.

Arrange lettuce leaves on a platter and lay salmon steaks on the lettuce. Alongside fish, place the beans, potatoes, and tomatoes, grouping each separately. (If made ahead, cool, cover, and chill up to overnight.) Offer sauce and lemon to add to taste. Makes 4 servings.

**Radish tartar sauce.** Mix 1 cup **unflavored yogurt** or sour cream, ¾ cup chopped **red radish,** ⅓ cup minced **green onion,** 2 tablespoons drained **capers,** and 1 tablespoon **prepared horseradish.** Add **salt** to taste.

*Peach-Blueberry Crackle Brûlée (page 198)*

Ideas for warm-weather menus brightened our August issue. Among our suggestions: a trio of cool soups, a dramatic five-tiered omelet, new ways to cook fresh trout, sparkling fruit fizzes from Italy, and assertive seasoning blends to flavor barbecued foods. A show-stopping dessert took the summer spotlight—a fruit-topped custard drizzled with a crackling web of caramelized sugar. We also explored the intriguing world of Japanese herbs, and how to choose, cultivate, and cook with them.

# Cooking with Japanese Herbs

BOTANICALLY SPEAKING, *Japanese herbs have some familiar cousins: parsley, mint, cabbage, radish, and chrysanthemum. But in terms of flavor, the six herbs we introduce here may surprise you. Anise, lemon, horseradish, and celery, in varying combinations, are some of the tastes you'll experience. All six herbs have a mild-to-robust spiciness that adds character to dishes they're used in—traditional Japanese foods or Western favorites-with-a-twist, like those shown here.*

*Japanese herbs are now grown in California and sold in Oriental markets in the West. And you can easily grow your own (see page 197).*

## HOW TO BUY & USE JAPANESE HERBS

Some of these herbs can be cooked, like mustard greens. But most are best raw or added to hot food at the last minute—to preserve their fresh, often volatile flavors. Here, we discuss them in terms of looks, selection, and traditional uses.

Oriental markets usually sell them by their Japanese names, but you may see English names, too (given here in parentheses).

## GREEN OR PURPLE SHISO (BEEFSTEAK)

**Looks.** Green or purple leaves are flat, broad, and slightly fuzzy; they have jagged edges.

**Selection.** Choose fresh-looking leaves; limp ones can't be perked up. Shiso wilts with excessive moisture and browns with age. Green shiso is often sold by the leaf, at 12 to 15 cents apiece. You'll find purple shiso in summer, in only a few markets, for 79 cents to $1 per bunch.

**Uses.** Serve raw, or add to hot foods at the last minute. With too much heat, shiso gets stringy. Purple shiso also bleeds with heat. The Japanese use green shiso in sushi, soup, salad, on sashimi, and alongside tempura. Purple is most often used in pickling, for its bright color. It tastes more fruity and "green" than green shiso and has less of a citrus flavor.

## MITSUBA (TREFOIL)

**Looks.** Long, white stalks are topped with flat leaves in clusters of three. These leaves are pale to bright green and small to fairly full, depending on the variety.

**Selection.** Avoid limp bunches. Choose crisp ones with strong stems and tender leaves. Older leaves start to yellow. A 2-ounce bunch costs 80 cents to $1.40.

**Uses.** Serve leaves and stalks raw or briefly wilted (with longer heating, mitsuba may get stringy). Traditional Japanese uses are in salads, savory custards, soups, one-pot dishes, tempura, sushi, and vinegared vegetables.

## SHUNGIKU (EDIBLE CHRYSANTHEMUM)

Shungiku's perfume is like that of ornamental chrysanthemum, but it can be eaten, while the ornamental cannot.

**Looks.** It's dark green and looks similar to ornamental chrysanthemum, but leaves are fuller and more deeply lobed.

**Selection.** Look for sturdy stalks with small, tender leaves. Plants wilt and yellow with age. An 8-ounce bunch costs 65 to 90 cents.

**Uses.** Serve raw or barely wilted. The Japanese use it cooked: blanched and chilled in salads, or hot in tempura, soups, and one-pot dishes—and as a cooked vegetable. If heated too intensely, though, leaves develop a bitter taste.

## KAIWARE DAIKON (DAIKON SPROUTS)

**Looks.** Each thin, white stalk has two tiny green, heart-shaped leaves on top.

**Selection.** Buy packages with crisp-looking sprouts. Leaves darken and become slippery with age and excessive moisture. Prices range from 75 cents to $1.15 for a 2- to 3-ounce package.

**Uses.** Serve raw, or add to hot foods at the last minute (overcooked, it gets stringy). Japanese uses include sushi, soup, and salads, and on sashimi and tofu.

## MIBUNA (NO ENGLISH NAME)

**Looks.** Leaves are long, slender, and light green, with smooth edges.

**Selection.** We've never seen it in a market. In the garden, pick crisp green leaves.

**Uses.** Serve raw or briefly cooked. In Japan, mibuna is pickled or used in soups.

## CLEANING & STORING

Before using the herbs, prepare them as we indicate here, then store if necessary.

**Green and purple shiso.** If still on stems, pick off leaves at base and discard stems. Rinse leaves and pat dry. To store, wrap leaves in a lightly dampened paper towel, seal in a plastic bag, and chill up to 1 week; dampen towel if it dries out.

**Mitsuba.** Pinch off and discard coarse part of stem, leaving about 2 inches of tender stem attached to clusters of leaves. Rinse and pat dry. To store, seal in a plastic bag and chill up to 1 week.

**Shungiku.** Pinch leaves from stalks; discard stalks. Rinse and pat dry. To store, seal in a plastic bag and chill up to 5 days.

**Kaiware daikon.** Store purchased sprouts in plastic package (no need to rinse). If homegrown, rinse and pat dry; seal in a plastic bag. Chill up to 4 days. Just before using, cut off and discard roots.

**Mibuna.** Pick green leaves on stems from stalks at the base; discard stalks. Rinse the leaves and pat dry. To store, wrap in paper towels, seal in a plastic bag, and chill up to 1 week.

## JAPANESE HERB PESTO

- 2 cups lightly packed, cleaned (preceding) shiso, mitsuba, shungiku, or mibuna
- 1 cup packed freshly grated parmesan cheese
  About ½ cup salad oil
- ½ pound dry pasta, cooked and hot

Whirl shiso, parmesan, and ½ cup oil in a blender or processor until puréed.

Mix with pasta. Or, to store, pack pesto sauce in a small jar, pour a thin layer of oil on top (to prevent darkening), cover, and chill up to 1 week. Freeze to store longer; let thaw and stir before using. Makes about 1 cup, 4 servings.

## JAPANESE HERB SPREAD

*Make the spread with butter to melt over hot cooked vegetables such as corn and peas. Or make it with cream cheese to use in tea sandwiches (recipes follow).*

In a blender or food processor, whirl ½ cup (¼ lb.) room temperature **butter** or cream cheese with ½ cup cleaned (preceding) and loosely packed **shiso**, mitsuba, shungiku, or mibuna **leaves** or kaiware daikon until herb is minced. If made ahead, cover and chill up to 1 week. Makes ½ to ⅔ cup.

Green shiso tastes like mint, citrus, and licorice; nest it under oysters on the half-shell (recipe below).

Mitsuba's flavor is between parsley and celery. Try some in clear Japanese-style soup (recipe below).

## TEA SANDWICHES WITH JAPANESE GREENS

Trim crusts from 6 thin slices **firm white sandwich bread,** then make into sandwiches with your choice of the following:

**Cream cheese and herbs.** Spread slices equally with **Japanese herb spread** (recipe precedes; make with cream cheese). Cut each slice into 4 triangles. Garnish each triangle with about ¼ teaspoon **tobiko** (flying fish roe) or red lumpfish caviar (optional), and 1 cleaned (preceding) **shiso,** mitsuba, shungiku, or mibuna **leaf** or a few sprigs kaiware daikon. Use small leaves (1 to 2 inches each) or tear larger ones in half. You'll need 2 tablespoons tobiko and 24 small leaves, total.

**Shiso and cheese.** Spread bread slices lightly with chopped **Major Grey chutney.** Cut each slice into 4 triangles. Top each triangle with 1 small (about 2 inches), cleaned (preceding) **shiso leaf** and 1 small slice **cheddar cheese.** You'll need 24 shiso leaves and ¼ pound cheese, total.

**Kaiware daikon.** Spread slices equally with 2 tablespoons **butter** or margarine at room temperature. Cut each slice into 4 triangles. Top each triangle with cleaned (preceding) **kaiware daikon** (1 cup lightly packed, total).

## OYSTERS ON A GREEN CUSHION

- 12 **small oysters in shells, scrubbed and shucked (if desired, have oysters shucked at the market and retain 12 half-shells)**
  **Crushed ice or rock salt**
- 12 **cleaned (preceding) shiso or shungiku leaves (about 2 inches each) or mitsuba sprigs, or 24 kaiware daikon pieces**
  **Mignonette sauce (recipe follows)**

If you shuck the oysters, cut oysters free from shells. Lay each oyster back in a half-shell with any of its juice; discard remaining shells. At this point, you can cover oysters (in a single layer) and chill them up to 1 day.

To serve, steady oysters in shells on a platter covered with crushed ice or salt. Slip a shiso or shungiku leaf or mitsuba sprig between each oyster and the shell, or top each with 2 pieces of kaiware daikon. Spoon sauce evenly over oysters. Makes 3 to 6 appetizer servings.

**Mignonette sauce.** In a bowl, stir together ⅓ cup **rice wine vinegar,** 2 tablespoons **water,** 1 tablespoon minced **shallot,** and ½ teaspoon **coarsely ground pepper.** Use, or cover and chill up to 1 day.

## CLEAR SOUP WITH JAPANESE HERBS

- 1 **quart regular-strength chicken broth (or use half bottled clam juice)**
- ½ **cup diced firm tofu**
- 2 **teaspoons lemon juice**
- ¼ **teaspoon Oriental sesame oil (optional)**
- ¼ **cup cleaned (preceding) and minced shiso, mitsuba, shungiku, or kaiware daikon**
- 4 **very thin lemon slices**
  **About 4 pieces kaiware daikon or 4 shiso, mitsuba, or shungiku leaves, cleaned (preceding)**
- 12 **matchstick-size pieces carrot**

In a 2- to 2½- quart pan over high heat, bring broth to a boil; remove from heat. Add tofu, lemon juice, and sesame oil.

Place equal portion of minced herb in 4 small soup bowls. Ladle hot broth equally into bowls. Top each with a

*(Continued on next page)*

Shungiku's robust "green" flavor works well with prawns and bacon in wilted-herb entrée (recipe below).

Kaiware daikon tastes slightly hot, like radishes. Put sprouts in creamy sauce (recipe below) for prime rib; top with more.

## …CLEAR SOUP WITH JAPANESE HERBS

lemon slice, whole pieces of the corresponding herb, and 3 pieces of carrot. Makes 4 servings.

## JAPANESE HERBS SALAD WITH ORANGES & CUCUMBER

- 2 cups mixed and cleaned (preceding) Japanese herbs (shiso, mitsuba, shungiku, kaiware daikon, mibuna)
- 1 quart butter lettuce, rinsed and crisped, large leaves torn in half
- 2 large oranges, peel and white membrane cut off, with fruit thinly sliced crosswise
- 1 small cucumber, peeled, seeded, and cut into matchstick pieces
  Orange dressing (recipe follows)
  Salt and pepper

In a salad bowl, mix herbs, lettuce, oranges, cucumber, and dressing. Add salt and pepper to taste. Serves 4 to 6.

**Orange dressing.** Mix 2 tablespoons *each* **orange juice** and **salad oil**, 2 teaspoons **lemon juice**, and ⅛ teaspoon **paprika**.

## WILTED HERBS WITH PRAWNS

- 4 slices bacon
- ½ cup slivered onion
- 1 pound large (30 to 35 per lb.) shrimp, shelled and deveined
- 8 cups packed, cleaned (preceding) shungiku, mitsuba, or mibuna
- 1 tablespoon red wine vinegar
- 1 to 2 teaspoons sugar

In a 10- to 12-inch frying pan, cook bacon over medium-high heat, turning occasionally, until brown and crisp. Drain bacon on paper towels, then crumble.

Add onion and shrimp to bacon fat in pan and cook on medium-high heat, stirring often, until shrimp are bright pink, about 5 minutes. Lift shrimp and any onions that cling to them from pan and keep warm in a low oven.

Add shungiku and crumbled bacon to onion in pan. Cook, stirring, until leaves are wilted, 3 to 4 minutes. Mix in vinegar and sugar to taste. Spoon onto a platter and top with shrimp. Makes 4 servings.

## KAIWARE DAIKON SAUCE

*This nippy sauce is good served with roast beef, broiled or fried fish, or as a salad dressing with crisp greens. Top with additional sprouts.*

- 1 package (2 oz.) or 1 cup packed 2-inch pieces kaiware daikon
- ¼ cup *each* mayonnaise and sour cream
- 2 teaspoons white wine vinegar
- 1½ to 2 teaspoons wasabi powder (Japanese horseradish) or 1 tablespoon prepared horseradish

In a blender or food processor, whirl kaiware daikon, mayonnaise, sour cream, vinegar, and wasabi powder until sprouts are minced. Serve at room temperature or cold. To store, cover and chill up to 3 days. Makes ¾ cup, 4 or 5 servings.

## MIBUNA SAUCE

Follow directions for **Kaiware Daikon Sauce** (recipe precedes), but use 1 cup cleaned (preceding), packed 2-inch pieces **mibuna**. Serve as suggested; do not top with additional leaves.

# Growing Japanese Herbs

DON'T BE DISCOURAGED if you can't find fresh Japanese herbs in a market. Seeds are readily available by mail (write to Reader Service, Sunset Books, for a list of sources), and plants are as easy to grow as their cabbage, mint, parsley, and radish relatives.

All but daikon can be seeded directly in the ground or started in flats and transplanted. They're good container plants. Shiso and shungiku reseed themselves readily; growing these in containers controls their spread.

Japanese cooks harvest these herbs when plants are young and the leaves tender. Start picking as soon as plants have enough leaves to spare. Even when plants are more mature, you can get tender leaves by harvesting from the newest growth.

## WHEN TO PLANT IN YOUR AREA

Some of these herbs are warm-season plants. Others do best in cool, mild temperatures. Daikon sprouts can be grown year-round, indoors or out, depending on where you live.

Grow mibuna, mitsuba, and shungiku at the same time you would normally grow cabbage, carrots, and radishes. In frost-free areas like Southern California, you can grow them outdoors from fall through late spring, avoiding only hottest midsummer weather.

In coastal northern California, Oregon, and Washington, where summers are mild but frosts are possible in winter, grow these plants spring through fall. In desert and hot inland areas, plant in fall and early spring. In intermountain regions, plant in late spring. Plant herbs in full sun. If your area gets spring hot spells, give plants afternoon shade.

Shiso is a warm-season plant. Sow after the last chance of frost in spring. In areas with long growing seasons, sow through September (in the desert, avoid planting May through July).

Seed-packet instructions may be in Japanese, so here are some tips on cultivation. All the herbs need regular watering and light feedings with a high-nitrogen fertilizer (except daikon).

**Daikon sprouts.** Grow these all year, indoors or out. For long, sturdy sprouts, grow them as shown above. They're ready to harvest in about 7 days in summer, up to 15 days in cool weather. In summer, sprouts need afternoon or full shade. In winter, grow in full sun.

You can also use a sprout planter. Premoisten the inner screen and fill the container with water so it just touches the screen. Sprinkle seeds onto the screen and set in a dark place. Add water, when necessary, so it always touches the screen; change water when it becomes cloudy.

Before harvesting sprouts, set planter in indirect light to green them up.

**Mibuna.** A member of the cabbage family, this grows very quickly from seed. Seeds germinate in about three days; harvest leaves in three to five weeks.

Sow seeds ¼ inch deep and 3 to 4 inches apart; thin to 1 to 1½ feet apart. Harvest leaves when young and tender. As plants mature, leaves become tough; pull up old ones and replant.

**Mitsuba.** Mitsuba is as easy to grow as its relatives, carrots and parsley. If you're planting in the ground, soil should be well drained. Scatter seeds and cover with ¼ inch of soil; seeds take at least a week to germinate. Thin plants to about 3 inches. Harvest leaves in 7 to 10 weeks.

**Shiso.** A relative of mint, shiso is a warm-weather annual that tolerates heat but needs deep watering. Give plants plenty of room if you want them to reach full size: they grow up to 3 feet tall. Sow seeds ¼ inch deep and 3 inches apart; thin to 6 to 12 inches apart. Seeds germinate in about three weeks. To encourage branching, pinch new growth. Harvest leaves after six to seven weeks.

**Shungiku.** This plant will develop decorative flowers, but leaves should be harvested before they form, so foliage is tender. Several varieties are available—the one in our photograph, with deeply serrated leaves; a moderately serrated type; and one that is thick leafed and smooth. Plants bolt prematurely in hot weather.

Sow seeds ¼ inch deep and thin to 5 to 6 inches apart. Harvest the entire plant when it's 4 to 5 inches tall—or allow it to grow to 4 feet tall and harvest tender young leaves and side shoots.

**1** *Partially fill container with potting mix. Then scatter seeds over moistened soil, cover with ¼ inch of soil, and water lightly.*

**2** *To make sprouts grow long, cover them up to their seed leaves with soil every few days (depending on how fast they grow).*

**3** *Harvest sprouts when at least 3 inches long by grabbing a few stems right below the seed leaves and pulling gently; rinse and dry.*

# Fruit & Custard Classic

GLISTENING STRANDS *of melted sugar form a crackly caramel net over fruit and custard in this stunning variation on crème brûlée. Not only is this dessert prettier than the classic; it's also easier to make.*

*First you bake a tender custard, flavored to complement the fruit you've chosen as a topping.*

*To caramelize sugar, you simply heat it* in a pan until it melts and turns a delicate amber color. Drizzle this hot liquid over fruit arranged on the cooled custard; the caramel takes just a few minutes to become crisp and brittle.

*As the caramel absorbs moisture from the dessert, it will quickly start to melt. Serve the dessert as soon as it's assembled, so you get to savor the contrasting textures.*

1 *Pour boiling water into larger pan to insulate custard so it cooks evenly.*

2 *Scatter blueberries over peach slices on cooled, baked custard.*

3 *Melt sugar, shaking pan, until it becomes a golden caramel liquid.*

4 *Drizzle hot caramel over top; it hardens in a few minutes.*

## PEACH-BLUEBERRY CRACKLE BRÛLÉE

- 5 large eggs
- 1¼ cups sugar
- 1¼ cups milk
- 1¼ cups whipping cream or light cream (half-and-half)
- 1 teaspoon grated lemon peel
- 1½ teaspoons vanilla
- ½ teaspoon almond extract
- ¼ cup orange-flavored liqueur such as Grand Marnier or triple sec
  Boiling water
- 2 medium-size firm-ripe peaches
- 1 tablespoon lemon juice
- ¼ cup blueberries

In a bowl, whisk eggs and ¾ cup of the sugar just until eggs are blended but not frothy. Gently whisk in milk, cream, lemon peel, vanilla, almond extract, and liqueur just to blend well.

Set a shallow 10-inch round (or shallow 1½-qt.) baking dish (such as a quiche or pie pan) in a larger pan (such as a roasting pan). Place both on center rack of a 350° oven. Pour egg mixture into the smaller dish, and pour boiling water into larger pan; water should be ⅓ to ½ the depth of the custard mixture.

Bake until custard jiggles only slightly in center when gently shaken, about 18 minutes. Protecting your hands, lift custard dish from hot water (you can support dish with 2 wide spatulas) and let cool on a rack. When cool, cover with plastic wrap and chill at least 1 hour or overnight.

Up to 1 hour before serving, half-fill a 3- to 4-quart pan with water. Bring to a boil over high heat. Immerse peaches in boiling water for 30 seconds; lift out with a slotted spoon. Let cool (to speed, immerse briefly in cold water), then pull skin from fruit with a knife. Cut peaches in half; cut each half into 4 wedges. Discard pits. Coat wedges with lemon juice to slow darkening. Drain off lemon juice.

Arrange peaches on custard, leaving a 1-inch border of custard inside dish rim. Scatter berries over peaches.

About 15 minutes before serving, put the remaining ½ cup sugar in an 8- to 10-inch frying pan (nonstick, if desired) over medium-high heat. Heat, tilting and shaking pan frequently, until sugar melts and becomes a pale amber syrup, about 8 minutes; watch closely, since it scorches easily. Remove at once from heat.

Tilt pan to pool caramel in 1 side. Stir slowly with a long-handled metal teaspoon until caramel thickens, 1½ to 2 minutes. Working quickly, pour syrup from spoon in a thin stream, crisscrossing fruit and custard to create a golden lace topping; use all the caramel. Let stand about 3 minutes for caramel to harden.

To serve, break through caramel with a spoon and ladle portions of fruit and custard onto dessert plates. Makes 6 to 8 servings.

## BERRY CRACKLE BRÛLÉE

Prepare **Peach-Blueberry Crackle Brûlée** (recipe precedes), but omit the lemon peel and almond extract and add 2 teaspoons grated **orange peel.**

Instead of peaches, blueberries, and lemon juice, use 2 cups **strawberries** (rinsed, hulled, and drained well) and ½ cup **raspberries** (rinsed and drained well). Arrange strawberries, tips up, in a single layer atop custard, leaving a 1-inch border of plain custard inside dish rim.

Tuck raspberries among the strawberries, then coat with caramel.

## CHERRY CRACKLE BRÛLÉE

Prepare **Peach-Blueberry Crackle Brûlée** (recipe precedes), but omit peaches, lemon juice, and blueberries. Instead, use 2 cups **pitted sweet cherries,** such as Bing. Arrange cherries atop custard, leaving a 1-inch border of plain custard inside dish rim, then coat with caramel.

*Break through a delicate golden web of crackly caramelized sugar to dish up smooth custard, juicy peaches, blueberries. Bake custard ahead; top with fruit and caramel just before serving—caramel melts on standing.*

# Cooking Fresh Trout

OOKED FROM COOL STREAMS or purchased from the market, fresh trout make excellent summer eating.

In these recipes, you cook the fish in a frying pan for either camp or kitchen preparation. To double the number of servings, simply use two pans with one recipe's worth in each.

Market trout from fresh-water farms are most commonly available dressed (gutted) with head and tail intact. The whole dressed fish is also sold boned. Other forms you are likely to encounter are boned and butterflied trout minus head and tail, and fillets of trout.

One dressed 10- to 11-inch trout—from head to tail—weighs about 8 to 10 ounces and makes an ample serving. If you're buying fish without a head and tail, purchase one weighing 7 to 9 ounces. Fillets (2 per person) should be 3 to 4 ounces each.

Select trout as you do all fish: the smell should be fresh, eyes clear and firm (not concave), and the body firm, not mushy. If you don't cook the fish immediately, store it in the coldest part of the refrigerator for no longer than a day or two.

## BREAKFAST TROUT FRY

½ cup firmly packed (3 oz.) chopped bacon

2 medium-size (¾ to 1 lb. total) thin-skinned potatoes, scrubbed and thinly sliced
Salad oil (optional)

1 small onion, sliced

½ teaspoon dry thyme leaves (optional)

2 whole 10- to 11-inch dressed trout with head and tail (8 to 10 oz. each), rinsed and patted dry

About 1 tablespoon all-purpose flour
Salt and pepper

In a 10- to 12-inch frying pan over medium heat, stir bacon occasionally until browned and crisp, about 8 minutes. Lift bacon from pan with a slotted spoon and set aside. Spoon out 2 tablespoons of the fat and set aside.

Add potatoes to pan and cook until they're brown on bottom, about 10 minutes (add salad oil, if necessary, to keep potatoes from sticking). Add onion and thyme; turn with a wide spatula to mix. Cook, turning occasionally, until potatoes are golden brown and tender when pierced, about 12 minutes. Stir in bacon. Pour mixture onto a platter; keep warm.

Coat fish with flour; shake off excess. Add reserved bacon fat to pan; place

*Cook mine next! After Dad browns potatoes, onion, and bacon, he'll set aside vegetables, then cook trout in sizzling fat.*

over medium heat, and add trout. Cook until browned on bottom, 2 to 3 minutes. With wide spatula, turn trout over and cook until other side is browned and fish is just opaque in thickest part (cut to test), 2 to 3 minutes more. Accompany trout with potato mixture; add salt and pepper to taste. Makes 2 servings.

## TROUT WITH VEGETABLE STEW

- 2 tablespoons butter or margarine
- 1 small onion, sliced
- 1 clove garlic, pressed or minced
- 1 small red bell pepper, stemmed, seeded, and cut in ⅛-inch strips
- 1 pound zucchini or yellow crookneck squash (or ½ lb. each), sliced into ⅛-inch rounds
- 1 tablespoon fresh tarragon leaves, chopped
- ½ teaspoon freshly ground pepper
- 3 whole 10- to 11-inch dressed trout with head and tail (8 to 10 oz. each), rinsed and patted dry
  Lemon wedges
  Salt

Melt butter in a 10- to 12-inch frying pan over medium heat. Add onion and garlic and cook, stirring often, until onion is limp, about 4 minutes. Add bell pepper, zucchini, tarragon, and pepper; cover and cook, stirring occasionally, until squash is tender-crisp, about 10 minutes.

Shake pan to make vegetables level, then lay trout on top; cover and cook until trout is just opaque in thickest part (cut to test), about 5 minutes. Transfer the trout and vegetables to a platter or plates. Accompany with lemon and salt to add to taste. Makes 3 servings.

## HOT TROUT SALAD

- 4 trout fillets (3 to 4 oz. each; if not available, have fish filleted at the market), rinsed and patted dry
- ⅓ cup chopped almonds
- 2 tablespoons butter or margarine
- 1 pound mushrooms, thinly sliced
- 2 tablespoons lemon juice
- 2 quarts lightly packed bite-size pieces tender romaine lettuce
- ½ cup lightly packed shredded parmesan cheese
- ¼ cup finely chopped fresh mint
  Dressing (recipe follows)
  Salt and pepper

Slice fillets crosswise into 1-inch-wide pieces; set aside.

*Whole trout were steamed on a stew of squash, bell peppers, and onions.*

In a 10- to 12-inch frying pan over medium heat, cook almonds, stirring occasionally, until light golden brown, about 6 minutes. Pour from pan and reserve.

Melt butter in the pan; add the mushrooms and cook, stirring occasionally, until liquid evaporates and mushrooms are lightly browned. Stir in lemon juice and shake pan to level mushrooms. Quickly lay trout pieces (push off a wide spatula) onto mushrooms. Cover and cook until trout is just opaque in center (cut to test), about 3 minutes. Remove from heat.

Mix lettuce with almonds, cheese, mint, and dressing, and spoon equal amounts on 4 dinner plates. Spoon equal amounts of the warm trout and mushrooms onto each salad. Add salt and pepper to taste. Makes 4 servings.

**Dressing.** In a bowl, combine 3 tablespoons **raspberry vinegar** or red wine vinegar, 1 tablespoon **salad oil**, and 1 teaspoon **Dijon mustard.**

# Omelet of the Year

**O**MELETS ARE FAST, *fun, and free-wheeling. That's why Betsy Allen and Don Mohr of Leucadia, California, settled on them as the competitive focus of their annual "Omelet Open" brunch.*

*They've found that about three dozen people can perform various functions for a smooth-running party. All hands are invited to cook, serve, or judge; there are no idle observers. Those who elect to whip up an omelet—either an old favorite or a new fantasy—bring ingredients and equipment. The first to respond to the invitation get dibs on the kitchen range. Others bring electric frying pans, woks, campstoves, or portable burners to set up in the garden.*

*Subcategories include beverages—blender fruit concoctions prevail—and coffee cakes that come ready to eat.*

*Guests arrive, with duties preassigned. To help keep order, a big poster noting all such details is on display.*

*The hosts have coffee, orange juice, and fresh strawberries ready. Judges evaluate the coffee cakes while cooking gets underway. Omelets and beverages are duplicated to make the needed number of servings. One sample goes to the judges, who stay segregated, slightly, until they come to their decisions. Winners are announced and rewarded, and the party moves on to a satisfied conclusion.*

*One omelet that caught our eye, and appetite, is this tiered creation. You can make meat and vegetable fillings ahead.*

## FIVE-TIER OMELET

10 large eggs
¼ cup water
About ¼ cup (⅛ lb.) butter or margarine
Sausage filling (recipe follows)
Zucchini filling (recipe follows)
Fresh salsa (recipe follows)
½ small ripe avocado (optional)

In a 4-cup glass measuring cup, beat eggs and water until blended.

Place a 7- to 8-inch nonstick omelet or frying pan on medium-high heat. When hot, add about 2 teaspoons butter and swirl over surface. Pour about ½ cup of the egg mixture into pan. As it begins to firm on bottom and bubble, pop bubbles so uncooked egg runs into holes. Also, with a rubber spatula, quickly and gently lift edges of cooked eggs to let uncooked mixture flow beneath; don't shake pan.

When eggs are almost set, push liquid on top to edges and under the omelet. Slide the set omelet, flat, into the center of a plate. Return pan to heat and add another 2 teaspoons butter. As butter melts, spoon half the sausage filling on top of the first omelet and put it in a 150° oven.

Make second omelet, following the same steps. While it is cooking, spread sausage filling into an even layer on the first omelet. When second omelet is cooked, slide it directly on top of the filling on the first omelet. (If you have a partner and 2 pans, cook 2 omelets at a time.)

Return pan to heat and add 2 more teaspoons butter; as it melts, spoon half the zucchini filling on top of second omelet and return stack to oven. Make third omelet; as it cooks, distribute zucchini and onions in an even layer on second omelet.

Slide the third omelet on top of the zucchini; cover the omelet stack with the rest of the sausage filling. Concurrently, make the fourth omelet; when it's cooked, add it to the stack and cover with the rest of the zucchini mixture. Keep warm.

Use remaining eggs to make fifth omelet; slide it on top of the stack and keep warm. Peel, pit, and slice avocado half. Arrange on top of stack. Cut five-tier omelet into wedges; add salsa to taste. Serves 4 to 6. —*Bob McAndrews, Olivenhain, Calif.*

**Sausage filling.** Pull casing off ½ pound hot or mild **Italian sausage.** Crumble meat in a 10- to 12-inch frying pan over medium-high heat. Add ½ pound **mushrooms,** rinsed and minced, and ¼ cup minced **parsley.** Stir often until meat is well browned. Stir in 2 medium-size ripe **tomatoes,** cored and chopped; and 1 small can (6 oz.) **tomato paste.**

Boil sauce, uncovered, stirring often, until so thick it no longer flows when you pull a spoon across pan bottom, about 15 minutes. If made ahead, cover and chill up to 2 days; reheat to continue. Use hot.

**Zucchini filling.** In a 10- to 12-inch frying pan over medium heat, combine 1 tablespoon **olive oil** or salad oil and 1 large **onion,** thinly sliced. Cook, stirring occasionally, until golden, about 20 minutes. Pour onions into a small bowl; set aside.

Trim ends from 3 medium-size **zucchini** (about 1 lb.); cut zucchini into ¼-inch-thick slices. Add 1 more tablespoon **olive oil** or salad oil to pan. Spread a single layer of zucchini slices (about ⅓) in pan; place over medium heat. Cook until slices are speckled with brown; turn as needed with a spatula. With a slotted spoon, transfer slices to onions. Repeat to cook remaining zucchini; you'll need 2 more tablespoons **olive oil** or salad oil.

If made ahead, cover and chill up to 2 days; reheat to continue. Use hot.

**Fresh salsa.** In a bowl, combine 1 large ripe **tomato,** cored and chopped; 1 small **onion,** finely chopped; ¼ cup minced **fresh coriander** (cilantro); 1 tablespoon **lemon juice;** and 1 small **fresh** or canned **jalapeño chili,** minced. Serve, or cover and chill up to 4 hours. Makes 1½ cups.

*Wedges of five-tier omelet, layered with sausage and zucchini-onion fillings, make a showy presentation. Salsa accompanies.*

# Cool Soups for Warm Days

SMOOTHLY PURÉE *cooked vegetables or ripe avocado with buttermilk, yogurt, or sour cream to make a refreshing cool soup. Serve as a first course or a light lunch with crusty bread and cheese.*

*The tangy avocado buttermilk bisque needs no cooking; it blends in seconds. Both the watercress and carrot soups can be served hot or cold.*

## AVOCADO BUTTERMILK DILL BISQUE

- 1 large ripe avocado, pitted and peeled
- 3 tablespoons lemon juice
- 2 tablespoons chopped fresh dill
- 2 cups buttermilk
- 2 cups regular-strength chicken broth
  Salt and white pepper
- ¼ pound small cooked peeled shrimp
  Dill sprigs

Cut 4 or 5 thin slices from avocado and coat with 1 tablespoon of the lemon juice; cover and chill to reserve for gar-nish. Cut remaining avocado in chunks.

In a blender or food processor, smoothly purée the remaining lemon juice, diced avocado, chopped dill, but-termilk, and broth, half at a time. Add salt and pepper to taste. If made ahead, cover and chill up to 4 hours. Pour into 4 or 5 shallow bowls. Garnish each bowl with an avocado slice, shrimp, and dill sprigs. Makes 4 or 5 servings.

## CREAMY POTATO WATERCRESS BISQUE

- 3 cups regular-strength chicken broth
- 2 large thin-skinned potatoes (1 lb. total), peeled and cut in 1-inch chunks
- 2 cups lightly packed watercress sprigs, rinsed and drained
- 1 cup sour cream
- 3 green onions, thinly sliced
- ⅛ teaspoon ground white pepper
  Salt
- ¼ pound thinly sliced cooked ham, cut in thin slivers

In a 3- to 4-quart pan, combine broth and potatoes. Bring to boiling. Cover and simmer until potatoes are tender when pierced, 15 to 20 minutes.

Reserve 4 or 5 sprigs of watercress for garnish. In a blender or food processor, smoothly purée broth mixture, remain-ing watercress, sour cream, onions, and pepper, half at a time. Add salt to taste.

To serve cold, cool, cover, and chill until cold, about 2 hours or up to over-night. To serve hot, return soup to pan and stir over medium heat just until hot.

Ladle soup into 4 or 5 shallow bowls. Garnish each with a mound of ham slivers and a watercress sprig. Makes 4 or 5 servings.

## CARROT YOGURT SOUP

- 2 tablespoons salad oil
- 1 large onion, chopped
- 1 clove garlic, pressed or minced
- 1 teaspoon curry powder
- 1 teaspoon all-purpose flour
- 3 cups regular-strength chicken broth
- 3 large carrots, peeled and sliced
- 1 cup unflavored yogurt
  Salt and cayenne
- ⅓ cup chopped salted roasted peanuts
  Carrot curls (directions follow), optional

In a 3- to 4-quart pan, combine oil, onion, and garlic. Stir over medium heat until onion is limp. Add curry powder and flour; stir about 30 seconds. Add broth and carrots. Cover and simmer until carrots are tender when pierced, 15 to 20 minutes. In a blender or food pro-cessor, whirl about half of the mixture at a time with ¾ cup of the yogurt until smoothly puréed. Add salt and cayenne to taste.

To serve cold, cool, cover, and chill about 2 hours or up to overnight. To serve hot, return soup to pan and stir over medium heat until hot. Ladle into 4 shallow bowls. Garnish each with a dol-lop of the remaining yogurt, a sprinkling of peanuts, and 1 or 2 carrot curls. Makes 4 servings.

**Carrot curls.** Peel 1 large **carrot.** Lay car-rot on a flat surface and run a vegetable peeler evenly and deeply down its length to make 4 or 8 strips. Loosely curl strips and immerse in **ice water** until crisp, about 10 minutes. If made ahead, chill up to overnight. Drain curls.

*Cool, creamy soups feature vegetables blended with tangy dairy products. Garnish adds substance: ham on the watercress, shrimp on the avocado, yogurt and peanuts on the carrot.*

# Salad Surprises

CORN AND POTATOES *take on a fresh new look in these salads. Ears of corn, cut in chunky wheels and splashed with a sweet-tart dressing, get picked up to eat. The grand old standby, potato salad, gets lightened with the addition of more vegetables and a yogurt dressing.*

## SWEET CORN COBLETS

  6  **medium-size ears of corn (about 4 lb. total)**
      **Water**
¾  **cup distilled white vinegar**
  1  **cup minced onion**
  2  **to 3 tablespoons sugar**
  1  **jar (2 oz.) chopped pimiento, drained**
  1  **teaspoon *each* mustard seed and crushed dried hot red chilies**
½  **teaspoon salt (optional)**

Remove and discard husks and silk from corn. With a heavy, sharp knife, cut corn crosswise into ¾-inch rounds (if needed, use a hammer or mallet to help drive knife through cob). In a 6- to 8-quart pan over high heat, bring 4 quarts of water to a boil, add corn pieces, cover, and cook until hot, 2 to 3 minutes. Drain corn and pour into a shallow, rimmed dish about 9 by 13 inches.

In the same pan used to cook corn, combine vinegar, onion, sugar, pimiento, mustard seed, chilies, and salt. Bring to a boil over high heat and cook, stirring, until sugar dissolves. Pour over corn; let stand until cool, spooning mixture over corn frequently.

If made ahead, cover and hold at room temperature or chill up to 6 hours. Pick up pieces and nibble kernels off cobs. Makes 8 to 10 servings.

*Pick up and nibble tart-sweet seasoned wheels of corn; the dish makes an ideal picnic salad for youngsters.*

## POTATO & VEGETABLE SALAD

      **Water**
  6  **medium-size russet or thin-skinned potatoes (about 2 lb. total)**
  1  **medium-size zucchini, ends trimmed**
  2  **medium-size peeled carrots**
½  **pound green beans, ends trimmed**
      **Yogurt dressing (recipe follows)**
      **Salt and pepper**

In a 6- to 8-quart pan, bring 4 quarts of water to boil over high heat. Add potatoes, reduce heat to medium, cover, and cook potatoes until tender when pierced, about 25 minutes. Drain and let cool.

Cut zucchini and carrots into ¼-inch slices. Cut beans into 1½-inch lengths.

In the same pan over high heat, bring 2 to 3 quarts water to a boil. Drop zucchini into water and cook until tender-crisp to bite, about 2 minutes. Lift out with a slotted spoon and immerse in bowl of ice water. Add carrots to boiling water and cook until tender-crisp to bite, about 5 minutes. Lift out with a slotted spoon and add to zucchini. Add beans to boiling water; cook until tender-crisp to bite, about 6 minutes. Drain and immerse in ice water. When vegetables are cool, drain and place in a large bowl.

Peel cool potatoes and cut into ½-inch cubes; add to other vegetables. Gently stir in yogurt dressing to coat all pieces. Add salt and pepper to taste. Serves 6 to 8. —*DeAndra Lewis, San Carlos, Calif.*

**Yogurt dressing.** Combine ⅓ cup *each* **unflavored yogurt** and **mayonnaise,** ½ cup chopped **onion,** 2 tablespoons minced **parsley,** and 1 tablespoon **lemon juice.**

# Seasoning Pastes for the Barbecue

AROMATIC AND BOLD, *spices from India flavor these grilled meats and seafood. Grind the seasonings in a blender, then use as marinades for the meats. Mix some of the reserved seasoning pastes with yogurt to make tempering cool sauces.*

*Accompany with sliced cucumbers and tomatoes and a rice pilaf.*

## SHRIMP WITH CHILI PASTE

> Chili paste (recipe follows)
> 1  cup unflavored yogurt
> 1½  pounds colossal shrimp (10 to 15 per lb.), shelled and deveined
> Lemon wedges

Mix ¼ cup of the chili paste with yogurt; cover and chill up to overnight.

In a bowl, mix the remaining chili paste with the shrimp. Cover and chill, turning occasionally, at least 4 hours or up to overnight.

Place 4 or 5 shrimp on each skewer, running skewer twice through each shrimp, near head and tail ends, as shown at right. Place skewers on a grill 4

to 6 inches above a solid bed of hot coals (you can hold your hand at grill level only 2 to 3 seconds). Cook, turning, until shrimp are opaque in center (cut to test), 4 to 6 minutes. Serve hot with yogurt sauce and lemon wedges. Makes 4 or 5 servings.

**Chili paste.** In a blender, combine ⅓ cup **lemon juice;** ¼ cup **salad oil;** 1 large **onion,** chopped; ½ cup lightly packed **cilantro** (coriander) **leaves;** 6 to 8 cloves **garlic;** 1 tablespoon chopped **fresh ginger;** and 1 or 2 **fresh jalapeño chilies,** seeded and stemmed. Whirl until smoothly puréed.

## LAMB CHOPS WITH SPICE PASTE

> Spice paste (recipe follows)
> 1  cup unflavored yogurt
> 12  lamb rib chops, each about 1 inch thick (about 3 lb. total)

Mix ¼ cup of the spice paste with the yogurt. Cover and chill up to overnight.

Trim excess surface fat from chops. In a 9- by 13-inch dish, coat lamb chops with remaining spice paste. Cover and chill at least 4 hours or up to overnight.

Place lamb on a grill 4 to 6 inches above a solid bed of hot coals (you can hold your hand at grill level only 2 to 3 seconds). Cook, turning, until brown on outside and still pink inside (cut to test), 8 to 10 minutes. Serve hot with yogurt sauce. Makes 4 servings.

**Spice paste.** In a 6- to 8-inch frying pan, combine 2 teaspoons *each* **cumin seed** and **coriander seed;** 1 teaspoon **black peppercorns;** 8 **whole cardamom,** pods removed; and 5 **whole cloves.** Cook over medium heat, shaking pan often, until spices are fragrant and lightly toasted, about 4 minutes. Pour spices into a blender and whirl until finely ground. Add ½ to 1 teaspoon **cayenne,** ¼ teaspoon **ground mace** (or nutmeg), ¼ teaspoon **ground cinnamon,** 2 tablespoons minced **fresh ginger,** 4 cloves **garlic,** and 1 cup **unflavored yogurt.** Whirl until smoothly puréed.

## PORK CHOPS WITH SPICED TOMATO PASTE

> Spiced tomato paste (recipe follows)
> 1  cup unflavored yogurt
> 8  pork loin chops, each about ½ inch thick (about 2 lb. total)

*Slide grilled shrimp off skewers to eat with the chili paste-seasoned yogurt.*

Mix ¼ cup spiced tomato paste with yogurt; cover and chill up to overnight.

Trim and discard excess surface fat from pork. In a 9- by 13-inch pan, mix remaining spiced tomato paste with pork. Cover and chill, turning occasionally, at least 4 hours or up to overnight (paste will coagulate when chilled; stir to soften and spread on meat just before putting on grill).

Place pork on grill 4 to 6 inches above a solid bed of medium-hot coals (you can hold hand at grill level 3 to 4 seconds). Cook, turning, until meat is brown on outside and no longer pink in thickest part at bone (cut to test), 5 to 7 minutes. Serve with yogurt sauce. Makes 4 servings.

**Spiced tomato paste.** In a blender, combine 1 large **onion,** chopped; ½ cup **wine vinegar;** 1 can (6 oz.) **tomato paste;** 3 tablespoons **salad oil;** 2 tablespoons chopped **fresh ginger;** 2 teaspoons **ground coriander;** ½ teaspoon *each* **cayenne** and **ground cumin;** and ¼ teaspoon *each* **ground mace** (or nutmeg), **ground cloves,** and **ground turmeric.**

*Assertive seasonings for shrimp include onion, cilantro, lemon, ginger, garlic, and chili whirled in the blender to a smooth paste; mixture also flavors yogurt for sauce.*

# Italian Coolers

Vibrant in hue *and flavor, these summer afternoon coolers are blend-as-you-go drinks based on fresh fruit and a sparkling beverage. The original inspiration comes from the Italians, who have a delicious habit of adding their muscat sparkling wines—or Asti Spumante—to fruit purées for delectable adult-style sodas.*

*You can share these drinks with all ages, replacing the wine with sparkling water or a light fruit-flavored soda to thin the purées to a sipping consistency.*

*Because bubbles diffuse quickly, beverages should be mixed just before drinking. You can organize the purées, however, up to 3 hours before serving. Choose several fruits to purée with orange juice—the juice makes the purées pourable and adds its own sweet touch. For peaches and apricots, which brown quickly when exposed to air, you add lemon juice to help preserve their bright color.*

*Present the purées in a collection of pitchers on a tray and let guests choose and sample from the whole lot.*

## SOME THOUGHTS ON SPARKLING WINES

Sparkling wines made from muscat grape varieties are on the sweet side; the best have the essence of freshly pressed grape juice and are refreshing rather than cloying. These wines are very popular in Italy, and many are imported here; they are often modestly priced. But these muscat wines are not just the domain of the Italian winemaker: at least one moderately priced one is made in California. Ask your wine merchant to recommend a brand with a fresh fruit flavor.

## ITALIAN SPARKLING FRUIT FIZZ

- 2 **cups prepared fruit (choices follow)**
- 6 **tablespoons orange juice**
  **Sugar (optional)**
- 1 **bottle (750 ml.) chilled sparkling muscat wine, or 1 bottle (32 oz.) chilled sparkling water or carbonated lemon-lime beverage**
  **Ice (optional)**

In a blender or food processor, whirl fruit and orange juice until very smoothly puréed. Add sugar to taste. (When making raspberry purée, pour purée into a fine strainer set over a bowl. Rub pulp to extract as much liquid as possible; discard the seeds.)

Pour the purée into a 3- to 4-cup serv-

*Offer colorful assortment of fruit purées to blend by the glass with sparkling wine, water, or beverage for fizzy delights.*

ing pitcher. If made ahead, cover and chill up to 3 hours. Stir before serving.

To make each serving (you can let guests serve themselves), fill a stemmed glass about ⅓ full with the fruit purée. Slowly, to avoid foaming over the rim, fill glass with sparkling wine or beverage. If the day is warm, keep the sparkling beverages on ice and have a few cubes to slip into glasses when purées begin to warm. Each batch of prepared fruit makes about 2¼ cups purée, enough for 10 to 12 servings in 8- to 10-ounce glasses.

**Prepared fruit.** For the richest, sweetest flavor, select fully ripened fruit.

*Apricot.* Rinse, halve, and pit 1 pound ripe **apricots;** mix with 2 tablespoons **lemon juice.**

*Kiwi fruit.* Peel 3 **kiwi fruit** (about 1 lb. total) and cut into chunks.

*Melon.* Peel and seed 1 small (about 2 lb.) **cantaloupe** or honeydew melon; cut enough into chunks to make 2 cups. Reserve remaining fruit to eat or use for other dishes.

*Peach.* Peel, halve, and pit about 4 medium-size (about 1½ lb.) ripe **peaches;** mix with 2 tablespoons **lemon juice.**

*Pineapple.* Cut peel and top off 1 small (about 3 lb.) **pineapple;** trim out any eyes that remain. Cut pineapple in half lengthwise; cut out and discard core. Cut enough pineapple into small chunks to make 2½ cups; reserve remaining fruit to eat or use in other dishes.

*Raspberry.* Gently rinse 2 cups **raspberries;** drain on paper towel.

*Strawberry.* Remove stems from about 2½ cups **strawberries;** rinse and drain on paper towels.

# Australia's Damper Loaf

EADEN might have described the original damper bread baked by convicts and other settlers in Australia's bush. No leavening, just flour and water, went into the dough baked in campfire ashes.

Today's damper, while still a simple, rustic loaf, is civilized enough for indoor consumption. It's basically a large biscuit with baking powder for leavening. Our version, inspired by Sylvester's bakery in southeastern Australia's wine-producing Hunter Valley, also uses yeast to give the bread a tangy flavor and a lighter texture. The loaf's soft interior and extra-crisp crust make a perfect sponge for butter and jam. Or serve it with soup.

Why the curious name? Some historians say the flour-and-water mixture was "damp." Others say damper is a corruption of William Dampier, a buccaneer and explorer of Australia, who reputedly ate nearly anything.

## AUSTRALIAN DAMPER BREAD

1 package active dry yeast
¼ cup warm water (110°)
1 cup warm milk (110°)
About 3 cups all-purpose flour
1 tablespoon baking powder
¾ teaspoon salt, or to taste
2 tablespoons butter or margarine

In a small bowl, soften yeast in water, about 5 minutes. Stir in milk; set aside.

In a bowl, mix 3 cups flour, baking powder, and salt. With a pastry blender or your fingers, cut or rub butter into flour mixture until fine crumbs form. Add milk mixture; stir until evenly moistened.

Scoop dough out onto a lightly floured board and knead until smooth, about 15 times; add flour if required to prevent sticking. Shape dough into a lumpy round loaf 5 to 6 inches in diameter. Dust lightly with flour, then place in a greased 8-inch round cake pan.

With a sharp knife or razor blade, cut an X about ½ inch deep and 3 inches long across center of loaf. Bake on bottom rack of a 375° oven until well browned, about 55 minutes. Remove from pan and let cool on a rack for 5 to 10 minutes, then serve warm. Makes 1 loaf, about 1½ pounds.

Break warm damper into chunks and serve with butter to accompany soup. Sylvester's bakery in Cessnock, New South Wales, sells about 22,000 damper loaves a week.

# More August Recipes

FIRE UP THE BARBECUE *to grill corn for an unusual soup and to cook the spicy spareribs.*

## GRILLED CORN SOUP WITH CHILI & CILANTRO CREAMS

*Bold streaks of color decorate and season this sweet corn bisque. Green cilantro and red chili flavor and color the creams floating on this simple but dramatic dish.*

*Dallas chef Stephen Pyles showed us this technique while he was demonstrating at Yosemite's annual Chefs' Holidays.*

- 4 **large ears corn, husks and silk removed**
- 3 **cups regular-strength chicken broth**
- 1 **large carrot, peeled and chopped**
- 1 **small stalk celery, chopped**
- 1 **small onion, chopped**
- 2 **cloves garlic**
- 1 **fresh jalapeño chili, stemmed, seeded, and chopped**
- ½ **cup whipping cream**
  **Salt**
  **Chili cream (recipe follows)**
  **Cilantro cream (recipe follows)**

Place corn on a grill 4 to 6 inches above a solid bed of medium coals (you can hold your hand at grill level only 4 to 5 seconds). Cover barbecue, open dampers, and cook, turning corn occasionally, until lightly browned on all sides, about 15 minutes. Remove from grill and let cool.

In a 3- to 4-quart pan, combine broth, carrot, celery, onion, garlic, and jalapeño. Bring to boiling, cover, and simmer for 5 minutes. Meanwhile cut corn off cob. Add corn to broth and simmer, covered, until vegetables are tender to bite, 5 to 10 minutes longer. Whirl soup, a portion at a time, in a blender until smoothly puréed. Pour soup through a fine wire strainer set over a bowl.

Return soup to pan; stir in cream and add salt to taste. (If made ahead, cool, cover, and chill up to overnight.) Serve soup hot or cold. To reheat, stir over low heat just until hot. Ladle into 4 wide, shallow bowls. Drizzle equal portions of chili and cilantro creams over each serving, as pictured above right. Serves 4.

**Chili cream.** Place 1 **dry ancho** or California **chili** in a 400° oven just until lightly toasted and fragrant, about 1 minute. Remove stems and seeds. Crumble chili into a bowl; cover with 1 cup hot **water;** soak until soft, about 10 minutes. Drain.

In a blender, combine chili, 2 tablespoons **milk,** and 2 tablespoons **sour cream;** whirl until puréed (if it sticks to blender sides, stop and push down). If needed, add a little milk to thin to about the same consistency as soup. (If made ahead, cover and chill up to overnight.)

**Cilantro cream.** In a blender, combine ½ cup lightly packed **cilantro** (coriander) **leaves,** washed and dried; 1 teaspoon **milk;** and 1½ tablespoons **sour cream;** whirl until puréed (if it sticks to blender sides, stop and push down). If needed, add a little milk to thin to about the same consistency as soup. (If made ahead, cover and chill up to overnight.)

## HOT-SWEET RIBS

*You cook these sweet, spicy ribs over indirect heat on the barbecue.*

- 1 **slab pork spareribs, 3½ to 4 pounds**
- ¼ **cup firmly packed brown sugar**
- 1 **teaspoon cayenne**
  **Hot-sweet sauce (recipe follows)**

Trim and discard excess fat from ribs. Mix together sugar and cayenne; rub onto both sides of slab.

Ignite 40 charcoal briquets on firegrate of a barbecue with lid. When coals are coated with gray ash, about 30 minutes, mound half on each side of the grate. Put a drip pan in the center. Add 5 or 6 briquets to each mound of coals. Place grill 5 to 6 inches above the grate.

*Special effects made with flavored creams accent basic corn soup.*

Lay pork, bonier side down, on grill over drip pan. Cover barbecue and open dampers; cook ribs 30 minutes. Brush top with about ⅓ of the sauce, and cook 15 minutes longer. Turn ribs, baste top with half the remaining sauce, and cook 15 minutes. Turn ribs again, basting top with remaining sauce, and cook until thickest part of meat at bone is gray (cut to test). Total cooking time is 1¼ to 1½ hours. Cut between bones to serve. Serves 3 or 4.

**Hot-sweet sauce.** To a 2- to 3-quart pan over medium heat, add ¼ cup **olive oil** or salad oil and 4 cloves **garlic,** minced or pressed; stir until golden, about 4 minutes. Stir in ½ cup firmly packed **brown sugar,** ½ cup *each* **red wine vinegar** and **regular-strength chicken broth,** ¼ cup **tomato paste,** 3 tablespoons **soy sauce,** and 2 teaspoons **dry mustard;** bring to boil. Cook on medium-high heat, stirring often, until reduced to 1 cup, about 15 minutes.

*Rice pilaf with peaches, cashews, green onions, and lemon is good hot or cool.*

## PEACH PILAF

> 1 tablespoon butter or margarine
> ¼ pound mushrooms, thinly sliced
> 1 cup long-grain white rice
> 1¾ cups or 1 can (14½ oz.) regular-strength chicken broth
> 4 green onions, ends trimmed
> 3 medium-size (about ¾ lb.) firm-ripe peaches
> About 1 tablespoon lemon juice
> ½ cup roasted, salted cashews
> Lemon wedges (optional)

In a 10- to 12-inch frying pan over medium-high heat, melt butter and add mushrooms. Cook, stirring occasionally, until mushrooms are lightly browned, about 5 minutes. Add rice and cook, stirring, about 2 minutes. Add broth, bring to boiling, cover, and simmer until rice is tender to bite, about 20 minutes.

Meanwhile, thinly slice 3 of the onions. Peel peaches, cut in half, discard pits, and cut fruit into ½-inch chunks. Mix with lemon juice to coat well. When rice is tender, gently stir in sliced onion, peaches, and cashews. Pour onto a serving platter; garnish with reserved onion and lemon wedges. Serve hot or at room temperature. Makes 6 servings. — *W.B. St. John, Sacramento.*

*Ripe tomatoes, potato are base for thick soup flavored with onion, garlic, basil.*

## TOMATO-POTATO SOUP

> 2 tablespoons butter or margarine
> 2 medium-size onions, minced
> 2 cloves garlic, pressed or minced
> 2 to 2½ pounds firm-ripe tomatoes, peeled and cored
> 1 large (8 oz.) russet potato, peeled and diced
> ¼ cup fresh basil leaves or 1 tablespoon dry basil
> 3 cups or 2 cans (14½ oz.) regular-strength chicken broth
> Unflavored yogurt (optional)
> Salt and pepper

In a 6- to 8-quart pan over medium-high heat, stir butter, onion, and garlic often until onion is golden, about 15 minutes. Meanwhile, in a food processor or blender, whirl tomatoes until coarsely puréed; pour into pan. Cook over medium-high heat, uncovered, until reduced by about a third. Also mince potato and basil in processor (in a blender, add ¼ cup broth); add with broth to pan. Simmer until potato is soft to bite, about 20 minutes.

Serve hot, at room temperature, or cold (cover and chill up to 2 days). Add yogurt, salt, and pepper to taste. Makes 4 servings, 1½ cups each. — *Jane A. Stone, Napa, Calif.*

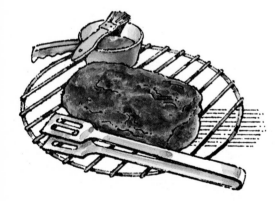

*Grilled beef brisket is glazed with sweet, tart marinade that becomes a thick sauce.*

## BARBECUED BEEF BRISKET WITH DOUBLE-DUTY MARINADE

> 1 center-cut beef brisket (about 5 lb.), excess fat trimmed off
> 1 small onion, minced
> ½ cup Worcestershire
> 2 tablespoons *each* soy sauce and liquid smoke
> ½ teaspoon cayenne (optional)
> Sauce (recipe follows)

Place beef in a large plastic bag and set in a pan. Combine onion, Worcestershire, soy, liquid smoke, and cayenne; pour over meat. Seal bag; chill overnight or up to 2 days, turning several times. Lift meat out; save marinade for sauce.

Lay brisket on a grill 4 to 6 inches over a solid bed of low coals (you should be able to hold your hand at grill level for about 6 seconds). Turn meat every 5 minutes, basting with sauce. Cook until a thermometer in center of thickest part reads 140°, about 25 minutes. Cut meat across grain in thin slanting slices; offer sauce. Serves 12 to 15. — *Irene Britton, San Jose, Calif.*

**Sauce.** Pour marinade into a 1- to 2-quart pan; add ½ cup **butter** or margarine, ½ cup each **catsup** and **red wine vinegar,** and 1 teaspoon **dry mustard.** Bring to a boil, stirring, on high heat; simmer until reduced to 1½ cups.

## LEEK QUICHE

- 2 cups sliced leeks, white and tender green parts (buy about 1½ lb.)
- 1 small green bell pepper, stemmed, seeded, and chopped
- ¼ teaspoon cayenne
- 1 tablespoon butter or margarine
- 4 medium-size firm-ripe Roma-type tomatoes
- 1 cup (4 oz.) shredded Swiss cheese
- 1 baked 9-inch pie crust
- 3 large eggs
- ½ cup milk

In a 10- to 12-inch pan over medium-high heat, cook leeks, bell pepper, and cayenne in butter, stirring often, until vegetables are limp, about 5 minutes.

Meanwhile, core, seed, and chop 3 tomatoes. Add to leek mixture and cook, stirring often, until liquid evaporates. Cool slightly, then stir in cheese. Spoon mixture into baked crust. Beat eggs with milk; pour over vegetables. Thinly slice remaining tomato; arrange over quiche. Bake in a 350° oven until center is firm when gently shaken, about 35 minutes. Let cool 10 minutes; cut into wedges. Serves 6.—*Doris G. Sherry, Corvallis, Ore.*

*Mild fresh leeks flavor vegetable quiche enriched by shredded Swiss cheese.*

## CORN & GREEN CHILI BAKE

- 1 medium-size onion, chopped
- 1 tablespoon olive or salad oil
- 3 cups fresh corn kernels
- 2 teaspoons chili powder
- 2 large cans (7 oz. each) whole green chilies
- 1 pound colby or longhorn cheese, shredded
- 7 large eggs
- 1 cup *each* sour cream and unflavored yogurt
   Purchased green chili salsa
   Salt and pepper

In a 10- to 12-inch pan over high heat, cook onion in oil, stirring often, until onion is lightly browned, about 6 minutes. Add corn and chili powder; stir often until corn is soft.

Split chilies open. Arrange half to cover the bottom of a buttered 9- by 13-inch baking dish. Sprinkle half the cheese over chilies. Cover with corn mixture. Cover corn with remaining chilies and top with remaining cheese. Beat together eggs, sour cream, and yogurt; pour over cheese. Bake in a 350° oven until top puffs and edges are browned, about 40 minutes. Let cool about 10 minutes, then cut into squares and serve with salsa, salt, and pepper to taste. Serves 10 to 12.—*Gladys Kent, Port Angeles, Wash.*

*Fresh corn, onions, canned chilies bake in sour cream, yogurt, and cheese custard.*

## FROZEN BLUEBERRY TRIFLE

- 1 (10¾ oz.) purchased pound cake, cut into ½-inch slices
- 2 cups blueberries (fresh or thawed unsweetened frozen)
- 2 tablespoons lemon juice
- 1½ cups whipping cream
- 2 large eggs
- 1 cup sugar
- 2 teaspoons grated lemon peel
- ½ cup milk

Line bottom of 9-inch cheesecake pan with removable bottom with cake slices cut and pressed in to fit snugly.

Mash 1½ cups blueberries and mix with lemon juice. With an electric mixer on high speed, whip cream until it holds soft peaks. In a separate bowl, also whip eggs, sugar, and lemon peel on high speed until a thick foam forms; stir in milk. Fold together blueberry mixture, whipped cream, and whipped egg mixture; pour over cake in pan. Cover and freeze until solid, at least 6 hours or up to 2 weeks.

Let dessert soften at room temperature about 10 minutes before cutting. Spoon remaining berries over portions. Serves 10 to 12.—*Jennifer Brinley, Santa Rosa, Calif.*

*Crushed blueberries settle to form ribbon layer in frozen trifle; top with whole berries.*

LANGDON SULLY'S *Broiled Pork Shoulders show a Chinese influence, though the method of serving them does not. A Chinese cook would use a similar marinade, but the pork would be slivered, mixed with some complementary vegetables, and quickly stir-fried. The diner could then employ chopsticks to deal delicately with the slivers.*

*The impatient American tends to prefer bigger bites managed with knife and fork. In fact, he is probably the fellow Chef Sully was talking about when he suggested eating the pork with Gusto.*

## BROILED PORK SHOULDERS

    4  pork shoulder steaks, each cut
       ¾ inch thick (about 2¼ lb.)
    1  beef bouillon cube
    ⅓  cup hot water
    1  teaspoon ground ginger
    1  tablespoon sugar
    ¼  cup honey
    ¼  cup soy sauce

Slash edge fat on steaks, just to meat, at 1-inch intervals. In a 9- by 13-inch baking pan, mash bouillon cube in water to soften, then stir in ginger, sugar, honey,

and soy sauce. Turn steaks over in mixture to coat all sides, then arrange in pan in a single layer; cover. Refrigerate at least 1 hour or up to overnight, turning meat once or twice.

Lift meat from marinade, drain briefly, and arrange on a rack in a broiler pan (about 12 by 15 inches). Broil about 3 inches from heat until both sides are browned and meat is no longer pink at bone (cut to test), about 15 minutes total. Baste with remaining marinade, using it all. Makes 4 servings.

*Langdon Sully*

*Vista, Calif.*

A GROWING RESPECT *for the opinions of dietitians requires that we skin chicken breasts before cooking them; after all, the deadly fat lies just beneath (and attached to) the skin. Unfortunately, so does a lot of the flavor, and cooks have had to devise ways to lend moistness and taste to the skinless meat. Most of these techniques involve wrapping it around butter or cheese—which, of course, returns some fat. Oh, well: the chef taketh away, and the chef giveth back.*

*Alan Kunz puts jack cheese inside his chicken rolls, then coats them in parmesan and butter. He tosses in jalapeños, cumin, and ground mild chili to wake the slumbering taste buds. The result is an Italo-Mexican Chicken Kiev.*

## MELTDOWN CHICKEN BUNDLES

    4  whole chicken breasts (1 lb. each),
       skinned, boned, and halved
    4  pickled jalapeño chilies
    ¼  pound jack cheese
    ¼  cup fine dry bread crumbs
    2  tablespoons freshly grated
       parmesan cheese
    1  teaspoon ground dried New Mex-
       ico or California chili (or regular
       chili powder)
    ¼  teaspoon ground cumin
    ¼  teaspoon pepper
    6  tablespoons butter or margarine,
       melted
       Salt

Place each breast half between 2 pieces of plastic wrap. With a flat mallet, pound meat until each piece is ¼ inch thick; set aside.

Stem and seed jalapeños, then cut each lengthwise into ¼-inch-wide strips. Cut jack cheese into 8 equal strips.

In an 8- or 9-inch wide pan, combine crumbs, parmesan cheese, ground chili, cumin, and pepper.

*"The Chinese diner employs chopsticks to deal delicately with slivers. The impatient American prefers bigger bites managed with knife and fork."*

*"The result is an Italo-Mexican Chicken Kiev."*

To assemble, unwrap chicken and on each piece place 1 strip of cheese and ⅛ of the jalapeños. Roll chicken around filling to enclose it; tuck thin ends of chicken under the roll. Coat rolls with melted butter, then with crumb mixture. Arrange rolls, seam side down, in a shallow 10- by 15-inch baking pan. Drizzle chicken evenly with any remaining butter. If made ahead, cover and chill up to overnight.

Bake, uncovered, in a 425° oven until meat in center is no longer pink (cut to test), about 15 minutes. Add salt to taste. Makes 8 servings.

*Alan A. Kunz*

Walnut Creek, Calif.

**S**OME COOKY BAKERS *exhibit a tendency to give aggressively cute names to their products. "Snicker doodles" is an example that comes all too readily to mind. We are grateful, then, to Ed Thyfault, who gives his creations the forthright name of Sweet Rich Cookies. That is just what they are.*

*"He gave his creation the forthright name of Sweet Rich Cookies."*

## SWEET RICH COOKIES

1 cup (½ lb.) butter or margarine
1 cup salad oil
 About 1½ cups granulated sugar
1 cup powdered sugar
2 large eggs
4¼ cups all-purpose flour
1 teaspoon baking soda
1 teaspoon cream of tartar
½ teaspoon salt (optional)

In a large mixing bowl, beat butter, oil, 1 cup of the granulated sugar, and powdered sugar until creamy. Then add eggs, 1 at a time, beating each in well.

Stir together flour, soda, cream of tartar, and, if desired, salt. Thoroughly blend dry ingredients into butter mixture.

Place about ½ cup granulated sugar in a small bowl. Shape dough into 1-inch balls, dropping each ball as shaped into the bowl and rolling it to coat with sugar. Place balls 3 to 4 inches apart on ungreased baking sheets. Dip the bottom of a flat-bottomed glass in the sugar and use it to flatten each ball to about ¼-inch thickness; dip glass again as required to prevent sticking.

Bake cookies in a 375° oven until edges are lightly browned, 10 to 12 minutes. (If you're baking more than 1 pan at a time, alternate pan positions halfway through.) Transfer cookies to racks to cool. Serve, or store airtight up to 4 days; freeze to store longer. Makes about 8 dozen.

*Ed Thyfault*

Seattle

**J**OHN GRAHAM *calls his recipe Blueberry Buckle. "Buckle," like "grunt" and "slump," is a term New Englanders have for desserts combining fruit and various batters. To our Western ears, streusel cake seems marginally more euphonious.*

## BLUEBERRY STREUSEL CAKE

¼ cup (⅛ lb.) butter or solid vegetable shortening
¾ cup sugar
1 large egg
½ teaspoon grated lemon peel
½ cup milk
2 cups all-purpose flour
2 teaspoons baking powder
¼ teaspoon salt
2 cups blueberries (fresh or thawed unsweetened frozen)
 Streusel (directions follow)
 Half-and-half (light cream) or vanilla ice cream

In a mixer bowl, beat butter and sugar together until thoroughly mixed. Beat in egg and lemon peel. Mix in milk. Stir together flour, baking powder, and salt. Add to batter and mix slowly to incorporate, then beat until well mixed. Stir in blueberries. Grease and flour a 9-inch square pan; spread batter in pan.

Evenly sprinkle streusel over top of batter. Bake in a 375° oven until top is well browned and a slender wooden pick inserted in the center comes out clean, 45 to 50 minutes.

Let cool on a rack for at least 20 minutes before cutting, or serve at room temperature. Cut into squares and offer half-and-half or scoops of ice cream to accompany each portion. Makes 8 or 9 servings.

**Streusel.** In a small bowl, combine ½ cup **sugar,** ⅓ cup **all-purpose flour,** ¼ cup (⅛ lb.) **butter** or margarine, and ½ teaspoon **ground cinnamon.** Rub mixture with your fingers until fine crumbs form, then mix in ⅓ cup chopped **pecans.** Squeeze mixture together to make lumps, then loosely break them apart.

*John M. Graham*

Claremont, Calif.

# August Menus

F AST, EASY MEALS *and little cooking— that's the ticket for hot August days. Choose quick-to-prepare main dishes, and serve seasonal fruit* au naturel *for dessert. For an evening picnic, pack dinner for two and select a scenic location. The salad entrée can easily be doubled.*

*Breakfast or brunch falls back on eggs for speed; enliven scrambled eggs with smoked salmon and cream cheese.*

*As you make frying pan quesadillas, let the family participate. Each person can cook his or her own—or appoint just one cook to supervise the project.*

---

### EVENING PICNIC ORIENTAL

**Mustard Shrimp**
**Chilled Lemon Noodles**
**Chilled Salad Greens**
**Strawberries with Gingered Vanilla Yogurt**
**Sweet Japanese Crackers**
**Iced Sake      Iced Tea**

---

*Perfectly suited to the home garden or a remote spot with a view, this simple-to-prepare picnic is ideal if you want dinner under control ahead of time. Pack each element of the salad separately—the marinated shrimp, the cold noodles with Oriental seasonings, and crisp greens. This not only keeps foods fresh but creates an inviting presentation as you spoon ingredients one on top of the other.*

*For dessert, dip fat strawberries into gingered vanilla yogurt; enjoy with purchased crisp, sweet Japanese crackers or cookies. Carry a thermos of chilled sake or tea to serve over ice.*

*You can start the meal a day ahead: cook and season shrimp and noodles, wash and crisp about 1 quart salad greens, and stir together the yogurt sauce. To transport any distance, pack containers in a refrigerated chest. Also chill the beverages, then pour into a thermos.*

*If you like strawberries best at room temperature, rinse and let drain while you pack, then package them for safe travel.*

## MUSTARD SHRIMP

- 2 **tablespoons butter or salad oil**
- 2 **cloves garlic, pressed or minced**
- ¼ **cup finely chopped onion**
- ⅛ **teaspoon cayenne**

*Warm summer evenings invite picnicking. This transportable meal features a three-part salad to assemble on site. Above, spoon mustard-flavored cold shrimp and dressing over lemon-seasoned buckwheat noodles that top crisp greens.*

- ¾ **pound large shrimp (30 to 35 per lb.), shelled and deveined**
- ¼ **cup dry sherry**
- ¼ **cup white wine vinegar**
- 1 **tablespoon Dijon mustard**
- 1 **tablespoon finely chopped fresh tarragon or 1 teaspoon dry tarragon**

Melt butter in a 10- to 12-inch frying pan over medium heat. Add garlic, onion, and cayenne; cook until onion is golden, about 5 minutes, stirring often. Add shrimp and cook, stirring, until opaque in center (cut to test), 4 to 5 minutes. Add sherry, vinegar, mustard, and tarragon; stir until boiling. Let cool, then cover and chill at least 1 hour or up to overnight before serving. Makes 2 servings.

## CHILLED LEMON NOODLES

Water
6 ounces dry thin buckwheat noodles or dry vermicelli
Lemon dressing (recipe follows)

In a 5- to 6-quart pan over high heat, bring 4 quarts water to boiling. Add noodles and cook, uncovered, stirring occasionally, until tender to bite, about 10 minutes. Drain; rinse with cold water until noodles are cool, about 2 minutes. Drain and mix with lemon dressing. Cover and chill until ready to serve or up to overnight. Makes 2 servings.

**Lemon dressing.** Stir together ¼ cup **lemon juice,** 2 tablespoons **soy sauce,** 2 teaspoons finely chopped **fresh ginger,** 2 teaspoons **sesame oil,** and 1 teaspoon **sugar.**

## STRAWBERRIES WITH GINGERED VANILLA YOGURT

In a bowl, stir together ¾ cup **vanilla-flavored yogurt** and ¼ teaspoon **ground ginger.** Serve as a dip for 1½ to 2 cups rinsed and drained large **strawberries.** Makes 2 servings.

### EGG & BAGEL BREAKFAST

Orange Juice
Cream Cheese Eggs with Smoked Salmon
Toasted Bagels
Raspberries & Cantaloupe
Iced Coffee
Sweetened Whipped Cream

*This speedy yet elegant meal gives new form to an old favorite—lox and bagels. Mix the cream cheese and salmon into the scrambled eggs while you toast the bagels.*

*Choose small melons and use each half as a bowl to hold a serving of raspberries. Before you start the eggs, cut and seed the cantaloupe, rinse and drain the berries, then put them in the melons.*

*Also juice oranges and brew extra-strong coffee—let the hot liquid start to cool while you whip some cream. Serve the coffee over ice; add the cream as an optional embellishment.*

## CREAM CHEESE EGGS WITH SMOKED SALMON

6 to 8 large eggs
1 green onion (root trimmed), thinly sliced, including top
4 ounces thinly sliced smoked salmon or lox, cut into thin strips
1 tablespoon butter or margarine
1 small package (3 oz.) cream cheese, cut into small pieces

In a bowl, beat eggs until blended, then stir in half the onion and all the salmon. Melt butter in a 10- to 12-inch frying pan over medium heat. Pour egg mixture into pan and stir frequently with a wide spatula until eggs begin to set but are still quite moist. Scatter cheese over eggs and continue to cook, stirring often, until eggs are set as you like. Spoon eggs onto plates and garnish with remaining onion. Makes 3 or 4 servings.

### FULL-MOON QUESADILLA DINNER

Full-Moon Quesadillas with Tomatillo Salsa
Cherry Tomatoes
Pickled Peperoncinis
Watermelon
Lime    Salt    Cayenne
Polvorone Cookies
Sangria    Mineral Water

*With traditional quesadillas, you fold tortillas into half-moons. In our variation, they remain flat. Simply sandwich the filling between tortillas, toast in a frying pan, then cut into wedges. Each person can tend to his or her own quesadilla, or you can cut each into wedges to share as they come out of the pan. To serve all at the same time,*

*Hot wedges of layered tortilla quesadilla have ham and melted cheese inside.*

*Dressed-up eggs, scrambled with smoked salmon and cream cheese, go with toasted bagels. Raspberries fill tiny cantaloupe halves.*

*transfer quesadillas from pan to oven as you cook them.*

*If you like, eat all foods with your fingers.*

*For simplicity, buy thinly sliced ham and cheese from the deli—or the supermarket deli. If you can find them, purchase crumbly and tender Mexican-style sugar cookies called* polvorones; *or serve regular sugar cookies.*

*Cut watermelon into wedges, then season as you eat with a squeeze of lime juice and a sprinkle of salt and cayenne. Or mix salt and cayenne in a small, shallow dish and dip melon lightly into it.*

## FULL-MOON QUESADILLAS WITH TOMATILLO SALSA

½ pound tomatillos, husks removed and rinsed, or 1 can (13 oz.) tomatillos, drained
½ pound jicama, peeled and rinsed, or 1 can (5 oz.) water chestnuts, drained
1 fresh jalapeño chili, stemmed, seeded, and finely chopped
⅓ cup lime juice
8 flour tortillas (8- to 10-inch diameter)
1 pound jack cheese, thinly sliced
½ pound thinly sliced cooked ham
2 teaspoons butter or margarine
Cilantro (optional)

Core fresh tomatillos. Finely chop tomatillos and jicama; combine in a bowl

*(Continued on next page)*

### ...FULL-MOON QUESADILLAS WITH TOMATILLO SALSA

with jalapeño and lime juice. Use, or cover and chill up to overnight. Makes 1¾ cups.

Lay 4 tortillas flat. Cover surface of each with an even layer of cheese and ham, using all, then put another tortilla on top; press lightly to make them stick together. As quesadillas wait to cook, cover with plastic wrap to keep from drying.

Place a 10- to 12-inch frying pan or 10- by 20-inch griddle over medium heat. When hot, add ½ teaspoon of the butter to the pan (or 1 teaspoon on a griddle); swirl or brush butter to coat cooking surface. Using a wide spatula for sup-port, place 1 quesadilla in pan (or 2 on griddle). Cook until lightly spotted with brown on the bottom, about 3 minutes. Turn with spatula and cook until bottom is lightly spotted with brown and cheese is melting (peek to check). Remove from pan. Keep warm as remaining quesa-dillas are cooked—or eat as they come from pan; cut into wedges to eat out of hand or with a fork. Accompany with salsa. Makes 4 servings.

# SEPTEMBER

*Curried Fish Fritter & Salad Platter (page 218)*

**F**or casual outdoor
entertaining in September, we suggested a Southeast Asian
variation on an old-fashioned fish fry, where guests build their
own salads and add sizzling curry-spiced seafood chunks hot
from the cooking pan. Or treat friends to a Moroccan feast
featuring honey-glazed lamb. Show off the season's harvest in a
colorful herb-flavored loaf bulging with vegetables, flavorful
appetizers and salads, and desserts displaying the
ripe fruits of late summer and early autumn.

# Fish-Fry Salad

ON A FAIR DAY, *let your garden be the stage for this curry-spiced variation on an old-fashioned fish fry. Its fresh flavors are influenced by Southeast Asia—and, with the salad base, the combination makes a wholesome main course.*

*The cook has company as chunks of curry-seasoned fish brown in oil. Guests build their own salads, adding freshly cooked fish fritters as they become available. Best of all, cooking takes place outdoors, where the odors of frying quickly dissipate.*

*It's a three-station menu, with all ingredients assembled before guests arrive. One station offers the self-serve iced chowder to sip while the cook gets started. At the second station are the fish, batter, and salad elements—you'll need an electrical outlet and an electric wok or cooking pan (or use a pan and a portable burner). At the third post, you can have beverages and the fruit dessert.*

---

### FISH-FRY SALAD FOR 8

**Cold Corn Chowder     Peanuts**
**Curried Fish Fritter & Salad Platter**
**Chili Cucumbers**
**Fresh Mango Fans**
**Thai Coffee or Tea**
**Beer     Sake**

---

*The day before, you can make the chowder, batter, peanut dressing, and chili cucumbers. Begin arranging fish and salad platters.*

*For Thai coffee or tea, make the beverage double strength (you can also do this step ahead) and chill. To serve, pour over ice; add evaporated milk and sugar to taste.*

*On the party day, finish the salad platter, cut mangoes (if necessary, they can be cut the day before), and set up your three serving stations in the shade.*

*Oriental markets, some supermarkets, and health-food stores carry rice sticks, hot red chili paste, and shiro miso. Oriental markets may have banana leaves (otherwise, use suggested alternatives).*

*The salad has five elements. Have them at hand as you begin to cook and serve: salad greens, rice sticks, fish, curry batter, and Indonesian-style peanut dressing. First, fry the rice sticks (they puff almost instantly and become fragile-crisp). Then place the sticks on greens. Guests serve themselves these foods as the salad base.*

*Corn chowder, nestled in ice to keep cold, is self-serve start for a garden party. Sip soup, munch peanuts, and chat with the cook.*

*Then, as fish is fried and hot, they can add it to the salad a few bites at a time. Anoint everything with the pungent dressing.*

## COLD CORN CHOWDER

3   large onions, diced
2   tablespoons salad oil
5   large ears corn, husked
1   medium-size (about ½ lb.) thin-skinned potato, scrubbed
¼   pound cooked ham
2   cups regular-strength chicken broth
2   cups milk
     Salt
     Ice cubes or crushed ice
3   green onions, ends trimmed

In a 5- to 6-quart pan on medium-high heat, cook onions in oil, stirring often, until they begin to brown, 15 to 20 minutes.

Meanwhile, cut corn kernels off the cobs with a sharp knife. In a food processor or blender, whirl kernels until coarsely chopped. Dice potato and ham into ¼-inch cubes. Add corn, potato, ham, and broth to onions. Cover, then bring mixture to a boil. Simmer just until potato cubes are tender when pierced, about 15 minutes; let cool. Stir in milk; chill, covered, until cold, at least 4 or up to 24 hours. Add salt to taste.

Pour soup into a bowl; nest in a larger bowl of ice. Thinly slice 2 green onions and sprinkle onto soup. Top soup with whole green onion, if desired. Serves 8.

## CURRIED FISH FRITTER & SALAD PLATTER

**Salad oil**
**Crisp spinach and peppers (directions follow)**
**Fish platter (directions follow)**
**Curry fritter batter (recipe follows)**
**Peanut dressing (recipe follows)**
½   **package (7 oz.) rice sticks**

Pour 2 to 2½ inches oil into an electric wok or deep electric pan (at least 3-qt.) and heat to 400° (use a thermometer).

As oil heats, arrange alongside it the spinach and peppers, the fish platter, the batter, the dressing, and a wide platter or basket lined with paper napkins.

Break rice sticks into 6 portions, each about 3 inches long. With chopsticks or tongs, add 1 portion of the sticks to hot oil. When sticks puff—in a few seconds—turn them over so they puff evenly. With a skimmer or slotted spoon, lift sticks from oil when they stop crackling; drain on towels. Skim out any small bits remaining in oil so they won't burn. Repeat to cook each portion; as cooked, place on spinach leaves.

Reduce oil heat to 375°. With a fork or chopsticks, add 1 of each kind of fish to batter; stir to coat, lift out, and briefly let excess batter drip into bowl. Add fish to oil, without crowding and without letting oil drop below 350°. Fry fish until brown, about 2 minutes; turn pieces once and push apart to keep from sticking.

Lift cooked fish from oil; drain briefly on napkins. Invite guests to fill individual plates with spinach, peppers, and rice sticks and top with several pieces of hot fish. Ladle dressing onto salads to taste. Repeat to cook remaining fish; add hot to individual salads. Makes 8 servings.—*Michael Roberts, Los Angeles.*

**Crisp spinach and peppers.** Pluck tender leaves from 1½ pounds **spinach;** discard yellowed leaves and stems. Immerse leaves in cool **water** to wash well; drain. Wrap leaves in paper towels, put in a plastic bag, and chill to crisp, 1 to 24 hours. Lay spinach on a large platter.

Stem, core, and seed 1 *each* medium-size **yellow and red bell peppers** (or 2 of either color). Cut peppers into long slivers and scatter over spinach. If done ahead, cover airtight and chill up to 4 hours.

**Fish platter.** Purchase ¾ pound *each* medium-large **shrimp** (about 40 to a lb.), **scallops,** and **white-fleshed fish,** boned and skinned, such as rockfish or orange roughy fillets. Also purchase 16 shucked **oysters** on the half-shell (or without shells, if desired), such as small Pacifics.

Shell and devein shrimp. Rinse shrimp, scallops, and fish. Cut scallops and white fish into 1-inch chunks.

Cut oysters away from their shells; rinse grit from oysters and shells, then lay oysters back into shells.

Use a large platter, or a wide, flat basket lined with plastic wrap or foil. Cover platter with washed and dried large **nontoxic leaves** such as banana, ti, or aspidistra. Arrange the fish, grouped by kind, on leaves. If made ahead, cover tightly with plastic wrap; chill up to 24 hours. Uncover, and scatter a few **ice cubes** over fish to keep cool until you cook.

**Curry fritter batter.** In a bowl, stir together until blended 1½ cups **canned coconut milk** (or 1 cup thawed frozen coconut milk and ½ cup water), 1 cup **all-purpose flour**, 2 **large eggs**, ¼ cup *each* **curry powder** and **soy sauce**, 3 tablespoons **water**, 2 tablespoons **hot red chili paste** or 1½ teaspoons cayenne, and 1½ teaspoons **ground cumin**. (If made ahead, cover and chill up to 24 hours.) Up to 15 minutes before using, stir 1 teaspoon **baking powder** into batter.

**Peanut dressing.** In a bowl, smoothly whisk together 1 cup **canned coconut milk** (or ⅔ cup thawed frozen coconut milk and ⅓ cup water), ½ cup **chunk-style peanut butter**, ¼ cup finely chopped **onion**, 3 tablespoons **shiro miso** (white miso) or 2 tablespoons soy sauce, ¼ cup **rice wine vinegar**, and 1½ tablespoons firmly packed **brown sugar**. (If made ahead, cover and chill up to 24 hours.)

## CHILI CUCUMBERS

  1  **cup water**
  ½  **cup rice wine vinegar**
  ½  **cup thinly sliced shallots**
  ⅓  **cup sugar**
  1  **teaspoon salt**
  2  **fresh jalapeño chilies, seeded, stemmed, and finely chopped**
  1  **European-style or 3 Japanese cucumbers (about 1 lb. total), ends trimmed, thinly sliced**

In a bowl, stir together water, vinegar, shallots, sugar, salt, and chilies; add cucumbers. Cover and chill until cold or up to 24 hours. Drain and serve. Makes 8 servings.

*Chef dishes up fish fritters coated in curry batter, then drains them briefly on a napkin-lined tray. Guest builds salad of hot fritters, peppers, spinach, and fried rice sticks; peanut dressing in pitcher goes over salad.*

## FRESH MANGO FANS

Rinse 4 large ripe **mangoes**. With a sharp knife, cut parallel to pit on each side to slice fruit free. Score meat side of each slice, cutting to—but not through—peel in a ½-inch grid. Push from peel side to pop fruit upward and fan out. (If made ahead, cover fruit and chill up to overnight.) Cut 2 **limes** into 4 wedges each. Arrange mangoes and lime wedges on a platter. Squeeze lime juice onto mangoes and bite from skin, or eat with knife and fork. Makes 8 servings.

# Vegetable-Patch Bread

LIKE AN OVERGROWN *vegetable plot, this herb-flavored bread brandishes a rampant assortment of fresh produce. Your garden or market is its starting point.*

*You precook the vegetables to soften their crunch and bring out flavor, then mix them into a dough. Use the full amount of salt to bring out the most flavor.*

*As it rises, the dough absorbs moisture from the cooked vegetables; unlike the procedure for a conventional dough, you add a fair amount of all-purpose flour after the first rise.*

*The hearty loaf, partly whole-wheat, tastes great alone or with a favorite soup.*

### CRAZY VEGETABLE-PATCH BREAD

1 package active dry yeast
¾ cup warm water
1 large egg
½ to 1 teaspoon salt
1 tablespoon sugar
1 tablespoon *each* minced fresh thyme and tarragon, or 1 teaspoon *each* dry thyme leaves and dry tarragon
¼ cup minced fresh basil leaves or 1½ tablespoons dry basil
1 tablespoon olive oil or salad oil
¼ cup grated parmesan cheese
1 cup whole-wheat flour
 About 3 cups all-purpose flour
 Crazy garden vegetables (directions follow)

In a large bowl, soften yeast in water about 5 minutes. Mix in egg, salt, sugar, thyme, tarragon, basil, oil, cheese, and whole-wheat flour. Add 1⅔ cups of the all-purpose flour. With a dough hook, electric mixer, or heavy spoon, mix well.

*If using a dough hook,* beat at high speed until dough is stretchy and pulls cleanly from bowl, 5 to 8 minutes; if dough feels sticky and still clings to bowl, add more all-purpose flour, 1 tablespoon at a time.

*If mixing by hand,* scrape dough onto a floured board. Knead, adding flour as required to prevent sticking, until dough is smooth and elastic, 8 to 12 minutes.

Gently mix vegetables with ½ cup all-purpose flour. On a floured board, gradually and gently knead vegetables into dough (do not mash them) until evenly distributed (dough will feel sticky); add a little flour if dough sticks to board. Place in an oiled bowl; turn over to grease top. Cover bowl with plastic wrap and let rise in a warm place until doubled, about 1½ hours.

On a well-floured board, sprinkle flour over dough. Gently knead to release air, gradually adding enough all-purpose flour (½ to ⅔ cup total) until dough is soft but not sticky. Shape into a round loaf 6 to 7 inches in diameter and place on a greased 12- by 15-inch baking sheet. Cover lightly with plastic wrap; let rise in a warm place until puffy, about 30 minutes.

Bake, uncovered, in a 350° oven until well browned, 40 to 45 minutes. Transfer to a rack. Serve warm or cool. To store, chill airtight up to 3 days or freeze for longer storage. Makes 1 loaf, about 1¾ pounds.

**Crazy garden vegetables.** Halve lengthwise 1 medium-size **onion;** slice crosswise ¾ inch thick. In a 10- to 12-inch frying pan, mix onion; 2 cloves **garlic,** minced or pressed; ½ cup 1-inch chunks **eggplant;** and 2 tablespoons **olive oil** or salad oil. Cook over medium heat, stirring often, until eggplant is barely tender when pressed, about 10 minutes. Add ⅓ cup 1-inch chunks **Roma-style tomatoes;** stir until tomatoes are slightly softened, 1 to 2 minutes. Let cool.

Slice lengthwise into ½- to ¾-inch strips *each* medium-size **red and green bell peppers,** stemmed and seeded (or use ½ of 1 kind). Diagonally slice into ½- to ¾-inch widths 1 small **carrot,** 1 small stalk **celery,** and 1 small **zucchini.** You'll also need ¾ cup **broccoli flowerets** and 2 large **green onions** in 4-inch lengths.

In a 1- to 2-quart pan, bring 3 cups **water** to a boil over high heat. Add 1 kind of vegetable at a time; boil carrots and broccoli 1 minute, zucchini and bell peppers 45 seconds, and celery and green onions 30 seconds. As vegetables are cooked, lift from pan with a slotted spoon and put in **ice water.** When cold, drain, pat dry, and combine with tomato mixture in pan.

*Gradually knead vegetables (coated with flour to help absorb moisture) into dough. Then let dough rise until volume doubles.*

*Add flour; gently knead into risen dough until no longer sticky. (During first rising, dough absorbs moisture from vegetables.)*

*Let round loaf rise again until puffy, then bake until deep golden. Serve bread warm, or make it ahead and freeze.*

Earthy, homespun loaf is flavored with fresh vegetables (eggplant, celery, carrot, bell peppers, onions, broccoli, tomato), fresh herbs, garlic, and parmesan cheese.

# Moroccan Feast

FLAVORS WEAVE *from one dish to the next in this petite Moroccan feast, creating a pleasantly exotic impression. Salty olives, sharp feta cheese, and purchased stuffed grape leaves (dolmas) make a simple first course of contrasting tastes.*

*Succulent lamb is simmered with spices, then baked with a honey glaze. Complementing it are mellow couscous studded with raisins and carrots and a cucumber-tomato salad refreshed by cool mint.*

*Tender shortbread cookies laden with toasted sesame seed are sweet morsels to nibble along with grapes. End, if you like, with a cup of intense Turkish- or Greek-style coffee or Italian espresso.*

### MOROCCAN FEAST

**Feta Cheese     Dolmas     Olives
Honey-glazed Lamb Shoulder
Ground Cumin     Salt     Pepper
Carrot & Raisin Couscous
Cucumber Tomato  & Mint Salad
Baguettes or Crusty Rolls
Sesame Seed Shortbread     Grapes**

*To get a head start, begin the day before: simmer the lamb to tenderness, make the glaze for basting the meat, start the vegetables for the couscous, and bake the cookies. Shop at a deli or supermarket deli section for salty olives (calamata or salt-cured) and the feta cheese. Dolmas are sometimes sold in the deli case; if not, they're available canned.*

*Moderately priced lamb shoulder (you may have to order it ahead) is an unwieldy cut that's almost impossible to carve; when it's cooked as follows, you simply pull or tear the meat from the bones. The couscous is the only dish that requires last-minute attention.*

*Serve ground cumin, salt, and pepper at the table as extra seasoning for the meat, couscous, and salad.*

## HONEY-GLAZED LAMB SHOULDER

1   **bone-in lamb shoulder (about 6 lb.), fat trimmed**
1   **quart regular-strength chicken broth**
2   **medium-size onions, chopped**
1   **tablespoon ground coriander**
3   **cinnamon sticks, each 2½ to 3 inches**
1½  **teaspoons pepper**
1   **teaspoon ground ginger**
½   **cup honey**
    **Mint sprigs (optional)**

In a 7- to 8-quart pan, add lamb shoulder (bones down), broth, onions, coriander, cinnamon, pepper, and ginger. Bring liquid to a boil over high heat. Reduce heat, cover, and simmer until meat is very tender when pierced, about 4 hours; meat should pull easily from bone.

Carefully support shoulder with 2 large slotted spoons and lift from broth; place, bones down, in a 9- by 13-inch baking pan. If made ahead, let cool, then cover and chill until next day. Let meat return to room temperature (takes about 1½ hours) before continuing.

Skim and discard fat from broth; also discard cinnamon. Pour broth through a colander into a bowl; set aside onions. Measure 2½ cups broth; save remainder for other uses—freeze, if desired. If made ahead, cover and chill onions and broth until next day. (The onions and 2 cups of the broth are used to make the couscous, following.)

In a 2- to 3-quart pan, mix ½ cup broth with honey. Boil, uncovered, until glaze is reduced to about ½ cup. Brush about ⅓ of the glaze over the top side of the lamb.

Put lamb in a 400° oven and bake, uncovered, until well browned and sizzling, about 30 minutes. Using about ½ of the remaining glaze, brush meat again; 10 minutes later, brush once more with the rest of the glaze. Transfer lamb to a large platter. Garnish with mint. Pull or tear chunks of meat from bones to eat. Makes 5 or 6 servings.

## CARROT & RAISIN COUSCOUS

In a 10- to 12-inch frying pan, combine **cooked onion** and the reserved 2 cups **broth** (both set aside from preceding recipe). Add 2 medium-size peeled **carrots**, thinly sliced, and ½ cup firmly packed **raisins**. Bring to a boil on high heat. Then simmer, covered, until carrots are tender to bite, about 10 minutes. (If made ahead, let stand up to 4 hours, or cover and chill overnight.) Bring back to boil to continue.

Add 2 cups **couscous** to hot liquid, stirring well; cover and remove at once from heat. Let couscous stand until liquid is absorbed, about 5 minutes. Stir with a fork to fluff; serve. Makes 5 or 6 servings.

## CUCUMBER, TOMATO & MINT SALAD

1   **large (about 1 lb.) European-style cucumber**
4   **small firm-ripe tomatoes (about 1 lb. total), cored**
4   **green onions (roots trimmed), thinly sliced, including tops**
⅓   **cup minced fresh mint leaves, or 5 teaspoons dry mint**
    **Lime vinaigrette (recipe follows)**

Cut cucumber into ¼-inch-thick slices. Cut tomatoes into ½-inch wedges; put both vegetables into a large bowl. Add green onions and mint. Pour vinaigrette over vegetables and stir gently. Cover and let stand at room temperature or in the refrigerator up to 1 hour to blend flavors. If made ahead, chill up to 4 hours. Makes 5 or 6 servings.

**Lime vinaigrette.** Mix together ¼ cup *each* **lime juice** and **olive** or salad **oil**, and 2 tablespoons **white wine vinegar**. Makes about ⅔ cup.

## SESAME SEED SHORTBREAD

½   **cup sesame seed**
½   **cup (¼ lb.) butter or margarine, at room temperature**
    **About ½ cup sugar**
1   **cup all-purpose flour**

In 10- to 12-inch frying pan over medium heat, stir sesame seed often until golden, about 10 minutes. Remove from heat and stir frequently until pan cools slightly.

In large bowl of an electric mixer, beat butter and ½ cup sugar until creamy. Add toasted sesame seed and flour; mix slowly until flour is well incorporated.

(To use a food processor, whirl butter, sugar, and flour just until butter is cut into tiny bits, then add seed and whirl until dough forms a ball.)

Pat dough firmly in an even layer into an 8- or 9-inch round cake pan with removable bottom.

With the tines of a fork, make impressions around edge of dough. Sprinkle dough with 1 to 2 tablespoons sugar.

Bake in a 350° oven until cooky is pale golden brown, 25 to 30 minutes. Remove from oven. Cut into 6 wedges; let cool in pan. Remove rim, and slide a thin spatula under cookies to release them from pan; serve. If made ahead, cover and store airtight up to 5 days. Freeze to store longer. Makes 6 servings.

# Burnet: How to Grow & Use

**A** PRETTY HERB, *fresh burnet (Poterium sanguisorba) gives a lacy look and a light cucumber flavor to foods it accompanies.*

*Though burnet is a fairly well-known herb, it's rarely seen in markets. But because it's easy to grow and prolific when established, you can use garden-grown leaves and stems liberally—as in the following recipes for cucumber salad and dainty tea sandwiches.*

*Native to Europe and western Asia, burnet is very much a part of the cuisine of France, where it's used as a seasoning for dressings, salads, soups, and sauces that benefit from its elusive cucumber taste.*

## BUYING SEEDS & GROWING BURNET

*Plant burnet seeds in the fall in an area that gets full sun. Or start with nursery seedlings in mild weather. With adequate moisture and good drainage, burnet thrives even in poor soil; it's a hardy perennial that self-sows freely.*

*Start cutting the herb when you get a big flush of leaves, as weather starts to warm—usually in spring or early summer. The plant grows to a height of 12 to 18 inches, bearing clusters of minute blossoms on the ends of stems. To keep plants vigorous and limit self-seeding, cut flowers (they are good to eat, too) as they appear.*

*Look for burnet in specialty nurseries. Or order by mail. J.L. Hudson, Seedsman (Box 1058, Redwood City, Calif. 94064), has seeds for $1 per packet plus 40 cents shipping (catalog $1). Taylor's Herb Gardens, Inc. (1535 Lone Oak Rd., Vista, Calif. 92083) sells plants and seeds; minimum order of six herbs, which you choose from a large selection, costs $18 postpaid, while seeds are 90 cents a packet postpaid (catalog $1).*

*If you want to try these recipes before your burnet is ready to harvest, you can substitute Italian parsley.*

## VINEGARED CUCUMBERS WITH BURNET

- 2 **medium-size cucumbers (or 1½ European-style cucumbers)**
- 1 **teaspoon salt**
- ¼ **cup white wine vinegar**
- 2 **tablespoons firmly packed minced burnet leaves or Italian parsley**
- 2 **teaspoons sugar**
- ½ **teaspoon dry dill weed**
- ⅛ **teaspoon pepper**
  **Burnet or Italian parsley sprigs**

Peel cucumbers and thinly slice. In a bowl, mix cucumber slices with salt. Cover and chill 30 minutes or up to 24 hours.

Drain accumulated liquid from cucumbers. Stir in vinegar, burnet, sugar, dill weed, and pepper. Mound cucumbers on a serving plate; garnish with burnet sprigs. Makes 4 to 6 servings.

## BURNET & BUTTER TEA SANDWICHES

- 2 **tablespoons firmly packed burnet leaves or Italian parsley**
- ⅓ **cup butter or margarine, at room temperature**
- 8 **slices firm-textured white bread**
- 24 **sprigs burnet or Italian parsley**

In a food processor or blender, whirl burnet leaves until minced. Add butter and whirl again until it turns pale green.

Trim crusts from bread; slice each piece of bread into 3 long fingers. Spread each finger with butter, using all. Place 1 sprig burnet lengthwise on each piece of buttered bread, cutting to fit the length. Makes 24 tea sandwiches.

## BURNET & SALMON TEA SANDWICHES

- ⅔ **cup sour cream**
- 1 **tablespoon prepared horseradish**
- 3 **tablespoons firmly packed burnet or Italian parsley leaves**
- 8 **slices firm-textured white bread**
  **About ¾ pound cooked salmon, fresh or canned**
- 32 **sprigs burnet or Italian parsley**

*Deeply toothed leaves have cucumber flavor and scent. Plants grow in a rosette shape.*

In a food processor or blender, whirl sour cream with horseradish and burnet leaves until leaves are minced and sour cream turns pale green; chill to firm, 2 hours or up to overnight.

Trim crusts from bread; slice each piece of bread into 4 triangles. Spread each piece of bread with sour cream mixture, using all. With your fingers, gently pull salmon apart into 32 equal-size pieces; remove and discard skin and bones. Place 1 piece salmon on each triangle; top each with 1 sprig burnet. Makes 32 tea sandwiches.

*Minced burnet echoes cool flavor of cucumber in vinegared salad; whole sprigs garnish.*

# Fresh Figs Meet New Friends

THE NATURAL SWEETNESS *of fresh figs works to advantage in these savory pairings. For an appetizer or first course, consider fanciful fig tulips with sherried cream cheese centers. Belgian endive and prosciutto make a sharp-salty contrast to figs and carrots in a salad. And hot figs give simple roast chicken a new character.*

*Use black or white (yellow-green color) figs, depending on what's available in your area.*

## CHEESE-FILLED FIG TULIPS

*Pick up to eat, or use a knife and fork.*

Place 12 **whole blanched almonds** in an 8- or 9-inch baking dish. Bake in a 350° oven until golden, about 10 minutes. Let cool; set aside.

Trim stem ends from 12 small ripe **figs,** then trim other ends flat. Make 3 cuts through stem end ⅔ of the way to bottom of fruit to form 6 "petals"; open petals slightly. In a bowl, beat 1 small package (3 oz.) **cream cheese** with 2 teaspoons **dry sherry** until smooth. Spoon evenly into figs. Top each tulip with a whole almond. If made ahead, cover and chill up to 1 day. Makes 6 or 12 appetizer servings.

*Fig tulips, filled with cream cheese and topped with almonds, make a light, simple appetizer to serve with dry sherry.*

## GINGERED FIG SALAD

*This recipe was inspired by the Pokolbin Cellar restaurant in Cessnock, Australia.*

- 1 medium-size head (5 oz.) Belgian endive, leaves separated, rinsed, and crisped
- 1 cup shredded carrots (shred lengthwise)
- 10 small or 5 large ripe figs (stems trimmed), sliced crosswise
- ⅛ pound (4 to 6 very thin slices) prosciutto or cooked ham
  Ginger dressing
  (recipe follows)
  Pepper

On a platter, arrange endive, carrots, figs, and prosciutto. Spoon dressing onto salad; add pepper to taste. Serves 4.

**Ginger dressing.** In a bowl, mix 3 tablespoons *each* **olive oil** and **white wine vinegar,** 2 teaspoons **Dijon mustard,** and 1½ tablespoons minced **crystallized ginger.**

## ROAST CHICKEN & FIGS

- 1 broiler-fryer chicken, 3 to 3½ pounds, quartered
- 1 teaspoon grated orange peel
- ½ cup *each* orange juice and regular-strength chicken broth
- 1 tablespoon honey
- 12 large or 24 small ripe figs, stems trimmed

Place chicken, skin up, in a 12- by 15-inch pan. Bake in a 375° oven for 40 minutes. Spoon off fat and discard.

In a bowl, mix orange peel, juice, broth, and honey. Add figs; mix gently to coat.

Spoon figs into pan alongside chicken. Spoon juice mixture over meat. Continue to bake until figs are hot and chicken is no longer pink at thigh bone (cut to test), about 10 more minutes.

Spoon sauce out of roasting pan into a 1- to 2-quart pan. Turn off oven; keep chicken and figs warm. Bring sauce to a boil over high heat. Boil until reduced to ½ cup, 3 to 5 minutes.

Place equal portions of chicken and figs on plates. Add sauce to taste. Serves 4.

# Spanish Salads

ROBUST FLAVORS *characterize these fish and vegetable salads from Catalonia, a region in northeastern Spain. Dressings are equally pungent: vinaigrettes feature balsamic, sherry, or wine vinegars; the purée combines anchovies and avocados; and the classic romesco sauce has almonds, red bell peppers, and garlic.*

*Like anchovies, the tuna and cod used in the two main-dish salads have bold flavors. Flanked by the lighter salads, they create a substantial buffet when accompanied with bread and butter and a crisp, dry white wine—perhaps a Spanish Parellada or a domestic Sauvignon Blanc.*

*Also consider the lighter salads as companions to other menus.*

## CATALAN TUNA SALAD

    2   heads (about 6 oz. each) butter
        lettuce, leaves rinsed and crisped
    2   cans (6 oz. each) albacore tuna,
        drained
    1   cup shredded carrots
    1   cup cucumber, cut into 2-inch-
        long, ¼-inch-wide slivers
    1   can (2 oz.) anchovy fillets, drained
        and minced
    ¾   cup niçoise olives
    4   large firm-ripe Roma-style
        tomatoes, cored and thinly sliced
        crosswise
    4   large hard-cooked eggs, peeled
        and halved
        Romesco sauce (recipe follows)
        Pepper

Line a platter with lettuce. In a bowl, break tuna into chunks, then gently mix with carrots, cucumber, anchovies, and olives; mound on lettuce. Arrange tomatoes and eggs alongside. Offer romesco sauce in a bowl and pepper to add to taste. Makes 4 to 6 main-dish servings. —*Marimar Torres, Sausalito, Calif.*

**Romesco sauce.** Place ½ cup **almonds** in an 8- or 9-inch-wide pan. Bake in a 350° oven until nuts are golden in center (break to test), about 15 minutes. Let cool, then finely grind in a food processor or blender. To container, add 1 medium-size **red bell pepper**, cored, seeded, and coarsely chopped; ¼ teaspoon **crushed dried hot red chilies**; ½ teaspoon **paprika**; 1 small clove **garlic**, coarsely chopped; 1 tablespoon **parsley leaves**; and ¼ cup **red wine vinegar**; whirl until smooth. With motor running, add ¼ cup **olive oil** in a thin stream.

## AVOCADO & TOMATO SALAD

    2   medium-size firm-ripe avocados
    2   medium-size firm-ripe tomatoes,
        cored, each cut into 6 equal wedges
   12   large fresh basil leaves
    1   can (2 oz.) anchovy fillets, drained
    3   tablespoons balsamic or red wine
        vinegar
    1   tablespoon olive oil
    ½   teaspoon pepper

Quarter each avocado; pit and peel. Set aside 2 pieces. On a platter, arrange remaining avocado, tomatoes, and basil.

In a blender or food processor, whirl the reserved avocado with anchovies, vinegar, oil, and pepper until smoothly puréed. Offer sauce in a small bowl to add to salad. Makes 4 to 6 salad servings.

## CATALAN SHREDDED CODFISH SALAD

    1   pound boned, semidry salt cod
        Water
    1   medium-size green bell pepper,
        cored, seeded, and thinly sliced
    4   green onions, thinly sliced
    ¼   cup minced parsley
    1   large firm-ripe tomato, cored and
        cut into thin wedges
    1   cup niçoise olives
        Dressing (recipe follows)

Place cod in a large bowl, cover with water, and chill at least 24 or up to 48 hours; change water several times. Drain and squeeze cod firmly to extract water. Discard any skin or bones. Tear cod into shreds. Mix with pepper, onions, parsley, tomato, olives, and dressing. Serve from a bowl, or drained, on a platter. Makes 4 main-dish servings.

**Dressing.** Mix ½ cup **olive oil**; ½ cup **red wine vinegar**; 3 cloves **garlic**, minced or pressed; and ½ teaspoon **pepper**.

## RED CABBAGE SALAD WITH ANCHOVIES

    ½   cup slivered almonds
    1   small head (1½ lb.) red cabbage,
        cored and shredded
    2   cups water
    ½   cup sherry vinegar or red wine
        vinegar
    ½   cup shredded carrots
    1   can (2 oz.) anchovy fillets, drained
    ½   cup olive oil
        Salt and pepper

*Spanish salad buffet includes (top to bottom) tuna with romesco sauce; tomato, avocado, and basil with anchovy dressing; salt cod salad; and marinated cabbage with nuts.*

In a 7- to 8-inch frying pan over medium heat, shake almonds often until golden, 3 to 4 minutes. Set aside to cool.

In a 4- to 5-quart pan, bring cabbage, water, and vinegar to a boil over high heat. Cover and simmer until cabbage is tender-crisp to bite, about 12 minutes. Let cool, uncovered. Cover and chill at least 3 hours or up to 2 days. Stir occasionally. Drain well; place in a bowl with carrots.

In a blender or food processor, whirl anchovies and oil until smooth. Pour over cabbage mixture and mix well. Top with almonds. Offer salt and pepper to season. Makes 4 to 6 salad servings.

# Puget Sound Gefillte Fish

ABUNDANT FRESH SALMON *from Puget Sound inspired Helen Gurvich to create this version of gefillte fish, a dish she serves in celebration of Rosh Hashana, the Jewish New Year. Traditionally, the dish is a mixture of ground whitefish, onions, eggs, and matzo meal, shaped into balls and poached in broth made from the fish trimmings. Made with the orange-red fish, gefillte fish has a pretty pale pink color.*

*We've streamlined the process to help busy cooks. Get a quick start with boned and skinned fish. If you chop the fish in a food processor, it takes only seconds, and you must be careful not to turn the mixture into a purée. Season fish, pat into balls, and poach in water or broth.*

*There are options for serving. You can offer the gefillte fish warm or cold on salad greens as a first course, or in the flavored broth as a soup. Either way, dill pickles and a sharp horseradish and dill sauce are classic companions.*

## SALMON GEFILLTE FISH

- ¾ **pound chilled boned and skinned salmon, cut into 1-inch chunks**
- ¾ **pound chilled boned and skinned white-flesh fish such as lingcod or rockfish, cut into 1-inch chunks**
- 1 **medium-size onion, coarsely chopped**
- 2 **large eggs**
  **About ⅓ cup matzo meal**
- 1½ **teaspoons pepper**
  **Salt**
  **Broth (recipe follows) or 2 quarts water**
- 1 **to 1½ quarts mixed salad greens, rinsed and crisped**
  **Dill pickle spears**
  **Horseradish sauce (recipe follows)**

Grind salmon and lingcod through the fine blade of a food chopper. (Or whirl ⅓ of fish at a time in a food processor until very finely chopped, about 20 seconds; do not purée.) Put fish in a large bowl, cover, and refrigerate.

Whirl onion in a food processor until smoothly puréed. (Or whirl onion and eggs in a blender until smoothly puréed.)

*Salmon's a surprise in this gefillte fish. Nestle the fish balls in salad greens with pickle spears; drizzle with horseradish-dill dressing.*

To fish add onion, eggs, ⅓ cup matzo meal, pepper, and ½ teaspoon salt; stir until blended. Mixture should be just firm enough to hold its shape when formed into a ball with your hands. If too soft, stir in 2 to 3 more tablespoons matzo meal.

With your hands, pat fish mixture, 2 tablespoons at a time, into smooth balls and set slightly apart. Rinse hands frequently in cool water to prevent sticking.

In a 5- to 6-quart pan over high heat, bring broth to a boil; adjust heat to simmer. Add enough gefillte fish balls to pan to make a single layer without crowding. Simmer, uncovered, until balls are opaque in center (cut to test), about 10 minutes.

Lift gefillte fish from pan with a slotted spoon; drain on paper towels in a warm place. Repeat to cook remaining balls.

Serve fish warm or chilled. If made ahead, cool, cover, and chill fish until cold, at least 3 hours or until next day.

Arrange salad greens on individual plates or a platter; lay fish on the greens and accompany with pickles, horseradish sauce, and salt to taste. Makes 4 to 6 servings, 4 or 6 balls each.—*Helen Gurvich, Seattle.*

**Broth.** In a 5- to 6-quart pan, combine 1 large **onion**, quartered; 2 large **carrots** and 2 stalks **celery**, *each* cut into 1-inch pieces; 1 tablespoon **black peppercorns**; 2 quarts **water**; and 3 **fish** or chicken **bouillon cubes**. Bring to a boil on high heat, cover, and simmer until vegetables are very soft, about 45 minutes. Pour broth through a colander into a bowl. Discard vegetables and return broth to pan.

**Horseradish sauce.** Combine ¾ cup **sour cream**, ¼ cup **prepared horseradish**, and 1 tablespoon chopped **fresh dill** or 1½ teaspoons dry dill weed.

## GEFILLTE FISH SOUP

Prepare **Salmon Gefillte Fish** (recipe precedes) and cook in the broth. Omit salad greens. When all the fish is cooked, pour the broth through a colander lined with several layers of cheesecloth into a bowl. Rinse pan, then return broth to it. Bring to boiling over high heat, then add cooked gefillte fish. Cover, remove from heat, and let stand until balls are heated through (cut to test), about 5 minutes.

Ladle soup into 4 to 6 bowls; garnish with **fresh dill sprigs** (optional). Add **horseradish sauce** and **salt** to taste. Accompany with **pickles.** Serves 4 to 6.

# More September Recipes

OTHER SEPTEMBER RECIPES *included a light vegetable bouillon and a dessert featuring fresh berries and peaches topped by foamy zabaglione.*

## FRENCH VEGETABLE BOUILLON

*Long, slow simmering gives this lean vegetable-based bouillon its rich, satisfying flavor. The last-minute addition of colorful vegetables cut into slivers creates a stunning appearance as well.*

*This elegant first-course soup was inspired from one created by Chef Marc Meneau at L'Espérance in Saint-Père-sous-Vézelay, France.*

- 2 **medium-size leeks (about 1 lb.)**
- 4 **large carrots, peeled**
- 2 **medium-size zucchini (about 1 lb.)**
- ¾ **pound green beans, ends trimmed**
- 1 **large tomato**
- 2½ **quarts regular-strength chicken broth or water**
- 3 **large stalks celery, cut into thirds**
- 1 **cup celery leaves**
- 1 **large onion, quartered**
- ¾ **cup parsley sprigs**
- 1 **bay leaf**
- ½ **teaspoon *each* dry thyme leaves and black peppercorns**
- ⅓ **cup fresh shelled peas (¼ lb. in pod)**

Trim and discard roots and tough tops from leeks. Thinly slice enough of the white part of leek to make ¼ cup; gently rinse. Set aside. Slice remaining leeks lengthwise and rinse thoroughly.

*Finely cut vegetables in clear bouillon make a dramatic presentation, add crisp texture.*

Slice carrots and zucchini into 2-inch chunks; cut 1 chunk of each into matchstick-size pieces and set aside. Cut 10 of the green beans in half and then lengthwise into thin slivers; set aside. Cut 2 thin outer slices with peel from tomato; cut each in half and then into triangles and set aside. If not serving bouillon same day, cover and chill reserved cut vegetables for up to 3 days.

In a 6- to 8-quart pan over high heat, combine broth with remaining leeks, carrots, zucchini, beans, tomato, celery and leaves, onion, parsley, bay leaf, thyme, and peppercorns; bring to a boil. Reduce heat, cover, and simmer gently for 4 hours; stir occasionally.

Line a colander with 2 or 3 thicknesses of damp cheesecloth (you need pieces large enough to hang over sides); place colander over a wide 4- to 5-quart pan.

Pour bouillon through cheesecloth and, using the back of a large spoon, push vegetables against sides of colander, extracting as much liquid as possible. As bouillon cools, draw together corners of cheesecloth and twist tightly to squeeze out even more liquid; discard vegetables and remove colander from pan. At this point, you can cover and chill soup for up to 3 days.

If desired, clarify bouillon (directions follow). If not, return bouillon to boiling. Reduce heat to low and add reserved leek, carrot, zucchini, beans, tomato, and peas. Cover and simmer gently until vegetables are barely tender when pierced, about 3 minutes. Ladle into bowls. Makes 4 to 6 servings.

**To clarify bouillon.** Beat 4 **large egg whites** until foamy. Bring bouillon to a boil, then whip egg whites into boiling liquid. Return to a full boil; remove from heat and let stand until slightly cooled.

Meanwhile, line a colander with 2 or 3 thicknesses of damp cheesecloth (you need pieces large enough to hang over sides); place colander over a wide 4- to 5-quart pan. Pour bouillon slowly through cheesecloth. Draw together corners of cloth and twist gently to extract as much liquid as possible; discard whites. For exceptionally clear bouillon, repeat steps once more.

## WARM FRUIT GRATIN

*Cloak late summer berries and peaches with a warm, foamy mantle of whole egg zabaglione, then broil briefly to make a*

*Broil zabaglione until the top turns dark gold. Watch carefully; it happens fast.*

*splendid, delicately crusted hot dessert.*

*For a lighter, frothier zabaglione, use an electric mixer; for a creamier, denser, but less voluminous topping, use a wire whip.*

- **About 5 cups fruit—a combination of hulled strawberries, blueberries, raspberries, and sliced peaches, or all of 1 fruit**
- **Zabaglione (recipe follows)**
- 2 **tablespoons powdered sugar**
- 2 **tablespoons sliced almonds**

Rinse strawberries, blueberries, and raspberries; drain. Divide berries and peaches equally among 4 to 6 shallow ovenproof soup bowls, each 4½ to 5½ inches wide inside the rim.

Position broiler rack so bowl tops will be about 4 inches below heat source. Set bowls aside and turn on broiler. Make zabaglione and pour it, hot, equally over fruit. Dust sugar on zabaglione, then sprinkle evenly with almonds.

Broil on positioned rack until the zabaglione turns a rich, golden brown, about 1 minute; watch carefully to avoid scorching. Repeat if all the bowls don't fit on rack at one time. Serve immediately. Makes 4 to 6 servings.

**Zabaglione.** In a round-bottom zabaglione pan or double boiler top, beat to blend 3 **large eggs,** 6 tablespoons **sugar,** and 2 tablespoons **fruity white wine** such as Johannisberg Riesling or Gewürztraminer. Place round-bottom pan over medium gas heat or high electric heat; set double boiler in simmering water. Beat rapidly with a whisk or electric mixer until foam is just thick enough to briefly hold a slight peak when beater is lifted, 3 to 5 minutes; volume triples or quadruples. Use hot.

*Tart apples, walnuts, raisins, sugar, and cinnamon flavor this quick bread.*

### ROCKY MOUNTAIN APPLE BREAD

- 4 large eggs
- 2 cups sugar
- ½ cup *each* buttermilk and mayonnaise
- 1 teaspoon vanilla
- 3½ cups all-purpose flour
- ¼ teaspoon salt
- 1 teaspoon baking powder
- ½ teaspoon baking soda
- 1 teaspoon ground cinnamon
- 2 medium-size tart green apples, such as Newtown Pippin
- 1 cup raisins
- 1 cup chopped walnuts

In a large bowl, beat eggs, sugar, buttermilk, mayonnaise, and vanilla until smooth. In another bowl, mix flour, salt, baking powder, baking soda, and cinnamon. Add to egg mixture and stir just until combined.

Core apples and chop. Add to batter with raisins and nuts; stir just to mix. Spread batter evenly in 2 greased and floured 5- by 9-inch loaf pans.

Bake in a 375° oven until a slender wooden pick inserted in center comes out clean, about 1 hour and 10 minutes. Let bread cool in pans on a rack for 10 minutes, then turn out onto rack to cool completely. Makes 2 loaves, 1¾ pounds each. —*Eleanor Hart, Aurora, Colo.*

*Grate fresh asiago or parmesan cheese to accompany pasta sauce and macaroni.*

### VEGETABLE PASTA SAUCE

- 1 large onion, chopped
- 1 clove garlic, minced or pressed
- 2 teaspoons *each* dry basil, dry tarragon, fennel seed, and dry oregano leaves
- 2 tablespoons olive oil or salad oil
- 1 cup ½-inch pieces zucchini
- ½ pound mushrooms, sliced
- 1 medium-size green pepper, stemmed, seeded, chopped
- 1 cup dry red wine
- 2 pounds (about 5 medium-size) ripe tomatoes, peeled, cored, and chopped
- 1 large can (12 oz.) tomato paste
- 1 tablespoon sugar

In a 4- to 5-quart pan over medium heat, cook onion, garlic, basil, tarragon, fennel, and oregano in oil, stirring often, until onion is limp, 10 to 15 minutes. Add zucchini, mushrooms, and green pepper. Cook until mushrooms are limp, stirring often, 10 to 15 minutes.

Add wine, tomatoes, tomato paste, and sugar to pan. Bring to a boil over high heat, then reduce heat to low, cover, and simmer until sauce is thick, stirring occasionally, about 45 minutes. Use hot; if made ahead, cool, cover, and chill up to 3 days. Makes about 7 cups, 10 servings. —*Darcy Henderson, Beaverton, Ore.*

*Zucchini and cheese matchsticks top pesto-zucchini soup; offer with ham.*

### PESTO-ZUCCHINI SOUP

- 3 pounds (about 10 medium-size) zucchini, ends trimmed
- 2 medium-size onions, chopped
- 3 tablespoons olive oil or salad oil
- 6 cups regular-strength chicken broth
- ¾ cup (7 oz.) homemade or purchased pesto
- ⅓ cup matchstick-size pieces or grated parmesan cheese
  Basil sprigs (optional)

Cut 1 zucchini into matchstick-size pieces; set aside. Slice remaining zucchini into rounds. In a 5- to 6-quart pan over medium-high heat, cook onions in oil until limp, stirring often, about 10 minutes. Add zucchini slices and 1 cup of broth. Bring to a boil, cover, and simmer until zucchini is very tender when pierced, about 15 minutes.

In a blender or food processor, whirl zucchini mixture, a portion at a time if needed, until smooth. Return purée to pan with remaining broth. Bring to a simmer over high heat, stirring. Remove from heat and stir in pesto. If made ahead, chill ungarnished soup up to two days; reheat to simmering to serve.

Ladle soup into bowls and top with julienned zucchini, parmesan, and basil. Makes 11 cups, 6 or 7 servings. —*Libia Foglesong, San Bruno, Calif.*

## MEXICAN-STYLE SQUID SALAD

*Some markets carry squid mantles (tubes) cleaned and ready to use. If they're not available, use shrimp.*

    **Water**
- 2 **pounds cleaned squid mantles (tubes), cut into 1-inch rings, or 2 pounds large shrimp (31 to 35 per lb.), shelled and deveined**
  **Chili dressing (recipe follows)**
- 1 **small red bell pepper, stemmed, seeded, and thinly sliced**
- ¾ **cup cooked corn kernels**
- 1 **small can (8¾ oz.) kidney beans, drained**
  **Romaine lettuce leaves**
  **Salt and pepper**

In a 4- to 5-quart pan, bring 1½ inches water to a boil over high heat. Add squid; cook until opaque, about 30 seconds (or cook shrimp until pink, 2 minutes). Drain; rinse with cold water.

In a bowl, mix squid, chili dressing, bell pepper, corn, and beans. Arrange lettuce on 4 to 6 dinner plates; spoon squid mixture onto lettuce. Add salt and pepper to taste. Serves 4 to 6. — *Roxanne Chan, Albany, Calif.*

**Chili dressing.** Mix ½ cup **salad oil**, ⅓ cup **lemon juice**, 1½ teaspoons *each* **dry oregano leaves** and **ground cumin**, and 1 or 2 **jalapeño** or serrano **chilies**, stemmed, seeded, and minced.

*Serve chili-spiked whole-meal squid salad with wheat rolls to round out menu.*

## SAVORY FRUIT SALAD

    **Water**
- ½ **pound edible-pod peas, ends and strings removed**
  **Ginger dressing (recipe follows)**
- 2 **medium-size Golden Delicious apples, cored and thinly sliced**
- 1 **honeydew melon, 3 to 3½ pounds, seeded, flesh cut into 1-inch balls or chunks**
- ½ **medium-size green bell pepper, stemmed, seeded, and thinly sliced**
- 2 **green onions, thinly sliced**
  **Butter lettuce leaves, rinsed and crisped**

In a 2- to 3-quart pan, bring 2 inches water to a boil over high heat. Add peas and cook until tender-crisp to bite, about 1 minute. Drain and rinse with cold water to cool quickly; drain.

To dressing in bowl add peas, apples, honeydew, bell pepper, and onions; mix gently to coat. Line a large platter or 6 salad plates with lettuce leaves and spoon melon mixture on top. Makes 6 servings. — *Helen Kennedy, Albuquerque.*

**Ginger dressing.** In a large bowl, mix ¼ cup *each* **white wine vinegar** and **salad oil** and 1 tablespoon *each* **honey, soy sauce,** and minced **fresh ginger.**

*Cut melon balls; mix with peas, onions, apples, bell pepper, and ginger dressing.*

## YAKIMA VALLEY PEACH KUCHEN

- ¼ **cup (⅛ lb.) butter or margarine**
- ¼ **teaspoon baking powder**
- 1 **cup all-purpose flour**
- ½ **cup firmly packed brown sugar**
- 2 **large eggs**
- 3 **medium-size peaches, peeled, pitted, and sliced**
- 1 **tablespoon lemon juice**
- ½ **teaspoon ground cinnamon**
- ½ **cup sour cream**

In a bowl, rub butter, baking powder, flour, and 1 tablespoon sugar until fine crumbs form. Lightly beat 1 egg, then add 1½ tablespoons of it to flour mixture and stir with a fork until evenly distributed. (Set aside remaining egg.) Press dough evenly over bottom of a 10-inch-diameter quiche or pie pan.

Mix peaches with lemon juice; arrange evenly over dough. Mix cinnamon and all but 1 tablespoon sugar; sprinkle over peaches. Bake on bottom rack of a 375° oven for 15 minutes.

In a bowl, beat sour cream and remaining sugar and eggs to blend. Pour over peaches and continue baking until custard jiggles very slightly in center when gently shaken, 20 to 25 minutes.

Serve warm or cool; to store, cover and chill up to 2 days. Serves 6. — *Liska Anne Crowley, Klickitat, Wash.*

*Warm peach kuchen flavored with brown sugar and spice is a wholesome dessert.*

**T**HERE IS HAUTE CUISINE *and there is hot cuisine; Reverends' Red Chili is a classic example of the latter. Prepared for a chili cook-off by the Cool L'eau Caliente Chili Compadres, it represents, according to A.D. Hawkins, years of cooking chili topped off by a week of intensive preparation and serving to dozens of chili aficionados. The chef rates it at three alarms (sweat on mustache, forehead, and the balding place on the back of your head) and suggests somewhat less seasoning for guests with tender palates.*

*The absence of beans is intentional; Mr. Hawkins believes (and half of the country's chiliheads agree) that beans are a desecration. If you must have them, cook them separately and give your guests the option. He also objurgates users of ground beef. If you can't get buffalo (actually bison) meat, use cubed lean beef chuck instead.*

*The name? It springs from the fact that two of the compadres are ministers. Considering that their ordination was accomplished by mail order rather than by the conventional laying on of hands, and taking into account the roguish name of their order, Irreverent Red Chili might be a more appropriate name.*

## REVERENDS' RED CHILI

 1 or 2 fresh or pickled jalapeño chilies
¼ cup olive oil or salad oil
 5 pounds boned buffalo stew meat or lean beef chuck, cut into ¾-inch cubes
 1 large onion, chopped
 4 cloves garlic, minced or pressed
 2 large firm-ripe tomatoes, cored, peeled, seeded, and chopped
 1 large can (15 oz.) tomato sauce
 1 can (12 oz.) beer
 2 teaspoons dry oregano leaves
 2 to 3 teaspoons coarsely ground black pepper
1½ tablespoons ground cumin
 1 tablespoon paprika
⅓ cup ground pasilla chili or ground New Mexico chili
   Water
   Salt

To prepare fresh jalapeños, hold each by the stem over a gas flame or almost touching an electric burner on high, turning until chili is charred on all sides. Let chilies stand until cool. Wearing gloves to protect hands (if you handle chilies with bare hands, then touch your eyes, they will burn), pull blistered skin from chilies. Cut chilies in half lengthwise and scrape out seeds and veins; cut off stems. Chop chilies finely; discard remainder. (Or cut off and discard stems from pickled chilies; chop chilies finely.)

Add oil to a 6- to 8-quart pan over medium-high heat. Add meat, a portion at a time, and cook until well browned on all sides. Add onion and garlic and stir often until onion is limp, about 5 minutes. Stir in tomatoes, tomato sauce, chopped jalapeños, beer, oregano, pepper, cumin, paprika, and ground pasilla chili; stir well.

Bring to a boil, cover, reduce heat, and simmer until meat is very tender when pierced, about 2½ hours; stir occasionally. If chili is thinner than you like, uncover and simmer until some of the liquid evaporates. If it's thicker, stir in water to thin and bring to boiling. Add salt to taste. Makes 8 or 9 servings, each about 1 cup.

*A. D. Hawkins*

*Redwood City, Calif.*

*"There is haute cuisine and there is hot cuisine."*

**V**EGETARIANISM *prohibits the eating of fish, flesh, or fowl on ethical, ascetic, or nutritional grounds, according to the Encyclopaedia Britannica, which goes on to say that there is a notable diversity of opinion among vegetarians concerning the use of milk, cheese, and eggs.*

*Historically, Americans have been as carnivorous as they could afford to be, with a few exceptions. Seventh Day Adventists are vegetarians out of religious belief; a little-recognized outgrowth of their dietary practice was the development of breakfast cereals in the last quarter of the last century. Recently, vegetarianism has experienced a modest revival on ecological grounds. These vegetarians regard the feeding of animals for meat as wasteful, believing direct human consumption of plants to be more economical for a planet*

*"Vegetarian Stan Terdin makes a delicious one-dish meal that he calls Non-Violent Linguine."*

with a rapidly rising population and limited farming land.

Vegetarian Stan Terdin makes a delicious one-dish meal that he calls Non-violent Linguine. It is essentially a linguine primavera *with the addition of avocado, mushrooms, and olives.*

## NON-VIOLENT LINGUINE

- 6 ounces dry linguine
  Water
- 2 tablespoons butter or margarine
- 1 large clove garlic, minced or pressed
- ½ cup chopped onion
- ½ cup sliced mushrooms
- ½ cup peeled, seeded, and diced tomato
- 2 tablespoons sliced ripe olives
- ½ cup dry white wine
- 1 tablespoon lemon juice
- 1 jar (6 oz.) marinated artichoke hearts, drained and sliced
- 1 small ripe avocado, pitted, peeled, and sliced
  Freshly grated parmesan cheese

In a 3- to 4-quart pan, cook linguine, uncovered, in 1½ to 2 quarts boiling water until tender to bite, about 3 minutes, then drain.

Meanwhile, melt butter in a 10- to 12-inch frying pan over medium heat; add garlic, onion, and mushrooms; stir occasionally until onion is limp, about 10 minutes. Stir in tomato, olives, wine, lemon juice, and artichoke hearts. Bring to a boil on high heat; cook, uncovered, until reduced by ⅓, about 4 minutes.

Add linguine and mix with 2 forks until well coated. Pour onto a platter or plates and top with avocado. Offer cheese to sprinkle onto individual portions. Serves 2 or 3.

*Mountain View, Calif.*

I N THE PAST, *Western chefs have given us muffins that incorporated blueberries, cranberries, apples, and oranges. This recipe, submitted by Henry Harbert, uses eggplant and cheddar cheese to flesh out and flavor bran muffins.*

*Eggplant lovers will appreciate a new way of eating the vegetable, while eggplant haters (there are more than a few) will never know what they are eating.*

## EGGPLANT CHEDDAR MUFFINS

- 1½ cups all-purpose flour
- 2½ teaspoons baking powder
- 2 teaspoons instant minced onion
- ½ teaspoon salt
- 1 large egg
- ½ cup salad oil
- ⅔ cup milk
- 1¼ cups bran cereal
- 1¼ cups peeled, shredded eggplant
- ⅔ cup shredded sharp cheddar cheese

In a small bowl, stir together the flour, baking powder, onion, and salt. In a large bowl, beat egg, oil, milk, cereal, eggplant, and cheese to blend. Add the flour mixture and stir until evenly moistened but still lumpy.

Spoon batter equally into 12 greased 2½-inch muffin cups (fill to rim). Bake in a 350° oven until well browned on top, about 1 hour. Let stand to cool at least 10 minutes, then serve. Makes 1 dozen.

*Everett, Wash.*

C HEESE SOUPS *are all too often thick, floury white sauces rendered even more glutinous by the addition of cheese*

during the latter stages of preparation. Frank Pugh's version is lighter, with a base of chicken broth and fresh tomatoes lightly perfumed by cilantro, a touch of garlic, and onion. The broth is poured over the shredded cheese right in the soup bowl. The cheese softens, turning into strings that trail from your spoon like Salvador Dali's soft watches.

## SONOMA CHEESE SOUP

- 2 tablespoons butter or margarine
- 1 large onion, chopped
- 4 cloves garlic, minced or pressed
- ¼ cup chopped fresh cilantro (coriander)
- 6 cups regular-strength chicken broth
- 4 medium-size firm-ripe tomatoes, cored, peeled, and chopped
  Salt and pepper
- 2 cups (½ lb.) shredded jack cheese
- 2 cups (½ lb.) shredded sharp cheddar cheese

In a 4- to 5-quart pan, melt butter over medium heat; add onion and garlic and stir often until onion is limp, 5 to 8 minutes. Stir in cilantro, broth, and tomatoes; bring to a boil, cover, reduce heat, and simmer for about 10 minutes to blend flavors. Season to taste with salt and pepper. Place equal portions of jack and cheddar cheeses in 8 large soup bowls. Ladle soup over cheese. Makes 8 servings.

*Santa Rosa, Calif.*

*"The cheese softens, turning into strings that trail from your spoon like Salvador Dali's soft watches."*

# September Menus

**S**UMMER MAY HAVE PEAKED *but it's far from over. Fruits and vegetables are still coming on strong, days are warm (perhaps far too hot!), and most cooks want to minimize time in the kitchen.*

*Stuffed sandwiches heat in just minutes to carry outside for a backyard picnic.*

*For a casual supper, consider curried rice laced with seafood. Or offer hot stir-fried beef on a bed of cool, crisp greens for a quick warm-weather entrée. Either of these choices makes a delightful meal to enjoy on terrace or patio.*

*Stuffed sandwich rolls bake in the oven until crisp. Cheese in the center melts around cooked chicken and bacon, holding the filling in place.*

*You can assemble the sandwiches well before serving. Heat them just before sitting down to eat; they take only a few minutes to warm. Serve them with a collection of fresh vegetables and offer large slices of juicy melon for dessert.*

## CHICKEN & CHEESE STUFFED SUBS

4   unsliced French sandwich rolls, each about 3 by 6 inches
4   slices crisp cooked bacon
8   ounces camembert, fontina, or jack cheese, cut into 16 equal chunks
    About 2 cups shredded cooked chicken
2   tablespoons melted butter or margarine

Slice off about ½ inch from each end of the rolls to get an opening almost as big as the center width. Using a long, thin knife, carefully cut inside rolls ¼ inch from the outer crust. Pull out loose inner bread and reserve for another use.

Fill each roll with 1 slice bacon, 4 chunks cheese, and about ½ cup shredded chicken; plug both ends of roll with the chicken. If made ahead, cover and chill up to 12 hours before serving.

Lay rolls on a 10- by 15-inch baking pan and generously brush with melted butter. (If made ahead, bring rolls to room temperature before baking.) Bake in a 450° oven until rolls are crisp and brown, 6 to 8 minutes. Remove from pan and cut each diagonally across the center.

On a large platter or 4 dinner plates, stand sandwiches up, flat ends down (see below). Serve hot. Makes 4 sandwiches, 2 pieces for each serving.— *Michael Roberts, Los Angeles.*

*Diagonally cut French rolls filled with chicken, bacon, and cheese are centerpiece of backyard picnic; serve with fresh vegetables and pickles. There's melon for dessert.*

## BACK-TO-SCHOOL
## SEAFOOD SUPPER

Shrimp & Crab Curry Rice
Butter Lettuce Salad
Crunchy Breadsticks
Chocolate Chip Pie    Vanilla Ice Cream
Chardonnay    Milk

*For a quick family supper, add cooked seafood (real or less costly imitation) to curried rice.*

*While the rice cooks, let the children mix the batter for the pie. It bakes while you eat; serve warm wedges with ice cream.*

## SHRIMP & CRAB CURRY RICE

½ cup (¼ lb.) butter or margarine
1 medium-size red onion, chopped
2 stalks celery, chopped
1 cup long-grain white rice
2 teaspoons curry powder
⅛ teaspoon cayenne
2 cups regular-strength chicken broth
½ pound shelled cooked crab or shredded imitation crab
½ pound tiny cooked shelled shrimp
3 tablespoons minced parsley
Salt and pepper

In a 10- to 12-inch frying pan over high heat, melt butter; add onion and celery. Cook, stirring occasionally, until onion is lightly browned, about 8 minutes. Add rice, curry, and cayenne; cook, stirring, about 2 minutes. Add broth, bring to boiling, cover, reduce heat to low, and simmer until rice is tender to bite, about 18 minutes.

Gently stir in crab, shrimp, and parsley; cook, stirring occasionally, just until seafood is warm, about 3 minutes. Pour mixture onto a serving platter and serve immediately. Makes 6 servings. — *Vel Gerth, Tacoma.*

*Hot stir-fried beef strips combine with cool salad greens; add carrot-lemon relish.*

## CHOCOLATE CHIP PIE

2 large eggs
½ cup (¼ lb.) butter or margarine, melted and cooled
1 cup sugar
1 teaspoon vanilla
2 tablespoons bourbon or water
¾ cup all-purpose flour
1 cup chopped walnuts or almonds
1 cup (6 oz.) semisweet chocolate baking chips
1 purchased 9-inch deep-dish pastry shell

Beat together eggs, butter, sugar, vanilla, and bourbon until well blended. Stir in flour, walnuts, and chocolate chips. Scrape batter into pastry shell.

Bake in a 350° oven until a wooden pick inserted in center comes out clean, about 1 hour. Serve warm or cool. If made ahead, cool, cover, and store at room temperature up to a day. Serves 6 to 8. — *Ruth Fotouhi, Sonoma, Calif.*

## HOT & COLD SALAD

Chili Beef Stir-Fry on Mixed Greens
Carrot & Lemon Relish
Baguette    Butter
Fruit Sorbet Soda    Chocolate Wafers
Beer    White Grape Juice

*Cook thin strips of hot-seasoned beef quickly over high heat and spoon immediately on top of crisp salad greens.*

*Make carrot and lemon relish (to serve with salad), and wash and crisp greens in advance. If you like, marinate meat up to a day ahead. To make sodas extra frosty, freeze glasses before filling.*

## CHILI BEEF STIR-FRY
## ON MIXED GREENS

1 pound boneless lean beef steak, such as top sirloin (about 1 in. thick), excess fat removed
1 medium-size fresh jalapeño chili, stemmed, seeded, and minced
2 cloves garlic, minced or pressed
½ to ¾ teaspoon hot chili oil or cayenne
1 tablespoon soy sauce
½ teaspoon sugar
About ⅓ cup salad oil
¼ cup rice vinegar (or ¼ cup distilled white vinegar plus 1 tablespoon sugar)
8 cups washed and crisped greens, torn into bite-size pieces; choose 1 or several: watercress sprigs, escarole, butter lettuce, arugula, radicchio, leaf lettuce
Salt and pepper

Cut beef across grain into ⅛-inch-thick slices about 3 inches long. In a bowl, mix beef, jalapeño, garlic, chili oil to taste, soy sauce, and sugar. Cover and chill for at least 30 minutes or until the next day.

Shortly before serving, stir together in a large bowl 3 tablespoons salad oil

*(Continued on next page)*

### ...CHILI BEEF STIR-FRY ON MIXED GREENS

and the vinegar. Add greens and mix to coat with dressing. Arrange on 4 dinner plates.

Place a 10- to 12-inch frying pan or wok over high heat until pan is hot. Add 1 tablespoon salad oil and half the beef mixture; stir-fry until beef is lightly browned, 2 to 3 minutes. Arrange equal portions of meat on greens on 2 of the plates. Repeat with remaining oil and beef. Add salt and pepper to taste. Makes 4 servings.

### CARROT & LEMON RELISH

Peel 1 large **carrot** and cut into ⅛- by ⅛- by 1½-inch sticks; place in a bowl. Cut 1 medium-size **lemon** in half lengthwise. Thinly slice a lemon half crosswise, discarding ends. Cut each slice into 3 equal wedges. Add to carrot.

Ream remaining lemon half and mix 2 tablespoons of the juice, 1 tablespoon **salad oil,** and 1 teaspoon **sugar** with carrots and lemon wedges. Cover and refrigerate at least 1 hour or up to 2 days. Serve cool. Makes 1⅔ cups, 4 servings.

### FRUIT SORBET SODA

**About 1 pint fruit sorbet (your favorite flavor)**
**About 1 bottle (28 oz.) chilled sparkling water**
4 **medium-size strawberries, washed and cut partway up from tip**

Add a large scoop sorbet to each of 4 chilled, stemmed 12- to 14-ounce glasses. Slowly pour about ¾ cup sparkling water over sorbet. Slide a strawberry onto the edge of each glass. Serve with a spoon and a straw, if desired. Serves 4.

# OCTOBER

*Fuyu-type persimmon wedges with hazelnut liqueur (page 237)*

Golden orange persimmons provided inspiration in October; we suggested ways to enjoy the ripe fruit and recipes to show off its special qualities. Ideas for entertaining included a Brazilian party buffet, a Russian menu, and a cook-it-yourself pancake party. Other articles featured ways to use wild venison, three hearty peasant breads, simple salads with pungent cheeses, dishes using subtle caramelized garlic, and marzipan candies shaped into Halloween witches and pumpkins.

# Persimmons: One of Fall's Great Pleasures

**B**RIGHT JEWELS *of the fall season, per-simmons please the eye whether seen as golden orange orbs on leafless limbs or mounded in glistening plenty at the market. They are also the source of some confusion.*

*A native persimmon, found in the Eastern states, is a seed-filled, rather small fruit that is too puckery to eat until the first frost. It turns soft and sweet and perishes rapidly. Rarely will you see a native persimmon in the West. What you do find are the big, showy Oriental kinds.*

*Although all Oriental persimmons are similar in their rich, very sweet flavor, they divide quite cleanly into two groups. The first—Fuyu is the predominant market variety—is good to eat while firm and ripe; the second, represented mainly by the Hachiya, is astringent and inedible unless soft-ripe.*

*The persimmons that are best when firm-ripe have flat bottoms. In addition to Fuyu, other flat-bottom varieties are Gosho (or Giant Fuyu) and Maru (or Chocolate, because brown streaks run through the fruit). These crisp persimmons are much easier for newcomers to the fruit to like. Even when very ripe, they retain more texture than Hachiya types do. They also keep their texture when cooked.*

*Hachiya-type persimmons have pointed tips. Similar varieties, mostly found in home gardens, are the Hyakume, Tam-opan, and Tanenashi. Hachiya-type fruit are too astringent (from tannins) to eat until soft and ripe. However, they are the most intensely flavored persimmons. Unless handled in specific ways during cooking, the sweet, creamy pulp will revert to bitter astringency. In baking, this behavior is neutralized by baking soda, but unless soda is added to the pulp before it is mixed with other ingredients, the resulting product will be gummy.*

*Crisp persimmons are the first to appear in the fall; soft-ripe ones usually linger into December.*

## RIPENESS: HOW TO DETERMINE

Feel a Hachiya-type persimmon. When it gives readily or is actually squishy when pressed and begins to look translucent with a slightly dull skin, the fruit is at the ideal eating stage.

Flat-bottom Fuyu-type persimmons are sweet and flavorful while firm and crisp. Color indicates ripeness. Fruit above is pale and immature; at right, shiny bright orange color signifies good eating.

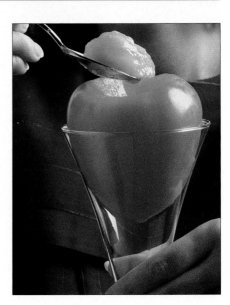

Pointed-tip Hachiya-type persimmons above are still firm, puckery tasting. Let fruit ripen until translucent and soft enough to scoop from skin. One way to serve: nest in a glass and eat with a spoon.

For Fuyu-type persimmons, color is the main clue. Fruit should be shiny, with a bright, deep orange color. It should feel solid, like an apple, but even when the fruit is riper and gives to gentle pressure, this variety makes excellent eating.

Frequently you will notice black streaks on the skin. These are harmless markings caused by bumps or branches whipping against the hard fruit on the tree.

## HOW TO STORE PERSIMMONS, HASTEN RIPENING

At room temperature, the fruit ripen slowly—one reason why many people like to keep piles of persimmons in bowls for fall decorations. To hasten ripening, especially of Hachiya types, enclose fruit in a paper or plastic bag with an apple for 3 to 5 days; check frequently.

In the refrigerator, you can store firm persimmons up to about 1 month; check occasionally for spoilage.

To freeze persimmons, fruit should be at a ready-to-eat stage; both types will be soft when thawed. Freeze whole fruit in a single layer; when solidly frozen, enclose in plastic bags. Or scoop soft Hachiya-type pulp from skin and pack in small containers; cover surface with plastic wrap (to reduce darkening) and freeze. Held at 0° or colder, fruit will keep up to the next season.

## Enjoying Persimmons

Raw or cooked, Oriental persimmons make a delicious contribution to the table. With more than brief heating, both types begin to lose their bright color; handled carefully or preserved (canned or frozen) as directed here and on page 239, they make attractive offerings year-round.

Two of the simplest and perhaps most stylish preparations are shown on the facing page and on page 235. Slice off stem end of a soft-ripe Hachiya-type persimmon and nestle in a stemmed glass. Serve chilled, if you like, to scoop from skin with a spoon; squeeze fresh lime juice over the fruit or splash with hazelnut-, almond-, or orange-flavored liqueur.

Or cut a Fuyu-type persimmon into wedges, starting from the bottom without cutting into the stem end. Peel back skin to create a petal effect (see page 235). Lay fruit stem side down on a plate. Serve with hazelnut-, almond-, or orange- flavored liqueur to pour over fruit; serve with knife and fork.

## Glazed Persimmon Wedges

*Spicy, glazed persimmon wedges are a sweet-savory counterpoint to baked ham or roasted pork.*

1¼ to 1½ **pounds (see chart above) crisp-ripe Fuyu-type persimmons**
¼ **cup (⅛ lb.) butter or margarine**
1 **teaspoon ground ginger**
½ **teaspoon ground cumin**
¼ **teaspoon curry powder**
3 **tablespoons lime juice**
1 **tablespoon raisins**

With a sharp knife or vegetable peeler, cut off persimmon stems and peel; slice the fruit into ½-inch-thick wedges, discarding any seeds.

In a 10- to 12-inch frying pan, combine butter, ginger, cumin, and curry powder; cook, uncovered, over medium

heat until mixture foams. Stir in persimmons and lime juice. Heat mixture until sizzling, then reduce heat to low and cook, turning fruit occasionally with a spatula until hot and lightly glazed, about 5 minutes.

Serve warm in a bowl; sprinkle with raisins. Makes 2 cups, 5 or 6 servings.

## Hachiya-Type Persimmon Syllabub

*Use the thick version as a dessert or sauce; sip the thin syllabub.*

*Orange-gold purée of Hachiya-type persimmons makes dessert syllabub.*

1½ **pounds (see chart above) soft-ripe Hachiya-type persimmons**
1 **cup *each* whipping cream and powdered sugar**
⅓ **cup dry sherry**
2 **teaspoons lemon juice**
1½ **cups milk (optional)**

Pull stems off persimmons, cut fruit in half, and scoop pulp from skin with a spoon; discard any seeds. You should have 2 cups pulp. In a food processor or blender, whirl persimmon pulp until puréed; set aside.

With an electric mixer, whip cream and sugar (scrape bowl sides often) until mixture will hold soft peak. Stir in persimmon purée, sherry, and lemon juice to taste. Serve, or cover and chill up to 1 day.

To serve as a dessert, stir persimmon mixture, then ladle into small bowls or wide-mouth wine glasses and eat with a spoon.

To serve syllabub as a beverage, stir milk into persimmon mixture. Pour into wine glasses or cups to sip. Makes 6 or 7 dessert servings, about ¾-cup size, or 6 beverage servings, about 1-cup size.

## How Many Persimmons Do You Need for Our Recipes?

| Hachiya-Type | Average diameter (inches) | Approx. number 1 lb. | Approx. number 2 lb. | Approx. number 3 lb. | Approx. number 4 lb. | Approx. number 5 lb. |
|---|---|---|---|---|---|---|
| Small | 2½ to 2¾ | 2 | 5 | 7 | 9 | 12 |
| Medium | About 3 | 2 | 4 | 6 | 8 | 10 |
| Large | 3¼ up | 1 to 2 | 4 | 5 | 6 | 8 |
| **Fuyu-Type** | | | | | | |
| Small | 2½ to 2¾ | 4 | 8 | 12 | 16 | 20 |
| Medium | About 3 | 3 | 6 to 7 | 10 | 13 | 17 |
| Large | 3¼ up | 2 | 4 | 6 | 8 | 10 |

*Thick persimmon purée gives moistness to Indian pudding. Firm Fuyu-type wedges decorate the top. Accompany with syllabub (page 237) if you wish.*

## BAKED HACHIYA-TYPE PERSIMMON INDIAN PUDDING

*If you like, accompany this pudding with a sauce of the thick syllabub and a garnish of persimmon chutney (right) and slices of crisp Fuyus.*

- ½ **pound (see chart, page 237) soft-ripe Hachiya-type persimmons**
- 2 **teaspoons baking soda**
- ¾ **cup sugar**
- ½ **cup (¼ lb.) butter or margarine**
- ¼ **cup dark molasses**
- 2 **large eggs**
- 1 **teaspoon vanilla**
- 1 **cup all-purpose flour**
- ¾ **cup cornmeal**
- ½ **teaspoon *each* ground cinnamon and ground ginger**
- ¼ **teaspoon ground allspice**
- 1 **cup raisins**
- ½ **cup chopped walnuts**

Pull stems off persimmons. Cut fruit in half and scoop pulp from skin with a spoon; discard any seeds. You should have 1 cup pulp. In a food processor or blender, purée pulp with baking soda; set aside.

With an electric mixer, beat together sugar, butter, and molasses until blended; add eggs and vanilla and beat until smooth. In a separate bowl, stir flour with cornmeal, cinnamon, ginger, and allspice. Gradually stir into creamy mixture with purée, raisins, and nuts.

Pour batter into a buttered 6- to 7-cup loaf pan or ring mold (no deeper than 3 inches); cover tightly with foil. Put pan in a larger pan and place in a 300° oven. To larger pan, add ¾ inch boiling water around loaf pan or ½ inch boiling water around ring mold. Bake until pudding is firm in center when lightly pressed, about 2 hours. Let stand 10 minutes, then run a knife around side of pan to release pudding. Invert onto a plate. Serve warm or cool, cut into slices. Makes 12 servings.

## PERSIMMON CHUTNEY

*Use crisp persimmons for a chunky chutney, soft persimmons for a smoother texture. The chutney goes well with curries, grilled cheese sandwiches, and ham, pork, duck, or goose.*

- 2 **pounds (see chart page 237) crisp-ripe to soft-ripe Fuyu-type persimmons; or 2 pounds (see chart) soft-ripe Hachiya-type persimmons**
- 3½ **cups water**
- ½ **pound (2 cups) dried apricots**
- 1½ **cups raisins**
- 2 **tablespoons minced fresh ginger or 1½ teaspoons ground ginger**
- 1 **tablespoon mustard seed**
- ¾ **teaspoon chili powder**
- 1½ **cups white wine vinegar**
- 1¼ **cups firmly packed brown sugar Salt**

*To prepare Fuyu-type persimmons,* cut off stems and peel with a sharp knife or vegetable peeler. Chop fruit, discarding any seeds; you need 4½ cups fruit.

*To prepare Hachiya-type persimmons,* pull off stems, then cut fruit in half and scoop pulp from skin with a spoon; you need 2⅔ cups fruit.

Set fruit aside.

*If using Fuyu-type persimmons,* in a 5- to 6-quart pan combine fruit with water, apricots, raisins, ginger, mustard seed, and chili powder. Bring to a boil, reduce heat to a simmer, then cover and cook 10 minutes. Add vinegar and sugar. Simmer, uncovered, stirring occasionally, then more frequently as mixture thickens, until most of the liquid evaporates and chutney is reduced to 7 cups, about 45 minutes; remove from heat.

*If using Hachiya-type persimmons,* in a 5- to 6-quart pan bring water, apricots, raisins, ginger, mustard, and chili to boiling; reduce heat to simmer, cover, and cook 10 minutes. Add vinegar and sugar, and simmer, uncovered, stirring occasionally until reduced to 4½ cups, about 55 minutes. Stir in Hachiya-type fruit and remove at once from heat.

Salt chutney to taste. Serve chutney warm, or store in covered jars in the refrigerator up to 1 month; or freeze in easy-to-use units.

*To can Fuyu-type chutney,* follow directions for canning on page 240; use ½-pint canning jars. Store in a cool, dark place.

Hachiya-type chutney is not suitable to can, as heating makes it very astringent.

Makes 3½ pints Fuyu-type chutney, 3 pints Hachiya-type chutney.

# Preserving Persimmons

ORIENTAL PERSIMMONS *make beautiful preserves, some to can and some to freeze. The methods and recipes you use depend upon the distinctly different behaviors of the two Oriental persimmon types described on page 236.*

*Hachiya-type persimmons—good to eat when soft-ripe—can be cooked only under certain conditions, because heat causes their flavor to deteriorate, but they freeze well. The versatile Fuyu types—delicious at either crisp or soft-ripe stages—are easier to work with; they can also be preserved by canning or freezing.*

*Here, we give directions for putting your persimmon crop or purchase to work in two kinds of jam, a jelly, a syrup, a nectar, brandied fruit, and pickles.*

## FREEZER PERSIMMON JAM

- 1½ pounds (see chart, page 237) soft-ripe Fuyu-type persimmons; or 1½ pounds (see chart) soft-ripe Hachiya-type persimmons
- 3 cups sugar
- 1 pouch (3 oz.) liquid pectin
- ¼ cup lemon juice

Cut or pull off stems from persimmons; discard stems. If Fuyu types are firm enough, peel with a knife. For soft fruit, cut in half and scoop out pulp. Discard any seeds and skin.

*If using Fuyu-type persimmons,* mash pulp, or coarsely chop using a knife or food processor (do not purée); you should have 1½ cups fruit.

*If using Hachiya-type persimmons,* cut pulp into about ½-inch chunks; you should have 2 cups fruit.

In a bowl, mix fruit and sugar; let stand for 10 minutes, stirring occasionally. Meanwhile, mix pectin and lemon juice; add to fruit and stir gently for 3 minutes (mixing vigorously traps air bubbles, making the jam cloudy). Fill ½-pint jars or freezer containers to ½ inch of rim. Cover, and let stand 12 to 16 hours at room temperature. You can store unopened jam in covered jars in the refrigerator up to 6 months, up to 1 month if opened. Or freeze to store longer; cover and chill thawed jam. Makes 4 cups.

*Preserved persimmon treats include (top) hot Fuyu pickles, brandied persimmons; (center) syrup, Fuyu jelly, freezer jam; (bottom) nectar, jelly, chutney.*

## SHORT-COOK FUYU-TYPE PERSIMMON JAM

*Hachiya persimmons are unsuitable for this recipe and other cooked preserves, because they become very astringent when heated.*

- 3 pounds (see chart, page 237) soft-ripe Fuyu-type persimmons
- 6 cups sugar
- ½ lemon juice
- 1 pouch (3 oz.) liquid pectin or 1 envelope (1¾ or 2 oz.) dry pectin

Cut or pull stems from persimmons; discard stems. If fruit is firm enough, peel with a knife. For soft fruit, cut in half and scoop out pulp. Cut large pieces of fruit into ½-inch chunks; discard the peel and any seeds.

*If using liquid pectin,* combine persimmon chunks with sugar and lemon juice in a 6- to 8-quart pan; set aside for 15 minutes. Place pan on high heat and bring persimmon mixture to a rolling

*(Continued on next page)*

boil that can't be stirred down; stir constantly. Remove from heat and add pectin; stir for 3 minutes. Skim off foam.

*If using dry pectin,* in pan mix pectin with persimmon chunks and lemon juice. Bring to a boil over high heat, stirring constantly. Still stirring, add sugar and return to a boil that cannot be stirred down; boil exactly 2 minutes, stirring. Remove from heat and skim off foam.

To store in the refrigerator, pour jam into serving-size jars; let cool, cover, and chill up to 6 months if jars are unopened, up to 1 month if opened.

To can jam, follow directions below on canning Fuyu-type persimmon mixtures; use ½-pint canning jars. Store in a cool, dark place. If jars do not seal, store in the refrigerator up to 6 months, up to 1 month if opened. Makes 7½ cups.

## How to Can Fuyu-Type Persimmon Mixtures

Immerse jars and jar rings in boiling water to cover. Hold at a gentle simmer at least 10 minutes. Heat lids in water according to manufacturer's directions. To use, drain jars on a clean towel.

Ladle hot persimmon mixture into jars, filling to within ¼ inch of rim. If mixture is thick, run a narrow spatula down between food and jar to release air bubbles. Wipe jar rims clean. Cover with hot lids; *firmly screw on rings, but do not force.*

Choose a deep pan with rack that will hold the jars side by side. Place jars on the rack, and add boiling water to cover jars by 1 to 2 inches. Bring water to simmering (180°); hold at simmer for 10 minutes.

Lift jars from water and set on a towel. *Don't tilt jars (even to drain water from lids).* Let stand until cool. Test seal by pressing center of lid. If it stays down, seal is good. Store in a cool, dark place.

If the jar is not sealed, store as directed in each recipe. Unopened jars will keep up to 6 months; opened jars, with more surfaces exposed to air, may develop mold if stored for more than 1 month.

## Fuyu-Type Persimmon Jelly

> About 2 pounds (see chart, page 237) crisp-ripe Fuyu-type persimmons
> 1 cup water
> 2 cups sugar
> 1 tablespoon lemon juice
> 1 thin slice fresh ginger, about 1½-inch diameter; or 1 cinnamon stick, 2 to 3 inches long
> 1 pouch (3 oz.) liquid pectin

Rinse persimmons. Cut or pull off stems and discard. Chop unpeeled fruit into ¾-inch pieces and discard any seeds; you need 6 cups fruit.

In a 3- to 4-quart pan, combine persimmons and water; bring to boiling. Reduce heat to simmering, cover, and simmer 10 minutes, stirring occasionally. Line a colander with 8 layers of wet cheesecloth; set colander in a bowl. Pour persimmon mixture into colander and let stand until liquid has drained into bowl; do not squeeze pulp through cheesecloth. Discard pulp.

You should have 1 cup juice; if you have more, boil in pan until reduced to 1 cup; if you have less, add water to make 1 cup.

In pan, mix persimmon juice with sugar, lemon juice, and ginger or cinnamon. Stirring constantly on high heat, bring to a rolling boil that can't be stirred down. Add pectin. Return to a rolling boil and boil for 1 minute, stirring. Remove from heat and quickly skim off foam.

To can jam, follow preceding directions on canning Fuyu-type persimmon mixtures, using ½-pint canning jars. Store in a cool, dark place. If jars do not seal, store them in the refrigerator up to 6 months, up to 1 month if opened. Makes 2 cups.

## Fuyu-Type Persimmon Syrup

*Pour over pancakes or ice cream, or into sparkling water or dry white wine to sip.*

Follow directions for **Fuyu-Type Persimmon Jelly** (preceding), combining fruit, water, sugar, lemon juice, and ginger or cinnamon in pan; omit liquid pectin.

Bring to a boil on high heat, stirring; reduce heat and boil gently until flavor of ginger or cinnamon permeates syrup, about 2 minutes. Remove from heat and skim off any foam.

To use syrup freshly cooked or after storing in the refrigerator, offer hot, cool, or reheated; store cool syrup, covered, in the refrigerator up to 1 month.

To can, pour syrup into hot, clean ½-pint jars to within ¼ inch of rim, following preceding directions on how to can Fuyu-type persimmon mixtures. If jars do not seal, store in the refrigerator up to 6 months, up to 1 month if opened. Or freeze in easy-to-use units. Shake to mix well before using. Makes 2 cups.

## Persimmon Nectar

*Hachiya types make a brighter nectar because they are only gently heated; Fuyu types fade more. Freeze to store.*

> About 3 pounds (see chart, page 237) soft-ripe Hachiya-type persimmons; or about 3 pounds (see chart) crisp to soft-ripe Fuyu-type persimmons
> Water
> 1 cup sugar
> ⅓ cup lemon juice

Cut or pull off stems from persimmons; discard stems. If Fuyu-types are firm enough, peel with a knife. For soft fruit, cut in half and scoop out pulp. Discard any seeds and skin.

*If using Hachiya-type persimmons,* purée pulp in a food processor or blender.

*If using Fuyu-type persimmons,* finely chop fruit, then place in a 4- to 5-quart pan with 5 cups water. Bring to a boil on high heat; cover and simmer fruit until soft enough to mash, about 20 minutes. Purée fruit with liquid in a food processor or blender.

Blend persimmon purée with sugar and lemon juice. Add enough water to Hachiya-type purée to make 2 quarts; add water to Fuyu-type purée to make 2½ quarts.

To serve nectar, cover and chill until cold; store nectar up to 1 month in the refrigerator. Or freeze in easy-to-use units.

*To can Fuyu-type nectar only,* pour syrup into hot, clean 1-pint canning jars to within ¼ inch of rim, following preceding directions on how to can Fuyu-type persimmon mixtures. If jars do not seal, store in the refrigerator up to 6 months, up to 1 month if opened. Or freeze in easy-to-use units. Shake to mix well before using.

Makes 2 quarts Hachiya nectar, 2½ quarts Fuyu nectar.

## FUYU-TYPE BRANDIED PERSIMMONS

*Spoon over pound cake or ice cream, or layer in trifle; sip any extra brandy-flavored syrup or serve over sliced fresh persimmons.*

- **4 to 5 pounds (see chart, page 237) crisp-ripe Fuyu-type persimmons**
- **1½ cups water**
- **1½ cups sugar**
- **½ cup brandy**
- **3 tablespoons lemon juice**

Pull or cut off stems from persimmons; discard stems. Peel fruit with a sharp knife or vegetable peeler and discard peel. Cut persimmons crosswise into ½-inch-thick rounds; discard any seeds.

In a 2- to 3-quart pan, bring water to a boil on high heat. Add ¼ of the fruit at a time to the water; cover and, when boiling resumes, cook 1 minute. Lift fruit from pan with a slotted spoon. Measure water and add enough to make 2 cups; return to pan and set aside.

Firmly pack persimmons into 4 hot jars, 1-pint size.

Add sugar to water and bring to a boil on high heat, stirring until sugar is dissolved. Remove from heat and add brandy and lemon juice.

Pour enough hot syrup into jars to fill within ¼ inch of rim (save extra syrup; suggestions for use follow recipe title).

To can fruit, follow preceding directions on how to can Fuyu-type persimmon mixtures. Store in a cool, dark place at least 2 weeks before serving; if unsealed, store in refrigerator up to 6 months, up to 1 month if opened. Makes 4 pints.

*Oriental persimmon harvest is ready to preserve. Hachiya types (bag and basket) must be soft-ripe to use; they can become astringent when cooked. Fuyu types (colander) are sweet, nonastringent while crisp or soft and retain flavor when cooked.*

## FUYU-TYPE PERSIMMON CHILI PICKLES

*Eat with lamb; cheddar, stilton, or blue cheese; or grilled cheese sandwiches.*

- **4 pounds (see chart, page 237) crisp-ripe Fuyu-type persimmons**
- **3 medium-size onions**
- **2 medium-size green bell peppers, stemmed and seeded**
- **8 medium-size cloves garlic**
- **12 small dried hot red chilies**
- **6 cups water**
- **2½ cups white wine vinegar**
- **1 tablespoon salt**
- **1 tablespoon pickling spices**

Cut or pull off stems from persimmons; discard stems. Peel fruit with a sharp knife or vegetable peeler and discard peel. Cut persimmons into 1-inch wedges, discarding any seeds. Cut the onions and bell peppers into 1-inch squares; set fruit and vegetables aside.

Peel and slightly crush the garlic; break each chili in half.

In a 4- to 6-quart pan, bring garlic, chili, water, vinegar, salt, and pickling spices to boiling on high heat. Add ¼ of the persimmons to boiling liquid; cover and, when rolling boil resumes, cook 30 seconds. Lift fruit from pan with a slotted spoon and set aside. Repeat to cook remaining fruit.

Pour ⅛ of the onions into each of 8 hot canning jars, 1-pint size. Add ⅛ of the persimmons to each jar, then top with ⅛ of the bell peppers. Bring cooking liquid to boiling and pour equally into each jar, filling to within ¼ inch of rim.

Can fruit, following preceding directions on canning Fuyu-type persimmon mixtures. Store in a cool, dark place at least 2 weeks before serving. If jars do not seal, store up to 6 months in the refrigerator, up to 1 month if opened. Makes 8 pints.

# Brazil's Party Dish—Feijoada

FROM HUMBLE BEGINNINGS as a meal made by Brazilian slaves, feijoada (fay-zhwah-dah) has evolved into a party food popular throughout Brazil. In this country, too, the stew of meats and black beans, with colorful accompaniments, makes appealing party fare.

Smoked meats simmer with beans to bring out rich flavors. You serve elements separately, with traditional side dishes: rice, kale, orange slices, chili salsa, and a crisp-soft topping called farofa—toasted dry manioc with onions and bananas.

For dessert, offer Brazil's intense, rich coconut custard, quindin, with pineapple. You'll find manioc (also called cassava) in markets catering to Brazilians and Africans (who call it gari). Or use farina instead; it's available in supermarkets with other hot breakfast cereals.

A chunk of carne seca (air-dried beef), sold here in Brazilian markets and gourmet food stores, adds authenticity, but harder, thinner beef jerky will do.

Feijoada preparation is most easily done over two days. A day or two ahead, cook beans and meat, make farofa and the custard, and wash kale. On party day, make salsa, chop and cook kale, cook rice, slice oranges, and reheat meat, beans, and farofa.

Brazilian buffet party for 12 includes, front to back: cooked meats (short ribs, tongue, sausages) with brown rice, kale, fresh salsa, farofa (a manioc-banana topping), a bowl of black beans, and orange slices.

### BRAZILIAN FEIJOADA

1 small (about 2½ lb.) smoked or corned beef tongue
½ pound Brazilian carne seca (dried beef) or beef jerky
    Water
1½ pounds (3 cups) dry black beans, sorted of debris and rinsed
5 pounds lean beef short ribs (fat trimmed), sawed into 2-inch lengths
½ pound *each* beef link sausage, Polish sausage (kielbasa), and linguisa (Portuguese-style sausage)
⅛ pound Canadian bacon (optional), cut into ½-inch cubes
8 cloves garlic, minced or pressed
2 bay leaves
2 large onions, chopped
2 tablespoons salad oil
⅓ cup minced parsley
    Fresh salsa (recipe follows)
    Brown rice (recipe follows)
    Farofa (recipe follows)
    Wilted kale (recipe follows)
    Sliced oranges (directions follow)

Place tongue and carne seca in a 10- to 12-quart pan. Cover with cold water, then bring to a boil over high heat. Drain and repeat. To meats in pan, add beans, 4½ quarts water, and ribs. Bring to a boil over high heat, then cover and simmer until tongue is very tender when pierced, about 2¾ hours. Add beef, Polish, and linguisa sausages and Canadian bacon; simmer until sausages are hot in center (cut to test), about 10 minutes longer. Skim fat off liquid and discard.

Lift out sausages and cut into 1-inch chunks; arrange on a large ovenproof platter. Lift out carne seca; cut into 1-inch pieces and place next to sausages. Lift out tongue. Cut off and discard skin, then cut meat into 1-inch chunks. Lift out ribs; arrange on platter with other meats. Cover tightly and keep warm in a 150° oven. (If made ahead, let cool completely, then cover and chill up to 2 days; reheat, covered, in a 350° oven until meat is hot to touch, about 30 minutes.)

Ladle 2 quarts broth from pan (there will still be broth on beans); reserve ¼ cup for salsa. Save balance of 2 quarts for other uses. With a slotted spoon, lift 1½ cups beans from pan; set aside.

In a 10- to 12-inch frying pan over medium-high heat, cook garlic, bay leaves, and onions in oil until onions are limp, about 10 minutes; stir often. Add parsley and reserved beans; mash beans with a spoon. Stir until mixture bubbles. Return bean mixture to large pan. (If made ahead, let cool, cover, and chill up to 2 days.) Stirring, bring beans to a boil over medium-high heat.

Pour bean mixture into a bowl. Arrange salsa, rice, farofa, kale, and oranges in separate dishes. To serve, spoon meats, rice, farofa, kale, and oranges onto plates. Ladle beans over meat; add salsa to taste. Makes 12 to 14 servings.—*Gisela Claper.*

**Fresh salsa.** Core and dice ½ pound firm-ripe **tomatoes**. Combine in a bowl with the ¼ cup **reserved bean broth;** 1 small, minced **onion;** 1 can (4 oz.) **diced green chilies;** 2 tablespoons minced **parsley;** 1 tablespoon *each* **lemon juice** and **white wine vinegar;** and ¼ teaspoon **pepper.**

**Brown rice.** In a 3- to 4-quart pan, bring 4½ cups **water** and 1 teaspoon **salt** (optional) to a boil over high heat. Add 2 cups **long-grain brown rice,** cover, and simmer until rice is tender to bite, about 40 minutes.

**Farofa.** In a 12- to 14-inch frying pan over medium-high heat, stir 1 large chopped **onion** with 3 tablespoons **butter** or margarine until limp, about 10 minutes.

Meanwhile, mash 2 medium-size ripe **bananas** until fairly smooth. Add 1 **large egg;** mix until blended.

To onion, add 1 pound (2½ cups) **manioc flour** (also called cassava or gari) or farina. Stir often until manioc is golden, about 20 minutes. Add egg mixture and stir to coat. Serve warm. If made ahead, cool, cover, and chill up to 2 days. To reheat, place in a shallow 2½-quart baking dish, cover, and bake in a 350° oven until hot in center, about 35 minutes.

*Fresh pineapple and ring of Brazilian coconut custard make a tart-sweet conclusion to the dinner.*

**Wilted kale.** Cut stems from 2½ pounds **kale** and discard. Wash leaves and chop. Place in a 5- to 6-quart pan with 2 cups **water.** Bring to a boil over high heat; stir often until leaves wilt, 3 to 5 minutes.

**Sliced oranges.** With a knife, cut peel and membrane from 5 medium-size **oranges.** Slice fruit crosswise ¼ inch thick.

## BRAZILIAN COCONUT CUSTARD

- 2 **large eggs**
- 10 **large egg yolks**
- 2 **cups sugar**
  **Water**
- ¼ **cup (⅛ lb.) butter or margarine, cut into 1-inch pieces**
- 1¼ **cups sweetened shredded coconut**
- 1 **small pineapple (about 3 lb.), peeled, cored, cut into wedges**

Place eggs, yolks, sugar, 1½ cups cold water, and butter in a blender or food processor; whirl until well combined. Add coconut; whirl just to mix.

Set a 5- to 6-cup ring mold in a larger rimmed baking pan (at least 2 inches deep). Pour egg mixture into ring mold. Place both pans in a 350° oven. Fill bottom pan with boiling water halfway up sides of mold. Bake until custard jiggles only slightly when gently shaken, about 50 minutes.

Lift mold from water and place on a rack; let cool completely. Invert a plate on top of mold; hold plate and mold together and invert custard onto plate. Lift off mold. Serve, or cover and chill up to 2 days. Cut into wedges; accompany with pineapple. Makes 12 to 14 servings.

# Three Hearty Peasant Breads

HEARTY FLAVORS AND TEXTURES *unite these peasant breads from three different countries. The first, a cheese-filled quick bread from southern Russia, is substantial enough to serve as an entrée.*

*The sour pumpernickel, a German bread that's good with soup and for making sandwiches, gets its crunch from sunflower, flax, and sesame seeds.*

*The dense French walnut loaf is one version of a bread often served with the cheese course in France.*

*Both the dense-textured pumpernickel and walnut doughs use yeast, but they are kneaded rather briefly—just until they feel smooth. Longer kneading, required to make wheat-flour doughs springy and elastic, isn't necessary, since both these breads contain a high proportion of rye flour. (Rye-based dough doesn't become as elastic as wheat-based dough.)*

## RUSSIAN CHEESE BREAD
### *Khachapuri*

*You need a total of 1½ pounds cheese. For boldest, most authentic flavor, use 1 pound goat cheese. Traditional accompaniments include parsley, cilantro, or green onions, and dry, fruity white wine.*

- ½ to 1 pound goat cheese, such as bûcheron or montrachet
- 1 to 2 packages (8 oz. each) neufchâtel cheese (if using 1 lb. goat cheese, use only 8 oz.)

About 3 cups all-purpose flour
- ½ teaspoon salt
- 1 teaspoon baking soda
- 1 tablespoon baking powder
- 1¾ cups sour cream
- 1 large egg yolk beaten with 1 teaspoon water

In a large bowl, mix goat cheese and neufchâtel until well combined; set aside.

In a large bowl, mix 3 cups of the flour, salt, baking soda, and baking powder. Add sour cream and stir until evenly blended. Gather dough into a ball and gently knead on a well-floured board until fairly smooth, 20 to 30 turns.

Divide dough in thirds; set aside 1 portion. On a well-floured board, roll remaining dough into a 14-inch round. Trim edges to make even; add scraps to reserved dough. Fold dough round in quarters; set in a greased 10-inch cast-iron frying pan (or other oven-safe frying pan). Unfold dough to line pan and extend beyond rim.

Evenly pat cheese mixture into dough-lined pan. On a floured board, roll remaining dough into a 9-inch round; set on top of the cheese filling. Brush dough top with yolk mixture. Fold extended rim down over dough top, crimp, and brush rim with yolk mixture. Prick top in 12 places with a fork. Bake in a 400° oven until well browned, about 30 minutes. Let stand 5 minutes, then run a

knife between pan and bread. Turn bread out of pan onto a plate, then turn upright onto a rack; cool for at least 10 minutes. Serve in wedges, warm or at room temperature. If made ahead, cool completely; chill airtight up to 2 days. Makes 9 or 10 servings.

## SOUR SUNFLOWER PUMPERNICKEL BREAD

*For sourest flavor, let the beer mixture ferment the maximum time. Cracked rye, flax seed, and sunflower seed are sold in some supermarkets and most health-food stores.*

- 2 packages active dry yeast
- ¾ cup warm water (110°)
- ¾ cup stout (dark, strong beer) at room temperature
- 1 tablespoon sugar
- ¾ cup cracked rye
- 1½ cups rye flour
- ¾ cup unsalted sunflower seed
- ¼ cup flax seed
- 1 teaspoon salt
- 2 tablespoons salad oil
  About 1½ cups all-purpose flour
- 3 tablespoons sesame seed

In a large bowl, let 1 package yeast soften in ½ cup of the water. Mix in beer, sugar, cracked rye, and ½ cup of the rye flour. Cover with plastic wrap and let stand at room temperature until bubbly and sour smelling, 15 to 48 hours.

In a bowl, soften remaining yeast in remaining water. Stir into beer mixture with sunflower seed, flax seed, salt, and oil; mix. Stir in 1½ cups all-purpose flour; add remaining rye flour and mix with hands until evenly moistened. On a well-floured board, gently knead briefly until smooth and no longer sticky; add flour to prevent sticking. Shape dough into a round about 6½ inches in diameter. Sprinkle sesame seed on board, then gently roll dough in the seed, pressing lightly, until all sides are coated. Place on greased 12- by 15-inch baking sheet. Cover lightly with plastic wrap and let rise in a warm place until puffy, about 40 minutes.

Bake in a 350° oven until well browned, about 40 minutes. Remove from pan to a rack and let cool completely. Serve, or store airtight up to 3 days; freeze to store longer. Makes 1 loaf, about 2 pounds.

*Spoon cheese filling into dough-lined frying pan to make Russian bread. Pat filling smooth and top with a dough round. Brush top with egg yolk and crimp to seal; bake.*

*Rustic country loaves include (from left) cheese-filled Russian quick bread, seed-crusted German pumpernickel, and French walnut loaves served with soft, ripe cheese.*

## FRENCH WALNUT BREAD
### *Pain aux Noix*

*Chef-owner Michel Lorain serves this at La Côte Saint Jacques in Joigny, France.*

- 1 **cup coarsely broken walnuts**
- 1 **package active dry yeast**
- 1 **cup warm water (110°)**
- ¾ **teaspoon salt**
- 1 **teaspoon sugar**
- 1½ **cups** *each* **rye flour and all-purpose flour**
- 1 **tablespoon melted butter or margarine**

Place walnuts in an 8- or 9-inch wide pan. Bake in a 350° oven until lightly toasted, 10 to 12 minutes; shake often. Let cool.

In a large bowl, soften yeast in water. Stir in salt, sugar, rye flour, 1⅓ cups all-purpose flour, and walnuts. Mix well.

Scrape dough out onto a board coated with remaining all-purpose flour. Knead briefly until smooth and no longer sticky when lightly touched. Divide dough in half. Shape each portion of dough into a 2- by 10-inch log; place loaves about 4 inches apart on a greased 12- by 15-inch baking sheet. Cover lightly with plastic wrap; let rise in a warm place until slightly puffy, 30 to 40 minutes.

Brush top of loaves with melted butter. Bake in a 425° oven until loaves are well browned, about 20 minutes. Remove from pan and let cool on a rack. Cut into thin slices to serve. Or store airtight up to 3 days; freeze to store longer. Makes 2 loaves, each about ¾ pound.

# Four Ways to Use Wild Venison

THE HUNTER *was successful. The freezer holds another season's worth of venison, and it's time to consider ways to use this special treat.*

*However, venison from the wild throws the cook a few challenges, because its quality is unpredictable. The diet of these free-roaming creatures varies, size differs considerably, age can only be estimated, and the amount of exercise each animal gets is anybody's guess. Dressing and handling venison also affect its taste and texture.*

*So each season, and with each deer, you may find yourself dealing with a seemingly different animal. These recipes are designed to get the best from any situation you encounter.*

*For scrappy or tough pieces, grind them to make the base of a flavorful meat loaf, which can also be served cold and be more elegantly called a terrine or pâté. You can also thinly slice any part of the venison and quickly stir-fry it for tender results.*

*Very lean, less tender cuts from the shoulder and leg make a fine stew. Tender cuts from the loin grill well. Chop sizes from one deer vary, but if cut the same thickness, they cook at about the same rate.*

*For best-quality meat with little loss of juices, thaw frozen venison in a microwave oven according to the manufacturer's directions. This takes only a few minutes. We also recommend that you rinse venison cuts and pat dry to remove any stale odors; scrape off any bone crumbs left from cutting up the carcass.*

## VENISON LOAF

 2 tablespoons butter or margarine
 1 large onion, finely chopped
 1 tablespoon minced fresh ginger
 1 teaspoon *each* fennel seed and dry marjoram leaves
 1 large carrot, peeled
   Water
 2 large eggs
 1½ pounds ground venison
 ½ pound ground lean pork
 1 cup fine dry bread crumbs
 ⅓ cup milk
 ¾ teaspoon *each* salt and pepper
 8 to 10 slices bacon

In a 10- to 12-inch frying pan, melt butter over medium heat. Add onion; stir often until golden, about 10 minutes. Add ginger, fennel, and marjoram. Scrape mixture into a large bowl; set aside to cool.

Meanwhile, cut carrot into 3-inch lengths; then cut each section lengthwise into ¼-inch-thick slices. Rinse frying pan; add ½ inch water and bring to a boil over high heat. Add carrots and cook, covered, until tender when pierced, about 5 minutes. Drain and set aside.

To cooled onion mixture, add eggs and beat to blend. Add venison, pork, crumbs, milk, salt, and pepper; mix well with your hands or a fork. Set aside 2 slices bacon; arrange remaining slices side by side across the width of a 5- by 9-inch loaf pan, lining it. Cut 2 reserved slices in half crosswise and use to line ends of pan.

Smoothly spread half of the meat mixture in the pan. Lay carrot slices parallel to length of pan, covering meat layer. Spread remaining meat mixture evenly over carrots. Fold bacon ends over meat and pat level.

Place loaf pan in a 9- by 13-inch pan. Put both pans into a 350° oven. Fill larger pan with 1 inch boiling water. Bake loaf until meat feels firm in center when pressed and edges begin to pull from pan sides, about 1 hour. Remove loaf pan from water and let meat cool at least 20 minutes.

Tilt pan to drain off juices. Invert a platter over pan; hold together and flip over. Lift pan off loaf. Serve loaf warm or cold. To chill it, lightly cover and refrigerate at least 2 hours. If made ahead, wrap airtight and chill up to 5 days. Cut into thick slices. Makes 8 to 10 servings.

## BARBECUED VENISON RIB CHOPS

 8 venison rib chops, cut ¾ to 1 inch thick (2 to 2½ lb. total)
 ¼ cup fresh rosemary leaves
   About 2 tablespoons olive oil
   Salt and pepper

Rinse venison and pat dry. Trim most of the rim fat from chops and discard. Sprinkle ½ the rosemary onto meat on 1 side of each chop. With a flat mallet, firmly pound meat to hold herb in place. Turn chops over and repeat. Lightly brush chops all over with oil.

Place chops on a grill 4 to 6 inches above a solid bed of hot coals (you can hold your hand at grill level for only 2 to

*Draped with bacon, venison loaf sports a layer of sliced carrots through its middle. Serve cold with pickles, bread, and butter.*

*Gently pound rosemary leaves into each chop, then brush lightly with oil. From one deer, chop sizes vary.*

3 seconds). Arrange smaller chops near outside edge of coals, larger ones in the center. Cook until browned and done as you like; turn as needed. Chops should be red (cut to test) for medium-rare, about 4 minutes total; pale red for medium, about 6 minutes total (well-done venison is dry and firm). Season with salt and pepper. Serves 4 to 6, depending on size of chops.

## BRAISED VENISON WITH VEGETABLES

2½ pounds fat-trimmed and boned venison round steak (or other leg or shoulder cut)
   About 3½ cups regular-strength beef or chicken broth
2 tablespoons olive or salad oil
3 tablespoons distilled white vinegar
1 large can (7 oz.) diced green chilies
1 tablespoon mustard seed
4 small (about 2-inch diameter) thin-skinned potatoes, scrubbed and cut in half
4 small (about 3 inch wide) turnips, peeled and cut in half
4 medium-size (about ¾ lb. total) carrots, peeled
2 tablespoons cornstarch mixed with 3 tablespoons water
   Mustard greens (recipe follows)
   Salt and pepper

Rinse venison, pat dry, and cut into 1½-inch cubes. In a 5- to 6-quart pan, combine venison, ½ cup broth, and oil. Cover and bring to a boil over high heat; reduce heat and simmer for 30 minutes. Remove lid and boil over high heat until meat starts to sizzle and brown, about 7 minutes; turn heat down to medium and stir frequently until drippings are dark brown and meat is glazed with brown.

Add 3 cups broth, vinegar, chilies, and mustard seed; stir to release browned bits in pan. Lay potatoes and turnips on top of meat, and then lay carrots on vegetables. Bring to a boil, cover, and simmer over low heat until meat and vegetables are tender when pierced, about 40 minutes.

With a slotted spoon, lift vegetables and meat from pan and arrange on a platter; keep warm. Skim and discard fat from pan juices. On high heat, boil the juices until reduced to about 2 cups. Stirring, add cornstarch mixture to juices. When boiling resumes, pour into a small bowl; keep warm. Cook mustard greens as directed below; add to platter. Serve stew with sauce, salt, and pepper to taste. Makes 4 to 6 servings.

**Mustard greens.** Wash 1 pound **mustard greens;** drain well. Break or cut off coarse stems and discard. Stack greens and cut into wide strips. If made ahead, enclose in a plastic bag and chill up to 6 hours.

After venison and vegetables (preceding) are cooked, bring ¼ cup **water** to boiling in a 4- to 5-quart pan over high heat. Add greens and stir until limp and wilted, about 3 minutes. Lift out with a slotted spoon and add to meat platter.

## VENISON STIR-FRY

   About ⅓ cup regular-strength beef or chicken broth
2 tablespoons soy sauce
3 tablespoons orange marmalade
1 tablespoon cornstarch
1 pound boneless venison, fat trimmed
2 tablespoons minced fresh ginger
3 tablespoons salad oil
1 medium-size onion, cut into 1-inch wedges
   About ¾ pound edible-pod peas, ends and strings removed

Combine ¼ cup broth, soy sauce, and marmalade. In another cup, mix remaining broth with cornstarch until blended.

Rinse venison and pat dry. Cut meat across the grain into ⅛-inch-thick slanting slices, each about 2 inches long. Mix pieces with ginger.

Place wok or 10- to 12-inch frying pan over high heat. When wok is hot, add 1 tablespoon oil. When oil is hot, add onion. Stir-fry until onion is lightly tinged with brown, about 2 minutes; pour onion from pan and set aside.

Add another 1 tablespoon oil to pan; when hot, add half the venison mixture and stir-fry until meat is lightly browned, about 2 minutes; add to onions. Repeat, using remaining 1 tablespoon of oil and venison mixture; add to meat and onions.

Pour marmalade mixture into wok, add peas, and stir until they turn bright green, about 2 minutes. Add meat, onions, and cornstarch mixture to pan; stir until boiling. Pour onto a platter. Makes 4 servings.

*Chinese pea pods simmer in sauce until tender-crisp; add cooked, sliced venison and stir-fried onions.*

# Quick Teamwork: Cheese & Salad

ASSERTIVE CHEESES *give these salads a pungent spark. All three have crisp bread companions; two feature fresh fruit.*

*Showy but quick to assemble, the salads fit easily into hectic schedules. Serve them for a first course or a light meal.*

## ROMAINE SALAD WITH BLUE CHEESE TOAST

- ½ cup sugar
- 1 cup pecan halves
- 4 slices sourdough bread (each about 4 by 5 inches, ½ inch thick)
- ¾ cup crumbled blue cheese (such as Roquefort or Stilton)
- 2 quarts romaine lettuce, washed, crisped, and torn into 2-inch pieces
  Blue cheese vinaigrette (recipe follows)

Place sugar and pecans in an 8- to 10-inch frying pan over medium-high heat. Cook, stirring often, until sugar is melted and amber in color, 6 to 8 minutes. Spread on a buttered 12-inch square of foil. Let cool, then break nuts apart.

Trim and discard crusts from bread, then cut each slice into 2 triangles. Place on a rack on a 12- by 15-inch baking sheet and bake in a 325° oven until very crisp, about 20 minutes. Lightly press cheese onto toast, then continue to bake until cheese is melted, about 5 minutes.

Mix romaine and pecans with vin-

*Pomegranate seeds and cheese shreds accent pear-spinach salad accompanied by a sharp cheddar cheese puff.*

aigrette in a bowl. Place equal portions of salad and toast on 4 salad plates. Serves 4.

**Blue cheese vinaigrette.** In a bowl, whisk together 3 tablespoons **red wine vinegar** and ⅓ cup **salad oil.** Stir in ½ cup **blue cheese** chunks. Add **pepper** to taste.

## PEAR-POMEGRANATE SALAD WITH CHEDDAR CHEESE PUFFS

- 3 medium-size soft-ripe pears
- 1 tablespoon lemon juice
- 2 cups lightly packed spinach leaves, washed and crisped
- ½ cup pomegranate seeds
- ⅓ cup long shreds sharp cheddar cheese
  Madeira dressing (recipe follows)
  Salt and pepper
  Cheddar cheese puffs (recipe follows)

Halve and core pears. Place in a bowl with lemon juice; turn gently to coat.

Place a pear half and an equal portion of spinach on each of 6 salad plates. Sprinkle with pomegranate seeds and cheese. Offer dressing and salt and pepper to add individually. Serve with cheddar cheese puffs. Makes 6 servings.

**Madeira dressing.** In a small bowl, whisk together 1½ tablespoons *each* **lemon juice** and minced **Major Grey chutney,** and 2 tablespoons *each* **salad oil** and **madeira.**

**Cheddar cheese puffs.** In a 1- to 2-quart pan over medium-high heat, bring ½ cup **water,** ¼ cup (⅛ lb.) **butter** or margarine, and ¼ teaspoon **salt** (optional) to a boil. Boil until butter melts. At once add ½ cup **all-purpose flour** and beat with a spoon until mixture forms a ball and leaves sides of pan. Remove from heat and add 2 **large eggs,** 1 at a time, beating after each until dough is glossy. Let cool 10 minutes.

*Blue cheese adds pungency to toast and romaine mixed with caramelized pecans.*

Spoon dough in 6 equal portions, about 3 inches apart, onto a greased 12- by 15-inch baking sheet. Place a ¾-inch cube of **sharp cheddar cheese** in center of each portion of dough. Pull dough over cheese to cover completely.

Bake in upper third of a 425° oven for 15 minutes. Reduce heat to 375°; bake until golden brown, about 10 minutes longer. Sprinkle with ¼ cup shredded **sharp cheddar cheese.** Bake until cheese melts, about 2 minutes. Serve hot.

If made ahead, cool on a rack, wrap airtight, and chill until next day. Reheat on baking sheet in a 350° oven until hot, about 8 minutes.

## GOAT CHEESE-APPLE SALAD

- 3 **medium-size red apples**
- 1 **tablespoon lemon juice**
- 6 **to 12 large butter lettuce leaves, washed and crisped**
  **Baguette batons (recipe follows)**
- 6 **round, firm, ripened goat cheeses (1½ to 3 oz. each) such as crottin or chavignon**
  **Honey-mustard dressing (recipe follows)**
  **Pepper**

Quarter and core apples; slice lengthwise ⅓ inch thick. Mix gently in a bowl with lemon juice. Arrange apples, lettuce, and baguette batons on 6 salad plates.

Place cheeses on a 12- by 15-inch baking sheet and broil 2 inches from heat until lightly browned, about 5 minutes. Place 1 cheese on lettuce on each plate. Offer honey-mustard dressing and pepper to season. Makes 6 servings.

**Baguette batons.** From a **slender baguette** (about 8 oz., 3-inch diameter) cut 2 portions, *each* 6 inches long. Cut each portion lengthwise into 9 equal pieces. Brush cut surfaces with 3 tablespoons melted **butter** or margarine. Place cut side up on a 12- by 15-inch baking sheet and bake in a 350° oven until golden, about 15 minutes.

**Honey-mustard dressing.** In a small bowl, whisk together 3 tablespoons *each* **salad oil** and **cider vinegar,** 1 tablespoon **honey,** and 1½ tablespoons **Dijon mustard.**

*Crunchy baguette batons and crisp apples contrast with soft, warm goat cheese.*

# Semi-Serious Pancakes

LACED WITH FALL FLAVORS *and served with a collection of condiments, pancakes are the focus of this casual cook-it-yourself party that takes the pressure off the hosts.*

*Try this menu for a weekend brunch, after a rousing football game, or even for a midnight gala following a play or movie.*

*The mainstays are three pancake batters: one studded with corn kernels, another loaded with crunchy wild rice, and a soufflé version mixed with red peppers. You cook some of the pancake ingredients the day before, then assemble the rest at the last minute—but make sure all the elements are measured and ready to go. Each recipe makes 4 servings.*

*For cooking, set up an electric griddle in the family room or dining room, or use frying pans on the stove. You can bake one of each pancake, experiment with several toppings, and then cook up batches of diners' favorites. Many of the toppings are purchased ready to eat and require little preparation.*

*Splurge on dessert. Pecan pie, caramel ice cream, and pears make choices for all.*

Guests flip their choice of flavored pancakes on the griddle.

---

## FALL PANCAKE PARTY FOR 12

**Fresh Corn Pancakes**
**Wild Rice Pancakes**
**Red Pepper Soufflé Pancakes**
Sour Cream      Chopped Onions
**Smoked Trout or Alaskan Cod**
**Chèvre      Salmon Caviar**
**Pickled Herring Sauce**
Salad Greens      Olive Oil      Vinegar
**Hot Pecan Pie      Caramel Ice Cream**
**Ripe Pears**
**Dry Gewürztraminer or**
**Dry Sparkling Wine**

---

Cook corn and rice up to a day ahead. The batters go together quickly. Group bowls of batter—each with a ladle—next to the griddle. Place several wide spatulas and a small bowl of oil with a brush alongside.

For the toppings, buy 2 or 3 cups sour cream, a medium-size red onion to slice thin, ¾ to 1 pound smoked fish (remove skin and any bones), ¾ to 1 pound unripened chèvre (goat cheese), 4 to 6 ounces salmon caviar, and ingredients for the herring sauce. Present each food in a separate dish, or arrange together on trays.

For individual salads, offer a large basket of washed and crisped salad greens (allow about 1½ cups lightly packed greens per person) and cruets of oil and vinegar. If you serve pecan pie, warm it slowly in the oven while guests enjoy the party.

**To cook pancakes,** heat an electric griddle to 400° or place 1 or 2 frying pans, 10- to 12-inch size, over medium heat. Lightly brush griddle with **salad oil.** For each pancake, ladle 2 to 3 tablespoons **batter** onto griddle, allowing about 1 inch between cakes (use a 2- to 3-tablespoon-size ladle or a ¼-cup measure, filling ½ to ¾ full). Quickly spread cakes to ¼-inch thickness with the back of ladle or spoon. Cook pancakes, turning once, until each side is golden, about 5 minutes total. Serve hot. Repeat with remaining batter.

## FRESH CORN PANCAKES

    1  medium-size red bell pepper,
       stemmed, seeded, and diced
    2  tablespoons butter or margarine
 1½  cups fresh or frozen corn kernels
    ½  cup minced onion
 ⅔  cup yellow cornmeal or polenta
 ⅓  cup regular-strength chicken broth
    4  large eggs
    3  tablespoons grated parmesan
       cheese
       Salt

In a 10- to 12-inch frying pan over medium-high heat, cook pepper in butter until limp and just beginning to brown, about 5 minutes; stir often. With a slotted spoon, set pepper aside.

Add corn and onion to pan, and cook in remaining butter until onion is limp and just beginning to brown, about 7 minutes; stir often.

Add corn mixture to a food processor or blender along with cornmeal, chicken broth, eggs, and cheese. Whirl mixture just enough to chop corn coarsely; do not purée. Stir in cooked pepper. Add salt to taste. (If made ahead, cover and chill up to 24 hours; stir before using.)

Cook pancakes as directed, preceding. Makes 2 to 2½ dozen pancakes.— *Michael Roberts, Los Angeles.*

## WILD RICE PANCAKES

    ½  cup minced onion
    1  tablespoon butter or margarine
 1⅛  cups water
 ⅔  cup wild rice (4-oz. package),
       rinsed and drained
    1  cup all-purpose flour
    1  teaspoon baking powder
    3  large eggs
 1¼  cups regular-strength chicken
       broth
       Salt

In a 2- to 3-quart pan on medium-high heat, cook onion in butter until limp and just beginning to brown, about 5 minutes; stir often.

Add water to pan and bring to boiling on high heat. Add rice; return to boiling. Cover pan and reduce heat; simmer until rice is tender to bite, about 50 minutes. Let rice cool to room temperature. (If made ahead, cover and chill up to overnight.) Drain any liquid off rice.

In a bowl, mix flour with baking powder. Add rice, eggs, and broth; stir until batter is evenly moistened. Add salt to taste. Cook pancakes as directed, preceding. Makes 2 to 2½ dozen pancakes.

*Top tiny autumn-flavor pancakes of red pepper, wild rice, and corn with savory condiments for a brunch-or-later party.*

## RED PEPPER SOUFFLÉ PANCAKES

- 1 jar (7 oz.) roasted red peppers, or ¾ cup roasted, peeled, stemmed, and seeded red bell peppers
- ½ cup chopped onion
- 1 tablespoon butter or margarine
- 6 large eggs, separated
- 2 tablespoons salty black olives, such as calamata, pitted
- ½ cup all-purpose flour
- ¾ teaspoon baking powder
- ¼ teaspoon baking soda
- ½ teaspoon cream of tartar
  Salt

In a food processor or blender, purée peppers; set aside. In a 10- to 12-inch frying pan over medium-high heat, cook onion in butter until slightly browned, about 5 minutes; stir often. Add onions to pepper purée along with egg yolks, olives, flour, baking powder, and baking soda. Whirl mixture just enough to blend ingredients.

In a large bowl, beat egg whites and cream of tartar with an electric mixer until whites form stiff, moist peaks. Gently but thoroughly fold pepper mixture into egg whites. Add salt to taste. Cook pancakes as directed (preceding). Makes 2 to 2½ dozen pancakes.

## PICKLED HERRING SAUCE

- 1 jar (6 oz.) pickled herring in vinegar, drained and chopped
- 1 tablespoon sherry vinegar or dry sherry
- ½ cup whipping cream (optional)

In a bowl, mix together chopped herring, sherry, and cream. Use, or cover and chill up to 2 days. Makes ⅔ to ¾ cup.

# Pesto without Basil

PESTO MEANS "POUNDED" in Italian. In culinary terms, it usually denotes a basil sauce made by pulverizing the ingredients in a mortar and pestle. To create the pesto variations given here, we've used other fresh herbs.

In a food processor or blender, grind together mint, cilantro, chili, and garlic with oil for a spicy hot yet refreshingly cool sauce. Or blend intensely flavored, small-leafed herbs such as thyme, oregano, marjoram, and tarragon with mild spinach leaves, cheese, and oil.

Keep the sauces in the refrigerator or freezer, ready for salads, pasta, or vegetables. The sauces darken slightly when stored; to help preserve color, cover top with a thin layer of oil.

## CILANTRO-MINT-CHILI PESTO

- 1 cup lightly packed fresh cilantro (coriander) leaves
- 1 cup lightly packed fresh mint leaves
- 2 or 3 fresh jalapeño chilies, seeded, stemmed, coarsely chopped
- 2 cloves garlic
- ½ cup salad oil
  Salt

In a blender or food processor, combine cilantro, mint, chilies, garlic, and oil; whirl until puréed. Add salt to taste. Use at once; or place in small jars, cover, and refrigerate up to 1 week or freeze up to 1 month (thaw to use). Makes ¾ cup.

## SPINACH-HERB PESTO

- 1½ cups lightly packed washed, drained spinach leaves
- ¼ cup lightly packed fresh tarragon, thyme, marjoram, or oregano leaves, tough stems discarded
- ½ cup lightly packed grated parmesan cheese
- ½ cup olive oil

Put spinach, tarragon, cheese, and oil in blender or food processor. Whirl until spinach is finely chopped. Use at once;

From the garden or market, gather fresh mint, cilantro, green chili, and garlic. Purée with oil to make pesto; use as a salad dressing over sliced tomatoes, cucumbers, and shrimp—or mix with pasta and hot cooked vegetables.

or place in small jars, cover, and refrigerate up to 1 week or freeze up to 1 month (thaw to use). Makes 1 cup.

## WAYS TO USE

**On pasta.** Mix 2 to 3 tablespoons **Cilantro-Mint-Chili Pesto** or Spinach-Herb Pesto with ¼ cup melted **butter** or margarine. Spoon over 4 cups hot, cooked (8 oz. dry, 12 to 14 oz. fresh), drained **capellini** or spaghetti; mix noodles with pesto. Add **salt, pepper,** more pesto, and grated **parmesan cheese** to taste. Makes 4 servings.

**On vegetables.** Mix 1 to 2 tablespoons **Cilantro-Mint-Chili Pesto** or Spinach-Herb Pesto with 2 tablespoons melted **butter** or margarine. Mix with 1 pound hot, cooked **green beans,** sliced summer squash, or peas. Makes 4 servings.

**As a dressing.** Mix 2 tablespoons **Cilantro-Mint-Chili Pesto** or Spinach-Herb Pesto with ¼ cup **salad oil** and 2 tablespoons **white wine vinegar.** Mix with **lettuce** (washed, crisped, torn into bite-size pieces). Or pour over sliced **tomatoes, cucumber,** and **avocados** or cold cooked **chicken** or seafood. Makes about ½ cup dressing.

# Turning Garlic Sweet & Unassertive

**T**WO WHOLE HEADS OF GARLIC? *There's that much in each of these recipes, but slow roasting disarms its hot, raw assertiveness and turns it into a subtle, surprisingly sweet condiment or seasoning.*

*The roasting procedure is simple. Cut garlic heads in half and bake them, cut side down, on an oiled pan. The surfaces of the cut cloves turn a rich brown and become almost sticky.*

*At this point, caramelized garlic is delicious as is, offered with roast meats, or to spread on toasted bread. Or use it to enhance these recipes for tamed aïoli, tantalizing prune and cream cheese appetizers, or aromatic pizza.*

## CARAMELIZED GARLIC CLOVES

Cut 2 large heads **garlic** (each about 2½ inches wide) in two crosswise about ⅓ from the root end. Pour 1 tablespoon **salad oil** in an 8- or 9-inch wide baking pan. Place garlic, cut side down, in pan. Bake in a 350° oven until center cloves are very soft when pressed and cut sides are browned, about 1 hour.

To serve, offer garlic warm, allowing ½ head for each serving. To eat or use in the following recipes, pluck cloves from head, or, to extract quickly, squeeze whole head to force out soft cloves. (Remove any bits of husk.) If made ahead, cover and chill up to 3 days; freeze for longer storage. Makes about ¼ cup.

## CARAMELIZED GARLIC AÏOLI

*Serve this mellow aïoli as a dip for cherry tomatoes, red or green bell pepper strips, or cold cooked artichokes or green beans.*

- About ¼ cup Caramelized Garlic Cloves (recipe precedes)
- 1½ tablespoons lemon juice
- 1 large egg
- ½ cup salad oil
- ½ cup olive oil
- 1 to 2 tablespoons water
- Salt

In a blender or food processor, combine garlic, lemon juice, and egg; whirl until smooth. Combine salad oil and olive oil in a glass measuring cup. With motor on medium-high, pour in blended oils in a thin, steady stream. As mixture thickens, add oil faster but not quickly enough to form a puddle.

When sauce is too thick to incorporate oil, stir in water by hand, a spoonful at a time. With motor on, add remaining oil slowly. (In a blender, with motor off, you may need to stir the mixture by hand to get it moving.) Add salt to taste.

Serve, or, if made ahead, cover and chill up to 4 days. Makes 1⅔ cups, about 12 servings.

## CARAMELIZED GARLIC & CREAM CHEESE PRUNES

- 30 pitted prunes (8 to 12 oz. total)
- ½ cup dry red wine
- 1 large package (8 oz.) cream cheese, at room temperature
- About ¼ cup Caramelized Garlic Cloves (recipe precedes)
- 15 slices bacon, cut in half

In a 1- to 1½-quart pan, combine prunes and wine. Bring to a simmer; cover and cook over low heat just until prunes are plump, 7 to 9 minutes.

With a mixer, blend cream cheese and garlic until smooth. Drain prunes and make a depression in center of each. Fill depression in each prune with about 1 teaspoon of the cheese mixture. Wrap a half-slice of bacon around each prune, bacon ends on bottom.

Set prunes, cheese side down, on a rack in a 10- by 15-inch broiler or baking pan. Broil about 4 inches from heat until bacon just begins to brown, 3 to 4 minutes. Turn over and continue broiling until bacon is crisp, 3 to 4 minutes longer. Let stand on pan until cheese firms slightly, about 2 minutes, then transfer to platter and serve warm with wooden picks. Makes 30 appetizers; allow 2 or 3 for a serving.

## CARAMELIZED GARLIC PIZZA

- About 3 tablespoons olive oil
- 1 loaf (1 lb.) frozen white bread dough, thawed
- About ¼ cup Caramelized Garlic Cloves (recipe precedes)
- 6 ounces sliced mozzarella cheese
- ¼ cup fresh basil leaves, cut in thin strips, or 2 tablespoons dry basil
- 3 ounces thinly sliced dry salami, cut in slivers
- ½ cup grated parmesan cheese

Drizzle 1 tablespoon of the oil over each of 2 baking pans, each 10 by 15 inches. Cut dough into 4 equal pieces. Put 2 pieces on each pan and shape into

*Mellow, sweet garlic seasons the aïoli dip for artichokes and other vegetables.*

*Garlic-laced cream cheese fills bacon-wrapped prunes. Serve warm with wooden picks.*

6-inch rounds. Pat a slight depression, 4 inches across, in center of each round. Brush dough with remaining oil. Let rise in a warm place until puffy, about 30 minutes.

Evenly distribute equal portions of caramelized garlic over the depression on each pizza. Lay mozzarella evenly over each round. Then sprinkle evenly with basil, salami, and parmesan. Bake in a 450° oven until crust is dark golden brown, 10 to 14 minutes. Alternate pan positions halfway through baking. Serve hot. Serves 4. — *Irene Chriss, Albany, Calif.*

# Four-Dish Russian Menu

THE MELLOW FLAVORS *of oven-braised brisket with slowly cooked vegetables and barley pilaf make these Russian dishes satisfying fare. Ingredients and techniques are familiar to Westerners, but some pairings on the menu may be surprising.*

### RUSSIAN MENU

**Pickles with Honey & Sour Cream**
**Oven-Braised Brisket**
**Sautéed Parsnips & Carrots**
**Barley & Onion Pilaf**
**Vanilla Ice Cream with Brandy**

*Together, these dishes create a dinner for 8. We were introduced to them at Bellevue, a Russian restaurant in Helsinki.*

## PICKLES WITH HONEY & SOUR CREAM

6 large (about 4 inch) whole kosher-style dill pickles, quartered lengthwise
1 cup sour cream
¼ cup honey

Place 3 pieces of pickle on each salad plate; spoon 2 tablespoons of sour cream alongside. Drizzle honey on cream. Eat with knife and fork, pushing pickles through cream and honey. Serves 8.

## OVEN-BRAISED BRISKET

2 tablespoons salad oil
1 center-cut piece beef brisket (2¾ to 3 lb.), excess fat trimmed off
4 large onions (about 2¾ lb.)
¼ cup (⅛ lb.) butter or margarine
1 can or jar (32 oz.) sauerkraut
1¾ cups regular-strength beef broth
Pepper
Parsley sprigs (optional)

Pour 1 tablespoon of the oil into a 5- to 6-quart ovenproof pan on medium-high heat. When oil is hot, add beef; cook until well browned on both sides, turning once, about 10 minutes total. Remove meat from pan and set aside.

While meat browns, thinly slice onions. After meat is removed, add 2 tablespoons of the butter, the remaining 1 tablespoon oil, and onions to pan; cook, stirring occasionally, until onions are very limp, about 25 minutes. Drain sauerkraut; stir into onions along with broth. Set beef on top of onion mixture. Cover and bake in a 350° oven until meat is very tender when pierced, 2½ to 2¾ hours. Turn meat several times.

At this point, you can let dish cool, then cover and chill until next day. To reheat, bring to a boil, covered, over medium heat; simmer until meat is hot in center, 10 to 15 minutes (cut to test).

To serve, lift meat onto a board and cut across the grain into ½-inch-thick slices. Season onion mixture to taste with pepper; lift with a slotted spoon from pan (reserve juices) and arrange in a wide band in center of a large platter. Overlap meat slices on top. Surround with Sautéed Parsnips & Carrots, if desired.

Boil pan juices, uncovered, over high heat until reduced to ¾ cup, about 2 minutes. Drain juices from platter into pan; boil again until reduced to ¾ cup. Add remaining 2 tablespoons butter; stir until mixed. Spoon sauce over meat; garnish with parsley. Serves 8.

## SAUTÉED PARSNIPS & CARROTS

5 *each* medium-size parsnips and carrots (about 1½ lb. of *each*)
7 tablespoons butter or margarine
⅓ cup minced parsley
Salt and pepper

Peel parsnips and carrots. Shred in long strips with an Oriental shredder, or coarsely shred or cut into julienne strips in a food processor or by hand.

In a 12- to 14-inch frying pan, melt half of the butter over medium-high heat. Add half of the parsnips and carrots; cook, turning often with a wide spatula, until vegetables are tender-crisp to bite, about 8 minutes. Spoon into a bowl and keep warm; repeat with remaining butter, parsnips and carrots. Stir in parsley, and season to taste with salt and pepper. Makes 8 servings.

## BARLEY & ONION PILAF

2 tablespoons butter or margarine
2 tablespoons salad oil
2 large onions (about 1½ lb.), halved lengthwise and thinly sliced
1½ cups pearl barley, rinsed
3¼ cups regular-strength beef broth
Salt and pepper
Parsley sprigs (optional)

In a 10- to 12-inch frying pan, melt butter in oil over medium-high heat. Add onions and cook, stirring, until limp and golden, 10 to 15 minutes.

Mix in barley and cook, stirring, until slightly toasted, about 3 minutes. Add broth and bring to a boil over high heat; reduce heat and simmer, covered, until broth is absorbed and barley is tender to bite, about 45 minutes. Season to taste with salt and pepper. Garnish with parsley. Makes 8 servings.

*Spoon shiny sauce of pan juices and butter over baked beef brisket on bed of sauerkraut and onions. Shredded parsnips and carrots surround meat; barley pilaf accompanies.*

# Marzipan Menagerie

ASSEMBLY-LINE *techniques make these Halloween confections quick to produce. An 8-ounce can of almond paste makes enough marzipan for examples of two separate shapes. Let the artist choose simple designs, such as moons, or more complex ones, such as witches.*

*To slice candies, use a thin, sharp knife (clean it often). And clean paintbrush well with water between color changes.*

## MARZIPAN HALLOWEEN CANDIES

1   **can (8 oz.) almond paste**
2   **tablespoons light corn syrup**
2   **cups sifted powdered sugar**
1   **large egg white**

In a food processor or with a mixer, thoroughly blend almond paste, syrup, and sugar; mixture should hold together readily when patted. If crumbly, beat in 1 to 2 teaspoons egg white, 1 at a time.

Divide marzipan into 2 equal portions. Color, flavor, shape, and slice each portion in 1 of the following ways. Use remaining egg white to join pieces or when decorating.

To decorate candies as shown, make square or round depressions with the corresponding end of a chopstick. For triangles and dots, use the pointed end of a punch-type can opener. Use a knife for thin lines. To color depressions, dip tools in egg white between each pressing, then paint designs with a small brush. Store candies airtight up to 1 week.

**Crescent moons.** Put ½ recipe **Marzipan** in a food processor or mixer bowl. Add 1 teaspoon grated **lemon peel** and 5 drops **yellow food coloring;** blend thoroughly. Roll into a 1¼-inch-diameter cylinder. Press the handle of a wooden spoon down the length of cylinder, making a groove ⅓ inch deep. Cut cylinder crosswise into ½-inch-thick slices; pinch each to make a curved half-moon. Makes about 18.

**Not-quite-black cats.** Put ½ recipe **Marzipan** in a food processor or mixer bowl; add 1½ teaspoons **unsweetened cocoa** and blend thoroughly. Pinch off about 1 teaspoon marzipan and set aside.

Roll remaining marzipan into a 1-inch-diameter cylinder. Press a chopstick down the length of cylinder, making a groove about ⅓ inch deep. Pinch edges of groove to make pointed ears. Cut cylinder crosswise into ½-inch-thick slices.

*Marzipan menagerie comes from almond paste dough. An adult can supervise slicing to make five fanciful shapes.*

Pat chin end of each piece to make round. Paint eyes with **green food coloring.** Roll reserved marzipan into tiny balls equal to the number of cats. Dip base of balls into egg white; press noses onto faces. Makes about 24.

**Haunted houses.** Divide ½ recipe **Marzipan** in 3 equal parts; join 2 parts and shape into a block 1 by 1 by about 5 inches. Put remaining part in a food processor or mixer bowl. Add 1 teaspoon **unsweetened cocoa** and blend thoroughly. Shape into a rectangle that is ¾ by 1¼ inches wide and half as long as the plain rectangle.

Cut chocolate rectangle diagonally through center to make 2 prisms. Brush the length of 1 side of plain rectangle with **egg white.** Set prisms, cut down and end to end, on top to make a roof; press gently. Cut marzipan crosswise into ½-inch thick slices. Paint windows with **red food coloring.** Makes about 20.

**Jack-o'-lanterns.** Put ½ recipe **Marzipan** in a food processor or mixer bowl, add 1 teaspoon **grated orange peel,** and mix well. Set aside 1½ tablespoons. To remainder add 3 drops *each* **red** and **yellow food coloring;** mix well. Remove orange marzipan from mixing container. Rinse and dry container, and put the reserved marzipan in it; add 4 drops

**green food coloring** and mix well.

Roll orange marzipan into a 1½-inch-diameter cylinder. Press a chopstick down its length, making a groove ¼ inch deep. Roll green marzipan into a cylinder as long as orange piece; pinch the length of 1 side of green cylinder to give it a V shape. Brush groove in orange cylinder with **egg white.** Lay green cylinder, V edge down, into groove on orange cylinder; press gently.

Cut cylinders crosswise into ⅓-inch-thick slices. Pat chin end of each to make round. Paint features with **green food coloring.** Makes about 15.

**Witches.** Put ½ recipe **Marzipan** in a food processor or mixer bowl, add ¼ teaspoon **anise extract** (optional); mix well. Divide marzipan in 3 equal pieces. Set aside 1 piece. Return 1 piece to mixing container; add 1 drop **red food coloring.** Mix; set aside. Rinse and dry container. Add 1 more piece marzipan and 12 drops **green food coloring;** mix.

Pinch off ½ teaspoon pink marzipan and set aside; roll remaining pink marzipan into a 1-inch-diameter cylinder. Shape green marzipan into a prism 1½ inches wide and as long. Brush top of the pink cylinder with **egg white.** Gently press the green cylinder onto egg white on pink one.

Cut marzipan crosswise into ⅓-inch-thick slices. Roll reserved pink marzipan into tiny balls equal in number to the marzipan slices. Dip base of balls in egg white and press onto slices for noses. Paint eyes with **green food coloring.** Press plain marzipan through a garlic press; attach to heads for hair, using egg white to glue. Makes about 10.

*Egg white cements separate parts together, seals food coloring into indentations made with pointed end of punch-type can opener.*

# More October Recipes

OTHER RECIPES *highlighted in October included a pumpkin soup served in mini-pumpkins, a salad that looks like a rose, an exceptional stew featuring oysters and artichokes, and seafood brochettes for a special occasion.*

## MINI-PUMPKIN SOUP

*Single-serving pumpkins make whimsical containers for soup. Hollow out the shells and cook the flesh with onion and pimientos for seasoning. These tiny pumpkins should be in grocery stores this month.*

- 6 mini-pumpkins (Munchkin or Jack Be Little), each ¾ to 1 pound
- 1 large onion, sliced
- 2 tablespoons butter or margarine
- 1 large jar (4 oz.) diced pimientos, drained
- ¼ teaspoon pepper
- 1¾ cups regular-strength chicken broth
- 1 cup milk
  Boiling water
  Whole or ground nutmeg

Cut through top of each pumpkin to make a lid about 3 inches in diameter. Trim undersides of lids so they're ½ inch

*Lift tiny pumpkin's lid to uncover soup. Top with freshly grated nutmeg to taste.*

thick; reserve pumpkin flesh. Scrape out and discard seeds and strings from pumpkins.

With a short, sharp knife, hollow out pumpkins to leave ½-inch-thick shells. Cut up any large pieces of pumpkin flesh. Set aside tops, shells, and flesh.

In a 3- to 4-quart pan over medium-high heat, cook onion in butter until limp, about 10 minutes; stir often. Add pimientos, pepper, broth, and pumpkin flesh. Bring to a boil over high heat, then simmer, covered, until pumpkin is very tender when pierced, about 15 minutes.

In a blender or food processor, whirl soup until smoothly puréed. Return to pan with milk. Over medium-high heat, stir soup until steaming.

Fill pumpkin shells with boiling water; drain. Place shells on plates; fill shells with soup. Top with lids. Offer nutmeg to grate into soup. Makes 6 servings.

## CONFETTI ROSE SALAD

*Loosely reshape butter lettuce leaves into a head to create the rose shape that distinguishes the look of this salad.*

- 4 large oranges
- ¾ pound thinly sliced cooked ham, cut into about ¼-inch squares
- 3 tablespoons salad oil
- 4 small heads (5 to 6 oz. each) butter lettuce, cored, rinsed, dried, and crisped
- 1 pound jicama, peeled and cut into thin (2 by 3 inch) wedges
- 16 cherry tomatoes, halved
- 4 hard-cooked eggs, peeled and coarsely chopped
- 1 can (3½ oz.) pitted ripe olives, diced
  Confetti dressing (recipe follows)
  Salt and pepper

Cut off and discard peel and white membrane from oranges. Slice fruit crosswise, then cut rounds in half. Set aside.

In a 10- to 12-inch frying pan, cook ham in oil over medium heat (or lower, if meat pops out of pan), stirring often until ham is lightly browned and crisp, about 15 minutes. Drain ham on paper towels.

Reserve for another use 2 or 3 of the largest lettuce leaves from each head. On each of 4 dinner plates, arrange 3 or 4 medium-large leaves from each head to form a cup. In center, arrange smaller leaves to resemble a rose. Arrange jicama, orange, and tomatoes around lettuce. Sprinkle ¼ of ham, egg, and olives over each salad, then moisten equally with dressing. Add salt and pepper to taste. Serves 4.—*Bill Maldonado, Pasadena, Calif.*

**Confetti dressing.** Mix ¾ cup **olive oil,** ¼ cup **white wine vinegar,** 1 tablespoon thinly sliced **chives** or green onions, and 1 teaspoon chopped **fresh thyme leaves** or ½ teaspoon dry thyme leaves.

## OYSTER & ARTICHOKE STEW

*They're not beautiful, but if you love oysters, they attract you to an occasional splurge. The same might be said of artichokes. Put them together, and they make this exceptional stew. You start with oysters in the shell, scrub them, then steam them open in the stew.*

- 4 medium-size (about 3-inch diameter) artichokes
  Water
- ¾ teaspoon dry thyme leaves
- ¾ teaspoon ground nutmeg
- ¼ cup (⅛ lb.) butter or margarine
- ½ cup chopped green onion
- ½ cup finely chopped parsley
- 2 large cloves garlic, minced or pressed
- ¼ to ½ teaspoon cayenne
- 3 bottles (8 oz. each) clam juice
- 2 dozen medium-size (about 4 inch long) Pacific or Eastern oysters, scrubbed
- 1 cup whipping cream

Rinse artichokes, then pull off and discard tough outer leaves. Put artichokes in a 5- to 6-quart pan with 2 quarts water and ½ teaspoon *each* of the thyme and nutmeg. Cover and bring to a boil on high heat; reduce heat and boil until artichoke bottoms are very tender when pierced, about 45 minutes. Drain artichokes and let cool. Scrape soft pulp from leaves and return pulp to pan; discard leaves. Scrape out and discard fuzzy centers of artichoke bottoms; cut off stems and add to pulp. Set bottoms aside.

To pulp in pan, add butter, green onion, parsley, garlic, remaining thyme and nutmeg, and cayenne. Cook, stirring, until butter melts. Add clam juice and 2 cups water and bring to a boil on high heat. Cover, reduce heat, and simmer to blend flavors, about 15 minutes.

Whirl artichoke broth, a portion at a time, in a blender until puréed, then rub firmly through a fine strainer set over a large bowl. Discard residue. Rinse and dry pan, then pour broth into pan. Bring liquid to boil over high heat, stirring occasionally; add oysters, cover, and simmer just until shells pop open slightly, 5 to 10 minutes.

Lift out oysters as they open, draining juices into pan. Protecting your hand, pry top shells free and place 6 oysters on bottom shells in each of 4 wide soup bowls; keep warm. Stir cream and artichoke bottoms into broth; bring to simmering. Ladle an artichoke bottom and broth into each bowl. To avoid shell bits, don't ladle from pan bottom. Serves 4.

## SEAFOOD BROCHETTES WITH TOMATO-BASIL CHAMPAGNE SAUCE

*For an occasion that merits a special meal, splurge on these show-stopping seafood brochettes.*

*The choice ingredients need only simple preparation. Large shrimp encircling scallops broil on skewers in a bed of onions and champagne. The broiler pan juices then cook with tomato and basil for an aromatic sauce.*

*Offer a steaming rice pilaf and tender cooked summer squash alongside. Serve the remaining champagne as a festive accompaniment.*

16 extra-jumbo shrimp (16 to 20 per lb.), shelled and deveined
16 small sea scallops (1¼ to 1½ inch wide; ¾ to 1 pound total), rinsed
1 small onion, thinly sliced
6 tablespoons butter or margarine
1 teaspoon minced fresh thyme leaves or ½ teaspoon dry thyme leaves
⅛ teaspoon ground turmeric

*Offer broiled seafood in tomato-champagne sauce for easy, fancy entrée.*

⅛ teaspoon ground white pepper
½ cup dry champagne or dry white wine
2 teaspoons fine dry bread crumbs
2 large firm-ripe tomatoes, cored and cut into ¾-inch-wide wedges
½ cup lightly packed fresh basil leaves or 2 tablespoons dry basil
½ teaspoon sugar
2 cloves garlic, minced
Salt
Basil sprigs (optional)

Insert an 8- to 12-inch skewer through tail of a shrimp; next, slide a scallop on skewer so it lies flat, then let shrimp curve around scallop and skewer the head end. Repeat with remaining shrimp and scallops, putting 3 or 4 pairs on each skewer.

Scatter onion evenly over a 10- by 15-inch baking or broiler pan. Set skewers on top of onion. Melt 2 tablespoons of the butter. Mix the melted butter, thyme, turmeric, and white pepper; brush tops of shrimp and scallops with half of the butter mixture. Pour the champagne into pan.

Broil 4 inches from heat until tops of shrimp are pink, 4 to 5 minutes. Turn brochettes over and brush with remaining butter mixture. Sprinkle seafood evenly with bread crumbs. Continue broiling until seafood is golden on top and white in thickest part (cut to test), 4 to 6 minutes. Set brochettes aside and keep warm.

Pour pan juices through a fine strainer into a 10- to 12-inch frying pan; discard onion. Add tomato wedges, basil, sugar, and garlic. Cook on high heat, turning tomatoes gently and occasionally, until hot, about 1 minute. Reduce heat to medium and add remaining 4 tablespoons butter, stirring constantly to incorporate it into sauce. Add salt to taste.

Spoon sauce and tomatoes onto a serving platter or 4 or 5 dinner plates. Set brochettes on sauce. Garnish with basil sprigs. Makes 4 or 5 servings.— *Sheryl Benesch, Guerneville, Calif.*

*Offer cream cheese flecked with radishes to spread on vegetables and crispbread.*

### RED RADISH CHEESE SPREAD

1 large package (8 oz.) cream cheese or neufchâtel cheese
½ cup (¼ lb.) butter or margarine
1 tablespoon prepared horseradish
1 teaspoon Worcestershire
   Salt or celery salt
1½ cups finely chopped red radishes
¼ cup finely chopped green onions
   Thin rye crispbread
   About 2 pounds rinsed, trimmed raw vegetables such as celery, cucumber, radishes (choose 1 or several)

Let cheese and butter warm to room temperature. In a small bowl, beat cheese, butter, horseradish, and Worcestershire with an electric mixer until creamy. Beat in salt to taste.

With a spoon or fork, stir in chopped radishes and green onions until well distributed. Transfer to a small serving bowl. Serve, or cover and chill as long as 4 hours. If made ahead, let mixture warm to room temperature.

Offer radish cheese to spread onto crispbread and raw vegetables. Makes 2½ cups spread, enough for 10 to 12 appetizer servings. —*Jane Ingraham, Laguna Beach, Calif.*

*Diced tomatoes garnish cheese and chili egg custard; season with salsa to taste.*

### HUEVOS RANCHEROS CUSTARD

2 cans (7 oz. each) whole green chilies, split
2 cups (8 oz.) shredded longhorn cheese
2 cups (8 oz.) shredded jack cheese
   Pepper
3 large eggs
1 cup sour cream
1 medium-size firm-ripe tomato, cored and diced
   Prepared salsa (optional)

Arrange half of the chilies, spread open, in a single layer on the bottom of a shallow 2½- to 3-quart baking dish. Evenly sprinkle half of the longhorn and jack cheeses over chilies. Lightly sprinkle with pepper. Repeat layers, using remaining chilies and cheeses.

In a bowl, beat together eggs and sour cream until blended. Pour evenly over chilies and cheese. Bake in a 350° oven until custard is set and jiggles only slightly in center when gently shaken and edges have begun to brown, about 30 minutes. Let cool 5 to 10 minutes. Garnish with a band of diced tomatoes on top. To serve, cut through all the layers with a knife or spoon. Offer salsa to pour over individual portions. Makes 8 to 10 servings. —*Kathy Degiorgio, Honolulu.*

*Lightly flavor this vegetable salad with oil, vinegar, mustard, basil, salt, pepper.*

### BROCCOLI, PASTA & BEAN SALAD

1 pound broccoli
   Water
2 cups large dry pasta shells
1 can (1 lb.) kidney beans, rinsed and drained
½ cup olive oil
¼ cup red wine vinegar
1 tablespoon Dijon mustard
½ teaspoon dry basil
   Salt and pepper

Trim tough ends off broccoli stalks and discard. Thinly slice tender part of stalks crosswise, then cut, if needed, into ½- by 1-inch pieces. Cut flowerets into pieces roughly the same size. In a 5- to 6-quart pan, bring about 3 quarts water to boiling over high heat. Add pasta; cook until just barely tender to bite, 10 to 12 minutes. Drop in broccoli and cook just until broccoli turns bright green, 1 to 2 minutes longer. Drain; rinse with cold water to cool. Drain well. In a large bowl, mix pasta, broccoli, and beans.

Combine oil, vinegar, mustard, and basil. Add to pasta mixture and stir gently. Season to taste with salt and pepper. Serve, or cover and chill up to 2 hours. Makes 6 to 8 servings. —*J. Heflin, Kirkland, Wash.*

## OAT-WHEAT WAFFLES

- ¾ cup all-purpose flour
- ¾ cup whole-wheat flour
- ½ cup instant rolled oats
- 4 teaspoons baking powder
- 1 tablespoon sugar
- ¼ teaspoon salt (optional)
- 6 tablespoons salad oil
- 2 large eggs, separated
- 2 cups milk
  Unflavored or fruit yogurt and
  sliced bananas, or butter and syrup
  Freshly grated or ground nutmeg
  (optional)

In a bowl, mix all-purpose flour, whole-wheat flour, oats, baking powder, sugar, and salt. Add oil, egg yolks, and milk; stir until smooth. In a small bowl, whip egg whites until they hold stiff, moist peaks; fold into batter.

Heat a greased waffle iron to 375° or medium-high; half-fill with batter. Cook batter until crisp and golden, 4 to 5 minutes. Lift out waffle and repeat to bake remaining waffles.

Serve hot. Offer yogurt and bananas, or butter and syrup to spoon over waffles. Dust with freshly grated nutmeg. Makes 7 or 8 waffles (8-inch size). —*Irene Lilja, Corvallis, Ore.*

*Top oat-and-wheat waffle with orange yogurt, banana, and grated nutmeg.*

## CURRY CHICKEN WITH CURRANTS

- 3 pounds chicken thighs
  About ¾ cup all-purpose flour
- 2 tablespoons salad oil
- 1 large onion, chopped
- 1 large bell pepper, stemmed, seeded, and chopped
- 2 cloves garlic, pressed or minced
- 1 tablespoon curry powder
- 1 can (14½ oz.) tomatoes
- 1 teaspoon liquid hot pepper seasoning
- ½ cup currants
  Salt
- ½ cup chopped salted almonds

Coat chicken with flour; shake off excess.

Pour oil into a 12- to 14-inch frying pan over medium-high heat. Cook chicken, a portion at a time (do not crowd pan), turning until browned on all sides; remove from pan. Add onion, bell pepper, garlic, and curry powder; stir over low heat until vegetables are limp, about 5 minutes.

Add tomatoes (break up with a spoon), including juices, hot pepper seasoning, chicken, and currants. Cover and simmer over low heat until chicken is tender when pierced, 35 to 45 minutes. Add salt to taste. Skim and discard fat. Spoon onto dish and sprinkle with almonds. Makes 4 to 6 servings. —*Gladys Kent, Port Angeles, Wash.*

*Brown chicken thighs, then braise with curry powder, tomatoes, and vegetables.*

## WHITE & DARK CHOCOLATE BROWNIES

- ¾ cup all-purpose flour
- ¼ teaspoon baking soda
- ¼ teaspoon salt (optional)
- ⅓ cup butter or margarine
- ¾ cup sugar
- 2 tablespoons water
- 1 cup (6 oz.) semisweet chocolate baking chips
- 1 teaspoon vanilla
- 2 large eggs
- 1 cup (6 oz.) chilled white chocolate baking chips

In a bowl, mix flour, soda, and salt.

In a 2- to 3-quart pan, combine butter, sugar, and water. Bring to a boil, stirring, over high heat. Remove from heat and add semisweet chocolate chips and vanilla. Stir until chocolate melts and mixture is smooth. Add eggs, 1 at a time, beating well after each. Stir in flour mixture. Let cool to room temperature. Stir in white chocolate chips. Spread into a greased 8- or 9-inch square baking pan. Bake in a 350° oven until sides are firm and center springs back when gently pressed, 35 to 40 minutes. Cool on a rack. Cut into pieces. Serve warm or cool. If made ahead, cover and store at room temperature until the next day. Serves 9 to 12. —*Mary B. Brock, Grass Valley, Calif.*

*Chewy dark chocolate brownies are studded with white chocolate chips.*

# Chefs of 🍴 the West®

## The Art of Cooking . . . by men . . . for men

THE BIRCHES OF RUSSIA *don't have much in common with the beaches of Baja California; likewise, Russia's root-cellar cuisine, which relies heavily on beets, cabbage, and potatoes, bears little resemblance to Mexico's sunstruck peppers and tomatoes. In an inspired moment, though, Joseph Moehler managed to reconcile the two in his Baja Borscht. Leon Trotsky, who ended his days in Mexico, might not have found it to his taste, but Westerners will find it to theirs.*

*Beef, broth, and beets supply the Russian elements. Chayote, cilantro, taco sauce, and tomatillos bring southern sun and heat to what might otherwise be an earthy and stolid (though satisfying) soup.*

*"In an inspired moment, Russia and Mexico meet in Baja Borscht."*

## BAJA BORSCHT

- 1 to 1½ pounds lean boneless beef chuck, trimmed of excess fat
- 2 tablespoons olive oil or salad oil
- 1 medium-size red onion, chopped
- 2 large cloves garlic, minced or pressed
- ⅓ cup finely chopped fresh cilantro (coriander)
- 5 cups or 3 cans (14½ oz. each) regular-strength beef broth
- 1 cup water
- 4 medium-size beets without tops (about 1¼ lb.), peeled and shredded
- 2 large carrots (about ½ lb.), peeled and shredded
- 1 medium-size chayote (about ½ lb.), peeled and shredded
- 3 medium-size tomatillos (about ¼ lb.), husked, cored, and diced
- 2 tablespoons lime juice
  About ¾ cup bottled red taco sauce
  About 3 cups finely shredded romaine lettuce
  About 1 cup sour cream
  Salt and pepper

Cut beef into ¾-inch cubes. Pour oil into a 5- to 6-quart pan over medium-high heat; when hot, add meat and cook until browned on all sides. Add onion and garlic and stir often until onion is limp, about 10 minutes.

Add cilantro, broth, and water; bring to a boil over high heat. Cover, reduce heat, and simmer until meat is tender when pierced, 1½ to 2 hours.

Stir in beets, carrots, chayote, tomatillos, lime juice, and 1 tablespoon taco sauce. Cover, bring to a boil on high heat, then reduce heat and simmer until very tender to bite, 15 to 20 minutes.

To serve, ladle soup into individual bowls. Add lettuce, sour cream, additional taco sauce, and salt and pepper to taste. Makes 2½ to 3 quarts, 6 to 8 servings.

*Alpine, Calif.*

THE BOOK OF PROVERBS, *the Old Testament's fountainhead of practical wisdom, counsels, "Do not look upon the wine when it is red....At the last it biteth like a serpent and stingeth like an adder." The same warning applies to Johnny Lee Newcomb's Salsa Diabola. The tomato sauce at first leads your taste buds on with a slight suggestion of sweetness; then comes the moment of truth, when the jalapeños, cayenne, and pepper spread like a grass fire in a high wind.*

*That is, of course, just what the iron palate of the Mexican food addict wants. Moreover, such stimulation jells perfectly with Proverbs XXI:6 — "Give strong drink unto him that is ready to perish, and wine unto those that be of heavy hearts."*

## SALSA DIABOLA

- 2 tablespoons salad oil
- 2 large onions, chopped
- 6 large firm-ripe tomatoes, cored, peeled, and diced
- 6 small fresh jalapeño chilies, stemmed, seeded, and diced
- 6 medium-size Fresno (yellow wax) chilies, stemmed, seeded, and diced
- 2 medium-size red or green bell peppers, stemmed, seeded, and diced
- 1 tablespoon coarsely ground black pepper
- 1 teaspoon cayenne
- 2 large cans (15 oz. each) tomato sauce
- ⅓ cup (½ of 6-oz. can) tomato paste
- 1 tablespoon chopped fresh cilantro (coriander)
- 1 tablespoon distilled white vinegar

In a 5- to 6-quart pan over medium heat, combine oil, onions, tomatoes, jalapeños, Fresno chilies, bell peppers, black pepper, and cayenne. Cover and cook, stirring occasionally, until vegetables are soft when pressed, about 20 minutes. Stir in tomato sauce, tomato paste, cilantro, and vinegar. Cook uncovered, stirring occasionally, until sauce reduces to about 9 cups, about 20 minutes. Let cool and serve. To store, ladle into small containers, cover, and chill up to 1 week; freeze to store longer. Makes 9 cups.

*Johnny Lee Newcomb*

*Avery, Idaho*

**T**HE PETER ROCKS *of Walnut Creek, California, regularly meet up with seven other couples, all of whom happen to love eating liver. They gather from time to time to indulge this inexplicable passion; the host is supposed to prepare the liver according to a new, preferably original recipe. Because Mr. Rock's recipe involves flaming brandy, it's a good showoff dish for tabletop preparation.*

*Realistically, you may not be able to find eight couples who savor liver, so we've adapted the dish to serve a few less.*

## LIVER LOVERS' FLAMBÉE

1½  **pounds calf's liver, sliced about ¼ inch thick**
½  **cup brandy**
4  **to 6 tablespoons butter or margarine**
2  **large onions, thinly sliced**
2  **cloves garlic, minced or pressed**
1  **tablespoon Dijon mustard**
½  **cup whipping cream**
2  **tablespoons chopped parsley**

Trim coarse membrane from liver and discard; rinse liver and pat dry. Place slices in a shallow dish and pour ¼ cup of the brandy over liver; set aside.

Melt 2 tablespoons of the butter in a 10- to 12-inch frying pan over medium heat. Add onions and garlic and stir often until onions are limp and lightly browned, 20 to 25 minutes. Remove onion mixture from pan and keep warm.

Turn heat to medium-high and melt 2 more tablespoons butter in pan. Lift liver

from brandy (reserve brandy) and arrange in the pan without crowding. Cook until slices are browned on both sides but still pink in the center (cut to test), 1½ to 2 minutes total. Lift from pan and keep warm. Repeat to cook remaining liver, adding more butter as needed.

Remove pan from heat and return all liver to pan. Warm remaining ¼ cup brandy in a small, long-handled cup or pan just until sizzling at edges. Hold over liver (do not place pan beneath a vent or flammable material) and set brandy aflame with a match; pour, flaming, over liver. Shake pan until flames die; lift out liver onto a platter; keep warm.

To the pan, add brandy marinade, mustard, and cream. Bring to a boil over high heat, stirring to scrape browned bits from pan; continue to stir until large, shiny bubbles form, 4 to 5 minutes. Pour sauce over liver, and top with onion mixture and parsley. Makes 4 to 6 servings.

*Peter Rock*

*Walnut Creek, Calif.*

**M**EAT LOAF *is sometimes derided as the prototypical proletarian main course, the sort of food you might find in a faded-blue-collar diner. No more: the history of eating follows a cyclical, not linear, track and meat loaf's in again—as are diners and faded blues. If the words "meat loaf" offend your sensibilities, just rephrase it as* pâté de campagne.

*Stephen Moore commandeers his family's kitchen from Friday sunset through*

*"If 'meat loaf' offends your sensibilities, just rephrase it as pâté de campagne."*

*Sunday night. He often obliges his family by making a dish that combines two of their favorites: meat loaf and teriyaki. Feel free to drizzle bottled teriyaki sauce over your serving, but the meat loaf contains plenty of teriyaki flavor even if you take it plain.*

## TERIYAKI MEAT LOAF

2  **tablespoons salad oil**
1  **medium-size onion, finely chopped**
1  **medium-size carrot, shredded**
¼  **cup thinly sliced green onions, including tops**
½  **cup finely diced celery**
2  **cloves garlic, minced or pressed**
1  **teaspoon grated fresh ginger**
½  **cup milk**
½  **cup tomato-based chili sauce**
1  **tablespoon firmly packed brown sugar**
¼  **cup soy sauce**
1  **tablespoon chili powder**
2  **large eggs**
1½  **pounds ground lean beef**
½  **pound ground lean pork**
1  **cup panko (Japanese-style coarse bread crumbs) or fine dry bread crumbs**

In a 10- to 12-inch frying pan over medium heat, combine oil, chopped onion, carrot, green onions, celery, garlic, and ginger. Cook, stirring often, until onion is limp, about 10 minutes. Add milk, chili sauce, sugar, soy sauce, and chili powder; cook, stirring, until bubbling, 1 to 2 minutes longer. Remove from heat and let stand until cool enough to touch.

In a large bowl, beat eggs to blend, then add beef, pork, panko, and the vegetable mixture; mix with a fork or your hands until well blended.

In the center of a 9- by 13-inch baking pan, shape meat mixture into a 6- by 12-inch loaf. Bake in a 375° oven for about 1 hour, until meatloaf is browned and no longer pink in center (cut to test). During the final 15 minutes, baste several times with pan drippings.

Remove from oven and let stand 10 to 15 minutes. Supporting it with 2 wide spatulas, transfer loaf to a platter; cut into thick slices. Serve hot or cold. Makes 8 or 9 servings.

*Bothell, Wash.*

# October Menus

Autumn days call for a salute to the change of seasons. On a pleasant fall day, take advantage of the weather and enjoy homemade bread, soup, and cheese at a tailgate picnic or meal in the park. In honor of newly lost tree foliage, our weekend brunch focuses on pastries shaped like fallen leaves; use frozen puff pastry to get a quick start. On a blustery evening, let the aroma of chicken roasting with fall vegetables fill the house.

---

### A LOAF OF BREAD

Clear Vegetable Soup
Stilton, Münster, or Sharp Cheddar
Cheese
Celery Bread
Green Onions    Celery Sticks
Italia or Tokay Grapes
Sugar Cookies
Merlot or Boysenberry-Apple Juice

---

Celery bread and wine go well with pungent and mild cheeses, light soup, muscat-flavored grapes, and crisp cookies.

Purchased frozen dough speeds the bread-making process; add sautéed onion and celery to the dough, shape the loaf, and bake it.

To accompany the bread, offer green onions and celery, with one or more types of cheese, a total of at least ¾ to 1 pound.

### CLEAR VEGETABLE SOUP

    7  cups regular-strength beef broth
1½  cups small cauliflowerets
    1  medium-size red or green bell
       pepper, stemmed, seeded, and
       chopped
    1  medium-size onion, chopped
    ¼  cup tiny alphabet-shaped pasta
       Pepper

In a 3- to 4-quart pan, bring broth, cauliflower, bell pepper, onion, and pasta to a boil over high heat. Cover and simmer until cauliflower is tender to bite, about 10 minutes. Season to taste with pepper. Serve, or ladle into a wide-mouth thermos to transport. If made ahead, cover and chill up to 2 days. To reheat, bring to a boil over high heat, stirring. Makes about 9 cups, 4 to 6 servings.

### CELERY BREAD

    1  cup thinly sliced celery (including
       some leaves)
    ⅔  cup minced onion
    2  tablespoons butter or margarine
    ½  teaspoon celery seed
    ¼  teaspoon pepper
    1  loaf (1 lb.) frozen white bread
       dough, thawed

In a 10- to 12-inch frying pan over medium heat, cook celery and onion in butter until limp and golden, 10 to 15 minutes; stir often. Stir in celery seed and pepper. Remove from heat; let cool to lukewarm.

On a board, gently knead vegetables into dough. Shape into a round about 5 inches in diameter; place on a greased 10- by 15-inch baking sheet. Cover and let rise in a warm place until puffy, about 45 minutes.

Bake, uncovered, in a 350° oven until well browned, about 35 minutes. Remove from pan to a rack and let cool. Makes 1 loaf, about 1¼ pounds.

*Pregame spread combines celery bread, cheeses, fruit and vegetables, light soup.*

*For fall breakfast, serve leaf-shaped, jam-glazed pastry with nuts, pears, Canadian bacon.*

## AUTUMN LEAVES BRUNCH

**Ricotta-filled Hazelnut Leaves**
**Warm Hazelnuts**
**Bartlett Pears      Red Delicious Apples**
**Canadian Bacon or Ham**
**Coffee      Spiced Milk**

*To celebrate fall, cut purchased puff pastry into leaf shapes, fill, and bake. Serve with warm nuts. Heat cardamom-flavored milk (use whole cracked pods) for kids. Adults can mix it with coffee.*

*If you like, make the pastries a day ahead. Plan on 1 pear or apple and 1 to 2 ounces of Canadian bacon per person.*

### RICOTTA-FILLED HAZELNUT LEAVES

1   package (17¾ oz.) frozen puff
     pastry sheets, thawed
     Ricotta-apricot filling (recipe
     follows)
½   cup apricot jam

Cut out a leaf-shaped paper pattern about 5 inches long and 4 inches wide. Unfold puff pastry; using pattern as a guide, cut dough with a pastry wheel or knife to make 8 leaves. Discard pastry scraps. With wheel or knife, score a line ¾ inch from the edge all the way around each leaf. Evenly space leaves on 2 bak-ing sheets, each 10 by 15 inches. Bake in a 350° oven for 10 minutes.

Remove leaves from oven. Retrace scoring (do not cut through pastries) and smoothly spoon equal portions of ricotta filling onto each leaf over area inside scoring. Then smoothly spoon the jam equally over filling on each pastry. Return to oven and bake until pastries are golden, 15 to 20 minutes longer. Serve warm.

If made ahead, let pastries cool on racks, then cover and chill up to 1 day. To reheat, return to baking sheets and bake in a 350° oven until hot to touch, about 10 minutes. Makes 4 to 8 servings.

**Ricotta-apricot filling.** In a bowl, mix 1 cup **ricotta cheese** with 1 **large egg,** ½ cup chopped **dried apricots,** 3 table-spoons firmly packed **brown sugar,** and ¼ teaspoon **almond extract.**

## WARM HAZELNUTS

Place 1 cup **hazelnuts** in a 5- by 9-inch loaf pan; bake in 350° oven next to pas-tries (preceding) until nuts are golden in center (break 1 to check), about 15 min-utes. Serve warm. Makes 4 to 8 servings.

## ROAST CHICKEN DINNER

**Oven-Baked Barley Pilaf**
**Roast Chicken with Beets,**
**Squash & Onions**
**Date Bars**
**Cidre Bouché or Apple Cider**

*Everything cooks in the oven for this easily prepared meal. Cidre bouché (French hard cider) makes a good accompaniment; look for it in wine shops.*

*Bake the date bars first. While they cool, cook the chicken, vegetables, and pilaf.*

## OVEN-BAKED BARLEY PILAF

Rinse and drain 1 cup **pearl barley** and place in a 1½-quart casserole. In a 1- to 2-quart pan, bring 2¼ cups **regular-strength chicken broth** to a boil over high heat. Add to barley, cover, and bake in a 375° oven until barley is tender to bite, about 50 minutes; stir once halfway through cooking.

Just before serving, mix in 2 table-spoons minced **parsley.** Serves 4.

*Oven-dinner chicken sits amid herbs, roasted vegetables. Barley was baked alongside.*

## ROAST CHICKEN WITH BEETS, SQUASH & ONIONS

*To eat the onions, cut them in half and scoop their soft centers from the peels.*

- 4 small (about 1½-inch size) beets without tops, scrubbed
- 8 small onions (about 1-inch size), unpeeled, rinsed
- ¼ cup olive oil
- 2 teaspoons *each* fresh (or 1 teaspoon dry) thyme and rosemary leaves
- 1 whole broiler-fryer chicken, 3½ to 4 pounds
- ¾ pound banana or Hubbard squash, cut into 2-inch chunks
- Fresh thyme or rosemary sprigs

Place beets and onions in separate corners of a shallow 12- by 15-inch roasting pan. In a bowl, mix oil, thyme, and rosemary leaves; brush some over vegetables. Bake in a 375° oven for 10 minutes.

Reserve chicken giblets for other uses. Rinse chicken and pat dry; pull off and discard lumps of fat. Place bird breast up in center of pan. Place squash in an empty corner. Brush meat and vegetables with remaining oil mixture. Bake, basting with pan juices, until chicken is well browned and beets are tender when pierced, about 45 minutes.

Trim root ends from beets. Lift chicken and vegetables to a platter and garnish with thyme sprigs. Serves 4.

## DATE BARS

- 1 package (8 oz.) chopped pitted dates
- ½ cup water
- ½ cup granulated sugar
- 1 teaspoon grated lemon peel
- 1 cup all-purpose flour
- ¼ teaspoon baking soda
- ⅓ cup firmly packed brown sugar
- ½ cup (¼ lb.) butter or margarine, cut into pieces
- ¾ cup regular rolled oats
- ¼ cup sour cream

In a 1- to 2-quart pan, bring dates, water, granulated sugar, and lemon peel to a boil over medium heat. Cover and simmer, stirring occasionally, until mixture is thick, 10 to 15 minutes. Let cool.

In a food processor or bowl, whirl or mix flour, soda, and brown sugar. Add butter and whirl, or cut in with a pastry blender until butter is the size of peas. Mix in oats. Add sour cream and whirl, or stir just until combined (dough should be lumpy).

Press half of dough into bottom of a greased 9-inch square pan. Evenly spread date mixture on top, then evenly sprinkle with remaining dough.

Bake, uncovered, in a 350° oven until golden, about 30 minutes. Let cool in pan on a rack. Serve—or, if made ahead, cover and store up to 3 days. Cut into 12 equal bars. Makes 6 to 12 servings.— *Louise Lawson, Walnut Creek, Calif.*

# NOVEMBER

*London Broil (page 273)*

**M**eats have been getting
leaner in recent years, and today's lean beef, pork, and lamb
make old calorie and nutrient charts—and many cook books—
out of date. Our fact-packed 12-page article offered new
strategies for meat shopping, and new cooking techniques
that retain tenderness and flavor. Also in November we
featured 27 make-ahead dishes for a potluck Thanksgiving,
party appetizers, recipe ideas from France and South America,
and festive desserts for holiday entertaining.

# Lean Meat: Shopping Strategies

W E'RE HEARING MORE *about it today, but meat has actually been getting leaner for some time. Years ago, when Westerners first began to prefer lighter diets, ranchers began breeding for leaner meat, favoring more muscular, larger-framed animals that reach market weight earlier.*

*Compared to 30 years ago, beef cattle have 40 percent less fat, yielding meat that's 8 to 10 percent leaner. Hogs have 50 percent less fat, and pork is 6 to 8 percent leaner. Lambs have almost doubled in weight, producing more lean meat in relation to fat.*

*Old charts listing nutrients and calories in meat are obsolete, and not only because meat has changed. A comprehensive update of existing nutritional information on meats, begun in the late 1970s, is nearly finished, and it's far more detailed and accurate than anything available before.*

*For one thing, we now know how important the cut of meat is—how widely fat*

content varies from place to place on the same animal. Pork tenderloin, for example, is one of the leanest meats, with about 140 calories in a trimmed, cooked 3-ounce serving; a same-weight portion of pork sparerib meat has about 340 calories. A chart on page 271 gives the new calorie counts and fat and cholesterol values for a sampling of meat cuts.

Most people realize how important it is to cut back on fat in the diet. The problem, as cooks have discovered, is that meats can lose tenderness and flavor as they become leaner. And the wrong cooking method can put the fat right back on the plate again.

In Sunset's own kitchens, we've done extensive testing to discover the best ways to cook lean meats without adding high-calorie ingredients. Cooked with the appropriate techniques, these meats can be made almost as tender and succulent as fatter cuts. On pages 272 through 276, we explain six basic cooking techniques we've found give good results. By varying meats, seasonings, and serving accompaniments, you can use these six techniques to produce a whole repertoire of low-calorie meat dishes.

But our lean-meat strategy really begins with a new way of looking at meat cuts in the market—assessing their yield of lean meat and its potential for lighter meals.

On the pages that follow, we show you

which cuts of beef, veal, pork, and lamb usually offer a good proportion of lean meat. Most of the meats need some further cutting at home, and we tell you how to do it. When you cut meat at home, you can often trim off extra fat and still save over the price of ready-to-cook packaged meats—and you can use the bones and trimmings for making soup.

When you don't have time to do your own cutting, you can buy meats already sliced thin for scaloppine, cut into strips for stir-frying, or cubed for skewers.

## SHOPPING FOR BEEF

New, leaner breeds of cattle are also being fed differently, and for shorter periods. Less time in feed lots results in meat with less marbling (the tiny streaks of fat you see interlaced with lean muscle).

Marbling is still the main indicator of quality used in the U.S. Department of Agriculture's grading standards for beef. Of the three top grades, *Prime* is the fattiest, followed by *Choice*, then *Good*— although the difference in fat content between well-trimmed *Choice* and *Good* beef is now quite small. Very little *Prime* beef is produced today, and most of that is sold to restaurants. If all beef were graded (it's not: grading is optional, paid

*He's cutting out tender "eye" muscle from the thick chuck blade. First he removed flatiron from atop blade bone.*

## BEEF: Five economic lean cuts

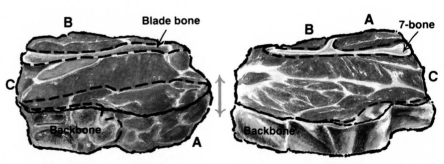

***Chuck blade.*** *Eye muscle (A) and flatiron (B) are tenderest. Turn boned pieces on side and slice across grain (shown by arrow) for thin steaks, stir-fry strips, or scaloppine; or cut into cubes. What remains (C) is best braised.*

***Chuck 7-bone.*** *Top blade (A) and mock tender (B) are tenderest. Cut these and parts of (C) with least connective tissue cross-grain into thin slices or strips. It's best to braise the remainder.*

for by packers who choose to use the service; all meat, however, is inspected for wholesomeness), most beef sold in the West today would be rated *Good.*

The tenderest roasts and steaks come from the loin and rib sections. However, many parts of the less expensive round and chuck can be tender and succulent if prepared by our techniques. The leanest beef comes from the round, but carefully trimmed cuts from the loin, rib, and chuck can also be low in fat.

The beef cuts described here are usually economical sources of lean meat. You can divide these larger cuts for several different meals, freezing what you plan to use later. More expensive cuts of boneless lean meat include the all-tender rib eye and tenderloin roasts and flank steak.

**Chuck: blade and 7-bone roasts.** Both have a lot of seam fat, but it's easily trimmed away. Blade cuts include some of the tender "eye" muscle (a continuation of the rib eye) and usually have a little more separable fat than 7-bone roasts.

To have pieces thick enough to cut as directed below, buy a 4- to 5-pound roast. Select the blade roast with the smallest blade bone and largest eye.

Choose the 7-bone roast with the longest 7-bone; cuts nearest the neck have a shorter bone but less tender meat. The grain runs perpendicular to the surface of these cuts; after trimming away the fat and connective tissue, turn meat and slice parallel to the original cut.

**Chuck: boneless shoulder.** The whole muscle, weighing 10 to 12 pounds, is usually divided to make several roasts or thick steaks. In California, they're often called cross-rib roasts, and the tapering end is often sold as diamond or Diamond Jim roast. Most of the meat is tender when cut across the grain.

**Round.** You can buy parts of the round separately as top round steak (often called London broil), eye of round roast, or bottom round pot roast. The full-cut steak, a cross-section of the leg, includes some of all three parts. Round steaks are usually not cut exactly across the grain; the cooked meat will be most tender if cut in slanting slices. In eye of round roasts, the grain always runs lengthwise.

To use a full-cut steak for several meals, choose one that's 1 to 2 inches thick. It provides top round thick enough for London broil, with enough meat left for several other meals. Separate the three parts along the natural

seams. If top round has an extra strip of meat on top, remove it and add to bottom round meat.

**Round tip roast.** Often called sirloin tip, this boneless cut is usually split down the middle into two 3½- to 4-pound roasts. Both roasts are equally lean and tender, but one side has a seam through it and the other is more solid and a little more versatile. Untie or remove netting. You might cut a London broil steak off the widest end. The tapering end has a little more connective tissue, but the whole piece is quite tender.

**Triangle tip (tri-tip).** This boneless cut, weighing 1½ to 2 pounds, is a muscle from the bottom sirloin. It is often sliced and sold as culotte steaks. The whole piece is tender when cut cross-grain. Cut into steaks, or grill whole.

## SHOPPING FOR VEAL

Veal may come from animals as young as a week or as old as five months. The color of the meat depends on the animal's diet. A calf raised solely on milk or milk replacers produces meat that's grayish white to creamy pink in color. As the diet is supplemented with grass and grain, the meat becomes pinker.

*(Continued on next page)*

## ...and how to use them

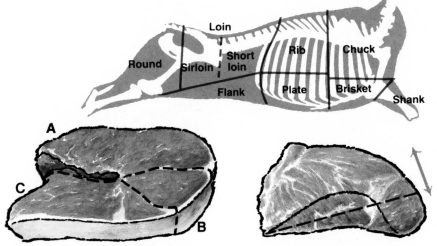

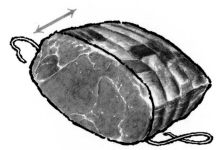

***Chuck boneless shoulder.*** *Untie roast. For London broil, cut thick slice of widest end. Use most compact part for roast or to slice. Cut remaining meat into strips or cubes; braise parts with most connective tissue.*

***Full-cut round steak.*** *Top round (A) is tenderest; use for London broil, cubes. Cut slices or strips from (A) or less tender eye (B), slanting slices to cross meat's grain. Bottom round (C) is best braised.*

***Triangle tip (bottom sirloin).*** *Slice off wide end at an angle directly across grain and cut steaks or slices at same angle; cut irregularly shaped ends into strips to stir-fry. Or grill whole, like London broil.*

What little meat the very youngest animals have on their bones is quite bland in flavor. Premium-quality veal usually comes from animals fed mainly on milk and milk replacers for four months or longer. This meat is creamy pink, with a smooth, firm texture; most of it is sold under brand names of companies that raise the animals.

Veal has little surface fat and almost no marbling. A 3-ounce serving of most cuts, cooked and trimmed, has less than 200 calories. Veal is fairly tender, although some cuts have quite a lot of connective tissue. Bone-in cuts are similar to beef cuts, but smaller; they're usually called chops rather than steaks. Boneless slices are called cutlets.

Butchers typically use most of the veal shoulder and leg for cutlets and scaloppine. They cut the loin and rib sections into chops and cutlets. Irregular pieces from any part may be cubed and sold as stew. Although harder to find, boned roasts from leg and shoulder are good sources of lean meat.

**Boneless veal stew.** To use this meat in ways other than braising, look for cubes that are uniformly 1 to 1½ inches thick, with little tough connective tissue showing.

To cut strips for stir-frying, partially freeze the cubes, then slice across the grain, discarding connective tissue. For scaloppine, trim cubes, then pound in same direction as grain (see page 276).

## SHOPPING FOR PORK

In the past, most pork leg and shoulder meat was cured and most of the loin sold fresh. That's still true, but more fresh boneless leg is being offered today; meat dealers often cut and package it as bone-

*On leg-end roast, remove tenderloin, a boneless strip of meat inside rib cage. Then cut away ribs. At base of ribs, work knife down to vertebrae to free meat.*

**PORK:** Leanest cuts come from leg & loin. You can cut up a loin roast into several meals

Shoulder

Loin

Leg (ham)

Side

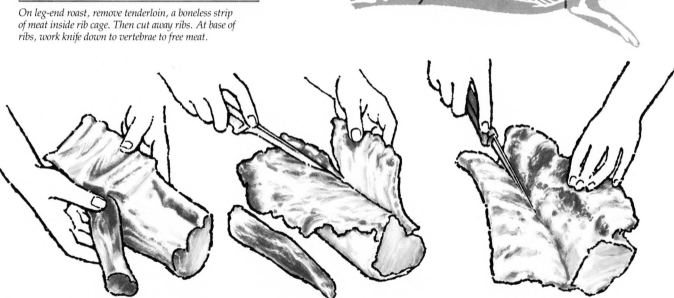

*Center-cut pork loin is usually cut and sold as two roasts. Shoulder-end roast (forward of knife) is a little easier to bone. Leg-end roast includes part of tenderloin.*

*On shoulder-end roast, work close to bones, cutting ribs away from the meat.*

less slices, strips, or cubes for skewers.

Hogs are usually marketed when five to six months old. There's little variation in the meat's quality, so USDA grades are not used for retail cuts. The loin is the tenderest section, but cuts from the leg are almost as tender.

The leanest cuts come from the leg and loin. When you want boneless meat for several different meals, a center-cut loin roast is a good choice; it's sold in most markets, and you can often save by boning it yourself. Although not always available, the tenderloin and boneless leg are also good sources of lean meat.

**Center-cut pork loin.** Buy it bone-in or already boned. Usually the whole center cut is divided into two roasts, each weighing 3 to 5 pounds with bone. For either roast, ask your meatman to remove the chine bone. For pork chops, simply cut between ribs. From a boned roast, you might use part of the meat as a mini-roast; the remaining meat can be cut in slices, strips, or cubes.

## SHOPPING FOR LAMB

Lamb is defined as meat from an animal less than a year old; six to nine months is the typical age.

The vast majority of America's lambs are raised in the West. Today's breeds grow to nearly twice the size of lambs produced in other countries and have more lean meat in proportion to bone mass and fat. The meat of American lamb is firmer and a little subtler in flavor.

The term "spring lamb" has no real significance, as the supply is constant. In California, lambing season is October and November; the young animals are raised over winter, when pastures are green. In areas where pasture grasses stay green in summer, lambs are born in spring.

The USDA's grading program for lamb has been modified in recent years to conform to the leaner animals being produced. About 90 percent of lamb sold in retail stores is graded *Choice*.

Lamb's fat is mostly on the outside of pieces and in layers between muscles; how well the fat is trimmed before cooking and how the meat is prepared chiefly determine cooked lamb's calorie count. The range for a 3-ounce serving of cooked, trimmed lamb is from about 155 calories for leg roasts to 235 calories for some braised chops. The leg is the best source of lean meat.

*(Continued on next page)*

*Thin-pounded slices of pork tenderloin cook in less than a minute in hot fry pan.*

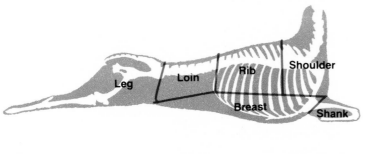

# LAMB:
Today's cuts are larger as well as leaner. You can subdivide

*To take apart a boned leg, turn cut side up; remove muscles intact, pulling meat apart along natural seams (use a knife to free meat from connective tissue, fat, skin). Muscles correspond to beef round. Remove top round (A), then eye (B), heel (C), end of tenderloin (D), end of flank (E), top sirloin (F), bottom sirloin (G). Bottom round (H) extends under (C), (F), and (G).*

*Use top round (A) or top sirloin (F) for small roast or cutlets. Trim bottom sirloin (G) evenly thick to grill like London broil. Cut remaining pieces for shish kebabs, stir-fry strips, scaloppine, braising.*

Individual cuts of American lamb are all larger than they were in the past. A full-cut leg, which includes the sirloin, often weighs 8 to 10 pounds—too large for most families. Typically, butchers now sell the sirloin portion separately; what's left is called a ¾ (or short-cut) leg. Or they may divide the leg three ways into a sirloin portion, shank portion, and center roasts.

**Leg roasts.** A full-cut leg is especially versatile and can provide lean meat for up to six different meals. Ask the meat-man to bone it for you. You might have the shank removed first; simmered with beans or vegetables, it makes a small meal. Follow directions on page 269 to divide the balance of the leg for different meals.

Imported lamb cuts, smaller than their domestic counterparts, are often sold frozen. If you want to use a frozen leg for several meals, ask your meat dealer to saw it so you can thaw just the part you need. You might have 2 or 3 steaks cut from the large end, have the shank removed, and leave the center section whole to roast.

## KEEPING MEAT SAFE & LABELS HONEST

All meat-processing plants in this country operate under government surveillance. Federal requirements are meant to ensure that meat will not contain harmful residues of drugs; animals also undergo pre- and post-slaughter inspections.

Still, some question the use of any drugs in livestock. About four out of five food animals are given some drugs during their lifetimes—to stimulate growth, to help them utilize their feed more efficiently, and to treat disease. In general, fewer drugs are used now than in the past. The synthetic hormone DES, once widely used to promote growth, has been banned because of evidence that it causes cancer.

## How to Read a Meat Label

Meats labeled with fanciful names such as "breakfast steak" or "California roast" have frustrated shoppers for years. But a new uniform meat labeling program, adopted by most retail food stores nationwide, now identifies the meat, states the part of the animal from which it was taken, and gives the standard retail name for the cut. In addition, a retailer may show on the label or with a separate sticker any other familiar name for the cut. Look for the following information on today's meat label:

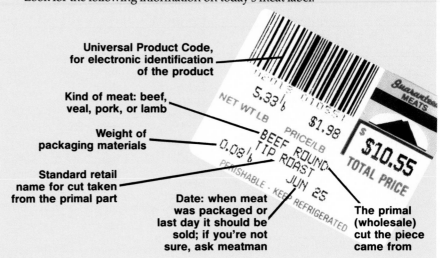

**Universal Product Code, for electronic identification of the product**

**Kind of meat: beef, veal, pork, or lamb**

**Weight of packaging materials**

**Standard retail name for cut taken from the primal part**

**Date: when meat was packaged or last day it should be sold; if you're not sure, ask meatman**

**The primal (wholesale) cut the piece came from**

A few markets are selling meats labeled "natural." As the term is defined—meaning any product that has no artificial color, flavor, or other ingredients and is not more than minimally processed—all fresh meat is natural, and the appearance of this word is no guarantee it is drug-free. But it has recently been given a little more meaning; labels marked "natural" must now explain the use of the term.

A few market animals are being raised today without drugs, and the USDA has approved labels that make specific claims about how the animals were raised. Some typical claims are "raised without the use of antibiotics or hormones" or "fed grain grown without the use of pesticides." Anyone using such phrases on a label must have records to verify them.

Labels such as "lite," "lean," and "low-fat" have also been redefined. Any meat

product called "extra-lean" may have no more than 5 percent fat by weight; a "lean" or "low-fat" product may have no more than 10 percent fat. A product may be called "light," "lite," "leaner," or "lower fat" if it has at least 25 percent less fat than most comparable products; the label must state its fat content versus that of the standard product.

Meats labeled ground beef or hamburger may have no more than 30 percent fat and must be pure beef—all from skeletal muscles (no variety meats). But they may have added seasonings if declared on the label. If called ground chuck or ground round, meat must be entirely from those cuts and may contain no more than 30 percent fat. Any product that makes a claim about fat content must state the percentage of fat it contains.

# Lean Meat: A Nutrition Scorecard

OUR CHART COMPARES the calories, fat, and cholesterol of some typical meat cuts. The figures are from the U.S. Department of Agriculture's new and comprehensive analysis of the nutrient content of meat.

Notice how many cuts, when cooked and trimmed of knife-separable fat, have fewer than 10 grams of fat in a 3-ounce serving. Although nutritionists differ on how much is too much, many agree with the American Heart Association's recommendation that not more than 30 percent of calories come from fat.

How does that 30 percent translate into grams of fat? Allow 9 calories for each gram of fat. If you consume 2,000 calories a day, about 67 grams of fat supplies 30 percent of your calories. A 1,500-calorie diet allows about 50 grams of fat. Allow 5 grams for each 1 teaspoon butter, margarine, oil, mayonnaise, or meat fat you eat or use in preparing a meat dish.

Cholesterol is found in both lean and fat meats, so fatty and lean cuts have about the same amounts. But if you are trying to control your blood cholesterol level, limit intake of saturated fats, which tend to increase circulating cholesterol. The American Heart Association recommends limiting cholesterol to 300 milligrams or less a day. A 3-ounce serving of most meats has 60 to 90 milligrams, roughly a quarter of the recommended amount.

Because meat is so nutrient-dense, a 3-ounce serving provides 20 to 30 grams of protein, 40 to 60 percent of the recommended daily allowance for an average adult. The body doesn't store protein, so it needs a new supply daily: only about 56 grams a day for a 154-pound man, 44 grams for a 121-pound woman.

Three ounces of meat also supplies some important B vitamins as well as zinc and iron—minerals often lacking in meatless diets. The iron in red meats is in a form that's especially usable by the body, and meat even helps it utilize iron from other sources.

The USDA's *Dietary Guidelines for Americans* recommends two roughly 3-ounce servings of lean meat, poultry, fish, or an alternative such as eggs or dry beans each day. Two small servings are more efficient than one large serving. Excess protein over the body's need is burned for energy or stored as fat.

To yield a 3-ounce serving, you need about 4 ounces of boneless raw meat, 4 to 8 ounces of many bone-in cuts, as much as 16 ounces of very bony cuts.

| Meat cuts* | | Calories | Total fat (grams) | Cholesterol (milligrams) |
|---|---|---|---|---|
| **Beef** (all grades) | | | | |
| Eye of round, roasted | | 155 | 5.5 | 59 |
| Top round, broiled | | 162 | 5.3 | 72 |
| Round tip, roasted | These beef cuts | 162 | 6.4 | 69 |
| Tenderloin, broiled | are lower | 174 | 7.9 | 72 |
| Sirloin steak, broiled | in calories | 177 | 7.4 | 76 |
| Liver, pan-fried | | 184 | 6.8 | 410 |
| Porterhouse steak, broiled | | 185 | 9.2 | 68 |
| Bottom round, braised | | 189 | 8.2 | 81 |
| Rib, roasted | | 207 | 11.9 | 68 |
| Flank steak, broiled | | 207 | 12.7 | 60 |
| Brisket (flat portion), braised | | 223 | 13.5 | 77 |
| Lean ground beef, broiled (medium) | | 228 | 15.2 | 74 |
| Chuck blade, braised | | 230 | 13.0 | 90 |
| Regular ground beef, broiled (medium) | | 248 | 17.9 | 77 |
| Shortribs, braised | | 251 | 15.4 | 79 |
| **Pork** | | | | |
| Tenderloin, roasted | These pork cuts | 141 | 4.1 | 79 |
| Leg, rump portion, roasted | are lower | 187 | 9.1 | 81 |
| Loin, center-cut, broiled | in calories | 196 | 8.9 | 83 |
| Loin, center rib chop, broiled | | 219 | 12.7 | 80 |
| Shoulder, blade (butt), braised | | 250 | 15.0 | 99 |
| Loin, blade (country ribs), broiled | | 255 | 18.3 | 85 |
| Spareribs, braised (lean and fat) | | 338 | 25.8 | 103 |
| **Lamb** | | | | |
| Leg (shank portion), roasted | | 153 | 5.7 | 74 |
| Foreshank, braised | Most lamb cuts | 159 | 5.1 | 88 |
| Leg, (sirloin portion), roasted | are low | 174 | 7.8 | 78 |
| Shoulder, blade chop, broiled | in calories | 181 | 9.5 | 77 |
| Loin chop, broiled | | 183 | 8.2 | 80 |
| Rib, rack, roasted | | 197 | 11.4 | 74 |
| Shoulder, arm chop, braised | | 237 | 12.0 | 103 |
| **Veal** | | | | |
| Rib, roasted | All veal cuts | 143 | 5.5 | 108 |
| Leg cutlet, pan-fried | are low | 155 | 3.9 | 112 |
| Shoulder, arm steak, braised | in calories | 166 | 4.1 | 135 |
| Shoulder, blade steak, braised | | 167 | 4.9 | 139 |
| Sirloin chop, braised | | 168 | 5.1 | 128 |
| Loin chop, braised | | 185 | 7.2 | 138 |

*Figures for each cut are for 3-ounce cooked servings with knife-separable fat removed.

# Lean Meat: Six Cooking Techniques

MEATS CAN LOSE TENDERNESS *as they become leaner. And the wrong cooking method can add unwanted fat.*

## HOW COOKING AFFECTS MEAT

What makes meat tender or tough? Juicy or dry? Flavorful or bland? The answers lie in the structure of muscles and connective tissues (such as tendons and gristle) and how they respond to cooking.

Muscles consist of long, thin fibers held together in bundles by connective tissue. In young animals, the muscles are thin; later, they become thicker and tougher. But younger animals often have a higher ratio of connective tissue to muscle. In any animal, muscles that are used least are most tender. Usually, muscles along the back get the least action, while those in the shoulder and legs get the most.

When cutting meat, you can often remove tendons and gristle along with fat. Meats that appear coarse-grained have thicker muscles and often lots of connective tissue laced through them. Fine-grained meats have thinner muscles, with less connective tissue, and are usually more tender. Within many cuts, such as chuck blade, you'll find both coarse- and fine-grained meat.

The most direct ways to tenderize meats are physical. Slicing it thinly across muscle fibers makes it easier to chew. Pounding meat slices, scoring the surface, and putting slices through a mechanical tenderizer are all ways to break down fibers; grinding breaks them down even more, and also changes texture.

When preparing less tender cuts, determine the direction in which muscle fibers run and slice perpendicular to it. This is critical in cutting strips for stir-frying and slices for scaloppine, as well as for slicing roasts and thick steaks. Marinades containing wine, vinegar, or citrus juice also soften muscle fibers but work only on the surface. We use them to add flavor, not to tenderize.

The flavor of cooked meats is influenced by the age of the animal, what it was fed, and how the meat was stored after slaughter. Within muscles and surrounding them, even when not visible, are fat deposits. These melt during cooking, lubricating fibers and making meat seem more tender and flavorful. Our recipes use light sauces with lean meats to help compensate for the lack of fatty juices.

Changes that take place during cooking also result in characteristic flavors. High temperatures that give a brown crust to the meat's surface concentrate flavor there. As meat cooks, its color also changes predictably, so color can be a gauge of doneness. As the meat's internal temperature rises from about 130° to 170°, the fibers shorten and bond together in solid masses, squeezing out liquid from within the cells. At 170°, most of the juices have been exuded. Lean meats, especially, are more tender and juicy to eat when served rare.

We've been told for years that pork must be well cooked to kill any trichinae parasite. But, when roasted to the 160° or 170° recommended in the past, today's lean pork is tough and tasteless. The parasite is actually destroyed at 137°; it's safe to cook pork to an internal temperature of 150° (use a meat thermometer in the thickest part.)

Connective tissue breaks down most effectively at temperatures close to the boiling point of water, and in liquid. When meat has a lot of connective tissue, it needs to simmer until both muscle fibers and connective tissue begin to disintegrate—as with our braising method.

In Sunset's kitchens, we've tested six techniques to cook lean meats to make them as tender and succulent as fatter cuts without adding high-calorie ingredients.

---

## 1. KEBAB CUBES:

*Bright vegetables add color, texture*

*Buy meat already cubed, or cut cubes from any fairly tender cut of meat.*

For 4 servings, you need 1 pound **boneless lean meat** (see chart, page 276); a **marinade** (choices follow); 8 tiny **onions** (each about 1-inch diameter), boiled until tender, or 1 small onion, cut into about 1-inch squares (optional); and 2 medium-size **yellow**, green, or red **bell peppers,** stemmed, seeded, and cut into about 1-inch squares (optional).

Cut meat into 1- to 1¼-inch cubes. In a bowl, mix meat cubes and marinade. Cover and chill, stirring occasionally, 1 hour or until the next day.

Lift meat from marinade; reserve marinade. Thread ¼ of the cubes alternately with onions and pepper pieces

onto each of 4 skewers; push ingredients close together.

Lay skewers on a rack in a 12- by 15-inch broiler pan, and broil 4 inches from heat. Or lay on a barbecue grill 4 to 6 inches above a solid bed of hot coals (you can hold your hand at grill level for only 2 to 3 seconds). Or place on grill of a gas or electric barbecue over high heat, pre-

heated as manufacturer directs.

Turn skewers every 2 to 3 minutes to brown all sides; if desired, brush skewers with marinade on each turn. For medium-rare meat, cook 8 to 12 minutes total (cut to test; pork will still be slightly pink). Makes 4 servings.

**Fajita marinade.** In a bowl, mix 2 tablespoons **lime juice;** ¼ cup **water;** 1 clove **garlic,** pressed or minced; ½ teaspoon **ground cumin;** and 1 teaspoon **ground coriander.**

**Lemon-soy marinade.** In a bowl, mix 3 tablespoons **soy sauce;** ¼ cup **lemon juice;** 2 cloves **garlic,** pressed or minced; and 1 tablespoon finely chopped **fresh ginger** (or ¼ teaspoon ground ginger).

**Orange-anise marinade.** In a bowl, mix 2 tablespoons thawed **frozen orange juice concentrate,** ⅓ cup **dry red wine,** and ½ teaspoon **anise seed** (crushed) or fennel seed (finely chopped).

## 2. LONDON BROIL:

### *Cook rare for succulent slices*

*Thick, boneless steaks are broiled or bar-becued to rare, then sliced cross-grain into thin strips. Serve hot or chilled.*

For 4 servings, you need about 1 pound **boneless beef steak** or lamb bottom sir-loin (see chart, page 276) cut 1 to 2 inches thick and a **marinade** (choose fajita, lemon-soy, or orange-anise, facing page).

To cut a London broil steak from a large roast, such as round tip, take a 1- to 2-inch-thick slice from its widest end.

Put meat in an 8- to 9-inch-wide bak-ing dish and pour marinade over meat; turn meat to coat. Cover and chill 1 hour or until the next day. (Or omit marinat-ing and brush cooking steaks with marinade.)

*To barbecue,* surround an 8- to 9-inch drip pan with 60 ash-covered ignited charcoal briquets. Add 12 more briquets to coals. Set grill 5 to 6 inches above firegrate; place meat on grill over drip pan.

For rare steaks, cook and turn until well browned on each side. Allow about 20 minutes for 1-inch-thick steaks, about 35 minutes for 1½-inch steaks, about 45 minutes for 2-inch steaks (120° on a meat thermometer inserted in thickest part).

*To broil,* place meat on a rack over an 8- to 9-inch-wide pan. Broil meats up to 1½ inches thick about 4 inches from heat until browned on top, 7 to 10 minutes; turn and broil until browned on other side but still rare in center (cut to test), 7 to 10 minutes longer. Broil meats 1½ to 2 inches thick about 6 inches from heat until a meat thermometer inserted into center registers 120° for rare, 10 to 14 minutes per side.

To serve, cut thin, slanting slices of meat across the grain. Makes 4 servings.

## 3. MINI-ROASTS:

### *Just right for small meals*

*Lean meats are moist and tender when roasted just to rare—less than an hour for these ¾- to 1½-pound cuts. Roasting to the internal temperature specified is very important; just a few degrees can make an immense difference in taste and texture. Be sure to use an accurate meat thermometer. Check temperature often: degrees increase by the minute. Choose a cut that's compact and not more than about 3 inches thick.*

You need a ¾- to 1½-pound **roast** (see chart, page 276) and a **glaze** (two choices follow).

Some cuts are compact; if not, use clean cord to tie meat in an evenly thick shape. Thick roasts take longer to cook than slender pieces of the same weight.

Spread glaze evenly over roast. Place meat on a rack over a foil-lined 8- to 9-inch-wide pan or 12- by 15-inch broil-ing pan.

Roast beef or lamb in a 425° oven until a thermometer inserted in thickest part registers 135° for rare, 25 to 45 minutes. After 25 minutes, check temperature every 5 to 10 minutes.

Cook pork in a 350° oven until a ther-mometer inserted in the thickest part registers 150° (slightly pink in center), 35 to 55 minutes. After 25 minutes, check temperature every 5 to 10 minutes.

To serve, slice meat thinly across the grain. Makes 3 to 6 servings.

**Honey-pepper glaze.** In a bowl, mix 2 tablespoons **honey** and 2 teaspoons **coarsely ground black pepper.**

**Chutney glaze.** In a bowl, stir until evenly mixed 2 to 3 tablespoons finely chopped **chutney.**

## 4. BRAISED CUBES:

*No flouring, no frying, more flavor*

*Using a technique called "sweating," you can brown meat and onions with very little fat. You can do this step a day ahead. Next day, reheat the tender meat cubes and serve with rice or vegetables. Or turn them into a quick stew, a curry, a soup, or chili con carne (recipes on page 277).*

For 4 servings, you need 1 pound **boneless lean meat** (see chart, page 276); 2 medium-size **onions,** thinly sliced; 2 cloves **garlic,** pressed or minced; ½ cup **water;** 1 tablespoon **salad oil;** and 1 to 4 cups **regular-strength chicken** or beef **broth.**

Buy meat cut for stew, or cut boneless meat into ¾- to 1-inch cubes; trim off and discard any fat.

In a 5- to 6-quart pan with a tight-fitting lid, combine meat, onions, garlic, water, and oil. Cover pan and simmer over low heat, stirring occasionally, for 30 minutes (add more water if it cooks away).

Uncover pan; stir often over medium-high heat until liquid almost cooks away. Reduce heat to medium; stir until juices evaporate and brown (the meat browns very little). This step takes 15 to 45 minutes *total*, depending upon meat and how you regulate heat. Add 1 cup of the broth; stir to free browned bits in pan.

Simmer, covered, until meat is very tender when pierced, 45 minutes to 1½ hours. Add broth, if needed, to keep about ½-inch of liquid in pan. (If made ahead, cool, cover, and refrigerate up to 3 days. Reheat meat, adding broth if needed.)

Serve hot as is, or use in one of the recipes on page 277. Makes 4 servings.

## 5. STIR-FRY STRIPS:

*Quick, useful for almost any cut*

*Because you cut the strips thinly and across the grain, even the less tender cuts can be used for stir-frying. Vary cooking sauces and presentation to turn simple meat strips into a variety of dishes.*

For 2 servings, you need 8 ounces **boneless lean meat** (see chart page 276), 1 to 2 teaspoons **salad oil,** and **seasoning sauce** (choices on facing page). To increase servings, double ingredients; cook half the meat at a time, using half the oil. Cook full amount of vegetables or fruit at once.

To cut the meat strips from a large piece, such as a roast, first slice it with the grain into pieces about 1 inch thick.

Then slice meat across the grain into ¹⁄₁₆- to ⅛-inch-thick strips (for easiest slicing, freeze meat until firm but not solid). Discard any fat or tough connective tissue.

Place wok or 10- to 12-inch frying pan over high heat until a few drops of water sizzle and dance on surface. Add oil, rotating pan to coat bottom. When oil is hot, add meat to pan. Cook, stirring, until meat changes color outside but is still pink inside, 1 to 2 minutes. Put meat in a bowl.

Add seasoning sauce to pan and stir,

scraping browned bits free from pan, until sauce boils and thickens. Stir in meat, and serve in any of the ways suggested, following. Makes 2 servings.

**Barbecued stir-fried strips.** For seasoning sauce, mix ⅓ cup **regular-strength beef broth;** 1 tablespoon *each* **red wine vinegar, Worcestershire,** and firmly packed **brown sugar;** 1 clove **garlic,** minced or pressed; 1 teaspoon **cornstarch;** and ½ teaspoon **dry mustard.**

*Serving suggestions:* Serve over toasted buns with lettuce, tomatoes, and onions. Or serve over crisp salad greens or hot pasta.

**Ginger-sherry stir-fried strips.** For seasoning sauce, stir together ¼ cup *each* **dry sherry** and **regular-strength beef broth;** 1 tablespoon **soy sauce;** 1 teaspoon chopped **fresh ginger;** 1 clove **garlic,** minced or pressed; 1 teaspoon **cornstarch;** and ⅛ to ¼ teaspoon **crushed dried hot red chilies.**

Stir-fry meat strips as directed. After removing cooked meat from pan, add to pan 1 small **yellow** or red **bell pepper,** stemmed, seeded, and cut into ¼-inch slices; cook, stirring, for about 1 minute. Add sauce to pan; cook as directed (preceding); add meat. Remove from heat; stir in ¼ cup thinly sliced **green onions.**

*Serving suggestions:* Serve with hot rice or on a bed of finely shredded napa cabbage.

**Rosemary-pear stir-fried strips.** For seasoning sauce, mix ½ cup canned **pear nectar,** 2 to 3 teaspoons **white wine vinegar,** 1 teaspoon chopped **fresh rosemary** (or ½ teaspoon dry rosemary), ¼ teaspoon **coarsely ground pepper,** and ¾ teaspoon **cornstarch.**

Stir-fry meat strips as directed. Remove from pan and add ¼ cup firmly packed chopped **bacon;** stir over medium heat until crisp, about 5 minutes. Lift bacon from pan, drain on paper towels, and reserve; discard all but ½ teaspoon fat. Stem 1 large firm-ripe **pear;** cut into ¼-inch wedges. Return pan to high heat; when hot, add pear; stir until tender when pierced, 2 to 3 minutes. Return bacon to pan, add sauce, and cook as directed on facing page; add meat.

*Serving suggestions:* Serve on a bed of lightly cooked sliced mustard greens or kale. Or serve with rice.

# How to Handle Meat at Home

A package of meat gets forgotten in the refrigerator. A casserole is left all night on the kitchen counter. We've all had these or similar experiences. No one wants to take chances involving "food poisoning," but there's a lot of confusion about what is and isn't safe.

Understanding the differences between organisms that cause foods to spoil and those that cause food-borne illness can help us judge meat's safety. The food spoilers continue to multiply even at refrigerator temperatures. They eventually cause the meat to rot or spoil; when that happens, it's usually very obvious. Spoiled meats look and smell awful: throw them out.

But organisms that commonly cause food-borne illness can't be seen, smelled, or tasted. They're present all around us, in the intestines and skin of humans and animals, and in soil and air. Though they thrive at normal room temperatures and warmer, most grow very slowly or not at all at refrigerator temperatures. The best way to keep foods safe from these organisms is to keep them from multiplying enough to cause illness. (Follow precautions with poultry, fish, and dairy products as well.)

**Keep meats cold.** Pick up meats last when shopping and get them into your refrigerator quickly; use an ice chest if you might be delayed getting home. Never leave raw meats at room temperature longer than 3 hours. Thaw frozen meats and poultry in the refrigerator. If you need them faster, thaw in a watertight bag under cold water and change water often, or thaw in a microwave oven as the manufacturer directs.

**Guard against cross-contamination.** Salmonella bacteria, often present on raw meats, are easily destroyed in cooking but can cause big problems when transferred to other foods that are eaten without cooking. As a prevention, thoroughly clean anything—a cutting surface, dish, knife, or your hands—that has been in contact with raw meat before touching other foods.

After using a cutting board to cut raw meat, scrub it with hot, soapy water and rinse well before using it again to cut other foods. Periodically, you can also wipe meat-cutting boards with a solution of household bleach.

**Handle meat as little as possible.** Use gloves if you have any infection on your hands. Unless the wrapping is torn, refrigerate meat in its original wrapper.

**Keep hot foods hot.** If you need to delay serving cooked foods, don't hold them at warm (under 140°) temperatures for more than 3 hours. It is best not to interrupt cooking, giving bacteria a chance to grow before cooking is complete.

**Put cooked leftovers into the refrigerator** as soon as they have stopped steaming. Don't cool on the kitchen counter. Divide large amounts of food into small portions in shallow containers to cool more quickly. Reheat leftovers.

**How long can you store meat and poultry?** It depends on how they're handled in the store and how long they've been in the meat case, but here are guidelines: Keep roasts and chops up to 5 days (veal is best used within 3 days). Store ground meat, and meats in small pieces no more than 2 days. Use cooked meat or poultry dishes in about 5 days.

**If your freezer fails.** A well-insulated freezer filled with foods will keep them frozen about 2 days. If it's half-full, foods should stay frozen for about a day. Don't open to check. If power will be off for a longer time, find a locker, store, or friend to accept your food temporarily. Meats that still feel cold to touch are usually safe to refreeze. If they feel only cool, it's best to cook them right away. Discard any meat that has an unusual odor.

**If your refrigerator fails.** Unless your kitchen is very warm, meats keep 4 to 6 hours with the door closed. If there's a delay in getting power, add block ice to a refrigerator to keep it cool.

## 6. SCALOPPINE:

*Pound for tenderness, quicker cooking*

*Purchase meats cut for scaloppine, or cut and pound slices.*

For every 2 servings, you need 8 ounces **boneless lean meat** (see chart at right), 1 to 2 teaspoons **salad oil**, a **savory sauce** (choices follow), and **salt** and **pepper**.

Slice meat across the grain into slices about ½ inch thick.

Place slices between sheets of plastic wrap and pound firmly and evenly with a flat-surfaced mallet until slices are ⅛ to ¹⁄₁₆ inch thick.

Brush about 1 teaspoon of the oil in a 10- to 12-inch frying pan and place over high heat until a drop of water sizzles and hops around in the pan. Arrange as many meat slices in pan as you can fit without crowding. Cook just until meat changes color around edges, 10 to 15 seconds. With a wide spatula, turn slices over. Cook just until meat changes color on bottom, 10 to 15 seconds longer. Remove meat from pan and arrange on serving plate; keep warm. (Meat should be slightly pink in center: cut to test.) Repeat until all meat is cooked, brushing pan with oil as needed to prevent sticking.

Remove pan from heat. Pour sauce (choices follow) into pan and scrape to release browned bits. Return pan to heat; bring sauce to boiling and pour over meat. Add salt and pepper to taste. Makes 2 servings.

**Mustard-tarragon sauce.** In a bowl, mix ⅓ cup **regular-strength beef broth**, 1 teaspoon **red wine vinegar**, 1 teaspoon **Dijon mustard**, ½ teaspoon **cornstarch**, and ½ teaspoon chopped **fresh tarragon** (or ¼ teaspoon dry tarragon).

**Wine-blue cheese sauce.** In a bowl, mix ⅓ cup **regular-strength beef broth**, 2 tablespoons **dry red wine**, 1 teaspoon **cornstarch**, and ¼ teaspoon **Worcestershire**. Pour heated sauce over meat, then sprinkle with 1 to 2 tablespoons crumbled **blue cheese.**

**Thyme sauce.** In a bowl, mix ⅓ cup **regular-strength chicken broth**, 1 teaspoon chopped **fresh thyme** (or ½ teaspoon dry thyme leaves), and ½ teaspoon **cornstarch.**

**Tapenade-tomato sauce.** In a bowl, mix ½ tablespoon chopped canned **anchovies** or 1 teaspoon anchovy paste; ¼ cup chopped pitted **black ripe olives;** 1 tablespoon drained **capers;** 1 clove **garlic,** pressed or minced; 1 teaspoon **Dijon mustard;** and 1 small ripe **tomato,** peeled, cored, and chopped (about ⅔ cup).

### What Cooking Techniques can you use for each cut of meat?

| | Kebab cubes | London broil | Mini-roasts | Braised cubes | Stir-fry strips | Scaloppine |
|---|---|---|---|---|---|---|
| **Beef** | | | | | | |
| Chuck: blade roast (see page 266) | ■ | | | ■ | ■ | ■ |
| Chuck: boneless shoulder (see page 267) | ■ | | | ■ | ■ | ■ |
| Chuck: 7-bone roast (see page 266) | ■ | | | ■ | ■ | ■ |
| Flank: flank steak | | ■ | | | ■ | ■ |
| Loin: tenderloin roast | ■ | | ■ | | ■ | ■ |
| Rib: rib eye roast | ■ | | ■ | | ■ | ■ |
| Round: bottom round (see page 267) | ■ | | | ■ | ■ | ■ |
| Round: eye round roast (see page 267) | ■ | | ■ | ■ | ■ | ■ |
| Round: tip roast (see page 267) | ■ | | ■ | | ■ | ■ |
| Round: top round (see page 267) | ■ | ■ | ■ | | ■ | ■ |
| Sirloin: bottom triangle (see page 267) | ■ | ■ | ■ | | ■ | ■ |
| **Veal** | | | | | | |
| Leg: boned roast | ■ | | ■ | | ■ | ■ |
| Shoulder: boned roast | ■ | | | ■ | ■ | |
| Stew meat | | | | ■ | | |
| **Pork** | | | | | | |
| Leg: boned roast | ■ | | ■ | | ■ | ■ |
| Loin: center-cut roast (see page 268) | ■ | | ■ | | ■ | ■ |
| Loin: tenderloin | ■ | | | | ■ | ■ |
| **Lamb** | | | | | | |
| Leg: full-cut, boned (see page 269) | ■ | | ■ | | ■ | ■ |
| Leg: ¾-cut, boned | ■ | | ■ | | ■ | ■ |
| Shoulder: boned | ■ | | | ■ | ■ | |

# Lean Meat: More Recipes

**R**ICH IN FLAVOR *but low in fat, these recipes use lean cuts of meat (see chart on facing page) and a minimum of oil, so you can serve a hearty-tasting soup, curry, ragout, or chili that's light in calories.*

*Each recipe begins with tender chunks of slowly cooked meat you can prepare a day or more ahead; directions for braising beef, veal, lamb, or pork are on page 274. Once the meat is cooked to succulence, it takes less than a half-hour to assemble these well-seasoned dishes.*

*Mediterranean ragout boasts cubed meat braised to tenderness in flavorful sauce.*

## BRAISED MEAT & CRISP VEGETABLE SOUP

- 6 cups regular-strength chicken or beef broth
- 1 large carrot, cut into ⅛-inch-thick slices
- 2 cups broccoli flowerets
- 1 medium-size red bell pepper, stemmed, seeded, and cut into ⅜-inch squares
- 1 medium-size zucchini (ends trimmed), cut into ⅛-inch-thick slices
- 2 green onions (ends trimmed), thinly sliced
- 2 tablespoons finely chopped fresh basil leaves or 1 tablespoon dry basil leaves
  Braised meat cubes (recipe on page 274)

In a 5- to 6-quart pan over high heat, bring broth and carrot to a boil. Cover and simmer until carrot is tender-crisp when pierced, about 3 minutes. Add broccoli, pepper, zucchini, onions, basil, and meat; simmer, covered, until broccoli is tender-crisp when pierced, about 8 minutes. Makes 4 to 6 servings.

## BRAISED MEAT CURRY

- 2 teaspoons ground coriander
- 1½ teaspoons ground cumin
- ½ teaspoon ground turmeric
- ⅛ teaspoon *each* ground cinnamon, nutmeg, and cayenne
- 1 large onion, thinly sliced
- 2 tablespoons salad oil
- 2 tablespoons minced fresh ginger
- 3 cloves garlic, pressed or minced
  Braised meat cubes (recipe on page 274)
- ¼ cup currants or raisins
- ½ to 1 cup regular-strength chicken broth
- 1 cup unflavored yogurt (optional)
  Hot cooked rice

In a 5- to 6-quart pan, combine coriander, cumin, turmeric, cinnamon, nutmeg, and cayenne; stir over medium heat until spices darken slightly, about 5 minutes. Add onion, oil, ginger, and garlic; stir often until onion is limp.

Add meat, currants, and enough broth to give desired consistency. Bring to boiling over high heat; cover and simmer until hot, about 5 minutes. Spoon yogurt over individual portions; serve with rice. Makes 3 or 4 servings.

## MEDITERRANEAN RAGOUT

- 3 medium-size firm-ripe tomatoes, cored and chopped
- 3 cloves garlic, pressed or minced
- 1 tablespoon olive oil or salad oil
- 2 teaspoons dry oregano leaves
- ½ teaspoon dry rosemary, crushed
  Braised meat cubes (recipe on page 274)
- 1 package (9 oz.) frozen artichoke hearts, thawed and drained
- 1 cup pitted black ripe olives
- 2 tablespoons drained capers
- ½ teaspoon anchovy paste or 1 teaspoon chopped canned anchovy fillets
- 1 tablespoon red wine vinegar
- ¼ cup cored and diced firm-ripe tomatoes (optional)

In a 5- to 6-quart pan over medium heat, combine chopped tomatoes, garlic, oil, oregano, and rosemary; cook, stirring, until tomatoes are dry, 20 to 30 minutes. Add braised meat cubes, artichoke hearts, olives, capers, and anchovy paste; stir to free browned bits in pan. Bring to a boil over high heat. Cover and simmer until hot, about 5 minutes. Stir in vinegar. Top with diced tomatoes. Makes 4 servings.

## GREEN CHILI WITH BRAISED MEAT

- 1 tablespoon salad oil
- 1 large onion, thinly sliced
- ½ teaspoon ground cumin
  Braised meat cubes (recipe on page 274)
- 2 cups regular-strength chicken broth
- 1 can (7 oz.) whole green chilies, drained, cut into thin slices
- 1 can (15 oz.) white beans, drained
  About 1 to 2 tablespoons prepared green salsa
  Coarsely chopped fresh cilantro (coriander)

In a 5- to 6-quart pan over medium heat, combine oil, onion, and cumin; stir often until onion is limp, about 10 minutes.

Add meat, broth, chilies, beans, and green salsa to taste. Stirring, bring to a boil over high heat. Cover and simmer until hot, about 5 minutes. Garnish with cilantro; add salsa. Serves 4.

# The Potluck Thanksgiving

**T**HIS YEAR, TAKE IT EASY. *Have a potluck Thanksgiving.*

*According to the many Western families we talked to, potluck Thanksgivings are not only a whiz to assemble, they're also fun. Everyone shares in the activities. And, with proper planning, cleanup is fast.*

*How do you proceed? First, take a head count. Next, work out a menu, ranging from a loose framework to a detailed plan, then assign duties (including number of portions to produce) and establish the ground rules. Most popular requests are to ask guests to bring dishes ready to serve— hot or cold—and to take the empty containers home afterward.*

*With these rules in mind, we propose 27 make-ahead dishes that travel well. They're all pictured below. Basically, there are 3 menus, each featuring 9 interchangeable dishes. You can pick and choose among the offerings from appetizers through desserts, or substitute some of your family's favorite dishes.*

**APPETIZERS**

1 Clam-stuffed Shells

2 Gorgonzola and Belgian Endive

3 Shrimp on Palm Pedestals

**SOUPS**

4 Tomatillo and Chili Broth

Curried Yam and Apple Bisque 5

22 Cranberry-Port Relish

Cranberry Borscht 6

**SALADS**

7 Apple Chard Salad

Tricolor Celery Heart Salad 8

9 Red Radish Rafts

**GREEN VEGETABLES**

10 Broccoli Milanese

11 Green Beans with Braised Oriental Mushrooms

2 Artichokes and Spinach au Gratin

*You can build three different Thanksgiving menus from these 27 interchangeable, make-ahead dishes.*

Each dish makes 8 servings; if your group is smaller, keep in mind that the leftovers hold up well. Paired with a 10- to 12-pound turkey, you have a meal that will more than satisfy 8 hungry diners.

If you expect 16 to sit down for Thanksgiving dinner, just make each recipe twice or select 2 dishes in the same category. To multiply servings for larger groups, use the same formula.

Hosts often plead: don't expect to find room in my holiday refrigerator! This menu's cold or room-temperature foods are simple to manage: just keep them cold in insulated chests or bags.

As no household has unlimited oven space, make sure it is well understood how the space is to be used. Usually it's easiest to heat foods at home and carry them in insulated containers. But it is very important that hot foods not be held at serving temperature for more than 3 hours. Beyond this limit, there is always the possibility that bacteria capable of causing

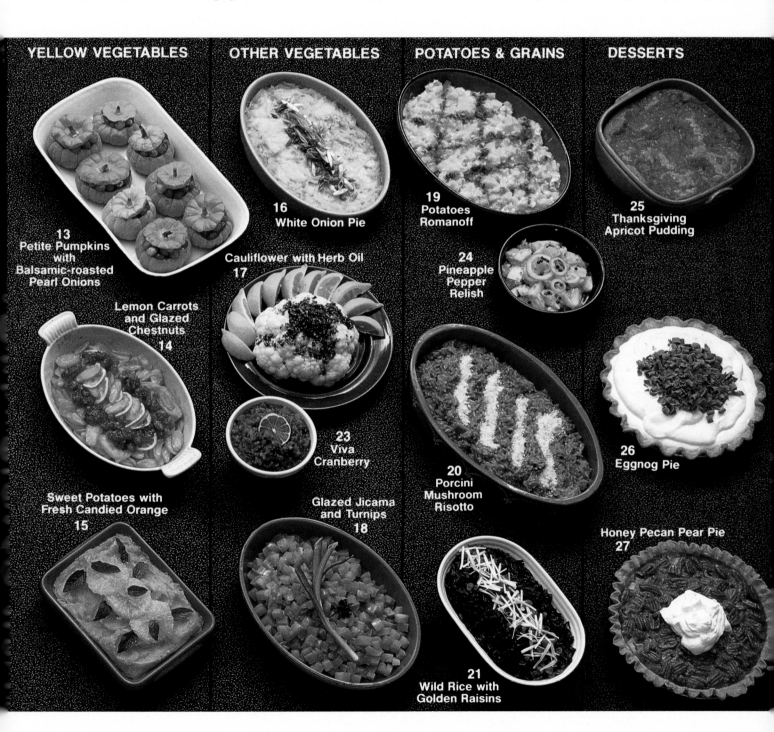

**YELLOW VEGETABLES**

13
Petite Pumpkins with Balsamic-roasted Pearl Onions

Lemon Carrots and Glazed Chestnuts
14

Sweet Potatoes with Fresh Candied Orange
15

**OTHER VEGETABLES**

16
White Onion Pie

Cauliflower with Herb Oil
17

23
Viva Cranberry

Glazed Jicama and Turnips
18

**POTATOES & GRAINS**

19
Potatoes Romanoff

24
Pineapple Pepper Relish

20
Porcini Mushroom Risotto

21
Wild Rice with Golden Raisins

**DESSERTS**

25
Thanksgiving Apricot Pudding

26
Eggnog Pie

Honey Pecan Pear Pie
27

*illness will develop in sufficient numbers to be dangerous (for some details on how to handle food properly, see page 275).*

*As you will note in many of the recipes, dishes can be reheated in the microwave oven—either before or, if manageable for the host, after arrival for dinner.*

## APPETIZERS

*Showy, simple, quick,
& refreshing ways
to start the meal*

### 1. CLAM-STUFFED SHELLS

*If you can't find giant pasta shells, use the large-size shells, about 1½ inches long; you need about 150.*

- 32 giant pasta shells, each about 2½ inches long (about 8 oz. total)
- 1 tablespoon salad oil
- 2 large packages (8 oz. each) cream cheese, at room temperature
- 3 cloves garlic, pressed or minced
- 2 tablespoons prepared horseradish
- ¼ cup chopped parsley
- 4 cans (6½ oz. each) chopped clams, drained
  Salt and coarsely ground pepper
  Parsley sprigs

In a 5- to 6-quart pan, bring about 3 quarts water to boiling. Stir in pasta. Boil, uncovered, until pasta is just barely tender to bite, about 15 minutes; drain. Fill pan with about 2 quarts cold water. Add pasta and oil; when cool, drain in a colander, shaking gently to remove water lodged in curves of shells.

With a mixer, beat cheese, garlic, and horseradish until creamy. Stir in chopped parsley, clams, and salt and pepper to taste. With 1 hand, hold open a pasta shell; with the other hand, spoon in clam mixture to fill. Arrange on a serving platter; sprinkle liberally with pepper.

Serve, or cover and chill up until the next day; garnish with parsley. To transport, carry in an insulated chest. Makes 8 appetizer servings.—*Mary Baier, Fair Oaks, Calif.*

### 2. GORGONZOLA & BELGIAN ENDIVE

- 4 or 5 medium-size heads (about 2 oz. each) Belgian endive
  About ½ pound gorgonzola or blue-veined cheese

Rinse endive heads, wrap in paper towels, enclose in a plastic bag, and chill at least 30 minutes or until next day. To transport endive and cheese, carry both in an insulated bag.

Place cheese in the center of a tray. Cut endive leaves free at base and arrange on plate with tips out, overlapping leaves around the cheese. Let individuals serve themselves, cutting off a small bit of cheese and putting it in a leaf to eat. Makes 8 appetizer servings.

### 3. SHRIMP ON PALM PEDESTALS

- 1 can (14 oz.) hearts of palm, drained and rinsed
- ¼ cup mayonnaise
- 1 teaspoon minced fresh dill weed or ¼ teaspoon dry dill weed
- 1 teaspoon lemon juice
- ¼ pound tiny cooked shelled shrimp
  Dill sprigs (optional)

Cut hearts of palm into ¾-inch lengths and set with a cut end up on a small tray.

Mix mayonnaise, dill, and lemon juice. On top of each palm piece, place an equal amount of dill mayonnaise. Set 1 shrimp and 1 tiny dill sprig on top of each palm piece. Serve, or cover and chill until next day; to transport, carry in an insulated chest. Makes 8 appetizer servings.

## SOUPS

*Light broth to thick,
smooth bisque*

*The first two are best served hot; the cranberry borscht is served cold.*

### 4. TOMATILLO & CHILI BROTH

- 6 cups regular-strength chicken broth
- 1 fresh jalapeño chili, stemmed, seeded, and minced
- ¾ pound tomatillos, husked, rinsed, cored, and finely chopped
- ¼ cup lime juice
  About ⅓ cup fresh cilantro (coriander) leaves

In a 3- to 4-quart pan on high heat, bring broth to boiling with chili and tomatillos. Simmer, uncovered, for 3 to 4 minutes. Add lime juice.

Serve hot. If made ahead, let cool, then cover and chill up until next day. Reheat to simmering. Transport in a thermos. Pour into a tureen and top with cilantro. Ladle into small bowls. Makes 8 servings, about 1 cup each.

### 5. CURRIED YAM & APPLE BISQUE

- 2 tablespoons butter or margarine
- 1 large onion, chopped
- 2 large Golden Delicious apples, peeled, cored, and chopped
- 1 clove garlic
- 2 teaspoons curry powder
- ½ teaspoon ground coriander
- 7 cups regular-strength chicken broth
- 1 cup dry sherry
- 2 pounds (about 3 medium-size) sweet potatoes or yams, peeled and cut into 1-inch cubes
  Salt
  Unflavored yogurt (optional)
  Golden raisins (optional)

In a 5- to 6-quart pan, melt butter over medium heat. Add onion, apples, and garlic; stir until onion is limp, about 10 minutes. Add curry and coriander; stir and cook until spices are fragrant, about 30 seconds.

Add broth, sherry, and sweet potatoes. Bring to boiling. Reduce heat, cover, and simmer until potatoes are tender when pierced, about 20 minutes. In a blender, purée soup, a portion at a time, until smooth. Add salt to taste.

Serve hot. If made ahead, cool, cover, and chill until the next day. Stir over low heat until hot. Transport in a thermos. If desired, garnish each serving with a dollop of yogurt and a few raisins. Makes 8 servings, about 1½ cups each.

## 6. CRANBERRY BORSCHT

1 can (1 lb.) diced beets
2 cups cranberry juice cocktail
1¾ cups or 1 can (14½ oz.) regular-strength chicken broth
¼ cup finely chopped green onions
¼ cup finely chopped celery
About ½ cup sour cream
About 1 tablespoon finely shredded orange peel
Freshly grated nutmeg

In a blender, smoothly purée beets with their liquid. Pour into a 3- to 4-quart pan; add cranberry juice, chicken broth, green onions, and celery. Bring to a boil on high heat; cover and simmer 5 minutes. Remove from heat, uncover, and let cool. Cover and chill at least 3 hours. Serve cold or chill up until next day. Transport in a thermos.

To serve, present in a tureen or ladle into small bowls. Spoon sour cream into soup, and top with orange peel and grated nutmeg. Makes 8 servings, about ¾ cup each.—*Lois Dowling, Tacoma.*

---

# SALADS

*Colorful & long lasting;
some are cooked*

*An option to consider is your favorite salad of leafy greens with a light dressing—or try one of the salads on page 289. Add one of them to the menu, or use instead the following choices.*

## 7. APPLE CHARD SALAD

About 2 pounds Swiss chard
5 tablespoons water
6 tablespoons cider vinegar or white wine vinegar
2 medium-size Red or Golden Delicious apples
½ cup olive oil
Salt and pepper
¼ cup pecan halves

Wash and drain chard; trim off tips of stems and discard. Finely sliver remaining stems; also finely sliver leaves but keep separate.

In a 5- to 6-quart pan, combine stems, 3 tablespoons water, and 1 tablespoon vinegar. Place on high heat and stir often until stems are crisp and lighter in color, 3 to 4 minutes. Pour from pan into a bowl. (Stems may darken slightly on standing.)

Set aside 3 cups of the slivered leaves. Rinse pan and add 2 tablespoons water and remaining leaves; stir over high heat just until barely wilted, about 3 minutes. Pour from pan and let cool.

Cut apples in quarters, core, and thinly slice. Reserve 4 slices for garnish, then cut remaining apple into thin slivers. Mix slices and slivers with 5 tablespoons vinegar and oil. To hold until next day, cover stems, cooked leaves, raw leaves, and apples separately; chill.

To serve, mix stems, leaves, and slivered apples together in a bowl; season to taste with salt and pepper. Sprinkle salad with pecans and top with apple slices. To transport, cover and carry in an insulated chest. Makes 8 servings.—*Roxanne Chan, Albany, Calif.*

## 8. TRICOLOR CELERY HEART SALAD

3 celery hearts (each about 2-inch diameter)
½ cup regular-strength chicken broth
6 tablespoons white wine vinegar
¼ cup salad oil
1 teaspoon dry basil leaves
½ teaspoon dry oregano leaves
¼ teaspoon pepper
¼ teaspoon salt
12 green onions
¼ cup niçoise olives
2 to 3 tablespoons finely chopped canned pimientos or canned roasted peppers

Rinse celery hearts and drain, then trim to 6 inches in length; reserve stalks for other uses. With a vegetable peeler, pare as many of the coarse strings as possible from outer stalks on hearts. Also pare base to remove any discoloration.

Cut each heart lengthwise in quarters; tie a string around the middle of each quarter to hold together. Place in a 5- to

6-quart pan. Add broth, vinegar, oil, basil, oregano, pepper, and salt. Bring to a boil on high heat, cover, and simmer on low heat until celery is tender when pierced, 15 to 20 minutes (after about 8 minutes, transfer celery on pan bottom to top). Remove from heat, uncover, and let cool. If made ahead, cover and chill up until next day.

Meanwhile, rinse onions and trim off and discard roots and tips of stems.

In a 10- to 12-inch frying pan, bring about ½ inch water to boiling. Immerse green onions in water just until slightly wilted, about 1½ minutes. At once, immerse in ice water until cool. Drain; if made ahead, cover and chill up until next day.

Snip string from celery. Lift each heart from marinade, and tie a wilted green onion around it. Arrange on a platter. Add olives and pimiento to dressing. To transport, cover celery, and pour marinade into a container and cover. To serve, pour marinade over celery. Makes 8 servings.—*Claire Kellogg, Beavercreek, Ore.*

## 9. RED RADISH RAFTS

4 medium-size (about 1½ lb. total) yellow, red, or green bell peppers
1 cup finely chopped red radish
1 to 1½ cups (5 to 7 oz.) finely chopped peeled daikon
½ cup minced red onion
⅓ cup seasoned rice vinegar (or ⅓ cup white wine vinegar plus 2 teaspoons sugar)
Salt and pepper
3 or 4 red radishes

Cut peppers in half lengthwise; cut out seeds and stems. Lay, cut side down, in a 10- by 15-inch baking pan. Broil about 2 inches from heat until charred, about 8 minutes. Let cool, then pull off and discard charred skin that comes away easily.

In a bowl, combine chopped red radish, daikon, and onion. Add vinegar and mix; season with salt and pepper to taste. Arrange peppers, cut side up, and fill equally with radish mixture. Serve, or cover and chill until the next day; transport in an insulated chest or at room temperature. Thinly slice remaining radishes and use to garnish salads. Makes 8 servings.

## GREEN VEGETABLES

### *Ways to keep them green and fresh*

*Because green vegetables fade and lose their pretty color when kept hot for even a short period, the broccoli and green bean dishes are designed to be served at room temperature. If you aren't going to make them ahead or transport them, both dishes can be cooked and served hot. The spinach-filled artichokes hold their color better; bake or reheat them in the microwave oven.*

### 10. BROCCOLI MILANESE

    ½  cup olive oil
    3  cloves garlic, minced or pressed
    ½  cup fine dry bread crumbs
    ¼  cup minced parsley
    ½  teaspoon grated lemon peel
    2  pounds broccoli
    2  tablespoons lemon juice
       Salt and pepper

In a 7- to 8-inch frying pan over medium-high heat, combine ¼ cup olive oil and garlic; stir often until garlic is pale gold; do not brown, as the flavor will be bitter. Add bread crumbs and stir until they taste richly toasted. Stir in parsley and lemon peel. Let cool, then package airtight and hold for up to a day.

Rinse broccoli, trim and discard tough ends. Cut stalks, through flowerets, into sections no thicker than ½ inch. In a 5- to 6-quart pan, bring about 3 inches water to boiling on high heat. Add broccoli and cook, uncovered, at a gentle boil until stalks are just tender when pierced, 6 to 8 minutes.

If made ahead, drain broccoli and immerse at once in ice water until cool. Drain well; cover and chill up until next day. Also mix remaining ¼ cup oil with lemon juice; cover and let stand up until next day. To transport, cover broccoli in a serving dish; carry seasoned crumbs and oil and lemon dressing in separate containers.

To serve, pour dressing over broccoli and sprinkle with crumbs. Makes 8 servings. —*Tracy King, Eagle Rock, Calif.*

### 11. GREEN BEANS WITH BRAISED ORIENTAL MUSHROOMS

    2  ounces dried shiitake mushrooms
       Water
    3  tablespoons soy sauce
    3  tablespoons dry sherry
    1  tablespoon sugar
    4  slices fresh ginger (each about the size of a quarter)
    5  teaspoons Oriental sesame oil
    2  pounds green beans, ends trimmed

Soak mushrooms in hot water to cover until soft and pliable, about 20 minutes; then trim off and discard tough stems.

In a 1- to 2-quart pan, combine mushrooms, 2 tablespoons soy, 2 tablespoons sherry, sugar, ginger, and 1 cup water. Bring to boil on high heat; reduce heat and simmer, covered, over low heat until mushrooms have absorbed all the liquid, about 15 minutes. Stir in remaining soy, sherry, and 2 teaspoons sesame oil.

Meanwhile, in a 5- to 6-quart pan bring 3 quarts water to boiling on high heat. Push beans into water. Cook, uncovered, until beans are bright green and just tender to bite, 3 to 5 minutes; drain. (If made ahead, immerse in cold water until cool; drain, cover, and chill up until next day.)

Mix beans with 3 teaspoons sesame oil and arrange in a serving dish. To transport, cover beans and mushrooms in separate containers. To present, spoon mushrooms and juices in a band across the beans. Serve warm or at room temperature. Makes 8 servings.

### 12. ARTICHOKES & SPINACH AU GRATIN

    8  large artichokes, each about 3½-inch diameter
       About ½ cup vinegar
    1  tablespoon *each* dry thyme leaves, coriander seed, dry basil leaves, and black peppercorns
    ½  teaspoon crushed dried hot red chilies
       Spinach filling (recipe follows)
    1  cup shredded gruyère or Swiss cheese

With a sharp knife, cut off about the top ⅔ of each artichoke. Also cut off stems flush with bottoms, and peel lightly to remove coarse fibers. Snap coarse outer leaves back, pulling them away from the fleshy base until all coarse leaves are removed. Drop artichokes as trimmed into a bowl with about 1 quart water and ¼ cup vinegar.

In a 4- to 5-quart pan, combine 2 quarts water, the remaining ¼ cup vinegar, thyme, coriander, basil, peppercorns, and chilies. Bring to boiling on high heat. Drain artichokes and add to pan. Cover and boil gently until artichoke bottoms are tender when pierced, about 30 minutes. Let cool in broth; drain. Pull and discard small leaves and fuzzy center from each artichoke. Spoon spinach into each, mounding to use all the filling.

Set artichokes in a shallow 9- by 13-inch dish. If made ahead, cover and chill up until next day. Sprinkle cheese onto artichokes, mounding to use it all. Bake artichokes, uncovered, in a 350° oven until hot, about 30 minutes. Or cover loosely with plastic wrap and heat in a microwave oven on full power (100 percent) until hot, about 15 minutes. To transport, cover artichokes and carry in an insulated chest. Makes 8 servings.

**Spinach filling.** Thaw 2 packages (10 oz. each) **frozen leaf spinach.** With your hands, squeeze spinach tightly to remove as much liquid as possible. Coarsely chop the leaves and set aside.

Mince 1 large **onion.** Melt 5 tablespoons **butter** or margarine in a 10- to 12-inch frying pan over medium-high heat. Add onion and stir often until lightly browned, about 5 minutes. Stir in 2 tablespoons **all-purpose flour,** then 1 cup **regular-strength chicken broth** and 6 tablespoons **half-and-half** (light cream) or whipping cream, and ¼ teaspoon **ground nutmeg.** Stir and boil about 1 minute. Add spinach and stir to mix well. Remove from heat and add **salt** and **pepper** to taste. Use hot or cool.

## YELLOW VEGETABLES

### *Traditional choices with a light touch*

*Tiny pumpkins stuffed with equally diminutive onions look enchanting, taste great. Chestnuts, a traditional favorite, team up with carrots for a mellow dish. And the delectable sweet potato dish, remarkably, contains no fat.*

*Create a grand feast with few chores. Host family did turkey, dressing, and gravy. Guests brought assigned dishes ready to serve hot or cold.*

## 13. PETITE PUMPKINS WITH BALSAMIC-ROASTED PEARL ONIONS

*If you can't get the mini-pumpkins, use 4 acorn or golden acorn squash (each about 1½ lb.). Cut squash in half lengthwise, seed, and put cut side down in a 12- by-17-inch pan. Add 1 cup water and bake, covered, in a 375° oven until tender when pierced, about 1 hour. Fill with onions and continue as directed, following:*

8  mini-pumpkins (Jack Be Little or Munchkin) or sweet dumpling squash (each 6 to 7 oz.)

6  cups (about 2¼ lb.) or 3 packages (12 oz. each) pearl onions (about ¾-inch diameter); or 3 packages (10-oz. size) frozen tiny onions
   Water

½  cup balsamic or red wine vinegar
   About 4 tablespoons (⅛ lb.) butter or margarine

1  tablespoon sugar
   Salt

Rinse pumpkins, then set slightly apart in a 10- by 15-inch baking pan. Bake, uncovered, in a 375° oven until soft when pressed, about 40 minutes. Let cool. With a small, sharp knife, cut off tops, making them large enough to use as lids; set tops aside. With a small spoon, scoop seeds from pumpkins and discard.

Peel fresh onions (to make peeling easier, put onions in a large bowl; add boiling water to cover, then drain and peel). Put onions (fresh or frozen) in a 9- by 13-inch baking pan. Add vinegar and 2 tablespoons butter. Bake, uncovered, in a 400° oven, stirring every 10 minutes or so, until vinegar is almost gone, about 1 hour. Mix sugar into onions and continue to bake until lightly glazed, about 10 minutes; stir several times. Add salt to taste.

Spoon onions into pumpkin shells, filling equally and using all (the onions will mound up). Add a dot of butter to each pumpkin, then set lid on top. Set pumpkins closely together in a shallow 9- by 13-inch baking dish. If made ahead, cover and chill up until next day.

Bake, covered, in 375° oven until hot, about 15 minutes if warm, or 25 minutes if chilled. Or cover loosely with plastic wrap, and heat in a microwave oven on full power (100 percent) until hot, about 12 minutes. To transport, cover and carry in an insulated chest. Serves 8.

## 14. LEMON CARROTS & GLAZED CHESTNUTS

3  pounds carrots
   Water

2  tablespoons butter or margarine
   Salt

1  lemon

¾  cup canned chestnuts in syrup (including syrup)

Peel carrots and cut in long diagonal slices about ¼ inch thick. Place in a 3- to 4-quart pan and add 4 cups water. Bring to a boil, cover, and simmer until carrots are just barely tender when pierced, about 5 minutes. Drain, reserving 2 tablespoons of the water. Return the reserved water to the pan with carrots; add butter and salt to taste.

Cut lemon in half lengthwise, then very thinly slice crosswise; pick out seeds and discard. Mix lemon with carrots and pour into a shallow 2-quart baking dish. Spoon chestnuts in syrup onto carrots. If made ahead, cover and chill up until next day.

Cover carrots and bake in a 350° oven for 15 minutes. Uncover and bake until carrots are very tender when pierced, about 10 minutes; several times, tilt pan to gather juices and spoon over carrots to keep moist. If you let carrots cool, you can cover with plastic wrap and reheat in a microwave oven on full power (100 percent) until hot, about 15 minutes. To transport, cover and carry in an insulated chest. Makes 8 servings.

## 15. SWEET POTATOES WITH FRESH CANDIED ORANGE

3½  to 4 pounds (about 6 medium-size) sweet potatoes or yams, scrubbed

4  large (about 3 inch diameter) oranges
   Water

½  cup sugar

¼  cup orange-flavor liqueur

1  cup orange juice (optional)

3  or 4 cross-cut orange slices (optional)
   Fresh mint leaves (optional)

Set potatoes in a 10- by 15-inch pan and bake in a 350° oven until soft when pressed, about 1 hour. Let cool, peel, and put in a large bowl; set aside.

With a vegetable peeler, pare orange part of peel only from the four oranges. With a knife, cut peel into long, very thin strips (about 1/16 inch wide). Juice oranges and set juice aside.

To remove bitterness from peel, place in a 4- to 5-quart pan and add 3 cups water. Bring to boiling on high heat; drain. Add 3 more cups water, bring to boiling, and drain. Repeat boiling step a third time, then drain peel. To candy the peel, add sugar and 1 cup water to pan. Boil on high heat, uncovered, until water is almost gone; watch carefully to avoid scorching. Add ½ cup orange juice (use juice reamed from 4 oranges) and boil until liquid is almost gone; watch carefully to avoid scorching. Then add liqueur and boil until liquid is almost gone; watch carefully to avoid scorching.

Add ¼ cup orange juice (use juice reamed from 4 oranges) and stir until boiling. Remove from heat and set aside about 2 tablespoons of the candied peel. Add remaining orange juice (use juice reamed from 4 oranges) and boil on high heat, uncovered, until reduced to 1 cup. Pour mixture into potatoes and mash to blend well. Sweet potatoes are inclined to be drier, so add as much of the optional 1 cup orange juice as needed to give a moist, smooth texture.

Spoon potato mixture into a shallow 2½- to 3-quart baking dish. If made ahead, cover and chill potatoes and reserved candied peel up until next day.

Bake, uncovered, in a 350° oven until hot, about 1 hour; or heat in a microwave oven on full power (100 percent) until hot, about 25 minutes. To transport, cover and carry in an insulated chest; also bring reserved candied peel, orange slices, and mint leaves. To present, arrange orange slices on potatoes, and spoon candied peel over fruit; garnish with mint leaves. Makes 8 servings.

## OTHER VEGETABLES

*Onion, cauliflower
& turnips with a surprise*

*This broad category yields three Thanksgiving dinner options: sautéed onions to bake in a pie, cauliflower to enjoy hot or cold with a flavorful herb dressing, and an intriguing combination of turnips and jicama with its tender-crisp texture.*

## 16. WHITE ONION PIE

*Although you assemble the pie ahead, so the bread will have time to absorb the milk-egg mixture, you bake it just before serving or transporting. Also, carry along green onions to garnish the pie before serving it.*

4 **large onions (about 2 lb. total), sliced**
2 **tablespoons butter or margarine**
  **Salt**
4 **slices white bread**
½ **cup grated parmesan cheese**
2 **large eggs**
¼ **teaspoon pepper**
1 **cup milk**
2 **to 4 tablespoons slivered green onions**

In a 10- to 12-inch frying pan over medium-high heat, cook onions in 1 tablespoon of the butter, stirring frequently until slightly browned, about 30 minutes. Add salt to taste.

Meanwhile, toast the bread and spread with remaining butter. Tear or cut toast into ½-inch cubes and scatter over bottom of a buttered shallow 1½-quart (about 8- by 12-inch oval) pan or dish. Evenly spoon onions over bread; sprinkle onions with cheese.

Beat eggs and pepper to blend with milk. Pour milk mixture over onions. Cover and chill for at least 6 hours or until next day. Uncover and bake in a 350° oven until filling in center jiggles only slightly when pan is gently shaken, about 25 minutes.

To transport, cover and carry in an insulated chest. Also bring along slivered onions. Sprinkle onions on top of casserole. Makes 8 servings.—*Fran P. Thoman, Saratoga, Calif.*

## 17. CAULIFLOWER WITH HERB OIL

1 **large head (about 2¼ lb.) cauliflower**
2 **lemons, cut into wedges**
½ **cup extra-virgin olive oil**
¼ **cup thinly sliced chives or green onions**
1 **tablespoon minced fresh thyme or 1 teaspoon dry thyme leaves**
1 **teaspoon grated lemon peel**
  **Several whole chives or 1 or 2 green onions, ends trimmed**
  **Salt and pepper**

Trim wilted leaves off cauliflower. Rinse head. Set cauliflower on a rack above about 1 inch boiling water in a deep 6- to 8-quart pan. Cover and steam until tender when pierced in thickest part, about 15 minutes. (If made ahead, immerse in cold water until cool; drain.) Place cauliflower in a serving dish. Arrange lemon wedges beside cauliflower.

Stir together oil, sliced chives, thyme, and lemon peel. If made ahead, cover and chill cauliflower and oil mixture separately until the next day; to transport, carry separately. Pour oil mixture over cauliflower. Garnish with whole chives. Cut head into wedges, leaving wedges in place. Squeeze lemon onto each serving, and add salt and pepper to taste. Serve warm, at room temperature, or cold. Makes 8 servings.

## 18. GLAZED JICAMA & TURNIPS

2 **tablespoons butter or margarine**
1½ **pounds jicama, peeled and cut into ½-inch cubes (about 4 cups)**
2½ **cups regular-strength beef broth**
1 **whole star anise or 1 teaspoon anise seed (optional)**
2 **tablespoons sugar**
1 **tablespoon soy sauce**
2 **green onions, ends trimmed**
1½ **pounds turnips, peeled and cut into ½-inch cubes (about 4 cups)**

In a 4- to 5-quart pan, combine butter, jicama, broth, anise, sugar, soy, and 1 green onion. Bring to boiling on high heat, cover, and simmer over low heat for 15 minutes. Add turnips and continue cooking, stirring occasionally, until jicama is tender but still slightly crisp, turnip is tender when pierced, and most of the liquid has evaporated, 30 to 40 minutes. Spoon mixture into a shallow 2- to 3-quart casserole.

If made ahead, cool, cover, and chill up until the next day. Loosely cover with plastic wrap and reheat in a microwave oven at full power (100 percent) until hot, stirring occasionally, about 15 minutes. Or bake, covered, in a 350° oven until hot, about 45 minutes. Stir, then garnish with remaining onion. Makes 8 servings.

## POTATOES OR GRAINS

*A little turkey gravy
enhances these dishes*

### 19. POTATOES ROMANOFF

- 3 large russet potatoes (about 2 lb. total), scrubbed
- 2 cups large-curd cottage cheese
- 1 cup sour cream
- 1 clove garlic, minced or pressed
- ¼ cup finely chopped green onions
  Salt
- 1 cup (4 oz.) shredded sharp cheddar cheese
  Paprika

Cut potatoes into quarters and put into a 3- to 4-quart pan. Cover with water; bring to boiling on high heat. Cover and boil gently until tender when pierced, about 25 minutes. Drain and let cool.

Peel potatoes and cut into ¼-inch cubes into a large bowl. Add cottage cheese, sour cream, garlic, onions, and salt to taste; mix well. Spoon into a shallow 2- to 2½-quart (or 8- by 12- inch oval) casserole and spread out evenly. Sprinkle with shredded cheese, and dust with paprika in a decorative pattern. If made ahead, cover and chill up until next day.

Bake, covered, in a 350° oven until hot, about 1 hour. Or cover with plastic wrap and reheat in a microwave oven on full power (100 percent) until hot, about 20 minutes. To transport, cover and carry in an insulated chest. Makes 8 servings.— *Lisa Johnson, Albuquerque.*

### 20. PORCINI MUSHROOM RISOTTO

- 2 ounces dried porcini mushrooms (cèpes)
- 3 cups hot water
  About 3 cups regular-strength beef broth
- ⅓ cup butter or margarine
- 2 tablespoons olive oil
- 1 large onion, chopped
- 2 cloves garlic, pressed or minced
- 2 cups arborio or pearl (short-grain) rice
  About 1 cup grated parmesan cheese

Soak mushrooms in water until soft, 20 to 30 minutes. Squeeze and rub to work out any grit. Lift from water, squeezing dry. Coarsely chop mushrooms. Pour soaking water (be careful not to disturb sediment on bottom of bowl) through a fine strainer into a 1-quart glass measuring cup. Add broth to make 6 cups.

Place butter and olive oil in a 5- to 6-quart pan over medium heat. Add onion and stir often until limp and golden, about 10 minutes. Add garlic and rice; stir until rice looks opaque, about 5 minutes. Add broth mixture and chopped mushrooms.

Cook, stirring occasionally, until mixture comes to a boil. Adjust heat so rice boils gently; cook, uncovered, stirring occasionally, until rice is tender to bite and most of the liquid has been absorbed, 20 to 25 minutes. Toward end of cooking time, stir rice often to prevent sticking. Remove from heat and stir in half the parmesan cheese. Transfer mixture to a buttered shallow 2- to 3-quart baking dish.

If made ahead, cool, cover, and chill until the next day. Loosely cover with plastic wrap and reheat in a microwave oven at full power (100 percent) until hot, about 20 minutes. Or bake, covered, in a 350° oven until hot, about 1¼ hours. Sprinkle with remaining cheese. Makes 8 servings.

### 21. WILD RICE WITH GOLDEN RAISINS

- ¼ cup (⅛ lb.) butter or margarine
- ½ cup golden raisins
- 1 large onion, minced
- 1 teaspoon dry thyme leaves
- 6 cups regular-strength beef or chicken broth
- 1¾ cups wild rice
- 2 tablespoons dry sherry (optional)
- 2 to 3 tablespoons slivered green onions

Melt butter in a 3- to 4-quart pan on medium-high heat. Add raisins and stir until they puff. Lift raisins out with a slotted spoon and set aside.

Add onion and thyme to pan and stir often until onion is lightly browned, about 10 minutes. Add broth and bring to boil.

Rinse rice in a strainer under running water. Add to broth, bring to a boil on high heat, cover, and simmer until tender to bite, about 1¾ hours; stir occasionally. Add sherry the last 10 minutes. Pour rice into 2-quart baking dish. (If made ahead, let cool, cover, and chill up to 24 hours.)

Bake, uncovered, in a 350° oven for 15 minutes; if made ahead, bake, covered, until hot, about 1 hour. Uncover; put raisins on rice; bake 10 minutes. Or loosely cover with plastic wrap and reheat in a microwave oven on full power (100 percent) until hot, about 20 minutes. Add raisins; heat 2 to 3 minutes. To transport, cover and carry in an insulated chest. Garnish with green onions. Serves 8.

## RELISHES

*Lively fruited complements
for the holiday bird*

*One relish is cooked; two are raw. All have vivid, lively flavors.*

### 22. CRANBERRY-PORT RELISH

- 3 cups (12-oz. package) fresh or frozen cranberries
- 1 medium-size onion, minced
- ⅓ cup cider vinegar
- 1 cup golden raisins
- 1 cup sugar
- 1½ cups port
- ½ teaspoon ground nutmeg
- 1 teaspoon *each* ground ginger and ground cinnamon

In a 3- to 4-quart pan, combine cranberries, onion, vinegar, raisins, sugar, port, nutmeg, ginger, and cinnamon. Bring to a boil over high heat, stirring occasionally. Simmer, uncovered, until mixture is thick and reduced to 3 cups, about 30 minutes; stir often to prevent scorching. Let cool. Serve, or cover and chill up to 2 weeks. Cover to transport. Makes about 3 cups, 8 servings.

## 23. VIVA CRANBERRY

- 3 cups (12-oz. package) fresh or frozen cranberries
- 1 fresh jalapeño chili, stemmed, seeded, and minced
- ¾ cup finely chopped onion
- 2 tablespoons minced fresh ginger
- ⅓ cup minced fresh cilantro (coriander)
- 5 tablespoons lime juice
- 2 teaspoons grated orange peel
- ¼ cup tequila (optional)
- 3 tablespoons orange-flavor liqueur
  Salt

In a food processor or with a food chopper, finely chop or grind cranberries with chili. Mix with onion, ginger, cilantro, lime juice, orange peel, tequila, orange liqueur, and salt to taste. Serve, or cover and chill up to 1 week. Cover to transport. Makes about 3 cups, 8 servings.

## 24. PINEAPPLE PEPPER RELISH

- 3 cups ½-inch cubes pineapple
- ¾ cup chopped red onion
- 3 tablespoons drained canned green peppercorns
- ¼ cup lime juice

Combine pineapple, onion, peppercorns, and lime juice. Serve, or cover and chill up until the next day. Cover to transport. Makes 3⅔ cups, 8 servings.

# DESSERTS

*Two to serve warm,*
*one to serve cold*

## 25. THANKSGIVING APRICOT PUDDING

- 1 cup all-purpose flour
- ⅔ cup firmly packed brown sugar
- 1½ teaspoons baking powder
- ½ cup milk
  Apricot sauce (directions follow)
  Whipped cream or vanilla ice cream

In a bowl, stir together flour, sugar, and baking powder. Add milk and stir until evenly moistened. Scrape the batter into a greased 9-inch-square baking dish and spread level. Pour apricot sauce over the batter. Bake in a 350° oven until the cake layer that forms on top is richly browned and firm to touch, about 35 minutes.

Serve the pudding warm, or let cool, cover, and let stand until next day. Then serve at room temperature, or cover and reheat in 350° oven until hot, about 20 minutes. Or loosely cover with plastic wrap and heat in a microwave oven on full power (100 percent) until hot, about 4 minutes.

To transport, cover and carry in an insulated chest. Spoon into bowls and top with whipped cream or ice cream. Makes 8 servings. —*Roxie Kamian, Walnut Creek, Calif.*

**Apricot sauce.** In a 1½- to 2-quart pan, combine 1 cup finely chopped **dried apricots**, 2 cups **water**, ⅔ cup firmly packed **brown sugar**, 2 tablespoons **butter** or margarine, and ¼ teaspoon *each* **ground cinnamon** and **ground allspice**. Bring to a boil on high heat; turn heat to medium and stir often for 2 to 3 minutes. Use hot.

## 26. EGGNOG PIE

- ¾ cup water
- 2 envelopes (4¾ teaspoons) unflavored gelatin
- 1 cup half-and-half (light cream)
- 3 large eggs
- ¾ cup sugar
- ⅛ teaspoon grated nutmeg
- 1 cup whipping cream
- 4 to 6 tablespoons light rum
- 1 baked 9-inch pie shell
  About 1 cup semisweet chocolate curls or grated semisweet chocolate

In 1- to 2-quart pan, combine water and gelatin. Let stand until gelatin is softened, about 5 minutes. Place on medium heat and stir often until gelatin dissolves. Remove from heat and add half-and-half. Cover and chill until mixture just begins to get syrupy.

Separate eggs, putting yolks in a small bowl, whites in a large bowl. With an electric mixer on high speed, whip whites until foamy, then beat in ½ cup sugar until whites will hold soft, curving peaks.

Beat yolks with nutmeg and remaining ¼ cup sugar until slightly thickened and lighter in color. Whip cream until it holds soft peaks. Fold whites, yolks, cream and rum to taste into the gelatin mixture. If the mixture is not stiff enough to hold soft mounds, cover and chill until it does; check frequently, as it should not be too stiff to spoon in soft puffs. Mound mixture into pie shell. Set pie on a tray, and cover with a large inverted bowl. Chill at least 3 hours or until next day.

Transport in an insulated chest, packing to protect filling and crust. To serve, spoon chocolate onto pie, and cut into wedges. —*Patt Hudler, Aptos, Calif.*

## 27. HONEY PECAN PEAR PIE

- 1 pastry shell for deep-dish 9-inch pie
- ¼ cup (⅛ lb.) melted butter or margarine
- 1 cup honey
- 3 large eggs
- ½ teaspoon grated orange peel
- 1 teaspoon vanilla
- 2 cups pecans in large pieces
- 1 medium-size ripe pear
  Whipped cream or vanilla ice cream

Bake pastry shell in a 350° oven until pale gold color, about 8 minutes.

Meanwhile, beat together until well blended the butter, honey, eggs, orange peel, and vanilla; stir in the nuts. Peel pear, core, and cut into about ½-inch cubes. Distribute pear over bottom of pie shell (may be hot or cool). Pour honey mixture over fruit. Bake on the lowest rack of a 325° oven until filling is set when pan is gently jiggled, about 45 minutes. If top begins to brown excessively, drape pie loosely with a sheet of foil until pie finishes baking. Let cool in pan on a rack. If made ahead, cover loosely and let stand until next day. To transport, pack so crust is protected. Cut into wedges and top with whipped cream. Makes 8 servings. —*Ann Rawlings, Paisley, Ore.*

# Holiday Appetizers

PUNGENT FLAVORS —*sharp olives, goat cheese, and chilies—lend distinction to these appetizers. You can make the olive bread and cheese spread ahead, then toast the bread just before serving. The crab and cheese quesadillas are best made at party time; they go together quickly.*

## OLIVE BREAD WITH CHEESE SPREAD

*We enjoyed this at Stephanie's Restaurant in Melbourne, Australia.*

  All-purpose flour
⅓ cup *each* drained, halved, and pitted calamata olives; and sliced and drained pimiento-stuffed green olives
1 loaf (1 lb.) frozen white bread dough, thawed
  Cheese spread (recipe follows)

On a lightly floured board, gently knead calamata and green olives into bread dough until evenly distributed; add flour as required to prevent sticking. Shape dough into a smooth, round loaf about 5 inches across and place on a greased 12- by 15-inch baking sheet. Cover lightly with plastic wrap and let rise in a warm place until puffy, about 40 minutes.

Bake in a 350° oven until well browned, about 45 minutes. Cool on a rack. If made ahead, store airtight up to 2 days.

Cut bread into ⅓-inch-thick slices. Place in a single layer on two baking sheets (each 12 by 15 inches). Bake in a 350° oven until golden, about 25 minutes. Switch positions of pans halfway through baking. Serve hot or cool; spread with cheese. Serves 5 or 6.

**Cheese spread.** In a bowl, mix together 1 small package (3 oz.) **cream cheese** and 3 ounces (⅓ cup) **goat cheese** such as montrachet or bûcheron. If made ahead, cover and chill up to 2 days.

## CRABBY JACK QUESADILLAS

¼ pound shelled cooked crab
2 cups shredded jack cheese
1 cup thinly sliced green onions
10 flour tortillas, each 7 to 8 inches wide
  Fresh cilantro (coriander) sprigs
  Chili-cilantro sauce (recipe follows)

*Crisp quesadillas, filled with jack cheese and crab, are baked. Serve them warm with chili-spiked cilantro sauce and a dry white wine such as Sauvignon Blanc.*

In a bowl, mix crab, cheese, and onions. Place 5 tortillas in a single layer on 2 baking sheets, each 14 by 17 inches. Evenly cover tortillas with crab mixture to within ¾ inch of edges. Top each with 1 of the remaining tortillas.

Bake in a 450° oven until cheese melts and tortillas are lightly browned, 7 to 9 minutes. Slide quesadillas onto a board and cut each into 6 wedges. Arrange on a platter and garnish with cilantro sprigs. Offer with chili-cilantro sauce to add to each serving. Makes 10 servings. —*Peter Morency, San Francisco.*

**Chili-cilantro sauce.** Place 4 medium-size fresh **Anaheim chilies** on a 12- by 15-inch baking sheet; broil 2 inches below heat, turning often, until brown and blistered on all sides, about 5 minutes. Let cool on pan, then pull off and discard skin, stems, and seeds. Coarsely chop chilies.

In a blender or food processor, whirl until smooth chilies; ¼ cup **dry white wine;** 1 medium-size **shallot,** chopped; and 1 tablespoon **lemon juice.** Pour into a 2- to 3-quart pan, bring to a boil over high heat, and boil, stirring, until reduced to ⅓ cup, 5 to 10 minutes.

Return mixture to blender or food processor. Add 1 cup firmly packed fresh **cilantro** (coriander) and whirl until smooth; scrape container sides several times. With motor running, slowly add ¼ cup (⅛ lb.) hot melted **butter** or margarine until incorporated; scrape container sides once or twice. Serve warm.

# Bourride: Bouillabaisse's Country Cousin

RELATIVELY UNKNOWN *outside France, bourride, a fish soup from Provence, deserves wider recognition. Like many specialties from this region of Southern France, bourride's straightforward presentation belies its richness of flavor.*

*You begin by simmering rockfish trimmings with seasonings to make broth, then strain the broth and poach fish fillets in it. At the table, serve broth and fish with a pungent sauce made with garlic, red bell pepper, cayenne, saffron, and olive oil.*

*To get a whole rockfish, give your fish market several days' advance notice.*

## BOURRIDE
### *Provençal Fish Soup*

*You'll need fish bones and trimmings to make broth; ask your market to save them when filleting the fish. Buy 1 big fish—or 2 or 3 small ones, the same or different species.*

- 1 **to 3 whole rockfish (about 4 lb. total), such as rock cod, Pacific snapper, or lingcod, filleted; save head, tail, bones, skin**
- 2 **quarts water**
- 1 **large onion, sliced**
- 2 **tablespoons packed fresh thyme sprigs or 2 teaspoons dry thyme leaves**
- ½ **teaspoon fennel seed**
- 2 **bay leaves**
- 12 **black peppercorns**
- 1 **piece, 1 by 7 inches, orange peel (orange part only)**
  **Rouille (recipe follows)**
  **Salt and pepper**
  **Toast (directions follow)**
  **Shredded parmesan cheese**

Cut fish fillets into 6 equal portions; rinse, cover, and chill. In a 5- to 6-quart pan over high heat, bring to boil water, fish head, tail, bones, skin, onion, thyme, fennel, bay, peppercorns, and orange peel. Cover and simmer 1½ hours.

Pour broth through a fine strainer into a bowl, pressing juice from trimmings and seasonings. Discard fish scraps and seasonings; return broth to pan. Prepare rouille, using 1 tablespoon of the fish broth; set aside.

Season broth to taste with salt and pepper, then bring to a simmer over high heat. Add fish fillets, cover, and simmer gently until fillets are opaque in center (cut 1 to test), about 5 minutes.

At the table, let diners assemble the bourride. Place a toast slice in a wide soup bowl. Using a wide spatula, carefully lift a fillet from broth and place on top of toast. Ladle some broth on top, then add rouille and cheese to taste. Makes 6 servings.

**Rouille.** In a blender or food processor, whirl until fairly smooth 1 **large egg yolk;** ½ medium-size **red bell pepper,** stemmed, seeded, and chopped; 1 clove **garlic,** minced or pressed; ¼ teaspoon **cayenne;** ⅛ teaspoon **saffron threads;** 2 tablespoons **soft bread crumbs;** and reserved 1 tablespoon **fish broth.** With motor running, gradually add ½ cup **olive oil** until incorporated. Season to taste with **salt.**

**Toast.** Diagonally cut 1 **sourdough baguette** (1 lb.) into ¾-inch-thick slices. Lightly brush cut sides with **olive oil** (takes about ⅓ cup). Set in a single layer on a 14- by 17-inch baking sheet. Bake in a 375° oven until golden, about 20 minutes. Use hot or cold.

*To assemble soup, place toast in a wide bowl; top with fish fillet, broth, and sauce with garlic, saffron, and bell pepper; then add parmesan shreds.*

# Crisp Green Salads

CRISP REFRESHING SALADS *provide a welcome addition in a month of bountiful holiday meals. Choose a spinach salad topped with a hot dressing of Italian sausage, fennel seed, and tart balsamic vinegar. Or present a light cabbage slaw dressed with cumin and orange juice but no oil. Your third choice is salad "flowers" composed of mixed greens.*

## WARM SPINACH & SAUSAGE SALAD

- ¾ pound spinach, rinsed well, stemmed, and crisped
- 1 large yellow or red bell pepper, stemmed, seeded, and cut into thin strips
- 3 green onions (ends trimmed), cut into 3-inch lengths and slivered
- ½ pound mild or hot Italian sausage, casings removed
- ½ teaspoon fennel seed
- ⅓ cup balsamic vinegar
  Salt and pepper

Place spinach, bell pepper, and onions in a large salad bowl. In a 10- to 12-inch frying pan, cook sausage over medium-high heat, stirring and breaking up with a spoon, until brown, about 10 minutes.

Add fennel seed and vinegar to pan. Stir until browned bits are loosened, then pour dressing and sausage over salad and mix. Season to taste with salt and pepper. Makes 6 servings.

## ORANGE & CABBAGE SLAW

- 1 head (about ¾ lb.) Savoy cabbage
- 4 medium-size oranges
- 1 cup golden raisins
- 1 teaspoon ground cumin
  Salt
- ½ cup roasted peanuts

Core and rinse cabbage; pat dry. Separate several large outer leaves and use to line a salad bowl; cover and chill. Shred remaining cabbage; set aside.

Juice 2 of the oranges and put juice in a large bowl. Cut off and discard peel and white membrane from remaining oranges. Over bowl, cut fruit into segments between membranes. Add fruit to

*Spoon warm sausage dressing with balsamic vinegar over spinach, bell pepper, and onion.*

bowl, then squeeze juice from membrane into bowl; discard membrane. Gently mix in shredded cabbage, raisins, and cumin. Season to taste with salt. (At this point, you can cover and chill up to 3 hours.)

Spoon salad and dressing into leaf-lined bowl; sprinkle with peanuts. Serve in individual salad bowls. Makes 6 to 8 servings. —*Kathleen Ritchie, Truckee, Calif.*

## SALAD FLOWERS WITH PISTACHIO DRESSING

- ¼ cup shelled whole pistachios or pine nuts
- 2 heads (2¼ oz. each) limestone lettuce, or 2 small heads (4 to 5 oz. each) butter lettuce
- 1 large head (about 5 oz.) radicchio, leaves separated, rinsed, and crisped
- 2 medium-size heads Belgian endive, leaves separated, rinsed, and crisped

- ¼ cup raspberry or red wine vinegar
- ¼ cup salad oil
- ¼ teaspoon *each* sugar and grated lemon peel
  Salt and pepper

Place pistachios in an 8- or 9-inch-square pan and bake in a 350° oven until golden brown in center (break 1 to test), 3 to 5 minutes. Let cool.

Plunge whole lettuces into water to rinse, then gently shake and pat dry. Cut out core and place lettuces apart on a large platter. Pull out leaves slightly to separate. Tuck radicchio and endive between lettuce leaves. Sprinkle pistachios onto leaves.

In a small bowl, mix vinegar, oil, sugar, and lemon peel. Spoon evenly over salad flowers; season to taste with salt and pepper. Makes 4 to 6 servings.

# Vinegar & Ham—A French Secret

**T**HE SHARP BITE *of vinegar, tempered by ham, seasons these three traditional dishes from the Auvergne region of south-central France. All have lively character but are otherwise quite diverse.*

*In the lentil salad, made with red wine vinegar, well-smoked ham exerts more influence; serve it for lunch or a light supper.*

*In this version of* pot-au-feu *(meat and vegetable stew), ham replaces beef, the traditional choice. You simmer the ham with winter vegetables and flavor the broth with tart-sweet balsamic vinegar. Look for this vinegar in well-stocked supermarkets or fancy food stores.*

*The pan-fried trout, dressed with a piquant white wine vinegar sauce, get only a subtle accent from ham.*

## VINEGAR-SEASONED LENTIL SALAD
### Salade Tiède de Lentilles du Puy

*Black Forest and Westphalian ham are available in most delicatessens and well-stocked grocery stores. These smoky meats can be expensive, but a little goes a long way. Buy a chunk, rather than thin slices, so you can cut the meat into sticks as described.*

- ⅓ pound cooked smoked ham, such as Black Forest or Westphalian (fat trimmed off), cut into ¼- by 3-inch matchstick pieces
- 2 tablespoons salad oil
- 2 large onions, sliced
- 2 cups (12 oz.) lentils, cleaned of debris and rinsed
- ½ teaspoon pepper
- 3 cups water
- ⅔ cup red wine vinegar
- ½ cup minced parsley
  Butter lettuce leaves, washed and crisped
  Parsley sprigs

In a 10- to 12-inch pan over high heat, brown ham in 1 tablespoon of the oil, stirring often. Reduce heat to medium. Add onions and the remaining oil. Cook until onions are golden and very limp, about 15 minutes; stir often.

Stir in lentils, pepper, and water. Bring to a boil over high heat, then reduce heat and simmer, covered, until lentils are barely tender to bite, 25 to 30 minutes.

Stir in vinegar and simmer, covered, until lentils are just tender to bite, about 5 more minutes; stir often. Stir in minced parsley. Let cool. (If made ahead, cover and chill up to 2 days; bring to room temperature before serving.)

Spoon into lettuce leaves, then garnish with parsley sprigs. Makes 6 servings.

## AUVERGNE HAM & VEGETABLE STEW
### Pot-au-Feu de l'Auvergne

*Because of its attractive crinkly appearance, Savoy cabbage is the first choice for this hearty winter stew—but if it's not available, use regular green cabbage instead. Cook and present the cabbage whole, then slice to serve.*

- 3 medium-size onions
- 24 whole cloves
- 1 smoked picnic ham, bone in (also called butt or shoulder), 4 to 5 pounds, fat trimmed
- 1 teaspoon pepper
- 3 quarts water
- 1 pound slender carrots
- 1 pound small turnips (about 2½-inch diameter), ends trimmed; peeled, if desired
- ½ pound small red thin-skinned potatoes (about 2½-inch diameter), scrubbed
- 1 package (10 oz.) frozen baby lima beans
- 1 small head (1 lb.) Savoy or regular green cabbage, cored
- ⅓ cup balsamic vinegar or red wine vinegar
  Coarsely ground mustard

Cut onions in half lengthwise and stud each half with 4 cloves. In an 8- to 10-quart pan, bring ham, pepper, onions, and water to a boil over high heat. Cover and simmer for 1 hour.

Add carrots, turnips, potatoes, and beans to pan; add cabbage, pushing it down into broth. Return to a boil, then simmer, covered, until cabbage is tender when pierced, about 20 minutes more.

With 2 slotted spoons, lift vegetables and ham out of pan and place on a rimmed platter (lift carrots gently so they won't break). Skim and discard fat from broth, then stir in vinegar. Pour broth into a tureen.

To serve, slice ham and cut cabbage into wedges. Spoon meat and vegeta-bles into wide soup bowls; offer broth to pour over each serving, and mustard to season to taste. Serves 8 to 10.

## TROUT WITH LEEKS & VINEGAR
### Truite aux Poireaux et au Vinaigre

*Choose trout that smell fresh and have clear, convex eyes. For the ham, use leftover meat or buy a thick slice from a delicatessen or a grocery's service meat department.*

- 1 pound leeks
- 2 bottles (8 oz. each) clam juice
- ⅓ cup (2 oz.) diced cooked ham, fat trimmed
- ⅓ cup white wine vinegar
- 4 whole trout (1½ to 2 lb. total), cleaned and fins removed
  All-purpose flour
- 3 tablespoons butter or margarine
  Pepper

Trim off and discard root ends and upper half of the green tops of leeks. Remove tough outer leaves. Split leeks lengthwise, rinse well under cold running water, then cut them lengthwise into ½-inch-thick sections. Group pieces in 8 equal portions; securely tie each bundle of sections with cotton string.

In a 10- to 12-inch frying pan, bring clam juice, leeks, and ham to a boil over high heat. Reduce heat, cover, and simmer until leeks are tender when pierced, about 5 minutes.

Gently stir vinegar into leek mixture. Lift leeks from juice, place on a warm rimmed platter, and keep warm. Increase heat to high and boil broth until reduced to 1 cup, 8 to 10 minutes.

Meanwhile, coat trout with all-purpose flour and shake off excess. Place butter in a 12- to 14-inch frying pan and cook over medium-high heat until it melts. Add trout and cook, turning once, until browned on outside and no longer translucent in center (cut the largest fish to test), about 8 minutes.

Place trout on platter between leek bundles. Spoon ham and reduced broth over fish. Season to taste with pepper. To serve, lift fish and leeks to plates and spoon sauce and ham on top. Makes 4 servings.

# Taking the Bite Out of Belgian Endive

**E**LEGANT RAW, *Belgian endive has excellent flavor when cooked, too. Heat tempers the characteristic bitter bite of these tapered heads of cream-colored leaves.*

*Braise small heads to eat as a vegetable. Endive makes a delicious light bisque, too. Or wrap braised heads with a fish fillet to make a handsome entrée.*

## BRAISED BELGIAN ENDIVE WITH BACON

    2  slices bacon, cut into ½-inch pieces
    8  heads Belgian endive (2 oz. each)
    ¼  cup water

In a 10- to 12-inch frying pan over medium heat, cook bacon, stirring often, until crisp, about 5 minutes. Lift out with a slotted spoon. Add endive and water to pan. Cover tightly and cook, turning endive occasionally, until tender when pierced, 15 to 20 minutes. Transfer to serving dish and sprinkle with bacon. Makes 4 or 8 servings.

## BELGIAN ENDIVE BISQUE

    6  ounces Belgian endive, cut
       crosswise into ¼-inch slices
    3  tablespoons butter or margarine
    2  medium-size carrots, peeled and
       chopped
    1  large onion, chopped
    3  tablespoons all-purpose flour
    5  cups regular-strength chicken
       broth
       Salt and white pepper

Set aside ½ cup of the endive. In a 3- to 4-quart pan, melt butter over medium heat. Add carrots, onion, and remaining endive; stir until onion is limp, 8 to 10 minutes. Add flour; stir until it coats vegetables. Stir in broth. Bring to a boil. Cover and simmer until carrots are tender when pierced, 10 to 15 minutes. In a blender, smoothly purée soup, a portion at a time.

Return soup to pan. Stir over medium heat until hot. Add salt and pepper to taste. Ladle into a tureen or bowls. Offer remaining endive to sprinkle into each portion. Makes 4 to 6 servings.

## SOLE-WRAPPED BELGIAN ENDIVE ROLLS

    1  tablespoon butter or margarine
    8  heads Belgian endive (2 oz. each)
    ¼  cup water
    8  thin, skinned sole fillets
       (2 to 3 oz. each)
       Salt and white pepper
    ⅓  cup chopped shallots
    ¼  teaspoon dry tarragon
    1  cup dry white wine
    1  cup regular-strength chicken broth
    ½  cup whipping cream

In a 10- to 12-inch frying pan, melt butter over medium heat. Add endive and water. Cover and cook, turning often, until endive is tender when pierced, 15 to 20 minutes; set aside.

Lightly sprinkle fillets with salt and pepper. Lay an endive head on 1 end of

*Spoon tarragon and shallot reduction sauce over fish and Belgian endive rolls.*

each fillet; roll up. Set rolls, seam side down, in a buttered shallow 2- to 2½-quart baking dish. Cover and bake in a 400° oven just until fish is opaque in thickest part (cut to test), 10 to 15 minutes.

Meanwhile, in the pan used to cook endive, combine shallots, tarragon, wine, and broth. Boil, uncovered, over high heat until reduced by half, about 10 minutes. When fish is done, drain juices from baking dish into wine mixture; add cream. Boil until reduced to ¾ cup. Spoon over fish. Makes 4 servings.

*Wrap thin fish fillets around braised endive. Set in a buttered baking dish and oven-steam just until fish is done. After baking, use the pan juices to enrich the sauce.*

# Getting Young Cooks Started

A RECIPE SIMPLE ENOUGH to be remembered easily but good enough to produce a real treat may inspire youthful chefs to repeat performances.

Here are two such recipes. They require a minimum of tools and ingredients, and most ingredient quantities are whole numbers, easy for a child to remember. The recipes were tested—and approved—by several novice cooks, four through eight years of age.

Makings for the egg-filled flaky pastry can be kept on hand; the hamburger cutouts can be made when hamburgers are on the family menu—or when friends come for lunch.

An adult should supervise use of the oven.

It's not just play. Children learn to handle pastry, crack an egg, do some measuring, use a cooky cutter, cook hamburgers—and, maybe, clean up.

## COOKY-CUTTER HAMBURGER

Press cooky cutter (choose a simple shape) through **ground beef** patted about ½ inch thick. Use same cutter on 2 slices of **bread**. Pan-fry or broil meat (an adult's help may be necessary). Then toast bread and put meat between the

Use cooky cutter to give shape to ground beef patty; use same cutter for bread to make matching bun—toast to make crisp.

two slices; add **mustard** or catsup if you want.

## EGG, CHEESE, OR PEAR NESTS

On toaster-oven pan (or 8- or 9-inch pie pan), press out center of 1 thawed **frozen patty shell** until it's about 4 inches across; don't press rim. Bake in 400° oven for 12 minutes to start browning. Remove, using pot holder, and press center of pastry flat with the back of a

spoon. Crack 1 large **egg** into hot pastry. Sprinkle lightly with **salt** and **pepper.** Return to oven, using pot holder. Bake until pastry is brown and egg yolk is solid, 8 to 10 minutes.

Instead of an egg, you could add 1 slice of cheese (about 1 oz. of jack, Swiss, mozzarella, or cheddar), or put cheese on top of the egg. Or instead of egg or cheese, you could add 4 slices of peeled and cored pear (sprinkle pear with 1 teaspoon each lemon juice and sugar). Bake until pastry is brown.

Start with a puff pastry shell (the kind that comes frozen) to make a nest that you can bake and fill with eggs and cheese, then bake again to make a sandwich nest.

# Quinoa: Mother Grain of the Incas

CONSIDERED the "mother grain" in ancient Inca civilization, quinoa (pronounced keen-wa), a tiny millet-like seed used as a grain, is finding its way into health-food stores throughout the West—at $3.50 to $4 per pound.

Indigenous to the Andes Mountains of South America, quinoa was introduced into Colorado only a decade ago. It is now being cultivated most successfully in that state and in New Mexico; research is progressing to determine varieties most adaptable to the West.

Quinoa's delicate flavor and couscous-like texture make it an easy addition to our own menus. It's high in protein—16 percent compared to 7½ percent in rice, for which it is easily substituted—and ranks a little higher in protein quality than soybeans. Because it's low in gluten, it can be enjoyed by many who cannot eat wheat products.

Quinoa expands about four times when cooked. Before cooking, always rinse the grain well to remove a slightly bitter coating. When the seeds are toasted before cooking, the mild flavor becomes slightly peanut-like. Use the toasted grain as described here—or as you would chopped nuts or seeds, to add texture.

## TOASTED QUINOA

Pour 1 cup **quinoa** into a fine strainer; rinse thoroughly under cool running **water.** Put rinsed quinoa into a 10- to 12-inch frying pan over medium heat; cook, shaking pan occasionally, until quinoa dries and turns golden brown, about 15 minutes. Pour toasted quinoa from pan and let cool. Use in the recipes that follow; to store, cover airtight and keep in a cool place up to 1 month. Makes 1 cup.

## COOKED QUINOA

- 2 **cups water, regular-strength chicken broth, or regular-strength beef broth**
- 1 **cup quinoa, rinsed, or toasted (recipe precedes)**
- ¼ **to ½ teaspoon salt (optional)**

Bring water to a boil in a 3- to 4-quart pan; stir in quinoa and salt. Cover and simmer gently on low heat until liquid is absorbed, 15 to 20 minutes. Serve, or cool, cover, and chill up to 2 days. Makes about 4 cups, 4 to 8 servings.

**Curry quinoa.** Make **Cooked Quinoa,** preceding, using broth, but omit salt. Stir 1 teaspoon **curry powder** into the broth.

**Spicy hot cereal.** Make **Cooked Quinoa,** preceding, using water. Omit salt and add ½ teaspoon **ground cinnamon** and ¼ cup **currants** or raisins to the water.

## QUINOA & WHOLE-WHEAT MUFFINS

- ⅓ **cup Toasted Quinoa (recipe precedes)**
- 1 **cup all-purpose flour**
- 1 **cup whole-wheat flour**
- 1 **tablespoon baking powder**
- ½ **teaspoon salt**
- 1 **large egg, slightly beaten**
- ⅓ **cup firmly packed brown sugar**
- ¼ **cup (⅛ lb.) melted butter or margarine**
- 1 **cup milk**

Set aside 2 teaspoons of the quinoa. In a bowl, combine remaining quinoa, all-purpose flour, whole-wheat flour, baking powder, and salt. In another bowl, whisk together egg, sugar, butter, and milk.

Pour liquid mixture into flour mixture; stir just to combine. Spoon batter into greased or paper-lined muffin cups (2½ inches wide), filling each to the top. Sprinkle reserved quinoa evenly over the batter.

Bake in a 375° oven until tops of muffins are golden, about 30 minutes. Remove from pan; serve, or cool on a rack, then wrap and store in a cool place until the next day. Makes 10 to 12 muffins.

## QUINOA PILAF

- ⅓ **cup firmly packed chopped bacon Salad oil (optional)**
- 1 **cup sliced mushrooms**
- ⅓ **cup finely chopped onion**
- 1 **cup regular-strength beef broth**
- ½ **cup Toasted Quinoa (recipe precedes)**
- ⅓ **cup shredded carrot**
- ⅓ **cup finely chopped green pepper**

*Curry-seasoned quinoa, cooked in chicken broth, accompanies grilled pork chop and zucchini.*

In a 10- to 12-inch frying pan over medium heat, cook bacon, stirring occasionally, until crisp around edges, 6 to 8 minutes. With a slotted spoon, lift bacon pieces from pan and set aside. Spoon off and discard all but 2 tablespoons of the bacon fat (or add salad oil to equal 2 tablespoons).

Add mushrooms and onion to pan and cook, stirring occasionally, until liquid cooks away and mushrooms are golden. Add broth, quinoa, carrots, and green pepper; bring to boiling over high heat. Cover and simmer until liquid is absorbed, about 15 minutes. Take off heat, remove lid, and let stand 2 minutes. Stir with a fork to separate grains. Spoon onto serving dish; sprinkle with cooked bacon. Makes about 2½ cups, 3 or 4 servings.

# Cakes Loaded with Nuts

THE WONDERFUL AROMA of almonds toasting makes these cakes just as much a treat to prepare as to eat. Loaded with almonds, they're rich in nutty flavor and fragrance.

Our first tender coffee cake uses ground almonds in place of flour and gets its volume from whipped eggs.

Ground almonds combine with flour in the next recipe to make a torte with the texture of a coarse pound cake. Serve it with fruit for a light breakfast treat—or bring it out as a dessert with just a touch of sweetness.

For best value, look for whole unblanched or blanched almonds sold in bulk or in 1- and 2-pound bags.

Toasted almonds decorate this torte made with more ground toasted almonds. The lightly sweet cake is good for dessert—or try it at breakfast, too.

## GROUND ALMOND STREUSEL COFFEE CAKE

        Whole toasted almonds (directions follow)
6   large eggs, separated
¾   cup sugar
1   teaspoon baking powder
¼   teaspoon salt
¼   teaspoon almond extract
        Streusel topping

In a blender, whirl 1 cup of the toasted almonds, ½ cup at a time, stirring every 15 seconds, until very finely ground. Watch carefully—if blended too much, nuts will turn to butter. In large bowl of an electric mixer, beat egg yolks with half the sugar until thick and light in color. Add baking powder, salt, almond extract, and ground almonds; blend well. In another large bowl, whip egg whites with clean beaters until foamy; gradually add remaining sugar and continue to whip until whites will hold stiff peaks; fold into nut mixture.

Butter a 3-inch deep (or deeper) 9- to 10-inch cheesecake pan with removable bottom. Spread batter in pan, mounding it slightly higher in the center. Drop streusel topping by teaspoonfuls evenly over top of batter.

Bake in a 325° oven until cake feels set in center when lightly touched or a slender wooden pick inserted in center (not streusel) comes out clean, 50 to 55 minutes. Place on a rack (cake settles as it cools) for 10 minutes; remove pan sides. Serve warm or cool, in wedges. Serves 10 to 12.

**Whole toasted almonds.** Spread 1½ cups whole **unblanched** or blanched **almonds** in an 8- or 9-inch-wide pan. Bake in a 350° oven until light brown inside (cut 1 open to test), 15 to 20 minutes; shake pan occasionally.

**Streusel topping.** In a blender or food processor, or with a knife, coarsely chop ½ cup **whole toasted almonds** (directions precede). Add ¼ cup (⅛ lb.) **butter** or margarine, and ⅓ cup firmly packed **brown sugar.** Process or rub with your fingers until crumbly and evenly mixed.

## GROUND ALMOND TORTE

1   cup whole toasted almonds (directions precede)
¾   cup (⅜ lb.) butter or margarine
¾   cup sugar
2   large eggs
½   teaspoon vanilla
¼   teaspoon almond extract
¾   cup all-purpose flour

In a blender, whirl ⅔ cup of the toasted almonds, half at a time, stirring every 15 seconds, until very finely ground. Watch carefully—if blended too much, nuts will turn to butter.

In large bowl of an electric mixer, beat butter and sugar until creamy. Add eggs, 1 at a time, beating well after each addition. Beat in vanilla and almond extract. On low speed, thoroughly mix in flour and ground almonds.

Scrape into a buttered 8- or 9-inch tart or cake pan with a removable bottom; smooth surface of batter with a spatula. Arrange remaining whole toasted almonds on top.

Bake in a 350° oven until center springs back when gently touched or a slender wooden pick inserted in center comes out clean, 25 to 30 minutes. Cool on a rack 10 minutes. Remove pan sides. Serve warm or cool, in wedges. Serves 10 to 12.

# Plain Custard Up to Some New Tricks

LIKE TO TRY *an interesting variation on an old favorite? Just dress plain custard with new flavors. Here are three suggestions, all delicious and easy to make.*

*Following the style of classic Mexican flan, the pumpkin and double-caramelized custards bake in caramel-lined pans. To allow the caramelized sugar time to dissolve into a sauce after baking, both flans need to be made at least 4 hours ahead. The melted sauce lets the dessert free when it's inverted onto a serving dish.*

*Orange-flavored liqueur and sliced oranges also add a delicate fruitiness to a basic baked custard.*

## SPICED PUMPKIN FLAN

1¼  cups sugar
¼  teaspoon salt (optional)
1  teaspoon ground cinnamon
1  cup canned pumpkin
5  large eggs
1¾  cups half-and-half (light cream) or canned evaporated milk
1½  teaspoons vanilla
  Ginger whipped cream (directions follow), optional

In an 8- to 10-inch frying pan, melt ½ cup sugar over medium heat, shaking pan often. When all sugar is melted and turns a dark amber color, 3 to 4 minutes, immediately pour caramelized sugar into an 8- or 9-inch-square metal baking pan. Using hot pads to protect hands, tilt pan quickly to let syrup coat bottom (it does not need to coat bottom completely). Set aside.

In a bowl, combine remaining ¾ cup sugar, salt, cinnamon, pumpkin, and eggs; mix well. Stir in half-and-half and vanilla. Pour into caramel-coated pan. Set pan in another baking pan slightly larger than the one used for flan. Place in a 350° oven. Carefully pour boiling water into outer pan so it is about 1 inch deep.

Bake until flan appears set in center when gently shaken, about 45 minutes. Remove from hot water and chill at least 4 hours or until the next day (cover pan when flan is cold).

To serve, cut around custard to loosen from pan. Invert a rimmed serving platter over flan. Holding platter in place, quickly invert flan; custard and sauce will slowly flow out. Cut into squares. Serve ginger whipped cream to spoon on each serving. Makes 9 servings.— *Carmela Meely, Walnut Creek, Calif.*

**Ginger whipped cream.** In a small bowl, beat 1 cup **whipping cream,** ½ teaspoon **ground ginger,** and 2 tablespoons **powdered sugar** until cream holds soft peaks. Transfer to serving bowl.

## DOUBLE CARAMELIZED FLAN

1  cup sugar
2  cups milk
6  large eggs
1  teaspoon vanilla

In an 8- to 10-inch frying pan, melt sugar over medium heat, shaking often until sugar melts and turns a dark amber color, 3 to 4 minutes. At once, pour about ⅓ of the caramelized sugar into a 9-inch pie pan at least 1¼ inches deep. Using hot pads to protect hands, quickly tilt pan to coat bottom with syrup (it does not need to coat bottom completely). Set aside.

Add milk to the remaining caramelized sugar in frying pan. Stir over medium-low heat until sugar liquefies again, 5 to 8 minutes; do not boil milk. In a bowl, beat eggs and vanilla to blend. Whisk in milk mixture. Pour egg mixture through a fine strainer into the caramel-coated pan. Set pan in a slightly larger baking pan. Place in a 350° oven. Fill outer pan with about 1 inch boiling water.

Bake until custard appears set in center when gently shaken, about 15 minutes. Lift out of water and chill at least 4 hours or until the next day (cover when cold).

To serve, cut around custard to loosen from pan. Cover with a rimmed serving plate. Holding plate in place, quickly invert; custard will slip out and sauce will slowly flow over it. Cut into wedges. Makes 6 servings.

## ORANGE BAKED CUSTARD

3  large oranges
⅔  cup sugar
1¾  cups half-and-half (light cream)
6  large eggs
½  cup orange-flavored liqueur
1  teaspoon vanilla
¼  cup sweetened grated coconut

With a vegetable peeler, cut 4 thin strips of peel (orange part only) from 1 orange (each strip should measure about ½ by 4 inches). Set oranges aside.

In a 1- to 2-quart pan, bruise orange peel with sugar, using a wooden spoon; add half-and-half. Stir over low heat just until mixture is hot to touch; remove from heat. Remove and discard orange peel.

In a bowl, beat together eggs, ¼ cup orange liqueur, and vanilla. Whisk in hot milk. Pour mixture through a fine strainer into a shallow 1- to 1½-quart baking dish. Set in a baking pan slightly larger than the custard dish. Place in a 350° oven. Fill pan with about 1 inch of boiling water. Bake until custard appears set in center when gently shaken, 25 to 35 minutes.

Meanwhile, spread coconut evenly in a 9-inch-wide pan. Bake in the same 350° oven, stirring occasionally, until golden, 5 to 10 minutes. Remove from oven and cool; if made ahead, store airtight up to 3 days. When custard is done, remove from hot water. Cool, cover, and chill until cold, at least 2 hours or until the next day.

Meanwhile, cut peel and white membrane off oranges. Thinly slice fruit crosswise. Mix orange slices with remaining ¼ cup orange liqueur. Transfer to serving bowl. Cover and chill until cold, at least 1 hour or until the next day.

To serve, garnish custard with 3 orange slices and sprinkle coconut in a ring over custard. Spoon out custard; offer orange slices to add to portions. Makes 6 servings.—*Marian Wilcox, Clarkdale, Ariz.*

*Fresh orange slices and toasted coconut garnish liqueur-flavored baked custard.*

# Kiwi Cake, Tart & Seviche

**P**RICES FOR KIWI FRUIT *are apt to be very attractive in late fall. The domestic harvest is underway, and this fruit is often a bargain, compared to the alternate-season crop shipped from New Zealand.*

*Since the fuzzy brown-skinned fruit has lost its novelty status, it's time to use it more often and less self-consciously, particularly when it's a good value.*

*Used fresh, as in this cooling seviche and simple, handsome tart, kiwi fruit shows off its melon-strawberry-banana flavor and brilliant green flesh studded with black seeds.*

*Cooked kiwi fruit's color fades, but in this tender tea cake the fruit's characteristic flavor remains. Enjoy the cake with tea, as dessert, or even for breakfast or brunch.*

*How do you know when kiwi fruit is ready to use? Hold it in your palm and press gently; if it gives slightly, like a ripe peach, it's at the ideal stage for eating. To ripen firm fruit, enclose in a bag and hold at room temperature until the fruit softens; this may take up to a week.*

## SEVICHE WITH KIWI FRUIT

- 2 medium-size oranges
- ¾ cup lemon juice
- 1 pound boned and skinned firm-texture white fish such as rockfish or sole
- 3 medium-size (about ¾ lb.) firm-ripe kiwi fruit
- 1 small red onion
  Jalapeño vinaigrette (recipe follows)
  About 2 cups watercress sprigs, washed and crisped
  Salt

Cut oranges in half and ream to make ¾ cup juice; reserve any extra fruit for other uses. Cut peel from 1 of the reamed orange halves into pieces about ¼ inch wide and 1 inch long; discard remaining peel. Put orange juice, cut peel, and lemon juice into a deep bowl.

Cut fish into pieces ¼ inch wide and 1 inch long; mix with juices. Cover and chill, stirring every 3 to 4 hours, until fish pieces are opaque in center (cut to test), at least 10 hours or until next day.

With a knife, pare skin from kiwi fruit; cut fruit crosswise into ¼-inch-thick slices. (Or cut in half lengthwise, then slice halves.) Thinly slice onion and separate into rings. Place fruit and onion in a bowl. With a slotted spoon, lift fish

and peel from citrus juices and add to kiwi mixture; reserve ¼ cup of the juices. Add jalapeño vinaigrette; stir gently to mix.

Arrange watercress equally on 4 or 8 salad plates. Spoon kiwi mixture with dressing onto plates. Add salt to taste. Makes 4 entrée or 8 appetizer servings.

**Jalapeño vinaigrette.** Combine the ¼ cup **reserved citrus juices** used to marinate the fish with 2 tablespoons **olive** or salad **oil**, 1 tablespoon drained **capers**, 2 to 3 teaspoons minced fresh **jalapeño chili.**

## WINE-GLAZED KIWI CHEESE TART

- ⅓ cup granulated sugar
- 1 tablespoon cornstarch
- 1 tablespoon lemon juice
- ⅓ cup fruity white wine
- 1 large package (8 oz.) cream cheese, at room temperature
- ⅓ cup powdered sugar
- 1 teaspoon vanilla
  Butter pastry (recipe follows)
- 7 medium-size (about 1¾ lb.) firm-ripe kiwi fruit

In a 1- to 2-quart pan, stir together granulated sugar and cornstarch; add lemon juice and wine. Stirring, bring to a boil on high heat; set aside to cool.

With an electric mixer or food processor, beat cream cheese, powdered sugar, and vanilla until very smoothly mixed. Spread cream cheese mixture evenly over bottom of butter pastry.

With a knife, pare skin from kiwi fruit and cut fruit crosswise into ¼-inch-thick slices. Arrange slices, overlapping them neatly to fit tart and cover cheese.

Spoon or gently brush the wine mixture over the fruit. Serve at room temperature or chilled; to chill, cover without touching glaze, and refrigerate at least 1 hour, or until next day. Makes 8 to 10 servings. —*Lynda Arsenault, Visalia, Calif.*

**Butter pastry.** In a food processor or with your fingers, mix 1⅓ cups **all-purpose flour** and ¼ cup **sugar**. Add ½ cup (¼ lb.) cold **butter** or margarine, cut into

chunks. Whirl or rub until mixture forms fine crumbs. Add 1 large **egg;** process or stir with a fork until dough holds together. Press dough evenly over bottom and sides of an 11-inch tart pan with removable bottom. Bake in a 300° oven until golden brown, about 40 minutes. Cool. If made ahead, cover and let stand until next day.

## KIWI TEA CAKE

> About 6 medium-size (about 1½ lb.) firm-ripe kiwi fruit
- 1 cup granulated sugar
- 1 teaspoon grated lemon peel
- 1 large egg
- ½ cup salad oil
- 1½ cups all-purpose flour
- ½ teaspoon *each* baking powder and salt
- ½ teaspoon baking soda
- 1 cup powdered sugar
- 6 to 8 teaspoons lemon juice

With a knife, pare skin from kiwi fruit.

If you want fruit slices to use as garnish later, cut 4 or 5 rounds (about ¼ inch thick) from center of 1 kiwi fruit. Enclose in plastic wrap and chill up to 1 day.

Chop enough remaining fruit to make 1½ cups; reserve extra fruit to eat. Put chopped fruit in a 2- to 3-quart pan, add granulated sugar and lemon peel. Bring to a boil on high heat, stirring; cook until fruit turns a paler green color. Let cool.

In a large bowl, beat eggs and oil until well mixed. Stir together flour, baking powder, and salt. Add baking soda to cooked kiwi and stir until small bubbles form, then pour into egg mixture. Add flour mixture and stir until dry ingredients are moistened. Spoon batter into well-buttered 5- by 9-inch loaf pan.

Bake in a 350° oven until cake just begins to pull away from pan sides and a slender wooden pick inserted in center comes out clean, about 55 minutes. Let cool in pan 10 minutes, then invert onto a rack to cool completely. If made ahead, wrap airtight and chill up to 1 week; freeze to store longer, up to 1 month (thaw wrapped).

Place cake, baked top up, on a plate. Mix powdered sugar with lemon juice until smooth. Spoon icing over top of cake; lay reserved kiwi slices (rounds or half-slices) on icing. Cut into about ½-inch slices. Makes 8 to 10 servings.

# Two Pear Desserts

THE DELICATE FLAVOR *of pears plays different roles in these two desserts: with bold ingredients, it provides an elegant undertone; with mild companions, it's a light, refreshing star.*

*In the first dish, which is quick to make and relatively lean, hot tangerine and ginger sauce contrasts tartly with sweet poached pears. In a richer, subtler dessert, pears top cheesecake flavored with pear liqueur and cloves. For either, use Anjou or Bosc pears; both are plentiful in late fall.*

## POACHED PEARS IN CITRUS SAUCE

- ¾ **cup sugar**
  **Water**
- ⅓ **cup thawed frozen tangerine juice concentrate**
- ¼ **cup lemon juice**
- ¼ **cup chopped crystallized ginger**
- 1 **tablespoon very finely shredded orange peel**
- 6 **medium-size firm-ripe Anjou or Bosc pears, peeled**
- 1 **tablespoon cornstarch**
  **Fresh orange or tangerine segments, white membrane removed**

In a 5- to 6-quart pan, combine sugar, 1 cup water, tangerine concentrate, lemon juice, ginger, and peel. Bring to a boil over high heat. Add pears, rotating in sauce. Cover and simmer until fruit is tender when pierced, 10 to 15 minutes; turn halfway through cooking. Lift pears from sauce and put on individual dessert plates.

In a small bowl, stir together cornstarch and 1 tablespoon water until smooth. Mix into sauce. Stir over high heat until sauce boils. Pour equal portions over pears. Garnish with orange segments. Serves 6.

## PEAR & HAZELNUT CHEESECAKE

    **Hazelnut crust (recipe follows)**
- 2 **large packages (8 oz. each) cream cheese**
- 1½ **cups sugar**
- 1¾ **cups sour cream**
- 4 **large eggs**
- ½ **cup pear-flavor liqueur**
- ½ **teaspoon ground cloves**
- 1 **teaspoon vanilla**
- 3 **medium-size firm-ripe Anjou or Bosc pears**

*Circle of pear slices and cluster of hazelnuts top pear-flavored cheesecake. Cake serves a dozen; you can make it a day ahead.*

- ½ **cup water**
- 2 **tablespoons lemon juice**
- 2 **teaspoons whole cloves**

Press crust evenly over bottom and 1½ inches up sides of a 9-inch cheesecake pan that's at least 3 inches deep and has a removable bottom. Bake in a 350° oven until golden, 25 to 30 minutes. Remove from oven and lower heat to 300°.

Meanwhile, in large bowl of an electric mixer, beat cream cheese and 1 cup of the sugar until smooth. Beat in sour cream, then eggs, 1 at a time, just until blended. Stir in liqueur, ground cloves, and vanilla.

Pour into crust (batter will be above crust top) and bake until cheesecake is just golden and jiggles only slightly when gently shaken, about 1 hour. Cool on a rack for 5 minutes. Run a knife between cake and pan rim; do not remove rim. Let cool completely. Cover and chill until cold, at least 3 hours or until next day.

While cheesecake bakes, peel pears, halve, and core. In a 3- to 4-quart pan,

bring remaining ½ cup sugar, water, lemon juice, and whole cloves to a boil over high heat. Add pears, cover, and simmer until fruit is tender when pierced, 3 to 5 minutes; turn halfway through cooking. Remove pan from heat and let pears cool in syrup. Cover and chill until cold, at least 2 hours or until next day.

Up to 2 hours before serving, remove pan rim from cheesecake. Lift pears from syrup and slice lengthwise ⅓ inch thick; discard syrup. Arrange slices in circle on top of cheesecake. In center, place reserved hazelnuts. Serve cold. Makes 12 servings.

**Hazelnut crust.** Place ¾ cup **hazelnuts** in a 9-inch-wide baking pan and bake in a 350° oven until golden, about 15 minutes. Let cool. Reserve ¼ cup to top cheesecake; finely chop remaining nuts.

In a bowl, use your fingers to mix ½ cup (¼ lb.) **butter** or margarine with 1½ cups **all-purpose flour** and 2 tablespoons **sugar** until fine crumbs form. Mix in chopped nuts. Lightly beat 1 **large egg;** stir into flour mixture. Press into a ball.

# Smooth & Sinfully Rich—Tartufo

INCREDIBLY SMOOTH, *sinfully rich, white chocolate* tartufo *is a dessert lover's dream come true. Digging into this frozen Italian confection reveals a toasted hazelnut filling laced with hazelnut liqueur. You can also make the filling with pistachios or almonds*

*The dessert takes time to prepare, but the effort is worth it. Tartufo can be made ahead and kept frozen for up to 3 weeks.*

## WHITE CHOCOLATE-HAZELNUT TARTUFO

- ¾ cup hazelnuts
- 3 large egg yolks
- ⅓ cup *each* sugar and water
- 9 ounces white chocolate
- 1 cup whipping cream
- 2 tablespoons hazelnut-flavor liqueur

Place hazelnuts in an 8- or 9-inch-wide pan. Bake in a 350° oven until lightly toasted beneath skins, shaking pan occasionally, 18 to 20 minutes. Pour nuts onto a towel and rub with cloth to remove most of the skins; lift out nuts.

In a deep bowl with an electric mixer, beat egg yolks until light colored and thick. Next, combine sugar and water in a 1- to 1½-quart pan. Bring to boiling on high heat. Cook until the syrup reaches 234°; to read, tilt pan so syrup covers end of thermometer. At once, beat yolks on high speed and pour syrup into them in a slow, steady stream (avoid beaters). Continue to beat until mixture is very thick and has cooled, 3 to 5 minutes.

Place 6 ounces white chocolate, cut into chunks, in top of a double boiler set over simmering water. Stir chocolate occasionally just until melted. Immediately pour into egg yolk mixture and stir to blend thoroughly. Gradually add cream, beating rapidly until slightly thickened, about 3 minutes. Fill 6 muffin cups (about 2½-inch diameter) half-full with white chocolate mixture. Measure out ½ cup of the remaining white chocolate mixture and set aside. Cover chocolate mixture in the muffin pan and the balance in the bowl and freeze until firm, 3 to 4 hours.

Put the reserved ½ cup chocolate mixture, ½ cup hazelnuts, and liqueur in a blender or food processor. Whirl until smoothly puréed. Put in a bowl; cover and freeze until firm, 3 to 4 hours.

Using a small ice cream scoop or melon ball cutter, evenly divide frozen hazelnut mixture into 6 balls; set 1 on top of each chocolate-filled muffin cup. Working quickly, scoop equal portions of remaining frozen white chocolate mixture on top of each nut ball. Using back of scoop, pat mixture evenly around top and sides so filling is completely enclosed. Return muffin pan to freezer until dessert is firm, about 1 hour.

Finely grate the remaining 3 ounces of chocolate, then mound in the center of a large piece of waxed paper.

Working quickly, run a knife around edge of 1 tartufo in muffin cup to loosen; lift out. Set tartufo in mound of grated chocolate. Place your hands underneath paper and lift up, patting gently, to coat all sides with chocolate. At once set coated ball in a chilled 8- or 9-inch-wide pan and put in freezer. Repeat to coat remaining tartufo with chocolate; do not let balls touch. If uncoated tartufo gets too soft to handle, freeze until firm. Freeze coated tartufo until firm, at least 1 hour.

Serve, or cover airtight and store up to 3 weeks. To present, coarsely chop remaining hazelnuts and sprinkle onto each ball. Makes 6 servings.

## WHITE CHOCOLATE-ALMOND TARTUFO

Follow the directions for **White Chocolate Hazelnut Tartufo** (recipe precedes), but instead of hazelnuts use ¾ cup **whole blanched almonds**; toast in a 350° oven for about 10 minutes. Substitute **almond-flavor liqueur** for the hazelnut liqueur.

## WHITE CHOCOLATE-PISTACHIO TARTUFO

Follow the directions for **White Chocolate Hazelnut Tartufo** (recipe precedes), but instead of hazelnuts use ¾ cup **roasted unsalted shelled pistachios** (about 1½ cups nuts in the shell). Omit toasting step. Substitute **orange-flavor liqueur** for the hazelnut liqueur.

*Decadent white chocolate tartufo yields sweet surprise: intense hazelnut filling accented with hazelnut liqueur.*

# More November Recipes

OTHER NOVEMBER ARTICLES *offered a fresh-tasting soup based on canned tomato purée, a hearty Mexican main-dish soup, an unusual salad, and a versatile seasoning blend from the Middle East.*

## FAUX-FRESH TOMATO SOUP

*It may sound like heresy, but fresh isn't always the answer. In this warming soup, canned tomato purée forms the base; dried or fresh basil brings out a fresh flavor.*

*First you build a smooth foundation with onions and carrots, cooked slowly and gently to bring out their sweetest flavor.*

*You also dress up servings of the hot puréed soup with crisp rounds of home-made cheese croutons; some float in the soup, with extras served alongside.*

- 2 **tablespoons butter or margarine**
- 1 **medium-size onion, chopped**
- 1 **large carrot, peeled and chopped**
- 4 **cups regular-strength chicken broth**
- 1 **can (15 oz.) tomato purée**
- 3 **tablespoons dry basil leaves or ⅓ cup chopped fresh basil**
- ¾ **teaspoon sugar**
- ½ **teaspoon ground white pepper**
  **Cheese croutons (directions follow)**

In a 3- to 4-quart pan, melt the butter over medium-low heat. Add the onion and carrot and cook, stirring occasionally, until both the onion and carrot are sweet tasting and tender when pierced, about 30 minutes.

Stir broth, tomato purée, basil, sugar, and pepper into pan. Bring to a boil on high heat. Cover and simmer to blend flavors, about 15 minutes. With a slotted spoon, scoop vegetables and a little of the broth into a food processor (or pour mixture, a portion at a time, into a blender); whirl until smoothly puréed. Pour vegetable mixture back into the pan; heat until steaming. Ladle into 4 bowls; top each serving with 2 cheese croutons. Accompany with remaining croutons. Makes 6 cups, 4 servings.— *Nicole Perzik, Saratoga, Calif.*

**Cheese croutons.** Slice 1 slender **baguette** (about ½ lb.) crosswise into ¼-inch-thick slices. Thinly spread each slice of bread with **butter** or margarine and lay buttered side up; you'll need about ¼ cup (⅛ lb.) butter total.

Top slices equally with shredded **gruyère** or Swiss **cheese** (use ¼ lb. total).

*Hot tomato soup, topped with crisp cheese croutons, is a surprisingly fresh-tasting blend of basil and canned tomato purée. Offer with raw vegetables.*

Sprinkle evenly with **dry basil leaves**, using about 1 teaspoon total, then sprinkle lightly with **coarse salt** (such as rock or kosher salt, about ½ teaspoon total).

Line 2 baking pans, each 10 by 15 inches, with wire racks. Set bread slices, cheese side up, slightly apart on racks. Bake in a 250° oven until cheese is melted, about 30 minutes. For even cooking, alternate pan positions halfway through baking. Serve hot or at room temperature.

## POZOLE

*In the Southwest, pozole is often made with dried or partially cooked frozen hominy, but our version uses more readily available canned hominy.*

- 2 **large cans (49½ oz. each) regular-strength chicken broth**
- 3 **pounds meaty ham hocks, cut into 1-inch-thick slices**
- 2 **pounds chicken drumsticks and thighs**
- 1 **teaspoon dry oregano leaves**
- ½ **teaspoon cumin seed**
- 2 **large onions, cut into chunks**
- 1 **large can (29 oz.) yellow hominy, drained**
  **Condiments (suggestions follow)**
  **Crisp tortilla strips (recipe follows)**
  **Purchased green chili salsa**

In a 6- to 8-quart pan, combine broth, ham, chicken, oregano, cumin seed, and onions. Bring to a boil over high heat; reduce heat, cover, and simmer until meat is tender when pierced, about 2 hours. Lift out meat and set aside. Pour broth through a fine strainer; return strained broth to pan. When ham and chicken are cool enough to handle, discard skin, bones, and fat; tear meat into chunks; return to broth. (At this point, you can cover and chill up to 2 days.)

Skim and discard fat from broth; bring broth to a simmer. Stir in hominy; cover and cook for 30 minutes. Serve hot; offer

*(Continued on next page)*

Pozole, a meaty regional stew from the Southwest, uses traditional ingredients.

### ...POZOLE

condiments, tortillas, and salsa to add to each portion. Makes 8 to 10 servings.

**Condiments.** Arrange in separate bowls 2 or 3 **limes,** cut into wedges; 2 small packages (3 oz. each) **cream cheese,** diced; 2 cups shredded **iceberg lettuce;** 1 to 1½ cups thinly sliced **green onions** (including tops); and 2 large **red bell peppers,** stemmed, seeded, and slivered.

**Crisp tortilla strips.** Stack 8 to 10 **corn tortillas** (6- to 7-inch diameter); cut into ¼-inch-wide strips. In a 3- to 4-quart pan, heat about 1 inch **salad oil** to 375° (use a deep-frying thermometer). Fry strips a handful at a time, stirring often, until crisp and lightly browned, about 1 minute. Lift out with a slotted spoon and drain on paper towels. Sprinkle with **salt.**

### SQUID BOATS ON CABBAGE BEDS

*Edible geometric elegance characterizes this luncheon salad arrangement. Coarse minced cabbage combines with smooth squid mantles and crisp Belgian endive for interesting textural contrasts.*

*Serve the lightly dressed salad for a first course, or for lunch—with bread and butter and a glass of dry white wine.*

*In many fish markets, squid mantles are sold ready to use. If not, you'll need to buy whole squid and clean them at home.*

- 12 **squid mantles (tubes; about ½ lb.), cleaned, or about 1½ pounds whole squid, cleaned (directions follow)**
- 2 **small packages (3 oz. each) cream cheese, at room temperature**
- 5 **tablespoons minced parsley**
- ¼ **cup freshly grated parmesan cheese**
- ¼ **cup** *each* **salad oil and lemon juice**
- 2 **cups minced red cabbage**
- 12 **large Belgian endive leaves, washed and crisped**
- ½ **pound tiny cooked shelled shrimp Salt and pepper**

In a 10- to 12-inch frying pan, bring 1 inch water to a boil over high heat. Add squid; cook until opaque, about 30 seconds. Drain; immerse in cold water until cool. Drain again.

In a food processor or in the small bowl of an electric mixer, whirl or beat cream cheese, 4 tablespoons parsley, and parmesan cheese until smoothly puréed or well mixed, scraping down sides of container to blend.

Using kitchen scissors, slit open each squid mantle, starting at the large end of tube and ending ½ inch from pointed end. Fill mantles equally with cream cheese mixture, using all. If made ahead, cover and chill up to 4 hours.

Mix together oil, lemon juice, and remaining parsley. Add about ⅔ of the oil and lemon juice dressing to the minced cabbage; reserve remaining dressing. Stir cabbage, then evenly divide among 4 salad plates and spread to form a bed.

Nestle each filled squid mantle into an endive leaf; arrange 3 filled leaves on each plate, tips out. Sprinkle squid tentacles (if used) and shrimp over filled squid. Drizzle remaining dressing onto salads. Add salt and pepper to taste. Makes 4 servings.

**To clean squid,** pull off and discard thin speckled membrane from the mantle. Gently pull body (end with tentacles) from mantle and set aside.

Cheese-filled squid mantles in Belgian endive leaves rest on bed of minced red cabbage; tiny shrimp top the salad.

Pull out and discard the long, transparent, sword-shaped shell from inside mantle. Squeeze out and discard contents of mantle; rinse mantle inside and out.

Turn body upside down to spread tentacles open. Squeeze body gently from beneath to pop out the beak in the center; discard beak. Cut off and discard portion with eyes and ink sac. Rinse tentacles thoroughly.

## SYRIAN ZAHTAR

*Tart and faintly woodsy in taste, sumac is a versatile seasoning often used in Middle Eastern cookery. Although not well known in the West, sumac is worth getting to know because of its unusual flavor and the way it tingles refreshingly on the tongue.*

*You can find dry ground sumac in well-stocked spice shops and some Middle Eastern markets and delicatessens. It is derived from the dark reddish purple berries of a nonpoisonous Asian species of sumac (Rhus genus). The sour tasting berries are*

*dried and coarsely ground. Blended with thyme, the ground berries become* zahtar *(za'atar in Arabic); with additional spices, the mixture is called* Syrian zahtar.

- ¼ **cup dry ground sumac**
- 2 **teaspoons dry thyme leaves**
- 1 **teaspoon cumin seed or ground cumin**
- ½ **teaspoon paprika**
- ¼ **teaspoon salt**

In a blender, combine sumac, thyme, cumin, paprika, and salt. Whirl until a fine powder. Use or store airtight. Makes about 5¼ tablespoons.

**A few ways to use Syrian zahtar.** Brush bread dough with olive oil and sprinkle generously with Syrian zahtar before baking. Add the blend to unflavored yogurt, drained yogurt cheese *(labneh)*, or cream cheese. Or dust on meat, poultry, or fish and sauté, barbecue, or cook in the oven. Use the herb blend to season salads dressed with oil-and-vinegar, or sandwiches made with feta cheese, tomato, and cucumber.

*Sumac spice blend adds pleasant tang and aroma to a pocket-bread sandwich.*

# Looking Out for Food Safety

CAN I STUFF MY TURKEY ahead of time? Why did the can of green beans squirt and smell funny when I opened it? The grocery bag with the milk got left in the car overnight; is the milk spoiled?

Food-safety questions like these keep phones ringing in *Sunset's* home economics department—particularly during the holidays, when cooking and eating are a big part of the festivities.

But food safety is an issue not just at home, nor is it limited to the busy holiday season. In fact, it makes headlines year-round, with reports on frightening—and sometimes serious—outbreaks of salmonellosis, botulism, and other food-borne illnesses. We also hear about unsanitary conditions in some foodprocessing plants, pesticide and chemical contamination, and food tampering.

You can practice proper food hygiene in your own kitchen, but how do you know what's happened to foods before you get them home?

**Who's looking out for you?** Who sets safety guidelines, and who enforces them? And whom should you call when you suspect a problem? The answers lie in a network of federal, state, and local agencies.

Start with your state's Cooperative Extension Service. One of its many mandates is to work with the USDA and FDA (they set food-safety standards) to teach proper foodhandling techniques. If a *Sunset* editor has questions on food safety, she turns to this service for help. You can, too; look for the telephone number under the county government listings in your telephone directory.

In restaurants and other places where foods are prepared or handled after processing and packaging (school lunch programs, hospital meals, cafeterias, grocery stores), on-site inspections are done by the environmental health services program within the county's publichealth department. If you suspect a problem in your area, these are the people to call.

The USDA and FDA wield the regulatory clout. Their inspectors have the authority to impound foods and stop production if safety standards aren't met. Violators face stiff fines, even imprisonment. States may have their own system for inspection and regulation; if so, they must meet or exceed federal standards.

**Can all risks be eliminated?** Frankly, no—these harmful bacteria are a natural part of our environment. But we *can* keep them under control.

On page 275, we tell you how to handle meats safely; the same rules apply to all fresh foods, raw or cooked. Most processed foods—canned, frozen, dried—aren't suspect. But if cans are opened (even a pinprick), frozen foods thawed, or dried foods rehydrated, handle them just as you would fresh foods. And when in doubt (for instance, when a can or carton is swollen), throw the product out. Play it safe: that's the basic premise of food safety.

Baked apple bits hide under bread pudding's top. Serve with milk or cream.

## PAN DULCE

- 2 **tablespoons butter or margarine**
- 1 **medium-size tart apple, such as Granny Smith**
- ⅓ **cup firmly packed brown sugar**
- 4 **large eggs**
- 2 **cups milk**
- 1½ **teaspoons vanilla**
- ½ **teaspoon ground cinnamon**
- ¼ **teaspoon ground nutmeg**
- 2 **cups ½-inch cubes day-old sweet Italian or French bread**

In a shallow 6-cup baking dish, melt butter in a 350° oven. Core and dice apple; add to melted butter. Set aside 1 tablespoon sugar, and stir the rest with the apple. Bake apple, uncovered, until

juices have almost evaporated, about 15 minutes.

Meanwhile, in a bowl, mix the 1 tablespoon sugar, eggs, milk, vanilla, cinnamon, and nutmeg.

Quickly scatter bread cubes over apple, then pour egg mixture over cubes, moistening evenly. Return pudding to oven and bake until the center feels firm when you touch it and does not jiggle when dish is gently shaken, about 30 minutes. Let stand at least 10 minutes. Serve hot or cool. Makes 4 or 5 servings. —*Lorna M. Hall, Albuquerque.*

Onions cook with turmeric and cayenne to season napa cabbage and tomatoes.

## SPICED NAPA CABBAGE WITH TOMATOES

- 2 **tablespoons olive or salad oil**
- 1 **medium-size onion, thinly sliced**
- 2 **garlic cloves, minced or pressed**
- ½ **teaspoon ground turmeric**
- ¼ **teaspoon cayenne**
- ¾ **pound napa cabbage (about 1 small head), thinly shredded**
- 2 **medium-size firm-ripe tomatoes, cored and chopped**
- 2 **limes, each cut into 6 wedges**
  **About 1 cup unflavored yogurt**
  **Salt and pepper**

To a 10- to 12-inch frying pan over medium-high heat, add oil, onion, garlic, turmeric, and cayenne. Stirring often, cook onion until limp, about 5 minutes. Add cabbage and tomatoes; stir often on high heat until most of the liquid has evaporated and cabbage is wilted, about 15 minutes.

Pour the cabbage and tomatoes onto a warm platter; surround with the lime wedges. Spoon unflavored yogurt into a small bowl. To each portion of the hot vegetables, add lime juice, unflavored yogurt, and salt and pepper to taste. Makes 4 to 6 servings. —*Leila Advani, Santa Clara, Calif.*

Polenta, and broiled chicken thighs with vegetables, bake in two dishes, one oven.

## CHICKEN & SAUCE WITH POLENTA

- 8 **chicken thighs (about 2 lb. total)**
- 1 **small onion, chopped**
- 1 **small green bell pepper, stemmed, seeded, and chopped**
- 1 **can (14 oz.) stewed tomatoes**
- 1 **can (8 oz.) tomato sauce**
- ½ **cup dry red wine**
- 2 **teaspoons dry oregano leaves**
- 1 **teaspoon dry basil leaves**
- 3½ **cups regular-strength chicken broth**
- 1 **cup polenta**
- ¼ **cup grated parmesan cheese**

Arrange thighs slightly apart in a 9- by 13-inch pan; broil 4 inches from heat

until browned, about 7 minutes on each side. Set thighs aside; to pan, add onion, pepper, tomatoes, tomato sauce, wine, oregano, and basil; mix well.

In a 9-inch-square baking pan, stir together broth and polenta. Put vegetable and polenta pans in a 450° oven. Bake until vegetables are very soft and form a thick sauce and polenta liquid is absorbed, about 45 minutes; stir mixtures several times. Set thighs onto sauce and sprinkle cheese over polenta; bake for 15 minutes. Serve chicken and sauce over portions of polenta. Makes 4 to 6 servings. —*Marie Bergamini, Walnut Creek, Calif.*

## MEXICAN CAULIFLOWER SOUP

- 2 tablespoons butter or margarine
- 1 medium-size onion, chopped
- 1 small can (4 oz.) diced green chilies
- 1 teaspoon ground cumin
- 2 cups regular-strength chicken broth
- 1 head (about 2 lb.) cauliflower
- 4 stalks celery, chopped
- 2½ to 3 cups milk (or use part or all regular-strength chicken broth)
- ¼ cup minced green onions
  Salt and pepper

In a 4- to 5-quart pan over medium-high heat, melt butter and add onion, chilies, and cumin. Stir often until onion is limp, about 5 minutes. Add 2 cups broth; reduce heat to low; cover.

Trim leaves from cauliflower and discard. Rinse cauliflower, coarsely chop, and add to broth with celery. Bring to boiling on high heat. Cover and simmer until cauliflower is tender when pierced, about 20 minutes. Smoothly purée ½ the soup in a blender. Return purée to pan; thin with milk, as desired. Stir over medium-high heat until hot. Pour soup into bowls, top portions with green onion, and add salt and pepper to taste. Serves 6 or 7. —*Robin Saltonstall, Boulder, Colo.*

*Chilies lend Mexican spark to soup you thicken with cauliflower purée.*

## SKEWERED FISH NORTHWEST-STYLE

- ¼ cup *each* Worcestershire, soy sauce, and dry white wine
- 2 tablespoons olive or salad oil
- ½ pound boned and skinned halibut or other firm-texture white fish
- ½ pound sea scallops
- 15 small (about 1-inch caps) button mushrooms
- 1 medium-size green bell pepper, stemmed, seeded, and cut into 1-inch pieces

In a bowl, mix together Worcestershire, soy sauce, wine, and oil. Rinse and cut halibut and scallops into about 1-inch cubes and add to bowl; mix. Cover and chill at least 10 minutes or as long as 4 hours; mix occasionally.

Rinse mushrooms. Thread halibut, scallops, mushrooms, and bell pepper pieces equally onto 5 thin skewers, alternating ingredients until all are used; reserve the fish marinade. Arrange skewers slightly apart on a rack on a 13-by 15-inch broiler pan. Broil 3 inches from heat until fish is just opaque in center (cut to test), about 8 minutes total; turn once and brush with marinade. Makes 4 servings. —*Micki Kent, Bainbridge Island, Wash.*

*Broil skewers of fish and vegetables, basting with fish marinade as they cook.*

## CRANBERRY LINZER TORTE

- ¼ cup water
- 1 package (12 oz.) or 3 cups fresh or frozen cranberries
- 1 cup sugar
- 1 tablespoon grated orange peel
  Linzer crust (recipe follows)

In a 2- to 2½-quart pan over high heat, bring water, cranberries, sugar, and peel to boiling. Boil, uncovered, until mixture is the consistency of soft jam, about 4 minutes; let cool.

Pour cranberry mixture into crust. Break reserved dough into almond-size lumps and scatter over filling. Bake in a 350° oven until crust is richly browned at edges, about 45 minutes. Serve warm or cool. Makes 8 servings. —*Lulu Karp, Berkeley, Calif.*

**Linzer crust.** In a food processor, whirl 1 cup **almonds** until finely ground. To almonds, add 1½ cups **all-purpose flour,** 1 cup (½ lb.) **butter** or margarine, 1 cup **sugar,** 2 **large egg yolks,** 1 tablespoon grated **orange peel,** 1 tablespoon **unsweetened cocoa,** 2 teaspoons **ground cinnamon,** ½ teaspoon **ground cloves.** Whirl until well mixed. Press ¾ of dough into a 9-inch cake pan with removable bottom; make edges about 1½ inches high. Reserve the remaining dough to use as topping.

*Richly browned, thick orange-almond crust surrounds tart cranberry filling.*

COMPETING WITH *an eggplant or a tomato, jicama will never win a beauty contest, but beneath its drab skin lies a white flesh of delicate flavor and unquenchable crispness. Although it is usually eaten raw, this firm, nutty root retains its texture when cooked, much like the water chestnut (with which jicama is sometimes confused). More remarkable still, the crispness remains even when the jicama is pickled; not even boiling vinegar can soften its proud spirit. Compared with the audible crunch of pickled jicama spears, the finest dill pickle is mere mush.*

*The touch of red chilies and the sprigs of cilantro pay homage to Mexico, jicama's native home. There, it's often sold by street vendors, usually as slices bathed in lime juice and sprinkled with salt and chili powder.*

## PICKLED JICAMA

1½ to 2 pounds jicama, scrubbed
2 tablespoons salt
  Water
1 teaspoon mustard seed
1 teaspoon dry dill weed
½ teaspoon crushed dried hot red chilies
4 sprigs fresh cilantro (coriander)
1½ cups distilled white vinegar
½ cup finely chopped onion
⅓ cup sugar

Peel jicama and cut into sticks about ½ inch thick and 5 inches long. Place sticks in a glass or stainless steel bowl, sprinkle with 1 tablespoon of the salt, and add enough water to cover. Stir until salt is dissolved, then let stand at least 1 or up to 2 hours; drain.

Pack jicama upright into 2 wide-mouthed 1-pint jars. In each jar, put half the mustard seed, dill weed, chilies, and cilantro.

In a 2- to 3-quart pan, bring to a boil the vinegar, remaining 1 tablespoon salt, onion, and sugar. Boil, uncovered, for 1 minute, then pour hot mixture into jars to cover jicama. Let cool, then cover tightly and chill at least until next day or up to 1 month. Makes 2 pints.

*Sacramento*

*"Jicama will never win a beauty contest, but beneath its drab skin…"*

NOSTALGIA WORKS *for some people: François Villon achieved immortality by lamenting the snows of yesteryear, Samuel Woodworth grew dewy-eyed over the old oaken bucket, and a whole generation sighed over yesterday's gardenias and last year's crop of kisses. Harry Lockwood, however, keeps his eyes firmly fixed on the future, especially when he's cooking Tomorrow's Potatoes.*

*Why the name? You prepare the potatoes one day to bake and serve the next (although you can rush matters with no loss of character—except perhaps as an organized cook—and plunge right ahead).*

*Shredding the boiled potatoes produces a vegetable dish that artfully combines the textures of potatoes au gratin with that of lumpy mashed potatoes now in vogue.*

## TOMORROW'S POTATOES

2 pounds russet potatoes, scrubbed
1½ cups (6 oz.) shredded sharp cheddar cheese
6 green onions (roots trimmed), thinly sliced
1½ cups sour cream
  Salt and pepper
  Paprika

Place potatoes in a 3- to 4-quart pan and add 2 inches water. Cover and bring to a boil over high heat; reduce heat and boil gently until potatoes are tender when pierced, about 45 minutes. Drain, let cool, then peel and coarsely shred.

In a large bowl, combine shredded potatoes, cheese, onions, and sour cream. Season to taste with salt and pepper. Butter a shallow 2-quart casserole; pour in mixture. If made ahead, cover and chill up until next day.

Bake, uncovered, in a 350° oven until hot and golden on top, about 1 hour. Sprinkle with paprika. Serves 5 or 6.

*Harry Lockwood*

*Troutdale, Ore.*

MANY WESTERN DINERS *who pride themselves on the breadth and discrimination of their palates are perfectly happy to eat no bread but sourdough French. This is not a bad decision by any means, but it shuts off a whole universe of other breads, such as Lyle Farrow's Walnut Bread.*

*This is not a dense, sweet, banana-nut or tea-sandwich sort of bread to load with cream cheese, but an honest, light loaf to spread with butter (and possibly jam), then serve as a buttress to a light meal or as toast for breakfast. The yeast dough is started the night before.*

## WALNUT BREAD

About 4½ cups all-purpose flour
2 cups warm water (110°)
2 packages active dry yeast
4 teaspoons sugar
1 cup chopped walnuts
½ cup milk
⅓ cup honey
½ cup (¼ lb.) butter or margarine, melted
1 teaspoon salt
1 cup whole-wheat flour
1½ cups rye flour

Stir together 2 cups all-purpose flour, water, yeast, and sugar. Cover with plastic wrap and let stand at least 18 or up to 24 hours.

Put nuts in an 8- or 9-inch-wide pan. Bake in a 350° oven, shaking occasionally, until lightly toasted, about 10 minutes. Let cool; if made ahead, set aside.

Stir milk, honey, butter, salt, whole-wheat flour, rye flour, and nuts; beat until well blended. With a spoon or a dough hook, beat in 2 more cups all-purpose flour.

*If mixing by hand,* scrape onto a floured board and knead until dough is smooth and satiny, 15 to 20 minutes; add as little flour as possible to keep dough from sticking. Place dough in a greased bowl.

*If using a dough hook,* beat until dough is stretchy and begins to pull from bowl, then add all-purpose flour, 1 tablespoon at a time, until dough pulls fairly cleanly from bowl. Remove dough hook.

*"Diners who eat no bread but sourdough French...shut off a whole universe of other breads."*

Cover bowl with plastic wrap and let dough rise in a warm place until doubled, about 1 hour. Punch dough down, knead briefly to expel air, then divide dough into 3 equal portions. Shape each portion into a round loaf; place well apart on greased baking sheets (you will need 2 pans: 1 pan 12 by 15 inches and 1 pan 9 by 11 inches). Cover lightly with plastic wrap and let rise until puffy, about 45 minutes.

Bake loaves, uncovered, in a 350° oven until richly browned, about 35 minutes. Let cool on racks; serve warm or cool. To store, wrap cool loaves airtight and keep up to 3 days; freeze to store longer. Makes 3 loaves, about 1 pound each.

*Lyle Farrow*

Los Gatos, Calif.

CLEVER COOKS *have devised many ways of stretching expensive seafood to serve a number of guests. Some add celery, greens, macaroni, even fruit to make salads, while others use seafood helpers such as rice, linguine, and vegetables to create casseroles, gumbos, and other mixed blessings. Too often the clenched hand of economy is evident in such preparations, especially when the chunks of protein are widely dispersed.*

*Not so with J. Harry MacArthur's recipe; he uses chicken to stretch his seafood. By blending a large amount of chicken with a modest quantity of seafood and heating them together with a lavish sauce of reduced cream, wine, and cognac, he convinces fellow diners that they have stuffed themselves with shrimp and scallops—and some chicken, too.*

### CALIFORNIA CHICKEN SEAFOOD

½ pound medium-size shrimp (43 to 50 per lb.)
Shrimp stock (recipe follows)
2 tablespoons butter or margarine
1 tablespoon salad oil
3 whole chicken breasts (about 1 lb. each), skinned, boned, and halved
¼ pound scallops, rinsed well and drained
¾ cup whipping cream
¼ cup cognac or brandy
Several whole chives
Salt and pepper

*"He uses chicken to stretch his seafood."*

Rinse, shell, and devein shrimp. Save shells for stock. Set aside shrimp.

Heat butter and oil in a 10- to 12-inch frying pan over medium-high heat; add breasts and cook, turning as needed, until golden brown and meat in center is no longer pink (cut to test), 8 to 10 minutes. Lift out chicken and keep warm.

If using sea scallops, cut them into ½-inch chunks. Add scallops and shrimp to pan and stir often on medium-high heat until shrimp turn pink, 3 to 5 minutes. Lift out and set aside. Add shrimp stock, cream, and cognac to pan and boil on high heat; stir frequently until sauce is reduced to about ¾ cup and large bubbles form, 5 to 8 minutes.

Reduce heat to medium and return chicken and seafood to pan, turning to coat with sauce. Arrange on a serving dish. Garnish with chives; season to taste with salt and pepper. Makes 6 servings.

**Shrimp stock.** In a 2- to 3-quart pan, combine reserved **shrimp shells** (preceding), 1 cup **dry white wine,** and 1 cup **regular-strength chicken broth.** Boil, uncovered, over high heat until liquid is reduced to about 1 cup. Pour through a fine strainer; discard shells. Return shrimp stock to pan and boil until reduced to about ½ cup. Use hot or cold.

*James Harry MacArthur*

Ventura, Calif.

# November Menus

A S THE HOLIDAY BUSTLE *draws near, simple family meals built around one great dish have wide appeal—especially when the main dish is easy to cook and has familiar, homespun flavors.*

*For a leisurely Sunday dinner, slip the one-pan lamb stew into the oven for a few carefree hours while the meal slowly cooks to succulence.*

*Risotto, a creamy-textured rice dish, is typically served as a side dish, but—when you add vegetables—it also makes a fine family entrée.*

*The hearty bean and pasta soup also needs little attention; it simmers on top of the range until the beans are tender. If you like, make the soup ahead.*

## ROASTING-PAN LAMB STEW

Oven-braised Norwegian Lamb Stew
Red Cabbage & Apple Slaw
Thin Crispbread     Butter
Lemon Sorbet     Crisp Ginger Cookies
Sparkling Water & Juice Cooler
Beer     Coffee

*You braise this lamb dish entirely in the oven. Start by browning the meat in a big roasting pan in a hot oven. Next, add the broth and vegetables, cover tightly, and bake until everything is tender. Thicken the plentiful pan juices for sauce.*

*You'll need to start the lamb stew about 3 hours before you plan to serve. Shortly before the stew is done, assemble the slaw.*

## OVEN-BRAISED NORWEGIAN LAMB STEW

  2  **tablespoons salad oil**
  2  **pounds boneless, fat-trimmed lamb shoulder, cut into 1½-inch cubes**
  4  **medium-size leeks (about 2 lb. total)**
  3  **cups regular-strength beef broth**
  4  **small carrots, peeled**
  8  **small thin-skinned potatoes (2 inches wide), scrubbed, with a band of peel cut from the middle of each**
  4  **large stalks celery, cut in half crosswise**
  1  **head (1½ to 2 lb.) cauliflower**
     **Parsley sprigs**
  3  **tablespoons cornstarch**
 ⅓  **cup whipping cream**
  2  **tablespoons water**
     **Salt and pepper**

*She's pouring hot, cream-smoothed pan juices over oven-braised lamb and vegetables.*

Mix oil with lamb in an 11- by 17-inch roasting pan; spread meat so pieces are slightly apart. Bake in a 450° oven until browned, 30 to 45 minutes.

Meanwhile, trim root ends and dark green tops from leeks and discard. Split leeks lengthwise and rinse well.

When meat is brown, bring broth to boiling in a 1½- to 2-quart pan over high heat. Remove roasting pan from oven and push meat to one end of pan. Arrange leeks, carrots, potatoes, celery, and cauliflower in empty space. Pour hot broth over vegetables and meat.

Cover tightly with foil and return to oven. Reduce oven temperature to 350°

and cook until meat is very tender when pierced, about 2 hours. Remove from oven and, with a slotted spatula or spoon, transfer meat and vegetables to a warm serving platter. Garnish with parsley, cover, and keep warm.

Mix cornstarch, cream, and water until smooth. Stir cornstarch mixture into pan juices and set pan directly over 2 burners. Stir over high heat until sauce thickens and boils. Add salt and pepper to taste. Pour into a bowl or pitcher. Serve vegetables and meat in rimmed plates or wide bowls, and pour sauce over top. Serves 4.

## RED CABBAGE & APPLE SLAW

6 cups finely shredded red cabbage
1 large Golden Delicious apple, cored and diced
6 tablespoons salad oil
3 tablespoons cider vinegar
1 teaspoon Dijon mustard
1 teaspoon caraway seed
  Salt and pepper

In a large bowl, combine cabbage and apple. Stir together oil, vinegar, mustard, and caraway. Mix with cabbage. Add salt and pepper to taste. Serves 4.

### RISOTTO FEAST

**Escarole & Butter Lettuce
with Oil & Vinegar Dressing
Vegetable Risotto
Orange Slices with Nutmeg
Sauvignon Blanc    Sparkling Water**

*Risotto is rice slowly cooked with broth and cheese to develop a rich, creamy texture. This vegetable-laced version can stand alone as a main dish, or you can add chunks of leftover holiday turkey.*

*Wash and crisp salad greens at least 30 minutes before serving. While risotto cooks, assemble salad and slice oranges. If desired, marinate fruit with orange-flavor liqueur and sprinkle lightly with nutmeg.*

## VEGETABLE RISOTTO

2 tablespoons olive oil
1 large red bell pepper, stemmed, seeded, and diced
2 medium-size (about ½ lb. total) zucchini, diced
¼ cup (⅛ lb.) butter or margarine
1 large onion, chopped
1 clove garlic, pressed or minced
1½ cups short-grain white (pearl) rice
4 to 4⅓ cups regular-strength chicken broth
1 package (9 oz.) frozen artichoke hearts, thawed
2 cups diced cooked turkey (optional)
  About 1 cup freshly shredded or grated parmesan cheese
  Salt and pepper

Pour oil into a 12-inch frying pan or 5- to 6-quart pan and place over high heat. Add red pepper and zucchini; stir until vegetables are tender-crisp, about 5 minutes. Lift out vegetables and set aside.

Add butter, onion, and garlic to pan; stir often over medium heat until onion is soft and golden. Add rice and stir often until it is opaque and looks milky, about 10 minutes. Mix in 4 cups broth; cook, stirring occasionally, until mixture comes to a boil. Adjust heat so rice boils gently; cook, uncovered, stirring occasionally, for 10 minutes.

Stir in artichoke hearts, turkey (if used), red pepper, and zucchini. Reduce heat to low and continue to cook, stirring often, until rice is tender and most of the liquid is absorbed, 10 to 15 minutes more (if liquid evaporates before rice is done, add a little more broth).

Remove from heat and gently mix in ¼ cup of the cheese and salt and pepper to taste. Scoop into a warm serving dish and sprinkle with ¼ cup of the parmesan; offer remaining cheese to sprinkle over each serving. Makes 4 main-dish servings.

### SUPER SOUP SUPPER

**Fresh Fennel      Olives
White Bean, Pasta & Sausage Soup
Crusty Bread      Butter
Ripe Pears    Bel Paese Cheese
Chianti      Milk**

*A big bowl of hot, thick soup is a comforting meal for a cool evening. This one is full of spicy sausage, creamy white beans, and tender pasta shells.*

*For predinner nibbles, offer about ¼ pound raw vegetables such as fennel, celery, or radishes and 1 cup plain or marinated olives.*

*Make the soup up to a day ahead or at least 2½ hours before serving. For dessert, serve the cheese to eat on slices of pear.*

*(Continued on next page)*

*Thick with beans and pasta, hearty soup goes into bowls for casual supper.*

## WHITE BEAN, PASTA & SAUSAGE SOUP

½ pound hot Italian sausage
1 large onion, chopped
3 cloves garlic, pressed or minced
1 large carrot, peeled and chopped
2 tablespoons dried currants
6 cups regular-strength chicken broth
3 cups water
1 teaspoon dry basil

1½ cups (8 oz.) dried Great Northern or small white beans, sorted for debris and rinsed
1 can (14½ oz.) pear-shaped tomatoes
1 cup dry large shell pasta
Freshly grated parmesan cheese

Remove casings from sausages and crumble large chunks into a 5- to 6-quart pan. Cook over high heat, stirring occasionally, until lightly browned. Drain off all but 2 tablespoons of the fat. Add onion, garlic, and carrot; stir until onion is limp. Add currants, broth, water, basil, and beans. Cover and bring to a boil. Reduce heat and simmer until beans are soft when pressed, 2 to 2½ hours.

Coarsely chop tomatoes (cut through them in the can with a knife) and add with liquid and pasta to pan. Cover and simmer until pasta is barely tender to bite, about 10 minutes. Skim off and discard fat. (If made ahead, cool, cover, and chill until the next day; reheat, covered, over medium-high heat, stirring occasionally.)

Pour into a tureen. Offer cheese to add to each portion. Makes 4 to 6 servings.

# DECEMBER

*Gingerbread reindeer (page 316)*

A Scandinavian smörgåsbord party led off our holiday entertaining ideas, with a tempting array of make-ahead dishes and a dozen kinds of Christmas cookies. For other festive gatherings, we offered quick appetizers, handsome roasts, elegant pheasant, and showpiece desserts. Gift ideas from the kitchen featured a fila-wrapped torta for Christmas morning, fanciful gingerbread creations, and fruits steeped in mellow liqueur.

# Smörgåsbord Party for 36

I**T'S AN EXTRAVAGANT ARRAY** —*but with careful planning, it's really quite achievable."* That's how Maud Hallin of San Francisco describes the smörgåsbord party she gives to share her Swedish heritage with friends. Like her, you can pick and choose among components of this lavish-seeming menu, deciding which recipes to make and which foods to buy.

The menu serves 3 dozen guests. This gives you flexibility for party planning. Stage one big party for 3 dozen, or have several smaller gatherings. Sometimes Ms. Hallin has two parties, back to back.

All or part of the following dishes can be made ahead. You can serve all or part of any dish at one time; or select a few dishes to present on separate occasions.

Foods that are prepared once but served at more than one party must be refrigerated between events; foods to be served cold must be kept cold at all times so they will stay fresh and safe to eat.

Using each recipe's yield as a guide, you can easily fill in with substitutes purchased from a delicatessen, particularly a Scandinavian one.

Herring choices in the market can be confusing. Atlantic salted herring is sold whole or in fillets; both forms are sold in bulk at delicatessens or Scandinavian markets and need to be desalted before using. Or use seasoned herring in jars found in the refrigerated section; drain fish and reseason it as directed in recipes. Matjes herring are young, tender herring available canned with various seasonings. Swedish anchovies, available in cans, are a form of herring, not to be confused with the skinny, saltier anchovies from Spain and Italy.

Recipes follow for the dishes marked with an asterisk. Or purchase similar dishes; each recipe gives a yield you can use as a buying guide.

## MATJES HERRING WITH GRAVLAX SAUCE

*To serve 36, make this recipe twice. Just spoon the herring onto the plate to serve.*

    2   cans (8 oz. each) wine-flavored
        matjes herring pieces or fillets,
        drained; cut fillets in ½-inch-
        wide pieces
        Gravlax sauce (recipe follows)
        Mild Swedish or Dijon mustard

Arrange herring pieces in 1 layer on a platter. Spoon gravlax sauce down the center of the herring. Dot with mustard. Makes about 2½ cups, 18 servings.

**Gravlax sauce.** Mix together 1 cup minced **fresh dill sprigs,** ½ cup **Swedish** or Dijon **mustard,** ¼ cup **salad oil,** 2 tablespoons **red wine vinegar,** and 2 tablespoons **sugar.** Use, or cover and chill up to 1 week.

## MATJES HERRING WITH HORSERADISH & BEETS

*As suggested in the previous recipe, make this recipe twice to serve 3 dozen.*

    2   cans (5 or 6 oz. each) matjes herring
        fillets, drained and cut into ½-inch-
        wide slices
        Horseradish sauce (recipe on
        page 312)
    1   can or jar (about 1 lb.) sliced
        pickled beets, drained and cut into
        ¼-inch cubes
    ⅓   cup minced chives

Arrange herring pieces in 1 layer on platter. Spoon sauce down center of herring.

*(Continued on page 312)*

---

### A HERRING COLLECTION

*Refresh salt herring or drain seasoned herring and add new flavors. Matjes herring are the young and tender fish.*

**Matjes Herring with Gravlax Sauce***
**Matjes Herring with Horseradish
& Beets***
**Glassblower's Herring***
**Spiced Herring***
**Danish Herring Salad***

### HOT & COLD FISH PLATES

*Smoked mackerel or trout flavors a pâté. The two hot dishes, assembled ahead, are ready to bake. Swedish anchovies, baked with the potatoes for Jansson's Temptation, are actually herring, too. They are far less salty than the skinny anchovy fillets from Southern Europe, but both work.*

**Smoked Mackerel Pâté***
**Hot Tomato Sprats***
**Jansson's Temptation***

### MEATS & CHEESE

*Typically, these foods end up on bread as open-faced sandwiches. Buy cheese in a chunk, allowing 1 or 2 ounces as a serving; Jarlsberg is a good alternative to cheddar.*

**Swedish Liver Pâté***
**Spiced Rolled Veal***
**White Cheddar Cheese**
**Assorted Mustards**

### THE MAIN PLATE

*Bake a ham or buy baked ham to slice; you'll need about 2 ounces per serving. Boil tiny potatoes (at least 1 per person), or heat canned tiny Swedish potatoes (¼ cup per serving) and season with fresh dill and butter; keep warm in a chafing dish. Bake beans, using a favorite recipe, or heat purchased beans; allow about ¼ cup per person.*

**Cold Baked Ham**
**Danish Pickled Cucumbers***
**Swedish Cabbage & Apples***
**Tiny Boiled Potatoes**
**Baked Beans**

### A BASKET OF BREADS

*Have several types of rye bread—plain, caraway, or orange (limpa) in hearty loaves. Crispbread comes in many flavors and can be paper-thin to cracker-thick.*

**Rye Bread    Crispbread
Butter**

### SWEET CHOICES

*Allow 2 or 3 cookies per person; offer several kinds. Good make-ahead recipes start on page 318. Shine apples with a cloth.*

**Homemade Cookies
Big Bowl of Red Apples**

*Take just a little taste and see! A classic smörgasbord offers many choices; with small quantities, even the young and the timid can sample traditional Swedish dishes.*

## ...MATJES HERRING WITH HORSERADISH & BEETS

Top decoratively with beets and chives. Makes about 4 cups, 18 servings.

**Horseradish sauce.** In a bowl, mix ½ cup peeled, cored, and minced **tart green apple**; 1 cup **sour cream**; 2 tablespoons grated **fresh horseradish** (or 3 tablespoons prepared horseradish), and ¼ to ½ teaspoon **ground white pepper.** Use, or cover and chill until next day.

## GLASSBLOWER'S HERRING

 1  **small red onion, thinly sliced crosswise and separated into rings**
 1  **large carrot, peeled and cut diagonally into thin slices**
12  **thin slices peeled fresh horseradish**
 9  **bay leaves**
 1  **tablespoon mustard seed**
 1  **tablespoon whole allspice**
10  **ounces (1½ cups) prepared salt herring fillets (recipe follows), cut diagonally into ½-inch-wide strips; or 1 jar (6 oz.) purchased prepared herring pieces, drained**
    **About 2½ cups pickling liquid (recipe follows)**

In a 4-cup clear glass container with straight sides, layer ingredients in this order: ½ the onion, ⅓ the carrot, ½ the horseradish, ⅓ of the bay leaves, ½ the mustard seed, ½ the allspice, and ½ the herring. Repeat. Top with remaining carrot and bay leaves.

Pour enough pickling liquid over herring to cover, about 2½ cups. Set a bowl or plate on top with a weight in it to keep herring submerged in the pickling liquid. Cover and chill at least 2 days. Serve, or store, chilled, up to 2 weeks. Makes about 2½ cups, 36 servings.

**Prepared salt herring fillets.** In a bowl, cover **Atlantic salted herring fillets** with **cold water** and stir; drain. Rinse repeatedly until water is nearly clear. Add water to herring (use about 2 quarts water for every 3 lb. fillets), cover, and chill at least 10 hours or until the next day; drain.

**Pickling liquid.** In a 4- to 5-quart pan, mix 4 cups **distilled white vinegar**, 3½ cups **water,** and 3 cups **sugar.** Bring to a boil, stirring to dissolve sugar. Let cool to use; store, covered, indefinitely in the refrigerator. Makes 8 cups.

## SPICED HERRING

 1  **small onion, thinly sliced crosswise and separated into rings**
 1  **teaspoon** *each* **whole cloves, whole allspice, and white or black peppercorns**
 6  **bay leaves**
 1  **teaspoon dry aromatic hops (optional)**
 4  **thin slices fresh ginger (each about the size of a quarter)**
10  **ounces (1½ cups) prepared salt herring fillets (recipe precedes), cut diagonally into ½-inch-wide strips; or 1 jar (6 oz.) purchased prepared herring pieces, drained**
    **About 1 cup pickling liquid (recipe precedes)**

In a 4-cup clear glass container with straight sides, layer ½ of the ingredients in this order: onion, cloves, allspice, peppercorns, bay leaves, hops, ginger, and herring. Repeat with remaining ingredients, but put all the remaining spices on top. Pour enough pickling liquid over spiced herring to cover. Set a bowl or plate on top with a weight in it to keep the herring submerged in the pickling liquid. Cover airtight and chill at least 2 days. Serve, or chill up to 2 weeks. Makes about 3 cups, 36 servings.

## DANISH HERRING SALAD

*If you aren't presenting the full buffet, or serving within 4 days, cut this recipe in half.*

 2  **jars or cans (1 lb. each) sliced pickled beets**
 ½  **pound prepared salt herring fillets (see preceding), or 1 jar (6 oz.) purchased prepared herring**
    **Beet salad dressing (recipe follows)**
 4  **medium-size tart green apples, cored and cut into ¼-inch cubes**
 2  **medium-size cooked thin-skinned potatoes, peeled and cut into ¼-inch cubes**
 ½  **cup minced dill pickle**
    **Salt and pepper**
 2  **hard-cooked eggs**

Drain juice from beets; reserve juice for dressing and cut beets into ¼-inch cubes. Cut herring into ¼-inch cubes.

In a large bowl, mix pickled beet salad dressing with diced beets, herring, apples, potatoes, and pickle; add salt and pepper to taste. Cover and chill at least 6 hours, or up to 4 days.

To serve, spoon herring salad into a bowl. Press egg white and yolk separately through a fine strainer. Make a

design on the salad with the egg. Serve, or cover and chill up to 24 hours. Makes about 3 quarts, 36 servings.

**Beet salad dressing.** Melt 3 tablespoons **butter** or margarine in a 2- to 3-quart pan over medium heat. Add ¼ cup **all-purpose flour** and stir until lightly browned. Whisking, slowly add 2 cups **half-and-half** (light cream). Cook, stirring, until mixture boils, about 5 minutes. Stir in the reserved 1 cup **pickled beet juice** (see preceding), ⅔ cup **cider vinegar,** ¼ to ⅓ cup mild **Swedish** or Dijon **mustard,** and ½ teaspoon **white pepper.** Let cool.

## SMOKED MACKEREL PÂTÉ

*To serve 36, double the recipe, or make 1 each of mackerel and trout.*

 ¾  **pound smoked mackerel or trout**
 1  **large package (8 oz.) cream cheese**
    **White pepper**
    **Croutons (recipe follows)**

Lift bones from fish and discard. Pull off skin and discard. In a bowl, mix together mackerel and cream cheese with a fork. Add pepper to taste. Put in a small bowl and serve at room temperature, or cover and chill up to 5 days. Spread on croutons. Makes about 2 cups, 18 servings.

**Croutons.** Slice 1 slender **baguette** (½ lb.) crosswise into ¼-inch-thick slices. Place in 2 baking pans, each 10 by 15 inches. Bake, uncovered, in a 200° oven until dry but still white, about 20 minutes. Let cool to serve; if made ahead, wrap airtight and store up to 5 days.

## HOT TOMATO SPRATS

 2  **medium-size onions (about 1 lb. total), chopped**
 2  **tablespoons salad oil**
 1  **cup** *each* **catsup and whipping cream**
 2  **cans (3 oz. each) Swedish anchovy fillets, drained; or 1 can (2 oz.) anchovy fillets, drained**
 1  **tablespoon** *each* **fine dry bread crumbs and melted butter or margarine**

In a 10- to 12-inch pan, cook and stir onions in oil over medium-high heat until limp and golden, about 10 minutes. Add catsup, cream, and anchovies. Stirring, bring mixture to a boil.

Reduce heat to a simmer and continue cooking until thickened and reduced to

3 cups, about 15 minutes. Pour mixture into 1 shallow 1-quart casserole, or 2 shallow 2-cup casseroles. (If made ahead, let cool, cover airtight, and freeze; use a foil pan, if you like. Thaw to continue.) Sprinkle crumbs and butter over the tomato sprats. Bake on an upper rack in a 400° oven until mixture is hot and crumbs are lightly browned, about 20 minutes. Makes 36 servings; 1 small casserole serves 18.

## JANSSON'S TEMPTATION

- 2 **pounds russet potatoes, peeled and thinly sliced**
- 1 **can (3 oz.) Swedish anchovy fillets, drained; or 1 can (2 oz.) anchovy fillets, drained**
- 2 **large onions, chopped**
- 1⅔ **cups whipping cream**
- 2 **tablespoons butter or margarine**
- 2 **tablespoons fine dry bread crumbs**
  **Salt**

In each of 2 shallow, 9- or 10-inch-diameter casseroles, layer the following ingredients in this order: ¼ of the potatoes, ½ the anchovies, ½ the onions, ¼ of the potatoes. Pour whipping cream equally over ingredients in both casseroles; cover. Bake in a 350° oven until potatoes are tender to bite, about 1 hour. Cool, cover, and chill up to 2 days; or freeze (thaw to continue). Dot potatoes with butter and crumbs. On the top rack of a 400° oven, bake uncovered until golden, about 30 minutes. Salt to taste. Makes 36 servings; 1 small casserole serves 18.

## SWEDISH LIVER PÂTÉ

- 1 **pound beef liver**
- ½ **pound bacon, coarsely chopped**
- 1 **large onion, peeled and quartered**
- 1 **can (3 oz.) Swedish anchovy fillets, drained and cut in chunks**
- ½ **cup all-purpose flour**
- 1 **tablespoon sugar**
- 1 **large egg**
- ⅔ **cup milk**
- ¾ **teaspoon pepper**
- ½ **teaspoon** *each* **minced fresh marjoram and fresh thyme; or ¼ teaspoon** *each* **dry marjoram and thyme leaves**
  **Chopped parsley**

Trim and discard tough membrane from liver; rinse liver, pat dry, and cut in chunks. Grind liver, bacon, onion, and anchovies through the medium blade of a food chopper; or whirl, a portion at a time, in a food processor just until finely ground.

In a large bowl mix flour and sugar, then add egg and milk and beat until blended. Stir in pepper, marjoram, thyme, and liver mixture; mix well.

Pour mixture into 4 loaf pans, 2½- by 5-inch-size; cover with foil. Place in a larger pan, set in a 400° oven, and fill larger pan with about 1 inch of boiling water. Bake until liver mixture feels firm when pressed lightly in center, about 45 minutes. Remove from oven. Lift loaves out of water bath. Cool, cover, and chill thoroughly, at least 4 hours or up to 3 days; or freeze (thaw to continue). To unmold, dip pans to rim in hot water until sides begin to liquefy. Invert onto a serving plate. Garnish with parsley. Makes 36 servings; each loaf serves 9.

## SPICED ROLLED VEAL

*Use saltpeter if you want roll to be pink.*

- 2 **tablespoons whole allspice**
- 2 **teaspoons dry juniper berries**
- 2 **teaspoons black peppercorns**
- 1 **veal breast, 4 to 5 pounds, boned, with fat trimmed**
- 2 **tablespoons sugar**
- 1 **teaspoon saltpeter, optional**
- ¾ **pound salt pork, thinly sliced**
- 4 **to 6 cups regular-strength chicken broth**

In a food processor, grind together allspice, juniper berries, and peppercorns. Lay veal flat, smooth side down. Sprinkle evenly with ground spices, sugar, and saltpeter; top with a single layer of saltpork, placing pieces side by side. Starting from a narrow end, roll veal up like a jelly roll. Place roll on a single layer of cheesecloth cut big enough to enclose roll; wrap cloth around meat, then tie roll snugly at about 1-inch intervals with string. Gather cloth at each end of roll and tie to enclose meat.

In a 4- to 5-quart pan, bring broth to a boil on high heat. Add veal; cover and bring to a boil. Cover and simmer gently until veal registers 155° on a thermometer inserted into center (prop roll above broth to test), about 1 hour.

Lift roll from broth, set in a pan, and cover airtight; reserve broth for other uses. In another pan, set several heavy weights (such as canned foods); set pan on the veal to weight it evenly. Chill at least 6 hours or up to 2 days. Remove weights and cloth. (If made ahead, wrap and freeze. Thaw in refrigerator.) Slice thinly. Makes 36 servings.

## DANISH PICKLED CUCUMBERS

- 6 **large (about 4 lb. total) cucumbers**
- 3 **cups cider vinegar**
- 2 **cups water**
- ⅔ **cup sugar**
- ¼ **cup mustard seed**
- 2 **teaspoons** *each* **whole cloves, whole allspice, white peppercorns, and dill seed**
- 6 **large shallots, chopped**
- 2 **teaspoons salt**

Peel cucumbers and cut in half lengthwise. Scoop out and discard seeds. Cut cucumbers crosswise into ½-inch-thick slices. Divide slices equally between 2 jars, each 1-quart size.

In a 2- to 3-quart pan, combine vinegar, water, sugar, mustard seed, cloves, allspice, peppercorns, dill seed, shallots, and salt. Bring mixture to a boil, stirring to dissolve sugar; cool to room temperature. Pour over cucumbers. Cover and chill at least 24 hours or up to 7 days. Makes about 2 quarts, 36 servings.

## SWEDISH CABBAGE & APPLES

- 2 **large onions, chopped**
- 2 **heads red cabbage (about 3 lb. each), finely shredded**
- 6 **tart green apples, peeled, cored, and chopped**
- ½ **cup (¼ lb.) butter or margarine**
- 2 **cups dry red wine**
- ⅔ **cup firmly packed brown sugar**
- ½ **cup cider vinegar**
- ⅓ **cup red currant jelly**
- 1 **teaspoon ground allspice**
- ½ **teaspoon ground cloves**
  **Salt**

In an 8- to 10-quart pan on medium heat, cook onion and apples in butter until onion is very limp, about 30 minutes; stir occasionally. Increase heat to medium-high, add cabbage, and stir until cabbage wilts but is still tender-crisp to bite, 10 to 12 minutes. Stir in wine, sugar, vinegar, jelly, allspice, and cloves; bring to a boil.

Serve hot or warm. (If made ahead, cool, cover, and chill up to 7 days. Reheat.) Makes about 4 quarts, or 36 servings.

# Gingerbread Architecture

THE BASIC BUILDING MATERIAL *for this selection of fantasy gingerbread structures is a strong, good-tasting ginger cooky dough that bakes to sturdiness in flat slabs or slightly contoured pieces. Your creation can be quite imaginative, as stark or full of curlicues as you like, provided you adhere to the strengths and limitations of this construction material. The designs on these pages were produced by Westerners of varying ages and skills.*

*You'll find the recipes for cooky dough and icing below; you need icing to decorate or glue the cookies together. Here we offer techniques for creating and controlling the structural elements—how to make patterns, how to shape the dough, how to use icing to embellish and cement the pieces together, and how to add decorations to the finished product.*

## TO MAKE PATTERNS

Draw outlines on pasteboard or heavy paper, then cut out. To test your design's structural integrity, fit the pieces together with tape; if the pasteboard wobbles, so will thin gingerbread.

Your dimensions are limited to the 12- by 15-inch size of a large baking sheet. Lay the pattern pieces out on your baking sheets to estimate how much dough you'll need. Maximum thickness for dough is ⅜ inch. For houses larger than 6 inches square, or for heavy, load-bearing walls, use ¼-inch-thick cooky slabs. Smaller houses and decorative overlays can use ⅛-inch-thick slabs.

See the photographs on page 317 for basic construction techniques.

## TO DECORATE COOKY SLABS

Use a pastry bag with a plain or decorating tip to apply icing cement (recipe below) to unassembled sections of cooky. Let dry until set, at least 30 minutes, before assembling.

You can also paint the slabs by spreading a thin layer of icing onto them; you may need to thin it with a few drops of water to make it spread smoothly. If you want, you can tint portions of the icing, too: add a few drops of food coloring.

## TO ASSEMBLE STRUCTURES

Use a knife or a pastry bag with a small, plain tip to apply icing cement generously (but not enough to ooze or run) to 1 side of a piece, such as the edge of a wall. Butt an uniced piece against the icing, as dictated by your pattern, and hold pieces together briefly until the icing sets. To improve the stability of your structure, apply icing to its bottom edge and set it on a firm, flat surface—a rectangle of gingerbread, a board, or a platter. (If you want to be able to lift the building up to hide or reveal treats inside, don't cement the bottom edge to a supporting base.)

Continue to apply icing, holding joined pieces together until set, until

*(Continued on page 316)*

## Sturdy & Good-Tasting, This Is the Basic Building Gingerbread

### GINGERBREAD COOKY BUILDING SLABS

- 1½ cups whipping cream
- 1 teaspoon vanilla
- 2½ cups firmly packed brown sugar
- 2 tablespoons baking soda
- 1 tablespoon ground ginger
- 2 teaspoons ground cinnamon
- 1⅓ cups light or dark molasses
- 9 cups all-purpose flour
  Icing cement

Whip cream and vanilla until cream holds soft peaks. In a large bowl, mix sugar, baking soda, ginger, and cinnamon. Stir in molasses and cream. Gradually add flour, mixing well.

On a lightly floured board, roll out a portion of dough until it's flat but still thick enough to pick up easily without tearing. Place it on a greased and floured 12- by 15-inch rimless baking sheet.

Finish rolling dough on pan, supporting the rolling pin on equally thick wooden strips placed along opposite edges of pan. Use about 2 cups dough for each ⅛-inch-thick slab, about 4 cups for each ¼-inch slab, and about 6 cups for each ⅜-inch slab. If cookies are not evenly thick, the thin areas bake darker in color and are more brittle.

You can bake up to 2 pans of dough at a time in 1 oven. Bake dough until fairly firm when pressed in center—in a 300° oven, allow about 1 hour for ⅛-inch-thick slabs; in a 275° oven, allow about 1¾ hours for ¼-inch slabs and about 2¼ hours for ⅜-inch slabs.

After 30 minutes, remove pans from oven and place pattern pieces close together on the dough; with a sharp knife, cut around pattern edges; lift off pattern and scraps. (Later, bake the scraps to eat.) Return both pans to oven, switching their positions, and finish baking. Meanwhile, roll out remaining dough to make cones (page 317, bottom) and other special features.

When done, carefully loosen cookies with a spatula; cool on pan until firm, about 5 minutes. Transfer to a rack to cool. Decorate and assemble structure with icing cement or wrap pieces airtight and store up to 1 month; cookies keep crisp longer, but do not taste as fresh. Makes about 9 cups dough, or 4½ slabs ⅛ inch thick, 2½ slabs ¼ inch thick, or 1½ slabs ⅜ inch thick. Each full slab is 10 by 15 inches.

**Icing cement.** With an electric mixer, beat 2 **large egg whites,** ⅛ teaspoon **cream of tartar,** and 2 teaspoons **water** until frothy. Mix in 3 cups sifted **powdered sugar;** beat on high speed until icing is stiff, 5 to 10 minutes. Use, or cover up to 8 hours. Makes about 1½ cups.

Three structural elements—cone, slabs, and cutouts—come together in gingerbread barn.

Built from blueprints for real house, gingerbread model was Judy Tuck's gift to owners, Susan and Pat McBaine.

Two-story Southwest pueblo needs extra support: first-floor walls are thicker, and cinnamon sticks running structure's width serve as "vigas".

Lucia maids of SWEA (a Swedish group) admire Viking ship curved with technique used for making gingerbread cones (page 317).

project is assembled. If there are any gaps, you can fill them neatly by piping or spreading icing into or over them. If icing smudges, wipe with a damp cloth.

**To build higher.** When you build more than 1 story on a house, as in the pueblo on page 315, make the bottom story ⅛ inch thicker than the upper level.

**To attach decorations,** dab undersides with a little icing cement and hold in place until set. You can use this technique to add hard candies, licorice whips, candy canes, chocolate-drop candies, cutout cookies, or a variety of other things.

**Other details.** Many of our architects used some of the cooky dough for cutouts to populate or adorn their designs. Feel free to make designs on the dough before cooking; it will hold the impressions on its surface as it bakes. Simply cut partly through the dough with a knife, or impress floured objects (such as fork tines or heads of screws) in it, then remove.

## To Display Your Masterpiece

Keep gingerbread in a dry place. In a humid atmosphere, the cooky will absorb moisture and soften quickly; a bad place to display a gingerbread crea-tion in winter is close to windows that steam up.

You might cover the structure with plastic wrap at night to help extend its longevity and to keep off dust. Some of our experiments were still strong and upright after a year of being loosely sealed under plastic wrap.

To eat, gingerbread structures that are dust-free and still crisp or only slightly softened are enjoyable to break apart as an attention-getting party dessert, perhaps to go with ice cream or fruit. One favorite trick is to fill a structure with more cookies, confections, or dried or fresh fruit; it becomes a treasure trove of prizes for guests to take home.

*Behind candy columns is a gingerbread Parthenon, built by Robert Mueller of Berkeley.*

## Gingerbread Reindeer

To make the gingerbread reindeer on page 309, use the pattern below. On heavy paper or pasteboard, draw this pattern on a ¼-inch grid. Cut out pattern. Roll Gingerbread Cooky Building Slabs (page 314) ¼ inch thick. Bake dough. Trim off tiny corner of dough, measure thickness, and adjust notches in your pattern to fit thickness exactly. Then cut out cookies, as directed, using pattern. When cookies are cool, pipe a dot of icing cement (recipe on page 314) on each side of head to make eyes; let dry. If desired, tint icing that joins reindeer by mixing in unsweetened cocoa.

To assemble, pipe icing into 2 leg notches and set body in place. Stand upright and adjust legs to make it steady; hold until icing sets. Attach antlers with icing; hold until set.

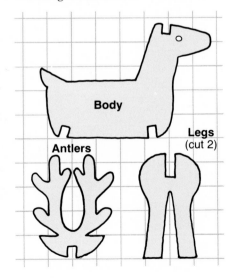

Roll dough on pan, supporting ends of rolling pin on strips of wood lath—as thick as you want dough, and long enough to run pan's length. This ensures uniform thickness for uniform baking.

Cut around patterns arranged on partially baked dough; remove extras. Continue to bake until the dough is cooked; it will harden as it cools.

Pipe icing along edge of piece to be joined; butt pieces together and hold in place briefly to set.

For a cylinder, use icing to glue cooky strips onto foil-wrapped can or cardboard tube; pipe more icing between pieces.

For a cone, fit a round of dough over a foil-covered cardboard cone; cut out folds, and pinch edges together. Rim any overhang. Bake for the full time.

# Christmas Cookies

A MENAGERIE OF COOKIES, *this collection of twelve choices is wildly delectable. From the dozens of cookies that result, you have ample variety and supply to make gift packs, offer to guests, or just simply enjoy with a cup of coffee or tea when you take a short break from holiday activities.*

*Dig out your cooky-making tools—presses, cutters—or use your hands to shape rounds, crescents, triangles, bars, and strips. Flavor with nuts, seeds, sweet spices, chocolate, jam—even cranberries.*

## TIPS FOR THE COOKY BAKER

*To use a food processor,* often an alternative in these recipes, you need one with a large bowl if the recipe calls for 3 to 4 cups of flour.

*To keep dough easy to handle,* chill to firm if the recipe so directs.

*To help cookies bake evenly* when the oven is full, alternate position of pans halfway through baking.

*To keep cookies fresh,* store as directed. Different types need different care.

## SALLY'S FAVORITE

| | |
|---|---|
| 1 | cup (½ lb.) butter or margarine, at room temperature |
| 1 | cup granulated sugar |
| 1 | cup firmly packed brown sugar |
| 1 | large egg |
| 1 | cup salad oil |
| 1 | teaspoon vanilla |
| 1 | cup regular rolled oats |
| 1 | cup finely crushed corn flakes |
| ½ | cup sweetened shredded coconut |
| ½ | cup chopped walnuts or pecans |
| 3½ | cups all-purpose flour |
| 1 | teaspoon baking soda |
| | About 70 walnut or pecan halves |

In large bowl of an electric mixer or with a spoon, blend together butter, granulated sugar, brown sugar, and egg. Add oil and vanilla; mix well and set aside.

In a food processor (or a blender, a portion at a time), whirl together rolled oats, corn flakes, coconut, and chopped nuts until finely chopped. Stir in flour and baking soda.

Add dry mixture to sugar mixture; stir to mix, then beat to blend well. Form dough into balls, each about 5-teaspoon size (1 heaping tablespoon).

Place balls 2 inches apart on 12- by 15-inch ungreased baking sheets. With a fork, press balls to flatten, making a crisscross pattern; dip fork in water as needed to prevent sticking. Press a nut half on top of each cooky.

Bake in a 350° oven until cookies are firm to touch, 16 to 18 minutes. Let cool on pans about 1 minute, then transfer

Sally's Favorite

Meringue Nut Sticks

Sugar & Spice Cutouts

Peppermint Christmas Trees

Chocolate Hazelnut Biscotti

Sesame Moons

Mocha Morsels

White Chocolate & Cranberry Rounds

Pecan Crunch Gems

Almond Triangles

Brandied Toffee Lace

Walnut-Lemon Packets

*A dozen kinds of Christmas cookies offer ample variety for holiday entertaining and gift-giving.*

with a wide spatula to racks; let cool. Serve, or store airtight up to 1 week; freeze to store longer. Makes about 5 dozen. —*Sally Ellenberger, Palo Alto, Calif.*

## SESAME MOONS

- 6 **tablespoons sesame seed**
- 1 **cup (½ lb.) butter or margarine, at room temperature**
- 2 **cups powdered sugar, sifted**
- 1 **teaspoon vanilla**
- 2 **cups all-purpose flour**

In a 6- to 8-inch frying pan over medium heat, toast sesame seed, shaking pan often, until golden, 2 to 3 minutes; set aside.

In a large bowl, beat the butter, ½ cup of the powdered sugar, and vanilla until creamy. Add flour and ¼ cup of the sesame seed; mix until well blended.

Pinch off dough in 1-inch balls and roll each into a 2½-inch log. Place logs about 2 inches apart on ungreased 12- by 15-inch baking sheets; shape into crescents. Bake in a 350° oven until lightly browned, 18 to 20 minutes. Transfer to racks and let cool for 10 minutes. Roll in remaining powdered sugar, then press tops in remaining sesame seed; let cool. Serve, or store airtight up to 2 days; freeze to store longer. Makes about 3 dozen.

## MOCHA MORSELS

- ½ **cup whole blanched almonds**
- 2 **cups (12 oz.) semisweet chocolate baking chips**
- 2 **tablespoons butter or margarine**
- ½ **cup sugar**
- 2 **tablespoons whipping cream**
- 2 **tablespoons coffee-flavor liqueur**
- 2 **large eggs**
  **Mocha crust (recipe follows)**

Place almonds in an 8- or 9-inch-wide pan. Bake in a 350° oven until lightly toasted, 10 to 12 minutes. Let cool, then chop finely and set aside.

In a 1- to 1½-quart pan, stir chocolate with butter over lowest heat until melted. In a large bowl, combine chocolate mixture, sugar, cream, and liqueur until well blended; beat in eggs and almonds. Fill each mocha crustlined muffin cup equally with about 1 heaping teaspoon chocolate mixture. Bake in a

350° oven until tops look dry, 20 to 25 minutes. Let cool in pan 10 minutes, then transfer to racks to cool. Serve, or store airtight in the refrigerator for up to 2 days; freeze to store longer. Makes 4 dozen.

**Mocha crust.** In a food processor or with your fingers, whirl or rub together 1¾ cups **all-purpose flour**, ⅓ cup **unsweetened cocoa**, ¼ cup **sugar**, and ¾ cup (⅜ lb.) **butter** or margarine, cut up, until dough is a coarse meal. Add ⅓ cup chilled **strong coffee**, and stir just until dough holds together.

Divide dough into 4 pieces; wrap each airtight and chill until cold, at least 1 hour. Divide 1 dough piece into 12 equal portions. Press each piece of dough over bottom and up sides of greased tiny muffin cups (about 1½-inch diameter). Repeat with remaining dough. Note: if you have only 1 pan, wash, dry, and grease it again before baking next batch.

## WHITE CHOCOLATE & CRANBERRY ROUNDS

- 1 **cup (½ lb.) butter or margarine, at room temperature**
- 1½ **cups sugar**
- 2 **teaspoons baking soda**
- 1 **large egg**
- 1½ **cups all-purpose flour**
- 1½ **cups quick-cooking rolled oats**
- 6 **ounces (about 1¼ cups) coarsely chopped white chocolate, or white chocolate baking chips**
- 1½ **cups fresh or frozen cranberries**

With an electric mixer or with a spoon, beat butter, sugar, and baking soda in a large bowl until creamy; beat in egg. Add flour, oats, and chocolate; mix well.

Spoon lumps of dough, each about 5-teaspoon size (1 heaping tablespoon), 2 inches apart on greased 12- by 15-inch baking sheets. Press 3 or 4 cranberries into each cooky. Bake in a 350° oven until light golden, 10 to 12 minutes.

Let cool on pans until firm to touch, about 2 minutes. With a wide spatula, transfer to racks; let cool. Serve, or store airtight in the refrigerator up to 2 days; freeze to store longer. Makes about 3 dozen.

## MERINGUE NUT STICKS

- 3 **cups (about 1 lb.) almonds**
- 4 **large eggs**
- 2 **cups granulated sugar**
- 1 **teaspoon grated lemon peel**
- 2 **teaspoons vanilla**
- 1¾ **cups sifted powdered sugar**

Put almonds in a 10- by 15-inch baking pan. Bake in a 375° oven until nuts are lightly brown in center (break to test), about 12 minutes. Let cool. Whirl, a portion at a time, in a food processor or blender until finely ground. Put ground nuts into a large bowl.

Separate 3 of the eggs; put whites in a deep bowl. To ground almonds add yolks, remaining whole egg, granulated sugar, lemon peel, and vanilla. Work mixture with your hands until it sticks together.

Divide dough into 6 equal parts. Squeezing, shape 1 portion into a rope, then roll on an unfloured board until it is 13 inches long. Lay rope on a well-greased 12- by 15-inch baking sheet; flatten to make a strip about 1½ inches wide and ⅓ inch thick. Push edge with a long spatula or ruler to make straight.

Repeat procedure to shape remaining dough; place 3 strips 1½ inches apart on each baking sheet.

In a large bowl, whip the egg whites with an electric mixer on high speed until foamy. Gradually add powdered sugar, beating on high speed until meringue will hold slightly curving peaks. Spoon ⅙ of meringue (about 3 tablespoons) along the length of each strip of dough, then spread with a small spatula to completely cover top of strip.

Bake in a 200° oven for 10 minutes. Quickly remove from oven and, with a sharp knife or pastry scraper, cut strips diagonally into ¾-inch-wide pieces. Leave cut cookies in place and return to oven. Bake until topping is a very pale beige, about 40 minutes longer.

Remove from oven and let cookies cool on pan about 5 minutes. Then, with a knife, cut meringue flush with edges of each strip and cut through strip again to separate cookies. With a wide spatula, transfer cookies to racks to cool. Serve, or store airtight up to 1 week; freeze to store longer. Makes about 7 dozen. —*Lillian Jordan, Visalia, Calif.*

## Sugar & Spice Cutouts

1 cup pecans or walnuts
3½ cups all-purpose flour
1 teaspoon *each* baking powder and ground cinnamon
½ teaspoon *each* ground ginger and ground allspice
¼ teaspoon ground nutmeg
1 cup (½ lb.) butter or margarine, at room temperature
1½ cups sugar
2 large eggs
  Orange frosting (recipe follows)

In a food processor or blender, whirl nuts until finely ground. Mix with flour, baking powder, cinnamon, ginger, allspice, and nutmeg.

In a large bowl with an electric mixer or in a large food processor, beat or whirl butter and sugar until creamy; beat in eggs. Add flour mixture and blend thoroughly. Cover and chill dough until cold, at least 2 hours or as long as 3 days.

On a well-floured board, roll out ¼ of dough ⅜ inch thick. With floured cooky cutters (about 2½-inch diameter), cut shapes and place pieces 1 inch apart on ungreased 12- by 15-inch baking sheets.

As pans are filled, bake in a 350° oven until edges of cookies are golden brown, about 14 minutes. With a wide spatula, transfer to racks and let cool. With a small spatula, lightly spread frosting on each cooky. Let stand until frosting is dry to touch. Serve, or store airtight up to 1 week; freeze to store longer. Makes about 6 dozen. —*Hannah Kodatt, Mesa, Ariz.*

**Orange frosting.** Mix together 1½ cups sifted **powdered sugar**, ½ teaspoon grated **orange peel**, and about 1½ tablespoons **water** or orange-flavor liqueur. Frosting may thicken as you use it; if so, add a few drops extra liquid as needed.

## Peppermint Christmas Trees

1 cup (½ lb.) butter or margarine, at room temperature
¾ cup sugar
1 large egg
½ teaspoon *each* vanilla and peppermint extract
2¼ cups all-purpose flour
¼ teaspoon baking powder
  Green food coloring, optional
  Green-colored sugar

In a large bowl, beat butter and sugar until fluffy. Beat in egg, vanilla, and pep-

permint extract. Add flour, baking powder, and a few drops of food coloring; mix well. Place dough in a cooky press fitted with a tree plate; pack in firmly. Force out onto ungreased 12- by 15-inch baking sheets, spacing apart. Sprinkle with colored sugar.

Bake in a 375° oven until edges are golden, 10 to 12 minutes. Quickly transfer to racks and cool. Serve, or store airtight up to 2 days; freeze to store longer. Makes about 6 dozen.

## Chocolate Hazelnut Biscotti

1 cup hazelnuts
½ cup (¼ lb.) butter or margarine, at room temperature
¾ cup sugar
1 tablespoon grated orange peel
3 large eggs
1 teaspoon vanilla
3 cups all-purpose flour
1 tablespoon baking powder
½ teaspoon salt
1 cup (6 oz.) semisweet chocolate baking chips

Place hazelnuts in an 8- or 9-inch-wide pan. Bake in a 350° oven until lightly toasted beneath skins, shaking pan occasionally, 18 to 20 minutes. Pour nuts onto a towel and rub with cloth to remove most of the skins; lift out nuts, coarsely chop, and set aside.

In a large bowl, beat butter, sugar, and orange peel until fluffy. Add eggs, 1 at a time, beating well after each addition. Stir in vanilla. Combine flour, baking powder, and salt; add to butter mixture and stir to blend thoroughly. Mix in nuts.

Divide dough into 3 pieces. Shape each into a long roll, about 1½ inches in diameter. Place rolls, 2 inches apart, on a greased 12- by 15-inch baking sheet; flatten rolls to about ½-inch thickness. Bake in a 350° oven for 15 minutes.

Remove from oven and cut rolls crosswise into ¾-inch-thick slices; lay cut side down on pan (at this point, you will need another greased baking sheet to bake cookies all at once). Return to oven and continue baking until biscotti look dry and are lightly browned, about 15 minutes. Transfer to racks to cool.

In a 1- to 1½-quart pan, stir chocolate over lowest heat just until melted. Spread on top and sides of 1 end of each biscotti. When chocolate firms, serve, or store airtight up to 2 days; freeze to store longer. Makes about 4 dozen.

## Brandied Toffee Lace

½ cup (¼ lb.) butter or margarine
1 cup quick-cooking rolled oats
½ cup firmly packed brown sugar
⅓ cup all-purpose flour
5 tablespoons whipping cream
1 cup (6 oz.) semisweet chocolate baking chips
2 tablespoons brandy

In a 1- to 1½-quart pan, melt butter. Remove from heat and stir in oats, brown sugar, flour, and 2 tablespoons cream; stir often as using to keep well mixed. Drop dough in 1 teaspoon portions, placing 6 well apart on each greased 12- by 15-inch baking sheet. Bake in a 350° oven until lightly browned, 7 to 9 minutes.

Remove from oven and let stand until cookies are firm, about 3 minutes. With the tip of a pointed knife, ease each cooky free, then lift onto racks to cool. Repeat to bake remaining batter.

In another 1- to 1½-quart pan, stir remaining cream, chocolate, and brandy over lowest heat just until chocolate melts. Chill until mixture is slightly thickened, 10 to 12 minutes. With a small knife or spatula, gently spread the back of a cooky with chocolate mixture and top with a second cooky. Repeat with remaining cookies and chocolate.

Serve, or store airtight in the refrigerator for up to 2 days; freeze to store longer. Makes about 2 dozen. —*Georgianna Smith, Redwood City, Calif.*

## Pecan Crunch Gems

1 cup (½ lb.) butter or margarine, at room temperature
10 tablespoons sugar
1 teaspoon vanilla
2 cups all-purpose flour
¾ cup coarsely crushed potato chips
½ cup finely chopped pecans
¼ cup raspberry or apricot jam

In a large bowl beat butter, ½ cup of the sugar, and vanilla until fluffy. Stir in flour, potato chips, and pecans; mix until thoroughly blended.

Roll dough into 1¼-inch balls. Place 2 inches apart on ungreased 12- by 15-inch baking sheets. Flatten each ball with back of a teaspoon that has been dipped in remaining sugar. Neatly dot each cooky center with ¼ teaspoon jam.

Bake in a 350° oven until lightly browned, 16 to 18 minutes. Serve, or store airtight at room temperature for up to 2 days; freeze to store longer. Makes about 3½ dozen. —*Emilie Serpa, Daly City, Calif.*

## ALMOND TRIANGLES OR SQUARES

2½ cups all-purpose flour
1 cup (½ lb.) butter or margarine, cut into chunks
1 large egg
  Almond filling (recipe follows)
1 cup sliced almonds

In food processor or with your fingers, whirl or rub flour and butter until fine crumbs. Add egg and whirl until dough forms a ball (or stir with a fork, then press together). Evenly press dough over bottom and ¼ inch up sides of a 9- by 13-inch baking pan. Pour almond filling over dough and spread evenly. Sprinkle sliced almonds over filling and gently press onto surface of filling. Bake in a 350° oven until almond slices are golden brown, about 40 minutes.

Let cool in pan, then cut pastry into about 2-inch squares (to make triangles, cut squares diagonally). Remove from pan with a spatula and serve, or store airtight in the refrigerator up to 2 weeks; freeze to store longer. Makes about 2 dozen squares or about 4 dozen triangles. —*Faye Massey, La Cañada, Calif.*

**Almond filling.** With an electric mixer or food processor, mix or whirl together until thoroughly blended 2 **large eggs,** 1 cup **sugar,** and 8 ounces (1 cup packed) **almond paste,** in small pieces.

## WALNUT-LEMON PACKETS

1 cup (½ lb.) butter or margarine, at room temperature
1 large package (8 oz.) cream cheese, at room temperature
1 teaspoon grated lemon peel
½ teaspoon vanilla
2 cups all-purpose flour
  Walnut filling (recipe follows)
1 large egg yolk
  About ¼ cup powdered sugar

In a food processor or with an electric mixer, whirl or mix together butter, cream cheese, lemon peel, and vanilla. Add flour and whirl or mix until well blended. Cover and chill pastry until cold, at least 2 hours or up to 3 days.

On a well-floured board, roll out ¼ of dough to make a 10- by 12½-inch rectangle (dough will be almost transparent); turn dough over frequently and flour board to prevent sticking. Using a ruler to guide, cut dough into 2½-inch squares. Place 1 teaspoon walnut filling onto the center of each square. Fold diagonally opposite corners to the center over filling, dab corners with egg yolk, and press gently together to secure. Transfer each packet to ungreased 12- by 15-inch baking sheets, spacing packets at least 1 inch apart. Repeat to shape remaining dough.

As each pan is filled, bake cookies in a 375° oven until lightly browned, 14 to 16 minutes. With a wide spatula, transfer to racks and dust with sugar; let cool.

Serve, or store airtight up to 1 week; freeze to store longer. Makes about 8 dozen. —*Dorothy Jones, Duarte, Calif.*

**Walnut filling.** In a food processor or blender, whirl 2½ cups **walnuts** (a portion at a time) until finely ground. With an electric mixer on high speed, whip 2 large **egg whites** and 2 teaspoons **lemon juice** in a deep bowl until whites are foamy. Gradually add 1 cup **sugar,** beating at high speed until whites will hold stiff peaks. Stir in walnuts.

## Where to Call to Ask Questions about Food

**B**READ WON'T RISE? Need to defrost your turkey fast? Many food manufacturers provide toll-free hot lines to answer questions about their products.

You can check if a company has such a number by dialing (800) 555-1212 (a free call). Many companies *don't,* so sometimes you'll get a number, sometimes you won't. But two directories can make your search easier.

The free *Consumer's Resource Handbook* gives numbers (some toll-free), addresses, and advice on when and how to make a product complaint. To order a copy, write to Handbook, Consumer Information Center, Pueblo, Colo. 81009. Allow four to six weeks for delivery.

The *AT&T Toll-Free 800 Consumer Directory,* which includes many hot line numbers—but not always under con-venient names—is available at AT&T phone center stores for $9.95. To order, call (800) 426-8686; shipping costs will be added.

To get you started, here are hot lines with hours and time zone for a dozen major food companies. Except where noted, all are area code 800.

**Arm & Hammer:** 524-1328; 9 A.M. to 4 P.M. weekdays, Eastern time zone.
**Borden, Inc.:** 848-9570; 8:30 to 5 weekdays, Eastern.
**Butterball Turkey:** 323-4848 through December 24; 8 to 8 weekdays, Central (6 to 6 on Thanksgiving and 8 to 6 on December 24). The rest of the year, call (312) 572-4831 from 8:15 to 4:30 weekdays, Central.
**Dole:** 232-8888 in California, 232-8800 elsewhere; 8 to 6 weekdays, Pacific.

**Fleischmann's Yeast, Inc.:** 227-6202; 7 to 6 weekdays, Pacific.
**Kraft, Inc.:** 447-1167 in northern California; 8 to 4 weekdays, Pacific. Elsewhere call (312) 998-2000; 8 to 5 weekdays, Central.
**Lawry's Foods, Inc.:** 952-9797; 8 to 5 weekdays, Pacific.
**Morton Salt:** 972-5215 in California, 227-1140 in Idaho, Nevada, Oregon, Utah, and Washington; 7:30 to 4:30 weekdays, Pacific and Central.
**Nabisco Brands, Inc.:** 932-7800; 9 to 4:30 weekdays, Eastern.
**Pet, Inc.:** 325-7130; 24 hours daily.
**The Pillsbury Company:** 328-4466; 8 to 6 weekdays, Central.
**USDA Food Safety** (meat and poultry): 535-4555; 10 to 4 weekdays (9 to 5 November 2 through 27), Eastern.

# Brunch Bundle

Aʀᴛᴇʀ ᴛʜᴇ ᴘᴀᴄᴋᴀɢᴇꜱ *have been opened on Christmas morning, delight the family with one more attractive gift: this stunning, fila-swathed breakfast torta.*

*The torta—a baked egg and ricotta casserole chock-full of sausage, red bell pepper, zucchini, and fontina cheese—is encased in paper-thin layers of buttered fila dough, then baked again. A bright ribbon tied around it marks the festive occasion.*

*You can make the torta a day ahead. At the last minute, quickly wrap with fila (it doesn't take long); then bake. Fila will dry out if left standing too long.*

### FILA-WRAPPED SAUSAGE TORTA

 1 **pound mild Italian sausage**
 1 **clove garlic, minced or pressed**
 1 **large onion, chopped**
 1 **large red or green bell pepper, stemmed, seeded, and chopped**
10 **large eggs**
 2 **cups (1 lb.) ricotta cheese**
 ½ **cup all-purpose flour**
 1 **teaspoon baking powder**
 ½ **teaspoon pepper**
 2 **medium-size (about ¾ lb.) zucchini, ends trimmed, cut into ⅛-inch-thick slices**
 ¾ **pound fontina cheese, shredded**
 5 **sheets (12- by 17-inch) fila dough**
 3 **tablespoons butter or margarine, melted**

Remove casings and crumble sausage into a 10- to 12-inch frying pan. Cook over medium-high heat, stirring often, until lightly browned, 10 to 12 minutes. Drain off and discard all but 3 tablespoons of fat. Add garlic, onion, and bell pepper; cook, stirring occasionally, until onions are golden, 8 to 10 minutes. Set aside.

In a large bowl, with an electric mixer beat eggs, ricotta, flour, baking powder, and pepper until smoothly blended. Stir in sausage mixture, zucchini, and fontina cheese. Pour into a buttered and floured 2½-quart soufflé dish. Bake, uncovered, in a 375° oven until top is golden brown and feels firm in center when pressed, 55 to 65 minutes.

Remove from oven and let stand at least 30 minutes. Run a knife around edge of torta; invert onto a baking sheet. (At this point, you can cover and chill a day. Let cold torta stand at room temperature for about 1 hour before wrapping.)

To arrange fila, lay 1 sheet out flat; brush lightly with butter. Overlap the narrow side of the first sheet by half with a narrow side of a second sheet to make a 24-inch-long strip; butter the second sheet.

To form the cross (see step 2), place a third sheet across the center of the 24-inch-strip with 1 narrow side extending out about 8 inches; brush lightly with butter. Overlap a fourth sheet, crossing center of the long strip, with 1 narrow side extending out in the opposite direction by the same distance (each leg of the cross should extend out about 8 inches from the center square). Brush fourth sheet lightly with butter. Brush last fila sheet with butter; set aside.

Set torta in the center of the cross.

Gently lift 1 side of fila at a time up and around torta, gathering all 4 sides at top (an extra pair of hands helps). Pinch center of reserved buttered fila sheet and gently lift up; set pointed end in center of gathered top. Wrap a 1-inch strip of foil around base of fila ruffle to hold it upright.

Brush filled portion of fila with remaining butter. Using 2 wide spatulas, lift package onto a 12- by 15-inch baking sheet. Cut a 10-inch square of foil and loosely cup over ruffled top. Bake on lowest rack of a 375° oven for 45 minutes; remove foil and continue to bake until top is golden, 5 to 10 minutes longer. Using spatulas, transfer package to a platter. Cut into wedges to serve. Makes 10 to 12 servings.

*Pour filling into buttered and floured soufflé dish to bake; cool baked torta before proceeding.*

*Lift cross of buttered fila, made by overlapping 4 fila sheets, up and over torta, gathering on top.*

*Pinch center of reserved fila sheet; invert and tuck into center of gathers to add height.*

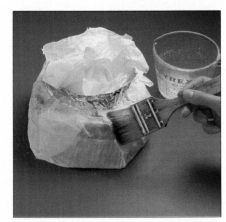

*Brush sides of wrapped torta with melted butter; foil strip holds the ruffle steadily upright.*

*Christmas morning, present this edible, gift-wrapped package. A slice reveals a savory sausage-and-egg filling surrounded by layers of flaky fila.*

# Holiday Roast Showpieces

**H**ANDSOME, SAVORY, AND QUICK *to pre-pare, these three roasts meet the de-mands of your hectic holiday schedule. Each carves easily to serve eight or more.*

*Peppercorns and juniper berries season beef and vegetables that roast together. The lamb leg (have it boned at the market) conceals a simple sage-flavored stuffing. Fresh ginger and tangerine juice brighten flavors of pork roast and sauce.*

## PEPPERED BEEF RIB ROAST WITH PEPPERS

- 2 tablespoons black peppercorns
- ¼ cup dry juniper berries
- 1 center-cut beef standing rib roast, about 8 pounds
- 1 tablespoon salad oil
- 1¼ pounds small onions (about 1-inch diameter), unpeeled

- 4 large red or green bell peppers, halved and seeded
- 8 medium-size fresh Anaheim chilies
- ½ cup *each* gin and regular-strength beef broth (or use 1 cup broth)

In a blender or food processor, whirl peppercorns and juniper berries until coarsely ground. Rub beef all over with half the oil, then with half the seasonings.

Set beef, fat up, on a V-shaped rack in a deep 12- by 17-inch roasting pan. Place onions in pan. Roast in a 325° oven for 1 hour, then add bell peppers and chilies to pan. Lightly brush all vegetables with remaining oil, then sprinkle with remaining peppercorn mixture.

Cook, basting vegetables once or twice with pan juices, until a meat thermometer inserted in thickest part of meat indicates desired doneness: 130° for rare, about 1½ hours longer; 140° for

medium, 2 hours longer; and 150° for well done, 2¼ hours longer.

Lift meat and vegetables to a board or platter and keep warm. Tilt pan; skim off and discard fat.

Add gin to pan, place over high heat, and carefully ignite (not beneath a vent, fan, or overhang). When flames subside, add broth and bring to a boil, stirring to loosen browned bits in pan. Pour into a serving dish.

Carve meat as shown below. Offer sauce to spoon over meat and vegetables. Makes 8 servings.

## SAGE-STUFFED LEG OF LAMB

- 1 large onion, minced
- 2 large stalks celery, including some leaves, finely chopped
- 3 tablespoons olive oil or salad oil

*Pat pepper, juniper berries onto oiled beef; oil makes spices stick to meat.*

*Ignite gin in pan drippings to burn off alcohol; add regular-strength broth for sauce.*

*Carve pepper- and juniper-crusted beef ribs to go with roasted vegetables. Together, they make an impressive, colorful array. To carve, steady four-rib roast by holding a bone tip, then slice parallel to rib. Every other slice gets a bone.*

1 tablespoon ground sage or 3 tablespoons minced fresh sage leaves
  Pepper
1½ cups coarse soft white bread
  crumbs
  Salt
1 leg of lamb, 5 to 6 pounds, boned
  but not tied
1 cup dry red wine
  Celery leaves (optional)

*Flatten boned leg of lamb; cover with sea-soned herb-bread filling.*

*Roll meat; then tie to enclose filling, tucking in ends.*

In a 10- to 12-inch frying pan over medium heat, frequently stir onion and celery
in oil until vegetables are very limp
and golden, about 20 minutes. Stir in
sage, ½ teaspoon pepper, and crumbs.
Remove from heat and add salt to taste.

Lay lamb flat, boned side up, between
sheets of plastic wrap. Pound with a flat
mallet until meat is evenly 1 inch thick.
Pat stuffing over meat to within 1½
inches of edges. Roll up meat from a
narrow side, then tie snugly with string
at 1½-inch intervals, tucking in ends of
meat. Place lamb, seam down, on a rack
in a shallow 12- by 15-inch roasting pan.

Roast in a 400° oven until a meat thermometer inserted in thickest part of
meat indicates desired doneness, 140°
for rare, 55 to 60 minutes; 150° for medium, about 1 hour; 160° for well done,
1 to 1¼ hours.

Lift meat to a board or platter and
keep warm. Tilt pan; skim off and discard fat. Add wine to pan and bring to a
boil over high heat, stirring to loosen
browned bits; pour into a serving dish.
Discard string; garnish meat with celery
leaves. Thickly slice roast crosswise and
offer sauce to season portions. Makes 8
to 10 servings.

*After roasting lamb, slice to reveal moist, aromatic stuffing. Serve with wine sauce.*

## ROAST PORK WITH
## POMEGRANATE-PRUNE RELISH

1 center-cut boneless pork loin, 3 to
  3½ pounds
⅓ cup minced fresh ginger
1 can (6 oz.) frozen tangerine juice
  concentrate
2 tablespoons distilled white vinegar
1 pound (2½ cups) pitted dry prunes
1 large pomegranate
  Small fresh tangerines or kumquats
  (optional)

Place pork, fat up, on a narrow rack in a
shallow 12- by 15-inch roasting pan.
Roast in a 375° oven until a meat thermometer inserted in thickest part
reaches 145°, 50 to 60 minutes.

Meanwhile, in a 2- to 3-quart pan,

combine ginger, juice concentrate, vinegar, and prunes. Bring to a boil over high
heat, stirring. Cover and simmer until
prunes are slightly softened, about 10
minutes; stir often. Remove from heat.

Halve pomegranate. Immerse in a
bowl of water; break apart to remove
seeds. Discard skin, pith, and water. Set
seeds aside.

After meat has reached 145°, tilt pan to
skim off and discard fat. Pour prune
mixture over pork, spooning liquid over
roast and pushing prunes into pan. Bake
until thermometer reaches 155°, 10 to 15
minutes longer. Lift pork to a platter;
garnish with tangerines. Stir pomegranate seeds into prune mixture, then
spoon into a dish. Slice meat crosswise;
accompany with fruit. Serves 8 to 10.

*Prunes and pomegranates, baked with meat, complement succulent pork loin.*

# If You've Been Intimidated By Pheasant

**F**OR AN ELEGANT, INTIMATE *occasion, try a farm-raised pheasant. Check your supermarket's freezer section for frozen birds, usually sold whole. Some grocers or meat markets may stock fresh pheasants, whole or parts, or will order them.*

*Pheasant, a rather small bird, usually weighs about 2½ pounds; one serves three generously. However, at $10 to $18 per bird, it is pricey compared to chicken.*

*Properly cooked, the white, lean meat is mild, moist, and tender. Overcooked meat turns tough, dry, and stringy. These three recipes enhance this delicate flavor and fine texture.*

*Two dishes use the whole pheasant: in one, you split, marinate, and grill it; in the other, you roast it, then serve with hot fruit. In the third, you pound breast meat thin, then sauté and serve with green pistachio butter and red cranberry sauce.*

## BARBECUED BUTTERFLIED PHEASANT WITH WHITE TERIYAKI SAUCE

- 1 **pheasant, about 2½ pounds**
- ½ **cup sake or dry white wine**
- ¼ **cup rice wine vinegar or distilled white vinegar**
- 1 **tablespoon sugar**
- 2 **tablespoons minced fresh ginger**
- ½ **teaspoon Oriental sesame oil (optional)**
- **Salt and pepper**
- **Watercress (optional)**
- **Gingered wild rice (recipe follows)**

Rinse pheasant and pat dry. Reserve neck and giblets for other uses.

To butterfly pheasant, lay bird breast down on a cutting board. With poultry shears or a large, heavy knife and mallet, split pheasant lengthwise along backbone. Firmly pull bird open, cracking bones as needed to lay it as flat as possible.

Rinse bird and pat dry. With a small, sharp knife, pierce breast in 6 to 8 places. Put pheasant, breast down, in a 9- by 13-inch baking dish.

Mix together sake, vinegar, sugar, and ginger; pour over pheasant. Cover and chill for at least 4 hours or up to overnight; turn pheasant at least twice.

On firegrate in a covered barbecue, ignite 60 charcoal briquets. When coals are coated with light gray ash (about 35 minutes), push half to each side of the grate; position grill 4 to 6 inches above.

Lift pheasant from marinade and place on center of grill, *not* over coals. Put on lid and open drafts. Turn bird every 10 minutes and baste generously with marinade. Cook until breast meat is white with a touch of pink at the breastbone, about 30 minutes. To test, make a cut to the bone parallel to the wing joint; meat should look moist, not soft and wet.

Transfer pheasant to platter; brush with sesame oil. Cut into serving pieces, add salt and pepper to taste, garnish with watercress. Serve with gingered rice. Makes 3 or 4 servings. —*Joann Mass, Knightsen, Calif.*

**Gingered wild rice.** Pour ¾ cup **wild rice** into a fine strainer and rinse under running water. To a 1½- to 2-quart pan, add rice, 1½ cups **regular-strength chicken broth,** and ½ cup **sake** or dry white wine. Bring to a boil over high heat, reduce heat to medium low, and cover. Simmer, stirring occasionally, until rice is tender to bite and absorbs liquid, about 50 minutes. Stir in 2 teaspoons **slivered pickled ginger,** drained. Serves 3 or 4.

Grilled and butterflied pheasant, served with wild rice, plays up bird's delicate flavor.

## OVEN-ROASTED PHEASANT

  1  **pheasant, about 2½ pounds**
  ½  **cup regular-strength chicken broth**
  2  **tablespoons butter or margarine**
  2  **tablespoons orange marmalade**
  ½  **cup firmly packed dried apricots**
  2  **tablespoons orange-flavor liqueur
     or water**
1½  **to 2 cups seedless green grapes**

Rinse pheasant and pat dry. Reserve neck and giblets for other uses. Arrange bird, breast down, on a rack in an 11- by 14-inch roasting pan.

In a 1½ to 2-quart pan over high heat, boil broth, butter, and marmalade, uncovered, until slightly thickened, about 3 minutes. Brush bird with some of this orange syrup.

Roast pheasant in a 450° oven. When back is golden brown, about 15 minutes, turn bird breast up. Baste again with syrup. Continue to bake until breast is brown and meat is white with a touch of pink at bone, about 15 minutes more. To test, make a cut to bone parallel to wing joint; meat should look moist, not soft and wet. While bird roasts, bring marmalade mixture to a boil over high heat; add apricots and orange liqueur. Simmer, covered, until apricots are soft and plump, about 10 minutes. Stir in grapes; heat until warm.

Set roasted bird on a platter and top with apricot mixture. Carve bird, and spoon fruit and syrup onto individual portions. Makes 3 or 4 servings.

*Cranberries and pistachio butter brighten pheasant breast.*

*Use poultry shears to split pheasant lengthwise along backbone. Pull bird open.*

## PHEASANT BREASTS WITH PISTACHIO BUTTER & CRANBERRIES

  2  **pheasant breast halves (about 6 oz. each), breastbone removed (may have wing joint attached)**
  ½  **teaspoon coarsely ground pepper**
  2  **tablespoons butter or margarine
     Pistachio butter (recipe follows)**
  ¾  **cup fresh or frozen cranberries**
  1  **tablespoon sugar
     Parsley, Italian or curly (optional)**

Rinse breast halves and pat dry. If wing joints are attached, cut them off and save. Pull off and discard all skin and fat from breast halves. Place meat between pieces of plastic wrap. With a flat-surfaced mallet, firmly pound meat until it is ¼ to ⅛ inch thick. Sprinkle meat with pepper.

In a 10- to 12-inch frying pan over medium-high heat, melt butter. When butter sizzles, add meat and wing pieces; cook until breasts are lightly browned on both sides but still slightly pink in center (cut to test), about 4 minutes total. Place 1 breast half on each heated dinner plate; top each serving equally with pistachio butter; keep warm.

To pan with wing sections, add cranberries and sugar. Turn heat to low and stir often until berries just begin to pop, about 1 minute. Spoon cranberries equally onto breast pieces beside pistachio butter. To each plate, add a wing joint and garnish with parsley. Makes 2 servings.

**Pistachio butter.** Mince ¼ cup **roasted, salted pistachios.** Mix well with 2 tablespoons softened **butter** or margarine, 1 tablespoon minced Italian or curly **parsley,** ¼ teaspoon grated **lime peel,** and 1 teaspoon **lime juice.**

# "Sculpted" Ice Cream Desserts

**I**T'S EASY TO TRANSFORM *ice cream or sorbet into a festive yule log or Christmas wreath. You just sculpt purchased, frozen desserts, and the only cooking required is for the simple sauces and garnishes.*

*For the wreath, you mound scoops of sorbet into a big ring. To make the log, you lay cylindrical pints of ice cream end to end, then frost with more softened ice cream. Garnish both desserts with chocolate leaves or with nontoxic real leaves.*

*Both desserts can be made up to a week ahead; garnish when ready to serve. Each yields about a dozen portions.*

## RASPBERRY SORBET WREATH

> 4 pints raspberry sorbet or sherbet, or 2 pints *each* vanilla ice cream and raspberry sorbet or sherbet
> Chocolate leaves (recipe follows)
> Cranberry sauce (recipe follows)

Set a 12- to 16-inch-diameter rimmed platter into freezer until cold, at least 15 minutes. If sorbet is very hard, set in refrigerator to soften slightly, 5 to 10 minutes. (If you have a microwave, you can place sorbet, 1 container at a time, in the oven and heat at 50 percent power until slightly softened. Check after 10 seconds. If needed, continue at 10-second intervals up to 30 seconds until firm-soft.)

With an ice cream scoop, make small balls (1½- to 2-inch-diameter) of sorbet and set on chilled platter in a 10- to 11-inch-wide ring. Make another circle of scoops inside the outer ring; scoop remaining sorbet on top of the 2 rings, as pictured below. Work quickly; if sorbet begins to melt, return platter and sorbet to freezer to firm before continuing.

Freeze completed wreath until firm, at least 30 minutes. If made ahead, cover airtight once firm and store up to 1 week.

Garnish with chocolate leaves and a few cranberries removed from the sauce. To serve, lift several scoops for each portion. Offer cool or cold cranberry sauce to spoon on top. Makes 10 to 12 servings.

**Chocolate leaves.** Rinse and pat dry 15 to 18 sturdy, **nontoxic leaves** (2 to 3 inches long), such as camellia or citrus. In the top of a double boiler set over hot (just below simmering) water, stir ½ cup **semisweet chocolate** or white chocolate **baking chips** just until melted. Remove from heat but leave over hot water; stir occasionally to keep chocolate evenly .smooth (white chocolate tends to be thicker).

With a small brush, paint an ⅛-inch-thick layer of chocolate over the *backs* of the leaves, leaving an ⅛- to ¼-inch unpainted border. Set leaves, chocolate side up, in a single layer on a flat pan and chill or freeze until chocolate hardens, at least 15 minutes or up to overnight. When firm, peel away real leaf. If made ahead, place chocolate leaves in a single layer on a pan; cover and chill or freeze up to 1 week.

**Cranberry sauce.** In a 1½- to 2-quart pan, mix 1 cup **fresh** or frozen **cranberries,** ½ cup **sugar,** and ½ cup **orange juice.** Simmer, covered, on low heat; stir occasionally until berries are translucent, 5 to 10 minutes. Cool. Stir in ¼ cup **orange-flavor liqueur** or orange juice. If made ahead, chill up to 1 week. Serve cool or cold.

## ICE CREAM YULE LOG

> 3 pints coffee, nut, or vanilla ice cream (in cylindrical containers about 4 inches tall)
> 2 pints chocolate ice cream
> ½ cup sliced almonds
> Chocolate leaves (recipe precedes)
> Mocha fudge sauce (recipe follows)

Set a 12- to 16-inch-long platter into the freezer until it is very cold, at least 30 minutes.

Fill a 1-quart measuring cup or small bowl half-full with hot water. Dip each container of coffee ice cream, 1 at a time, into water to just below the container's rim; hold just until ice cream begins to melt around sides, 5 to 15 seconds. Slide spatula inside carton around sides, then ease ice cream out onto chilled platter. Lay pints end to end; push together to form log. Smooth joints with a spatula.

*Scoops of raspberry sorbet with white chocolate leaves form festive wreath.*

*Sculpted frozen yule log assembles quickly from pints of coffee ice cream covered in chocolate ice cream.*

Return log (on platter) to freezer until surface is firm, at least 15 minutes. Cover if stored until next day. Dip containers of chocolate ice cream in hot water, 1 at a time, and slide ice cream out into a large bowl. Cut into about 2-inch chunks and let soften in the refrigerator, stirring occasionally, until the consistency of thick frosting, 10 to 20 minutes. (If you have a microwave, you can put ice cream in a nonmetal bowl and heat at 50 percent power just until soft. Check after 20 seconds; continue at 10-second intervals up to 60 seconds, stirring to soften evenly without turning runny.)

Working quickly, spread chocolate ice cream over frozen log on platter; do not frost ends. Freeze until firm, at least 1 hour. (If made ahead, wrap when firm and store in freezer up to 1 week.)

Place almonds in an 8- or 9-inch-wide pan. Bake in a 350° oven, shaking pan occasionally, until nuts are golden, 8 to 10 minutes. Let cool. If made ahead, wrap and store up to 1 week.

To serve, garnish log on platter with some of the almonds and leaves; arrange remaining nuts and leaves around platter rim. Let stand at room temperature 5 to 10 minutes to soften slightly, then cut into ¾-inch slices. Offer mocha sauce to spoon onto slices. Makes 12 to 16 servings.

**Mocha fudge sauce.** In a 1- to 1½-quart pan, combine 1½ cups (9 oz.) **semisweet chocolate baking chips** and ¾ cup **whipping cream.** Stir over low heat just until melted. Stir in 3 tablespoons **coffee-flavor liqueur** or strong coffee. Serve warm. If made ahead, cool, cover, and chill up to 1 week. Stir over low heat to warm.

*Chocolate leaves: paint back of real, nontoxic leaves (we used camellia) thickly with melted chocolate. Chill until firm; peel away real leaf.*

# Quick Appetizers

IF THE CUPBOARDS ARE BARE *when un-expected guests drop by, consider stocking supplies to make these five fast appetizers.*

*Lox and the cheeses will keep up to 1 week in the refrigerator. Carrots, beans, and jicama last about 4 days chilled; use them for dinner if guests don't stop by. Other ingredients are shelf stable.*

## VEGETABLE STICK BOUQUET FOR DIPPING

- 3 **tablespoons sesame seed**
- 3 **tablespoons soy sauce**
- ¼ **teaspoons** *each* **ground allspice and anise seed**
- ⅓ **pound green beans**
- 1 **large carrot**
- ⅓ **pound jicama, peeled**

Place sesame seed in a 6- to 8-inch frying pan and shake often over medium heat until golden, 4 to 5 minutes. Place in a very small bowl. In another very small bowl, mix soy, allspice, and anise seed; set both bowls aside. Trim ends from green beans. Cut carrot and jicama, into sticks about the same size as green beans. Set jicama aside.

In a 1- to 2-quart pan, bring 2 cups water to a boil over high heat. Add carrot sticks and cook until just tender-crisp to bite, about 1½ minutes. Lift from pan with a slotted spoon and place in ice water until cold; drain. Repeat process with beans.

Place beans, carrots, and jicama upright in a small container. Dip vegetables in soy mixture, then in sesame. Serves 4.

## HOT NUTS

- ¼ **teaspoon garlic powder**
- 2 **teaspoons hot chili oil**
- 3 **tablespoons brown sugar, firmly packed**
- 3 **tablespoons** *each* **soy sauce and cider vinegar**
- 1 **jar (12 oz.) unsalted dry-roasted peanuts**

In a bowl, mix garlic powder, hot chili oil, brown sugar, soy sauce, cider vinegar, and peanuts.

Line a 10- by 15-inch rimmed baking pan with foil; grease foil. Spread nut mixture evenly in pan. Bake in a 325° oven until liquid has evaporated, about 20 minutes; stir twice. Cool, then break apart. Serve, or store airtight up to 1 week. Nuts get sticky when exposed to air for more than a few hours. Makes 3 cups, 6 to 8 servings.

*Indonesian-style peanuts taste spicy; offer with orange juice.*

*Vegetable bouquet features green beans, carrots, and jicama.*

**Lox, cream cheese, and pistachios**

They're a winning combination. For 4 servings, place 2 small packages (3 oz. each) **cream cheese** in a small serving bowl; mash slightly. Sprinkle with ¼ cup coarsely chopped roasted **pistachios**. Accompany with 3 to 4 ounces sliced **lox** (smoked salmon) and **sesame crackers** (at least 4 per person). Garnish salmon with fresh **dill sprigs.**

**Pungent, nutty, sweet snack**

Serve with Amontillado sherry. For each serving, allow at least 1 ounce **goat cheese**, 3 **crackers**, 2 tablespoons **hazelnuts**, 1 **date**, and 1 piece **short-bread**. To toast nuts, put in an 8- or 9-inch-wide pan; bake in a 350° oven until golden in center, 10 to 15 minutes.

**Oriental party mix**

Goes well with sake. To make about 2⅓ cups or 4 servings, combine ½ cup **roasted peanuts**, 1⅓ cups (3½-oz. package) **Japanese rice crackers**, 3 tablespoons chopped **crystallized ginger**, and ¼ cup ¼- by 2-inch strips **nori** (seaweed). Serve immediately, since nori softens upon standing. Buy ingredients in groceries or Asian markets.

# Light & Mild Chinese Soups

A DEPARTURE *from soup's more familiar appearance at the beginning of a meal, these broths from China are designed as palate cleansers, to follow the main course. At many Chinese banquets, soups served in this fashion are lean in body, mild and delicate in flavor. Here we offer two to try with your next dinner; offer as a first course, or serve after the entrée.*

## CHICKEN CLOUD SOUP

- 1 **whole chicken breast (¾ to 1 lb.)**
- 6 **cups regular-strength chicken broth**
- 4 **slices fresh ginger (each about the size of a quarter)**
- 2 **green onions**
- 2 **large egg whites**
- 2 **tablespoons dry sherry**
- 1 **tablespoon cornstarch**
- ⅛ **teaspoon white pepper**
- ¼ **to ½ teaspoon salt (optional)**
- 1 **medium-size firm-ripe tomato, cored and cut in ½-inch wedges**
- 7 **cups lightly packed spinach leaves**

Bone and skin chicken. Reserve skin and bones; cut meat into chunks. In a 3- to 4-quart pan, combine 5⅔ cups broth, chicken bones and skin, ginger, and green onions. Bring to a boil over high heat. Cover and simmer about 30 minutes. Lift out and discard bones, skin, ginger, onion.

Meanwhile, in a food processor, combine chicken, egg whites, ⅓ cup broth, sherry, cornstarch, pepper, and salt; process until mixture forms a well-blended, paste-like purée. (Or mince chicken with a knife; add egg whites, broth, sherry, cornstarch, pepper, and salt; beat with an electric mixer on high speed until paste-like.) Slide chicken mixture in a single mass into hot broth; cover and simmer until meat is white in thickest part (cut to test), 10 to 15 minutes. Push tomato and spinach leaves into broth; cook just until spinach is wilted, 3 to 5 minutes longer.

With a slotted spoon, lift chicken cloud into serving bowl. Pour broth and vegetables over chicken. To serve, break up chicken cloud with a spoon and put some into each individual bowl; add soup. Serves 6 to 8.

*Egg crêpe noodles, tomato, broccoli, and bamboo shoots add color to soup.*

## EGG CRÊPE & VEGETABLE SOUP

- 6 **cups regular-strength chicken broth**
- 4 **slices fresh ginger (each about the size of a quarter)**
- 2 **green onions**
- 2 **tablespoons dry sherry**
- 1 **small kohlrabi (about 2½ inch diameter) or 2 pieces (each 1 by 3 inches) broccoli stalk**
- 3 **large leaves napa cabbage, cut crosswise into ½-inch-wide strips**
- 1 **can (8 oz.) sliced bamboo shoots, drained**
- 1 **medium-size firm-ripe tomato, cored and cut into ½-inch cubes**
  **Egg crêpe noodles (recipe follows)**
- 1 **teaspoon Oriental sesame oil**
- ⅛ **teaspoon white pepper**

In 3- to 4-quart pan, combine broth, ginger, onions, and sherry. Bring to a boil over high heat. Simmer, covered, for 30 minutes. Discard ginger and onions.

Meanwhile, peel kohlrabi or broccoli and slice lengthwise as thinly as possible. Cut slices into ½- by 3-inch strips. Add kohlrabi, cabbage, and bamboo shoots to broth; bring to a boil over high heat. Boil, uncovered, until cabbage wilts, about 1 minute. Add tomato and noodles. Cook until hot, about 1 minute. Add oil and pepper. Ladle into bowls. Serves 6 to 8.

**Egg crêpe noodles.** Beat 2 **large eggs** with 1 tablespoon **water.** Over medium heat, set a 10- or 11-inch nonstick frying pan that measures about 7 inches across the bottom; when pan is hot, brush inside with **salad oil.** Add ¼ cup egg mixture all at once; tilt pan to coat bottom with a thin, even layer. Cook until crêpe feels dry on top, about 30 seconds, and turn out of pan; repeat process. Cut crêpes into ½-inch-wide strips. (If made ahead, cool, cover, and chill up to next day.)

# Desserts from Ready-Made Eggnog

READY-MADE EGGNOG, *sold during the holidays, makes a flavorful base for these three desserts. All can be made ahead. To have an out-of-season supply of eggnog for cooking, you can freeze it in the carton up to nine months. Thaw in the refrigerator, and shake before using.*

## EGGNOG LAYER CAKE

- 4 large eggs, separated (reserve yolks for filling, following)
- 1 cup granulated sugar
- ½ cup (¼ lb.) butter or margarine
- 2¼ cups sifted cake flour
- 1 tablespoon baking powder
- 1 cup commercial eggnog
- ¼ cup finely chopped walnuts
  Eggnog filling (recipe follows)
- 2 cups whipping cream
- ¼ cup powdered sugar
  Ground nutmeg

In the large bowl of an electric mixer, whip egg whites until foamy. Beating at high speed, gradually add ½ cup granulated sugar. Continue to beat until whites hold stiff peaks; set aside. In another large bowl, beat butter and remaining granulated sugar until fluffy. Mix flour and baking powder; beat into butter mixture alternately with eggnog until blended. Stir in nuts; fold in whites.

Spread batter evenly in 2 well-greased and floured 9-inch-diameter cake pans. Bake in a 350° oven until a slender wooden pick inserted in center comes out clean, 30 to 35 minutes. Let cool in pans on racks for 10 minutes, then run a knife between cake and pan edges; turn cakes out onto racks and let cool.

Cut each layer horizontally into 2 equal pieces. Center 1 piece on a cake plate. Slide strips of waxed paper under edge of cake to keep plate clean as you frost cake. Spread top of cake with ⅓ of the filling, to within ¼ inch of edge. Set another layer on filling. Repeat to fill and stack remaining layers; leave top of cake bare.

In a bowl, whip cream with powdered sugar until stiff. Spread a little more than ½ the cream over sides and top of cake. Put remaining cream into a pastry bag fitted with a large star tip; pipe puffs of cream onto top of cake (or spoon puffs of cream onto cake). Sprinkle cake top with nutmeg. Carefully pull out waxed paper and discard. Serve, or, if made ahead, tent cake with foil or inverted bowl, not touching cake; chill up to 2 days. Serves 12. —*Mary Word, Fresno, Calif.*

**Eggnog filling.** In a 2- to 3-quart pan, stir together ¾ cup **sugar** and ¼ cup **cornstarch** (mash any lumps). Smoothly stir in 2¼ cups **commercial eggnog**. Bring to a boil over medium heat, stirring. Whisk some hot liquid into 4 **large egg yolks;** return mixture to pan and stir 2 minutes longer. Remove from heat, stir in ¼ cup **rum** (or more eggnog). Let cool, then lay plastic wrap on filling to cover; chill until cold, at least 2 hours or until next day.

## EGGNOG-TAPIOCA

*Add chocolate only after pudding is cold.*

- 1 quart commercial eggnog
- 5 tablespoons quick-cooking tapioca
- ⅓ cup dark rum (optional)
  Chocolate curls (optional)

In a 2- to 3-quart pan, stir eggnog into tapioca; let stand 5 minutes. Bring to a boil over medium heat, stirring. Remove from heat and let stand, stirring occasionally, for 20 minutes. Mix in rum.

Divide pudding among 6 serving dishes. Serve; or let cool, stirring occasionally. Lay plastic wrap on pudding to cover; chill until cold, at least 2 hours or up to 2 days. Top with chocolate curls. Serves 6. —*Nancy Lynn, Los Gatos, Calif.*

## EGGNOG GELATO

- 3 cups commercial eggnog
- 4 large egg yolks

In a 2- to 3-quart pan, whisk eggnog with yolks. Stir over medium-low heat until thick enough to coat a metal spoon in a thin, even layer, about 10 minutes. (Do not scald; custard curdles.)

Let cool. Cover and chill until cold, at least 2 hours or up to overnight. Freeze in an ice cream maker (self-refrigerated or with 1 part salt and 8 parts ice), as manufacturer directs. Serve, or freeze airtight for longer storage. Makes 1 quart.

*Cream-frosted cake has eggnog filling sandwiched between layers.*

# Spirited Fruit Gifts

**B**ERIBBONED BOTTLES *of fruit liqueur and jars filled with layers of steeped dried fruits make welcome holiday gifts.*

*Both the fragrant orange nectar and the fruits need at least a week to blend flavors. Serve the liquid as an after-dinner cordial, pour over sliced fruit or ice cream, or use it to flavor hot cocoa or other beverages that go well with orange. Serve the steeped fruits as is, or spoon them over vanilla or eggnog ice cream.*

*For holiday gifts, offer spirited fruits and orange cordial. Both easy-to-assemble recipes can be made weeks ahead.*

## GOLDEN-ORANGE NECTAR

> 3 **large oranges, thinly sliced**
> 3⅓ **cups sugar**
> 1 **vanilla bean (6 to 7 inches long), split lengthwise**
> 2 **cups milk**
> 2 **cups light rum or vodka**

In a large glass bowl, combine oranges, sugar, and vanilla bean; mix to coat oranges. Cover and let stand at room temperature, stirring occasionally, until sugar dissolves, at least 4 hours or until the next day. Add milk and rum; mix well. Cover and let stand at room temperature for 1 week; stir daily.

Pour mixture into a colander or large strainer set over a large bowl; let drain, then gently press liquid out of oranges. Discard fruit. Rinse vanilla bean, let dry, and save for other uses.

Line the colander with a 12-inch-diameter coffee filter or double thickness of white paper towels. (Liquid may be cloudier with towels; strain twice, if desired.)

Set colander over another large bowl. Pour about ¼ of the liquid into the filter. Let drain; allow 1 to 1½ hours. Or cover and let drain overnight. (Do not force liquid through filter.) Pour filtered liqueur into small bottles and cap with a cork or lid.

Replace filter, and strain in batches until all liquid is filtered; to speed up the process, use 2 bowls. Serve, or store in a cool place up to 6 months. Makes 4½ to 5 cups.

## BEGGARS IN RUM

> 1½ **cups (12 oz.) pitted prunes**
> 1 **cup golden raisins**
> 1½ **cups (8 oz.) dried figs**
> 1 **cup (6 oz.) dried apricots**
> 1 **cup dark raisins**
>   **About 1⅓ cups rum**
> 1⅓ **cups water**
> 1 **cup sugar**

In each of 3 wide-mouth, 1-pint jars, layer ⅓ prunes, golden raisins, figs, apricots, and dark raisins. Add ⅓ cup rum to each.

In a 1- to 1½ quart pan, mix water and sugar; bring to a boil over high heat. Pour hot syrup into each jar; fill to within ½ inch of top. Cover; let stand until fruits are plump, at least 1 week. Check after 2 days; if fruit is dry on top, add rum to cover. Serve, or store in a dark, cool place up to 2 months. Makes 3 pints.

*Add milk to orange mixture; it coagulates, separating out solids. Filtering yields a clear liquid.*

*Ladle hot syrup into jars filled with layered dried fruits and rum. Fruits absorb liquid, turn soft and plump.*

# More December Recipes

*I*N DECEMBER, *our food pages also offered a simple-to-make Italian appetizer for holiday entertaining; a pair of refreshing and low-calorie asparagus salads; and a versatile hot chocolate mix to prepare for gifts.*

## POLENTA DIAMONDS

*Two classics from Italy—polenta and gorgonzola cheese—work together in these easy-to-make appetizers. You cook coarse-ground polenta (or regular corn-meal) until thick, then spread it evenly in a pan. Stud the polenta with cheese and cut it in the pan to make bite-size diamonds. Just broil to heat, pick up to eat.*

  2  **tablespoons butter or margarine**
  1  **medium-size onion, finely chopped**
5½ **cups regular-strength chicken broth**
1¾ **cups polenta or yellow cornmeal**
  ½ **to ¾ pound gorgonzola cheese**

Melt butter in a 4- to 5-quart pan on medium-high heat. Add onion and cook uncovered, stirring often, until it just begins to brown, about 7 minutes. Add 4 cups broth, cover, and bring to a boil on high heat.

Mix polenta with remaining 1½ cups broth. Using a long-handled spoon, stir polenta mixture into the boiling broth. Cook, stirring, until thick; mixture spatters and is hot, so be careful. Reduce heat to low; stir until polenta is stiff enough to cease flowing about 10 seconds after the spoon is drawn across the pan bottom, 15 to 20 minutes.

At once, pour the hot polenta into a buttered 10- by 15-inch pan and quickly spread in an even layer.

Cut cheese into ¼-inch-thick sticks. Set in parallel rows about 1 inch apart on the polenta, pressing cheese partway into polenta. When polenta is cool, use a long knife or cleaver and cut through polenta between bands of cheese to make rows about 1 inch wide. Cut across rows diagonally at 1-inch intervals to make diamond shapes. (If made ahead, cover and chill up to 2 days; let come to room temperature before proceeding.)

To serve, broil polenta 6 inches from heat until cheese is sizzling, about 5 minutes. If needed, run a knife along

existing cuts to separate. With a wide spatula, transfer pieces to a tray. Serve hot or at room temperature. Makes about 100 pieces. Allow 6 or 7 for a serving.

## ASPARAGUS WITH TOMATILLOS

*Now that asparagus is grown all over the world, it's available almost year-round. In this first-course salad, the green spears are simply dressed with a salsa mixture of tomato and tart tomatillos. Parmesan cheese and lemon juice add the finishing touches.*

*Squeeze lemon on asparagus dressed with tomatillos and cheese.*

  1  **pound asparagus**
  3  **tablespoons olive oil**
  4  **large tomatillos (about 1½-inch diameter), husks removed, cored, and finely diced**
  1  **small firm-ripe Roma-type tomato, cored and finely diced**
  ¼  **cup finely shredded parmesan cheese**
     **Lemon wedges**
     **Salt and pepper**

Snap off and discard tough ends of asparagus. Peel stalks, if desired. In a deep 10- to 12-inch frying pan, bring about 1 inch water to boiling over high heat. Add asparagus; cook, uncovered, until barely tender when pierced, 3 to 5 minutes. Drain and immerse in ice water. When cool, drain and arrange equal portions of asparagus on 4 salad plates.

In a bowl, mix oil, tomatillos, and tomato. Spoon ¼ of the dressing in a band over each plate of asparagus. Sprinkle dressing with parmesan cheese. Garnish each salad with a lemon wedge; sprinkle with salt and pepper to taste. Makes 4 servings.

## STIR-FRIED ASPARAGUS & SCALLOPS ON COOL PASTA

*Here, scallops and sliced asparagus are combined with a light rice vinegar dressing and thin noodles.*

    8   ounces dry capellini or coil
        vermicelli
    1   pound asparagus
    3   tablespoons salad oil
    3   tablespoons water
    1   clove garlic, pressed or minced
    1   tablespoon minced fresh ginger
    ½   pound bay scallops or sea scallops,
        cut into ½-inch chunks, rinsed
        and drained
    ½   cup rice vinegar (or white wine vin-
        egar plus 1 teaspoon sugar)
    2   tablespoons sugar
    1   teaspoon soy sauce
    1   teaspoon Oriental sesame oil

In a 5- to 6-quart pan, bring 3 quarts water to boiling over high heat. Add noodles and cook, uncovered, just until barely tender to bite, 3 to 5 minutes. Drain and rinse with cold water until cool; drain well. Place noodles in a shallow dish.

Snap off and discard tough ends of asparagus. Cut asparagus diagonally into ¼-inch-thick slices 1½ to 2 inches long.

Place a wok or 10- to 12-inch frying pan over high heat. Add 1 tablespoon salad oil and asparagus; stir-fry to coat with oil. Add water; cover and cook just until tender-crisp, 2 to 3 minutes. Pour asparagus onto the pasta.

Add remaining 2 tablespoons salad oil, garlic, ginger, and scallops to pan. Stir-fry over high heat until scallops are opaque in center (cut to test), 2 to 3 minutes. Add rice vinegar, sugar, soy sauce, and Oriental sesame oil; stir just until sugar dissolves. Pour scallop mixture over noodles. Serve, or cover and chill up to 4 hours. Makes 4 to 6 servings.

## INSTANT HOT CHOCOLATE MIX

*Instead of cocoa, which must be cooked a few minutes to dissolve well, this extra-easy hot drink mix uses chocolate chips, which melt quickly in boiling water.*

*Your choice of chocolate determines the flavor; try semisweet, mint, milk, or white chocolate. Or use part butterscotch or peanut butter chips. You can also add malted milk powder, instant coffee, orange peel, or spices.*

*With adult supervision, children can easily prepare this mix. It makes a great gift for relatives, teachers, or friends.*

    3   cups instant nonfat dry milk
    2   cups (12 oz.) semisweet, mint, or
        milk chocolate baking chips
    1½  cups miniature marshmallows
        (optional)
        Boiling water

Put half of the dry milk in a blender or food processor, add half the chips, and whirl until finely ground. If using a blender, stop motor once to scrape mixture away from blades; do not continue mixing after finely ground or mixture may clump.

Pour mixture into a bowl and repeat to grind remaining milk and chips. Stir in marshmallows. Spoon into a jar (or jars) and cover tightly.

*Stocking-stuffer beverage mix pleases Grandpa; all he does is add boiling water to chocolate blend and stir. One recipe makes enough for 15 servings.*

Use, or store airtight up to 6 months. For each serving of chocolate milk, place ⅓ cup (about 3 heaping tablespoons) mix into a mug. Add ¾ cup boiling water and stir until well combined. Makes 4 to 5 cups mix, enough for 12 to 15 servings.

## HOT MALTED CHOCOLATE MIX

Follow directions for **Instant Hot Chocolate Mix** (preceding; do not use mint chips), decreasing **dry milk** to 1½ cups and adding 1½ cups **malted milk powder** with it.

## HOT MOCHA MIX

Follow directions for **Instant Hot Chocolate Mix** (preceding), adding ½ cup **instant coffee powder** with the dry milk.

## ORANGE-CINNAMON HOT CHOCOLATE MIX

Follow directions for **Instant Hot Chocolate Mix** (preceding; do not use mint chips); thoroughly stir in with marshmallows 1 tablespoon grated **orange peel** and 2 teaspoons **ground cinnamon.** Store 6 weeks at room temperature, up to 3 months chilled.

## BUTTERSCOTCH OR PEANUT BUTTER HOT CHOCOLATE MIX

Follow directions for **Instant Hot Chocolate Mix** (preceding), decreasing **semisweet chocolate baking chips** to 1 cup and adding with them 1 cup (6 oz.) **butterscotch** or peanut butter **baking chips.**

## HOT SPICED WHITE CHOCOLATE MIX

Follow directions for **Instant Hot Chocolate Mix** (preceding), but omit **semisweet chocolate chips** and use 2 cups (12 oz.) **white chocolate baking chips.** With the chips, grind 1 teaspoon **ground cardamom** or ground mace.

*Warm mustard sauce tops hot ham slices, spinach; try sprinkled with mustard seed.*

### HAM & SPINACH WITH MUSTARD SAUCE

- 2 packages (10 oz. each) thawed frozen leaf spinach
- ¾ pound cooked ham, cut into ⅜- to ½-inch-thick slices
- 2 tablespoons butter or margarine
- ⅓ cup finely chopped onion
- 1½ tablespoons all-purpose flour
- ½ cup *each* regular-strength chicken broth and milk
- 2 tablespoons Dijon mustard
- 1 teaspoon *each* dry mustard, firmly packed brown sugar, and Worcestershire

In a 10- to 12-inch frying pan over high heat, stir spinach until hot, about 5 minutes. Transfer to a serving platter; keep warm.

Arrange a single layer of ham slices in pan; cook until lightly browned on each side, about 8 minutes total. As browned, place ham on spinach; add remaining ham to pan and repeat.

Rinse pan; put on medium-high heat. Add butter and onion; cook, stirring, until onion is limp, about 3 minutes. Stir in flour. Gradually mix in milk and broth; cook, stirring, until boiling. Stir in Dijon mustard, dry mustard, sugar, and Worcestershire. Pour over ham. Makes 3 or 4 servings.—*Roxanne E. Chan, Albany, Calif.*

*Oven-browning is a neat, easy way to make these appetizer-size meatballs.*

### CRANBERRY APPETIZER MEATBALLS

- 1½ pounds ground lean beef
- 2 large eggs
- 1 cup fine dry bread crumbs
- ⅓ cup *each* minced parsley, minced onion, and catsup
- 1 tablespoon prepared horseradish
- 1 clove garlic, pressed or minced
  Cranberry sauce (recipe follows)

In a bowl, thoroughly mix together beef, eggs, crumbs, parsley, onion, catsup, horseradish, and garlic. Shape mixture into 1½-inch balls; set slightly apart in a 10- by 15-inch baking pan. Bake, uncovered, in a 450° oven, stirring once, until meatballs are lightly browned, about 15 minutes. Pour off and discard fat.

Pour cranberry sauce over meatballs. Reduce heat to 350° and bake, uncovered, stirring occasionally, until sauce bubbles, about 18 minutes. Keep warm while serving. Makes about 50 meatballs, 10 to 12 appetizer servings.—*T. Walker, San Francisco.*

**Cranberry sauce.** In a bowl, mash 1 can (16 oz.) **jellied cranberry sauce** with 1 bottle (12 oz.) or 1¼ cups **tomato-based chili sauce** and 2 tablespoons firmly packed **brown sugar.**

*Chicken soup, Southwest-style, includes hominy, green chilies, and sliced olives.*

### CHICKEN POSOLE

- 2 large onions, chopped
- 2 cloves garlic, pressed or minced
- 1 tablespoon dry oregano leaves
- ½ teaspoon ground cumin
- 2 tablespoons salad oil
- 1 cut-up broiler-fryer chicken (3 to 3½ lb.), skin removed
- 6 cups regular-strength chicken broth
- 2 cans (4 oz. each) diced green chilies
- 1 can (29 oz.) hominy, drained
- 1 can (2¼ oz.) sliced ripe olives, drained

In a 5- to 6-quart pan over medium heat, stir onions, garlic, oregano, cumin, and oil until onion is limp, about 5 minutes. Set chicken breasts aside; add remaining chicken, broth, chilies, and hominy to pan; bring to boiling over high heat. Cover pan; simmer 10 minutes. Add breasts and cover; remove from heat and let stand until breasts are white in thickest part (cut to test), about 20 minutes.

Lift chicken from liquid. When cool enough to handle, tear into bite-size pieces; discard bones. Skim fat from broth. Return chicken to broth; add olives. Bring to boiling over high heat. Pour into a tureen. Makes 6 or 7 servings.—*Loretta Peña, Lakeside, Ariz.*

## Winter Salad

- 2 large eggs
- 1 small red apple, cored
- 1 small head (8 to 9 oz.) romaine lettuce, washed, crisped, and torn into bite-size pieces
- 1 cup ¼-inch cubes jack cheese
- 3 tablespoons white wine vinegar
- 3 tablespoons salad oil or mayonnaise
- 3 tablespoons crumbled blue cheese

Put eggs into a 1- to 1½-quart pan and add water to cover by 1 inch; bring to boiling over high heat. Cover pan and remove from heat; let stand 20 minutes. Drain eggs and cover with cold water; let stand until cool. Peel eggs and cut into wedges.

Chop apple into ¼-inch cubes. In a salad bowl, combine apple, lettuce, and jack cheese.

In small bowl, stir together vinegar, salad oil, and blue cheese. Pour over salad; mix to coat leaves with dressing. Arrange egg wedges on top of salad. Makes 5 or 6 servings.—*Peggy Deen, Corvallis, Ore.*

*Romaine salad with apple, jack cheese, cooked eggs has blue cheese dressing.*

## Ginger-Sweet Potato Salad

- 2 pounds (about 4 medium-size) sweet potatoes or yams
- 1 cup sliced green onion
- 1 cup thinly sliced celery
- ½ cup chopped dry-roasted almonds
- ⅓ cup cream sherry
- ⅓ cup lemon juice
- ¼ cup salad oil
- 1 tablespoon *each* honey and minced or grated fresh ginger (or ½ teaspoon ground ginger)
  Salt and pepper

Scrub sweet potatoes; place in a 5- to 6-quart pan and cover with 1 inch of water. Bring to boiling over high heat, then simmer, uncovered, until potatoes are just tender when pierced, 30 to 40 minutes. Drain and let cool; peel and cut into ½-inch cubes.

In a salad bowl, combine green onion, celery, almonds, cream sherry, lemon juice, oil, honey, and ginger. Add sweet potatoes and gently stir to coat evenly with dressing mixture. Serve, or cover the salad and chill up to 6 hours. Add salt and pepper to taste. Makes 6 to 8 servings.—*Gladys Kent, Port Angeles, Wash.*

*Potato salad created with golden sweet potatoes or yams suits winter menus.*

## White Chocolate Mousse

- ½ cup milk
- 1 cup (6 oz.) finely chopped white chocolate or white chocolate baking bits
- 1 teaspoon vanilla
- 2 large egg whites
- 1 cup whipping cream
- 2 tablespoons sugar
  Bittersweet chocolate, cut into curls or grated

Put milk and white chocolate in a metal bowl. Bring 1 inch of water to boiling in a 3- to 4-quart pan. Nest bowl over water; turn heat to low. Stir often until chocolate melts. Remove from heat and stir in vanilla. Let cool to room temperature.

In a small, deep bowl, whip egg whites on high speed with an electric mixer until foamy, then gradually beat in sugar until whites hold soft peaks. Fold into chocolate mixture.

Pour cream into the egg white bowl; beat with the mixer on high speed until cream holds soft peaks. Fold into the chocolate mixture. Cover and chill until cold, at least 1 or up to 6 hours.

Spoon the mousse into 6 goblets or dessert bowls. Garnish with bittersweet chocolate curls. Serves 6.—*Carmela M. Meely, Walnut Creek, Calif.*

*Two-chocolate dessert: base is white mousse; curls on top are bittersweet.*

## Chefs of ✪ the West®

### The Art of Cooking . . . by men . . . for men

THE EXOTIC CUISINES *of Thailand and Vietnam aren't yet as familiar as those of China, but they're gaining fast. All these schools of cooking use a wide variety of spices and seasonings to enhance simple, often inexpensive ingredients. They are alike, too, in their quickness to marry with foods from other lands. This soup, for instance, contains jalapeño, tomato, and a garnish of avocado—none of which are native to the Far East.*

*Yet for all their common traits, each cuisine has its own unique array of flavors. One dear to the Thais and Vietnamese is lemon grass. It's the principal source of the haunting, elusive play between flavor and fragrance that characterizes both these cuisines.*

*This peculiar grass (Cymbopogon citratus), never found growing in the wild, furnishes a flavor very like lemon peel. Yet the plant doesn't take up as much space as a lemon tree—an important consideration in a tiny village garden.*

*Most Oriental markets and many larger supermarkets now sell lemon grass fresh; the bulbous stalk with leaves is about the size of a green onion. If you don't see it, ask your grocer for help.*

"One flavor dear to the Thais and Vietnamese is lemon grass."

### CHICKEN & LEMON GRASS SOUP

|   |   |
|---|---|
| 1 | stalk fresh lemon grass |
| 1 | large can (49½ oz.) or 6 cups regular-strength chicken broth |
| ⅛ | teaspoon freshly ground black pepper |
| 1 | fresh jalapeño chili, stemmed, seeded, and minced |
| 1 | clove garlic, minced or pressed |
| ½ | cup thinly sliced green onions, including tops |
| ½ | cup chopped fresh cilantro (coriander) |
| 1 | medium-size firm-ripe tomato, cored, seeded, and coarsely chopped |
| 2 | to 3 cups bite-size pieces cooked chicken |
| 1 | medium-size firm-ripe avocado, peeled, pitted, and chopped |

Trim and discard root end and leaves from lemon grass; peel and discard coarse outer layers of stalk. In a 4- to 5-quart pan, combine lemon grass, broth, pepper, chili, and garlic.

Bring to a boil over high heat, cover, and simmer for 30 minutes. Discard lemon grass. Stir in the green onion, cilantro, tomato, and chicken.

Evenly divide the chopped avocado among 6 soup bowls, then ladle soup over the avocado. Makes 6 servings, about 1⅓ cups each.

*Tom Feed Hensinger*

*Aurora, Colo.*

CHARLES LUCAS' *Pecan Wine Cakes (cookies, actually) derive their richness from finely chopped pecans. Not overly sweet, the little cakes are delicately flavored with sherry, anise extract, and lemon peel. Offer them as companions for ice cream or fruit, or alone with coffee or tea. Any not consumed right away can be stored in the cooky jar, then surreptitiously removed and savored in solitude.*

### PECAN WINE CAKES

|   |   |
|---|---|
| ½ | cup (¼ lb.) butter or margarine |
| ⅓ | cup sugar |
| 2 | large egg yolks |
| ¼ | teaspoon grated lemon peel |
| ¼ | teaspoon anise extract |
| 4 | teaspoons dry sherry |
| 1 | cup all-purpose flour |
| 1 | cup finely chopped pecans |

With an electric mixer, beat butter and sugar until well blended. Beat in egg yolks, lemon peel, anise extract, and sherry until fluffy. Add flour and ½ cup of the nuts; beat until well mixed.

Mound remaining ½ cup nuts on a sheet of waxed paper. To shape each cooky, drop 1 tablespoon of dough into nuts and roll to coat evenly. Put nut-covered pieces about 2 inches apart on a greased baking sheet; flatten until about ¼ inch thick. Bake in a 350° oven until golden brown, about 25 minutes. Let cool 1 to 2 minutes, then transfer with a spatula to racks to cool completely. Serve, or store airtight up to 3 days; freeze to store longer. Makes about 2 dozen.

*Charles Lucas*

*Lynwood, Calif.*

PAELLA, *Spain's version of gumbo, pilaf, risotto, and a host of other rice-based dishes from other lands, differs in the blend of ingredients cooked with the grain. The name paella (say pie-ay-ya) applies to both the dish and the wide, shallow, two-handled pan in which it is traditionally prepared. For those of us working on the kitchen range, it's easier to use a deeper, narrower pan that fits the burner.*

*The dish begins with a bed of rice perfumed with a touch of saffron, then flavored with onion, pimiento, and tomato. Nestled in the rice are various meats and seafoods; the mix depends upon individual preference and availability. Typical combinations include chicken, pork, ham, sausage, squid, and sea critters in the shell—shrimp, clams, mussels, and oysters.*

*John Endresen's version varies from the norm, using brown rice rather than white and shellfish minus the shells.*

*Obviously, this isn't a peasant dish (unless the peasant has a well-stocked farm by the sea). Instead, think of it as showy yet easy-to-make dinner-party fare.*

## ENDRESEN'S PAELLA

2  to 3 tablespoons olive oil
8  small (about 1½-inch-diameter) onions, quartered
1  pound boneless lean pork shoulder or butt, cut into ½-inch cubes
8  chicken thighs (about 1¾ lb.), skinned
   About ¾ pound chorizo sausages, casings removed
2  cups long-grain brown rice
1/16  teaspoon powdered saffron
4  cups hot water
6  chicken bouillon cubes
1  can (16 oz.) stewed tomatoes

*"Obviously, this isn't a peasant dish...think of it as showy."*

1  jar (4 oz.) sliced pimientos, drained
½  cup chopped parsley
1  pound tiny cooked, shelled shrimp
1  jar (10 oz.) small Pacific oysters, optional

In a 6- to 8-quart pan over medium heat, combine 2 tablespoons oil and onions; stir often until onions are lightly browned, about 5 minutes. Lift out onions and set aside. Add pork cubes to pan and stir often until browned, about 20 minutes; lift out and set aside.

Add chicken to pan and brown well on all sides, adding more oil if needed to prevent sticking, about 15 minutes. Lift out and set aside. Add chorizo to pan and crumble with a spoon; stir often until browned, about 15 minutes. Spoon out and discard all but 3 tablespoons of drippings. Add rice to remaining drippings and chorizo; stir until rice is opaque, about 8 minutes.

Meanwhile, moisten saffron with about 2 tablespoons of hot water. Add saffron liquid to pan, along with remaining water, bouillon cubes, onions, and pork (include any juices); stir well.

Bring to a boil on high heat, then cover and simmer 20 minutes. Stir in chicken thighs (with any juices) and tomatoes with their liquid; cover, and continue to simmer until rice is tender to bite, about 30 minutes more.

Add pimientos, parsley, shrimp, and oysters and their liquid. Stir gently to mix well; cover and let stand over lowest heat for 5 minutes to blend flavors. Ladle into wide soup plates. Makes 8 to 10 servings.

*Seattle*

WHAT'S HAPPENED *to omelets? After extensive sleuthing in restaurants, watching short-order chefs and sampling their products, Ronald Cook decided that most omelets consist of a rubbery yellow mass imprisoning some sort of filling in a purely custodial relationship. No melding of flavors, no flair for presentation.*

*To remedy the situation and brighten his breakfast scene, Ronald Cook invented this "unomelet": soft-scrambled eggs blended with cheddar cheese and Mexican seasonings, then topped with marinated artichokes, sour cream, and salsa.*

*The unomelet makes a splendid, easy-to-prepare brunch dish, but timing is critical;*

*"To remedy the situation and brighten his breakfast scene...the 'unomelet'"*

*seat your guests at the table and give them some juice or coffee to keep them busy while you prepare the meal. Before you start, be sure you have all ingredients cracked and beaten, shredded and chopped.*

## THE UNOMELET

6  tablespoons sour cream
1  teaspoon chili powder
½  teaspoon *each* dry oregano leaves and ground cumin
¼  teaspoon celery salt
2  tablespoons butter or margarine
1  small onion, chopped
8  large eggs
¼  cup shredded sharp cheddar cheese
1  jar (6 oz.) or ¾ cup marinated artichokes, well drained
   Prepared green chili salsa

Stir together sour cream, chili powder, oregano, cumin, and celery salt; set aside.

Melt butter in a 10- to 11-inch frying pan over medium heat; add onion and stir often until limp, about 10 minutes. Meanwhile, beat eggs in a bowl until combined. Pour eggs over onions; lift cooked eggs with a spatula from pan bottom to allow uncooked portion to flow underneath.

Cook just until eggs are set but still moist.

Divide eggs among 4 warm plates; top each portion equally with cheese, artichokes, and sour cream mixture. Offer salsa to taste. Makes 4 servings.

*Santa Cruz, Calif.*

# December Menus

IT'S THAT BUSY TIME OF YEAR *when celebrating begins to fill your calendar. Keeping in mind that time is minimal, we've devised three satisfying yet simple-to-prepare menus.*

*After trimming the tree, reward your family with crusty calzone. Our last two menus, a quick-to-fix holiday breakfast and a dinner suited for company, depend on the oven to do most of the work.*

### FIRESIDE SUPPER

**Mushroom & Prosciutto Calzone**
**Spinach Salad**
**Amaretti Cookies**
**Red Seedless Grapes**
**Chianti     Milk**

*These serving-size calzone are easy to eat out of hand at a casual feast by the fire.*

*To speed preparation, make the calzone filling a day ahead. Get dough started at least 2 hours before serving. Rinse spinach, discarding stems and coarse leaves; drain well, then assemble the salad while the calzone bakes.*

## MUSHROOM & PROSCIUTTO CALZONE

- 1 package active dry yeast
- 1 cup warm water (110°)
- 2½ cups all-purpose flour
  - About ½ cup cornmeal
- 1 tablespoon sugar
- ½ teaspoon salt
- 2½ tablespoons olive oil
  - Mushroom filling (recipe follows)

In a small bowl, soften yeast in water, about 5 minutes. In a large bowl, mix flour, ½ cup cornmeal, sugar, and salt. Add yeast mixture and 2 tablespoons oil. Stir with a fork until evenly moistened and dough holds together. Scrape dough out onto a lightly floured board and knead until a smooth, compact ball, about 15 turns. Place dough in a greased bowl; turn over to grease top. Cover and let rise in a warm place until doubled, about 1 hour.

When dough has risen, punch down and divide into 6 equal pieces. Roll out each on a lightly floured board to make an 8-inch round. Spoon ⅙ of the filling over half of each dough circle to within ½ inch of edge. Fold other half over the filling, pressing edges firmly together; seal and crimp edges.

With a wide spatula, transfer calzone to greased and cornmeal-dusted 12- by 15-inch baking sheets. With a fork, prick tops of turnovers and brush lightly with remaining oil. Bake in a 425° oven until richly browned, 18 to 20 minutes. Serve hot. Serves 6.

**Mushroom filling.** In a 10- to 12-inch frying pan, combine 2 tablespoons **oil from dried tomatoes packed in oil** or olive oil; 1 clove **garlic,** pressed or minced; 1 large **onion,** sliced; 1 pound **mushrooms,** sliced; and 2 ounces thinly sliced **prosciutto,** chopped. Stir often over medium-high heat until onion is golden and mushrooms are brown, 15 to 18 minutes. Remove from heat; cool briefly. Add 2 tablespoons **dried tomatoes packed in oil** (optional), drained and cut into thin slivers; 2 tablespoons minced **parsley;** ½ pound **jack cheese,** cut into ½-inch cubes; and ⅓ cup grated **parmesan cheese.** If made ahead, cool, cover, and chill until the next day.

### CHRISTMAS BREAKFAST STARTER

**Cranberry-Walnut Scones**
**Whipped Honey-Orange Cream Cheese**
**Oven-Fried Bacon**
**Sparkling Compote**
**Hot Cocoa**

*On this December morning, enjoy cranberry scones with honey and orange-flavored cream cheese.*

*You can bake the scones and bacon together in the same oven.*

*Use orange peel to flavor the scones and the whipped cream cheese. Orange segments go into a sparkling fruit compote. Cut segments free from membranes and*

*Fireside supper of mushroom and prosciutto calzone, spinach salad, cookies, and grapes will satisfy hearty appetites.*

*mix with peeled, sliced kiwi fruit and canned sliced pears in their own juice; to serve 4 to 6, you'll need 4 medium-size oranges, 2 medium-size kiwi fruit, and 1 can (1 lb.) sliced pears. Spoon into champagne flutes, and fill with sparkling apple cider or with sparkling wine.*

## CRANBERRY-WALNUT SCONES

>     3  cups all-purpose flour
>     ½  cup sugar
>     1  tablespoon baking powder
>     ½  teaspoon *each* baking soda and salt
>     ¾  cup (⅜ lb.) butter or margarine, cut into small pieces
>     1  cup fresh or frozen cranberries
>     ½  cup chopped walnuts
>   1½  teaspoons grated orange peel
>     1  cup buttermilk
>        About 1 tablespoon whipping cream or milk
>     1  tablespoon sugar mixed with ¼ teaspoon ground cinnamon and ⅛ teaspoon ground allspice

In a large bowl, stir together flour, ½ cup sugar, baking powder, baking soda, and salt. Using a pastry blender or your fingers, cut or rub butter into flour mixture until coarse crumbs form; stir in cranberries, walnuts, and orange peel. Add buttermilk and mix with a fork just until dough is evenly moistened.

Gather dough into a ball and place on a floured board. Roll or pat into a ¾-inch-thick circle. Using a 2½-inch-diameter cutter, cut into rounds. Place on a greased 12- by 15-inch baking sheet, spacing 1½ inches apart. Reroll and cut scraps. Brush tops of scones with cream; sprinkle with sugar-spice mixture.

Bake on a lower rack in a 400° oven until tops are lightly browned, 14 to 16 minutes. Serve warm. Makes 1 dozen, 4 to 6 servings.

## WHIPPED HONEY-ORANGE CREAM CHEESE

In a small bowl, beat 1 large package (8 oz.) **cream cheese** (at room temperature), 2 tablespoons **honey**, and 1 tablespoon grated **orange peel** until light and fluffy. Serve, or cover and chill up to 2 days. Makes about 1¼ cups, 4 to 6 servings.

*Wake up to this simple yet festive breakfast: cranberry scones, flavored cream cheese, bacon, sparkling compote, and hot cocoa.*

## OVEN-FRIED BACON

Line a 10- by 15-inch rimmed baking pan with foil; place a wire rack over pan. Lay 12 to 14 strips (about 1 lb.) **bacon,** slightly overlapping, on rack. Bake on upper rack in a 400° oven until brown and crisp, 14 to 16 minutes. Serves 4 to 6.

---

### IMPROMPTU COMPANY DINNER

**Artichoke, Endive & Shrimp Salad**
**Baked Pork Chops Dijon**
**Best-Ever Crispy Potatoes**
**Steamed Broccoli**
**Apple Turnovers**
**Merlot     Mineral Water**

---

*About an hour is all you need to prepare this dinner for last-minute entertaining. Here, a mustard dressing works two ways. Drizzle on salads and spread over pork chops before baking. Buy apple turnovers at the bakery, or bake frozen ones.*

*Start potatoes first. Make dressing and crisp greens. About 20 minutes before potatoes are done, place chops in same oven. Then cook broccoli and dress salad.*

## ARTICHOKE, ENDIVE & SHRIMP SALAD

>     2  heads Belgian endive (about 4 oz. each), leaves separated
>     2  cups watercress sprigs, washed and crisped
>     1  can (8½ oz.) artichoke hearts packed in water, drained and cut into quarters
>     ½  pound tiny cooked shelled shrimp
>        Mustard dressing (recipe follows)

Arrange equal portions of Belgian endive, watercress, and artichoke hearts in rows on each of 6 salad plates; scatter shrimp over vegetables. Drizzle about 2 tablespoons mustard dressing over each salad. Makes 6 first-course servings.

**Mustard dressing.** In a bowl, whisk together ¾ cup **olive** or salad **oil,** ½ cup **red wine vinegar,** ¼ cup **Dijon mustard,** 2 tablespoons minced **chives,** 2 teaspoons **dry tarragon,** and ¼ teaspoon **freshly ground pepper.** Makes 1½ cups.

## BAKED PORK CHOPS DIJON

>     6  loin pork chops (about 2½ lb.), cut ¾ inch thick
>     ¾  cup mustard dressing (recipe precedes)

Arrange chops in a foil-lined 10- by 15-inch rimmed baking pan. Spread 1 tablespoon of dressing over top of each chop.

Bake, uncovered, on the upper rack of a 475° oven for 10 minutes. Turn chops over, spread each with 1 more tablespoon of dressing, and continue to bake until browned and no longer pink at bone (cut to test), 8 to 10 minutes. Serves 4 to 6.

## BEST-EVER CRISPY POTATOES

>     2  tablespoons *each* olive oil and butter or margarine
>     5  large russet potatoes (about 3¼ lb. total), peeled and cut into 1-inch chunks
>     1  large onion, cut into eighths
>     4  cloves garlic, cut into halves
>        Salt

Place oil and butter in a rimmed 10- by 15-inch baking pan. Scatter potatoes, onions, and garlic in pan. Bake on lower rack of a 475° oven until golden brown and crispy, 1 to 1¼ hours, stirring occasionally. Add salt to taste. Serves 4 to 6.

# Articles Index

# Index of Recipe Titles

# General Index

## Photographers

**Victor Budnik:** 185. **Glenn Christiansen:** 7, 9, 10, 11, 12, 13, 14, 15, 16, 100, 101, 102, 103, 104, 105, 203, 217, 218, 219, 265, 266, 268, 269, 270, 277. **Peter Christiansen:** 204, 214, 215, 224, 227, 244, 245, 252, 257, 298, 300 (bottom), 301, 306, 307, 311, 315 (bottom right), 322, 323, 330, 331. **Stephen Cridland:** 76, 243. **Norman A. Plate:** 1, 4, 18, 19, 29, 30, 31, 32, 56, 57, 58, 59 (top right), 77, 78, 79, 90, 109, 111, 125, 127 (top right), 144, 183, 190, 191 (bottom right), 193, 198, 199, 205, 207, 209, 226, 232, 233, 250, 251, 293, 315 (top right), 328, 329, 333, 335, 340, 341. **Teri Sandison:** 191 top. **David Stubbs:** 17, 26, 27, 38, 39, 41, 85, 96, 97, 114, 115, 120, 124, 167, 169, 256, 316. **Darrow M. Watt:** 2, 5, 20, 21, 33, 34, 35, 42, 43, 48, 49, 51, 52, 53, 55, 59 (left), 60, 61, 62, 63, 64, 65, 66, 67, 72, 73, 75, 80, 81, 82, 83, 84, 86, 87, 88, 89, 91, 99, 106, 107, 108, 112, 113, 116, 117, 118, 119, 121, 122, 123, 126, 127 (bottom left), 128, 129, 134, 135, 137, 138, 139, 141, 143 (left), 145, 147, 148, 149, 150, 151, 152, 153, 154, 155, 160, 161, 163, 164, 165, 168, 170, 172, 173, 174, 175, 176, 177, 178, 179, 180, 181, 182, 184, 195, 196, 197, 200, 201, 206, 208, 220, 221, 223, 225, 235, 236, 237, 238, 239, 241, 242, 246, 247, 248, 249, 253, 254, 255, 262, 263, 278, 279, 283, 287, 288, 289, 291, 292, 294, 295, 297, 299, 309, 315 (bottom left, top right), 317, 318, 324, 325, 326, 327, 332, 334. **Doug Wilson:** 36, 37. **Tom Wyatt:** 300 (top left). **Nikolay Zurek:** 142, 143 (right).

If you are not already a subscriber to SUNSET magazine and would be interested in subscribing, please call SUNSET's subscriber service number, 415-321-3600.